Hollywood
Stunt Performers,
1910s–1970s

Hollywood Stunt Performers, 1910s–1970s

A Biographical Dictionary

Second Edition

GENE SCOTT FREESE

McFarland & Company, Inc., Publishers

Jefferson, North Carolina

LIBRARY OF CONGRESS CATALOGUING-IN-PUBLICATION DATA

Freese, Gene Scott, 1969–
[Hollywood stunt performers]
Hollywood stunt performers, 1910's-1970's : a biographical dictionary /
Gene Scott Freese. — Second edition.
p.   cm.
Includes bibliographical references and index.

ISBN 978-0-7864-7643-5 (softcover : acid free paper) ∞
ISBN 978-1-4766-1470-0 (ebook)

1. Stunt performers—United States—Biography—Dictionaries.   I. Title.
PN1995.9.S7F67 2014   791.4302'8092273—dc23   [B]   2014007740

BRITISH LIBRARY CATALOGUING DATA ARE AVAILABLE

On the cover: Harold Lloyd hangs from the hands
of a clock on *Safety Last*, Hal Roach Studios, 1923

Printed in the United States of America

*McFarland & Company, Inc., Publishers
Box 611, Jefferson, North Carolina 28640
www.mcfarlandpub.com*

Table of Contents

Acknowledgments

Many thanks to the stunt performers and actors I have encountered at nostalgic western film festivals and those who have answered questions through e-mail, regular mail, or phone. They include Budd Albright, Fritz Apking, Stephen Burnette, Bud Cardos, Roydon Clark, Louie Elias, Robert Fuller, Dan Haggerty, Robert Hoy, Whitey Hughes, Loren Janes, Dick Jones, Ron Nix, Joe Pronto, Burt Reynolds, William Smith, Neil Summers, Rodd Wolff, and Jack Young. The library archives of the Academy of Motion Pictures Arts and Sciences was a fine information resource.

Preface

The subject of this book is motion picture stunt performers who were active from the 1910s through the 1970s. Stunt personnel are an important part of the filmmaking process and cinema history, yet during this period they went without credit or recognition for their hard work. Behind the scenes they were often the most interesting people, elite athletes or specialists recruited for their individual or collective nerve and skill. All on-screen action with any level of risk is totally reliant on the presence of these experienced performers.

I became interested in the subject because action appealed to me. Stuntmen were often employed for small acting roles so two people would not be needed. These anonymous bit players became familiar and I sought out their names and backgrounds. The result is the formative research behind *Hollywood Stunt Performers*. There are no prior works assembling a combination of biographical and cinematic information for these important people, the first edition of this book included. That book, *Hollywood Stunt Performers: A Dictionary and Filmography of Over 600 Men and Women, 1922–1996* (McFarland, 1998), was a list of names, professional affiliations and films each stunt performer worked on. Very little biographical information was included for most people, and none at all for many. This book corrects that deficiency.

What this book does not cover is the history of the profession at the time the stunt performers herein were active. That is covered well in two interesting books: John Baxter's *Stunt* (1974) and Arthur Wise and Derek Ware's *Stunting in the Cinema* (1973).

I cover the stunt profession up until the end of the 1970s, choosing this as a cutoff point because stunt performers had begun receiving screen credit and there was a massive swarm of people wanting to be or claiming to be stunt performers. The style of film changed as well (and continues to change) with the advent of computer graphics. The bulk of my research utilized newspaper archives, obituaries, books, magazines, films, online databases, websites, and films at the Motion Picture Academy Library. In some cases I have been able to make contact with stunt performers who were active during this period.

Introduction

The movie *The Great Train Robbery* (1903) employed a man named Frank Hanaway as a train-robbing bandit. In the course of filming a chase, Hanaway fell off a horse for the camera without suffering permanent injury. In effect, Hanaway became the first movie stuntman.

Professional cowboys Art Acord, Hoot Gibson, and Tom Mix followed, hired for pictures due to their western riding ability. In the early days of silent film, stars such as Helen Holmes and Pearl White created a quandary for the motion picture studios. Audiences responded favorably to heroic feats of daring, but capturing these acts on film proved hazardous. Stars were putting themselves at great peril for the cameras. The studios didn't want to build up someone at the box office only to have their investment seriously injured or killed creating the very product they were selling. The answer emerged in the form of stunt doubles.

If an expendable, replaceable crew member were to step in during the star's most dangerous moments, a burgeoning and profitable career could be maintained. As it turned out, for the right price there was no shortage of daredevils willing to participate in action scenes. Major changes in transportation and ranching had forced many cowboys off the range. Movie studios recruited dozens of out-of-work horsemen from Gower Gulch (saloons at the corner of Gower and Sunset Boulevard in Hollywood) to work for dollars a day. For an extra few bucks they would gladly fall off a horse or jump from a boulder. Some of these men (such as the aforementioned Acord, Gibson, and Mix) proved handy and talented enough to graduate to stardom. Others saw stunting as the quickest entry point into filmmaking. John Ford, Raoul Walsh, and William Wellman learned enough about the camera to emerge from the stunt ranks to become directors.

The studios and top stars decided that it was in everyone's best interest if the public believed that the stars did their own action. Stuntmen and stuntwomen were sworn to secrecy. Athletic, prideful stars Douglas Fairbanks and Harold Lloyd had it written into their contracts that their doubles would be forbidden to reveal this subterfuge. That was fine with the early stunt performers, and a significant number of them weren't living to tell any trade secrets anyway. Stunt work involved a great deal of trial and error and fatalities up until the early 1930s were common as studios and directors demanded the impossible. The smartest of the stuntmen such as Richard Talmadge, Harvey Parry, Dave Sharpe, and Yakima Canutt began to keep track of what worked and what didn't. They realized the camera could be fooled and so could the audience with all manner of safe illusions.

This became most apparent in the simple fight scene, which once consisted of a single camera placement recording two men punching one another's arms and shoulders, then rolling around on the ground. The best of this type of fight was the legendary battle

1972-20

Budd Albright and Charlie Picerni, above the cannons, rappel down the face of a mountain on _Tobruk_ (1967).

between William Farnum and Tom Santschi on _The Spoilers_ (1914), but that sent both actors to the hospital. It wasn't until the early 1930s that Yakima Canutt and John Wayne realized that by utilizing camera placement and effective angles they could throw punches that missed by several inches but (on film) looked like direct hits with the proper reaction. Post-production editing and sound effects further enhanced these fights. By the late 1940s Jock Mahoney emphasized timing in fight scenes and was able to believably and safely fight multiple opponents coming at him from all angles. Canutt became a pioneer in designing stunt equipment and rigging that made stunts safer and easier. Horses were trained to fall rather than forced to fall. Canutt passed this knowledge down, and his innovations became industry standards.

Early stuntmen often took pride in the punishment their bodies could withstand, but the smartest realized that by padding sensitive areas they could repeat stunts that day and the next while being paid accordingly. It was impossible to earn money from a hospital bed. With better pay, elite athletes were attracted to the industry and began to replace the aging cowboys and boxers. By the late 1930s stunt performers began to unite regarding studio insurance policies and pay rates. Several bonded together, calling themselves the "Cousins." A common practice of the day was for assistant directors to simply promote inexperienced "bump men" from the ranks of extras to enact tough action scenes. Qualified stunt experts argued that this practice was inviting injury and costly reshoots for inferior action. The experienced stunt performers eventually prevailed but things weren't changed overnight.

Ultimately this cohesiveness resulted in the formation of the Stuntmen's Association of Motion Pictures in the early 1960s. This fraternal organization bonded together the top one hundred or so stuntmen to deal with the studios and primarily hire within their own ranks utilizing a stunt coordinator as opposed to the traditional assistant director or production manager. In 1967 the Stuntwomen's Association emerged as a logical offshoot, not only to represent the females but to guard against the practice of men doubling qualified women for the toughest action scenes. Soon to follow was the Black Stuntmen's Association representing minority talent and ending the controversial practice of "paint downs" where white stuntmen were put in dark makeup for doubling assignments.

In the late 1960s there was a federal crackdown on television violence. The networks minimized on-screen action, putting many in the unemployment line. This coincided with the decline of the western. Stunt performers were forced to learn new skills or lose their livelihood. Many of the older cowboy stuntmen retired as a new breed of cross-trained stuntmen emerged. Hal Needham, Ronnie Rondell, and Glenn Wilder started Stunts Unlimited with some of the top young stunt talent available. The old guard of the Stuntmen's Association was not happy and there was much political infighting, but eventually the groups ironed out their differences and began to work side by side.

The 1970s saw the profession blossom. The stunt-filled disaster epics *The Poseidon Adventure* (1972), *The Towering Inferno* (1974), and *Earthquake* (1974) as well as Burt Reynolds car-crash pictures such as *Smokey and the Bandit* (1977) dominated at the box office. Stuntmen and -women finally began to receive screen credit with *The Master Gunfighter* (1975), and names such as Hal Needham and Dar Robinson entered the realm of celebrity. The movies *Stunts* (1977), *Hooper* (1978), and *The Stunt Man* (1980) began to lift the illusion of stunt work as the profession reached a peak of public interest. Low-budget action films *Hollywood Man* (1976), *Black Oak Conspiracy* (1977), and *Texas Detour* (1978) featured lead characters who were movie stuntmen. Stunt competitions and specials aired regularly on network television. Pilot films for the prospective series *Stunt Seven* (1979) and *Stunts Unlimited* (1980) featured stuntmen as crime-fighting heroes. The Lee Majors television series *The Fall Guy* (1981–1986) enjoyed great popularity with its stuntman turned bounty hunter protagonist.

Change was in the air. The great interest in stunting caused a migration to Hollywood of would-be stunt performers, thoroughly watering down an already rapidly growing profession. Regional stunt organizations popped up around the country, as did training centers. Thousands began to call themselves professional stunt personnel without the appropriate background or expertise. The once small, tight-knit cluster of specialists now had to compete with daredevils trying to make a name for themselves and who were willing to try stunts for less than the established rate. Airbags replaced cardboard boxes as the landing spot in high-fall scenes; this meant that people could attempt jumps from hundreds of feet in the air at dangerously increased acceleration. More accidents and fatalities occurred. Self-promotion became the standard. The widespread use of drugs on Hollywood sets further threatened established safety measures.

The entire filmmaking process began to shift in the 1980s toward a fast-cut MTV-influenced style of filmmaking where the viewer is bombarded with rapid images that appear to be singular action. Stunts and fight scenes were rarely shown in their entirety, lessening the overall impressiveness of the stunt performance. The emergence of wire work, computer graphics, and digital effects threatened the stunt professional's livelihood. Now a stunt didn't even need to be performed for it to appear as if it had. Rugged location work was replaced with green screen technology. Unfortunately, the action presented is often extreme and cartoon-like in its non-believability. The digital invasion remains a work in progress.

For this book, effort has been made to track down the whereabouts or final destination of as many stunt performers as possible from the golden era of the silent films to the 1970s. Obviously not everyone who worked on a movie or television show is traceable. It was not an uncommon practice to use "stage" or professional names for the business, which makes finding biographical information difficult or next to impossible. In addition, many stuntwomen changed surnames with marriage, further clouding the trail. Some actors and actresses received their start in the industry as stunt performers and are present here as abbreviated entries. Also included for the sake of interest are a handful of stars that were reputed by the press or themselves to do their own stunts. Some of them were highly capable athletes who were only kept from doing all their own stunts by strong studio insurance policies. Effort is made to clear up what they did and did not do on screen.

Some stunt performers worked on hundreds of productions between film and television and there is no way to track down every credit. The truth is that would be difficult for the performers themselves, who may have been brought in for a day or two of work and sometimes didn't know who they were doubling let alone the title of the production. Credits shall reflect those films and television shows that are considered "action-heavy" or otherwise prestigious. B-westerns and lesser regarded serials will be mentioned but not discussed to any great degree. I would recommend Chuck Anderson's Old Corral website, Boyd Magers' *Western Clippings,* and the serial sites of Todd Gault and Jerry Blake for a more detailed view of these. Mention of a few early 1980s titles will be included for established performers, specifically those that began production in the late 1970s or are a throwback to an earlier era such as James Bond films, sequels, and the stunt-heavy television series *The Fall Guy.*

STUNT PERFORMERS

ART ACORD (1890–1931)

One of the industry's original pioneering stuntmen, 6'1" 185-pound Artemus Ward Acord came to motion pictures with the Bison Company after time with the Miller Brothers 101 Wild West Show. His experience as a cowboy on ranches in his native Utah aided his horsemanship for early films such as *Pride of the Range* (1910), *Two Brothers* (1910), and *The Invaders* (1912). On these he worked alongside his pal Hoot Gibson. Both concurrently had success on the rodeo circuit, with Acord winning the 1912 World Championship in bulldogging. In *The Squaw Man* (1914), Acord took part in what is believed to be the first filmed saloon brawl.

Acord was awarded the Croix de Guerre for bravery while serving with the U.S. Army during World War I. Upon returning to Hollywood he became one of the top silent picture cowboy stars at Universal Studios, occasionally under the moniker Buck Parvin. He had a clause in his contract that stipulated that no stunt double was to be used unless it was a stunt he had failed to perform. His fame did not carry over into the talkies and his reputation for heavy drinking and hellraising burned many professional bridges. He found himself mining in Chihuahua, Mexico, in the early 1930s. It was there that he died at the age of 40 of what was determined by authorities to be a suicidal ingestion of poison.

See: McKinney, Grange B. *Art Acord and the Movies*. Raleigh, NC: Wyatt Classics, 2000; Whitton, Douglas. "Mystery of Art Acord." *Favorite Westerns.* #10, April 1983.

PHIL ADAMS (1936–)

Phil Adams was born Philip Charles Granucci in Los Angeles. He used his mother's maiden name in pictures so he could be billed higher in cast lists. An athlete at John Burroughs High in Burbank, the 5'10" 160-pound Adams served in the U.S. Army and modeled for physique portraits. He is best known as one of the toughs confronting Sidney Poitier in *In the Heat of the Night* (1967) and as the "Disco Tarzan" character in *Thank God It's Friday* (1977). Adams doubled William Shatner and guest star Michael Pataki on the original *Star Trek* TV series, as well as Tom Laughlin in *The Trial of Billy Jack* (1974). War films dominate his credits.

He worked on *Lafayette Escadrille* (1958), *Darby's Rangers* (1958), *Battle of the Coral Sea* (1959), *Tobruk* (1967), *First to Fight* (1967), *The Green Berets* (1968), *Ice Station Zebra* (1968), *Hello, Dolly!* (1969), *Che!* (1969), *The Great Bank Robbery* (1969), *Tora! Tora! Tora!* (1970), *Catch 22* (1970), *Kelly's Heroes* (1970), *The Phynx* (1970), *Buck and the Preacher* (1972), *The Poseidon Adventure* (1972), *The Don Is Dead* (1973), *Freebie and the Bean* (1974), *Black Samson* (1974), *The Godfather Part II* (1974), *Day of the Locust* (1975), *Logan's Run* (1976), *Stunts* (1977), *Speedtrap* (1977), *Texas Detour* (1978), and *The Stunt Man* (1980). TV credits include *Alfred Hitchcock, McHale's Navy, Twelve O'Clock High,* and *The Invaders.* He is a member of the Stuntmen's Association.

BUDD ALBRIGHT (1936–)

Six foot, 160-pound Forrest Edwards Albright was born in Elkhart, Indiana. He was a diver at Willoughby High in Cleveland, Ohio, and after graduation he settled in Los Angeles where he worked at a Vic Tanny gym. Budd was a film and TV extra while starting the band the Exciters with actor Steve Rowland. Early jobs were photo doubling Warren Beatty and Robert Vaughn. On weekends he hung out with a group of dirt-biking stuntmen and was soon accepted as one of them. The movie *What Did You Do in the War, Daddy?* (1966) put Albright and other young stuntmen on the map, and he worked in many war films that followed. A high fall specialist, he rappelled and performed a double fall with Tony Brubaker on *Tobruk* (1967). On TV Albright doubled Christopher George on *The Rat Patrol* (1966–68) and Robert Wagner on *It Takes a Thief* (1968–70).

His other credits include *Spartacus* (1960), *Little Shepherd of Kingdom Come* (1961), *Palm Springs Weekend* (1963), *Beau Geste* (1966), *First to Fight* (1967), *Ice Station Zebra* (1968), *The Devil's Brigade* (1968), *Lonely Profession* (1969), *Patton* (1970), *There Was a Crooked Man...* (1970), and *Drive Hard, Drive Fast* (1973). TV credits include *Star Trek, Ironside, Outcasts, Bearcats, McCloud,* and *Name of the Game.* For two years he was the Belair Man in cigarette ads. Albright ended his stunt career in 1974 to pursue other interests, among them competitive car, boat, and bicycle racing.

See: Rowland, Steve. *Hollywood Heat.* Sussex, England: Book Guild, 2008; www.budd albright.com.

GILLIAN ALDAM

The first female to join the British Stunt Registry, 5'4" Gillian Aldam was a trapeze performer in the circus and specialized in aerial work. She was brought into the stunt business by Frank Maher. Aldam doubled Mary Ure descending a castle wall on *Where Eagles Dare* (1968) and worked throughout the James Bond franchise. Credits include *The Pink Panther* (1963), *Fahrenheit 451* (1966), *Casino Royale* (1967), *Witchfinder General* (1968), *The Wrecking Crew* (1969), *On Her Majesty's Secret Service* (1969), *The Looking Glass War* (1969), *Zeta One* (1969), *To Catch a Spy* (1971), *The Man with the Golden Gun* (1974), *The Eagle Has Landed* (1976), *The Spy Who Loved Me* (1977), *For Your Eyes Only* (1981), *A View to a Kill* (1985), and TV's *Danger Man* and *Secret Agent.*

See: Random, Eric. "Stunt Girl." *Photoplay.* July 1965.

ERIC ALDEN (1908–1962)

Eric Alden was born Franklin A. Almstead in Alameda County, California. He juggled athletics with an engineering degree from the Massachusetts Institute of Technology. Alden began as an actor but gravitated toward higher-paying stunt work. The husky (210-pound) Alden was a top fencer, doubling Basil Rathbone on *The Court Jester* (1956). Famed producer-director Cecil B. DeMille employed him on *North West Mounted Police* (1940), *Unconquered* (1947), *Samson and Delilah* (1949), *The Greatest Show on Earth* (1952),

The Ten Commandments (1956), and *The Buccaneer* (1958).

He also worked on *Hell Divers* (1931), *Gone with the Wind* (1939), *Seven Sinners* (1940), *Reap the Wild Wind* (1942), *The Spanish Main* (1945), *Monsieur Beaucaire* (1946), *The Perils of Pauline* (1947), *Joan of Arc* (1948), *Adventures of Don Juan* (1948), *Whispering Smith* (1948), *The Paleface* (1948), *At Sword's Point* (1952), *The Prisoner of Zenda* (1952), *Pony Express* (1953), *The War of the Worlds* (1953), *Arrowhead* (1953), *Casanova's Big Night* (1954), *Showdown at Abilene* (1956), *Omar Khayyam* (1957), *The Jayhawkers!* (1959), and *Last Train from Gun Hill* (1959). TV credits include *The Lone Ranger, Zorro, The Rebel,* and *Have Gun—Will Travel.* Alden died at the age of 53.

GENE ALSACE (1902–1967)

Colorado-born Gene Alsace entered films as an athletic trainer for MGM where he tightened the physiques of stars such as Joan Crawford. He did stunts for the studio, nearly losing his life in a filmed shipwreck off the coast of La Jolla in 1927. A former rodeo roper and horse specialist, Alsace was B-western star Tim McCoy's double and used the name Buck Coburn to play the lead in *Gunsmoke* (1935). It was his lone shot at stardom. Alsace returned to anonymous stunt work on *Captain Blood* (1935), *Adventures of Red Ryder* (1940), and *Texas* (1941). By 1944 he changed his name professionally to Rocky Camron, a variation on his birth name of Rockford Camron. The name change failed to elevate his career beyond B-western bits and stunts. Alsace died at the age of 64.

See: "Overheard in Hollywood." *San Antonio Express.* November 1, 1935; "Stunt Man Injured in Film Shipwreck." *Evening Tribune.* August 15, 1927.

ROD AMATEAU (1923–2003)

Rodney Amateau was born in New York City and moved to California in his teens. He entered films as a stuntman after World War II Army service, most notably doubling Mildred Dunnock being pushed down the stairs in her wheelchair on *Kiss of Death* (1947). Amateau doubled women in addition to short actors such as James Cagney, Edward G. Robinson, and Alan Ladd. He doubled Blake Edwards on *Leather Gloves* (1947),

Humphrey Bogart on *In a Lonely Place* (1950), and James Dean on *Rebel Without a Cause* (1955); in the latter, he took part in the knife fight and car sequences. He stunted on *Mighty Joe Young* (1949).

Amateau began writing, producing, and directing, including the western *The Bushwhackers* (1952), and was second unit director on several Henry Hathaway and Sam Peckinpah films. He directed the action sequences on *The Wilby Conspiracy* (1975) and continued working as a stunt coordinator on low-budget features. He was a producer and occasional director on the car crash–heavy TV series *The Dukes of Hazzard* (1979–85) on which his son J.P. Amateau was a stuntman. Amateau died from a cerebral hemorrhage at the age of 79.

See: McLellan, Dennis. "Rod Amateau, 79, Writer, Director, Producer of Sitcoms, Feature Films." *Los Angeles Times.* July 2, 2003.

TONY AMATO (1929–)

Professional boxer Tony "Wildcat" Amato was born in Guttenberg, New Jersey. At Fort Dix he won the First Army Middleweight Championship and he was sparring partner to light heavyweight champion Joey Maxim. As a professional, Amato amassed a record of 22–20–2 but his career ended due to a mild case of polio. After working as a longshoreman, Amato became a fight specialist stuntman on the New York City–filmed TV shows *Car 54*, *Naked City*, *The Defenders*, and *Hawk*. The last assignment led to bodyguard work for Burt Reynolds.

He worked on *How to Murder Your Wife* (1965), *A Lovely Way to Die* (1968), *The Detective* (1968), *What's So Bad About Feeling Good?* (1968), *Stiletto* (1969), *The Gang That Couldn't Shoot Straight* (1971), *The French Connection* (1971), *The Godfather* (1972), *The Valachi Papers* (1972), *Shamus* (1973), *The Godfather Part II* (1974), *King of the Gypsies* (1978), and *Superman* (1978). Amato has been inducted into the New Jersey Boxing Hall of Fame.

See: "Ex-Boxer Enjoying Life as Stunt-Man in Films." *Calgary Herald.* June 10, 1969; www.NJboxinghof.org.

BOB ANDERSON (1922–2012)

Robert James Gilbert Anderson was born in Gosport, Hampshire, England. He served in the Royal Marines during World War II, taught physical training, and was proficient in judo and gymnastics. He also took up fencing, becoming inter-service champion in the foil, epee, and saber. He was crowned British National and European Champ, earning a spot as an Olympic fencer for the 1952 Helsinki Games. The 6'1" Anderson trained Stewart Granger for *Scaramouche* (1952) and was hired for *The Master of Ballantrae* (1953), where he doubled Errol Flynn. He accidentally wounded Flynn in the thigh, but Flynn took responsibility. He worked with Flynn again on *Crossed Swords* (1954) and went on to train many other actors, from David Niven to Michael Caine. He was sword master for the National Shakespeare Theatre throughout the 1970s and coached Great Britain's National Fencing Team.

Anderson expanded his repertoire to become an all-around stuntman, performing a high fall on *From Russia with Love* (1963) and taking a spear hit for Charlton Heston on *Khartoum* (1966). He doubled Darth Vader and arranged the light saber fights with Peter Diamond on *Star Wars* (1977), *The Empire Strikes Back* (1980), and *Return of the Jedi* (1983). He doubled Sean Connery on *Highlander* (1986) and additionally worked on *Moonraker* (1958), *The Guns of Navarone* (1961), *Casino Royale* (1967), *Kidnapped* (1971), *Barry Lyndon* (1975), *One of Our Dinosaurs Is Missing* (1975), *Candleshoe* (1977), and *Superman II* (1980). TV credits include *Count of Monte Cristo*, *Secret Agent*, *Doctor Who*, and *The Protectors*. Even into his eighties he was still working on the *Lord of the Rings* and *Pirates of the Caribbean* films. Anderson died at the age of 89.

See: Ivie, Martin. "Bob Anderson: The Silver Blade." *Inside Stunts.* Fall, 2004; Murray, Will. "Duel Roles." *Starlog.* July 1998. Weber, Bruce. "Bob Anderson, Sword Master, Dies at 89." *New York Times.* January 2, 2012.

CARL ANDRE (1905–1972)

Carl Pierre Andre was born in France and raised in West Virginia, where the 180-pound six footer played football and basketball for Fairmont High. He turned down an athletic scholarship to study dentistry at the University of Maryland, where he was intercollegiate boxing champ. He began a dental practice in California, but was recruited to double Fredric March on *The Dark Angel* (1935). Andre liked the film business and found work as a wrangler, stand-in, and horseback double, working for several years with Joel Mc-Crea and Randolph Scott. His wife Claire also did stunts.

He worked on *Stella Dallas* (1937), *Three Blind Mice* (1938), *Sullivan's Travels* (1942), *Buffalo Bill* (1944), *O.S.S.* (1946), *The Paleface* (1948), *Samson and Delilah* (1949), *Dallas* (1950), *Colt .45* (1950), *Branded* (1950), *Warpath* (1951), *Fort Worth* (1951), *Carson City* (1952), *The World in His Arms* (1952), *Son of Paleface* (1952), *The Duel at Silver Creek* (1952), *Gunsmoke* (1953), *Law and Order* (1953), *The Great Sioux Uprising* (1953), *The Charge at Feather River* (1953), *The Man from the Alamo* (1953), *Thunder Over the Plains* (1953), *Siege at Red River* (1954), *They Rode West* (1954), *Dawn at Socorro* (1954), *Yellow Mountain* (1954), *The Violent Men* (1955), *Strange Lady in Town* (1955), *Man Without a Star* (1955), *Tall Man Riding* (1955), *The Rawhide Years* (1955), and *Three Violent People* (1956). Andre died at the age of 67.

See: Braden, Jerry. "Movie Stars Visiting Relatives Here." *Charleston Gazette.* January 19, 1953; "Dr. Andre Is Called Man of 1,000 Faces." *Charleston Daily Mail.* August 14, 1938.

DOROTHY ANDRE (1913–2002)

Horsewoman Dorothy Andre doubled Olivia de Havilland on *The Adventures of Robin Hood* (1938) and Dale Evans on TV's *The Roy Rogers Show* (1951–57). (Ironically she was riding Rogers' horse Trigger on *Robin Hood*.) She had a background in vaudeville. Her aunt Opal Ernie performed stunts, aiding Dorothy's entry into the profession. She worked on *The Great Gatsby* (1949), *Samson and Delilah* (1949), *Cattle Queen of Montana* (1954), *Santa Fe Passage* (1955), *The Ten Commandments* (1956), and *The Spiral Road* (1962). TV credits include *Wagon Train* and *June Allyson*. She switched from stunts to hairstyling, winning an Emmy Award.

See: Morse, Alice. "Local Stunt Woman Tells Love of Work." *Van Nuys News.* April 29, 1960.

PAT ANTHONY (1924–)

Cleveland, Ohio–born circus performer Pat Anthony specialized in wrestling exotic animals on screen. During World War II he was a combat jumper with the 11th Airborne Division. He got his start working with animals at the World Jungle Compound in Thousand Oaks, California, where he came to the attention of Hollywood. Anthony stood in for Victor Mature wrestling a lion on *Samson and Delilah* (1949), captured a tiger on *The Greatest Show on Earth* (1952), fought a wild hyena for Gregory Peck on *The Snows of Kilimanjaro* (1952), and doubled Robert Mitchum tangling with a mountain lion on *River of No Return* (1954). On Johnny Weissmuller's Jungle Jim films he suffered a serious mauling from a leopard. He left films in 1954 to tour with various circuses.

See: Biffle, Kent. "Cat Man Stitched Like Circus Tent." *Dallas Morning News.* March 26, 1964.

FRITZ APKING (1927–2006)

At 6'4" and 215 pounds, Fritz Apking had the distinction of physically being one of the biggest stuntmen in Hollywood. The Ohio-born Apking was quite agile for his size, having stood out as an athlete (football, basketball, track, and baseball) at Cincinnati's Reading High. After U.S Army service, Apking had a stellar football career at the University of Washington. The colorful Apking was rated as one of the best ends in the country, but he turned down a pro offer from the San Francisco 49ers to try his luck in Hollywood. He found the easiest path was utilizing his athletic skills to double tall actors such as Rock Hudson, Charlton Heston, Sterling Hayden, Vincent Price, Fess Parker, and George Kennedy in action scenes.

Apking landed an early break when he doubled Phil Carey for football scenes on John Ford's *The Long Gray Line* (1955). Ford was so impressed by Apking's toughness that he rewarded him with an acting part on *Mister Roberts* (1955). Apking was asked by the studio to change his name, so he opted to go by Fritz Ford in honor of the director who gave him his big break. He had one of his best roles as a heavy on the western *Revolt at Fort Laramie* (1957), a film highlighted by a fine fight with actor Robert Keys. On *Tomahawk Trail* (1957) Apking met Chuck Connors, a 6'5" former professional baseball and basketball player. Connors requested that Apking double him through the duration of his popular TV series *The Rifleman* (1958–63). This led to a working relationship that lasted more than twenty-five years as Apking served as his friend's regular stand-in and double. The highlight of their association was an extended fight in the 1962 *Rifleman* episode "I Take This Woman." One of Apking's most impressive stunts came on the World War II film *Bridge at Remagen* (1969), filmed in Prague. Apking, Hal Needham, and Gary McLarty were blown off a bridge into the River Moldau with a thousand-pound horse. Apking's stunt work tapered off with age, but he remained visible as a bit actor.

He worked on *The Desert Rats* (1953), *Gun*

Lion tamer Pat Anthony doubles Victor Mature on *Samson and Delilah* (1949).

Fury (1953), *Secret of the Incas* (1954), *Dangerous Mission* (1954), *Seminole Uprising* (1955), *Timberjack* (1955), *Onionhead* (1958), *Wreck of the Mary Deare* (1959), *The Big Operator* (1959), *Hell Is for Heroes* (1962), *Stage to Thunder Rock* (1964), *Tobruk* (1967), *Planet of the Apes* (1968), *Beneath the Planet of the Apes* (1970), *The Last Movie* (1971), *Soylent Green* (1973), *Doc Savage* (1975), and *F.I.S.T.* (1978). TV credits include *Annie Oakley, Zane Grey, Have Gun—Will Travel, Wagon Train, Death Valley Days, Batman, Hondo, I Spy, Felony Squad, The Rockford Files,* and *The Six Million Dollar Man.* Apking passed away at the age of 78.

See: Erardi, John. "Unknown Stuntman." *Cincinnati Enquirer.* December 2, 2001; Goodman, Rebecca. "Fred Apking Took Risks for a Living." *Cincinnati Enquirer.* September 1, 2006; Radcliffe, E.B. "Another Local Boy Makes Good." *Cincinnati Enquirer.* February 26, 1955.

RICHARD ARLEN
(1899–1976)

Leading man Richard Arlen did much of his own flying in the aviation classic *Wings* (1927), save for the daredevil dogfights and crack-ups that were executed by Dick Grace. Arlen played a stunt pilot on *Sky Bride* (1932), a boxer on *Leather Pushers* (1940), and a stunt driver on *Speed to Spare* (1948), examples of the many minor action flicks he headlined. Arlen had flown with the Royal Canadian Flying Corps in World War I, and during World War II was a flight instructor for the U.S. Air Force. Born in St. Paul, Minnesota, as Sylvanus Richard Van Mattimore, the 5'11", 160-pound Arlen spent time with the St. Paul Athletic Club as an amateur boxer and toiled in the oilfields of Oklahoma and Texas.

Arlen entered pictures as a double in a scene involving a Leatrice Joy car stunt on *Moonlighter* (1922). He got that job because he'd been working as a motorcycle messenger and was hit by a truck in front of the Paramount gates. A producer witnessed the accident and thought he'd make a good stuntman once his broken leg healed. Stuntmen included him in their "Devil May Care Club," voting Arlen as the star who threw the hardest movie punch. His best screen fights came on *Gun Smoke* (1931), *Let 'Em Have It* (1935), and *Wildcat* (1942) with Buster Crabbe. As an actor, he was proud of doing his own stunts and thought that asking for

a double in fight scenes demonstrated weakness. Arlen died from emphysema at the age of 76.

See: Bacon, James. "Arlen Upset Over Stars Virility Lack." *Milwaukee Sentinel.* October 3, 1956; "Best Film Puncher Title Goes to Arlen." *Pittsburgh Post-Gazette.* June 8, 1942; Brownlow, Kevin. *The Parade's Gone By.* Berkeley, Ca: University of California, 1968.

VIC ARMSTRONG (1946–)

Legendary British stuntman Vic Armstrong is best known for doubling Harrison Ford on *Raiders of the Lost Ark* (1981), *Indiana Jones and the Temple of Doom* (1984), and *Indiana Jones and the Lost Crusade* (1989). A side jump off a horse onto a tank on the latter film is regarded as one of filmdom's greatest leaps. Armstrong has the distinction of doubling three different James Bonds, performing action for George Lazenby on *On Her Majesty's Secret Service* (1969), Roger Moore on *Live and Let Die* (1973), and Sean Connery on *Never Say Never Again* (1983). He also doubled Christopher Reeve on *Superman* (1978) and *Superman II* (1980).

Victor Monroe Armstrong was born in Farnham Common, Buckinghamshire, England. His dad trained horses for the Olympic teams, and Armstrong became a jockey. He outgrew that vocation (eventually standing 6'1" and weighing 200 pounds) but was recruited to double Gregory Peck for a horse jump on *Arabesque* (1966). He was the first ninja to enter the volcano by rope on *You Only Live Twice* (1967). By the time he jumped out of a helicopter onto a hillside for Malcolm McDowell on *Figures in a Landscape* (1970), he was regarded as one of Britain's top stuntmen. Hailed by the Guinness Book of Records as the world's most prolific stunt double, he subbed for Jon Voight on *The Odessa File* (1974), George Segal and Ryan O'Neal on *A Bridge Too Far* (1977), Donald Sutherland on *Bear Island* (1979), and Timothy Dalton on *Flash Gordon* (1980).

Armstrong performed a hundred-foot fall off a viaduct on *Omen III: The Final Conflict* (1981). A year later he invented a fan-descender for a higher fall on *Green Ice* (1981). Adapted from military equipment, the descender slowed a fall and allowed stunt performers to safely jump from heights previously thought unattainable. The equipment revolutionized the way high falls were done. On *Never Say Never Again* (1983) he took a horse forty feet off a cliff into water, having spent weeks training the horse where to swim to safety. Armstrong married stuntwoman Wendy Leech, daughter of veteran stuntman George Leech. His brother Andy Armstrong is another noted stuntman.

Other credits include *Chitty Chitty Bang Bang* (1968), *Assassination Bureau* (1969), *Alfred the Great* (1969), *Ryan's Daughter* (1970), *When Eight Bells Toll* (1971), *Macbeth* (1971), *Mary, Queen of Scots* (1971), *Young Winston* (1972), *A Touch of Class* (1973), *Billy Two Hats* (1974), *Hennessy* (1975), *The Omen* (1976), *Return of a Man Called Horse* (1976), and *Escape to Athena* (1979). A member of the Stuntmen's Hall of Fame, he was stunt coordinator and second unit director on a number of later Bond films and must be included in any discussion of the all-time greats.

See: Armstrong, Vic, & Robert Sellers. *The True Adventures of the World's Greatest Stuntman.* London: Titan, 2012; Ross, John. "Vic Armstrong: An Original International Stuntman." *Inside Stunts.* Fall, 2005; www.vicarmstrong.com.

JAMES ARNETT

Colorado native M. James Arnett was Paul Newman's double for fifteen years, including on *Cool Hand Luke* (1967). He was stunt coordinator for the comic whorehouse shootout that saw stuntmen flying out all the windows on *The Life and Times of Judge Roy Bean* (1972). Arnett injured himself taking a fall on *Butch Cassidy and the Sundance Kid* (1969), likely preventing him from being one of the doubles for the iconic cliff jump. A college graduate with a degree in petroleum engineering, Arnett was one of the first coordinators and second unit directors to use computers to figure out complicated stunts.

He also worked on *WUSA* (1970), *Little Big Man* (1970), *Sometimes a Great Notion* (1970), *They Might Be Giants* (1971), *Pocket Money* (1972), *Sleeper* (1973), *The Mackintosh Man* (1973), *The Towering Inferno* (1974), *The Man Who Would Be King* (1975), *Jackson County Jail* (1976), *Airport '77* (1977), *Foul Play* (1978), *Delta Fox* (1978), *Steel* (1979), and *Smokey and the Bandit 2* (1980). TV credits include *Voyage to the Bottom of the Sea.* A member of Stunts Unlimited, his son Seth became a stuntman.

See: "Movie *Gas* Uses Stunts Rarely Ever Utilized." *Leader Post.* July 26, 1980.

DENNY ARNOLD
(1934–2001)

Dint "Denny" Arnold was born in Calgary, Alberta, Canada, and raised in Texas. Six feet tall and 190 pounds, he played running back and receiver for the University of Mississippi and briefly entered the NFL. A knee injury ended his football career. From there he tackled the pro rodeo circuit, becoming a champion bull rider and lifetime member of the Rodeo Cowboy Association. In 1966 he got his jaw broken after being kicked by a bull, leading him into films full-time. Arnold doubled Joe Don Baker, Johnny Cash, Ben Murphy, Reb Brown, Dan Haggerty, and Dick Butkus. He specialized in air rams and ratchets and performed a record long boat jump through an obstacle on *Gator* (1976).

He worked on *The Comancheros* (1961), *Return of the Seven* (1966), *Bullitt* (1968), *The Wild Bunch* (1969), *The Undefeated* (1969), *The Stalking Moon* (1969), *Support Your Local Sheriff* (1969), *A Time for Dying* (1969), *There Was a Crooked Man...* (1970), *Little Big Man* (1970), *Beneath the Planet of the Apes* (1970), *Big Jake* (1971), *The Omega Man* (1971), *A Gunfight* (1971), *The Culpepper Cattle Co.* (1972), *Conquest of the Planet of the Apes* (1972), *Magnificent Seven Ride* (1972), *Junior Bonner* (1972), *Soylent Green* (1973), *The Train Robbers* (1973), *The Stone Killer* (1973), *The Parallax View* (1974), *The Longest Yard* (1974), *McQ* (1974), *Chinatown* (1974), *Blazing Saddles* (1974), *Three the Hard Way* (1974), *Doc Savage* (1975), *The Hindenburg* (1975), *A Boy and His Dog* (1975), *W.W. and the Dixie Dance Kings* (1975), *Mother, Jugs, and Speed* (1976), *Vigilante Force* (1976), *Two-Minute Warning* (1976), *The Shootist* (1976), *Bound for Glory* (1976), *Gable and Lombard* (1976), *Hawmps!* (1976), *Close Encounters of the Third Kind* (1977), *Big Wednesday* (1978), *Blue Collar* (1978), *Apocalypse Now* (1979), *Prophecy* (1979), and *The Nude Bomb* (1980). TV credits include *High Chaparral, Bonanza, The FBI, Mod Squad, Adam–12, Alias Smith and Jones, Banacek, Hec Ramsey, Columbo, The Rookies, Gunsmoke, Kolchak: The Night Stalker, McCloud, The Six Million Dollar Man, Police Story, Kojak, Wonder Woman, Grizzly Adams, Baretta, Starsky and Hutch, The Incredible Hulk, BJ and the Bear, Vega$, Buck Rogers,* and *CHiPs.* The first Canadian inducted into the Stuntmen's Hall of Fame,

Arnold died at the age of 67 from a blood infection.

See: Cardwell, Jewel. "Denny Arnold Takes His Job on the Chin." *Advocate*. September 28, 1979; "He Flirts with Death as the Cameras Grind." *Bulletin*. November 17, 1980; www.snowcrest.net.

RICK ARNOLD

Rick Arnold worked as a stuntman for twenty-five years. The native Californian (6', 160 pounds) befriended Robert Fuller while serving with the U.S. Army in Korea. He was hired to double Fuller on the TV series *Laramie* (1959–63) and *Wagon Train* (1963–65) and the film *Incident at Phantom Hill* (1966), despite the fact Fuller often performed the bulk of his own stunt work. Noted for his jumping ability, Arnold also worked on *The Black Whip* (1956), *How the West Was Won* (1962), *Ballad of a Gunfighter* (1964), *Jeremiah Johnson* (1972), *Joe Kidd* (1972), and *Earthquake* (1974). TV credits include *Rawhide, Gunsmoke, The Virginian,* and *Laredo*. Arnold put together several charity stunt shows and toured with Lenny Geer's western variety show. A member of the Stuntmen's Association, he became a Teamster driver.

RAY AUSTIN (1932–)

London-born Ray Austin is best known for his work as a stunt arranger on the TV series *The Avengers* (1961–69) and *The Saint* (1962–69). He came to the States in the 1950s after two years in the British Army as a physical training instructor during the Korean War. He was Cary Grant's chauffeur and bodyguard, and Grant introduced him to stuntman Dave Sharpe. This led to stunt work on *North by Northwest* (1959), *Operation Petticoat* (1959), and *Spartacus* (1960) as well as the TV shows *Highway Patrol, Have Gun—Will Travel,* and *Peter Gunn*. When he returned to England, Austin worked on the TV series *Ivanhoe* and the films *Cleopatra* (1963), *Tarzan's Three Challenges* (1963), *Tom Jones* (1963) and *The Dirty Dozen* (1967). Back in the States, he became a prolific television director on shows such as *Magnum P.I.*

See: Murray, James. "Action Austin." *Cinefantastique*. July 1998; Noble, Peter. "From Chauffeur to Helmsman." *Screen International*. October 10, 1981; www.raymondaustin.com.

BILL BABCOCK (1927–)

New York–born "Wild" Bill Babcock was raised on a dairy farm. He served with the Army Air Force during World War II and as a Marine Corps frogman during the Korean War. Between wars he was a policeman, a cowboy, and a stuntman at Republic Studios. Babcock got his first break standing in for Roy Rogers. He joined the Rodeo Cowboy Association and spent four years at Corriganville as a trick rider with his horse Thunder. His stunt specialty was the Russian Cossack Death Drag. In 1959 he toured with Bob McCaw's Cavalcade recreating famous movie stunts such as the *Ben-Hur* chariot race. He worked on *Run Silent, Run Deep* (1958), *The Big Country* (1958), *Rio Bravo* (1959), *The Alamo* (1960), *The Misfits* (1961), *The Sons of Katie Elder* (1965), and *Big Jake* (1971). TV credits include *Roy Rogers, Gene Autry,* and *The Lone Ranger*.

See: Scott, Bob. "Looking Back on a Wild Past." *Journal & Courier*. November 28, 2007; www.ourbrowncounty.com.

FRANK BABICH (1934–)

Minnesota-born Frank R. Babich was working on his doctorate as a research psychologist at UCLA, doing groundbreaking RNA work with rodents and the chemical transfer of knowledge, when he began movie extra work. At the time he and his family were broke and applying for new grants, so movies helped fund studies that had already seen him published in *Science* magazine. Extra work led to action jobs on *Beau Geste* (1966) and *Tobruk* (1967). Ironically, given his research subject, he was attached to the stunt-heavy TV series *The Rat Patrol* (1966–68) as a stuntman for star Christopher George. Babich broke ribs performing a dive into the ocean on the show while shooting in Spain. He continued stunting on the TV shows *The Man from U.N.C.L.E., The Green Hornet, Star Trek,* and *Voyage to the Bottom of the Sea,* retiring from his profitable sideline after *Barquero* (1970) when a clamping down on screen violence made stunt work scarce.

See: McIntyre, Dave. "Extra Finds Fame." *Bakersfield Californian*. February 14, 1966; Rosser, Jenny. "Hog Lagoons, Land Deals New Dives for Ex-Stuntman." *Triangle Business Journal*. July 17, 2000; "UCLA Researcher Is Film Extra Here." *Yuma Daily Sun*. January 9, 1966.

CHUCK BAIL (1936–)

Charles Bail was born in the steel city of Pittsburgh, Pennsylvania, and had an after-school job stabling horses. He joined the U.S. Navy during the Korean War. He was a competitive boxer and swimmer and dabbled as a rodeo cowboy. In 1956 he worked for a Wild West show in the Orient as a bronc rider, trick roper, and archery specialist. It was there he met stuntmen Bill and Chuck Couch. After the show went bust, he ended up in Los Angeles as a TV extra on *Wagon Train*. He talked Reg Parton into giving him a stunt job on *The Texan* (1958–60) and never looked back. On TV Bail doubled Tom Tryon on *Texas John Slaughter* (1958–61), Robert Bray on *Stagecoach West* (1960–61), Max Baer, Jr., on *The Beverly Hillbillies* (1962–71), Peter Breck on *The Big Valley* (1965–69), and John Ericson on *Honey West* (1965–66). On the big screen he doubled Fess Parker on *The Jayhawkers!*

(1959), Tony Young on *Taggart* (1964), and Jim Hutton on *The Hallelujah Trail* (1965) and *The Green Berets* (1968). Bail stood 6'4" and weighed 230.

Bail worked in the low-budget motorcycle genre on *Hells Angels on Wheels* (1967) and *Savage Seven* (1968), where he met director Richard Rush. He gained experience as a second unit director on *Freebie and the Bean* (1974). Bail's contemporary Hal Needham is often credited with being the first stuntman to find success as a film director with *Smokey and the Bandit* (1977), but Bail actually beat him to it by making modest money on *Black Samson* (1974), *Cleopatra Jones and the Casino of Gold* (1975), and *The Gumball Rally* (1976). He gained a reputation as a man who could rescue a film, working several times without credit. Rush had him play a significant role as an engaging stunt coordinator in the standout film *The Stunt Man* (1980).

He also worked on *Ballad of a Gunfighter*

Chuck Bail performs a high fall off the roof of the Del Coronado Hotel on *The Stunt Man* (1980).

(1964), *The Glory Guys* (1965), *Getting Straight* (1970), *The Last Movie* (1971), *Werewolves on Wheels* (1971), and *Cleopatra Jones* (1973). TV credits include *Wanted—Dead or Alive, Gunsmoke, The Virginian, Daniel Boone, Batman, High Chaparral, Bonanza,* and *Kung Fu.* Bail is an inductee of the Stuntmen's Hall of Fame.

See: Albright, Brian. "Chuck Amuck!" *Shock Cinema.* June 2008.

BARRIE BAILEY (1917–2006)

Five-foot-two Barrie Bailey, born in New York, was a Powers Model and professional dancer before becoming a stuntwoman on more than 200 films. She doubled Paulette Goddard falling off a boat on *Reap the Wild Wind* (1942) and went through a plate glass window for Elizabeth Taylor on *Butterfield 8* (1960). She did stunts for Ava Gardner and Anne Baxter prior to relocating to the Las Vegas area where she continued to work as a stuntwoman and extra into her octogenarian years. Bailey died at the age of 88.

See: Gibson, Gwen. "Age Doesn't Faze 76 Year Old Stuntwoman." *Elyria Chronicle.* August 19, 1992; Lacy, Thomas. "This Senior Takes Falls for a Living." *Henderson Home News.* October 12, 1995.

BOB BAKER (1910–1975)

Cowboy star Bob Baker was born Stanley Leland Weed in Forest City, Iowa. He was raised in Colorado and Arizona, learning to ride on ranches. He competed in rodeos and served two hitches in the U.S. Army. His mother sent a letter on her lumberjack son's behalf when she saw that Universal was looking for a new singing cowboy star. Six-foot "Bob Baker" won the berth over Roy Rogers and showcased his riding talents upon his paint horse Apache on *Courage of the West* (1937). Over a dozen more modestly budgeted westerns followed, with a handy Baker increasingly doing his own stunts.

He was paired with Johnny Mack Brown in a series of films but his role was unsubstantial. He returned to Arizona to wait for his agent to negotiate a new contract. With the start of World War II the motion picture ranks were thinned and Baker returned to Hollywood for a season to work exclusively as a stuntman. He doubled Randolph Scott and J. Carrol Naish on *Gung Ho* (1943) and

Franchot Tone on *Phantom Lady* (1944). He was a stunt rider on *Ali Baba and the Forty Thieves* (1944). After two more stints with the Army and service in Korea, he worked as a policeman and leather crafter in Arizona. Baker died from a stroke at the age of 64 after a bout with cancer and a series of heart attacks.

See: Brooker, John. "Bob Baker Interview." *Western Clippings.* #82, March-April 2008.

JIM BANNON (1911–1984)

Born in Kansas City, Missouri, James Shorttell Bannon excelled in football and baseball at Rockhurst College and played competitive polo. Classified as 4-F during World War II due to an ulcer, he became a civilian flight instructor at Condor Field. Due to so many men being off to war, Bannon got recruited to be a stuntman on *Riders of the Deadline* (1943). He was a stunt double for Charles Starrett but was hesitant to mention that he doubled other actors so as not to embarrass them. On *The Man from Colorado* (1948) Bannon and Ace Hudkins dove out of the way of a collapsing building engulfed in flame.

The 6'3", 200-pound Bannon emerged as a star on the serial *Dangers of the Canadian Mounted* (1948) and the Red Ryder B-westerns. On *Fighting Redhead* (1949) he worked his own slam-bang fight scenes with Lane Bradford and John Hart. Bannon put on good fights as a TV heavy opposite Jock Mahoney on *The Range Rider* and Clayton Moore on *The Lone Ranger.* Even after starring as Red Ryder he did some doubling work for Wild Bill Elliott in the early 1950s. Bannon died from emphysema at the age of 73.

See: Bannon, Jim. *The Son That Rose in the West.* Devil's Hole, 1975.

BRUCE BARBOUR (1949–)

Bruce Paul Barbour was born in New York City but raised in El Paso, Texas. While still in high school his musician brother-in-law Mike Nesmith offered him the opportunity to work as his stand-in and double on the TV show *The Monkees* and the film *Head* (1968). Barbour took advantage of the opportunity, following up as a stunt double for Peter Lupus on TV's *Mission: Impossible* and Rick Ely on *Young Rebels* (1970–71). Barbour also worked on the Roger Corman productions *Piranha* (1978) and *Lady in Red* (1979). On

1980s TV the 6'2", 185-pound Barbour doubled Stacy Keach on *Mike Hammer*, Lee Van Cleef on *The Master*, and Robert Urich on *Spenser for Hire*.

Barbour's specialty was driving stunts, in particular executing a "high ski." This stunt involved putting a car onto two wheels while negotiating the road. He performed this on the TV series *CHiPs* (1977–83) and *The Dukes of Hazzard* (1979–85). He worked on *Hells Angels '69* (1969), *There Was a Crooked Man...* (1970), *The Towering Inferno* (1974), *Moving Violation* (1976), *Meteor* (1979), *The Electric Horseman* (1979), *1941* (1979), *The Nude Bomb* (1980), and *Smokey and the Bandit 2* (1980). Barbour is a member of the Stuntmen's Association.

See: Hoover, Sandi. "Hollywood Stuntman No Longer a Fall Guy at Home in Nevada." *Las Vegas Review-Journal*. January 2, 2012.

STAN BARRETT (1943–)

A native of St. Louis, Missouri, 5'9", 150-pound Stanley Wayne Barrett was an undefeated lightweight Golden Gloves boxing champ. He entered the U.S. Air Force and spent four years instructing pilots how to cope with altitude sickness and dive pressure in aerospace escape system simulations. He was studying pre-med at the University of Oregon when he landed a spot as an extra on *Shenandoah* (1965). Interacting with the stuntmen convinced him he could join them, and Barrett became a protégé of Hal Needham on *Hellfighters* (1968), *The Undefeated* (1969), and *Little Big Man* (1970). He was a karate black belt, a competitive motocross racer, stock car driver, and downhill skier. His wife was top-rated skier Penny McCoy.

Barrett began doubling Burt Reynolds on the TV series *Hawk* (1966) and *Dan August* (1970–71), an association that lasted several years and also included *Smokey and the Bandit* (1977) and *Hooper* (1978), on which he slid a motorcycle under a semi truck and flipped over a curb. Barrett doubled Paul Newman on *Sometimes a Great Notion* (1970), *The Life and Times of Judge Roy Bean* (1972), and *The Drowning Pool* (1975). Steve McQueen also utilized Barrett as his double.

In 1979 he was behind the wheel of a specially designed car that broke the sound barrier as he set a land speed record of 739.666 miles per hour. In the 1980s he became a successful driver on the stock car circuit. His son Stanton Barrett

followed in his footsteps as a top driver and stuntman. The elder Barrett also worked on *Fade-In* (1968), *The Green Berets* (1968), *The Great Bank Robbery* (1969), *The Good Guys and the Bad Guys* (1969), *Beneath the Planet of the Apes* (1970), *Airport '77* (1977), and *Stunts Unlimited* (1980).

See: Gritten, David. "Stunt Man Stan Barrett Breaks the On-Land Sound Barrier, But Fortunately, Nothing Else." *People*. January 7, 1980; "Stuntman Is Ready for Latest Role." *Gadsden Times*. February 11, 1981.

GEORGE BARROWS (1914–1994)

Six-foot George Dickinson Barrows hailed from New York City but was raised in California. He had an early interest in wrestling and kept in shape with weight workouts, leading to his recruitment with other muscleman types to appear in *Cleopatra* (1934). From there he was asked to double Johnny Weissmuller on *Tarzan and His Mate* (1934). He didn't have Weissmuller's height, but he was proportioned nearly the same at the time. He became a stock player at Paramount but made more money performing stunt work on the side. In addition to being a fine picture fighter and horseman, Barrows was an accomplished fencer.

During World War II he served with the U.S. Army's Corps of Engineers. At some point the husky (220 pounds) Barrows had the idea to build his own gorilla costume. He is best known for donning a diver's helmet in addition to the gorilla outfit to play the title space creature on the cheapie *Robot Monster* (1953). He played the title simian on *Gorilla at Large* (1954) and appeared as apes on many TV series such as *The Lucy Show*, *The Beverly Hillbillies*, *The Man from U.N.C.L.E.*, and *The Wild Wild West*. He began playing small character roles while still taking the occasional stunt assignment for Broderick Crawford, whom he closely resembled as he aged and beefed up.

He also worked on *The Adventures of Robin Hood* (1938), *The Hunchback of Notre Dame* (1939), *The Son of Monte Cristo* (1940), *They Died with Their Boots On* (1941), *Prince of Thieves* (1948), *Joan of Arc* (1948), *Adventures of Don Juan* (1948), *Wake of the Red Witch* (1948), *All the Brothers Were Valiant* (1953), *Demetrius and the Gladiators* (1954), *Prince Valiant* (1954), *The Buccaneer* (1958), and *The Jayhawkers!* (1959). He portrayed TV heavies on *Mike Hammer, Richard Diamond,* and *Peter Gunn.* Barrows died at the age of 80.

See: Goldrup, Jim & Tom. *Feature Players: Stories Behind the Faces Vol. 2.* Self, 1992; Handsaker, Gene. "Some Make a Living Just Being an Ape." *Milwaukee Journal.* October 5, 1966.

BOBBY BASS (1936–2001)

Bobby S. Bass was born in California and began training in the martial arts at a young age. As a teenager attending Morningside High, he won a number of judo tournaments. He met and befriended fellow judoka Gene LeBell, who would later be instrumental in introducing Bass to the stunt world. Bass served as a paratrooper with the 82nd Airborne Division and became a Green Beret and a Special Forces instructor. He kept up with his judo training at the Seinan Dojo under Kenneth Kuniyuki and resumed competing, eventually attaining a third degree black belt.

He started appearing on screen at the close of the 1960s on TV's *Star Trek,* where he doubled James Doohan. His skill with weapons and self-defense set him up in the film industry as a go-to man for expertise on both subjects. Bass taught weapons handling or fighting to a number of stars, including Mel Gibson, Michael Douglas, and Burt Reynolds. He popularized the head-butt for fight scenes. Bass doubled Jackie Gleason on *Smokey and the Bandit* (1977) and Brian Keith on *Hooper* (1978). On *Bandit* he drove a car under a truck and sheared the top off. He was known as an especially inventive stunt coordinator as evidenced by the multiple action set-ups on *Hooper.* Bass was 5'11" and weighed 225.

He additionally worked on *The Green Berets* (1968), *Che!* (1969), *Westworld* (1973), *The Don Is Dead* (1973), *No Mercy Man* (1973), *McQ* (1974), *Posse* (1975), *Rafferty and the Gold Dust Twins* (1975), *Bound for Glory* (1976), *Close Encounters of the Third Kind* (1977), *Who'll Stop the Rain* (1978), *Tom Horn* (1980), *The Ninth Configuration* (1980), *The Hunter* (1980), and *Smokey and the Bandit 2* (1980). TV work included

Actor Richard Benjamin smashes a breakaway bottle over the head of Bobby Bass during a saloon brawl on *Westworld* (1973).

Daniel Boone, Ironside, Alias Smith and Jones, S.W.A.T., and *Baretta.* A member of Stunts Unlimited, Bass died at the age of 65 after a battle with Parkinson's Disease.

See: Oliver, Myrna. "Bobby Bass, 65; Legendary Hollywood Stuntman." *Los Angeles Times.* November 11, 2001.

PAUL BAXLEY (1923–2011)

Paul Reginald Baxley was born in Casper, Wyoming, and raised in Los Angeles. He was a stand-out athlete at Eagle Rock High in track and football. In the latter he was named All-City quarterback. During World War II he served with the U.S. Marines as a scout and a sniper. He was awarded two Purple Hearts and a Bronze Star for his heroism on Iwo Jima. Baxley also fought at Kwajalein, Saipan, and Tinian and received a letter of commendation from the president of the United States. At the close of the war he served as an instructor at Paris Island.

At Santa Ana Junior College he quarterbacked the football team to a junior college national championship and was named All-American. He was briefly in camp on a pro contract with the San Francisco 49ers prior to becoming one of the stuntmen trained by Allen Pomeroy. He made his name as the catcher for Jock Mahoney's stairwell leap on *Adventures of Don Juan* (1948). One of his most eye-opening stunts involved eluding a heavy construction truck careening down a hillside on *The Ugly American* (1963).

For more than a decade the 5'10", 180-pound Baxley served as Alan Ladd's chief stunt double and fight partner on *Shane* (1953), *Hell Below Zero* (1954), *The McConnell Story* (1955), *The Badlanders* (1958), *Guns of the Timberland* (1960), and *The Carpetbaggers* (1964). Baxley doubled

Paul Baxley barely eludes a runaway construction truck on *The Ugly American* (1963).

Audie Murphy on *The Red Badge of Courage* (1951), James Dean on *Rebel Without a Cause* (1955) and *Giant* (1956), Jeffrey Hunter on *Gun for a Coward* (1957), Marlon Brando on *One-Eyed Jacks* (1961), *Mutiny on the Bounty* (1962), *Morituri* (1965), *The Chase* (1966), and *The Appaloosa* (1966), and Paul Newman on *The Left Handed Gun* (1958) and *Harper* (1966). On TV he doubled Darren McGavin on *Mike Hammer* (1958–59), *Riverboat* (1959–60), and *Kolchak: The Night Stalker* (1974–75), Robert Loggia on *T.H.E. Cat* (1966–67), and William Shatner on *Star Trek* (1966–69). He also doubled Tim Holt on B-westerns.

He worked on *Pirates of Monterey* (1947), *The Lady from Shanghai* (1947), *The Swordsman* (1948), *Black Arrow* (1948), *Knock on Any Door* (1949), *Comanche Territory* (1950), *Flame and the Arrow* (1950), *Winchester '73* (1950), *The West Point Story* (1950), *Kansas Raiders* (1950), *Strangers on a Train* (1951), *The Iron Mistress* (1952), *The Crimson Pirate* (1952), *Desert Legion* (1953), *Rob Roy* (1953), *King Richard and the Crusaders* (1954), *The Black Knight* (1954), *The Black Shield of Falworth* (1954), *Hell on Frisco Bay* (1955), *Santiago* (1956), *The Man in the Gray Flannel Suit* (1956), *The Vagabond King* (1956), *Around the World in Eighty Days* (1956), *The Wings of Eagles* (1957), *The Big Land* (1957), *Gunfight at the O.K. Corral* (1957), *Baby Face Nelson* (1957), *Last of the Badmen* (1957), *The Deep Six* (1958), *The Proud Rebel* (1958), *Some Like It Hot* (1959), *Spartacus* (1960), *Elmer Gantry* (1960), *All the Young Men* (1960), *Atlantis, the Lost Continent* (1961), *Captain Newman, M.D.* (1963), *PT 109* (1963), *It's a Mad, Mad, Mad, Mad World* (1963), *The Greatest Story Ever Told* (1965), *The Great Race* (1965), *The Third Day* (1965), *Harum Scarum* (1965), *Tobruk* (1967), *Coogan's Bluff* (1968), *Journey to Shiloh* (1968), *The Split* (1968), *The Great Bank Robbery* (1969), *Sam Whiskey* (1969), *Catch-22* (1970), *Suppose They Gave a War and Nobody Came* (1970), *Diamonds Are Forever* (1971), *What's Up, Doc?* (1972), *The Godfather* (1972), *Charley Varrick* (1973), *Cleopatra Jones* (1973), *Mr. Majestyk* (1974), *The Parallax View* (1974), *The Killing of a Chinese Bookie* (1976), *Telefon* (1977), *Zero to Sixty* (1978), and *The Champ* (1979). He coordinated the fight between Nick Nolte and William Smith on the TV mini-series *Rich Man, Poor Man* (1976), orchestrated car jumps on *The Dukes of Hazzard*

(1979–85), and worked on *Restless Gun, Laramie, Wagon Train, Jamie McPheeters, Get Christie Love,* and *Wonder Woman.* He was a member of the Stuntmen's Hall of Fame; his son Craig and nephew Gary followed him into the business. Baxley died at the age of 87.

See: "Alan Ladd Still Slugging Away at Foes in Movies." *Rock Hill Herald.* July 22, 1958; Hagner, John. "Profile." *Falling for Stars. Vol. 1, #4* April 1965.

FLOYD BAZE (1934–)

Raised on a horse ranch in Washington's Yakima Valley, Floyd Baze was an all-around rodeo performer riding broncos and wrestling steers. This led to work on the TV series *Stoney Burke* (1962–63) as a double for Jack Lord. Baze doubled Neville Brand on *Laredo* (1965–67) and worked on *Cat Ballou* (1965) and *Paint Your Wagon* (1969). His most memorable stunt was a wild four-and-a-half minute scene riding a bronc for Lee Marvin on *Monte Walsh* (1970), completely demolishing a town. Baze doubled William Holden on *Wild Rovers* (1971) and *The Revengers* (1972) and Robert Preston on *Junior Bonner* (1972). Between stunt jobs he worked construction, was a bodyguard for Debbie Reynolds, and worked security in a Las Vegas casino. He retired to raise thoroughbred horses.

See: Juillerat, Lee. "Former Hollywood Stuntman Still Tall in the Saddle." *Spokesman Review.* November 6, 2006; Mahar, Ted. "Rodeo Cowboy Holden's Stand-In." *Oregonian.* April 16, 1971.

TONY BEARD (1910–1983)

USC multi-sport letterman Tony Beard was born in Grass Valley, California. He earned seventeen letters at Sacramento High and five letters at Sacramento Junior College, and was one of only a handful of men to letter in four different sports at USC. A football All-American, he participated in baseball, track, and swimming. While working as a highway patrolman, he added a California State diving championship and a commendation for rescuing swimmers from an icy lake in the High Sierras. His outstanding athleticism attracted the attention of Hollywood and MGM.

He doubled on *San Francisco* (1936), *Test*

Floyd Baze doubles William Holden on a bucking horse on *The Wild Rovers* (1971).

Pilot (1938), *Gone with the Wind* (1939), and *Northwest Passage* (1940). For *Mutiny on the Bounty* (1935) he dove off the ship's mast. Beard regularly doubled Allan Jones and once subbed for John Wayne. Other credits include *Navy Blue and Gold* (1937), *Rosalie* (1937), and *The Boys from Syracuse* (1940). He retired from Hollywood to become bodyguard to the attorney general and sergeant-at-arms of the state assembly in Sacramento. Beard died at the age of 72.

See: "Assembly's Security Chief Retiring." *Press Telegram.* January 14, 1977; Huston, Ralph. "Beard Given Medal for Saving Four from Lake." *Los Angeles Times.* October 3, 1932; "Tony Beard, Sr., Former Sergeant-at-Arms of State Assembly Dies." *Los Angeles Times.* May 2, 1983.

CODY BEARPAW (1943–2000)

Cree Indian Cody Bearpaw was born in Canada and raised in Wyoming. Audie Murphy discovered him performing in a rodeo. Bearpaw was a popular country and western singer known as the All-Around Indian Cowboy. He fronted the band The Fugitives, opening for Marty Robbins, Johnny Paycheck, and Mel Tillis with crowd-pleasing songs like "Tall, Good-Looking, and Bulletproof." The muscular Bearpaw starred in *Devil and Leroy Bassett* (1973) but mostly worked as a stuntman on more than 120 films. He performed a fire fall on *The Towering Inferno* (1974) that earned recognition from his peers as the year's best individual stunt.

He worked on *To Hell and Back* (1955), *Bus Stop* (1956), *True Grit* (1969), *Little Big Man* (1970), *Gentle Savage* (1973), *High Plains Drifter* (1973), *Oklahoma Crude* (1973), *Thunderbolt and Lightfoot* (1974), and *Smokey and the Bandit* (1977). TV credits include *Gunsmoke, Bonanza, High Chapparal, Alias Smith and Jones, The Streets of San Francisco, Police Story, The Dukes of Hazzard,* and *The Fall Guy.* Bearpaw died from cancer at the age of 57.

See: Edwards, Joe. "Champion Stuntman

Cody Bearpaw Tries Hand at Country." *Press-Courier.* July 20, 1986.

KAY BELL (1914–1994)

Six-foot-three, 240-pound Dee Kay Bell doubled Victor Mature extensively on director Cecil B. DeMille's *Samson and Delilah* (1949). He was born in Hoquiam, Washington, and stood out athletically at Lincoln High. He became an All-American football player at Washington State and played professionally as a tackle for the Cleveland Rams, the Los Angeles Bulldogs, the Columbus Bulls, the Chicago Bears, and the New York Giants. During the off-season he worked as a deep sea diver. As professional wrestler Handsome Kay Bell he attracted the attention of Hollywood. After making the DeMille epic, Bell adopted Samson as his ring moniker. He retired from wrestling to work as a San Mateo County jailer, taking a hiatus for a stunt job on DeMille's *The Ten Commandments* (1956). Bell died from cancer at the age of 80.

See: Burton, Ron. "Ex-Footballer Admires Actors." *San Diego Union.* July 17, 1955; "Kay Bell, Football Player and Wrestler, 80." *New York Times.* October 29, 1994.

SPENCER GORDON BENNET (1893–1987)

Spencer Gordon Bennet is best known as a director of action-packed Republic and Columbia serials. He knew a thing or two about staging stunts, having broken into the business as a stuntman during the silent era. The 6'2" Brooklyn-born Bennet's first film saw him hired to jump into the Hudson River. He was paid one dollar for each foot he jumped, earning $62.50 for the stunt. The next few years were spent as a stuntman for Edison films. He was an assistant director and stuntman on *Perils of Pauline* (1914) and doubled Charles Hutchison on *Hurricane Hutch* (1921).

Bennet became the king of the serial directors, and his superb action held up well with the majors. Directing credits include *Secret Service in Darkest Africa* (1943), *The Masked Marvel* (1943), *Zorro's Black Whip* (1944), *Superman* (1948), *Batman and Robin* (1949), and *Roar of the Iron Horse* (1951). He was an avid handball player and took part in the Polar Bear Club's Atlantic Ocean swim

every New Year. A member of the Stuntmen's Hall of Fame, Bennet died at the age of 94.

See: Nevins, Francis. "Spencer Gordon Bennet." *Western Clippings.* #65, May-June 2005; "Spencer Gordon Bennet, Stunt Man and Director." *St. Petersburg Times.* October 13, 1987.

JOHN BENSON (1916–1997)

Six-foot, 170-pound John Benson was born in St. Paul, Minnesota. During World War II he was a flight instructor for the Royal Canadian Air Force before joining the U.S. Navy. He doubled Ingrid Bergman on *Joan of Arc* (1948) and Donald O'Connor on *The Buster Keaton Story* (1957), and did stunts for Jerry Lewis, Elvis Presley, Fred Astaire, David Niven, and Jack Webb. Credits include *Around the World in Eighty Days* (1956), *Gunfight at the O.K. Corral* (1957), *The Buccaneer* (1958), and *Spartacus* (1960). Once age crept in, he became a production manager and assistant director. A member of the Stuntmen's Association, Benson died at the age of 80.

See: "John D. Benson: Character Actor, Stuntman, Production Manager." *Los Angeles Times.* April 25, 1997.

LINDA BENSON (1943–)

At the age of fifteen, the 5'2" Benson won the 1959 U.S. Surfing Championship at Huntington Beach and the Makaha Championship in Hawaii. She was the first woman to surf Waimea Bay in Hawaii and went on to win five U.S. Championships. Encinitas-born Benson was hired as a surfing double for Sandra Dee on *Gidget Goes Hawaiian* (1961) and doubled Annette Funicello and Deborah Walley on Beach Party films such as *Muscle Beach Party* (1964), *Bikini Beach* (1964), and *Beach Blanket Bingo* (1965). She won over twenty titles in a decade of surfing and was inducted into the Huntington Beach Hall of Fame.

See: Warshaw, Matt. *The Encyclopedia of Surfing.* Orlando, Florida: Harcourt, 2005.

CLIFF BERGERE (1896–1980)

Clifford Bergere was born in Toledo, Ohio, and became a well-known race car driver labeled the "whirling dervish." He placed many times in the Indianapolis 500, and his automotive skills were utilized for wrecking cars on screen at a minimum of $250 a stunt. He made hundreds of films doubling for Robert Taylor, Wallace Beery, and George Bancroft. By the close of the 1930s he had totaled over 200 cars for the camera, inducing more than forty of them to roll over. For such acts he wore a safety harness, took out all the glass from the vehicle, and left the gas tank near empty.

At 6'1" and 185 pounds, Bergere did all manner of stunts, inspired by the leather jacket he once saw on stuntman Omer Locklear. Bergere smashed chariots on the original *Ben-Hur* (1925), worked on *Perils of Pauline* (1933), and once performed a horse-to-plane transfer via a rope ladder. On *Eagle's Talon* (1923) he completed the plane-to-train transfer for Fred Thomson that killed Gene Perkins. Bergere often doubled his near lookalike Jack Holt. A member of the Stuntmen's Hall of Fame, Bergere died at the age of 83.

See: Brownlow, Kevin. *The Parade's Gone By.* Berkeley, Ca. University of California, 1968; Othman, Frederick C. "Films Pay Stunter Extra If He Comes Closer to Tragedy." *Repository.* April 7, 1938; Peck, Phillips J. "Cliff Bergere, Stuntman, Says Racing Less Harrowing Than Movie Thrillers." *Miami News.* May 21, 1940.

BOB BICKSTON

Quick-draw artist Bob Bickston of the San Fernando Valley Peacemakers gun club starred in live Corriganville stunt shows as Wyatt Earp and Bat Masterson. When he wasn't performing for crowds, he was working as a stuntman or gun coach on *Rio Bravo* (1959) and *Warlock* (1959) and the TV shows *Cheyenne, Have Gun—Will Travel, Gunsmoke,* and *Tales of Wells Fargo.* Bickston often doubled Guy Williams on the TV series *Zorro* (1957–61). In 1959 he toured with the Cavalcade show, recreating famous movie stunts for live audiences. In 1968 he produced and starred in the low-budget western *Hangfire* (1968) at Apacheland in Arizona.

See: Lefler, Jack. "Gunslingers Becoming Sport But Hazards Still High." *Advocate.* September 7, 1958; "Pay Now Better for Winning West." *Hutchinson News.* June 4, 1959.

NORMAN BISHOP (1918–1997)

Former Los Angeles lifeguard and prizefighter Norman Bishop worked as an underwater specialist and marine technical director. He famously rescued Marilyn Monroe from rough water on the Bow River while working on *River of No Return* (1954). Bishop was one of the first scuba divers and tested the deep diving equipment used on *20,000 Leagues Under the Sea* (1954). He worked often on the TV series *Sea Hunt* (1958–61). Bishop played the Gorog monster on *The Bowery Boys Meet the Monsters* (1954) and worked on *The Monster that Challenged the World* (1957), *Spartacus* (1960), and *The Wild Bunch* (1969). He owned the Cheerio Restaurant at State Beach and later self-published his memoirs, which became a collector's item. He was an honorary member of the Stuntmen's Association.

See: Bishop, Norm, & Carol Garlovsky. *I Rescued Marilyn Monroe: And Other Adventures of a Singular Person.* Self-published, 1989; Rasmussen, Cecilia. "Real Stars of the Beach Man the Watchtowers." *Los Angeles Times.* September 25, 2005.

ELI BOJACK BLACKFEATHER (1943–2004)

Seminole Indian Eli Bojack Blackfeather Trevino was a specialist at being shot off a horse and primarily worked westerns such as *Flaming Star* (1960), *Cheyenne Autumn* (1964), and *Nevada Smith* (1966). He amassed more than 200 film credits including *Blackboard Jungle* (1955), *Giant* (1956), and *West Side Story* (1961). Honored by the Stuntmen's Hall of Fame, he was a strong voice in Native American affairs. Blackfeather died from pneumonia after having three strokes at the age of 61.

See: Bindell, Stan. "Eli Bojack Blackfeather Walks On." *News from Indian County* November 14, 2004; "Stuntman Trevino Also Had Talent for Helping Others." *Sacramento Bee.* October 2, 2004.

TOM BLAKE (1902–1994)

Legendary, influential surfer Thomas Edward Blake was born in Milwaukee, Wisconsin, and did not encounter an ocean wave until he moved west at the age of nineteen. He became a national champion AAU swimmer for the Los Angeles Athletic Club while supporting himself as a lifeguard at the Santa Monica Swim Club. As he gained an interest in surfing under Hawaiian legend Duke Kahanamoku, Blake began to split time between the islands and the West Coast. In 1928 he won the Pacific Coast Surf Riding Championship. He also earned money as a stuntman specializing in water-related action.

Blake wrestled a dead shark on *Where the Pavement Ends* (1922), but his most infamous assignment came on *Trail of '98* (1928), where two stuntmen perished in the icy rapids of Alaska's Copper River. The experience compelled Blake to work on developing safety equipment for the industry. Blake continued doing stunts for the next decade, most notably for Ramon Novarro and for Johnny Weissmuller as Tarzan. He doubled Clark Gable on *Strange Cargo* (1940) and worked on *Wake Island* (1942) and *Commandos Strike at Dawn* (1942). He joined the U.S. Coast Guard during World War II and never returned to filmmaking. The influential designer of hollow surfboards, paddleboards, the surf fin, and waterproof camera housing, Blake was inducted into the Surfing Hall of Fame and the Swimming Hall of Fame. He died at the age of 92.

See: Lynch, Gary, Malcolm Gault-Williams, and William K. Houpes, *Tom Blake: The Uncommon Journey of a Pioneer Waterman*. Corona del Mar, CA: Croul Family Foundation, 2001; Warshaw, Matt. *The Encyclopedia of Surfing*. Orlando, Florida: Harcourt, 2005.

MONTE BLUE (1887–1963)

Gerard Montgomery Blue was born in Indianapolis, Indiana, of Cherokee heritage. Six-foot-two and 185 pounds he played football and worked manual labor jobs such as railroader, steelworker, fireman, miner, forest ranger, lumberjack, construction worker, and cowboy. He became so adept at riding that he joined the Ringling Brothers Circus as a horseman. Finding his way to Hollywood and D.W. Griffith's studio, he was put to work as a stuntman on *Birth of a Nation* (1915) and *Intolerance* (1916). This led to doubling assignments at other studios for their cowboy stars. He doubled DeWolf Hopper on *Don Quixote* (1916) and Sir Herbert Beerbohm Tree on *Macbeth* (1916).

Blue gained notice as a hard-galloping anti-hero on *Hands Up!* (1917) and became a silent star with *Orphans of the Storm* (1921). Stardom was fleeting, and he later achieved character actor status in the sound era specializing in villains. He had memorable fights with Guy Oliver on *Cum-*

berland Romance (1920) and *Moonlight and Honeysuckle* (1921) and Herman Brix on *Hawk of the Wilderness* (1938). Blue died from a heart attack at the age of 76.

See: Blue, Monte. "My Biggest Thrill in Movies." *Boston Globe*. August 5, 1925; "Monte Blue Knows Ups and Downs of Various Trades Besides Acting." *Evening Independent*. March 9, 1926; "Monte Blue, Veteran Film Actor Dies at 76." *Los Angeles Times*. February 19, 1963.

JOE BONOMO (1901–1978)

Joe Bonomo was born in Coney Island, New York, and followed a weightlifting routine that saw him build his body to award-winning dimensions. He excelled at a variety of athletics at the New York Military Academy and Erasmus High, later playing football professionally for the Coney Island Hiltons. First place in an Apollo Physique contest won him a stunt doubling assignment for Lon Chaney on *A Light in the Dark* (1922). Despite his thick body, Bonomo was agile and an accomplished tumbler and dancer. After performing stunts on the East Coast, he headed to Hollywood to double Chaney on *The Hunchback of Notre Dame* (1923).

The 5'11", 200-pound Bonomo doubled Charles Hutchison on *Hurricane Hutch* (1921) and Bill Desmond on *Beast of Paradise* (1923), and worked in the ring with Gene Tunney on *The Fighting Marine* (1926). Top fights came against Milton Sills on *Sea Tiger* (1927), Jack Hoxie on *Heroes of the Wild* (1927), and Tom Tyler on *Phantom of the West* (1931). Throughout his early Hollywood years the barrel-chested Bonomo supplemented his movie work by appearing as a professional wrestler known as Joe Atlas. He was a member of The Black Cats, the group of daring silent film stuntmen who risked their lives day in and day out. After a decade, Bonomo claimed that only he and Harvey Parry survived. Bonomo won leads on the serials *The Great Circus Mystery* (1925) and *Chinatown Mystery* (1928) and landed the role of Tarzan before an injury kept him from playing the part. He was one of a handful of stuntmen who escaped death while others perished on the Copper River rapids while making *Trail of '98* (1928).

He worked on *King of Kings* (1927), *Noah's Ark* (1928), *The Sign of the Cross* (1932), *Island of Lost Souls* (1933), and *Cleopatra* (1934) until a broken hip ended his ability to pull off his gags. Bonomo retired and went into a successful publishing business with his exercise routines. An honorary member of the Stuntmen's Association and an inductee of the Stuntmen's Hall of Fame, Bonomo died from pneumonia at the age of 76.

See: Bonomo, Joe. *The Strongman.* Bonomo, 1968; "Joe Bonomo, Star of Silent Films; Began as Stuntman." *New York Times.* April 1, 1978; Russell, Bill. "Joe Bonomo: Cowboy Strongman." *Western Clippings.* #92, November/December 2009.

MAY R. BOSS (1930–)

Top female horsewoman May Raymond Boss performed at Madison Square Garden as a rodeo trick rider and was a charter member of the Stuntwomen's Association. Although she started with horses, she became known for fight scenes, including boxing her "son" Jay Leno on *Americathon* (1979). The 5'4" Arizona native doubled Mamie Van Doren on *Born Reckless* (1958), Virginia Mayo on *Fort Dobbs* (1958), Rita Hayworth on *They Came to Cordura* (1959), Sandra Dee on *Tammy Tell Me True* (1961), Carol Lynley and Dorothy Malone on *The Last Sunset* (1961), Doris Day on *Send Me No Flowers* (1964), and Bette Davis on *Return from Witch Mountain* (1978). Inducted into the Stuntmen's Hall of Fame, she was awarded the Helen Gibson Award for her lifetime in stunts.

She also worked on *The Story of Will Rogers* (1952), *Westbound* (1959), *How the West Was Won* (1962), *It's a Mad, Mad, Mad, Mad World* (1963), *Savage Sam* (1963), *Roustabout* (1964), *Marnie* (1964), *Mary Poppins* (1964), *The Hallelujah Trail* (1965), *Nevada Smith* (1966), *The Way West* (1967), *Mackenna's Gold* (1969), *The Good Guys and the Bad Guys* (1969), *Soylent Green* (1973), *Cleopatra Jones* (1973), *Blazing Saddles* (1974), *Earthquake* (1974), *The Master Gunfighter* (1975), *Logan's Run* (1976), *Two-Minute Warning* (1976), *Return of a Man Called Horse* (1976), *Drum* (1976), *Airport '77* (1977), *Goin' South* (1978), *Concorde, Airport '79* (1979), *1941* (1979), and *Mountain Men* (1980). TV credits include *Gunsmoke, The Monroes, Mannix, Cannon, The Rockford Files, Police Woman, Wonder Woman, The Bionic Woman, Starsky and Hutch,* and *Charlie's Angels.* Her son Clay became a stuntman.

See: Holter, Peggy Magner. "Stuntwomen."

Playgirl. April, 1976; "Stunt Rider Prefers Denim to Chintz." *Omaha World Herald.* September 19, 1956.

LANE BRADFORD (1922–1973)

Lane Bradford was born Myrtland Viviene LaVarre, Jr. in Yonkers, New York. He was the son of veteran screen heavy, John Merton, a solid fight man. Bradford was arguably an even more intense and fierce bad guy, frightening audiences with his lantern jaw, hawk nose, and perpetual five o'clock shadow. He began as a riding and fighting western stuntman, doubling Bill Elliott on *North from the Lone Star* (1941), *Bullets for Bandits* (1942), and *Valley of Vanishing Men* (1942). Bradford took time out for military service during World War II and returned to double Buster Crabbe on *Ghosts of Hidden Valley* (1946). He graduated to cowboy thug on dozens of films where he squared off against virtually all the major and minor western stars.

Before a fight, the six-foot, 190-pound Bradford looked like he wanted to do serious damage to his opponent. He brought great energy to the screen and made a formidable foe for any hero. Bradford was quite adept at taking a punch, staggering a few feet, then throwing himself into some piece of furniture from the force of the blow. Often he wound up with his shirt ripped open. Notable battles came against Jim Bannon on *Fighting Redhead* (1949), Tony Curtis on *The Rawhide Years* (1956), and Jock Mahoney on *Showdown at Abilene* (1956). He fought Clayton Moore many times on TV's *The Lone Ranger* and guested on more than a dozen episodes each of *Gunsmoke* and *Bonanza.* Bradford died in Honolulu of a cerebral hemorrhage following a massive heart attack at the age of 50.

BOB BRADSHAW (1918–2008)

Robert Bradshaw was born in Xiamen, China, and traveled around the United States by rail during the Depression. He became an ambassador to the beauty of the western location Sedona, Arizona, after moving there in 1945 to work as a cowpuncher, tour guide, set builder, location manager, and movie stuntman. Because of his horseback skills, he got behind-the-scenes work as a wrangler on *She Wore a Yellow Ribbon* (1949). He doubled James Stewart on *Broken Arrow*

(1950), Zachary Scott on *Shotgun* (1955), and James Best on *Firecreek* (1968), and was a riding double or extra on *Station West* (1948), *Gun Fury* (1953), *Johnny Guitar* (1954), *Apache* (1954), *Drum Beat* (1954), *Stranger on Horseback* (1955), *The Last Wagon* (1956), *3:10 to Yuma* (1957), *Yellowstone Kelly* (1959), and *Wild Rovers* (1971).

Bradshaw built a western town beneath Coffee Pot Rock: The Bradshaw Ranch became a prime filming location for the area. He was responsible for bringing movies such as *The Rounders* (1965) and *Stay Away, Joe* (1968) into Sedona. In addition to stunt work, Bradshaw was a Marlboro Man and filmed many commercials in the red rocks. He wrote and published several books with photographs documenting the history of filmmaking in Sedona. Bradshaw died at the age of 90.

See: Bradshaw, Bob. *Westerns of the Red Rock Country*. Sedona, AZ: Bradshaw, 1991; www.bradshawgallery.com; Bradshaw, Bob, and Kathleen Francis. *Sedona Man: The Life and Adventures of Arizona Cowboy Bob Bradshaw*. Sedona, AZ: Bradshaw, 2002.

BUFF BRADY (1918–2004)

John "Buff" Brady was born in Butte, Montana, the son of rodeo performer Big Buffalo Brady. Although he rode bulls and broncos, the younger Brady became known as a trick rider and roper who incorporated gymnastics into his act. He could somersault backwards while twirling his rope and even perform the move off the back of a horse. He appeared often at the Pendleton Round-Up and Madison Square Garden. In Hollywood he played one of the rowdy Hannassey brothers on *The Big Country* (1958) and Will Rogers on *W.C. Fields and Me* (1976). Brady doubled Roy Rogers on his TV show and stood in for Rex Allen, Stewart Granger, and Dean Martin.

The 5'10", 175-pound Brady worked on *Westward Ho, the Wagons!* (1956), *The Brothers Karamazov* (1958), *The Horse Soldiers* (1959), *Pork Chop Hill* (1959), *Yellowstone Kelly* (1959), *Spartacus* (1960), *The Alamo* (1960), *El Cid* (1961), *Bullet for a Badman* (1964), *The Hallelujah Trail* (1965), *The Rare Breed* (1966), *Camelot* (1967), *Mackenna's Gold* (1969), *Paint Your Wagon* (1969), *There Was a Crooked Man...* (1970), *The Great Northfield Minnesota Raid* (1972), *Earthquake* (1974), and *The Towering Inferno* (1974).

TV credits include *Wagon Train, Have Gun—Will Travel, Stoney Burke,* and *Laredo*. He was inducted into the National Cowboy Hall of Fame, the Rodeo Hall of Fame, and the Stuntmen's Hall of Fame. A member of the Stuntmen's Association, Brady died at the age of 86.

See: Allen, Mike. *Ellensburg Daily Record*. "Rodeo and Movie Star Has Ellensburg Roots." August 27, 2001.

BOB BRALVER (1941–)

UCLA athlete Robert Bralver wrote a research paper for his Masters in physical education on the physics behind the speed of a professional baseball swing. He began doing stunts in the mid–1960s, doubling on TV for Robert Culp on *I Spy* (1965–68), DeForest Kelley on *Star Trek* (1966–69), and Martin Landau on *Mission: Impossible* (1966–69). On *Trek* he was cast as one of the doomed "red shirt" crewmen. He worked as a junior high P.E. teacher while building his stunt résumé with TV work on *The Man from U.N.C.L.E., The Girl from U.N.C.L.E., Adam-12, Search, Kung Fu, Emergency, McCloud, Cannon, Switch,* and *The Six Million Dollar Man*.

He worked on *Earthquake* (1974), *Avalanche* (1978), *Beyond the Poseidon Adventure* (1979), *Star Trek: The Motion Picture* (1979), and *The Nude Bomb* (1980). He was stunt coordinator on the TV series *Kojak* (1976–78), *Battlestar Galactica* (1978–79), and *The Fall Guy* (1981–82) and went from directing second units to first. His son Stephen played professional baseball and followed his dad into stunts.

See: www.stephenbralver.com;

X BRANDS (1927–2000)

X Brands is best known as the co-star of the fondly remembered *Yancy Derringer* (1958–59) where he played Jock Mahoney's loyal Indian friend Pahoo-Ka-Ta-Wah. Mahoney and Brands did all their own stunt work on the show, working especially well on the fluid exchange of knives and guns. Brands often portrayed Indians on TV shows such as *Rawhide, Cheyenne, Wagon Train, Gunsmoke,* and *High Chaparral,* though he was not a true Native American. As a villainous character player, he had a fine saloon brawl with John Bromfield on the western *Frontier Gambler* (1956).

Born in Kansas City, Missouri, and raised in California, Jay X Brands had a rodeo background. He served with the U.S. Navy in World War II and Korea. His credits include *Hondo* (1953), *The Wild One* (1953), *The Conqueror* (1956), *Escort West* (1958), *Beau Geste* (1966), and the TV series *Cowboy G-Men* and *Judge Roy Bean*. He doubled Bill Williams on TV's *Kit Carson* (1954–55) and Lee Van Cleef on *The Grand Duel* (1972). When parts dried up, he became a pilot and flight instructor at Van Nuys Airport. Brands died at the age of 72.

See: Anderson, Bob. "Pahoo Ka-Ta-Wah: Wolf Who Stands in Water." *Trail Dust.* Fall/Winter 1993.

PETER BRAYHAM (1936–2006)

Six-foot-one, 200-pound Peter Brayham most famously jumped a car over London's Tower Bridge doubling John Wayne on *Brannigan* (1975). He doubled Oliver Reed on *The Devils* (1971) and *Sitting Target* (1972) and James Coburn on *Cross of Iron* (1975) and *Sky Riders* (1976). Actors Michael Caine and Louis Jourdan also utilized Brayham's talents. A professional fencing instructor, swimmer, and amateur boxer, Brayham worked on *The Guns of Navarone* (1961), *From Russia with Love* (1963), *Goldfinger* (1964), *You Only Live Twice* (1967), *Straw Dogs* (1971), and *Live and Let Die* (1973). TV credits include *Danger Man, The Prisoner, The Sweeney,* and *The Professionals.* Brayham died from a heart attack at the age of 70.

See: "Same Old John Wayne." *Brandon Sun.* August 23, 1974.

HURLEY "RED" BREEN (1909–1963)

Michael Hurley Breen boxed out of the Hollywood Athletic Club as a featherweight and bantamweight in the late 1920s. Although he frequently lost, his fights were known as exciting bouts. He worked as a stand-in and stunt double for James Cagney for nine years, covering screen fights on *Frisco Kid* (1935) and *The Oklahoma Kid* (1939). Outside of his Cagney assignments, Breen took a memorable balcony fall during the massive saloon brawl on *Dodge City* (1939). He left Cagney to join the U.S. Navy during World War II. After the war he became a stand-in and double for Shemp Howard of the Three Stooges on Columbia shorts. Breen died at the age of 54.

See: "Hurley Breen." *Variety.* September 18, 1963; "Navy Takes Three of Cagney's Aides." *St. Petersburg Times.* February 22, 1942.

WALTER BRENNAN (1894–1974)

A three-time Oscar winner for Best Supporting Actor, Walter Andrew Brennan got his start as a stuntman and riding extra for $7.50 a day under the name Phillip Space, as in he was merely "filling up space." Early stunt credits include *Lorraine of the Lions* (1925), *Ridin' Rowdy* (1927), and *Destry Rides Again* (1932). Legend has it that Brennan lost his front teeth in a stunt accident in the early 1930s. Pal Gary Cooper took to calling him "Cripple" because Brennan's body was so banged up from stunts.

Brennan was born in Swampscott, Massachusetts, and played football at Cambridge. Moving to California, he was a lumberjack prior to service with an artillery unit in World War I. He estimated he had made close to 300 films. The actor died from emphysema at the age of 80.

See: Rosenfield, John. "Walter Brennan Can't Get a Commission." *Dallas Morning News.* March 30, 1943.

ROY BRENT (1903–1979)

Chicago-born Manierre Alexander Williamson worked in carnivals and served with the U.S. Navy during World War I. After playing semi-pro baseball, he landed in Hollywood as Roy Brent. He stunted on Christie comedies, worked as a technical advisor on baseball films, and stood in for Spencer Tracy on *Dante's Inferno* (1935). He secured henchman parts on *Daredevils of the Red Circle* (1939), *Adventures of Red Ryder* (1940), *Spy Smasher* (1942), *Wolves of the Range* (1943), *Captain America* (1943), *The Fighting Seabees* (1944), *Desert Hawk* (1944), and *Zorro's Black Whip* (1944). Brent died from emphysema at the age of 75.

See: Moyer, Donn. *Cowpokes and Cowbelles of the Movies and Early TV.* Wild West, 2003.

WILFORD BRIMLEY (1934–)

Portly Utah-born character actor Anthony Wilford Brimley achieved popularity in 1980s films such as *The Natural* (1984) and *Cocoon* (1985). He came across as a kind, grandfatherly type. Many were surprised to learn of his rugged background as a U.S. Marine, blacksmith, horse wrangler, stuntman, and bodyguard for Howard Hughes. For twenty years he shod horses at ranches, race tracks, and movie studios, picking up work as a riding extra in the mid–1960s. He cashed stunt paychecks as Bill Brimley on *Bandolero!* (1968), *True Grit* (1969), and *Lawman* (1971) as well as the TV series *Gunsmoke* and *Custer*.

See: Thomas, Bob. "Wilford Brimley Not the Average Actor." *Cedar Rapids Gazette*. May 25, 1984.

CHARLES BRONSON (1921–2003)

When he became a superstar at the unlikely age of fifty, Charles Bronson was not averse to parading around a still fantastically muscled physique. He also took great pride in doing as much of his stunt work as insurance companies would allow. He always did his own fights, at which he excelled. His bare-knuckle brawls with stuntmen Robert Tessier and Nick Dimitri on *Hard Times* (1975) are regarded as two of the best ever put on film. Stunt coordinator Max Kleven said, "The stuntmen regard Charlie as a life member of their own craft. He is a good athlete and keeps himself at the peak of condition. He's a physical actor and knows how to do fights better than anybody else in the movies."

Charles Bronson was born Charles Dennis Buchinsky in Ehrenfeld, Pennsylvania. He toiled in the coal mines, escaping the inevitable Black Lung only when he was drafted by the U.S. Army during World War II. Bronson boxed in the service and was a tail gunner on a B-29, earning a Purple Heart in combat. It was his skill in the boxing ring that saw him cast on his first film *You're in the Navy Now* (1951). He briefly showed up to be judo flipped by Katharine Hepburn on *Pat and Mike* (1952). The 5'8", 170-pound Bronson established himself as a stunt fighter on *House of Wax* (1953) and *Drum Beat* (1954), going on to play granite-faced henchmen and anti-heroes for the next twenty years in classic action films such as *The Magnificent Seven* (1960) and *The Dirty Dozen* (1967).

After attaining success in Europe on Sergio Leone's *Once Upon a Time in the West* (1969), Bronson returned to the States to become a top action star. Publicity played up his toughness and physical skills. A short film on the making of *St. Ives* (1976) emphasized that Bronson did many of his own stunts, including hanging over an elevator shaft. Bronson kept fit with a workout routine that incorporated many stunt skills such as rope-climbing, archery, and knife-throwing. Bronson died of pneumonia and Alzheimer's Disease at the age of 81.

See: "Bronson Does Stunts." *Aberdeen Daily News*. September 9, 1976; Whitney, Steven. *Charles Bronson: Superstar*. New York: Dell, 1975.

DOYLE BROOKS (1923–1986)

John Doyle Brooks from Batesville, Arkansas, began his career at an air show benefit in his hometown when he dove from a passing plane forty feet into the White River. He doubled James Brown and played Indians on the TV series *The Adventures of Rin Tin Tin* (1954–59), making public appearances throughout the decade. A fast-draw expert, he worked on *Tension at Table Rock* (1956) before settling in as a stuntman on the series *Naked City* (1958–63) and *Tallahassee 7000* (1961). When he wasn't doubling *Naked City* star Paul Burke or *Tallahassee 7000*'s Walter Matthau, he was handling action for the guest stars. For a time he was the White Knight of TV commercials. Brooks died at the age of 62.

See: Battelle, Phyllis. *Omaha World Herald*. "Risking Neck Day's Work for Stuntman." November 26, 1958.

JOE BROOKS (1923–2007)

Joe Brooks is best known to TV audiences as the near-sighted lookout Trooper Vanderbilt on the comedy western *F Troop* (1965–1967) and as the convertible driver who taunts Barry Newman on *Vanishing Point* (1971). Los Angeles–born John Joseph Brooks, Jr., was an extra prior to World War II military service in the South Pacific. He did stunts and bits on *All-American* (1953), *East of Eden* (1955), *Tall Man Riding* (1955), *The Sea Chase* (1955), *The Enemy Below* (1957), *The*

Young Lions (1958), *Flaming Star* (1960), and *Support Your Local Gunfighter* (1971). He later became an assistant director, often handling crowd scenes. Brooks died at the age of 83.

See: Johnson, John. "Hollywood's Aging Stuntmen Dust Off the Old Days." *Baltimore Sun.* February 11, 1992.

CALVIN BROWN (1936–)

Six-foot-two and 200 pounds, Calvin Brown was a native of Farmersville, Louisiana, and a multi-sport athlete in baseball and basketball at Grambling University. In 1958 he relocated to California and began working as a Hollywood extra for $11 a day. He was converted to stuntman on *Drums of Africa* (1962) when he was asked if he'd fall out of a tree for $100. He performed the stunt a total of six times and walked away that day with $600. Realizing the money to be made and the complete lack of black stuntmen in Hollywood, he set about making a name for himself. He trained at Paul Stader's gym, learning the proper way to perform fights and falls.

His big break came as the stunt double for Bill Cosby on *I Spy* (1965–68). Initially he had to prove himself to resentful white stuntmen, as he was taking work that would have typically been done in black face. He proved himself and began working on other sets, most notably TV's *The Wild Wild West* and *Mission: Impossible,* where he doubled Greg Morris. He doubled Jim Brown, Sidney Poitier, Woody Strode, Ossie Davis, Harry Belafonte, Bernie Casey, Raymond St. Jacques, Julius Harris, Moses Gunn, William Marshall, Yaphet Kotto, and Richard Roundtree. Still, he faced a difficult road finding acceptance in Hollywood. A broken leg suffered doubling Jim Brown on *The Split* (1968) necessitated a leg cast for two years. He began recommending other athletic blacks within the industry who might be able to handle the job. Along with Eddie Smith he formed the Black Stuntmen's Association in 1968, recruiting a group of local cavalry re-enactors named the Buffalo Soldiers. He trained the group of prospective stuntmen, many of whom went on to work regularly in the 1970s black action genre.

He worked on *Will Penny* (1968), *They Call Me Mr. Tibbs* (1970), *Tick ... Tick ... Tick* (1970), *Man and Boy* (1972), *Across 110th Street* (1972), *The New Centurions* (1972), *Freebie and the Bean* (1974), *Newman's Law* (1974), *Uptown Saturday Night* (1974), *Hustle* (1975), *Mandingo* (1975), *Report to the Commissioner* (1975), *Let's Do It Again* (1975), *Drum* (1976), *Rocky* (1976), *Two-Minute Warning* (1976), and the TV mini-series *Roots* (1977). His brother Jophery became a top stuntman.

COURTNEY BROWN (1931–2007)

Courtney Brown was born in Buffalo, New York, and raised in Los Angeles where he became interested in deep water diving in the early 1950s. A friendship with Zale Perry brought him to the attention of the producers of the TV series *Sea Hunt* (1958–61), and Brown was hired to double Lloyd Bridges for the duration of the show. Brown doubled Mark Stevens on *September Storm* (1960) and was with Ivan Tors' Florida-based productions for the TV series *Flipper* (1964–67) and *Gentle Ben* (1967–69). He worked on *Spartacus* (1960), *Thunderball* (1965), *Darker Than Amber* (1970), *Live and Let Die* (1973), *Murph the Surf* (1975), *Stunt Seven* (1979), and the TV series *The Six Million Dollar Man.* He was once married to aquatic stuntwoman Wende Wagner.

See: www.internationallegendsofdiving.com.

JERRY BROWN (1915–1979)

Jerry Brown was born in Brownwood, Texas, as Raymond Smith. He changed his name professionally after working on *The Charge of the Light Brigade* (1936). Horseman Jerry Brown might not be as famous as the jumping and falling stunt horse that carried his name. The bay horse Jerry Brown that he trained was one of the most popular western horses in Hollywood and won a Craven Award in 1951. Stuntman Jerry Brown worked at Glen Randall's ranch between stunt assignments. In addition to riding horses, the 5'9", 165-pound was often cast as a stagecoach driver. He was the Corinthian charioteer on *Ben-Hur* (1959).

He worked on *The Fighting Kentuckian* (1949), *The Kid from Texas* (1950), *Rio Grande* (1950), *Column South* (1953), *Man with the Steel Whip* (1954), *The Last Command* (1955), *Around the World in Eighty Days* (1956), *Westward Ho, the Wagons!* (1956), *Spartacus* (1960), *El Cid* (1961), *Taras Bulba* (1962), *Fall of the Roman*

Empire (1964), *A Distant Trumpet* (1964), *The War Lord* (1965), *Stagecoach* (1966), *The Great Bank Robbery* (1969), *Skin Game* (1971), *Oklahoma Crude* (1973), *99 and 44/100 percent Dead* (1974), and *Blazing Saddles* (1974). TV credits include *Gunsmoke, Cimarron Strip,* and *Alias Smith and Jones.* He was a member of the Stuntmen's Association and an inductee of the Stuntmen's Hall of Fame.

See: Payne, William A. "Movie Stunt Record Set By *Dundee* Fall." *Dallas Morning News.* April 16, 1964.

JOPHERY BROWN (1945–)

Born in Grambling, Louisiana, 6'2", 190-pound Jophery Clifford Brown was the younger brother of stuntman Calvin Brown. Jophery played football, basketball, and baseball at Grambling High and continued with basketball and baseball for Grambling University. As a professional baseball player he made the major leagues in 1968 pitching for the Chicago Cubs. Brown tore a rotator cuff the next spring and his career was suddenly over. He started doing minor stunt work on the TV series *I Spy* (1965–68) with his brother and trained with the Black Stuntmen's Association. His first job as a stunt coordinator came on the baseball film *The Bingo Long Traveling All-Stars* (1976).

Brown performed a fire burn on *Papillon* (1973), doubled Jim Brown escaping a phone booth smashed by a truck on *Three the Hard Way* (1974), jumped off a cliff for James Earl Jones on *Swashbuckler* (1976), and overturned a semi on *Convoy* (1978). Well known for his vehicular work, he doubled Mr. T on TV's *The A-Team* (1983–87) and perfected spiraling auto crashes. He did a major car flip on *Action Jackson* (1988) and made the bus leap over an unfinished freeway on *Speed* (1994). Brown was stunt coordinator on *Scarface* (1983) and doubled Yaphet Kotto, Morgan Freeman, Sidney Poitier, Denzel Washington, Danny Glover, and Gregory Hines. Other credits include *Coffy* (1973), *Live and Let Die* (1973), *Uptown Saturday Night* (1974), *Let's Do It Again* (1975), *Drum* (1976), *Bound for Glory* (1976), *Smokey and the Bandit* (1977), *Hooper* (1978), *Foul Play* (1978), *The Hunter* (1980), *Smokey and the Bandit 2* (1980), and *Stunts Unlimited* (1980). A member of Stunts Unlimited, Brown was awarded a Taurus Life Achievement Award in 2010.

See: Ross, John. "Jophery Brown: This Guy's Something Else." *Inside Stunts.* Summer, 2007.

WINNIE BROWN

Arizona-born horse wrangler and ranch owner Winna "Winnie" Brown began making western shorts. By the early 1920s she was one of film's top stuntwomen, doubling Norma Talmadge on *Ashes of Vengeance* (1923), Constance Talmadge on *Dangerous Maid* (1923), Pola Negri on *Bella Donna* (1923), and Colleen Moore on *Through the Dark* (1924). She did stunts for Mary Pickford and Priscilla Dean and doubled Joseph Schildkraut on *Song of Love* (1923) but soon after disappeared from the business.

See: "Doubles Risk Lives Daily for Pictures." *Morning Star.* July 2, 1925; Slide, Anthony. *Hollywood Unknowns.* Jackson, MS: University Press, 2012.

RICOU BROWNING (1930–)

Ricou Browning was born in Fort Pierce, Florida, and learned to swim and fancy dive at a young age. He appeared in sports shorts for Grantland Rice and worked in underwater shows at Weeki Wachee and Wakulla Springs. Browning entered the U.S. Air Force and starred on their swim team prior to competing for Florida State University. The producers of *Creature from the Black Lagoon* (1954) discovered Browning while scouting locations and asked him to wear the Gill Man costume for underwater scenes. The assignment created a cult legend in Browning, who donned the costume again for *Revenge of the Creature* (1955) and *The Creature Walks Among Us* (1956). Other players wore the Gill Man outfit for land scenes, but Browning excelled in the water.

Acquiring a solid reputation, the six-foot, 185-pound Browning began working on the TV shows *Sea Hunt* (1958–61), *Aquanauts* (1960–61), and *Malibu Run* (1961) as a double for the villainous guest stars. In the early 1960s he founded Underwater Studios and developed the TV series *Flipper* (1964–67), beginning a long association with producer Ivan Tors. Browning was a stuntman and second unit director on the Bond films *Thunderball* (1965) and *Never Say Never Again* (1983). He worked on *20,000 Leagues Under the Sea* (1954), *Jupiter's Darling* (1955),

September Storm (1960), *Lady in Cement* (1968), *Day of the Dolphin* (1973), *Lucky Lady* (1975), and *Black Sunday* (1977). TV credits include *Primus, The Six Million Dollar Man,* and *The Bionic Woman*. His son Ricou, Jr., became a stuntman and marine coordinator.

See: Luening, Bill. "Creature No Wan Off-Screen Star." *Lakeland Ledger*. October 31, 1983; Michalski, Michael. "Dangerous When Wet." *Scarlet Street*. #46, October 2002; Weaver, Tom. "Creature Man." *Starlog*. #167, June 1991; www. internationallegendsofdiving.com.

TONY BRUBAKER

Anthony Brubaker was an all-around San Fernando Valley athlete with backgrounds in football, boxing, polo, and the professional rodeo circuit. Six-three and weighing 220 pounds, he broke horses for a living before entering the movie business as a double for Otis Young on the series *Outcasts* (1968–69), Lou Gossett, Jr. on *Young Rebels* (1970–71), and Greg Morris on *Mission: Impossible* (1970–73). He made his name with a dicey run along a narrow ledge and sixteen-foot leap onto another stuntman on *There Was a Crooked Man...* (1970), but even that wasn't enough to guarantee consistent work. He gained notoriety when the Black Stuntmen's Association lobbied against Warner Brothers for hiring a white stuntman to double Lou Gossett on *Skin Game* (1971). Eddie Smith argued that Brubaker was available and more than capable. Established white stuntmen were not happy losing work to up-and-coming black stuntmen, but eventually the business became integrated with the likes of Brubaker and

Tony Brubaker, lower right, is among the stunt performers dodging falling debris on *Earthquake* (1974).

Bob Minor leading the way as members of the Stuntmen's Association.

Brubaker doubled Jim Brown on *Black Gunn* (1972) and *Slaughter's Big Rip-Off* (1973), Sidney Poitier on *Buck and the Preacher* (1972), *Uptown Saturday Night* (1974), and *A Piece of the Action* (1977), Fred Williamson on *Soul of Nigger Charley* (1973) and *Death Journey* (1976), and Rosey Grier on *The Glove* (1978). On 1980s TV he doubled Mr. T on *The A-Team* and Michael Dorn on *Star Trek: The Next Generation*. He doubled Danny Glover on the *Lethal Weapon* films. Brubaker was a top fight man, going against Sean Connery on *The Next Man* (1976), Arnold Schwarzenegger on *Conan the Barbarian* (1982), and Sylvester Stallone on *Rocky III* (1982). He doubled boxing champ Archie Moore during a great fight with Charles Bronson atop an ice-covered train on *Breakheart Pass* (1976).

He worked on *Tobruk* (1967), *Cotton Comes to Harlem* (1970), *Come Back, Charleston Blue* (1972), *Conquest of the Planet of the Apes* (1972), *Westworld* (1973), *99 and 44/100 percent Dead* (1974), *Black Samson* (1974), *Three Tough Guys* (1974), *The Towering Inferno* (1974), *Earthquake* (1974), *Rollerball* (1975), *Friday Foster* (1975), *Drum* (1976), *Dr. Black, Mr. Hyde* (1976), *The Last Hard Men* (1976), *Two-Minute Warning* (1976), *Return from Witch Mountain* (1978), *Buck Rogers in the 25th Century* (1979), *Freedom Road* (1979), *Smokey and the Bandit 2* (1980), and *The Nude Bomb* (1980). TV credits include *Kung Fu, The Rockford Files, The Six Million Dollar Man, Baretta, The Bionic Woman, Wonder Woman, The Incredible Hulk,* and *The Fall Guy*. Brubaker is an inductee of the Stuntmen's Hall of Fame.

See: Boas, Philip. "Movie Stuntman Yearns to Ride into Yesteryear: Love for Horses Sent Brubaker to Hollywood." *Daily News.* January 7, 1987; King, Susan. "Tribute to the Unknown Stuntmen." *Los Angeles Times.* June 1, 2002.

GEORGE BRUGGEMAN (1904–1967)

Georges Bruggeman from Antwerp, Belgium, entered Hollywood by scaling the studio wall at Paramount. He was a Greek God on *Manhattan Cocktail* (1928); that same year he won the forerunner to the Mr. California bodybuilding title when he was awarded The Most Perfectly Developed Body of 1928. This led to doubling

Johnny Weissmuller on *Tarzan the Ape Man* (1932) as well as Buster Crabbe, Clark Gable, and Richard Greene. He worked on *Noah's Ark* (1928), *Cleopatra* (1934), *The Adventures of Robin Hood* (1938), *The Wizard of Oz* (1939), *The Sea Wolf* (1941), *O.S.S.* (1946), *Monsieur Beaucaire* (1946), *Joan of Arc* (1948), *Ivanhoe* (1952), *The Stranger Wore a Gun* (1953), *Demetrius and the Gladiators* (1954), *Prince Valiant* (1954), *Around the World in Eighty Days* (1956), *Omar Khayyam* (1957), *The Buccaneer* (1958), and *Spartacus* (1960).

See: "Screen Life in Hollywood." *Joplin Globe.* November 11, 1928.

JERRY BRUTSCHE (1939–)

Gerald Eugene Brutsche was born in Los Angeles. A motorcycle specialist, he is credited as the coordinator for the bike chase on *Electra Glide in Blue* (1973). On TV the 5'6", 140-pound stunter doubled Irene Ryan on *The Beverly Hillbillies* (1963–70) and Don Knotts on *The Andy Griffith Show.* He doubled Knotts on *The Shakiest Gun in the West* (1968) and *No Deposit, No Return* (1976) and subbed for Robert Blake on *In Cold Blood* (1967), Bud Cort on *Brewster McCloud* (1970), and Michael J. Pollard on *Little Fauss and Big Halsey* (1970). He doubled many child actors, including Kurt Russell on the TV series *Travels of Jamie McPheeters* (1964–65). One of his most interesting stunts involved folding into a spinning dryer on *St. Ives* (1976).

He worked on *Beach Party* (1963), *Beach Blanket Bingo* (1965), *How to Stuff a Wild Bikini* (1965), *Harper* (1966), *Hot Rods to Hell* (1967), *Gunn* (1967), *Perils of Pauline* (1967), *Finian's Rainbow* (1968), *The Good Guys and the Bad Guys* (1969), *The Great Bank Robbery* (1969), *Sidehackers* (1969), *Hell's Belles* (1969), *Tora! Tora! Tora!* (1970), *Soldier Blue* (1970), *What's Up, Doc?* (1972), *The Poseidon Adventure* (1972), *Dillinger* (1973), *Magnum Force* (1973), *99 and 44/100 percent Dead* (1974), *Earthquake* (1974), *Lucky Lady* (1975), *Rooster Cogburn* (1975), *Marathon Man* (1976), *Swashbuckler* (1976), *Mr. Billion* (1977), *Close Encounters of the Third Kind* (1977), *Herbie Goes to Monte Carlo* (1977), *The Deer Hunter* (1978), *Every Which Way But Loose* (1978), *1941* (1979), *The Nude Bomb* (1980), and *Any Which Way You Can* (1980). TV credits include *Honey West* and *Starsky and Hutch.* A member of the Stuntmen's Association, he married stuntwoman Kevin N. Johnston.

BOB BRYANT (1919–2000)

Robert R. Bryant was born in Frederick, Oklahoma, and raised in Olton, Texas. Six-foot-three and 225 pounds, he was a Golden Gloves boxer and was a standout football lineman for Santa Ana Junior College and the Texas Tech Red Raiders prior to World War II military service. Upon returning home he played tackle professionally for the San Francisco 49ers from 1946 to 1949 and the Calgary Stampeders during 1952 and 1953. He was known for his aggressiveness. His football off-seasons were spent in Hollywood working as a stuntman. He was an assistant football line coach for the University of Arizona in the early 1950s.

Bryant's early stunt training came via Allen Pomeroy. His first film was *The Killers* (1946), and other early credits include *Pirates of Monterey* (1947), and *The Fighting Kentuckian* (1949). He worked many westerns for Republic and served as a double for Jeff Chandler on *Broken Arrow* (1950) and Victor Mature on *The Robe* (1953). His best known work came playing the title monster on *Curse of the Faceless Man* (1958). In *The Alligator People* (1959), he doubled Lon Chaney, Jr. TV credits include *Wagon Train, Bonanza, The Virginian,* and *Gunsmoke.* Retiring to open a saddle-making business, Bryant died from heart complications at the age of 81.

See: Parla, Paul. "Quintillus Remembers *Curse of the Faceless Man.*" December 1996.

KEN BUCKLE

After service as a guardsman during World War II, British stuntman Ken Buckle got his start with Jock Easton's Stunt Team. The 6'2", 215-pound Buckle received the benefits of training from visiting stunt coordinator Yakima Canutt in the early 1950s. Buckle performed jousting stunts on *Ivanhoe* (1952), doubled Gert Frobe on *Goldfinger* (1964), and jumped a motorcycle over a racetrack parapet on *Those Magnificent Men in Their Flying Machines* (1965).He worked on *Alexander the Great* (1956), *Zarak* (1956), *The Vikings* (1958), *Swiss Family Robinson* (1960), *Exodus* (1960), *The Longest Day* (1962), *Lawrence of Arabia* (1962), *Cleopatra* (1962), *From Russia with Love* (1963), *The Long Ships* (1964), *Battle of the Bulge* (1965), *Cast a Giant Shadow* (1965), *Khartoum* (1966), *The Long Duel* (1967), *Casino Royale* (1967), *The Dirty Dozen* (1967), *The Last Valley* (1971), *When Eight Bells Toll* (1971), *Macbeth* (1971), *Young Winston* (1972), and *The Sea Wolves* (1980).

DICK BULLOCK (1939–1971)

Five-foot-ten, 165-pound Frederick Bullock was a member of the Stuntmen's Association who made the break to Stunts Unlimited. His most notable stunt was a stirrup drag into the tongue of a wagon on *The Undefeated* (1969). He worked on *The Green Berets* (1968), *Chubasco* (1968), *Hellfighters* (1968), *Che!* (1969), *The Good Guys and the Bad Guys* (1969), *Chisum* (1970), *Beneath the Planet of the Apes* (1970), *Support Your Local Gunfighter* (1971), *Chrome and Hot Leather* (1971), *Something Big* (1971), and *Molly and Lawless John* (1972). A rising talent in the industry, Bullock died at the age of 32 in a Kansas auto accident.

EARL BUNN (1890–1954)

One-legged, one-eyed stuntman Earl Dewitt Bunn was injured by shelling and mustard gas in World War I. The injuries didn't stop the Amsterdam, New York, native from making his way to Hollywood as a double for John Barrymore on *The Sea Beast* (1926) and *Moby Dick* (1930). Bunn was best known as a sharpshooter, firing live rounds of ammunition at stars. He could shoot a glass out of a person's hand. At Republic Studios he drove in chase scenes and showed up for brawls whenever a peg-legged character was needed. He worked on *The Hurricane* (1937), *SOS Coast Guard* (1937), *Dick Tracy Returns* (1938), *Daredevils of the Red Circle* (1939), *Dick Tracy's G-Men* (1939), *King of the Royal Mounted* (1940), *Adventures of Captain Marvel* (1941), *King of the Texas Rangers* (1941), *Valley of the Sun* (1942), and *Two Yanks in Trinidad* (1942).

See: Lindeman, Edith. "Earl Bunn Shoots With Aim Guaranteed to Miss Stars." *Richmond Times.* March 19, 1939.

JIM BURK (1932–2009)

James Haskell Burk was born in Newhall, California. He was active in rodeo at Pierce Junior College and spent two years with the U.S. Army during the Korean War. His stepdad was horse wrangler Jim Louckes, who helped get him into the business doubling Buddy Baer on *Flame of Araby* (1951). Best known as one of the Hannassey brothers on *The Big Country* (1958), the lantern-jawed, 6'4", 225-pound Burk doubled big men Chuck Connors, Charlton Heston, Sean Connery, Gregory Peck, James Arness, Bo Svenson, and Tom Selleck. He doubled John Wayne on *Hellfighters* (1968), *True Grit* (1969), *Chisum* (1970), *The Cowboys* (1972), and *The Shootist* (1976). Burk is Rooster Cogburn charging a horse across the meadow while spinning a Winchester in the *True Grit* climax. He and his horse Detonator were part of the fourteen-rider horse fall seen in *The Alamo* (1960).

A top fight man, Burk memorably squared off against Merlin Olsen on *The Undefeated* (1969), Paul Newman on *Sometimes a Great Notion* (1970), and Jack Nicholson on *Chinatown* (1974). He doubled Forrest Tucker for the climactic fight with John Wayne on *Chisum* (1970) and took part in major brouhahas on *McLintock!* (1963), *The War Wagon* (1967), *The Trial of Billy Jack* (1974), *Convoy* (1978), and *Bronco Billy* (1980). On TV he filled in for James Arness' epic battle with Jim Davis on the *Gunsmoke* episode "Railroad." Burk crafted leather, designing saddles and custom stunt bags carried by many stuntmen of the day.

He worked on *Pony Express* (1953), *Arrowhead* (1953), *Pork Chop Hill* (1959), *The Horse Soldiers* (1959), *The Comancheros* (1961), *Geronimo* (1962), *The Hallelujah Trail* (1965), *Stagecoach* (1966), *The Way West* (1967), *The Green Berets* (1968), *Mackenna's Gold* (1968), *The Devil's Brigade* (1968), *Rio Lobo* (1970), *The Animals* (1970), *One More Train to Rob* (1971), *Big Jake* (1971), *Life and Times of Judge Roy Bean* (1972), *The Train Robbers* (1973), *Oklahoma Crude* (1973), *The Stone Killer* (1973), *The Outfit* (1973), *Three the Hard Way* (1974), *Take a Hard Ride* (1975), *The Man Who Would Be King* (1975), *Crazy Mama* (1975), *Gator* (1976), *Final Chapter—Walking Tall* (1977), *Hooper* (1978), *Prophecy* (1979), *Tom Horn* (1980), *The Long Riders* (1980), and *Mountain Men* (1980). TV credits include *Tales of Wells Fargo, Wagon Train, Lancer, Mission: Impossible, Mannix, Hec Ramsey, M*A*S*H,* and *Fantasy Island.* A member of Stunts Unlimited and an inductee of the Stuntmen's Hall of Fame, Burk died of heart failure at the age of 76.

See: "Empty Saddles." *Western Clippings.* #90, July-August 2009; Lilley, Tim. *Campfire Conversations.* Akron, OH: Big Trail, 2007.

RON BURKE

Six-foot-one, 175-pound Ron Burke grew up in the business as an extra. An expert swimmer and scuba diver, he was intrigued by the money he saw the stuntmen making and pursued that as a career. Burke most notably portrayed an undersea monster on *Destination Inner Space* (1966) and doubled John Smith on *Hot Rod Girl* (1956) and the TV series *Laramie* (1959–63). On *The Disorderly Orderly* (1964) he wore a full body cast for a memorable stunt.

He worked on *Rebel Without a Cause* (1955), *Giant* (1956), *Lafayette Escadrille* (1958), *Spartacus* (1960), *Incident at Phantom Hill* (1966), *A Fine Madness* (1966), *Warning Shot* (1967), *Welcome to Hard Times* (1967), *Hot Rods to Hell* (1967), *The Boston Strangler* (1968), *The Great Bank Robbery* (1969), *Catch–22* (1970), *Airport '77* (1977), *One Man Jury* (1978), and *Prophecy* (1979). TV credits include *Twilight Zone, The Virginian, Laredo, Batman, The Green Hornet, I Spy, Star Trek, Mannix, Dragnet, Adam–12, Emergency, McCloud, Police Story,* and *Petrocelli.* Burke was a member of the Stuntmen's Association.

See: Parla, Paul and Donna. *Filmfax.* "Monster Man." August 1997.

STEPHEN BURNETTE (1942–)

The son of western character player Smiley Burnette, Stephen "Smiley" Burnette grew up watching stuntmen Jock Mahoney and Al Wyatt work on his dad's Durango Kid films. This planted the seed for his future. He doubled David Stollery of *The Adventures of Spin and Marty* (1955–57) and worked behind the scenes on his father's touring show. Burnette served with the U.S. Navy, which stood him well for his participation on the naval war films *Tora! Tora! Tora!* (1970) and *Midway* (1976). He did fast draw at Corriganville and was part of the first Universal Studios stunt show. Burnette has the distinction of working on *Planet of the Apes* (1968) and all of its sequels.

He worked on *4 for Texas* (1963), *Cheyenne Autumn* (1964), *The Hallelujah Trail* (1965),

Beau Geste (1966), *Night of the Grizzly* (1966), *The Rare Breed* (1966), *Harper* (1966), *The War Wagon* (1967), *Tobruk* (1967), *Bonnie and Clyde* (1967), *Firecreek* (1968), *Hang 'Em High* (1968), *The Wild Bunch* (1969), *Paint Your Wagon* (1969), *There Was a Crooked Man...* (1970), *Airport* (1970), *The Cheyenne Social Club* (1970), *Dirty Harry* (1971), *Billy Jack* (1971), *Joe Kidd* (1972), *The Godfather* (1972), *The Sting* (1973), *Dillinger* (1973), *The Parallax View* (1974), *The Front Page* (1974), *Earthquake* (1974), *The Towering Inferno* (1974), *The Apple Dumpling Gang* (1975), *Blazing Saddles* (1974), *Mother, Jugs, and Speed* (1976), *The Big Bus* (1976), *Two-Minute Warning* (1976), *Logan's Run* (1976), *Silver Streak* (1976), *The Shootist* (1976), *The Gauntlet* (1977), *Smokey and the Bandit* (1977), *Capricorn One* (1978), *1941* (1979), *The Jerk* (1979), *Tom Horn* (1980), *The Long Riders* (1980), and *Smokey and the Bandit 2* (1980). TV credits include *Laramie, Combat, Wagon Train, Daniel Boone, Death Valley Days, Bonanza, Gunsmoke, The Virginian, Laredo, Honey West, F Troop, Get Smart, The Big Valley, The Rat Patrol, Cimarron Strip, High Chaparral, Lancer, It Takes a Thief, Mod Squad, Ironside, Adam–12, Mannix, Mission: Impossible, Alias Smith and Jones, Kung Fu, Emergency, The Rockford Files, The Six Million Dollar Man, The Bionic Woman, Police Story, Police Woman, Baretta, Little House on the Prairie, Grizzly Adams, Wonder Woman, Charlie's Angels, CHiPs, The Incredible Hulk, Battlestar Galactica, Buck Rogers, BJ and the Bear,* and *The Dukes of Hazzard.*

See: www.smileyburnette.org.

POLLY BURSON (1919–2006)

Known as "The Queen of Western Stuntwomen," 5'5" Polly Burson was born Pauline Shelton in Ontario, Oregon. Her parents were rodeo riders. Polly toured France and the Far East in a Wild West show as a trick rider then won the Powder Puff Derby. She is best known for a horse-to-train transfer doubling Betty Hutton on *The Perils of Pauline* (1947). Becoming adept at high work, she went over a waterfall for Yvonne De Carlo on *Raw Edge* (1956) and took a sixty-foot fall into a net for Kim Novak on *Vertigo* (1958). Burson doubled Barbara Stanwyck on TV's *The Big Valley* (1965–69) and was a charter member of the Stuntwomen's Association in 1967.

She doubled Paulette Goddard on *Unconquered* (1947), Lucille Ball on *Fancy Pants* (1950), Betty Hutton on *The Greatest Show on Earth* (1952), Jean Peters on *Niagara* (1953), Julie Adams on *Creature from the Black Lagoon* (1954), Dorothy Malone on *Pillars of the Sky* (1956), and Sophia Loren on *Heller in Pink Tights* (1960). Her toughest stunt was doubling Loren for a Mazeppa ride lying flat on the back of a horse that was running on a treadmill for the shot. She doubled Kim Darby for a fall into a snake pit on *True Grit* (1969) and subbed for Bette Davis, Jennifer Jones, Anne Baxter, Greer Garson, Mary Moore, Susan Cabot, Felicia Farr, Mala Powers, and Doris Day. Burson injured her back in 1969 and began working less. On *Earthquake* (1974) she broke a leg when a flood wiped out the porch she was on. Marriages to stuntmen Wayne Burson and Jerry Gatlin did not last.

She worked on *The Crimson Ghost* (1946), *Winchester '73* (1950), *Westward the Women* (1951), *A Ticket to Tomahawk* (1951), *Scarlet Angel* (1952), *Bend of the River* (1952), *Gunsmoke* (1953), *Wings of the Hawk* (1953), *Destry* (1954), *The Rains of Ranchipur* (1955), *The Ten Commandments* (1956), *Night Passage* (1957), *Some Like it Hot* (1959), *The Jayhawkers!* (1959), *Spartacus* (1960), *Hell Bent for Leather* (1960), *How the West Was Won* (1962), *McLintock!* (1963), *Cheyenne Autumn* (1964), *Seven Women* (1966), and *El Dorado* (1967). A Golden Boot Award honoree, she was an inductee of the Pro Rodeo Hall of Fame, the National Cowgirl Hall of Fame, and the Stuntmen's Hall of Fame. Burson died at the age of 86.

See: De Witt, Barbara. "Those Stunts Were No Act for Hollywood's Horse Women." *Chicago Tribune.* March 16, 1995; Lilley, Tim. *Campfire Conversations Complete.* Big Trail, 2010; McLellan, Dennis. "Polly Burson, 86, Pioneering Stunt Woman, Rodeo Rider." *Los Angeles Times.* April 16, 2006; Wiener, David Jon. *Burns, Falls, and Crashes.* Jefferson, NC: McFarland, 1996.

WAYNE BURSON (1920–1997)

Horse specialist Wayne Harold Burson was born Wayne Woodmansee in Moscow, Colorado. A former all-around rodeo competitor, he doubled Van Heflin on *Shane* (1953), Ronald Reagan on *Cattle Queen of Montana* (1954), and Kirk Douglas on *Spartacus* (1960). Others doubled include Gene Autry, Roy Rogers, Henry Fonda,

Polly Burson, doubling Yvonne De Carlo, goes over a waterfall on the Universal back lot on *Raw Edge* (1956). The stuntman is likely Rory Calhoun's regular double Reg Parton.

Glenn Ford, and Jimmy Wakely. On TV, Burson doubled Jay Silverheels on *The Lone Ranger* (1949–57) and worked on *Tales of Wells Fargo* (1957–62) with Dale Robertson. At one point in the 1950s Burson was the industry's highest-paid stuntman.

Burson trained *The Lone Ranger* horses Silver and Scout and quit stunting in the 1960s to become a trainer of thoroughbred race horses. He was married to top stuntwoman Patty Burson and she kept his name professionally even after they were divorced. Credits include *Bronco Buster* (1952), *The Cimarron Kid* (1951), *Destry* (1954), *Backlash* (1956), *The Burning Hills* (1956), *Gunman's Walk* (1958), and the TV shows *Have Gun—Will Travel* and *Bat Masterson*. An inductee of the Stuntmen's Hall of Fame, Burson died from congestive heart failure at the age of 76.

See: Menges, Jack. "From Hollywood to Horses." *Oakland Tribune.* March 10, 1977; "Wayne Burson, Ex-Hollywood Stuntman Dies at 76." *Oregonian.* May 9, 1997.

BILLY BURTON

William H. Burton was born in Tehachapi, California and grew up in the shadow of MGM Studios in Culver City. A 170-pound six-footer, he was wrestling steers in the rodeo prior to his first film assignment playing an Arab horseman on *Beau Geste* (1966). Burton was soon doubling Wayne Maunder on the TV series *Custer* (1967) and *Lancer* (1968–70), Frank Sinatra for horse falls on *Dirty Dingus Magee* (1970), and Ryan O'Neal for the tough car work on *The Driver* (1978). In addition to being cast as one of Kirk Douglas' deputies on *Posse* (1975), he doubled Bruce Dern.

Burton was a Professional Rodeo Association cowboy and a competitive motocross racer. He excelled in a series of all-around stunt competitions in the late 1970s, winning $13,000 and a high performance Trans-Am as his first place reward. His peers nicknamed him Billy America. In later years he doubled Roger Moore as James Bond on *Octopussy* (1983) and Warren Beatty on *Dick Tracy* (1990) while moving into second unit directing.

He worked on *The Pink Jungle* (1968), *The Great Bank Robbery* (1969), *The Undefeated* (1969), *Tell Them Willie Boy Is Here* (1969), *The Good Guys and the Bad Guys* (1969), *Beneath the Planet of the Apes* (1970), *Little Fauss and Big*

Halsey (1970), *Little Big Man* (1970), *Angel Unchained* (1970), *Something Big* (1971), *Star Spangled Girl* (1971), *Culpepper Cattle Co.* (1972), *Boxcar Bertha* (1972), *Ulzana's Raid* (1972), *Pat Garrett and Billy the Kid* (1973), *Blazing Saddles* (1974), *Three the Hard Way* (1974), *Earthquake* (1974), *A Boy and His Dog* (1975), *Bite the Bullet* (1975), *Crazy Mama* (1975), *The Killer Elite* (1975), *The Man Who Would Be King* (1975), *Street People* (1975), *Moonshine County Express* (1977), *Game of Death* (1978), *Hooper* (1978), *Comes a Horseman* (1978), *Hot Lead and Cold Feet* (1978), *The Long Riders* (1980), *Smokey and the Bandit 2* (1980), and *Heaven's Gate* (1980). He was stunt coordinator on the mini-series *The Macahans* (1976), *Centennial* (1978), *The Blue and the Gray* (1982), and *Lonesome Dove* (1989). TV credits include *Gunsmoke, Mannix, Mission: Impossible, The Immortal, Bearcats,* and *Barnaby Jones.* He was a member of Stunts Unlimited; his children William, David, and Heather became stunt performers.

See: Blanchard, Nina. *How to Break into Motion Pictures, Television, Commercials, & Modeling.* NY: Doubleday, 1978; "Stuntmen Compete in Sports Spectacular." *Joplin Globe.* January 15, 1977; Waxman, Sharon. "Lost Cowboys." *Milwaukee Journal Sentinel.* November 21, 2003.

HAL BURTON (1942–)

Harold David Burton was raised in Santa Monica, California, and was bull riding in the rodeo arena while still in his teens. An excellent horseman, 5'10", 175-pound Burton was hired to double Michael Landon on *Bonanza* in 1967 and continued in that capacity through 1973. He also doubled guest stars John Saxon and Dabney Coleman. Burton followed Landon onto *Little House on the Prairie* (1974–83) and regularly weight-trained with him at Vince's Gym. A member of the Stuntmen's Association, Burton doubled William Devane and worked on films from *The Nickel Ride* (1975) to *Tombstone* (1993).

See: "Knowing the Ropes." *L.A. Daily News.* September 5, 1994.

ARCHIE BUTLER (1911–1977)

Trick and bareback riding rodeo veteran Archie Butler was a constant presence on the TV series *The Rifleman* (1958–63) as a background player and double for Paul Fix. Butler later worked for director Sam Peckinpah on *Major Dundee* (1965) and *The Wild Bunch* (1969). He entered the stunt field in the 1930s, logging credits on *Under Two Flags* (1936), *The Hunchback of Notre Dame* (1939), *Across the Wide Missouri* (1951), *Westward the Women* (1951), and *Firecreek* (1968). On TV he can also be seen on *Wyatt Earp, The Big Valley,* and *Bonanza.* Between Hollywood assignments he worked at a pack station in the High Sierras. Butler died at the age of 65.

DICK BUTLER (1937–)

Richard E. Butler was raised in Long Beach, California, and starred in football as a quarterback for Wilson High. Six feet tall and 215 pounds, he played center and linebacker for the UCLA Bruins football squad from 1955 to 1958. That led to gladiatorial work on *Spartacus* (1960) and pursuit of the stunt profession. An early stunt assignment came on *It's a Mad, Mad, Mad, Mad World* (1963). Butler's highest profile stunts came doubling Sean Connery during the majority of the Mustang Mach 1 car chase on *Diamonds Are Forever* (1971) and Robert Shaw on *Jaws* (1975). He also doubled Gene Hackman and Brian Keith.

In 1972 Butler was accidentally run over by a boat while working in the water of San Francisco Bay on a *The Streets of San Francisco* episode. He suffered injuries to his head, back, chest, and legs. Series star Michael Douglas jumped into the water and helped keep him afloat until rescue crews could arrive. Butler completely recovered and went on to coordinate the TV cop dramas *Police Story* (1973–77) and *Police Woman* (1974–78).

He worked on *The Great Bank Robbery* (1969), *Conquest of the Planet of the Apes* (1972), *What's Up, Doc?* (1972), *Slither* (1973), *Battle for the Planet of the Apes* (1973), *The Towering Inferno* (1974), *Freaky Friday* (1977), *Black Sunday* (1977), *Stunts* (1977), and *Superman* (1978). TV credits include *Maverick, Daniel Boone, Adam–12, Joe Forrester,* and *Matt Helm.* Butler is a member of the Stuntmen's Association.

See: Teele, Jack. "Sports About Town." *Press Telegram.* September 18, 1958.

CARROLL BYRD

The daughter of *Dick Tracy* star Ralph Byrd and actress Virginia Carroll, Carroll Byrd grew up riding show horses and was able to persuade action director William Witney to allow her to do her first film stunt at the age of fourteen. She continued stunting while attending Canoga Park High and Pierce College. Her best known work came on the TV shows *Wagon Train* (1957–65) and *The Fugitive* (1963–67). Film credits include *Master of the World* (1961), directed by Witney, and *Pete 'n' Tillie* (1972), where she doubled Geraldine Page for a fight with Carol Burnett. The 5'7" Byrd also doubled Shirley Knight and performed in Universal Studio stunt shows.

See: *San Antonio Express.* "Stunt Girl Trades Jeans for Script." February 2, 1964.

DAVID CADIENTE (1937–2010)

John David Cadiente made a name for himself in the Los Angeles area as a hustling basketball guard at Valley College where he was named to the All-Metro Team in 1958. Known as David "Duke" Cadiente, he landed one of his first parts as a boxer on the Elvis Presley film *Kid Galahad* (1962). He became a recognizable extra and bit player appearing as islanders, Asians, Mexicans, and Indians. His roles often called for athleticism. He played a wave enthusiast on *Ride the Wild Surf* (1964) and began to gravitate toward stunt work as he built up action credits on *The Professionals* (1966), *Harper* (1966), and *The Green Berets* (1968).

He worked on *Donovan's Reef* (1963), *King Rat* (1965), *Seven Women* (1966), *Gambit* (1966), *Stay Away, Joe* (1968), *True Grit* (1969), *Che!* (1969), *The Great Bank Robbery* (1969), *There Was a Crooked Man...* (1970), and *Blazing Saddles* (1974). Cadiente's career was heavy on TV work as he was fire safety coordinator for Burbank Studios. TV credits include *Adventures in Paradise, Hawaiian Eye, Gallant Men, Daniel Boone, The Virginian, The Wild Wild West, Star Trek, Bearcats, Kung Fu, The Rockford Files, Wonder Woman, Charlie's Angels, Vega$,* and *Fantasy Island.* His son Jeff became a stuntman.

See: "Fireman Injured." *St. Joseph News.* July 29, 1982.

HANK CALIA (1934–)

Henry A. Calia trained with Lennie Geer and performed in the original Universal Studio stunt show. A high fall specialist, 5'7", 180-pound

Calia doubled short, stocky types such as Ed Asner and Robert Blake. He worked on TV's *The Virginian* and in the movies *The Appaloosa* (1966), *The Green Berets* (1968), *Che!* (1969), *Beneath the Planet of the Apes* (1970), *Conquest of the Planet of the Apes* (1972), *Battle for the Planet of the Apes* (1973), *Freebie and the Bean* (1974), *The Towering Inferno* (1974), *Earthquake* (1974), *The Stunt Man* (1980), and *Heaven's Gate* (1980). A member of the Stuntmen's Association, he was married to stuntwoman Teri McComas.

ROD CAMERON (1910–1983)

Six-foot-five, 215-pound Rod Cameron was born Nathan Roderick Cox in Calgary, Alberta, Canada, and was raised in New Jersey. "Rod Cameron" was the center on his high school basketball team and played tackle for a semi-pro football team, the New York Steamrollers. He was an excellent swimmer, diver, and ice hockey player, but failed the physical to become a Royal Canadian Mountie. After time spent outdoors as a sandhog and construction worker, Cameron ended up in California digging a tunnel near Palm Springs. He entered films as a stuntman working in that capacity on *Rangers of Fortune* (1940) and *The Forest Rangers* (1942). Some sources claim he doubled Buck Jones, which Cameron denied in interviews.

He distinguished himself as a two-fisted Republic serial star, playing Rex Bennett in both *G-Men vs. the Black Dragon* (1942) and *Secret Service in Darkest Africa* (1943). This latter served as Steven Spielberg's inspiration for *Raiders of the Lost Ark* (1981) and Indiana Jones. The granite-jawed Cameron was a rugged, virile B-movie and TV star, occasionally dubbed "the poor man's John Wayne." He had good fight scenes with Tom Tyler on *Boss of Boomtown* (1944), George Montgomery on *Belle Starr's Daughter* (1948) and *Dakota Lil* (1950), and Fred Graham on *Fort Osage* (1952). Cameron died of cancer at the age of 73.

See: Aaker, Everett. *Encyclopedia of Early Television Crime Fighters.* Jefferson, NC: McFarland, 2006.

DICK CANGEY (1933–2003)

Pennsylvania-born Dick Cangey pursued a career as a boxer, amassing a record of forty-three wins and only three defeats fighting out of Cleveland, Ohio. His career was interrupted by service with the U.S. Army. Cangey moved to California and took a job as a bar bouncer. There he met actor Peter Breck, who offered him a job as his stand-in on the TV series *The Big Valley* (1965–66). The husky Cangey befriended Robert Conrad and showed up with regularity as one of the stuntmen on *The Wild Wild West* (1966–69). As a stuntman, Cangey was limited to fight work, but that he did with commendable skill. Conrad continued to hire Cangey throughout the next decade.

See: Cangey, Dick. *Inside* The Wild Wild West. Cangey, 1996; "Cangey Scores as Stunt Man." *Youngstown Vindicator.* August 24, 1968.

JOE CANUTT (1937–)

Born in Los Angeles, Harry Joe Canutt is the son of Yakima Canutt, the greatest rodeo cowboy and movie stuntman who ever lived. Those were big boots to fill, but young Joe did all right for himself. As boys, he and brother Tap were practicing stunts on the sly in an effort to emulate their father's movie exploits. They'd practice saddle falls on the river banks or jump off the roof of their house into old mattresses. As they grew into young men, Yak began to bring them onto the movie sets as extras, and they were soon doing stunt work and making their old man proud.

Six-foot-four, 195-pound Joe took time off for service as a U.S. Navy diver and was a member of the Professional Rodeo Cowboy Association. He earned prize money but wasn't the bronc rider his father was and began to concentrate on his movie career. He made his name doubling Charlton Heston during the famous chariot race on *Ben-Hur* (1959), especially when he did an unplanned vault over the front of the chariot and managed to somehow hang on and pull himself back in. The fantastic accident was kept in the film and became one of the greatest known stunts in movie history. Joe worked with Heston throughout his career as double and coordinator on all his major action films, including such epics as *El Cid* (1961), *Major Dundee* (1965), *The War Lord* (1965), *Khartoum* (1966), *Julius Caesar* (1970), and *Antony and Cleopatra* (1972). He fought Heston on *Planet of the Apes* (1968).

On Sam Peckinpah's *The Wild Bunch* (1969), Canutt took part in some of the biggest

Joe Canutt does a full burn in his special fire suit on *The War Lord* (1965).

stunts. He performed a Running W for Ernest Borgnine and was blown off the bridge into the river with half a dozen men and horses. Canutt is sometimes credited with making the famous cliff jump on *Butch Cassidy and the Sundance Kid* (1969). He may have done the beginning of the jump on location, but the jump that ended up on film was done later at a studio lake by Howard Curtis and Mickey Gilbert. Canutt was stunt co-ordinator on *Patton* (1970) and performed a helicopter-to-plane transfer on *Airport '75* (1974). He was a leading proponent of safe stunt equipment, especially in regard to fire stunts. He and Tap devised the somersault harness for saddle falls, among other stunt equipment.

He worked on *20,000 Leagues Under the Sea* (1954), *The Prodigal* (1955), *Forbidden Planet* (1956), *Westward Ho, the Wagons!* (1956), *The Guns of Fort Petticoat* (1957), *Pork Chop Hill* (1959), *Spartacus* (1960), *The Alamo* (1960), *The Comancheros* (1961), *McLintock!* (1963), *The Great Race* (1965), *Shenandoah* (1965), *The Rare Breed* (1966), *Texas Across the River* (1966), *El Dorado* (1967), *Camelot* (1967), *Bandolero!* (1968), *The Scalphunters* (1968), *Will Penny* (1968), *Mackenna's Gold* (1969), *The Cheyenne Social Club* (1970), *Dirty Dingus Magee* (1970), *Macho Callahan* (1970), *Diamonds Are Forever* (1971), *The Omega Man* (1971), *Jeremiah Johnson* (1972), *Across 110th Street* (1972), *Skyjacked* (1972), *Papillon* (1973), *Soylent Green* (1973), *99 and 44/100 percent Dead* (1974), *Earthquake* (1974), *Doc Savage* (1975), *The Drowning Pool* (1975), *The Last Hard Men* (1976), *Breakheart Pass* (1976), *MacArthur* (1977), and *Mountain Men* (1980). TV credits include *Gunsmoke, Wagon Train, Zorro, The Virginian,* and *Daniel Boone.* Canutt was a member of the Stuntmen's Association and an inductee of the Stuntmen's Hall of Fame.

See: Foster, Jeremy. "All the Work, None of the Credit." *Santa Ynez Valley Journal.* July 16, 2009.

TAP CANUTT (1932–)

The oldest son of Yakima Canutt, Tap Canutt was born Edward Clay Canutt in Los Angeles. He started in the business with a horse fall for Randolph Scott on *Hangman's Knot* (1952) prior to service in the Korean War. He doubled Stephen Boyd on *Fall of the Roman Empire*

(1964), Lee Marvin on *Cat Ballou* (1965), Adam West on *The Outlaws Is Coming* (1965), James Coburn on *The Last Hard Men* (1976), and Guy Williams on the TV series *Zorro* (1957–61). On *The Wild Bunch* (1969) he jumped through candy glass, tumbled down a sand dune in a group fall, and was blown off the bridge in the famous action sequence. A 1959 episode of *26 Men* was a pilot for a proposed series titled *Tumbleweed Ranger* that would have starred Canutt. His favored falling horse was named Gypsy.

He worked on *Only the Valiant* (1951), *The Stranger Wore a Gun* (1953), *The Last Command* (1955), *Friendly Persuasion* (1956), *Westward Ho, the Wagons!* (1956), *The Guns of Fort Petticoat* (1957), *Spartacus* (1960), *The Alamo* (1960), *El Cid* (1961), *The Comancheros* (1961), *It's a Mad, Mad, Mad, Mad World* (1963), *McLintock!* (1963), *The War Lord* (1965), *Khartoum* (1966), *Camelot* (1967), *Counterpoint* (1968), *Bandolero!* (1968), *Planet of the Apes* (1968), *The Good Guys and the Bad Guys* (1969), *The Undefeated* (1969), *Beneath the Planet of the Apes* (1970), *Rio Lobo* (1970), *A Man Called Horse* (1970), *The Omega Man* (1971), *The Cowboys* (1972), *Joe Kidd* (1972), *Planet Earth* (1974), *The Master Gunfighter* (1975), and *Mountain Men* (1980). TV credits include *Daniel Boone.* He was a member of the Stuntmen's Association and an inductee of the Stuntmen's Hall of Fame.

See: Mitchum, Petrina Day & Audrey Paiva. *Hollywood Hoofbeats.* BowTie, 2005.

YAKIMA CANUTT (1895–1986)

Six-foot-three, 210-pound Enos Edward Canutt was born in Colfax, Washington, near the Snake River Hills. He was raised on a ranch and briefly worked as a lumberjack. His great love was the rodeo, and he began competing successfully while in his teens. He acquired the name Yakima from his fellow rodeo pals at the Pendleton Round-Up in Oregon. Canutt served with the U.S. Navy at the end of World War I even as he won a succession of rodeo titles such as the Police Gazette Championship and the Roosevelt Trophy. Canutt became the four-time All-Around Cowboy Champion of the World, and his rodeo success attracted the attention of Hollywood.

Canutt started as a part-time stuntman during the rodeo off-season, but by the mid–1920s was headlining his own silent films. His top film

Yakima Canutt gets airborne from a Bob Steele punch on _Under Texas Skies_ (1940).

from that era was _The Devil Horse_ (1926), containing a memorable stunt with Yak thrashed around by the horse Rex without letting go. He had contracted a severe case of pneumonia that affected his vocal cords in the Navy, so with the advent of sound he stepped back from starring roles to play western heavies and do stunts. He worked with John Wayne and became known throughout the industry as the Father of the Modern Fight Scene thanks to creating the Pass System. Outside of his battles with Wayne, he had a great fight with Bob Livingston on _Heart of the Rockies_ (1938) and a notable one with Bob Steele on _Under Texas Skies_ (1940).

Yak could lay claim to performing what many consider the single greatest stunt in film history when he leapt onto a six-up team of horses and was dragged under a moving coach's wheels at top speed on _Stagecoach_ (1939). Then doubling John Wayne he leapt out to the lead horse to recover the reins. Canutt performed variations of that stunt on _Riders of the Dawn_ (1937) and _Zorro's Fighting Legion_ (1939), which might be

the most impressive of all. In addition to Wayne, he doubled Errol Flynn, Clark Gable, Henry Fonda, Victor McLaglen, Ray "Crash" Corrigan, Bob Livingston, Lon Chaney, Jr., Fred Thomson, and Tom Tyler.

Major Canutt stunts involved driving an exploding ammunition wagon on _Man of Conquest_ (1939) and escaping the burning of Atlanta on _Gone with the Wind_ (1939). On _Dark Command_ (1940) he went off a cliff with horses, a wagon, and other stuntmen. On many occasions he performed daring stunts that had never been attempted. On _Boom Town_ (1940) he had a rearing horse fall on him, and the saddle horn impaled his belly. On _Idaho_ (1943) he broke both his ankles jumping off a wagon. In light of these injuries, he moved into second unit directing, where he has the distinction of staging the amazing chariot race action sequence on _Ben-Hur_ (1959). He followed this masterpiece with more epic action on _Spartacus_ (1960), _El Cid_ (1961), and _Khartoum_ (1966). Sons Joe and Tap followed him into the business, becoming two of the top stuntmen of the early 1960s. Son-in-law Tom Dittman was an active stuntman in the late 1960s. In 1966 Yak was awarded a special Oscar for his lasting contributions to the motion picture industry.

He worked on *Thundering Herd* (1923), *Last of the Mohicans* (1932), *Elinor Norton* (1934), *The Farmer Takes a Wife* (1935), *Dante's Inferno* (1935), *The Last Days of Pompeii* (1935), *Fighting Marines* (1935), *The Charge of the Light Brigade* (1936), *Trail of the Lonesome Pine* (1936), *San Francisco* (1936), *Nancy Steele Is Missing* (1937), *In Old Chicago* (1937), *Ali Baba Goes to Town* (1937), *The Painted Stallion* (1937), *SOS Coast Guard* (1937), *Zorro Rides Again* (1937), *Gunsmoke Ranch* (1937), *The Lone Ranger* (1938), *Dick Tracy Returns* (1938), *Army Girl* (1938), *Daredevils of the Red Circle* (1939), *Dodge City* (1939), *Jesse James* (1939), *Captain Fury* (1939), *Virginia City* (1940), *One Million B.C.* (1940), *They Died with Their Boots On* (1941), *Gentleman Jim* (1942), *Spy Smasher* (1942), *Valley of the Sun* (1942), *Perils of Nyoka* (1942), *For Whom the Bell Tolls* (1943), *In Old Oklahoma* (1943), *Dakota* (1945), *The Doolins of Oklahoma* (1949), *Rocky Mountain* (1950), *Only the Valiant* (1951), *Ivanhoe* (1952), *Knights of the Round Table* (1953), *The Naked Spur* (1953), *King Richard and the Crusaders* (1954), *The Far Horizons* (1955), *Helen of Troy* (1955), *Westward Ho, the Wagons!* (1956), *Old Yeller* (1957), *Rio Bravo* (1959), *Swiss Family Robinson* (1960), *Fall of the Roman Empire* (1964), *Cat Ballou* (1965), *The Flim-Flam Man* (1967), *Where Eagles Dare* (1968), *A Man Called Horse* (1970), *Rio Lobo* (1970), and *Breakheart Pass* (1976). A screen legend, Yak was inducted into the Stuntmen's Hall of Fame, the Cowboy Hall of Fame, the Rodeo Hall of Fame, and the National Western Heritage Museum. He was an honorary member of the Stuntmen's Association and a Golden Boot honoree.

See: Canutt, Yakima, and John Crawford. *My Rodeo Years*. Jefferson, NC: McFarland, 2010; Canutt, Yakima, and Oliver Drake. *Stunt Man*. New York: Walker & Co, 1979; Ross, John. "Life of Yakima Canutt." *Inside Stunts*. Winter-Spring 2005.

JOHN "BUD" CARDOS (1929–)

John "Bud" Cardos was born in St. Louis, Missouri, but grew up in California as a child

actor. As a young man he lived in Big Bear, California, wrangling and occasionally stunting on Gene Autry and Roy Rogers films. After military service he moved to the San Fernando Valley and learned the stunt trade from Buster Wiles. He worked on TV doing stunts for *Wagon Train, Bonanza, Maverick, 26 Men, Daniel Boone,* and *High Chaparral* while participating in small rodeos. One of his more interesting assignments came as a bird wrangler on *The Birds* (1963).

Cardos wore many hats on low-budget films. He doubled Cameron Mitchell (for a fire stunt) on *Nightmare in Wax* (1966), Adam Roarke on *Hells Angels on Wheels* (1967), and Jim Davis on *Five Bloody Graves* (1969). Cardos did motorcycle stunts on *Savage Seven* (1968) and *Satan's Sadists* (1969), where he had a big fight scene with Gary Kent. On *The Female Bunch* (1969) he did a horse drag wrapped in barbed wire. Cardos directed second unit shots for Sam Peckinpah on *The Wild Bunch* (1969), performed a well-regarded car chase on *Jud* (1971), and set up (what appears to be) a plane crash into a house on *Kingdom of the Spiders* (1977). He was often brought onto first units to finish troubled films.

See: Albright, Brian. *Wild Beyond Belief.* Jefferson, NC: McFarland, 2008; Kent, Gary. *Shadows and Light: Journeys with Outlaws in Revolutionary Hollywood.* Austin, Texas: Dalton, 2009; Plante, Bob. "John 'Bud' Cardos." *Psychotronic Video.* #24, 1997.

AL CARMICHAEL (1928–)

Albert Reinhold Carmichael was born in Boston and raised in California. He was a football star at Gardena High and with the U.S. Marines El Toro squad. He made his name upon his return from the military at Santa Ana College and USC, where he was the 1953 Rose Bowl hero, scoring the game's only points. He garnered All-American mention. Six-foot-one, 200-pound Carmichael was drafted first round into the NFL as a halfback, pass receiver, and kickoff return specialist for the Green Bay Packers, setting several Packer special teams records. He set an NFL record with a 106-yard kickoff return and scored the first touchdown in AFL history as a member of the Denver Broncos in 1960.

Carmichael was recruited as a stunt double for Burt Lancaster on *Jim Thorpe—All American*

(1951), *Elmer Gantry* (1960), and *Birdman of Alcatraz* (1962). He was one of the doubles for Kirk Douglas on *Spartacus* (1960) and worked on TV's *Rawhide*. In all, he worked on more than fifty films as a stuntman including *Saturday's Hero* (1951), *All-American* (1953), *Pork Chop Hill* (1959), *It Started with a Kiss* (1959), *The Big Operator* (1959), *Son of Flubber* (1962), and *How the West Was Won* (1962). Carmichael was inducted into the Green Bay Packers Hall of Fame, the Junior College Hall of Fame, the All-Service Hall of Fame, and the Orange County Sports Hall of Fame.

See: Crowe, Jerry. "Carmichael Goes Extra Yard in Autobiography." *Los Angeles Times*. October 3, 2006; Digiovanna, Mike. "Tapping His Potential." *Los Angeles Times*. October 21, 1992; Moss, Irv. "Carmichael Scored Broncos' First TD." *Denver Post*. August 10, 2010.

JOHNNY CARPENTER (1914–2003)

Arkansas-born Jasper Carpenter was raised on a farm and played baseball at the University of Arkansas. He was signed by the Chicago White Sox organization but broke his back in a hit-and-run accident, ending his sports career. Carpenter landed in Los Angeles, working at a stable where his horseback skills gained notice and got him work on *National Velvet* (1944). A saddle fall specialist, he doubled Jimmy Ellison on *I Killed Geronimo* (1950) and played the Tucson Kid on *Cattle Queen* (1951). He had the lead on *Badman's Gold* (1951) and went on to write, produce, and star in his own low-budget 1950s westerns with titles such as *Son of the Renegade* (1953) and *Lawless Rider* (1954). On *Outlaw Treasure* (1955) and *I Killed Wild Bill Hickok* (1956) he used the pseu-

Kenne Duncan takes a punch from Johnny Carpenter on *Badman's Gold* (1951).

donym John Forbes. Two of the titles were directed by Yakima Canutt and Richard Talmadge. They were the last of the series westerns.

He worked on *Red Canyon* (1949), *The Kid from Texas* (1950), *Comanche Territory* (1950), *Cave of Outlaws* (1951), *The Duel at Silver Creek* (1952), *Law and Order* (1953), *Backlash* (1956), and *Red Sundown* (1956). TV credits include *Wild Bill Hickok, Judge Roy Bean, Death Valley Days,* and *The Rifleman.* For many years Carpenter ran the Heaven on Earth Ranch for disabled children. His brother Frank "Big Red" Carpenter also performed stunts. An inductee of the Stuntmen's Hall of Fame, Carpenter died at the age of 88.

See: McLellan, Dennis. "Johnny Carpenter: Actor Ran Ranch for Disabled Kids." *San Francisco Chronicle.* March 7, 2003.

BARTLETT CARRE (1897–1971)

Bartlett A. Carre was born in Melrose, Massachusetts. A silent movie stuntman, he is best known for doubling Slim Summerville on *All Quiet on the Western Front* (1930). Carre worked often with Buck Jones and remained active in 1930s B-westerns before graduating to assistant director, production manager, and producer. Carre was in those occupations until the 1960s. He directed the film *Gun Smoke* (1935). An honorary member of the Stuntmen's Association, he died from a respiratory ailment at the age of 73.

FRED CARSON (1923–2001)

Fred Carson was born in Harlingen, Texas, and learned fancy gun handling skills at the age of nine from a genuine Texas Ranger. A rodeo cowboy and horse trainer, he doubled Anthony Quinn on *Viva Zapata!* (1952) and Victor Mature on *The Robe* (1953), *Demetrius and the Gladiators* (1954), and *The Egyptian* (1954). He also subbed for Rory Calhoun, Jeff Chandler, Rock Hudson, Rod Cameron, Claude Akins, Clint Eastwood, Cesar Romero, John Carroll, Jeff York, and Michael Forest. The 6'4", 205-pound Carson was with Michael Ansara on the TV series *Broken Arrow* (1956–58) and occasionally doubled Clint Walker on *Cheyenne* (1955–62).

Carson was regarded as one of the top fight men in the profession, best exemplified by the tooth-and-nail struggle between the characters Geronimo and Cochise on *Battle at Apache Pass*

(1952), where Carson doubled Jay Silverheels and made a twenty-seven-foot leap off a boulder. He doubled Richard Boone for a fight with Kirk Douglas on *Man Without a Star* (1955), a film on which he taught star Douglas a myriad of gun tricks. Carson was handy on a motorcycle, doubling Marlon Brando riding on *The Wild One* (1953). His career was interrupted when he broke a hip doing a high fall in the early 1950s, but he recovered to maintain his status as one of the top stuntmen in the business. His brother Ted Smile also worked as a stuntman.

He worked on *Fort Apache* (1948), *Kansas Raiders* (1950), *Frenchie* (1950), *The Kid from Texas* (1950), *Stage to Tucson* (1950), *Ten Tall Men* (1951), *Against All Flags* (1952), *The World in His Arms* (1952), *Wings of the Hawk* (1953), *The Charge at Feather River* (1953), *Column South* (1953), *Seminole* (1953), *Destry* (1954), *Sign of the Pagan* (1954), *Pillars of the Sky* (1956), *Gun Duel in Durango* (1957), *The Buccaneer* (1958), *Escort West* (1958), *Timbuktu* (1959), *Last Train from Gun Hill* (1959), *4 for Texas* (1963), *The Rare Breed* (1965), *Ride Beyond Vengeance* (1966), *Guns for San Sebastian* (1968), *More Dead Than Alive* (1969), *There Was a Crooked Man...* (1970), *Flap* (1970), *Skin Game* (1971), *The Master Gunfighter* (1975), and *F.I.S.T.* (1978). He was a member of the Stuntmen's Association and an inductee of the Stuntmen's Hall of Fame.

See: *Daily Review.* "Ex-Stuntman Teaches Stars Gun Handling." August 31, 1955; www.victormature.org.

MICKEY CARUSO (1937–2004)

Five-foot-ten, 195-pound Frank James Caruso was a standout athlete at Glendale High. "Mickey" was named All Football League as a center and linebacker. He played baseball and football at Glendale Junior College, earning Junior College All-American Honors and a scholarship to the University of Utah. Running into scholastic difficulties, he turned to semi-pro football, spending eight years in the Western League. He played linebacker for the Eagle Rock Athletic Club, the Valley All-Stars, the Valley Eagles, and the Hartford Charter Oaks in the Continental Football League. In 1964 and 1965 Caruso was named Most Valuable Player and he was a four-time All-Star. He was known for his fiery toughness and ferocious hitting.

When his football career ended, he moved into stunt work as a member of the Stuntmen's Association with the same hard-headed fearlessness. He had screen fights with Jim Kelly on *Enter the Dragon* (1973), William Smith on *Invasion of the Bee Girls* (1973), and Yul Brynner on *The Ultimate Warrior* (1975). He played a supporting role on the football film *Semi-Tough* (1977). Caruso was a top fire man, plummeting out of a burning tree on the TV movie *Fire* (1977), but his battered body suffered from phlebitis and he eventually retired.

He worked on *Conquest of the Planet of the Apes* (1972), *Battle for the Planet of the Apes* (1973), *The Towering Inferno* (1974), *The Longest Yard* (1974), *Earthquake* (1974), *Mr. Ricco* (1975), *Two-Minute Warning* (1976), *Black Sunday* (1977), *Smokey and the Bandit* (1977), *The Swarm* (1978), and *Lady in Red* (1979). On TV he appeared on *The Virginian, Men from Shiloh, Longstreet, The Rockford Files, The Six Million Dollar Man, Matt Helm, Police Woman,* and *Charlie's Angels.* Caruso died from heart failure at the age of 67.

See: Rich, Charlie. "Frank 'Mickey' James Caruso." *Glendale News Press.* December 31, 2004.

GORDON CARVETH (1897–1972)

Gordon John Carveth was an Illinois-born swimmer and Olympic diver for the Cleveland Athletic Association. Crowned champion long-distance swimmer of the Pacific Coast, he doubled Franchot Tone on *Five Graves to Cairo* (1943) and Bob Hope on *Road to Morocco* (1942) and *Son of Paleface* (1952). His most visible part was getting knocked over a banister onto a breakaway table by Dick Powell on *Singing Marine* (1938). Carveth's specialty was racing motorcycles and turning over cars. Beauty queen turned stuntwoman Marcella Arnold was killed in a 1937 turnover with Carveth at the wheel on *Footloose Heiress* (1937).

Tragedy visited Carveth before when he took a boat down Alaskan rapids on *Trail of '98* (1928). Fellow stuntman Red Thompson, on the same boat as Carveth, lost his life in the stunt. On *Very Confidential* (1927) he paddled a canoe into the path of a speedboat, and multiple times he took canoes down the Feather River rapids for film cameras. Footage of a Carveth cliff dive was reused for *Nevada Smith* (1966), and he was paid accordingly.

Other credits include *Men on Call* (1931), *3 on a Honeymoon* (1934), *Professional Soldier* (1935), *Thank You, Jeeves* (1936), *Strike Me Pink* (1936), *High Tension* (1936), *Nancy Steele Is Missing* (1937), *Marine Raiders* (1944), *The Spanish Main* (1945), *Wild Harvest* (1947), and *Around the World in Eighty Days* (1956). He was profiled on the 1938 radio program *Daredevils of Hollywood.* He was an honorary member of the Stuntmen's Association.

See: Keavy, Hubbard. "Screen Life." *Sarasota Herald-Tribune.* April 25, 1937; "Specialists Have Varied Roles in Making Motion Pictures." *Salt Lake Tribune.* June 1, 1930.

JIMMY CASINO (1920–1999)

Five-foot-nine James J. Casino weighed in at 170 pounds when he entered the U.S. Navy during World War II. The Los Angeles-born middleweight champ of California captured the Navy's Boxing Championship and taught hand-to-hand combat in the service. He fought professionally as a light-heavy. For rugged actors Jeff Chandler and Richard Egan he served not only as a stand-in and stuntman but as a sparring partner at the gym. He was Egan's right hand man on the TV series *Empire* (1962–63). Casino gradually put on weight until he was all the way up to 270 pounds, making him an ideal double for stocky actors Ernest Borgnine, Peter Ustinov, and Zero Mostel. Despite the extra pounds, Casino was still game for performing all the action for William Conrad throughout the TV series *Cannon* (1971–76). For Conrad he hung from helicopters and leaped into the ocean off the Santa Monica Pier.

He worked on *Iron Man* (1951), *Meet Danny Wilson* (1952), *It's Always Fair Weather* (1955), *Foxfire* (1955), *The Jayhawkers!* (1959), *Birdman of Alcatraz* (1962), *Chubasco* (1968), *The Split* (1968), *Darker Than Amber* (1970), *There Was a Crooked Man...* (1970), *The Don Is Dead* (1973), *Young Frankenstein* (1974), *F.I.S.T.* (1978), *Movie, Movie* (1978), *Paradise Alley* (1978), and *Rocky 2* (1979). TV credits include *Mike Hammer, The Untouchables, Mission: Impossible,* and *Mannix.* He was a member of the Stuntmen's Association; his son John followed him into the profession.

See: "Cannon Lookalike Does His Hair Raising Stunts." *Rock Hill Herald.* June 30, 1973;

Polier, Rex. "TV's Strangest Casting: Retainer to the Stars." *Toledo Blade.* September 8, 1963.

JOHN CASON (1918–1961)

John Lacy Cason was a light-heavyweight (190 pounds) Golden Gloves champion in his native Texas and fought pro prior to service with the U.S. Marines during World War II. His fight skill landed him in Hollywood, where the six-footer had memorable B-western fights against Lash LaRue on *Mark of the Lash* (1948), Gene Autry on *Big Sombrero* (1949), Reed Hadley on *Rimfire* (1949), and Don "Red" Barry on *Red Desert* (1949). On TV he battled Gene Autry, Roy Rogers, and Clayton Moore countless times on *The Lone Ranger.* Cason could handle a horse and worked often as a stuntman. Cason doubled John Dennis on *From Here to Eternity* (1953), Van Heflin on *Count Three and Pray* (1955) and *They Came to Cordura* (1959), Rod Steiger on *Jubal* (1956), and Scott Brady on *The Storm Rider* (1957). On TV he doubled Bill Williams on *Kit Carson* (1951–54) and Jack Kelly on *Maverick* (1957–61).

He worked on *The Hairy Ape* (1944), *Wreck of the Hesperus* (1948), *Belle Starr's Daughter* (1948), *Gallant Legion* (1948), *Comanche Territory* (1950), *Texas Rangers* (1951), *Westward the Women* (1951), *Hellgate* (1952), *Gun Fury* (1953), *Thunder Over the Plains* (1953), *Saskatchewan* (1954), *Cattle Queen of Montana* (1954), *The Last Frontier* (1955), *3:10 to Yuma* (1957), *Cowboy* (1958), *Gunman's Walk* (1958), and *Cimarron* (1960). TV credits include *Roy Rogers, Gene Autry, The Cisco Kid, Cowboy G-Men, Judge Roy Bean, Annie Oakley, Wild Bill Hickok, Wyatt Earp, Sugarfoot, Bronco, Colt .45, Lawman, Bat Masterson, Laramie,* and *The Untouchables.* Cason died in an automobile wreck at the age of 42.

DAVID CASS (1942–)

David S. Cass was born in Fort Wayne, Indiana. He attended Brown Military Academy in San Diego, California, and graduated from Tucson's Pueblo High where he lettered in football and basketball. As a young man he was attending the University of Arizona while working at the Anaconda Copper Mine. He went to work as an Old Tucson Studios cowboy and got an introduction to John Wayne. This led to work on *McLintock!*

(1963) and pursuit of a movie career. The 6'4", 225-pound Cass is best known as Robert Mitchum's double on *The Good Guys and the Bad Guys* (1969), *Young Billy Young* (1969), and *Farewell My Love* (1975). He doubled Mitchum's son Jim on *Trackdown* (1976). On TV he doubled Robert Brown on *Here Come the Brides* (1968–70).

Cass had a starring role in the 1971 horror feature *Disciples of Death* (aka *Enter the Devil*), a film on which he is credited as screenwriter. He starred as a western sheriff in an industrial film titled *Shoot Out at Deep Hole* (1971) and the short *One Block Away* (1975). Cass was often seen as stunt heavies while a member of the Stuntmen's Association. On *The Island of Dr. Moreau* (1977) he was the Bear Man and went over a balcony with a real panther. He moved into second unit work and became a full-fledged director, handling many TV movie assignments.

He worked on *Shenandoah* (1965), *Heaven with a Gun* (1969), *The Stalking Moon* (1969), *Suppose They Gave a War and Nobody Came* (1970), *Dirty Dingus Magee* (1970), *Earthquake* (1974), *The Master Gunfighter* (1975), *Two-Minute Warning* (1976), *Mr. Billion* (1977), *The Jerk* (1979), *Lady in Red* (1979), *1941* (1979), and *Heaven's Gate* (1980). TV credits include *Branded, High Chaparral, Hondo, The Virginian, Dundee and the Culhane, Lancer, Bonanza, Gunsmoke, The FBI, Cannon, The Streets of San Francisco, The Rockford Files, Police Woman,* and the TV mini-series *How the West Was Won* (1978) and *Centennial* (1978).

See: "Industrial Film Being Shot." *San Antonio Express.* May 5, 1971; Keating, Micheline. "Rising Stars Back Home for *Dingus.*" *Tucson Daily Citizen.* March 7, 1970; "Movie Filming Nears Finish." *Del Rio News Herald.* May 7, 1971; "Two Tucson Talents Soar." *Tucson Daily Citizen.* February 8, 1969; www.drgoresfunhouse.com.

BILL CATCHING (1926–2007)

Six-foot-one, 175-pound Jerome P. Catching was born in San Antonio, Texas. "Bill" Catching made a career out of being a top cowboy stuntman, dating back to when he left his job at a Bandera, Texas, dude ranch to hitchhike to California for work as a wrangler and horse trainer. After service with the U.S. Navy in the South Pacific during World War II, he worked at Ralph McCutcheon's stables and wrangled horses at Columbia for Durango Kid and Gene Autry Films. It was at Columbia that Jock Mahoney and Al Wyatt got him into stunts.

Catching was especially busy on 1950s TV doubling Leo Carrillo on *The Cisco Kid* (1950–56), Roy Rogers on *The Roy Rogers Show* (1951–57), and Guy Madison on *Wild Bill Hickok* (1955–58). Catching doubled Robert Stack on the series *The Untouchables* (1959–63) and *Name of the Game* (1968–71), Chuck Connors on *Branded* (1965–66), Lee Majors on *The Big Valley* (1965–69), and Dennis Weaver on *McCloud* (1970–77). He was stunt coordinator for the first season of *The Wild Wild West* (1965–66) but left after feuding with star Robert Conrad, who wanted to do all his stunt work. Catching excelled at screen brawls, battling Burt Reynolds on *Operation CIA* (1965) and doubling Chuck Connors on *Ride Beyond Vengeance* (1966) and Bruce Dern on *The Cowboys* (1972). Catching also doubled Randolph Scott, Glenn Ford, Keith Larsen, Peter Lawford, and Efrem Zimbalist, Jr., in the course of some 1500 films and television shows.

He worked on *The Man from Colorado* (1948), *War Paint* (1953), *The Nebraskan* (1953), *They Rode West* (1954), *The Egyptian* (1954), *Prince Valiant* (1954), *The Man from Laramie* (1955), *North by Northwest* (1959), *Spartacus* (1960), *Sergeants Three* (1962), *Ride the High Country* (1962), *Six Black Horses* (1962), *4 for Texas* (1963), *Gunfight at Comanche Creek* (1963), *Major Dundee* (1965), *The Great Race* (1965), *The Rounders* (1965), *Glory Guys* (1965), *Guns for San Sebastian* (1968), *The Great Bank Robbery* (1969), *Support Your Local Sheriff* (1969), *Flap* (1970), *The Phynx* (1970), *The Poseidon Adventure* (1972), *Westworld* (1973), *Mean Streets* (1973), *Blazing Saddles* (1974), *Dirty Mary, Crazy Larry* (1974), *Earthquake* (1974), *The Hindenburg* (1975), *The Killer Elite* (1975), *Two-Minute Warning* (1976), and *Avalanche* (1978). TV credits include *Death Valley Days*, *Wyatt Earp*, *Brave Eagle*, *Cheyenne*, *Maverick*, *Bronco*, *Law of the Plainsman*, *Zane Grey*, *Lawman*, *Tombstone Territory*, *Rough Riders*, *Texas John Slaughter*, *Johnny Ringo*, *Sea Hunt*, *Laramie*, *The Westerner*, *Klondike*, *Whispering Smith*, *Wanted—Dead or Alive*, *Wagon Train*, *Rawhide*, *The Outer Limits*, *The Virginian*, *Laredo*, *Honey West*, *Hondo*, *The Monroes*, *Star Trek*, *The FBI*, *Mod Squad*, *Men from Shiloh*, *McCloud*, *Kung Fu*, *Movin' On*, and

Wonder Woman. Catching was stunt coordinator for the early episodes of the TV series *The Fall Guy*. A member of the Stuntmen's Association, an inductee into the Stuntmen's Hall of Fame, and a recipient of the Golden Boot Award, Catching died from cancer at the age of 81.

See: "Bill Catching: A Lifetime of Doubles." *Bonanza Gold.* January-February-March 2006; Dishner, Jackie. "Fall Guy." *Arizona Highways.* March 2001; "Empty Saddles." *Western Clippings.* #79, September-October 2007; Smith, Pam. "Friends and Family Mourn Local Stuntman." *Yuma Sun.* September 3, 2007.

JERRY CATRON

Jerry "Jack" Catron was a prolific stuntman during the 1960s. Six feet tall and 170 pounds he worked regularly doubling Mark Goddard on TV's *Lost in Space* (1965–68) and Dack Rambo on *Guns of Will Sonnett* (1967–69). He doubled Tab Hunter on *Hostile Guns* (1967), fought Lee Marvin on *Point Blank* (1967), and played the flashy character Sidewinder Bates on *WUSA* (1970) opposite Paul Newman. He worked on *How the West Was Won* (1962), *Palm Springs Weekend* (1963), *The Great Race* (1965), and *Darling Lili* (1970). TV credits include *Richard Diamond*, *Twilight Zone*, *The Big Valley*, *Star Trek*, *Batman*, *The Green Hornet*, *Voyage to the Bottom of the Sea*, *Land of the Giants,* and *Mannix*. A member of the Stuntmen's Association, Catron died when his hang glider hit a power line and he was electrocuted.

FRED CAVENS (1882–1962)

Belgium-born fencing legend Frederic Adolphe Cavens had a hand in many of the great cinematic sword duels and was behind the action on the TV's *Zorro* (1957–61). He was assisted in his work by his son Albert Cavens, who often doubled the principles. Early in his career it was the senior Cavens who doubled actors such as Fredric March on *Anthony Adverse* (1936). Cavens worked on swashbuckling choreography with Douglas Fairbanks on *Robin Hood* (1922) and *The Black Pirate* (1926), Errol Flynn on *Captain Blood* (1935), *The Adventures of Robin Hood* (1938), *The Sea Hawk* (1940), *Adventures of Don Juan* (1948), and *Against All Flags* (1952), and Tyrone Power on *The Mark of Zorro* (1940) and *The Black Swan* (1942).

One of his crowning achievements came on the extended duel for *Scaramouche* (1952). Cavens emphasized facial expression in conjunction with his routine moves for optimum screen excitement.

Cavens graduated from the Military Institute of Physical Education as a fencing master. He was a member of the French Army and engaged in several real-life duels. Among the actors Cavens coached were Basil Rathbone, John Barrymore, Leslie Howard, Wallace Beery, Robert Donat, Robert Montgomery, Reginald Owen, Jose Ferrer, Alan Ladd, Dale Robertson, Guy Williams, and John Wayne.

He worked on *King of Kings* (1927), *The Iron Mask* (1929), *The Count of Monte Cristo* (1934), *Romeo and Juliet* (1936), *The Three Musketeers* (1935), *The Prisoner of Zenda* (1937), *The Man in the Iron Mask* (1939), *Ali Baba and the Forty Thieves* (1944), *The Spanish Main* (1945), *The Exile* (1947), *Cyrano de Bergerac* (1950), *Anne of the Indies* (1951), *At Sword's Point* (1952), *The Robe* (1953), *Casanova's Big Night* (1954), *Son of Sinbad* (1955), *The Conqueror* (1956), and *Around the World in Eighty Days* (1956). A member of the Stuntmen's Hall of Fame, Cavens died from uremic poisoning at the age of 79.

See: "Famous Fencer Engaged for Fairbanks Picture." *Plain Dealer*. October 11, 1925.

LON CHANEY, JR. (1906–1973)

Six-foot-two, 230-pound Lon Chaney, Jr., was born in Oklahoma as Creighton Tull Chaney. He was the son of the famous silent film horror star. A tall and gangly youth, he was cut from the football squad at Hollywood High. As he matured he became more physically adept at amateur athletics such as swimming and wrestling. After his father's passing, Creighton Chaney was signed by RKO and starred in *The Last Frontier* (1932), a serial on which he doubled up on stunts as an Indian. Chaney worked as a stuntman between acting jobs for extra money, claiming he bulldogged steers, fell off cliffs, rode horses into rivers, and drove prairie schooners up and down hills. The majority of his early assignments cast him as stunt heavies fighting cowboy heroes Gene Autry, Tom Keene, and Tom Tyler, most notably on *Cheyenne Rides Again* (1937). Under studio pressure he adopted the stage name Lon Chaney, Jr., and his career perked up playing the massive simpleton Lenny on *Of Mice and Men* (1939).

At Universal Chaney played classic monster characters including the Wolf Man, Frankenstein's Monster and the Mummy. When he grew heavier due to a fondness for drink, stuntmen aided him in action scenes. Chaney still enjoyed doing his own fight scenes, putting on classic battles with Broderick Crawford on *North to the Klondike* (1942) and John Payne on *Captain China* (1950). On *Abbott and Costello Meet Frankenstein* (1948) Glenn Strange (playing the Monster) broke his foot, so Chaney donned the Frankenstein makeup to throw a stunt girl around. The monster roles brought him fame, but undermined him as an actor. Chaney died at 67 from a heart attack brought on by a battle with throat cancer and liver failure.

See: Neill, Frank. "In Hollywood." *Long Beach Independent*. June 22, 1949; Smith, Don G. *Lon Chaney, Jr.: Horror Film Star*. Jefferson, NC: McFarland, 1996.

DAVID CHOW (1929–2007)

Chinese martial artist David Tai Wei Chow is best known as the technical advisor on the first two seasons of TV's popular *Kung Fu* (1972–74). He fought star David Carradine in the climax of the 1971 pilot film. As a boy, Chow learned to defend himself with judo and kung fu in Japanese-occupied Shanghai. He came to the United States to attend college at UCLA. There the young entrepreneur began formally teaching students after winning the California Judo Championship. Chow was one of the martial artists consulted for the famous fight on *The Manchurian Candidate* (1962). He worked on *Blood Alley* (1955), *Confessions of an Opium Eater* (1962), *The Spiral Road* (1962), *The Ugly American* (1963), *Planet of the Apes* (1968), *The Wrecking Crew* (1969), *Conquest of the Planet of the Apes* (1972), *That Man Bolt* (1973), and *Three the Hard Way* (1974). TV credits include *Hawaiian Eye*, *Hong Kong*, *Bonanza*, *I Spy*, *The Wild Wild West*, and *Mannix*.

See: Pilato, Herbie J. "Technical Genius." *Inside Kung Fu*. 2007; Scott, Vernon. "Oriental Superman Guides *Kung Fu*." *Omaha World Herald*. February 23, 1973; Shirota, Jon. "Men Behind TV's *Kung Fu*." *Black Belt*. January 1973; Shively, Rick. "David Chow Promises Million Dollar Payoff." *Fighting Stars*. April 1974; Smith, Cecil. "David Chow's Mastery Links Business, Combat to Stage." *Advocate*. February 18, 1972.

CRAIG CHUDY (1937-)

Craig Warren Chudy was born in Chicago and raised in California. He was a football and track star on the hurdles at Narbonne High. Chudy attended UCLA on an athletic scholarship and was drafted by the San Francisco 49ers. After being cut by the Pittsburgh Steelers in 1962 he played semi-pro football for the Valley All Stars. Six-foot-three and 220 pounds, he worked on *John Goldfarb, Please Come Home* (1965), *Beau Geste* (1966), *Tobruk* (1967), *Darling Lili* (1970), *MASH* (1970), and *The Poseidon Adventure* (1972). TV credits include *Mission: Impossible, The Man from U.N.C.L.E., Mannix, Lost in Space, The Invaders,* and *Emergency.* He remains best known as the double for Kent McCord on *Adam–12* (1968–75).

See: Phillips, Mark. "Craig Chudy: Facing the Wave!" *Filmfax.* April-June 2006.

BILL CLARK (1919–1974)

Alabama-born Earl William Clark was long associated with the TV series *Bonanza* (1959–72), where the husky 6'2", 250-pound stuntman doubled Lorne Greene and Dan Blocker and guest stars such as Aldo Ray. In his younger days he doubled slender stars Jack Holt and Tyrone Power, but by the early 1950s was doubling Smiley Burnette. He worked on *Masterson of Kansas* (1954), *Canyon River* (1956), *Decision at Sundown* (1957), *The Sheepman* (1958), *Good Day for a Hanging* (1959), *Face of a Fugitive* (1959), and *Young Fury* (1965). He was the double for Peter Ustinov on *Viva Max!* (1968), a film on which he and Frank Orsatti were sent to the hospital after overshooting a station wagon jump. He should not be confused with another stuntman by the name of Bill Clark, who wrestled professionally under the name The Great John L. The *Bonanza* Bill Clark died at the age of 54 as a result of injuries sustained in a private plane crash.

See: McNulty, Sean. "Film Stuntman: Money Makes Him Tick." *San Antonio Light.* March 20, 1969.

BOBBY CLARK (1937-)

Bobby Clark attained cult status in the sci-fi genre as the alien reptile The Gorn on the 1967 *Star Trek* episode "Arena." His fight with William Shatner at Vasquez Rocks has become the stuff of legend thanks largely to the cumbersome costume he was forced to wear. A rodeo cowboy, construction worker, and tree trimmer, Clark spent eight years as a stuntman on TV's *Gunsmoke* but it is his *Trek* appearance for which he is remembered. He was as good on a motorcycle as he was on a horse. Other credits include *Hells Angels on Wheels* (1967), *Rough Night in Jericho* (1967), *2001—A Space Odyssey* (1968), *The Losers* (1970), *Cleopatra Jones* (1973), *Black Sunday* (1977), *The Car* (1977), and *The Driver* (1978). TV credits include *Rawhide, The Big Valley, Cimarron Strip, The Virginian, Lancer,* and *Kung Fu.*

See: Collington, Jason. "Trek Expo: The Gorn Identity." *Tulsa World.* June 24, 2005; Wiener, Jocelyn. "Don't Know the Gorn? Trek Fans Will Help." *Sacramento Bee.* September 30, 2007; www.scvhistory.com; www.startrek.com.

ROYDON CLARK (1928-)

Roydon Clark is best known for being the double for James Garner, an association that lasted several decades and included the TV shows *Maverick* (1957–62) and *The Rockford Files* (1974–80). For Warner Brothers TV he doubled Will Hutchins on *Sugarfoot* (1957–61) and Ty Hardin on *Bronco* (1958–62). Clark was one of the best fight men in the business, doubling Garner on *Duel at Diablo* (1966), Jacques Bergerac on *Thunder in the Sun* (1959), Claude Akins on *Ride Beyond Vengeance* (1966), and Joe Don Baker on *Walking Tall* (1973). On *Little Big Man* (1970) he doubled Richard Mulligan as General Custer at the Battle of Little Big Horn.

Six-foot-two, 190-pound Roydon Elwood Clark was born in Dalton, Pennsylvania, to a family of itinerant migrant workers. In California he tended livestock and baled hay at the Hudkins Brothers Ranch across from Warner Bros. Clark worked as a cowboy at the ranch and picked up gymnastic and acrobatic training in school. This led to stunt work at Republic for director Joe Kane. The studio originally envisioned Clark as a cowboy star. He doubled Errol Flynn, Clark Gable, Randolph Scott, Robert Mitchum, Jack Palance, Burt Lancaster, Rock Hudson, and Charlton Heston. He doubled John Wayne for long shots on *The Conqueror* (1956) and Sean Connery on *Indiana Jones and the Lost Crusade* (1989). Clark's falling horses were named Maverick and Nichols.

He worked on *Wake of the Red Witch* (1948), *The Fighting Kentuckian* (1949), *Montana* (1950), *Rogues of Sherwood Forest* (1950), *Colt .45* (1950), *Ride the Man Down* (1952), *Woman of the North Country* (1952), *Them!* (1954), *The Deep Six* (1958), *Yellowstone Kelly* (1959), *McLintock!* (1963), *A Distant Trumpet* (1964), *Quick Before It Melts* (1964), *Cat Ballou* (1965), *The Rare Breed* (1965), *Not with My Wife, You Don't* (1966), *Texas Across the River* (1966), *The Way West* (1967), *Camelot* (1967), *Bonnie and Clyde* (1967), *Hour of the Gun* (1967), *Bandolero!* (1968), *Ice Station Zebra* (1968), *The Devil's Brigade* (1968), *Hellfighters* (1968), *More Dead Than Alive* (1969), *Marlowe* (1969), *The Great Bank Robbery* (1969), *The Undefeated* (1969), *Support Your Local Sheriff* (1969), *One More Train to Rob* (1971), *Skin Game* (1971), *Support Your Local Gunfighter* (1971), *Conquest of the Planet of the Apes* (1972), *Slaughter's Big Rip-Off* (1973), *Battle for the Planet of the Apes* (1973), *Cleopatra Jones* (1973), *Earthquake* (1974), *The Towering Inferno* (1974), *Doc Savage* (1975), *Silent Movie* (1976), *The Shootist* (1976), and *1941* (1979). TV credits include *Cheyenne, Colt .45, Get Smart, Star Trek, Nichols, Medical Center, Quincy, BJ and the Bear, Buck Rogers,* and *Hart to Hart.* Clark is an inductee of the Stuntmen's Hall of Fame and a member of the Stuntmen's Association.

See: Lilley, Tim. *Campfire Conversations Complete.* Akron, OH: Big Trail, 2010.

STEVE CLEMENTE (1885–1950)

Mexican-born Steve Clemento Morro was an expert knife thrower who taught John Wayne how to handle a blade on *The Big Trail* (1930). He worked as a stuntman and bit player, often playing Indians and south-of-the-border bandits. He worked on *The Most Dangerous Game* (1932), *Mystery Ranch* (1932), *King Kong* (1933), *Under Two Flags* (1936), *White Fang* (1936), *Stagecoach* (1939), *Valley of the Sun* (1942), and *Perils of Nyoka* (1942).

TOMMY COATS (1899–1954)

B-western stuntman Thomas J. Coats came from the rodeo ranks as a bronc and bull rider and appeared in more than 120 serials and oaters. Hailing from Scotland, he got his start at Lone Star–

Monogram on early John Wayne films such as *Lucky Texan* (1934) and *Randy Rides Alone* (1934) and stayed mostly at Republic Studios. He worked on *King of the Royal Mounted* (1940), *Western Union* (1941), *King of the Texas Rangers* (1941), *Spy Smasher* (1942), and *Jesse James Rides Again* (1947), and taught Betty Hutton to ride for *Incendiary Blonde* (1945).

IRON EYES CODY (1907–1999)

Iron Eyes Cody was born Espera Oscar De-Coti in Gueydan, Louisiana, of Italian ancestry. This was not revealed until after his death as Cody lived nearly his entire life as a Native American. He adopted the role so well that he built a long career in Hollywood as a stuntman and technical advisor on motion pictures involving Indians. He even authored the official book on Indian sign language. In addition to horseback work, Cody was a top man with a bow and arrow. He achieved widespread fame as the old Indian who sheds a tear at the despoiling of nature in a popular TV commercial from the 1970s.

He worked on *The Big Trail* (1930), *Captain Blood* (1935), *The Charge of the Light Brigade* (1936), *Stagecoach* (1939), *Winners of the West* (1940), *They Died with Their Boots On* (1941), *The Sea Wolf* (1941), *Valley of the Sun* (1942), *Perils of Nyoka* (1942), *Fort Apache* (1948), *Blood on the Moon* (1948), *She Wore a Yellow Ribbon* (1949), *Wagon Master* (1950), and *The Searchers* (1956). His older brother J.W. Cody also performed stunts. Iron Eyes put his feet into cement at the Stuntmen's Hall of Fame and was a Golden Boot Award honoree. Cody died of natural causes at the age of 91.

See: Cody, Iron Eyes, & Collin Perry. *Iron Eyes: My Life as a Hollywood Indian.* New York: Everest, 1982.

JACK COFFER (1938–1967)

Jack Coffer was born Jackie Laure Foster in San Joaquin Valley, California, where he attended Sonora High and competed in junior rodeos. He learned rope work from Bob Folkerson, who brought him to Hollywood as a cowboy stuntman. Coffer doubled Robert Fuller on TV's *Laramie* (1959–63) and *Wagon Train* (1963–65), Dennis Weaver on *Gunsmoke* (1959–63), and Peter Brown on *Laredo* (1965–67). Films include *4 for*

Texas (1963), *Rio Conchos* (1964), *Mail Order Bride* (1964), *The Rare Breed* (1965), *Stagecoach* (1966), *Hot Rods to Hell* (1967), and *The Way West* (1967). His sister Gerry Coffer also did stunts. A member of the Stuntmen's Hall of Fame, Coffer died at the age of 28 in a vehicular accident while driving home from work.

See: "Jack Coffer Backs Star in New Television Series." *Union Democrat.* September 22, 1959.

DENNIS COLE (1940–2009)

Six-foot-two, 175-pound Dennis Cole was born in Detroit, Michigan, and earned a football scholarship to the University of Detroit. After time as a physique model, he got his professional start as a stand-in and stunt double for Troy Donahue on the TV series *Hawaiian Eye.* He worked on *The Comancheros* (1961), *How the West Was Won* (1962), *Palm Springs Weekend* (1963), and *A Distant Trumpet* (1964) before finding success as a star on the detective series *Felony Squad* (1966–68). He played a studio stuntman on the series *Bracken's World* (1969–70) and co-starred with Rod Taylor on the action-packed *Bearcats* (1971). Cole died from liver failure at the age of 69.

See: Scott, Vernon. "Ex-Stuntman Clicks in Role on Television." *Tipton Tribune.* March 3, 1970; Trott, Walt. "TV Star Dennis Cole Judging USAFE Plays." *European Stars and Stripes.* November 27, 1973; Vadeboncoeur, Jane. "Dennis Cole Takes One Step at a Time." *Syracuse Herald Journal.* April 23, 1967.

DON COLEMAN (1898–1985)

Lloyd Donald Coleman was born in Sheridan, Wyoming, and was raised breaking horses on a ranch. After World War I military service, he won the World Championship in bronc riding at Bozeman, Montana, in 1921. This led to a year-long job in New York modeling for a statue of Buffalo Bill that stands in Cody, Wyoming, at the entrance of Yellowstone National Park. In New York, Coleman worked on *Sainted Devil* (1924) with Rudolph Valentino and modeled for Arrow Collar ads.

Coleman made his way to Hollywood and stunted on *Beau Geste* (1926), *King of Kings* (1927), and *The Gaucho* (1927), in the latter for Douglas Fairbanks. He supported Leo Maloney on Pathe westerns such as *Apache Raider* (1928).

Maloney stepped back to direct Coleman on the action westerns *Black Ace* (1928), *Bronc Stomper* (1928), and *.45 Calibre War* (1929). Coleman did his own stunt work on these. The advent of sound finished off his Hollywood career, though he managed to work stunts on *The Big Trail* (1930) and *Billy the Kid* (1930).

See: Coleman, Don, & Herb Swilling. "Stunt Kings: All About Don Coleman." *Blazing West.* #1, 1984.

CHICK COLLINS (1898–1981)

John "Chick" Collins was considered a top fight man in the 1930s, doubling Fred Kohler on *Frisco Kid* (1935) and joining Duke Green for a memorable slugfest with James Cagney on *Something to Sing About* (1937). Born in Brooklyn, New York, Collins worked on barges in his youth and boxed professionally. His film career dates to the early 1920s, when he was hired by Buster Keaton as a stuntman on *Our Hospitality* (1923). Keaton liked having Collins around so they could play baseball together on the set. Collins doubled Fredric March on *Dr. Jekyll and Mr. Hyde* (1931) and Clark Gable on *China Seas* (1935).

He worked on *Seven Days Leave* (1930), *King Kong* (1933), *The Glass Key* (1935), *Ali Baba Goes to Town* (1937), *Nancy Steele Is Missing* (1937), *Mysterious Mr. Moto* (1938), *Dodge City* (1939), *Seven Sinners* (1940), *Sullivan's Travels* (1941), *Wild Harvest* (1947), and *Singin' in the Rain* (1952). He was an honorary member of the Stuntmen's Association.

GARY COMBS

Gary M. Combs was the son of wrangler Del Combs. A natural on a horse, he helped his dad teach *Wagon Train* actor Robert Horton to ride. Combs learned the stunt trade from Terry Wilson and Lenny Geer. He doubled Horton, then James Drury and Doug McClure on *The Virginian* and William Shatner on *Star Trek.* When westerns were in vogue the 5'11", 160-pound Combs was a top man, performing horse falls on Chuck Hayward's horse Iodine while doubling Glen Campbell and Robert Duvall on *True Grit* (1969). Combs became known for his toughness, stemming from an arrow he took to the eye during the making of *Little Big Man* (1970).

Combs doubled Steve McQueen from *Ne-*

vada Smith (1966) through Tom Horn (1980) and worked for Sam Peckinpah many times, including The Wild Bunch (1969), The Getaway (1972), Pat Garrett and Billy the Kid (1973) (doubling Kris Kristofferson), Bring Me the Head of Alfredo Garcia (1974), The Killer Elite (1975), and Convoy (1978). He doubled Peter Strauss on Soldier Blue (1970), Paul Newman on Life and Times of Judge Roy Bean (1972), Kurt Russell on Charley and the Angel (1973), Richard Jordan on Rooster Cogburn (1975), and Kirk Douglas on The Villain (1979). His son Gilbert followed him into the business.

He worked on Beau Geste (1966), El Dorado (1967), Hour of the Gun (1967), Bandolero! (1968), Hellfighters (1968), The Stone Killer (1973), Three the Hard Way (1974), The Trial of Billy Jack (1974), Mitchell (1975), A Boy and His Dog (1975), Midway (1976), Two-Minute Warning (1976), Smokey and the Bandit (1977), Moonshine County Express (1977), Hooper (1978), The Hunter (1980), and Smokey and the Bandit 2 (1980). Combs is an inductee of the Stuntmen's Hall of Fame and an original member of Stunts Unlimited.

See: Lilley, Tim. Campfire Conversations Complete. Akron, OH: Big Trail, 2010; "Stuntmen Compete in Sports Spectacular." Joplin Globe. January 15, 1977.

JACK CONNER

Horse master Jack Conner and his mare Daisy performed a spectacular stunt on The Unforgiven (1960) as they charge a rifle-wielding Burt Lancaster in a doorway at full gallop. Conner hit the dirt and Daisy went onto the roof. Even more impressive were the fifty horses Conner trained to jump in a lake and swim across on Savage Sam (1963). Bronc-busting rodeo champ Conner was a veteran western man who became good friends with Tab Hunter on Gun Belt (1953). Hunter requested Conner as his double from then on for films such as Gunman's Walk (1958). Conner worked on The Man from the Alamo (1953) and They Came to Cordura (1959). When not filming, he and his wife trained race horses.

See: "Ex Rodeo Greats in Savage Sam." Republic Democrat. July 25, 1963; Hunter, Tab. Tab Hunter Confidential: The Making of a Movie Star. Chapel Hill, NC: Algonquin, 2006.

JIM "MATT" CONNORS (1946–2003)

Six-foot-four, 220-pound James Mathiasen Connors was an Olympic diver and swimming champ prior to becoming a double for James Arness on TV's Gunsmoke. He doubled Max Baer, Jr., for an epic fight with Forrest Tucker on Wild McCullochs (1975) and Jack Palance on Portrait of a Hitman (1977) and the TV series Bronk (1975–76). On TV he doubled Robert Reed for a seventy-foot plunge into water on the TV series Harry O. He worked on Butch Cassidy and the Sundance Kid (1969), MASH (1970), Ssssss (1973), The Trial of Billy Jack (1974), Blue Collar (1978), and Hooper (1978). He was a member of Stunts Unlimited.

ROBERT CONRAD (1935–)

Robert Conrad is best known as the star of the action-packed TV series The Wild Wild West (1965–69), which contained some of the most innovative, action-packed fight scenes ever seen. The athletic Conrad was front and center in the action, often performing his own stunt work on the show. Conrad has claimed he did all of his own stunts, which unfortunately is not true. Louie Elias, Chuck O'Brien, and Jimmy George can be identified on the series as Conrad doubles. They were under strict orders never to be caught on the set in Conrad's wardrobe, fostering the illusion to the press and the public that Conrad's proud claims were true. The handy Conrad did at least attempt to do all of his own stunts, clashing with original stunt coordinator Bill Catching and to a lesser extent Whitey Hughes over that subject.

Conrad was famously injured attempting to swing on a chandelier during a saloon brawl. Conrad missed kicking his target Jerry Laveroni, fell and fractured his skull on the floor. The mishap nearly killed Conrad and the show was shut down for an extended period, the exact reason stars have stuntmen. Conrad should be commended on his fight work and his early incorporation of martial arts moves onto the series. Conrad got his start as a stuntman at Ziv Studios on late 1950s TV shows. Conrad had a top-notch martial arts fight with Don Stroud on Sudden Death (1975), and the duo did a great deal of their own stunt work for an exciting speed boat chase on Live a Little, Steal a Lot (aka Murph the Surf) (1975).

Actors Robert Conrad and Don Stroud, who both got their start as stuntmen, perform their own speedboat chase on *Live a Little, Steal a Lot* (aka *Murph the Surf*) (1975). Chuck Courtney coordinated the action.

Five-foot-five, 160-pound Conrad Robert Falkowski was born in Chicago, Illinois. He had a background in acrobatics and participated in basketball and football in school. He worked as a dockworker before going to Hollywood to pursue an acting career. He found early success on the TV series *Hawaiian Eye* (1959–63). In the 1960s Conrad became interested in boxing and posted a 4–0–1 professional record. In the 1970s he famously advertised Eveready batteries, placing one atop his shoulder, looking into the camera and daring us to knock it off. Conrad has been inducted into the Stuntmen's Hall of Fame.

See: Dugas, David. "Conrad Enjoys Stunts." *Omaha World Herald.* August 10, 1975; Lowry, Cynthia. "Ex-Stunter Conrad Returning to Show." *Eureka Times Standard.* August 17, 1968; "Robert Conrad: Star and Stuntman." *Daily Review.* June 2, 1966; Weaver, Tom. "Night of the Stuntmen." *Starlog.* October 2006.

GENE COOGAN (1909–1972)

Gene Coogan was born in Essex, New Jersey, and traveled by rail to California with Lou Costello. The latter dabbled in stunt work and then moved on, but Coogan made a thirty-plus year career of it. A top water man, Coogan doubled Franchot Tone for a ninety foot dive from a ship's mast on *Mutiny on the Bounty* (1935). He worked with Robert Taylor on *Rogue Cop* (1954), *Many Rivers to Cross* (1955), and *The Law and Jake Wade* (1958). On TV he doubled Hugh O'Brian on *The Life and Legend of Wyatt Earp* (1955–61). He also worked on *Strange Cargo* (1940), *Battleground* (1949), *The Outriders* (1950), *Across the Wide Missouri* (1951), *Blood Alley* (1955), *The Marauders* (1955), *Harper* (1966), *Adventures of Bullwhip Griffin* (1967), *Support Your Local Sheriff* (1969), *True Grit* (1969), and the TV shows *Bonanza, The Untouchables,* and *High Chaparral.*

Coogan died as a result of falling asleep with a lit cigarette.

See: "Gene Coogan." *Variety.* February 2, 1972.

BILL COONTZ (1917–1978)

Iowa-born Willard B. Koontz went by the stage name Bill Foster when he was given screen credit. The six-footer was a regular stunt performer on the western TV series *The Cisco Kid, Wyatt Earp, Have Gun—Will Travel, The Rebel, Lawman, The Texan, Johnny Ringo, Rawhide, Wagon Train, Bonanza, The Virginian, Branded, The Big Valley, The Wild Wild West, Guns of Will Sonnett,* and *Gunsmoke.* He spent nearly twenty-five years in the industry doubling actors such as Lee Van Cleef, Jan Merlin, and Harold J. Stone. His final film was the Sam Peckinpah truck driving opus *Convoy* (1978) where he played the character Old Iguana.

He worked on *Gold Raiders* (1951), *Buffalo Bill in Tomahawk Territory* (1952), *Fearless Fagan* (1952), *Kansas Pacific* (1952), *Son of the Renegade* (1953), *Thunder Over the Plains* (1953), *The Lone Gun* (1954), *Sitting Bull* (1954), *Cattle Queen of Montana* (1954), *Seminole Uprising* (1955), *Wichita* (1955), *Apache Ambush* (1955), *The Oklahoman* (1957), *Badge of Marshal Brennan* (1957), *Ride Out for Revenge* (1957), *Man from God's Country* (1958), *Buchanan Rides Alone* (1958), *Ole Rex* (1961), *Showdown* (1963), *The Bounty Killer* (1965), *Ride Beyond Vengeance* (1966), *Heaven with a Gun* (1969), *Smoke in the Wind* (1971), *Dillinger* (1973), *Guns of a Stranger* (1973), *Gone with the West* (1975), and *Kingdom of the Spiders* (1977). Coontz died from cancer at the age of 60.

DEE COOPER (1920–1989)

Rodeo cowboy Dee Cooper was born in Muleshoe, Texas. He worked as a B-western henchman on the films of cowboy stars Lash LaRue, Whip Wilson, Eddie Dean, and Johnny Mack Brown and occasionally doubled these actors. When those jobs dried up he worked on TV and organized rodeos at Corriganville. During the late 1950s Cooper appeared in *Born Reckless* (1958), *Walk Like a Dragon* (1960), and *Gunpoint* (1966). In 1962 he leased the western town Paramount Ranch and was involved in the filming of

several minor films there, the last being *Shame Shame on the Bixby Boys* (1978). He also took part on *Texas Detour* (1978) and TV's *The Fall Guy.*

See: Yarbrough, Tinsley. "Hertz Paramount Ranch." *Western Clippings.* #15, January-February 1997.

GARY COOPER (1901–1961)

Born in Helena, Montana, Frank James Cooper grew up riding horses on his family's Montana ranch and served as a Yellowstone Park guide. "Gary" Cooper entered films in the mid–1920s as a nondescript stuntman and $10-a-day riding extra on *Vanishing American* (1925), *Trail Rider* (1925), *Thundering Herd* (1925), *Riders of the Purple Sage* (1925), *Wild Horse Mesa* (1925), *The Eagle* (1925), *Ben-Hur* (1925), and *Enchanted Hill* (1926), but his genuine western persona caught the right eye. The lanky, taciturn Cooper made a near perfect movie cowboy. In his first starring role *Arizona Bound* (1927) the 6'3", 185-pound actor performed a number of his own stunts for the camera, including a transfer from a horse to a stagecoach. He had leads in classic films such as *The Virginian* (1929), *The Plainsman* (1936), and *Beau Geste* (1939) and won two Best Actor Oscars.

Cooper was a solid fight man who required a minimum of doubling, memorably taking on the likes of William "Stage" Boyd on *The Spoilers* (1930), Forrest Tucker on *The Westerner* (1940), Marc Lawrence on *Cloak and Dagger* (1946), Larry Chance on *Distant Drums* (1951), Lloyd Bridges on *High Noon* (1952), and Jack Lord on *Man of the West* (1958). For years he was bothered by a bad back and hip, increasingly handing action scenes over to the likes of Slim Talbot and Ted Mapes. Cooper died of prostate cancer at the age of 60.

See: Meyers, Jeffrey. *Gary Cooper: American Hero.* Cooper Square, 2001.

JACK COOPER

Five-foot-nine, 170-pound British stuntman Jack Cooper dabbled in bodybuilding and wrestling and was a professional high diver prior to entering the world of stunts. He attracted immediate attention with a seventy-five-foot dive on *The Crimson Pirate* (1952) and followed with a sixty-foot dive into the sea over rocks on *Helen of*

Troy (1955), a sixty-foot fall on *Exodus* (1960), and a sixty-foot fall out a window on *Where Eagles Dare* (1968). He is best known for driving a Jaguar XK120 off the ferry bridge at Weymouth on *These Are the Damned* (1963) and for doubling Robert Shaw in the famous train compartment fight with Sean Connery on *From Russia with Love* (1963).

He worked on *Captain Horatio Hornblower* (1951), *Master of Ballantrae* (1953), *Zarak* (1956), *The Vikings* (1958), *The Guns of Navarone* (1961), *The Longest Day* (1962), *55 Days at Peking* (1963), *Cleopatra* (1963), *Those Magnificent Men in Their Flying Machines* (1965), *Battle of the Bulge* (1965), *Cast a Giant Shadow* (1966), *Khartoum* (1966), *Casino Royale* (1967), *You Only Live Twice* (1967), *Alfred the Great* (1969), *Ryan's Daughter* (1970), *You Can't Win 'Em All* (1970), *Live and Let Die* (1973), *Brannigan* (1975), *Return of the Pink Panther* (1975), *The Eagle Has Landed* (1976), *The Pink Panther Strikes Again* (1976), *The Spy Who Loved Me* (1977), *Ffolkes* (1979), *Moonraker* (1979), *Avalanche Express* (1979), *The Sea Wolves* (1980), and *Superman II* (1980). On TV he worked on *The Avengers*. Cooper was inducted into the Stuntmen's Hall of Fame.

KEN COOPER (1896–1989)

Virgil Kenneth Cooper was born in Olaton, Kentucky, and grew up on a farm. He migrated west to work as a cowboy in South Dakota and try his hand as a rodeo bronc rider. Cooper made it to Hollywood in the late 1920s, doubling Richard Dix on *Stingaree* (1934) and Bob Livingston on the Three Mesquiteer films. Cooper worked often with fellow rodeo champ Yakima Canutt. He was Gene Autry's chief double on *Phantom Empire* (1935) and many of his early B-westerns. He worked on *Beau Bandit* (1930), *Cimarron* (1931), *Elinor Norton* (1934), *The Plainsman* (1936), *Ali Baba Goes to Town* (1937), *The Lone Ranger* (1938), *Stagecoach* (1939), *Destry* (1954), and *The Ten Commandments* (1956). He was profiled on the 1938 radio program *Daredevils of Hollywood*.

BEN CORBETT (1892–1961)

Benjamin Ervin Corbett was born in Illinois and worked as a laborer prior to enlistment with the U.S. Cavalry. He took to horse work and learned trick and Roman riding. As Smiley Cor-

bett he was active in the Pendleton Rodeo as a contestant in bronc riding and bulldogging events and served as a rodeo clown. During this period he befriended a fellow rodeo cowboy named Yakima Canutt. Around 1915 Corbett made his way to Hollywood where he became known as a horse fall specialist. Canutt eventually followed him into the movies, with Corbett showing Yak around the studios.

Corbett doubled William Duncan and Antonio Moreno in silent films and worked often with Hoot Gibson, Ken Maynard, and Tim McCoy. He was featured as comic relief in a number of mid–1920s two-reel shorts but settled into a career as a stuntman and nondescript B-western henchman. In the 1930s Corbett headed up the Riding Actors Association of Hollywood in an attempt to get the studios to agree to higher wages and better working conditions. He made many pictures with directors Arthur Rosson and Michael Curtiz and became a technical advisor on cavalry matters. Even as he aged, he was still taking rough saddle falls on films like *Santa Fe Trail* (1940).

He worked on *Lightning Bryce* (1919), *Beau Bandit* (1930), *Squaw Man* (1931), *The Charge of the Light Brigade* (1936), *Conquest* (1937), *Army Girl* (1938), *The Texans* (1938), *The Adventures of Marco Polo* (1938), *The Adventures of Robin Hood* (1938), *Union Pacific* (1939), *Dodge City* (1939), *Kit Carson* (1940), *Virginia City* (1940), *Santa Fe Trail* (1940), *They Died with Their Boots On* (1941), *Buffalo Bill* (1944), *Saratoga Trunk* (1945), *The Man from Colorado* (1948), *Silver River* (1948), *Fighting Man of the Plains* (1949), *Stampede* (1949), *Dallas* (1950), *Colt .45* (1950), *Springfield Rifle* (1952), *The Charge at Feather River* (1953), and *Drum Beat* (1954). He was a member of the Stuntmen's Hall of Fame.

See: "If Screen Shows a Perilous Fall, It's Probably a Benny Corbett Stunt." *Salt Lake Tribune.* October 14, 1940; "Screen Riders are Members of Novel Benefit Society." *Seattle Daily Times.* July 24, 1938.

ERIC CORD

Eric Cord was born Cal Niskasari, Jr., in Windsor, Ontario, Canada. He grew up playing hockey but distinguished himself foremost as a baseball player and track athlete, holding pole-vault and high jump records. In America he joined the U.S. Army and settled permanently in California after his tour of duty. He became a certified lifeguard and learned stunt work from a friend at the health club he frequented. Cord became a resident stuntman on the Universal Studios Western Stunt Show, taking part in more than 3,000 live shows.

The 5'11", 175-pound Cord worked on *Tobruk* (1967) and the TV shows *The Fugitive, The Virginian, Batman,* and *Kung Fu.* He studied martial arts and was one of the first stunt coordinators to bring karate into his films. Along with Emil Farkas he trained stuntmen and athletes how to incorporate karate onto the big screen through their enterprise Creative Action in the Martial Arts. Cord served as stunt coordinator on several low-budget martial arts films and doubled Ross Hagen on fun drive-in fare such as *Wonder Women* (1973). Others actors he doubled include John Saxon, William Shatner, Dennis Hopper, Jack Nicholson, Robert Duvall, Dabney Coleman, Stacy Keach, and Richard Dawson on *The Running Man* (1987).

He worked on *Sidehackers* (1969), *Chandler* (1971), *Super Fly* (1972), *99 and 44/100 percent Dead* (1974), *Earthquake* (1974), *The Towering Inferno* (1974), *The Great Waldo Pepper* (1975), *Midway* (1976), *Moving Violation* (1976), *Black Sunday* (1977), *Black Oak Conspiracy* (1977), *The Norseman* (1978), *The Glove* (1979), and *The Stunt Man* (1980). A member of the Stuntmen's Association, Cord was awarded a Silver Spur Award.

See: Ehrlich, Dan. "Kick-Ins, Knock-Downs, Spills, and Falls." *Fighting Stars.* February 1974; Romberg, Lucy. "Silver Spur Awards." *Inside Stunts.* Winter, 2007.

FRANK CORDELL (1898–1977)

Oklahoma-born Frank Cordell was known as an expert horseman and stuck primarily to westerns. The first time he was ever in an airplane came when he was whisked to a hospital after suffering bad burns during a prairie fire sequence on *The Texans* (1938). Cordell doubled Gary Cooper on *The Plainsman* (1936), *The Westerner* (1940), *Along Came Jones* (1945), and *Unconquered* (1947) and Victor Mature on *Samson and Delilah* (1949). Charlton Heston credited Cordell with teaching him to be a cowboy on the films *The Savage* (1952) and *Arrowhead* (1953).

Other credits include *Elinor Norton* (1934), *Under Two Flags* (1936), *High Sierra* (1941), *Buffalo Bill* (1944), *Duel in the Sun* (1946), *Sundowners* (1950), *High Lonesome* (1950), *Warpath* (1951), *The Lawless Breed* (1952), *Law and Order* (1953), *Gunsmoke* (1953), *The Man from Laramie* (1955), *The Ten Commandments* (1956), *The Tin Star* (1957), *The Buccaneer* (1958), *One Eyed Jacks* (1961), and *How the West Was Won* (1962). He was a member of the Stuntmen's Hall of Fame.

See: "Actors Burned in Filming of *Texan.*" *San Antonio Light.* March 1, 1938; Kahn, Alexander. "Hollywood Film Shop." *Redwood Journal.* April 26, 1938.

JOE CORNELIUS (1929–)

Southern England's flashy Heavyweight Wrestling Champion Joe "The Dazzler" Cornelius is best known for donning the monster suit on the much maligned Joan Crawford film *Trog* (1970). He had previously worked as a stuntman on *Khartoum* (1966), *The Dirty Dozen* (1967), *Casino Royale* (1967), *Oliver!* (1968), *File of the Golden Goose* (1969), *The McKenzie Break* (1970), *Cromwell* (1970) and TV's *The Avengers.* Cornelius was a Physical Training Instructor in the British Army and a member of the Lynn Boxing Club. His brother Billy also did stunts.

See: Cornelius, Joe. *Thumbs Up.* West Allen, 1984; Parla, Paul & Donna. "Trog: The Gentle Savage." *Movie Collectors World.* April 7, 1998.

RAY "CRASH" CORRIGAN (1902–1976)

Cowboy star Ray "Crash" Corrigan was born Raymond Bernard in Milwaukee, Wisconsin, and raised in Denver, Colorado. At 6'2" and a muscular 200 pounds he played football and won a perfect physique contest. This led to work as a fitness instructor to Hollywood stars and stunt jobs at MGM. He doubled Johnny Weissmuller on *Tarzan the Ape Man* (1932) and *Tarzan and His Mate* (1934) and Clark Gable on *Night Flight* (1933), and served as a stuntman on *She* (1935), *Dante's Inferno* (1935), and *Mutiny on the Bounty* (1935). He starred on the action serial *Undersea Kingdom* (1936) during which he adopted his character's name Crash Corrigan as his own for his next role on *The Painted Stallion* (1937).

Corrigan did a lot of stunt work in a gorilla

Ray Corrigan (left) squares off with Yakima Canutt on *Gunsmoke Ranch* (1937).

costume of his own design, even during the time he achieved B-western stardom as a member of the Three Mesquiteers and the Range Busters on entertaining films such as *Gunsmoke Ranch* (1937). For *Flash Gordon* (1936) he donned an alien adaptation of his gorilla outfit for a fight with Buster Crabbe. He appeared on *Darkest Africa* (1936), *The Phantom* (1943), *Monster and the Ape* (1945), and *The White Gorilla* (1945), playing simians. The gorilla costume was a profitable gig, though it was hot and demanding work that he tired of with age. Corrigan even portrayed an alien creature as late as 1958 in *It! The Terror from Beyond Space.*

At the height of his fame in the late 1930s Corrigan purchased a tract of land in the Simi Valley which he developed into a western town and movie set. He opened Corriganville Movie Ranch as a popular tourist trap with live stunt shows part of the attraction. Corrigan himself sometimes took part in the action. Many working stuntmen got their start at Corriganville with Corrigan as their tutor. Corrigan died from a heart attack at the age of 74.

See: "Ray 'Crash' Corrigan." *Wildest Westerns.* August 1961; Schneider, Jerry L. *Corriganville: The Story of Ray "Crash" Corrigan and His Movie Ranch.* Rialto, California: Corriganville Press, 2005.

LOU COSTELLO (1906–1959)

Best known as the short (5'4"), roly-poly half of the comedy duo Abbott and Costello, Lou Costello was born Louis Francis Cristillo in Paterson, New Jersey. In his youth he starred in baseball and basketball at Paterson High. He dabbled at boxing under the name Lou King. In 1927 he found work as a laborer at MGM and Warner Brothers. He volunteered to jump off a balcony for Dolores Del Rio on *The Trail of '98* (1928) and worked a barroom brawl on that film. He was a stunt extra on *The Cossacks* (1928), doubled George K. Arthur on *Circus Rookies* (1928), and took part in football scenes on *Brotherly Love* (1928).

Costello returned to the East Coast and became a comic on vaudeville stages, known for his physical stunts and pratfalls. He returned to Hollywood in the early 1940s with partner Bud Abbott and starred in nearly three dozen films. On his movies his stuntman was customarily Vic

Parks or his older brother Pat Costello, although Lou still enjoyed taking the occasional tumble himself. Costello died from a heart attack at the age of 52.

See: Costello, Chris. *Lou's on First: The Tragic Life of Hollywood's Greatest Clown.* Macmillan, 1982; "Lou Costello Thinks He's Stunt Man." *Eugene Register Guard.* September 28, 1941; "Lou Costello's Career Included Stunts Stint." *Sarasota Herald Tribune.* June 6, 1954.

BILL COUCH (1926–1999)

Born in Asheville, North Carolina, William J. Couch followed his older brother Chuck into circus aerial work, specializing on the high wire. Bill Couch was regarded as one of the best "high men" in the stunt business. He doubled Spencer Tracy and Buddy Hackett on *It's a Mad, Mad, Mad, Mad World* (1963), made a tremendous leap off a mountain on *The Devil's Brigade* (1968), floated through space on *Marooned* (1969), flew with makeshift wings around the Houston Astrodome on *Brewster McCloud* (1970), and was the suicidal man Clint Eastwood talked down from a height with a punch to the face on *Dirty Harry* (1971). On *King Kong* (1976) Couch leapt between two buildings in a gorilla suit. On TV he doubled George Nader on *Man and the Challenge* (1959–60), Lee Majors on the pilot for *The Six Million Dollar Man* (1973), and Lloyd Bridges on the TV movie *The Great Wallendas* (1978). His son Bill, Jr., also did stunts.

The 5'10", 170-pound Couch also worked on *Around the World in Eighty Days* (1956), *The Flying Fontaines* (1959), *Everything's Ducky* (1961), *The Silencers* (1966), *Not With My Wife, You Don't* (1966), *Camelot* (1967), *King's Pirate* (1967), *Counterpoint* (1968), *The Boston Strangler* (1968), *The Green Berets* (1968), *The Split* (1968), *The Love Bug* (1968), *The Wrecking Crew* (1969), *Butch Cassidy and the Sundance Kid* (1969), *The Undefeated* (1969), *Flap* (1970), *Deliverance* (1972), *Conquest of the Planet of the Apes* (1972), *Magnum Force* (1973), *Battle for the Planet of the Apes* (1973), *Blazing Saddles* (1974), *The Towering Inferno* (1974), *The Eiger Sanction* (1975), *Logan's Run* (1976), *Last Embrace* (1979), *Star Trek: The Motion Picture* (1979), *The Black Hole* (1979), and *Meteor* (1979). TV credits include *The Man from U.N.C.L.E., The Virginian, Mission: Impossible, The Wild Wild West, The Green Hornet,* and

Emergency. He was a member of the Stuntmen's Association and an inductee of the Stuntmen's Hall of Fame.

CHUCK COUCH (1922–1991)

Six-foot-one, 180-pound Charles Edward Couch was born in Asheville, North Carolina. Like his stuntman brother Bill, Chuck had a circus background as an aerialist. He was also a Golden Gloves champion and professional boxer, so he specialized in heights and fights. Couch won notice in the film industry doubling Cornel Wilde for a gutsy jump onto an ore car above the Grand Canyon on *Edge of Eternity* (1959). He followed that success by doubling Stephen Boyd on *Billy Rose's Jumbo* (1962) and Terry-Thomas on the comedy classic *It's a Mad, Mad, Mad, Mad World* (1963). On TV, Couch doubled Guy Williams on *Lost in Space,* Martin Landau on *Mission: Impossible,* and Jack Lord on *Hawaii Five-0* (1968–80).

Couch also doubled Ricardo Montalban on TV's *Star Trek.*

He worked on *The Greatest Show on Earth* (1952), *Phantom of the Rue Morgue* (1954), *Gorilla at Large* (1954), *The Buccaneer* (1958), *The Flying Fontaines* (1959), *Everything's Ducky* (1961), *Beau Geste* (1966), *The St. Valentine's Day Massacre* (1967), *Counterpoint* (1968), *The Green Berets* (1968), *Chubasco* (1968), *The Undefeated* (1969), and *Conquest of the Planet of the Apes* (1972). TV credits include *Wyatt Earp, Have Gun—Will Travel, Yancy Derringer, Johnny Ringo, The Aquanauts, Voyage to the Bottom of the Sea, Lost in Space, Honey West,* and *The Girl from U.N.C.L.E..* He was a member of the Stuntmen's Association and an inductee of the Stuntmen's Hall of Fame.

See: Miller, Robert C. "I've Banged My Head a Few Times." *Ukiah Daily Journal.* February 7, 1979; "Stunt Choreographer TV's Latest Title." *Titusville Herald.* July 30, 1960.

Chuck Couch and Guy Way double Cornel Wilde and Mickey Shaughnessy high above the Grand Canyon on *Edge of Eternity* (1959).

CHUCK COURTNEY
(1930–2000)

Born in Los Angeles, Charles Courtney, Jr., remains best known for fourteen appearances he made on the TV show *The Lone Ranger* (1950–55) as the masked man's young nephew Dan Reid. Courtney showcased his ability to ride and fight, which led to his being cast as the lead on the minor western *Born to the Saddle* (1953). Courtney starred in further cheapies such as *Teenage Thunder* (1957), *Teenage Monster* (1958), and the infamous cult film *Billy the Kid Versus Dracula* (1965) on which Courtney played Billy the Kid. By this period he was making far more money as a stuntman and began to concentrate his energies on that. The 5'9", 165-pound Courtney doubled Robert Conrad, Richard Jaeckel, Nick Adams, Tommy Kirk, Doug McClure, and his good friend Robert Fuller. Son Dustin and stepson Lincoln Simonds also became stuntmen.

He worked on *5 Against the House* (1955), *Away All Boats* (1956), *Westward Ho, the Wagons!* (1956), *The Lineup* (1958), *Spartacus* (1960), *Swiss Family Robinson* (1960), *McLintock!* (1963), *The War Lord* (1965), *Red Line 7000* (1965), *Incident at Phantom Hill* (1966), *El Dorado* (1967), *First to Fight* (1967), *The Green Berets* (1968), *Hellfighters* (1968), *Rio Lobo* (1970), *There Was a Crooked Man...* (1970), *The Omega Man* (1971), *The Cowboys* (1972), *Ulzana's Raid* (1972), and *Live a Little, Steal a Lot* (aka *Murph the Surf*) (1975). TV credits include *Tales of Wells Fargo, Laramie, Wagon Train, The Virginian, Laredo, Voyage to the Bottom of the Sea, The Wild Wild West, Get Smart, Star Trek, Mannix, It Takes a Thief, Mission: Impossible, Adam-12, Baa Baa Black Sheep*, and *A Man Called Sloane*. Courtney was a member of the Stuntmen's Association, an inductee of the Stuntmen's Hall of Fame, and a Golden Boot honoree. Courtney suffered a series of debilitating strokes and died at the age of 69 from a self-inflicted gunshot wound.

See: Libby, Bill. "Dying...It's a Living." *Argosy.* 1967.

MONTY COX (1940–)

Five-foot-eight, 160-pound Lamont Cox was born in Huntington, Indiana, and raised in Reno, Nevada. An abalone diver, world record–setting skydiver, and animal handler, he specialized in exotics such as Clarence the Cross-Eyed Lion. Cox wrestled lions and tigers on the TV series *Daktari* (1967–69) and trained animals for Ivan Tors on *Gentle Ben* (1967–69). He worked at Africa USA until it dissolved, then performed animal work on *When the North Wind Blows* (1974) and *Mountain Family Robinson* (1979). Cox trained the bear on *Grizzly* (1976) and controlled the tiger on *Apocalypse Now* (1979), but his crowning achievement came handling a variety of creatures on *Day of the Animals* (1977). As a stuntman he drove the lead boat on *Lucky Lady* (1975).

See: Gagnard, Frank. "Two Stunt People." *Times-Picayune.* May 16, 1977; Hagen, Bill. "Trainers Enjoy Work." *Brownsville Herald.* July 15, 1977; Michaelson, Maureen. "Hollywood Animal Trainers Monty Cox and Susan Backlinie Bring Out the Best in Beasts." *People.* September 10, 1979;

BUSTER CRABBE (1908–1983)

The undisputed king of action serials, Olympic swimming champion Buster Crabbe got his start in films as a stunt double for Joel McCrea on *The Most Dangerous Game* (1932). Crabbe executed a twenty-foot dive off an exploding ship and was paid $30 for the stunt. Crabbe was soon starring on the Tarzan knockoff *King of the Jungle* (1933) and playing Tarzan himself on the serial *Tarzan the Fearless* (1933). This led to serial roles in *Flash Gordon* (1936) and *Buck Rogers* (1939), audience favorites that unfortunately kept him away from higher-level studio films. Throughout the 1940s he was stuck fighting his way through Poverty Row westerns. His best fight came against fellow Olympic swimming champ Johnny Weissmuller on *Swamp Fire* (1946). On episodic TV Crabbe played an aging stuntman on a 1979 episode of *BJ and the Bear.*

Clarence Linden Crabbe was born in Oakland, California, and raised in Hawaii. Six-foot-one and 190 pounds, he won athletic letters at Punahou High in football, basketball, track, and swimming. His aquatic success continued through his athletic career at USC as a record-setting swimmer and rival of Weissmuller. Crabbe accumulated sixteen world records and thirty-five national records in the water. At the 1928 Olympic Games he took a Bronze medal in the 1500 meter freestyle and in 1932 took home

Olympic Gold in the 400 meter freestyle. An inductee of the International Swimming Hall of Fame, Crabbe died from a heart attack at the age of 75.

See: Vermilye, Jerry. *Buster Crabbe: A Biofilmography.* Jefferson, NC: McFarland, 2008; Whitezel, Karl. *Buster Crabbe: A Self Portrait.* Madison, NC: Empire, 1997; www.ishof.org.

GERRY CRAMPTON (1930–2009)

Robert Gerald Crampton was born in Fulham, London, England. His father taught him how to box, and he became adept at swimming and diving. After service in the Royal Armed Forces the 190-pound six-footer began bodybuilding, winning Britain's Mr. Body Beautiful and competing for many of the top bodybuilding titles in Europe, including Mr. London, Mr. England, Mr. Europe, and Mr. Universe. Determining a bleak financial future in muscle building, Crampton helped stuntman Bob Simmons stage a fight scene for *Fury at Smuggler's Bay* (1961). He was with the James Bond franchise as an assistant to Simmons on *Dr. No* (1962), *Goldfinger* (1964), *You Only Live Twice* (1967), and *Diamonds Are Forever* (1971).

Crampton doubled Rod Taylor, Richard Harris, Vince Edwards, and Jock Mahoney, fighting a leopard for the later on *Tarzan Goes to India* (1962. Crampton was permanently scarred by the leopard. Crampton was stunt coordinator on *The Dirty Dozen* (1967) and played one of the paratroopers who corners Charles Bronson in the latrine. He fought Rod Taylor on *High Commissioner* (1968) and doubled Peter Carsten for a cliff-side fight with Taylor on *Dark of the Sun* (1968). He worked often with Peter Sellers and served as his off-set minder.

He worked on *The Hill* (1965), *Heroes of Telemark* (1965), *Casino Royale* (1967), *Hammerhead* (1968), *Cromwell* (1970), *Man in the Wilderness* (1971), *Eyewitness* (1971), *Ghost in the Noonday Sun* (1973), *Hennessy* (1975), *Sholay* (1975), *The Eagle Has Landed* (1976), *The Spy Who Loved Me* (1977), and *Raiders of the Lost Ark* (1981). TV credits include *The Avengers*, *The Prisoner*, and *The Persuaders*. Known as Mr. Mayhem, he is one of the rare Brits to be honored by the Stuntmen's Hall of Fame.

See: "Gerry Crampton." *Daily Telegraph.*

February 13, 2009; Nash, Max. "Stuntman Crampton a Leaping Wonder." *Independent Press.* April 21, 1973.

NICK CRAVAT (1912–1994)

Nick Cravat was born in New York City as Nicholas Cuccia. He is best known as the gymnastic partner of Burt Lancaster. Together they formed the Lang and Cravat team and toured with the Kay Brothers Circus. When Lancaster became a movie star he brought his diminutive (5'4") pal along to co-star on *The Flame and the Arrow* (1950) and *The Crimson Pirate* (1952). On these entertaining films the duo showed off many of their acrobatics. On both films Cravat played a mute because of his thick accent.

Cravat also worked on *Ten Tall Men* (1951), *Veils of Bagdad* (1953), *King Richard and the Crusaders* (1954), *Cat Ballou* (1965), *The Way West* (1967), *The Scalphunters* (1968), *Airport* (1970), *Valdez Is Coming* (1971), and *Ulzana's Raid* (1972). On TV he was featured on *Count of Monte Cristo* (1956) and played a gremlin on the wing of an airplane on *Twilight Zone.* Cravat died from lung cancer at the age of 82.

See: www.nickcravat.com.

LES CRAWFORD (d. 2006)

Six-foot-one, 185-pound Leslie David Crawford was Roger Moore's long-time stand-in, double, and fight partner dating back to the TV series *Ivanhoe* (1958–59), *The Saint* (1962–69), and *The Persuaders* (1971–72). The association continued through Moore's first two Bond films *Live and Let Die* (1973) and *Man with the Golden Gun* (1974), with Crawford working as the stunt gaffer on the latter. He arranged the fight between Moore and Lee Marvin on *Shout at the Devil* (1976).

A veteran of the British Infantry, Crawford became an NCO with the Royal Green Jackets. He doubled Stanley Baker on *Innocent Bystanders* (1972), slugged it out with John Wayne on *Brannigan* (1975), and worked on the early Bond films *From Russia with Love* (1963), *On Her Majesty's Secret Service* (1969), and *Diamonds Are Forever* (1971). TV credits include *The Avengers, Danger Man,* and *The Baron,* where he doubled Steve Forrest.

See: Kleiner, Dick. "These Brawlers Quite

Gerry Crampton, doubling Peter Carsten, delivers a punch to actor Rod Taylor (or his double Louie Elias) on *Dark of the Sun* (1968).

Polite." *Fond Du Lac Reporter.* November 1, 1974; Moore, Roger. *My Word Is My Bond: A Memoir.* HarperCollins, 2009.

MARTHA CRAWFORD (1928–)

Martha Crawford was born in Dresden, Texas, and raised on the West Coast. Her stepdad Carl Crawford was a professional polo player, which put her around horses on a regular basis. She was soon showing horses as well as riding them, becoming confident enough in her natural abilities and acrobatic training to win a prime stunt doubling job for Anne Baxter on the western *Yellow Sky* (1948). Crawford's biggest stunt was jumping a horse through a studio-made fire for Eleanor Parker on *Interrupted Melody* (1955). She doubled Parker on *Man with the Golden Arm* (1955), *The King and Four Queens* (1956), and *The Seventh Sin* (1957).

Crawford doubled Martha Hyer on *Kiss of Fire* (1955), Claudette Colbert on *Texas Lady* (1955), Debra Paget on *Love Me Tender* (1956), Rhonda Fleming on *Gun Glory* (1957), Betsy Palmer on *The Tin Star* (1957), Patricia Owens on *The Law and Jake Wade* (1958), Shirley MacLaine on *The Sheepman* (1958), and Jean Simmons and Carroll Baker on *The Big Country* (1958). She worked on *The Rains of Ranchipur* (1955) and the TV series *Cheyenne*. Crawford was inducted into the Stuntmen's Hall of Fame and received a Golden Boot.

See: Crawford-Cantarini, Martha, and Chrystopher J. Spicer. *Fall Girl: My Life as a Hollywood Stunt Double.* Jefferson, NC: McFarland, 2010.

EVERETT CREACH (1933–1994)

Everett Louis Creach made his mark in the business as the stunt coordinator on *Tora! Tora! Tora!* (1970), where he blew up thirteen planes on the ground with stuntmen working in and out of the explosions. The pyrotechnics went off early and Creach himself was struck in the foot by a flying engine, making for thrilling footage. He had other jobs as a coordinator and second unit director on *Soldier Blue* (1970), *Marathon Man* (1976), and *The Driver* (1978). He doubled Michael

Douglas for motorcycles scenes on *Napoleon and Samantha* (1972).

The versatile Missouri-born Creach got his start as a horseback double for Roddy McDowall. Creach was on the Pierce College Rodeo team and became a member of the Professional Rodeo Cowboys Association. In 1960 he took part in a multi-state Pony Express publicity stunt. In 1964 he worked a live stunt show at the World's Fair. His varied career includes horse work on the John Ford westerns *She Wore a Yellow Ribbon* (1949), *Rio Grande* (1950), and *The Horse Soldiers* (1959), a fire stunt on *Beau Geste* (1966), being knocked through a saloon window on *The War Wagon* (1967), and making motorcycle jumps for Christopher Mitchum on *Big Jake* (1971). He raced motorcycles and cars throughout his career.

The 5'11", 180-pound Creach also worked on *How the West Was Won* (1962), *Confessions of an Opium Eater* (1962), *A Distant Trumpet* (1964), *Night of the Grizzly* (1966), *The Way West* (1967), *The Green Berets* (1968), *Chubasco* (1968), *Bullitt* (1968), *The Love Bug* (1968), *Hellfighters* (1968), *The Good Guys and the Bad Guys* (1969), *The Great Bank Robbery* (1969), *Little Fauss and Big Halsey* (1970), *Sometimes a Great Notion* (1970), *Dirty Harry* (1971), *Diamonds Are Forever* (1971), *Evel Knievel* (1971), *Wrath of God* (1972), *The Last American Hero* (1973), *Magnum Force* (1973), *Hit!* (1973), *The Towering Inferno* (1974), *Airport '75* (1974), *Sidecar Racers* (1975), *Family Plot* (1976), *Black Sunday* (1977), and *The Car* (1977). He was stunt coordinator for the cult TV movie *Gargoyles* (1972). TV credits include *The Girl from U.N.C.L.E., Kung Fu, The Six Million Dollar Man, Matt Helm,* and *BJ and the Bear.* Daughters Vicki and Laura followed him into the business. He was a member of the Stuntmen's Association and an inductee of the Stuntmen's Hall of Fame.

See: Hurst. P.B. *The Most Savage Film: Soldier Blue, Cinematic Violence, and the Horrors of War.* Jefferson, NC: McFarland, 2008; Musgrove, Nan. "Stuntman on the Bike Tracks." *Australian Women's Weekly.* June 26, 1974.

PADDY CREAN (1911–2003)

Patrick "Paddy" Crean was born in London to a prominent family and became a competitive fencer. Taking to the English boards, he played Shakespeare and gained a reputation for stage combat. With partner Rex Rickman he ran the Sophy School in London and taught fencing to stars Alec Guinness and John Gielgud. Crean was known for his intricately detailed choreography and blocking out of action beforehand using miniature swords.

He became valued by the film industry and was hired as a coach and fight double for Errol Flynn on *Master of Ballantrae* (1953), *Crossed Swords* (1954), and the unfinished *William Tell*. When called upon to double Flynn, he wore specially made boots to give him added height and custom latex cast in his shoulders. Crean also worked on *War and Peace* (1956), *The Vikings* (1958), *Sword of Sherwood Forest* (1960) and the TV series *Captain Gallant* with Buster Crabbe. In the early 1960s he moved to Canada for a position as sword-master at the Stratford Theatre in Ontario. He was the subject of the documentary film *The Fight Master*.

See: Crean, Patrick. *More Champagne, Darling.* Toronto: McGraw Hill, 1981; www.paddy-crean.com.

ROGER CREED (1915–1997)

Roger Vernon Creed, Jr., was born in Fulton, Kentucky, and raised in Oklahoma. He became a professional boxer and served with the U.S. Army during World War II. Creed is best known for doubling Bob Hope on *Fancy Pants* (1950) and *My Favorite Spy* (1951). In 1961, Creed starred in a TV pilot for a series based on the comic book hero *The Phantom*. He made news wires when he was named to be an official "stunt coordinator" on *There Was a Crooked Man...* (1970), the first time such a post had been acknowledged. Creed was coordinator for the fight between actors Rod Taylor and William Smith on *Darker Than Amber* (1970), although much of that brawl became ad-libbed.

Six-foot-one, 190-pound Creed also worked on *Nancy Steele Is Missing* (1937), *Sergeant York* (1941), *Fall In* (1942), *Five Graves to Cairo* (1943), *O.S.S.* (1946), *Joan of Arc* (1948), *Ghost of Zorro* (1949), *Armored Car Robbery* (1950), *The Savage* (1952), *East of Eden* (1955), *The Sea Chase* (1955), *Tall Man Riding* (1955), *The Ten Commandments* (1956), *Gunfight at the O.K. Corral* (1957), *Omar Khayyam* (1957), *The Buccaneer* (1958), *The President's Analyst* (1967), *Rosemary's Baby* (1968), *The Molly Maguires* (1970), *Which Way to the Front?* (1970), *Delta Factor* (1970), *The Grissom Gang* (1971), *Badge 373* (1973), *The Klansman* (1974), *The Front Page* (1974), *The Towering Inferno* (1974), *Young Frankenstein* (1974), *King Kong* (1976), *Moving Violation* (1976), *Damnation Alley* (1977), *Piranha* (1978), *Amityville Horror* (1979), *Meteor* (1979), *The Electric Horseman* (1979), and *Lady in Red* (1979). TV credits include *The Lone Ranger, Outlaws, Batman, The Wild Wild West, Adam–12, Young Rebels,* and *Harry O.* He was a member of the Stuntmen's Association and an inductee of the Stuntmen's Hall of Fame.

DICK CROCKETT (1915–1979)

Richard Dehart Crockett was born in Maywood, Illinois. He spent his early life as a vaudeville acrobat and circus performer and represented the Los Angeles Athletic Club in a national tumbling championship. He entered the films as a stand-in for Frank Albertson at MGM. One of his first big assignments came doubling Charles Laughton in *The Hunchback of Notre Dame* (1939). Crockett became known for his ability to perform high falls, but was also considered a top fight man. With his near-complete baldness, he seemed ageless for decades, always presenting the physique of a well-muscled gymnast. One of his favorite pastimes was playing handball with fellow stuntman Dave Sharpe. After each serve they would perform a front or back flip before completing the return.

He made a name for himself as the stunt supervisor on Blake Edwards' TV series *Peter Gunn* (1958–61), the first stuntman to get screen credit for that position. The 5'10", 175-pound Crockett began coordinating all Edwards' films including *The Great Race* (1965). He did several classic Inspector Clouseau *Pink Panther* films, which featured all-out comic brawls between Peter Sellers and his servant Burt Kwouk. Crockett doubled Sellers and Kwouk, as well as Jack Lemmon, Mickey Rooney, Bing Crosby, Jack Benny, George Burns, Lloyd Nolan, Alan Ladd, Rod Taylor, and Tony Curtis. He ran stunts on the TV shows *The Man from U.N.C.L.E.* and *Star Trek,* occasionally doubling William Shatner.

He also worked on *Adventures of Captain Marvel* (1941), *Panhandle* (1948), *The Thing from Another World* (1951), *Sealed Cargo* (1951), *Jalopy* (1953), *The Rains of Ranchipur* (1955), *Hell on*

Frisco Bay (1955), *Abbott and Costello Meet the Keystone Kops* (1955), *Around the World in Eighty Days* (1956), *Santiago* (1956), *Baby Face Nelson* (1957), *No Time for Sergeants* (1958), *Darby's Rangers* (1958), *Spartacus* (1960), *It's a Mad, Mad, Mad, Mad World* (1963), *Soldier in the Rain* (1963), *Quick Before it Melts* (1964), *What Did You Do in the War, Daddy?* (1966), *Batman* (1966), *Harper* (1966), *Gunn* (1967), *Coogan's Bluff* (1968), *Darling Lili* (1970), *Wild Rovers* (1971), *Diamonds Are Forever* (1971), *Dirty Harry* (1971), *The Getaway* (1972), *Across 110th Street* (1972), *The Don Is Dead* (1973), *Blazing Saddles* (1974), *The Towering Inferno* (1974), *Earthquake* (1974), and *The Hindenburg* (1975). TV credits include *Superman, Zane Grey, The Lineup, M Squad, One Step Beyond, The Girl from U.N.C.L.E., Batman, Tarzan, It Takes a Thief, Kung Fu, The Rookies, Matt Helm,* and *Police Woman.* A founding member of the Stuntmen's Association and an inductee of the Stuntmen's Hall of Fame, Crockett died from a heart attack at the age of 63.

See: "Dick Crockett." *Variety.* February 7, 1979; Johnson, Erskine. "Film Stuntman, Versatile Crew." *Logansport Press.* August 16, 1961; Scott, Vernon. "Good Stuntman Makes Fortune in Hollywood." *New Castle News.* April 13, 1961.

WORTH CROUCH (1915–1943)

Texas-born cowboy Worth Nelson Crouch distinguished himself in the rodeo arena as a champion bulldogger, appearing at Madison Square Garden. The model for the *Red Ryder* comic strip, he was making headway in his young stunt career as a double for John Wayne. Crouch was killed at the age of 27 when a caisson in which he was riding flipped over during the making of *We've Never Been Licked* (1943).

JOE CUNY

French-born Joseph John Cuny was one of the industry's earliest risk-takers. Originally a wild horse tamer, he performed a variety of stunts for Pearl White on *Perils of Pauline* (1914). This led to regular employment at Pathe Studios as their serial stunt ace. He doubled anonymously for action stars Eddie Polo and Charles Hutchison on *Hurricane Hutch* (1921), *Go Get 'Em Hutch* (1922), and *Speed* (1922). They took all the credit

while Cuny made only $5 for each dangerous stunt. By the 1930s he was all but forgotten in the business.

See: "Fearless Joe." *Daily Globe.* March 5, 1921.

BILLY CURTIS (1909–1988)

Four-foot-two, 75 pound Billy Curtis was born Luigi Curto in Springfield, Massachusetts, and began his career as a vaudeville acrobat and professional wrestler. He stood in and doubled for child stars Shirley Temple, Roddy McDowall, Mickey Rooney, Margaret O'Brien, Butch Jenkins, and Darryl Hickman. He made $1,500 for a 36-foot fall into a net for Bobby Driscoll on *The Window* (1949). On *The Thing from Another World* (1951) he played the small version of the shrinking alien. Curtis was a munchkin on *The Wizard of Oz* (1939) but set himself apart from his contemporaries with a starring role as a heroic cowboy on the all-midget western *The Terror of Tiny Town* (1939). Over thirty years later he had another leading role on *Little Cigars* (1973) and a memorable supporting part opposite Clint Eastwood on *High Plains Drifter* (1973).

He worked on *Hellzapoppin* (1941), *Saboteur* (1942), *Gog* (1954), *The Court Jester* (1956), *The Conqueror* (1956), *Friendly Persuasion* (1956), *The Incredible Shrinking Man* (1957), *Merry Andrew* (1958), *The Angry Red Planet* (1959), *How the West Was Won* (1962), *John Goldfarb, Please Come Home* (1965), *Planet of the Apes* (1968), and *Dirty Harry* (1971). TV credits include *Superman, I Spy, The Wild Wild West, Batman,* and *Star Trek.* He died from a heart attack at the age of 79.

See: Folkart, Burt. "Actor, Double; Billy Curtis: Midget Had Film Career." *Los Angeles Times.* November 12, 1988; "Half-Pint Tom Mix to Star in All-Midget Picture." *Reading Eagle.* May 23, 1938; Heffernan, Harold. "He Found Fountain of Youth in Movies." *Toledo Blade.* November 2, 1961.

HOWARD CURTIS (1927–1979)

Howard Metcalf Curtis was one of the best high men in the stunt business. Pennsylvania-born, he served at the tail end of World War II and competed as an athlete, diving for the U.S. Air Corps Swim Team and running track. Upon

Jophery Brown, Chuck Waters, and Howard Curtis (doubling for actors James Earl Jones, Genevieve Bujold, and Robert Shaw, respectively) do a spectacular wagon leap off a cliff on *Swashbuckler* (1976).

his discharge, the 170-pound six-footer enrolled at Oberlin College as a physical education major, competing in soccer, track, diving, and lacrosse. He taught phys ed at Ohio State and coached. On the side he became a professional diver and semi-pro lacrosse player. Curtis took a job at UCLA as an athletic director while winning archery, diving, and skydiving championships. In 1957 he became a professional stuntman, eventually quitting UCLA after making a name with his skydiving on the series *Ripcord* (1961–63).

Curtis doubled Steven Hill on TV's *Mission: Impossible* (1966–67) and Robert Wagner on *It Takes a Thief* (1968–70), *Switch* (1975–78), and *Hart to Hart* (1979). Curtis wasn't a perfect match for Wagner, but he excelled in the star's fight scenes. Curtis doubled Paul Newman for the famous jump off the cliff on *Butch Cassidy and the Sundance Kid* (1969). Robert Shaw utilized Curtis on *Jaws* (1975), *The Deep* (1977), and *Black Sunday* (1977), hanging from a helicopter in the latter. Curtis doubled Ed Nelson for the fight on *Soldier in the Rain* (1963) and Charles Bronson for the battle with Archie Moore atop an icy train on *Breakheart Pass* (1976). He also subbed for Efrem Zimbalist, Jr., Robert Taylor, Tony Curtis, Tab Hunter, Vince Edwards, Peter Lawford, Dennis Weaver, and Elvis Presley for a motorcycle crash on *Roustabout* (1964). His wife Pepper was a stunt woman. Curtis collected armor and firearms and wrote a book on antique helmets.

He worked on *Never So Few* (1959), *Captain Newman, M.D.* (1963), *The Great Race* (1965), *Beach Blanket Bingo* (1965), *Not With My Wife You Don't* (1966), *The Split* (1968), *The Great Bank Robbery* (1969), *Star Spangled Girl* (1971), *The Poseidon Adventure* (1972), *Cleopatra Jones* (1973), *99 and 44/100 percent Dead* (1974), *The Towering Inferno* (1974), *Earthquake* (1974), *Airport '75* (1974), *The Front Page* (1974), *The Great Waldo Pepper* (1975), *The Hindenburg* (1975), *Swashbuckler* (1976), *The Choirboys* (1977), *The Deer Hunter* (1978), *Moonraker* (1979), *The Black Hole* (1979), and *Stunt Seven* (1979). TV credits include *Voyage to the Bottom of the Sea, Honey West, Branded, Mission: Impossible, The FBI, Firehouse, The Rockford Files,* and *Emergency.* A member of the Stuntmen's Association and an inductee of the Stuntmen's Hall of Fame, Curtis died in a skydiving accident attempting to save an amateur diver who became tangled in his chute. He was 52 years old.

See: Hagner, John. "Profile." *Falling for Stars.* Vol 1 #3 March 1965; "Howard Curtis." *Variety.* September 12, 1979; "Stuntman Engulfed in Flames." *Midland Reporter.* February 2, 1975.

PEPPER CURTIS (1932–1982)

Five-foot-five Pepper Curtis was born Elizabeth Jo Goracke in Green Bay, Wisconsin. The wife of stuntman Howard Curtis, she allegedly divorced him in the early 1960s because he wanted her to parachute jump. She doubled Amanda Blake on TV's *Gunsmoke,* Mia Farrow on *Peyton Place,* and Angie Dickinson on *Police Woman.* Films had her doubling Carol Lynley and Stella Stevens on *The Poseidon Adventure* (1972) and Farrah Fawcett on *Logan's Run* (1976). On the latter she fell during the carousel sequence when a safety cable snapped, severely injuring her back. Other credits include *Three on a Couch* (1966), *Up the Sandbox* (1972), and the TV series *The Untouchables, Perry Mason,* and *Adam–12.* A charter member of the Stuntwomen's Association and an inductee of the Stuntmen's Hall of Fame, Curtis died from heart complications at the age of 49.

See: Marcus, Becky. *Manic Rescue.* Author House, 2005.

JOHN DAHEIM (1916–1991)

John Joseph Daheim specialized in playing brawlers and pugilists, memorably opposing Kirk Douglas in the ring on *Champion* (1949). He was stunt coordinator on *Spartacus* (1960) and played Gentleman Jim Corbett on *City of Bad Men* (1953). Daheim fought Elvis Presley on *Jailhouse Rock* (1957) and Steve McQueen on *Baby, the Rain Must Fall* (1965). He was sometimes billed as Johnny Day, the name he used to star in *Jeep Herders* (1945) and *Detour to Danger* (1946), low-budget films produced and directed by stuntmen Harvey Parry and Richard Talmadge. The latter concluded with a wild, non-stop twelve-minute brawl.

Daheim was born in Minneapolis, Minnesota, and entered stunts during the Depression. His first was a daring motorcycle leap for *I Like It That Way* (1934). Trouble was, Daheim had never been on a motorcycle before. He woke up in the hospital, but a $600 check convinced him he had found his calling. He doubled William Holden on *Texas* (1941), Robert Taylor on *Undercurrent*

(1946), George Raft on *Christmas Eve* (1947), Bob Steele on *Exposed* (1947), Lawrence Tierney on *Bodyguard* (1948), Tyrone Power on *The Mississippi Gambler* (1953), and James Mason on *20,000 Leagues Under the Sea* (1954). He also subbed for Tim Holt, Hugh O'Brian, Cameron Mitchell, and James Garner. By the 1970s he was one of the most well-respected second unit directors and stunt coordinators in Hollywood, handed the duties for coordinating the large-scale disaster epics *Earthquake* (1974), *The Hindenburg* (1975), and *Rollercoaster* (1977).

The 5'10", 170-pound actor-stuntman also worked on *Perils of Nyoka* (1942), *Two Yanks in Trinidad* (1942), *The Kansan* (1943), *G-Men vs. The Black Dragon* (1943), *Passage to Marseille* (1944), *Haunted Harbor* (1944), *The Spanish Main* (1945), *Crimson Ghost* (1946), *The Lady from Shanghai* (1947), *Raw Deal* (1948), *Station West* (1948), *G-Men Never Forget* (1948), *Ghost of Zorro* (1949), *Where the Sidewalk Ends* (1950), *Kiss Tomorrow Goodbye* (1950), *Strangers on a Train* (1951), *His Kind of Woman* (1951), *The Racket* (1951), *Macao* (1952), *Wings of the Hawk* (1953), *99 River Street* (1953), *The Man from the Alamo* (1953), *Seminole* (1953), *Taza, Son of Cochise* (1954), *Seven Brides for Seven Brothers* (1954), *Yankee Pasha* (1954), *To Hell and Back* (1955), *Headline Hunters* (1955), *The Conqueror* (1956), *Johnny Concho* (1956), *Night Passage* (1957), *The Badlanders* (1958), *Westbound* (1959), *Night of the Quarter Moon* (1959), *Elmer Gantry* (1960), *The Misfits* (1961), *It's a Mad, Mad, Mad, Mad World* (1963), *The Ugly American* (1963), *Advance to the Rear* (1964), *He Rides Tall* (1964), *Shenandoah* (1965), *Von Ryan's Express* (1965), *A Man Could Get Killed* (1966), *The Silencers* (1966), *Duel at Diablo* (1966), *In Like Flint* (1967), *Tobruk* (1967), *Gunn* (1967), *Counterpoint* (1968), *P.J.* (1968), *Support Your Local Sheriff* (1969), *Tell Them Willie Boy Is Here* (1969), *Support Your Local Gunfighter* (1971), *The Poseidon Adventure* (1972), *The Don Is Dead* (1973), and *Silver Streak* (1976). TV credits include *The Lone Ranger, Soldiers of Fortune, Maverick, Cheyenne, Mike Hammer, Mr. Lucky, Peter Gunn, Hawaiian Eye, 77 Sunset Strip, Rawhide, The Untouchables, Wagon Train, Laramie, The Fugitive, Gunsmoke, Daniel Boone, T.H.E. Cat, The FBI, The Virginian, Nichols,* and *The Rockford Files.* He was a member of the Stuntmen's Hall of Fame.

See: Sanford, Harry. "John Daheim." *Falling for Stars.* #2, 1974; Scott, John. "Stunt Man Has More Than 9 Lives." *Los Angeles Times.* February 23, 1967.

FRED DALE (1920–2004)

New York-born Fred Dale was the original double for Richard Boone on the TV western *Have Gun—Will Travel* (1957–59) until there arose a tough tree-climbing sequence. Extra Hal Needham stepped forward and climbed so impressively that Boone opted to give Needham a shot at being his double. Needham became a stunt legend and Dale went on to have a quiet career behind the scenes of the long-running series *Gunsmoke.* He also worked on *Halls of Montezuma* (1950), *The Desert Fox* (1951), *House of Bamboo* (1955), *Mackenna's Gold* (1969), *The Poseidon Adventure* (1972), *The Don Is Dead* (1973), *The Front Page* (1974), and *The Cat from Outer Space* (1978).

CAROL DANIELS (1935–)

Five-foot-five Carol Daniels was born Carol Dement in Los Angeles. She doubled Joan Taylor on TV's *The Rifleman* (1960–62), Mildred Natwick on *The Snoop Sisters* (1972–74), and Lee Meriwether on *Barnaby Jones* (1973–74). She also filled in for Brenda Vaccaro, Barbara Hershey, Barbara Luna, Donna Mills, Sean Young, Teri Garr, Charlotte Rampling, Michele Lee, Suzanne Pleshette, Kate Jackson, Genevieve Bujold, Janice Rule, Madlyn Rhue, Barbara Stanwyck, and Rachel Ward. Daniels was buried alive in ten tons of sand on the 1985 TV series *Shadow Chasers* and sued Warner Brothers for negligence.

She worked on *Hot Rod Girl* (1956), *Spartacus* (1960), *What Ever Happened to Baby Jane?* (1962), *It's a Mad, Mad, Mad, Mad World* (1963), *The Greatest Story Ever Told* (1965), *What Did You Do in the War, Daddy?* (1966), *The Graduate* (1967), *The Great Bank Robbery* (1969), *The Reivers* (1969), *Airport* (1970), *Sometimes a Great Notion* (1970), *The Poseidon Adventure* (1972), *Earthquake* (1974), *Airport '77* (1977), and *Capricorn One* (1978). TV credits include *Wanted—Dead or Alive, The Untouchables, Have Gun—Will Travel, Gunsmoke, Bonanza, Mannix, The Man from U.N.C.L.E., Star Trek, Ironside, The Streets of San Francisco,* and *Emergency.*

See: Prelutsky, Burt. "Superdame." *Los Angeles Times*. June 18, 1972; "Stunt Woman Sues Over Burial in Sand." *Orange County Register*. November 17, 1986.

BETTY DANKO (1903–1979)

Betty Danko was born Bertha Danko in New Jersey and took her first tumble down a set of stairs at age three. She was unhurt. Falls became her specialty as one of Hollywood's top stuntwomen. Danko is best known for riding the broomstick for Margaret Hamilton as the Wicked Witch on *The Wizard of Oz* (1939). Danko's legs were badly burned by pyrotechnics during the sky-writing sequence and spent two weeks in the hospital. Another big assignment came doubling Marie Windsor for the famous *Frenchie* (1950) fight with Shelley Winters.

Danko doubled Patsy Kelly, Joan Crawford, Irene Dunne, Maureen O'Sullivan, Madge Evans, Jean Arthur, Myrna Loy, Binnie Barnes, and Thelma Todd. She drove a car through a fence for Joan Blondell on *Perfect Specimen* (1937), jumped from a hayloft on *Murder He Says* (1945), and worked on *The Spanish Main* (1945) and *Soldiers Three* (1951). She was forced to give up her career when she was hit by a car that jumped a curb while she was waiting for a bus. This accident was no stunt, but real life.

See: "Filmland's Fatalists." *Oakland Tribune*. August 9, 1936; "Stunt Men Sub for Stars." *Trenton Evening Times*. March 2, 1944.

FRANKIE DARRO (1917–1976)

Frankie Darro was born Frank Johnson in Chicago, Illinois. He was the son of circus performer turned movie stuntman Frank Johnson. Frankie was trained as a tumbler and became a child star who did his own stunts. He was a sidekick to Tom Tyler on FBO westerns, and had leading parts on the Mascot serials *Burn 'Em Up Barnes* (1934) and *Phantom Empire* (1935). In the 1930s Darro played a succession of tough kids in films such as *Wild Boys of the Road* (1933) and enthusiastically performed his own fights. As he got older, the wiry 5'5" Darro was cast as a jockey on the Marx Brothers film *A Day at the Races* (1937).

During World War II Darro joined the U.S. Navy and was unable to obtain leading roles upon his discharge. He drifted into bit parts and stunt work, battling alcohol the remainder of his life. He doubled Leo Gorcey in late 1940s Bowery Boys films and most famously was inside Robby the Robot on *Forbidden Planet* (1956) until a liquid lunch nearly caused him to fall while wearing the Robot suit. Darro did stunts on *Wyoming Mail* (1950), *Across the Wide Missouri* (1951), *Westward the Women* (1951), *Siren of Bagdad* (1953), *The Ten Commandments* (1956), *Darby O'Gill and the Little People* (1959), and *The Notorious Landlady* (1962) where he doubled a wheelchair-bound geriatric taking a wild ride down a cliff. He appeared semi-regularly on *The Red Skelton Show* as an old woman who gets thrown around. An inductee of the Stuntmen's Hall of Fame, Darro died from a heart attack at the age of 59.

See: Gloske, John. *Tough Kid: The Life and Films of Frankie Darro*. Lulu, 2008; Johnson, Erskine. "Modern Day Movie Stuntmen Have to Be Versatile." *Corpus Christi Times*. August 16, 1961; "Tough Kid Star of the 1930s Stages Comeback as Robot." *Racine Journal*. April 30, 1955; www.frankiedarro.com.

JADIE DAVID (1950–)

Jadie David is a pioneering black stuntwoman. She could already ride, swim, and dive when stunt coordinator Bob Minor spotted her on a horse at Griffith Park. She doubled Pam Grier on the low-budget hits *Coffy* (1973) and *Foxy Brown* (1974) and Teresa Graves on TV's *Get Christie Love!* (1974–75). David performed a fire stunt on *Mandingo* (1975) without the benefit of a protective suit. David injured her back on *Rollercoaster* (1977) when she was thrown from the coaster. Other credits include *Legend of Nigger Charley* (1972), *Earthquake* (1974), *Sheba, Baby* (1975), *Friday Foster* (1975), *Dr. Black, Mr. Hyde* (1976), *Drum* (1976), *Convoy* (1978), *Hooper* (1978), and *Time After Time* (1979). A production safety consultant at Paramount, she is co-founder of the Alliance of Stunt Performers of Color.

See: Silden, Isobel. "Stunt Women." *Australian Women's Weekly*. February 17, 1982; www.diamondintheraw.com;

SID DAVIS (1916–2006)

Chicago-born Sid Davis grew up in Los Angeles and worked as a child extra. After a stint with the Merchant Marine, the 6'4" Davis became a stand-in and occasional double for John Wayne. He worked all of Wayne's films from 1941 to 1952. On *Red River* (1948) Davis filled in for Wayne during the Montgomery Clift fight when Wayne is knocked into the wagon. He was put into action for large-scale brawls on *Angel and the Badman* (1947) and *The Fighting Kentuckian* (1949). When not working for Wayne, Davis was with Leif Erickson, John Carroll, Raymond Burr, and Ben Johnson.

Davis was the filmmaker behind dozens of 1950s and 1960s socially conscious message films targeted toward school age children warning them about the dangers of life. His friend Wayne loaned Davis the money for the first of these short films, titled *The Dangerous Stranger*. When Davis paid him back, Wayne tore up the check. A distinguished mountain climber, Davis holds the record for reaching Mt. San Jacinto's summit 643 times. He died from lung cancer at the age of 90.

See: "Sid Davis." *New York Times.* November 9, 2006; "Sid Davis, 90, Producer of Cautionary Films for Classrooms in 50s and 60s." *Los Angeles Times.* November 8, 2006.

WALT DAVIS (1929–1981)

Michigan-born Walter Shymer Davis was a familiar bit player, often playing soldiers, cops, and guards. The 6'1" Davis was a resident stuntman on the World War II TV series *Combat* (1962–67) and doubled series star Rick Jason. He had more death scenes than anyone else on that show. Davis doubled Dick Van Dyke on *The Comic* (1969) and worked on *Light in the Forest* (1958), *South Pacific* (1958), *Li'l Abner* (1959), *Nevada Smith* (1966), *The President's Analyst* (1967), *Project X* (1968), *Paint Your Wagon* (1969), *The Cheyenne Social Club* (1970), and *F.I.S.T.* (1978). TV credits include *Batman, Star Trek, Mission: Impossible, Mannix, Alias Smith and Jones, Emergency, The Bionic Woman, Wonder Woman,* and *Hawaii Five-O.*

See: Davidsmeyer, Jo. Combat! *A Viewer's Companion to the WWII Series.* Strange New Worlds, 2008.

DEAN DAWSON (1948–)

Leather maker Dean Dawson from Fort Worth, Texas, learned the stunt trade from his stuntman uncle Rudy Robbins. He was the regular double for Dennis Weaver on the TV series *McCloud* (1970–77) and worked on *The Undefeated* (1969), *Pat Garrett and Billy the Kid* (1973), *The Longest Yard* (1974), and *Superman* (1978). After touring with Buffalo Bill's Wild West Show in the late 1970s, Dawson settled in Texas. He founded the Texas Stuntmen's Association and opened a stunt school in Bandera, Texas.

See: Alle, Sheila. "Learning to Take the Fall." *Dallas Morning News.* June 25, 1984; Clark, Barbara. "They Fall for Stunts." *Dallas Morning News.* October 29, 1978; Estelle, Mary, & Gott Salterelli. *Historic Hood County: An Illustrated History.* HPN, 2009.

VINCE DEADRICK (1932–)

Vincent Paul Deadrick was born in St. Louis, Missouri. He entered the U.S. Marine Corps and was stationed in Oahu, Hawaii. Upon his discharge he applied as a carpenter's apprentice at MGM Studios but became intrigued by the stuntmen when he watched a fight scene being put together. He trained on the side and landed a stand-in job for Steve McQueen on the TV series *Wanted—Dead or Alive* (1958–61). He befriended McQueen and asked for a shot at being his stunt double, which McQueen granted. Deadrick was with McQueen a total of seven years including *Hell Is for Heroes* (1962) and the famous fight on *Soldier in the Rain* (1963).

The 5'10", 185-pound Deadrick physically outgrew McQueen and moved on to double Lee Majors on the series *The Big Valley* (1965–69) and *The Six Million Dollar Man* (1974–78). Deadrick developed many innovative stunts and intricate jumps for the bionic man but suffered numerous injuries because he was doing backward falls that were shown in reverse to give the appearance of fantastic leaps. On one fall he landed in the bottom of a swimming pool and nearly killed himself. Deadrick doubled Conlan Carter on TV's *Combat* (1962–67), Roger Smith on *Mister Roberts* (1965–66), William Shatner and DeForest Kelley on *Star Trek* (1966–69), and Dennis Cole on *Bearcats* (1971). On *Used Cars* (1980) he doubled Jack Warden for a wild comic fight. Deadrick later doubled Lloyd Bridges on *Blown Away* (1994), a film coordinated by his son Vince, Jr.

He also worked on *The Enemy Below* (1957), *Tora! Tora! Tora!* (1970), *Soldier Blue* (1970), *Skin*

Game (1971), *Dirty Harry* (1971), *Diamonds Are Forever* (1971), *Hit!* (1973), *The Norseman* (1978), *Lady in Red* (1979), *The Glove* (1979), *Beyond the Poseidon Adventure* (1979), and *Any Which Way You Can* (1980). TV credits include *Batman, The Man from U.N.C.L.E., Mission: Impossible, Mannix, Gunsmoke,* and *The Fall Guy.* Deadrick is a member of the Stuntmen's Association.

See: Coccagnia, Ann. "Vince Deadrick, Sr.: Pull No Punches." *Inside Stunts.* Spring, 2008; Hendrickson, Paula. "Family Business." *Emmy.* December 2003.

LENNY DEE (1940–)

The son of a Canadian rancher, Lenny Dee was raised in Wyoming. He served with the U.S. Marine Corps in Korea, rode with the Hells Angels, and was an over-the-road truck driver. He was trained by Jock Mahoney and worked on *Rio Bravo* (1959), *The Comancheros* (1961), *Cat Ballou* (1965), *Firecreek* (1968), *Rio Lobo* (1970), *Chisum* (1970), and the TV series *Gunsmoke.* Dee doubled Jack Elam and was recognized by the Stuntmen's Hall of Fame. He worked three years doing a character called Grampa Grubb for Disney. In the 1970s he fronted Lenny Dee's Wild West Show and ran the Lazy D Riding Stables in Casa Grande, Arizona.

See: Dungan, Ron. "Stuntman Reflects on Wild Career." *Casa Grande Dispatch.* February 10, 1985; "Stuntman Falls for High School Ballet." *Prescott Courier.* November 4, 1991.

BABE DeFREEST (1907–1986)

Babe DeFreest was born in California as Thelma Elder. She was excellent on a horse, having been a presence on the rodeo circuit and a winner of the Powderpuff Classic. At Republic she doubled Linda Stirling on the action packed serials *Zorro's Black Whip* (1944) and *The Tiger Woman* (1944). She did stunts for Frances Gifford on *Tarzan Triumphs* (1943), as well as Mae West, Marlene Dietrich, Jean Carmen, Kay Aldridge, and Maria Montez. She also worked on *The Painted Stallion* (1937), *Gunsmoke Ranch* (1937), *Perils of Nyoka* (1942), *Daredevils of the West* (1943), *In Old Oklahoma* (1943), and *Frontier Gal* (1945). She was an honorary member of the Stuntwomen's Association and an inductee of the Stuntmen's Hall of Fame.

See: Lowry, Paul. "Babe DeFreest Feels Right at Home Riding Horses." *Los Angeles Times.* March 26, 1940.

PAULA DELL (1925–)

Five-foot-two Paula Dell was born Paula Unger in Denver, Colorado. She moved to California and attended Santa Monica High, spending time at Muscle Beach as an acrobat under the name Paula Boelsems. It was there that she taught an elephant how to water ski. She appeared in her first film while still a teen. Paula attended USC studying Physical Education and taught in the Los Angeles school system. On the side she became a professional circus performer with the De Wayne Brothers and toured in an act with stuntman Russ Saunders. Dell doubled Carol Channing on *Thoroughly Modern Millie* (1967), Julie Andrews on *Star!* (1968), and Jaclyn Smith on TV's *Charlie's Angels* (1976–81). She also doubled Lucille Ball and Eva Gabor.

She worked on *Billy Rose's Jumbo* (1962), *Son of Flubber* (1963), *In Harm's Way* (1965), *Camelot* (1967), *The Poseidon Adventure* (1972), *Blazing Saddles* (1974), *Earthquake* (1974), *The Towering Inferno* (1974), *Death Race 2000* (1975), *Silent Movie* (1976), *Logan's Run* (1976), *Swashbuckler* (1976), and *Freaky Friday* (1977). TV credits include *Gilligan's Island* and *I Spy.* A charter member of the Stuntwomen's Association and founder of the World Acrobatic Society, Dell is an inductee of the U.S. Sports Acrobatic Hall of Fame, the Stuntmen's Hall of Fame, and the Muscle Beach Hall of Fame.

See: Gabriel, Louis. *Santa Monica, 1940–2010.* Santa Monica Historical Society, 2011; www.beachstories.smgov.

ANGELO DeMEO (1930–1997)

Angelo DeMeo is primarily known for two long-running television shows. He doubled Rick Jason for the duration of the series *Combat* (1962–67) and Randolph Mantooth on *Emergency* (1972–78). The Brooklyn-born DeMeo was stunt coordinator for both shows. His career dates back to *Around the World in Eighty Days* (1956) and includes *Che!* (1969) and *Logan's Run* (1976) and the TV shows *Batman, The Six Million Dollar Man,* and *CHiPs.* DeMeo died of lung cancer at the age of 67.

See: Davidsmeyer, Jo. *Combat! A Viewer's Companion to the WWII Series.* Strange New Worlds, 2008.

VON DEMING (1931–)

Automotive expert Von Deming captured the West Coast Go-Kart championship and was billed as such for *Bikini Beach* (1964). He was in charge of the Jeeps with mounted guns on the TV series *The Rat Patrol* (1966–68). One of his most interesting assignments was customizing the motorcycles used for *The Losers* (1970), an action-packed Vietnam War film that had outlaw motorcyclists behind enemy lines. The 5'8" Deming doubled Nick Adams, Barbara Stanwyck, and Phyllis Diller, the latter leaping through traffic on *Eight on the Lam* (1967). He worked on *What Did You Do in the War, Daddy?* (1966), *Beau Geste* (1966), *Dark of the Sun* (1968), *Finian's Rainbow* (1968), *Macon County Line* (1974), *Eat My Dust* (1976), *Texas Detour* (1978), and *Smokey and the Bandit 2* (1980). On TV he doubled Julie Adams for a memorable fight with Barbara Stanwyck on *The Big Valley.*

See: Lumm, Sharon. "Film Anti-Stupidity, Not Anti-War." *San Antonio Light.* May 28, 1970; Pashkoff, Anne. "Trio Promote Offbeat *Losers.*" *San Antonio Express.* May 28, 1970.

GEORGE DeNORMAND (1903–1976)

George W. DeNormand was born in New York City. Some sources say that his birthplace was Pueblo, Colorado, where he was likely raised. He embarked on a life of adventure when he served in the U.S. Cavalry under Blackjack Pershing during Pershing's quest to find Pancho Villa in Mexico. As a soldier of fortune DeNormand flew biplanes for a Chinese warlord in aerial dogfights. He spent time as a middleweight prizefighter in the late 1920s. Though he was undistinguished professionally, he scored a victory over the man who beat heavyweight champion Jack Dempsey as an amateur.

DeNormand, 5'10" and 185 pounds, was the established stunt double for Spencer Tracy for many years, especially after his own hair went white. He doubled Buster Crabbe on *Tarzan the Fearless* (1933), Henry Hull on *WereWolf of London* (1935), Bela Lugosi on *The Raven* (1935), and Boris Karloff on *Bride of Frankenstein* (1935). On the serial *Daredevils of the Red Circle* (1939) he raced a motorcycle down a flooding tunnel for Charles Quigley. On TV he doubled Leo Carrillo on *The Cisco Kid* (1950–56). He also subbed for Tom Mix, Buck Jones, Ken Maynard, Clark Gable, Victor Jory, Pat O'Brien, Fredric March, Grant Withers, Lyle Talbot, Warren Hull, Ralph Byrd, Rod LaRocque, Tim McCoy, Charles Starrett, and Whip Wilson. DeNormand taught Tom Steele and Dave Sharpe the art of screen fighting and spent considerable time at Republic Studios. He was often seen as henchmen taking on the cowboy stars.

He worked on *Fighting Marines* (1935), *Professional Soldier* (1935), *Dick Tracy* (1937), *The Painted Stallion* (1937), *Dick Tracy Returns* (1938), *Flash Gordon's Trip to Mars* (1938), *The Lone Ranger Rides Again* (1939), *Dick Tracy's G-Men* (1939), *The Hunchback of Notre Dame* (1939), *Flowing Gold* (1940), *Commandos Strike at Dawn* (1942), *Fall In* (1942), *Lady Takes a Chance* (1943), *Batman* (1943), *Nevada* (1944), *Desert Hawk* (1944), *Superman* (1948), *Adventures of Sir Galahad* (1949), *The Doolins of Oklahoma* (1949), *The Man from Bitter Ridge* (1955), *A Lawless Street* (1955), *The Last Hurrah* (1958), *North to Alaska* (1960), *It's a Mad, Mad, Mad, Mad World* (1963), and *4 for Texas* (1963). He finished his career working as a TV extra. He was a member of the Stuntmen's Hall of Fame.

See: Harmon, Jim. "George DeNormand." *Filmfax.* July-September 2005; Harmon, Jim. "Last of the Frankensteins." *Monsters of the Movies.* #2, August 1974.

PATTY DeSAUTELS (1927–1992)

Five-foot-four Patty DeSautels was born Patricia Louise Puett. She ran track at Occidental College and found employment as a track timer at the Los Angeles Sports Arena. This led to work as a stuntwoman and movie dancer, despite the fact she had four children who often tagged along to the set. She doubled Debbie Reynolds on *Tammy and the Bachelor* (1957), *This Happy Feeling* (1958), and *The Perfect Furlough* (1958) and drove a car to the side of a cliff for Lana Turner on *Portrait in Black* (1960). Others doubled include Janet Leigh, June Allyson, and Mona Freeman. She worked on TV's *Peter Gunn.*

See: "A Nursery Goes Backstage." *Life Magazine.* August 16, 1954; Tinkham, Harley. "A Jill of All Trades Rivals the Men as an AAU Certified Timer." *Altoona Mirror.* February 7, 1961;

DICK DIAL (1931–1992)

Richard Emile Ashley Dial was born in Oklahoma City. He was an athlete at Classen High and the University of Oklahoma and was a champion Golden Gloves boxer, a ranked tennis pro, and a competitive sailor. He got his start on *The Ten Commandments* (1956) and *The Searchers* (1956), leading to a job doubling William Holden on *The Horse Soldiers* (1959). He is best known for his TV work, where he doubled Lloyd Bridges on *Sea Hunt* (1958–61), David Janssen on *The Fugitive* (1963–67), William Shatner on *Star Trek* (1967–68), and Peter Graves on *Mission: Impossible* (1967–70).

Six-foot-one and 185-ounds, Dial also worked on *Kid Galahad* (1962), *Von Ryan's Express* (1965), *The Great Race* (1965), *Murderers' Row* (1966), *In Like Flint* (1967), *They Call Me Mr. Tibbs* (1970), *The Towering Inferno* (1974), *Earthquake* (1974), *Airport '75* (1974), *The Hindenburg* (1975), *Breakout* (1975), *The Eiger Sanction* (1975), and the TV movie *Helter Skelter* (1976). TV credits include *Felony Squad, Voyage to the Bottom of the Sea, The Time Tunnel, Mannix, The Man from U.N.C.L.E., The Green Hornet,* and *Mod Squad.* He was a member of the Stuntmen's Association.

See: "Richard E.A. 'Dick' Dial, Jr." *Oklahoman.* January 30, 1992.

PETER DIAMOND (1929–2004)

Peter Alexander Diamond was born in Durham, England. He fenced in the British Army and studied for two years at the Royal Academy of Dramatic Art. He became the fight arranger on *Knights of the Round Table* (1953), where he met and trained with American stuntman Yakima Canutt. One of his first roles was fencing against Errol Flynn on *The Dark Avenger* (aka *The Warriors*) (1955). Five-foot-eleven and 175 pounds, Diamond was a stuntman for Hammer Films on the horror classics *Horror of Dracula* (1958) and *Dracula Has Risen from the Grave* (1968).

He was fight arranger for the light saber duels on the first three *Star Wars* films and played

the Tusken Raider in the 1977 original. In *Highlander* (1986), he portrayed the immortal Fasil. He arranged the clifftop duel on *The Princess Bride* (1987) and doubled Robert Duvall for a fight atop a train on *Seven Percent Solution* (1976). He worked on *From Russia with Love* (1963), *Brannigan* (1975), *The Spy Who Loved Me* (1977), *Superman II* (1980), and *Raiders of the Lost Ark* (1981). TV credits include *Danger Man, The Prisoner, The Avengers, The Saint,* and *Doctor Who.* Diamond died from a stroke at the age of 74.

See: www.peterdiamond.co.uk.

DICK DICKINSON (1896–1956)

Contortionist Milton Arthur Dickinson was born in Tipton, Iowa, and started as a $3-a-day stuntman for producer Mack Sennett. On *Molly O* (1922) he performed what Sennett called the greatest thrill ever put on camera: Doubling star Jack Mulhall, Dickinson transferred from an airplane to the top of a blimp, before making his way down the side to the fuselage underneath. This was done at 5,000 feet and without a parachute. Dickinson showed off the ability to twist his body into a pretzel on *You Can't Cheat an Honest Man* (1939). He spent the 1930s as a horse-riding stuntman on B-westerns before becoming a stand-in for Walter Brennan. He worked on *Lucky Devils* (1932), *The Hunchback of Notre Dame* (1939), and *Ali Baba and the Forty Thieves* (1944). Dickinson died at the age of 60.

See: "Brennan Works, Keeps Pals Busy." *Oregonian.* April 4, 1948; Coons, Robbin. "Dick Dickinson is Still an Expert Contortionist." *Big Spring Daily Herald.* August 4, 1943; Handsaker, Gene. "Mack Sennett's Alumni." *Greenville Record.* September 8, 1951.

MICK DILLON (1926–2006)

Michael Patrick Dillon was born in Epsom, Surrey, England. Growing up amidst a family of horsemen, he made his debut as a jockey at the age of 14. He went into National Hunt Racing and served with the Royal Air Force. His first film *Just My Luck* (1957) called upon his jockey skills. Dillon doubled Ringo Starr on *Help!* (1965), Buster Keaton running into a tree on *A Funny Thing Happened on the Way to the Forum* (1966), and David Hemmings falling from a horse on

Charge of the Light Brigade (1968). He was one of the stuntmen inside the costume portraying the title creature on *Gorgo* (1961). He also worked on *The Day of the Triffids* (1962), *Dr. Who and the Daleks* (1965), *How I Won the War* (1967), *You Only Live Twice* (1967), *Chitty Chitty Bang Bang* (1968), and *Dead Cert* (1974).

See: "Mick Dillon." *Daily Telegraph.* August 19, 2006.

JAMES DIME (1897–1981)

Yugoslavian-born James Dime was a professional boxer nicknamed "Sheik of Spring Street." He worked mostly in anonymity, though he made news reports when he was injured falling from a tower on *The Lives of a Bengal Lancer* (1935). He doubled Monte Blue on *Hawk of the Wilderness* (1938) and worked on *King of Kings* (1927), *King Kong* (1933), *The Buccaneer* (1938), *Captain Caution* (1940), *Reap the Wild Wind* (1942), *Frenchman's Creek* (1944), *The Spanish Main* (1945),

Sudan (1945), *Wake of the Red Witch* (1948), *Fortunes of Captain Blood* (1950), *Julius Caesar* (1953), *Prince Valiant* (1954), and *Around the World in Eighty Days* (1956).

See: "Sheik of Spring Street." *Los Angeles Times.* February 27, 1923.

NICK DIMITRI (1932–)

Nick Dimitri was born Nicholas Dimitri Siggelakis and was raised in Rockaway Beach, New York. He joined the U.S. Navy and served on the U.S.S. *Kula Gulf,* supplementing his military income with work as a bar bouncer. He became an award-winning physical instructor for American Health Studios and a title-holding bodybuilder as Mr. New York State. He joined a touring muscleman chorus that led to California's Muscle Beach and casting on the movie version of *Li'l Abner* (1959). Known for his strength and toughness, the 6′2″, 205-pound Dimitri wisely pared down his muscles for film and TV work.

Nick Dimitri (left) battles actor Charles Bronson with bare knuckles on *Hard Times* (1975).

He worked with William Smith on TV's *Laredo* (1965–67) and earned his reputation doubling Gary Raymond on the action-heavy World War II series *The Rat Patrol* (1966–68). He doubled Dean Martin on *The Ambushers* (1967), Sean Connery on *The Molly Maguires* (1970) and *The Next Man* (1976), Joe Namath on *C.C. & Company* (1970), and Mike Connors on TV's *Mannix*. He became known for his screen deaths and ability to emerge from exploding pyrotechnics on *Tora! Tora! Tora!* (1970) and *Sorcerer* (1977). In one year alone he was killed eighty-six times.

Dimitri was one of the best fight men in the business with work on *Darker Than Amber* (1970), *Grave of the Vampire* (1972), and *Any Which Way You Can* (1980). On these fights William Smith did everything that made it to the screen, save for a fire burn and stair fall on *Vampire*. As an actor, Dimitri was highly capable of handling tough guy dialogue. He received special billing portraying Angie Dickinson's undead husband on the cult TV-movie *The Norliss Tapes* (1973), but is best known for playing the veteran street fighter who takes on Charles Bronson in the outstanding climax of *Hard Times* (1975). This is one of the best fight scenes ever.

He worked on *Palm Springs Weekend* (1963), *Harlow* (1965), *What Did You Do in the War, Daddy?* (1966), *Murderers' Row* (1966), *Planet of the Apes* (1968), *Support Your Local Gunfighter* (1971), *Diamonds Are Forever* (1971), *Conquest of the Planet of the Apes* (1972), *Black Caesar* (1972), *Cleopatra Jones* (1973), *That Man Bolt* (1973), *The Don Is Dead* (1973), *Black Samson* (1974), *Black Eye* (1974), *Dirty Mary, Crazy Larry* (1974), *99 and 44/100 percent Dead* (1974), *The Towering Inferno* (1974), *Earthquake* (1974), *Adios Amigo* (1975), *The Master Gunfighter* (1975), *Lepke* (1975), *The Four Deuces* (1975), *Death Journey* (1976), *Futureworld* (1976), *Scorchy* (1976), *Silver Streak* (1976), *F.I.S.T.* (1978), *The Driver* (1978), *Stunt Seven* (1979), and *The Nude Bomb* (1980). On TV Dimitri was the go-to man on *The Rockford Files* when it came time to beat up James Garner. On *The Fall Guy* he could be seen in the opening credits taking a punch from Lee Majors. TV credits include *Sea Hunt, Maverick, 77 Sunset Strip, Rawhide, Route 66, Branded, Voyage to the Bottom of the Sea, Mission: Impossible, Search, Emergency, Kolchak: The Night Stalker, The Streets of San Francisco, Planet of the Apes, The Six Million Dollar Man, Matt Helm, City of Angels,* *Kojak,* and *Dukes of Hazzard.* A member of the Stuntmen's Association, Dimitri posed in the buff for the woman's magazine *Viva.*

See: Adams, Eddie. "Stunt Man." *Viva.* January 1974; Cox, Billy. "Sarasota Stuntman Says His Profession Overdue for Recognition." *Herald Tribune.* June 12, 2011; www.theodoresworld.net.

IVAN DIXON (1931–2008)

Ivan Nathaniel Dixon III is best known for playing Sgt. Kinchloe on the sitcom *Hogan's Heroes* (1965–70), although he had serious aspirations as a respected dramatic actor and director on the stage and screen. Born in New York City, the six-foot Dixon got his start as a stand-in for his friend Sidney Poitier on *Something of Value* (1957) and *Edge of the City* (1957). Given the lack of black stuntmen, Dixon filled in for Poitier on action scenes where he could, most famously braving the rapids with stuntman Bob Hoy on *The Defiant Ones* (1958). Dixon died from renal failure at the age of 76.

See: Page, Don. "Ivan Dixon's Curious Career." *Los Angeles Times.* June 22, 1967.

BENNIE DOBBINS (1932–1988)

Bennie R. Dobbins was born in Los Angeles, the son of horse wrangler Earl Dobbins. Bennie's grandfather Ben Dobbins had been a stuntman dating back to the first cowboy films. As a football end the 5'11", 180-pound Bennie made All-Valley Second Team for North Hollywood. In baseball he was an infielder for the North Hollywood Junior American Legion team. After a stint with the U.S. Marine Corps during the Korean War, he played professional baseball in the Boston Red Sox minor league organization. An injury ended his professional baseball hopes and he returned to Hollywood as a horse wrangler.

Dobbins began stunting at Warner Brothers, doubling contracted TV actors James Garner, Peter Brown, Van Williams, and Anthony Eisley on *Maverick, Lawman, Surfside Six, Bourbon Street Beat,* and *Hawaiian Eye.* He doubled Robert Loggia on *Elfego Baca* (1958–60) and remained with Van Williams for *The Green Hornet* (1966–67). As stunt coordinator of the fight scenes, Dobbins realized he was going to have to slow co-star Bruce Lee down for the camera to catch his martial art moves. The show lasted one season, but set into motion the rabid cult interest in Lee. In the 1970s and early 1980s Dobbins worked on several top action films as stunt coordinator for Charles Bronson and Arnold Schwarzenegger. He worked less as a stuntman after suffering a broken back jumping a car on *First Blood* (1982).

He worked on *Ride Lonesome* (1959), *Stagecoach* (1966), *Not With My Wife, You Don't* (1966), *Bonnie and Clyde* (1967), *Camelot* (1967), *A Covenant with Death* (1967), *Planet of the Apes* (1968), *Barquero* (1970), *Soldier Blue* (1970), *Sometimes a Great Notion* (1970), *Wild Rovers* (1971), *Dirty Harry* (1971), *The Poseidon Adventure* (1972), *The Seven-Ups* (1973), *Magnum Force* (1973), *Blazing Saddles* (1974), *99 and 44/100 percent Dead* (1974), *The Towering Inferno* (1974), *Earthquake* (1974), *The Sugarland Express* (1974), *The Master Gunfighter* (1975), *The Outlaw Josey Wales* (1976), *Family Plot* (1976), *The White Buffalo* (1977), *Rollercoaster* (1977), *F.I.S.T.* (1978), *Love and Bullets* (1979), and *Mountain Men* (1980). TV credits include *The Six Million Dollar Man*. A member of the Stuntmen's Association and an inductee of the Stuntmen's Hall of Fame, Dobbins died from a heart attack at the age of 55 while choreographing an Arnold Schwarzenegger fight scene on *Red Heat* (1988).

See: Gast, Peter. "*48 Hours:* High Tension Stunts in Nick Nolte's Crime Thriller." *Action Films.* February 1983.

GEORGE DOCKSTADER
(1914–1987)

George Dockstader provided a fleet of motorcycles and stunt work on those bikes for several decades on everything from *The Wild One* (1953) to *Electra Glide in Blue* (1973). Dockstader was born in Lindina, Wisconsin, and was barnstorming stunts in the 1930s where he would drive a car through a solid brick wall. He occasionally did stunts outside of auto and motorcycle work and doubled actor James Brown. He worked on *China* (1943), *Frenchman's Creek* (1944), *The Devil Thumbs a Ride* (1947), *Kansas City Confidential* (1952), *The Egyptian* (1954), *Hell's Outpost* (1954), *The Court Jester* (1956), *Dragstrip Girl* (1957), *Motorcycle Gang* (1957), *Psycho* (1960), *Beach Blanket Bingo* (1965), *Dr. Goldfoot and the Bikini Machine* (1965), *Wild Angels* (1966), *Blazing Saddles* (1974), *Every Which Way But Loose*

(1978), and *Any Which Way You Can* (1980). An inductee of the Stuntmen's Hall of Fame, Dockstader died at the age of 73. His son Scott did stunts.

See: "Riding Actors Give Points on Safety." *Harrisonburg Daily.* January 25, 1939.

ROSS DOLLARHIDE
(1921–1977)

Oregon-born Ross Dollarhide, Jr., was raised on a ranch and began competing in his teens as a bronc rider and calf roper. He won the 1953 World Steer Wrestling Championship and a World Championship in calf roping. He was forced to end his rodeo career due to injury but found a home in Hollywood. He was a background drover on the long-running western series *Rawhide* (1959–66) and worked on *Will Penny* (1968), *Paint Your Wagon* (1969), *Blazing Saddles* (1974), and the TV series *Cimarron Strip* and *Gunsmoke*. At the age of 55 Dollarhide was hired to double Rod Taylor on the TV series *Oregon Trail* (1977). He died on location from internal injuries he sustained in a horse fall. Dollarhide was inducted posthumously into the Professional Rodeo Hall of Fame.

See: www.dollarhide.org.

FRANK DONAHUE
(1918–2007)

Santa Monica–born Frank Donahue was a lifeguard, swimmer, and diver hired to double Jon Hall on *The Hurricane* (1937). He spent two years surfing in Hawaii before World War II, during which time he joined the U.S. Navy as a frogman. He dabbled in many professions, all centered on the ocean. He was a boatman, fisherman, dock worker, shark wrangler, and marine salvage expert. He returned to motion pictures as a Hollywood stuntman, working as a technical advisor on *The Frogmen* (1951), doubling Jeffrey Hunter on *Lure of the Wilderness* (1952), and diving on *20,000 Leagues Under the Sea* (1954).

Donahue made the news when he was bit by a shark in 1954, one of more than sixty he reined in that day. He'd take camera equipment and film these excursions to sell as action filler to the film studios. Donahue was one of the first to film surfers on the waves to see how the sport looked on film. He fashioned his water experiences into a treatment for Ziv Studios called *Underwater Legion*. Although his proposed pilot was turned down, parts of it became the TV series *Sea Hunt*. Donahue and his partners won a $250,000 lawsuit against Ziv for taking his idea. On screen he fought Hugh O'Brian on *The Fiend Who Walked the West* (1958) and also worked on *They Were Expendable* (1945), *Prince Valiant* (1954), and *Spartacus* (1960). He was the stepfather of stuntman Mike Donahue (aka Mike Donovan).

See: Paskowitz, Dorian. "Rolling with Frank." *Surfer's Journal.* Winter, 2006; "Stuntman Runs Into Wrong Shark, Goes to Hospital." *Portsmouth Times.* June 30, 1954; Rivenbark, Bob. "Bob Rivenbark Tags Stand-In Experience as Unforgettable." *Waycross Journal-Herald.* July 16, 1952.

EDDIE DONNO (1935–)

Born in Philadelphia, Edward Donno was a singer in the late 1950s and attained regional success with the song "Philadelphia, USA." Donno visited his friend Frankie Avalon in Texas during the making of *The Alamo* (1960) and was recruited to be a horse extra. John Wayne took a liking to him, and 5'8", 200-pound Donno was hired as a stuntman on *The Comancheros* (1961), *Donovan's Reef* (1963), *McLintock!* (1963), *The War Wagon* (1967), *The Green Berets* (1968), *Chisum* (1970), *Big Jake* (1971), and *The Train Robbers* (1973). Agile despite his bulky frame, Donno became a horse fall specialist who could land on a run. Donno doubled John Belushi for the driving scenes and stair fall on *The Blues Brothers* (1980). On *Welcome Home, Soldier Boys* (1972) he was thrown from a car going forty miles per hour.

He also worked on *Hells Angels on Wheels* (1967), *Savage Seven* (1968), *The Last Movie* (1971), *Cleopatra Jones* (1973), *Big Bad Mama* (1974), *Freebie and the Bean* (1974), *Race with the Devil* (1975), *The Killer Elite* (1975), and *The Gumball Rally* (1976). TV credits include *The Wild Wild West, The Big Valley, Batman, Daniel Boone,* and *Vega$*. Donno is a member of Stunts Unlimited and an inductee into the Stuntmen's Hall of Fame. His son Tony does stunts.

See: Lilley, Tim. *Campfire Conversations.* Akron, OH: Big Trail, 2007; Welkos, Robert. "It's a Life of Hard Knocks." *Los Angeles Times.* June 26, 2005.

MICKEY "MIKI" DORA (1934–2002)

Born Miklos Sandor Dora in Budapest, Hungary, Mickey Dora grew up on the beaches of Southern California. He was an innovative artist on a surfboard, with everyone on the beach mesmerized by his rides. Dora was also a character who fed into his own legend at every opportunity. He was into the waves themselves, competing in surf contests only enough to bring in money to fuel his Zen-like passion for the ocean. Stunt work in the movies provided him an income, although the popularity of the beach party films ultimately overcrowded his beloved waves.

Dora was the surfing double for James Darren on *Gidget* (1959), *Gidget Goes Hawaiian* (1961), and *Gidget Goes to Rome* (1963) and for Elvis Presley on *Blue Hawaii* (1961). He was set to star in *Ride the Wild Surf* (1964) and filmed surfing footage in Hawaii before being replaced in the lead part by Fabian. Dora surfed on *Beach Party* (1963), *Surf Party* (1964), *Muscle Beach Party* (1964), *Bikini Beach* (1964), *For Those Who Think Young* (1964), *Beach Blanket Bingo* (1965), *Ski Party* (1965), and *How to Stuff a Wild Bikini* (1965). He doubled Marlon Brando on *Bedtime Story* (1964) and Anthony Franciosa on *The Sweet Ride* (1968) before leaving Hollywood to live abroad. An inductee of the International Surfer Hall of Fame, Dora died from pancreatic cancer at the age of 67.

See: Rensin, David. *All for a Few Perfect Waves. The Audacious Life and Legend of Rebel Surfer Miki Dora.* New York: Harper Entertainment, 2008; *Surfer.* "Mickey Dora: Surf Stuntman." July 1965.

BOBBIE DORREE (1905–1974)

Austrian ice skater Bobbie Dorree worked at Republic Studios in the 1940s as a double for Dale Evans and the leading ladies of *Dakota* (1945) and *Wyoming* (1947). She was a noted figure skater in Europe and entertained at the Queen's Club in London prior to coming to the States to skate professionally with Ice-Capades and the Ice Frolics. In 1939 she appeared at the World's Fair in New York. Her first film *Lake Placid Serenade* (1945) showcased her skating talent. Credits include *Utah* (1945), *Bells of Rosarita* (1945), *Bells of San Angelo* (1947), *The Red Pony* (1949), *Jubilee Trail*

(1954), and *Timberjack* (1955). Dorree died from cancer at the age of 69.

See: "Geitner Will Screen *Lake Placid Serenade*." *Dunkirk Evening Observer*. May 12, 1945.

KIRK DOUGLAS (1916–)

Athletic leading man Kirk Douglas worked closely with stunt crews preparing bits of action in order to present himself most effectively on screen. In the course of a long career he mastered many skills of the stunt trade. He played a boxer on *Champion* (1949) and learned trapeze work on *Story of Three Loves* (1953), juggled for *The Juggler* (1953), did gun tricks on *Man Without a Star* (1955), and did trampoline vaults for fancy horse mounts on *The War Wagon* (1967). He did many of his own stunts on screen, except for the most dangerous or specialized. On *The Vikings* (1958) Douglas memorably ran the outstretched oars of a ship.

The 5'9" Douglas was born Issur Danielovitch Demsky in Amsterdam, New York. He was a champion 145-pound wrestler at St. Lawrence University and spent time with the U.S. Navy during World War II. Douglas did his own standout fights on *Spartacus* (1960) and *Lonely Are the Brave* (1962), although he garnered a reputation for being unable to hold back during scenes of roughhousing. Douglas is one of the few actors inducted into the Stuntmen's Hall of Fame.

See: Douglas, Kirk. *The Ragman's Son*. New York: Simon & Schuster, 1988; "Kirk Douglas Plays a Klutz." *Kingston Gleaner*. December 23, 1978; "Kirk Still Does His Own Stunts." *Pittsburgh Post Gazette*. October 25, 1986.

ANN DUNCAN (1924–1990)

Ann Duncan is best-known for a thirty-foot high fall she took for Patricia Medina on *Phantom of the Rue Morgue* (1954). She doubled Lynne Roberts on *Sons of Adventure* (1948), Susan Cabot on *Gunsmoke* (1953), Audrey Dalton on *Drum Beat* (1954), and Lars Henderson, Jr., on *Last Train from Gun Hill* (1959), as well as Barbara Stanwyck, Helen Hayes, Kathryn Grayson, Julie London, Merle Oberon, and Wanda Hendrix. TV credits include *The Cisco Kid, Alfred Hitchcock, 77 Sunset Strip,* and *Mr. Lucky*. She doubled Cara Williams on *Pete and Gladys* (1960–62).

See: Petersen, Clarence. "Indestructible Fall Girl of TV." *Milwaukee Sentinel*. September 3, 1961; Thrasher, Al. "Stuntwoman Works at Falling Down on Job." *Los Angeles Times*. November 16, 1959.

LEE DUNCAN (1939–)

Lee Duncan attended Jorden High in Long Beach, California. He was a fine athlete skilled in swimming, cycling, tennis, and a variety of dance. He landed one of the first doubling assignments for a leading black actor when he was hired to handle action for Greg Morris on TV's *Mission: Impossible* in the late 1960s. The six-foot, 200-pound Duncan shared this job with rising stuntmen Calvin Brown and Tony Brubaker in the days before the Black Stuntmen's Association became established. Duncan worked on *Che!* (1969), *Hit* (1972), *The Mack* (1973) and the TV series *Star Trek, The Wild Wild West,* and *Mod Squad*.

TED DUNCAN (1934–1991)

Ted Duncan's stunt specialty was cars, although his career dates back to doing underwater work on *Up Periscope* (1959). He had an acting part on the low-budget *Pit Stop* (1969) and worked on *The Love Bug* (1968), *Winning* (1969), *What's Up, Doc?* (1972), *The Last American Hero* (1973), *Magnum Force* (1973), *Freebie and the Bean* (1974), *The Sugarland Express* (1974), *Thunderbolt and Lightfoot* (1974), *Greased Lightning* (1977), *Stunts* (1977), *The Deer Hunter* (1978), *Meteor* (1979), and *The Stunt Man* (1980). A member of the Stuntmen's Hall of Fame, Duncan died from cancer at the age of 57.

JIMMIE DUNDEE (1900–1953)

Burly, dark-haired James Reed Dundee was born in Missouri. A professional boxer and race car driver, he came to Hollywood in 1921 and became known as "Mr. Lucky." He specialized in auto crack-ups and high falls and often worked for director Preston Sturges. For years Dundee headed up a Paramount stunt crew known as the Suicide Squad. It consisted of Chick Collins, Johnny Sinclair, and Billy Jones. He doubled George Brent on *Racket Busters* (1938), Cary Grant on *Bringing Up Baby* (1939), and William

Ted Duncan rolls a car on *Stunts* (1977).

Bendix on *China* (1943), and had screen fights with Alan Ladd on *Chicago Deadline* (1949) and Kirk Douglas on *Champion* (1949).

Dundee is best known for choreographing a standout fall through a skylight on *The Glass Key* (1942). *Galloping Ghost* (1931) saw him board a taxiing airplane while doubling Red Grange. For *Sons of the Legion* (1938) he rolled a car 450 feet. On *$1,000 a Touchdown* (1939) he rode a motorcycle off a pier. *Wake Island* (1942) had him blown up in a six-ton truck. On *Star Spangled Rhythm* (1943) he drove an Army Jeep across the piping of the Los Angeles aqueduct. For *The Story of Dr. Wassell* (1944) he drove an Army truck off a 100-foot embankment. On *My Son John* (1952) he overturned a taxi cab on the steps of the Lincoln Memorial.

He worked on *Wild Party* (1929), *The Glass Key* (1935), *High Tension* (1936), *The Buccaneer* (1938), *Union Pacific* (1939), *North West Mounted Police* (1940), *Sullivan's Travels* (1941), *Hold Back the Dawn* (1941), *Reap the Wild Wind* (1942), *The Blue Dahlia* (1946), *O.S.S.* (1946), *Perils of Pauline* (1947), *Wild Harvest* (1947), *Whispering Smith* (1948), *Branded* (1950), *Soldiers Three* (1951), *The Greatest Show on Earth* (1952), *Denver and Rio Grande* (1952), and *The War of the Worlds* (1953). A member of the Stuntmen's Hall of Fame, Dundee died at the age of 52 from leukemia.

See: "Danger Is a Stuntman's Business." *Lewiston Evening Journal.* July 8, 1944; "Jimmie Dundee." *Variety.* December 2, 1953; Johnson, Erskine. "Greatest of Movie Stuntmen Never Suffered a Scratch." *Trenton Evening Times.* December 9, 1953; Todd, John. "Stunt Man Jimmie Dundee Lists Most Daring Feats." *St. Petersburg Times.* August 20, 1943.

PETE DUNN (1922–1990)

Donald Larry Dunn was born in Metuchen, New Jersey, and raised in Arizona. The rodeo cowboy and military veteran attained minor cult status within sci-fi–horror genre fans by playing a mutant on *Invaders from Mars* (1953) and the title character on *The Monster of Piedras Blancas* (1958). He also worked on *Soldiers Three* (1951), *Kismet* (1955), *Giant* (1956), *The Land Unknown* (1957), *Mackenna's Gold* (1969), *Chisum* (1970), *The Poseidon Adventure* (1972), *Blazing Saddles* (1974), and *The Shootist* (1976). TV credits include *Cimarron City, Rawhide, Wagon Train, The Virginian,* and *Gunsmoke.* Dunn died from a heart attack at the age of 68.

See: Parla, Paul. "Greetings from Piedras Blancas." *Scary Monsters.* June 1996.

JOE DUNNE

British stuntman Joe Dunne, a former professional soccer player, doubled Peter Sellers on all the Pink Panther films of the 1970s. As stunt coordinator for Sellers, the 5'9", 180-pound Dunne devised some of the best comic gags, in particular Sellers' hop off the parallel bars and down an open stairwell on *The Pink Panther Strikes Again* (1976) and the golf cart being dumped off a dock on *Revenge of the Pink Panther* (1978). Dunne worked closely with Blake Edwards during the latter half of the director's career. He doubled Ringo Starr on *Help!* (1965), Rod Steiger on *Hennessy* (1975), and James Mason on *Ffolkes* (1979).

He worked on *The Guns of Navarone* (1961), *From Russia with Love* (1963), *Heroes of Telemark* (1965), *Thunderball* (1965), *The Dirty Dozen* (1967), *You Only Live Twice* (1967), *Kelly's Heroes* (1970), *Straw Dogs* (1971), *A Bridge Too Far* (1977), *Superman* (1978), *Prisoner of Zenda* (1979), and *Superman II* (1980). TV credits include *The Avengers* and *The Professionals.*

See: Salome, Lou. "Sellers' Stunt Double Speaks: I Took Falls for Inspector Clouseau." *Action Films.* February 1983.

LARRY DURAN (1925–2002)

Larry Duran was a U.S. Navy veteran and former professional boxer. Often sporting a shaved head, he played many Indians and ethnic villains. He is best known as a friend of Marlon Brando, the two having met on *Viva Zapata!* (1952). Duran found employment as Brando's stand-in, handler, and occasional double many times thereafter. Legend has it that Brando himself was the one who taught Duran to ride a motorcycle and fall from a horse. Brando rewarded

his pal with a supporting role on *One-Eyed Jacks* (1961). Duran's specialty was fight scenes. The 5'10", 160-pound Duran had memorable battles with Clint Eastwood in a pool room on *Coogan's Bluff* (1968), Robert Hooks in an elevator on *Trouble Man* (1972), and John Saxon in a meat locker on *The Glove* (1979). His son Richard followed him into stunt work, as did grandson Lawrence.

He worked on *The Wild One* (1953), *Guys and Dolls* (1955), *Around the World in Eighty Days* (1956), *The Young Lions* (1958), *The Magnificent Seven* (1960), *Mutiny on the Bounty* (1962), *4 for Texas* (1963), *The Ugly American* (1963), *The Hallelujah Trail* (1965), *The Sand Pebbles* (1966), *Project X* (1968), *Che!* (1969), *The Great Bank Robbery* (1969), *The Omega Man* (1971), *Dirty Harry* (1971), *Conquest of the Planet of the Apes* (1972), *Soylent Green* (1973), *Battle for the Planet of the Apes* (1973), *99 and 44/100 percent Dead* (1974), *The Towering Inferno* (1974), *Earthquake* (1974), *Every Which Way But Loose* (1978), and *Meteor* (1979). TV credits include *I Spy, The Man from U.N.C.L.E., Batman, Get Smart, Mission: Impossible, Kung Fu,* and *The Six Million Dollar Man.* He was a member of the Stuntmen's Association and the Stuntmen's Hall of Fame.

See: Johnson, Erskine. "Brando Is His Own Fall Guy on Set of *One-Eyed Jacks.*" *Corpus Christi Times.* January 20, 1959.

DICK DUROCK (1937–2009)

Six-foot-five, 215-pound Dick Durock was costumed in heavy green latex for his most famous role as the comic book hero in *Swamp Thing* (1982). He repeated the assignment on *Return of Swamp Thing* (1989) and a syndicated 1990s TV show that made Durock a cult hero among the sci-fi crowd. Durock was born in South Bend, Indiana, and raised in New Jersey, where he played football. He entered the U.S. Marines out of high school and gave acting a shot despite an unconventional appearance. In addition to his height and long limbs, Durock had a distinctively flat-nosed appearance that suggested he would never be a leading man. He trained at Paul Stader's Gym and displayed keen athletic skills for a big man. He could take a punch and do a back flip.

His first stunt jobs were doubling Guy Williams on TV's *Lost in Space,* and Max Baer, Jr., and Buddy Ebsen on *The Beverly Hillbillies,* and fighting William Shatner on *Star Trek*. He doubled Chuck Connors on *99 and 44/100 percent Dead* (1974) and Jack Palance on *One Man Jury* (1978). TV work involved doubling Bo Svenson on *Snoop Sisters*, Ken Howard on *Manhunter,* and Richard Kiel on *Switch*. On *The Six Million Dollar Man* he donned the costume of Bigfoot for Ted Cassidy and Andre the Giant. On *Battlestar Galactica* (1978–79) he played Cylon soldiers until being tapped to don the makeup for the Imperious Leader. Durock's willingness to be made up landed him the job of playing Frye's creature on a memorable episode of *The Incredible Hulk*.

He worked on *The Grissom Gang* (1971), *Conquest of the Planet of the Apes* (1972), *The Poseidon Adventure* (1972), *Battle for the Planet of the Apes* (1973), *Mr. Majestyk* (1974), *Doc Savage* (1975), *The Master Gunfighter* (1975), *The Enforcer* (1976), *F.I.S.T.* (1978), *1941* (1979), *Stunt Seven* (1979), *Bronco Billy* (1980), *The Nude Bomb* (1980), and *Any Which Way You Can* (1980). TV credits include *The Rockford Files, The Streets of San Francisco, Joe Forrester, Kojak, Little House on the Prairie, Quincy, Buck Rogers, BJ and the Bear,* and *The Fall Guy*. A member of the Stuntmen's Association, Durock died from pancreatic cancer at the age of 72.

See: Blasko, Erin. "South Bend Native, *Swamp Thing* Actor Fondly Recalled." *South Bend Tribune*. September 25, 2009; Murray, Will. "Full Vegetable Jacket." *Starlog*. May, 1989.

BREEZY EASON (1886–1956)

Barnes Reeves Eason was born and raised in Friars Point, Mississippi. An expert horseman, he became one of the finest purveyors of action the cinema has ever known. He started his film career as an actor and stuntman, then assistant director, stunt coordinator, and second unit director. He made his reputation inserting close-up detail shots into large-scale action. Eason filmed the chariot race on the original *Ben-Hur* (1925), the land rush on *Cimarron* (1930), the tank-cavalry chase on *Army Girl* (1938), the swashbuckling on *The Adventures of Robin Hood* (1938), the explosive battles on *Man of Conquest* (1939), the burning of Atlanta on *Gone with the Wind* (1939), and the epic fisticuffs between John Wayne and Randolph Scott on *The Spoilers* (1942). He earned accolades for the spectacular action on *The Charge of the Light Brigade* (1936), although there was a disregard for the health and safety of his crew and the horses they were using. Because of this film, the American Humane Association became an omnipotent presence on film productions.

Eason's own six-year-old son was killed on the set of *The Fox* (1921) when he was accidentally run over by a truck. There were other confirmed deaths of horses and men on Eason sets, and at least once Eason himself had to dive out of the way of a stunt gone wrong. This was reaffirmed with his handling of the action on *They Died with Their Boots On* (1941), where Jack Budlong was killed during a mass charge when he fell on his saber. At that point the increasingly safety-conscious studios had seen enough. Eason was eventually passed over by the studios in favor of an emerging Yakima Canutt for many bigger second unit jobs, although Eason did handle the sweeping action on *The Spanish Main* (1945) and *Duel in the Sun* (1946). Eason was known to perform stunt work himself for the cameras when he became exasperated with the inability or unwillingness of others to do so. Eason died from a heart attack at the age of 69.

See: Brownlow, Kevin. *The Parades Gone By*. Berkeley, Ca: Univ. of California, 1968; Goodman, Ezra. "Step Right Up and Call Him Breezy." *New York Times*. June 19, 1942; Nevins, Francis M. "Men Who Call the Shots." *Western Clippings*. #80, March-April 2007.

JOCK EASTON (1922–1990)

Scots-born World War II Special Air Service Captain Jock Easton was the leading figure in English stunts. He grew up working fairgrounds on the Wall of Death prior to joining the British Army. During World War II Easton was a parachutist in North Africa, where he earned the Military Cross. Captured in Italy, he was sent to a POW camp but escaped to Switzerland. Once again interred, he managed to escape into France and join up with the Resistance. After the war, Easton saw the opportunity to recruit former commandos for a stunt troupe. Consisting of approximately thirty war vets, Jock Easton's Stunt Team made a name for themselves on *Captain Horatio Hornblower* (1951) and *The Crimson Pirate* (1952). Easton doubled star Gregory Peck on the former. He found it tough to get his casting agency started due to the politics of the business and briefly left partner Joe Powell in charge while he volunteered for SAS missions in Malaya to hunt down jungle bandits.

Easton doubled Errol Flynn on *Master of Ballantrae* (1953), *Crossed Swords* (1954), and the unfinished *Story of William Tell* (1952). The two made all the media outlets in 1954 when they exchanged real punches with one another after a heated row. Easton doubled Christopher Lee for a fiery acid bath plunge on *The Curse of Frankenstein* (1957) and performed a cliff dive for David Niven on *The Guns of Navarone* (1961). Other credits include *Broken Journey* (1948), *Helen of Troy* (1955), *Alexander the Great* (1956), *The Abominable Snowman* (1957), *Steel Bayonet* (1957), and *Where Eagles Dare* (1968). Easton died from cancer at the age of 68.

See: Beckett, Belinda. "Daredevil Jock Loses Last Battle." *Evening Arga.* 1990; "Ex Parachutists Get Movie Stunting Jobs." *Lima News.* October 17, 1946.

CLINT EASTWOOD (1930–)

Film icon Clint Eastwood was never a stuntman, but he became popular with audiences for his ability to do many of his own stunts. These include a jump from a trestle bridge onto a moving bus on *Dirty Harry* (1971), riding the hood of a careening car on *Magnum Force* (1973), mountain climbing on *The Eiger Sanction* (1975), and handling a motorcycle during a helicopter chase sequence on *The Gauntlet* (1977). Eastwood worked closely with his stunt coordinator and double Buddy Van Horn to place himself on screen as often as possible in action scenes.

Eastwood threw a great screen punch and did his own fight scenes, registering one of his

Actor Clint Eastwood performs his own jump from a trestle onto a moving school bus on *Dirty Harry* (1971).

most notable battles against a small army of stunt-men on *Coogan's Bluff* (1968). On the popular comedy *Every Which Way But Loose* (1978) Eastwood played a champion bare-knuckle brawler and returned in the sequel *Any Which Way You Can* (1980), where he performed the screen's longest two-man fight without doubles with William Smith. It ranks with *The Quiet Man* (1952) as one of the cinema's greatest donnybrooks.

Born in San Francisco, Clinton Eastwood, Jr. played basketball at Oakland Tech and swam competitively, logging time as a lumberjack, steelworker, and lifeguard prior to service with the U.S. Army as a swim instructor. He dug swimming pools to supplement his early income as a Universal Studios contract player. He received movie fight tips from Jock Mahoney and became comfortable astride a horse after working with Guy Teague on TV's *Rawhide* (1959–66). The 6'4", 200-pound Eastwood attained international superstardom as the fast-drawing star of Sergio Leone's 1960s spaghetti westerns.

See: Bacon, James. "Eastwood Cited for Film Scene." *Waycross Journal Herald.* December 11, 1974; Munn, Michael. *Clint Eastwood: Hollywood Loner.* London: Robson, 1992; Schickel, Richard. *Clint Eastwood: A Biography.* Knopf, 1996.

GARY EDWARDS

Collegiate gymnast and diver Gary Edwards got into a fender bender with a stuntman and launched a new career as a result. He worked live stunt shows at Corriganville showcasing his skills with whips, guns, and high falls. Edwards worked with Nick Adams, Peter Brown, Dale Robertson, and James Garner on the TV shows *The Rebel, Lawman, Tales of Wells Fargo,* and *Maverick.* Films include *How the West Was Won* (1962), *It's a Mad, Mad, Mad, Mad World* (1963), and *The Greatest Story Ever Told* (1965). Edwards joined the U.S. Army in 1965 and became one half of the Richards Brothers Whip Act.

See: Crawford, Bill. "Cream of Fourth Army Talent to Go on Stage on Thursday." *Lawton Constitution.* May 26, 1965; "Accidents Thrill Hollywood Stuntman at Sill." *Lawton Constitution.* August 29, 1965.

BUD EKINS (1930–2007)

Motorcycle specialist Bud Ekins performed one of the most famous stunts in the history of film, the iconic jump over the barbed wire fence for Steve McQueen on *The Great Escape* (1963). It was the first film stunt Ekins ever performed. He was a pal of the star, who brought him to Germany for the filming. When the filmmakers wouldn't allow McQueen to attempt the jump, Ekins took over. He dug out a ramp to help him achieve the twelve feet of elevation he needed. Ekins made the sixty-five-foot jump at sixty miles per hour on a 400-pound Triumph. He also did the bike slide into the barbed wire fence for McQueen. A few years later he did some of McQueen's driving on *Bullitt* (1968) in addition to laying down a Triumph during the chase.

Born in Hollywood, James Sherwin Ekins was a legendary desert and off-road racer, winner of the Catalina Grand Prix, the Big Bear Hare and Hound, and the Big Bear Endurance Run. Colleagues referred to him as "King of the Desert." He represented the United States in the International Six-Day Trials and took home four gold medals. The 6'3", 190-pound Ekins founded the Baja 1000 and was well-known in Hollywood circles for running a motorcycle shop and teaching celebrities how to handle a motorcycle. Bud and his brother Dave doubled Clint Eastwood and Don Stroud for the motorcycle chase on *Coogan's Bluff* (1968) and Bud did the truck stunts on *Sorcerer* (1977).

He also worked on *Camelot* (1967), *Speedway* (1968), *The Love Bug* (1968), *Diamonds Are Forever* (1971), *Electra Glide in Blue* (1973), *Hex* (1973), *The Front Page* (1974), *Earthquake* (1974), *Race with the Devil* (1975), *Scorchy* (1976), *Animal House* (1978), *Zero to Sixty* (1978), and *1941* (1979). On TV he was stunt coordinator for *Then Came Bronson* (1969–70) and did bike stunts on *CHiPs* (1977–83). He was a member of the Stuntmen's Association and an inductee of the Stuntmen's Hall of Fame, the Off-Road Motorsports Hall of Fame, and the Motorcycle Hall of Fame. Ekins died in his sleep at the age of 77.

See; Havesi, Dennis. "Bud Ekins, Stunt Cyclist, Dies at 77." *New York Times.* October 12, 2007; McLellan, Dennis. "Bud Ekins, 77, Stuntman Did Famous Motorcycle Jump on *The Great Escape.*" *Los Angeles Times.* October 10, 2007; www.budanddaveekins.com.

PATTY ELDER (1936–1984)

Los Angeles–born Patricia Ruth Elder grew up on the beaches of Santa Monica and was one

Bud Ekins jumps a Triumph motorcycle over a barbed wire fence for Steve McQueen on *The Great Escape* (1963).

of the top all-around stuntwomen of her era. She doubled Barbra Streisand and Madeline Kahn on *What's Up, Doc?* (1972), Goldie Hawn on *The Sugarland Express* (1974), and Barbara Harris on *Freaky Friday* (1977). On TV she doubled Mary Ann Mobley on *Mission: Impossible*. She also worked on *Quick Before It Melts* (1964), *Hot Rods to Hell* (1967), *Chubasco* (1968), *Paint Your Wagon* (1969), *Ulzana's Raid* (1972), *99 and 44/100 percent Dead* (1974), *Earthquake* (1974), *The Outlaw Josey Wales* (1976), *Two-Minute Warning* (1976), and *Highpoint* (1979).

The five-foot-tall stunter was involved in a wagon mishap on *The Rare Breed* (1965) that she was lucky to walk away from. She and Stephanie Epper were supposed to be thrown clear but instead were slammed under an overturned wagon. By chance they landed in a dug-out camera pit which saved their lives. The stunt remains in the film as it happened. At one time she was married to stuntman Eddie Hice and she is the mother of stuntman Freddie Hice. A charter member of the Stuntwomen's Association and an inductee of the Stuntmen's Hall of Fame, Elder died age 48 after a lengthy illness.

See: "Three Escape with Lives as Stunt Goes Awry." *Evening Independent*. March 15, 1965; Thomas, Bob. *Free Lance Star*. "Stunt Women Want More Work." June 7, 1976.

ALICE ELDRIDGE (1916–2011)

Alice Eldridge was born in St. Louis, Missouri, and raised in Colorado as Alice B. Broderick. In Hollywood she was a stand-in and double for Lucille Ball on approximately forty films, among them *That Girl from Paris* (1937) and *Room Service* (1938). She worked on nearly thirty Hopalong Cassidy B-westerns where she was tutored in horse stunts by Yakima Canutt and

Cliff Lyons. She left the industry in the early 1940s.

See: Carter, Katie. "St. Louisian Alice Broderick, Actress in Hollywood's Golden Age." *St. Louis Examiner.* January 20, 2011.

LOUIE ELIAS (1933–)

Five-foot-nine, 170-pound Louie Nicholas Elias was born in Los Angeles. Rough'n'tumble Louie participated in track and field and was quarterback of the football squad for the John Burroughs Indians. He made the football team at UCLA in an open tryout and played sparingly in 1955 as a defensive back and running back on offense. He did get a chance to play in the 1956 Rose Bowl. The following season he received the Most Improved Player Award. He was captain of the UCLA rugby squad during the football off-season and began getting film jobs. His first picture was *The Enemy Below* (1957). Elias turned professional and played two seasons with the Toronto Argonauts and one season with the Ottawa Rough Riders in the Canadian Football League.

His movie career was set in motion with a high-profile assignment doubling Charles Mc-Graw being thrust into a giant vat on *Spartacus* (1960). Elias was a regular stuntman on the TV series *Combat* (1962–67) and doubled Robert Conrad on *The Wild Wild West* (1965–69), his real-life brother James Stacy on *Lancer* (1968–70), and Michael Douglas on *The Streets of San Francisco* (1971–74). He doubled Rod Taylor throughout his career, most notably the toughest action on *Dark of the Sun* (1968) and the TV series *Bearcats* (1971). Elias was adept at throwing his body around in fights, including being flipped onto bar tables. For *The Trial of Billy Jack* (1974) he did a two-story back fall onto the roof of a car. His best fight was against Alex Cord in a swimming pool on *Stiletto* (1969). Every week he could be seen falling from the guard tower during the opening credits of the TV series *F Troop* (1965–67). He was cast as one of Kirk Douglas' deputies on *Posse* (1975) and doubled David Canary getting blown through a window on that film.

He worked on *The Spiral Road* (1962), *Palm Springs Weekend* (1963), *John Goldfarb, Please Come Home* (1965), *Dr. Goldfoot and the Bikini Machine* (1965), *Tickle Me* (1965), *Batman* (1966), *Lord Love a Duck* (1966), *The Glass Bottom Boat* (1966), *Double Trouble* (1967), *Planet of the Apes* (1968), *Ice Station Zebra* (1968), *The Wild Bunch* (1969), *True Grit* (1969), *Darker Than Amber* (1970), *Vanishing Point* (1971), *Support Your Local Gunfighter* (1971), *Boxcar Bertha* (1972), *Sssssss* (1973), *The Train Robbers* (1973), *Westworld* (1973), *The Deadly Trackers* (1973), *The Front Page* (1974), *The Longest Yard* (1974), *Night Moves* (1975), *The Next Man* (1976), *Lord of the Rings* (1978), *The Norseman* (1978), and *The Apple Dumpling Gang Rides Again* (1979). TV credits include *The Untouchables, Gallant Men, Twilight Zone, The Outer Limits, Batman, T.H.E. Cat, I Spy, Mission: Impossible, Garrison's Gorillas, Star Trek, Cimarron Strip, Gunsmoke, The FBI, Emergency, Police Story, The Six Million Dollar Man, Police Woman, Kojak, Cannon, Starsky and Hutch, Baretta, Logan's Run, How the West Was Won, Charlie's Angels,* and *The Fall Guy.* Elias was a member of Stunts Unlimited.

See: McDaniel, Marlene. *Mr. Louie Elias: A Tribute.* Self, 2010; "Stuntman Indestructible." *Sumter Daily.* September 11, 1971.

JACK ELLENA (1931–2012)

Jack Duane Ellena was born in Susanville, California, and was a standout athlete at Lassen High. At UCLA he was an All-American in both football and wrestling. UPI named him lineman of the year, and he finished seventh in the Heisman Trophy voting during the Bruins' undefeated 1954 national championship season. He wrestled professionally and played tackle, linebacker, and fullback with the Los Angeles Rams until a knee injury ended his career in 1957. The 6'1", 225-pound Ellena worked on TV's *Adventures of Ozzie and Harriet* (1959–63), providing the requisite muscle for young Ricky and David Nelson to toss around. As Ricky's teenage idol singing career took off, Ellena became his bodyguard. Credits include *Ben-Hur* (1959), *The Chapman Report* (1962), *Cleopatra* (1963), *The Cincinnati Kid* (1965), and *Love and Kisses* (1965). TV credits include *Wagon Train* and *Combat.*

See: "All-America Football Star at UCLA." *Los Angeles Times.* April 7, 2012; "Jack Duane Ellena." *Desert Sun.* April 19, 2012.

Louie Elias (in midair) doubles Rod Taylor for a two-story jump on *Dark of the Sun* (1968). Taylor twisted his knee attempting the stunt.

RICHARD ELMORE
(1914–2010)

Richard Elmore was born in Staten Island, New York, and rode the rails to California to see the 1932 Olympics. A hockey background led to his casting as a skater on *Thin Ice* (1937). He served with the U.S. Army during World War II as a paratrooper. The 5'9" Elmore doubled Bob Newhart on *Hell Is for Heroes* (1962) and Eddie Albert on TV's *Green Acres*. He worked on *Gone with the Wind* (1939), *Unconquered* (1947), *The Desert Fox* (1951), *Fixed Bayonets* (1951), *The Court Jester* (1956), *Around the World in Eighty Days* (1956), *The Enemy Below* (1957), *In Love and War* (1958), *The Buccaneer* (1958), *Spartacus* (1960), *Captain Newman, M.D.* (1963), and *Concorde, Airport '79* (1979). TV credits include *Bonanza*, *Wagon Train*, and *Get Smart*. Elmore died in a car accident at the age of 95.

See: "Richard W. Elmore Obituary." *San Diego Union-Tribune*. February 14, 2010; Roberts, Ozzie. "Nothing Phony About the Life of This Ex-Stuntman." *San Diego Union-Tribune*. April 6, 2008.

RON ELY (1938–)

Ron Ely became famous playing Tarzan on TV, insisting at the time on doing all his own stunt work in the jungles of Brazil and Mexico. He swung from vines, wrestled lions and tigers, dove and swam in rivers, and did his own fights. The quest for realism resulted in great action, but at the expense of the show's leading man. Ely suffered a rash of injuries that significantly slowed production time. A publicity photo of Ely showed superimposed bandages covering the length of his body from the first season alone. Former Tarzan Jock Mahoney was brought in to guest on the show and help Ely master the stunts. The two subsequently put on great fight scenes. In the meantime, the producers took out a $3 million insurance policy on their star. The popular series ran from 1966 to 1968, ending in part due to the physical demands on cast and crew.

Ronald Pierce Ely was born in Hereford, Texas, and grew up playing football and working in the oilfields. In California the 6'4", 210-pound Ely landed a studio contract with 20th Century–Fox. During this time Ely served with the U.S. Air Force Reserve and was an amateur boxer. One of his earliest roles cast him as a deep sea diver on the TV series *Malibu Run* (1961), for which he learned to scuba dive. Ely did many of his own stunts for the action film *Doc Savage—The Man of Bronze* (1975).

See: Ely, Ron. "Tarzan Star Performs Own Stunts; His Scars Prove It." *Ogden Standard Examiner*. July 16, 1967; Essoe, Gabe. *Tarzan of the Movies*. New York: Cadillac, 1968; Irvin, Bill. "TV Tarzan Has Fans Convinced He's a Swinger." *Salt Lake Tribune*. February 1, 1967.

KENNY ENDOSO (1940–2010)

Five-foot-nine, 200-pound Kenneth Gordon Endoso was born in Hilo, Hawaii. A former baseball player and military veteran, he worked on *The President's Analyst* (1967), *Project X* (1968), *The Great Bank Robbery* (1969), *Diamonds Are Forever* (1971), *Freebie and the Bean* (1974), *Blazing Saddles* (1974), *Earthquake* (1974), *The Pack* (1977), *Go Tell the Spartans* (1978), *Buck Rogers in the 25th Century* (1979), *The Electric Horseman* (1979), *Meteor* (1979), and *The Stunt Man* (1980). TV credits include *Daniel Boone*, *Hawaii Five-O*, *Kung Fu*, and *The Six Million Dollar Man*. A member of Stunts Unlimited, Endoso died from cancer at the age of 70.

See: "Having a Ball." *Daily News*. July 27, 1988; "Kenny Endoso." *Los Angeles Times*. August 21, 2010.

ANDY EPPER (1943–2010)

The middle son of stuntman John Epper, 6'4", 230-pound Andrew William Epper didn't enjoy quite the luster in the industry that his brothers Tony and Gary held. He took part in the pool hall fight scene with Clint Eastwood on *Coogan's Bluff* (1968) and doubled William Finley for a high fall on *Phantom of the Paradise* (1974). He also worked on *Blazing Saddles* (1974), *Earthquake* (1974), *The Killer Elite* (1975), *Bound for Glory* (1976), *Every Which Way But Loose* (1978), *Smokey and the Bandit 2* (1980), and *The Long Riders* (1980). Epper died at the age of 66.

GARY EPPER (1944–2007)

Six-foot-one, 170-pound Gary Epper was born in Los Angeles and started at age seven as a horseback double on TV shows such as *My Friend*

Flicka and *Fury*. As an adult he doubled David Soul on the TV series *Here Come the Brides* (1968–70) and *Starsky and Hutch* (1976–79). Epper doubled Don Stroud on *Death Trap* (1976), made a tricky fifty-foot fall from a factory catwalk on *Soylent Green* (1973), and took part in the famous bar brawl on *The Ninth Configuration* (1980).

He worked on *It's a Mad, Mad, Mad, Mad World* (1963), *Shenandoah* (1965), *A Man Called Gannon* (1968), *Beneath the Planet of the Apes* (1970), *The Omega Man* (1971), *Conquest of the Planet of the Apes* (1972), *The Cowboys* (1972), *Magnum Force* (1973), *Battle for the Planet of the Apes* (1973), *99 and 44/100 percent Dead* (1974), *The Towering Inferno* (1974), *Blazing Saddles* (1974), *Earthquake* (1974), *Doc Savage* (1975), *The Hindenburg* (1975), *Rollerball* (1975), *Futureworld* (1976), *Bound for Glory* (1976), *Hooper* (1978), *Delta Fox* (1978), and *1941* (1979). TV credits include *Gallant Men*, *Combat*, *Gunsmoke*, *Bonanza*, *Voyage to the Bottom of the Sea*, *The Wild Wild West*, *The Rat Patrol*, *Hawaii Five-O*, *Mod Squad*, *Kung Fu*, *The Rockford Files*, *Wonder Woman*, *Charlie's Angels*, and *Vega$*. He was a member of the Stuntmen's Association and an inductee of the Stuntmen's Hall of Fame.

See: Wiener, David Jon. *Burns, Falls, and Crashes*. Jefferson, NC: McFarland, 1996.

JEANNIE EPPER (1941–)

California-born Jeannie Epper is arguably the most famous stuntwoman to ever put on pads. She is best known for doing all the running, jumping, falling, and fighting for Lynda Carter on TV's *Wonder Woman* (1975–79). Her career spans over seven decades and is the subject of a documentary entitled *Double Dare* (2004). She was the first of the Epper children to perform a stunt, riding a horse down a cliff at the age of nine. The 5'8" Epper began at Warner Brothers doubling Connie Stevens and Diane McBain on the TV shows *77 Sunset Strip* and *Hawaiian Eye*. Epper doubled Barbara Stanwyck and Linda Evans on *The Big Valley* (1965–69), Angie Dickinson on *Police Woman* (1974–78), Lindsay Wagner on *The Bionic Woman* (1976–78), and Kate Jackson and Tanya Roberts on *Charlie's Angels* (1976–81). Her best-known film stunts came doubling Kathleen Turner swinging across a gorge and going down a long mud slide on *Romancing the Stone* (1984).

A fight specialist, she knocked around Paul Newman on *Life and Times of Judge Roy Bean* (1972), punched it out with Pam Grier on *Coffy* (1973) and *Foxy Brown* (1974), and can be spotted in the biker brawl on *The Ninth Configuration* (1980). She stood in for Linda Evans for the famous TV fight with Joan Collins on *Dynasty*. Epper was a natural on a horse. On *Mackenna's Gold* (1969) she jumped horses off a raft into a raging river for Camilla Sparv to the tune of $2,000 a day. She doubled Jessica Walter on *Play Misty for Me* (1971), Jill Clayburgh on *Silver Streak* (1976), Melinda Dillon on *Close Encounters of the Third Kind* (1977), Lorraine Gray on *1941* (1979), Shirley MacLaine on *Terms of Endearment* (1983), as well as Diane Ladd, Sally Kellerman, and Louise Fletcher.

She worked on *Cheyenne Autumn* (1964), *The Hallelujah Trail* (1965), *Our Man Flint* (1966), *Hello, Dolly!* (1969), *Little Big Man* (1970), *The Poseidon Adventure* (1972), *Soylent Green* (1973), *The Don Is Dead* (1973), *Slither* (1973), *The Towering Inferno* (1974), *Blazing Saddles* (1974), *Day of the Locust* (1975), *Switchblade Sisters* (1975), *Drum* (1976), *Bound for Glory* (1976), *Logan's Run* (1976), *Black Sunday* (1977), *Avalanche Express* (1978), *The Jerk* (1979), and *Smokey and the Bandit 2* (1980). TV credits include *Maverick*, *Gunsmoke*, *Mannix*, *Emergency*, *The Rockford Files*, *Police Story*, *Barnaby Jones*, *Starsky and Hutch*, and *Vega$*. The mother of Eurlyne, Richard, and Kurtis Epper, she is a founder of Stuntwomen's Association, an inductee of the Stuntmen's Hall of Fame, and the recipient of a Lifetime Achievement from the Taurus World Stunt Awards.

See: Conley, Kevin. *The Full Burn*. Bloomsbury, 2008; Day, Carolyn. "Jeannie Epper: A Real-Life Wonder Woman." *Inside Stunts*. Winter, 2007.; Dela Cava, Marco R. "Epper Pulls Out All the Stunts." *USA Today*. October 19, 2007; Silden, Isobel. "Stunt Women." *Australian Women's Weekly*. February 17, 1982; Wiener, David Jon. *Burns, Falls, and Crashes*. Jefferson, NC: McFarland, 1996; Willson, Karen E. "Invisible Superheroes of Hollywood." *Starlog*. January 1980; www.wonderland.com.

JOHN EPPER (1906–1992)

Born Hans Emil Epper in Gossau, Switzerland, John Epper was the patriarch of the industry's most famous stunt family. An officer in the Swiss cavalry, he moved to the United States and found his way to the Main Street Gym in Los Angeles. The 6'2" Epper fought one professional boxing match and lost. He was working as an instructor at the Beverly Hills Riding Academy when he began wrangling horses for the movie studios. On location he was recruited to jump a horse over a car. He became one of the industry's top horsemen, specializing in Running Ws, pit falls, and cable jerk-offs. On *Prince Valiant* (1954) he performed seven bone-rattling jerk-offs in one day. On *How the West Was Won* (1962) he appeared as an Indian jumping a horse over a wagon. Epper doubled Errol Flynn on *The Charge of the Light Brigade* (1936), Robert Taylor on *Remember* (1939) and *King Richard and the Crusaders* (1954), Ronald Reagan on *Santa Fe Trail* (1940), Henry Fonda on *Fort Apache* (1948), Gary Cooper on *Springfield Rifle* (1952) and *Friendly Persuasion* (1956), Richard Egan on *Love Me Tender* (1956), and Randolph Scott on *Westbound* (1959).

He worked on *Cowboy and the Lady* (1938), *The Westerner* (1940), *Western Union* (1941), *Action in the North Atlantic* (1943), *Guadalcanal Diary* (1943), *Buffalo Bill* (1944), *They Were Expendable* (1945), *Frontier Gal* (1945), *The Foxes of Harrow* (1947), *Joan of Arc* (1948), *She Wore a Yellow Ribbon* (1949), *The Desert Fox* (1951), *At Sword's Point* (1952), *The Duel at Silver Creek* (1952), *Column South* (1953), *Broken Lance* (1954), *The Egyptian* (1954), *Westward Ho, the Wagons!* (1956), *These Thousand Hills* (1959), *Spartacus* (1960), *North to Alaska* (1960), *The Spiral Road* (1962), *The Man Who Shot Liberty Valance* (1962), *Cheyenne Autumn* (1964), *The Greatest Story Ever Told* (1965), *The War Lord* (1965), *The Professionals* (1966), *Camelot* (1967), and *The Scalphunters* (1968). TV credits include *Fury, My Friend Flicka, The Big Valley,* and *Daniel Boone.* An honorary member of the Stuntmen's Association and an inductee of the Stuntmen's Hall of Fame, Epper died from prostate cancer at the age of 86.

See: "John Epper, Stunt Double in Films." *Los Angeles Times.* December 5, 1992; Lilley, Tim. *Campfire Conversations.* Akron, OH: Big Trail, 2007; Wiener, David Jon. *Burns, Falls, and Crashes.* Jefferson, NC: McFarland, 1996.

MARGO EPPER (1936–)

Margo Marie Epper, the oldest of John Epper's daughters, doubled the Norma Bates mother character during the shower scene on Alfred Hitchcock's *Psycho* (1960). She was cast in the knife-carrying part because her broad shoulders and lean torso were similar to those of Anthony Perkins. A horseback specialist, the Los Angeles–born Epper doubled Lana Turner, Gloria Graham, Vanessa Redgrave, Karen Steele, Carol Channing, and Anne Francis.

She worked on *Auntie Mame* (1958), *The Hallelujah Trail* (1965), *Our Man Flint* (1966), *Camelot* (1967), *Hello, Dolly!* (1969), *Paint Your Wagon* (1969), *Life and Times of Judge Roy Bean* (1972), and *Soylent Green* (1973). TV credits include *My Friend Flicka, The Beverly Hillbillies,* and *The Big Valley.* A member of the stuntmen's Hall of Fame, she married stuntman Richard Hock. They are the parents of stuntman Johnny Hock.

See: Rebello, Stephen. *Alfred Hitchcock and the Making of* Psycho. Open Road, 2010.

STEPHANIE EPPER

The youngest daughter of stuntman John Epper was the busiest of the lot in the 1950s when she doubled child actors for horseback riding on the TV series *Fury* and *My Friend Flicka.* "Steffi" Epper grew into a fight scene specialist who worked regularly on TV's *Bonanza* and *Gunsmoke.* On the latter she doubled Amanda Blake as Miss Kitty. Epper doubled Barbara Bain throughout her run on *Mission: Impossible* and was Linda Evans' stunt woman for the epic three-minute hair-pulling, vase-smashing battle against Joan Collins on TV's *Dynasty* in 1982. Stephanie and fellow stuntwoman Patty Elder barely survived an incredible wagon stunt gone wrong on *The Rare Breed* (1965). She doubled Susan Clark on *Valdez Is Coming* (1971), making a noteworthy horse fall.

Other credits include *It's a Mad, Mad, Mad, Mad World* (1963), *Cheyenne Autumn* (1964), *Quick Before It Melts* (1964), *The War Lord* (1965), *The Great Race* (1965), *Hello, Dolly!* (1969), *There Was a Crooked Man...* (1970), *Little Big Man* (1970), *Life and Times of Judge Roy Bean* (1972), *The Great Northfield Minnesota Raid* (1972), *Soylent Green* (1973), *The Towering Inferno* (1974), *Earthquake* (1974), *Mame* (1974), *Blazing Saddles* (1974), *Foxy Brown* (1974), *Bound for Glory* (1976), *Texas Detour* (1978), and *Smokey and the Bandit 2* (1980). She is a charter member

Stephanie Epper, Patty Elder, and Hal Needham a moment before a stunt went wrong on *The Rare Breed* (1966).

of the Stuntwomen's Association and an inductee in the Stuntmen's Hall of Fame. Her daughter Kim Epper became a stunt performer.

TONY EPPER (1938–2012)

Six-foot-four, 220-pound John Anthony Epper was born in Los Angeles. He was the oldest son of noted horseman and stunt patriarch John Epper. Tony was a strapping, wavy-haired young buck who began riding a horse at age four and grew up learning the tools of the stunt trade. Around the area of his dad's ranch, Tony and his brothers Gary and Andy were known as "the terrors of Lone Ridge Avenue," galloping horses along the road and fighting anyone in their path. They'd ride their horses up to trains and practice transfers, as well as rent cars from Hertz to test all kinds of vehicular maneuvers. Hertz eventually

caught on and refused to rent any more cars to the Eppers.

An early break came doubling Gary Cooper on *They Came to Cordura* (1959). Epper went on to double Chuck Connors on the TV series *The Rifleman* and *Branded* before hooking up with Burt Lancaster. He served as Lancaster's double on *The Professionals* (1966), *The Scalphunters* (1968), *Valdez Is Coming* (1971), and *Ulzana's Raid* (1972), among others over a twenty-year period. On *The Professionals* he doubled Jack Palance as well. Epper doubled Charlton Heston on *Beneath the Planet of the Apes* (1970), Slim Pickens on *Blazing Saddles* (1974) and *1941* (1979), Paul Wexler on *Doc Savage* (1975), and Denny Miller on *Caboblanco* (1980). He was Ken Howard's stuntman on the TV series *Manhunter* (1974–75).

Epper was a top fight man and carried a tough guy reputation in real life. While filming *Ulzana's*

Raid in Nogales, Arizona, he got into a bar fight with five men. One of his assailants died. Chuck Connors testified at his trial as a character witness, and it was determined that Epper was acting in self-defense. As an actor he made an effective heavy and was memorably thrashed by Tommy Lee Jones on the mini-series *Lonesome Dove* (1989). He fought Marc Singer on *Beastmaster* (1982) and was cast as Steve the Tramp on *Dick Tracy* (1990), but he remained best known for his fearless stunts.

He also worked on *Spartacus* (1960), *Two Rode Together* (1961), *Mail Order Bride* (1964), *The Hallelujah Trail* (1965), *The War Lord* (1965), *In Like Flint* (1967), *Camelot* (1967), *Planet of the Apes* (1968), *More Dead Than Alive* (1969), *Support Your Local Sheriff* (1969), *Paint Your Wagon* (1969), *The Wild Bunch* (1969), *The Good Guys and the Bad Guys* (1969), *The Cheyenne Social Club* (1970), *Lawman* (1970), *Rio Lobo* (1970), *The Omega Man* (1971), *The Cowboys* (1972), *The Great Northfield Minnesota Raid* (1972), *Jeremiah Johnson* (1972), *Conquest of the Planet of the Apes* (1972), *Soylent Green* (1973), *99 and 44/100 percent Dead* (1974), *The Towering Inferno* (1974), *The Master Gunfighter* (1975), *Bound for Glory* (1976), *The Island of Dr. Moreau* (1977), *Every Which Way But Loose* (1978), *Hooper* (1978), *FM* (1978), *Corvette Summer* (1978), and *Beyond the Poseidon Adventure* (1979). TV credits include *Gallant Men, Daniel Boone, I Spy, Batman, The Green Hornet, Hondo, Cimarron Strip, High Chaparral, Gunsmoke, Kung Fu, Search, The Streets of San Francisco, Kolchak: The Night Stalker, Police Story, The Six Million Dollar Man, Buck Rogers,* and *The Fall Guy.* Epper was a member of Stunts Unlimited and an inductee into the Stuntmen's Hall of Fame. His son Danny became a stuntman. Epper died from cancer at the age of 73.

See: "Actor-Stuntman Tony Epper Dies at 73." *Variety.* July 30, 2012; Nashawaty, Chris. "Danger Is Their Middle Name." *Entertainment Weekly.* October 12, 2007; "Movie Stuntman Charge in Death." *Yuma Daily Sun.* April 16, 1972; "Stuntman Acquitted in Death." *Arizona Daily Sun.* March 24, 1973.

HENRY "BLACKIE" ESCALANTE (1915–2002)

Los Angeles–born Henry Acevedo Escalante was the grandson of Mariano Escalante, originator of the famed Escalante Brothers Circus. He became a noted circus tumbler and trapeze artist in his own right. "Blackie" Escalante doubled Johnny Weissmuller on Tarzan films and performed stunt work on *At the Circus* (1939), *Frenchman's Creek* (1944), *Appointment with Danger* (1951), *The Conqueror* (1956), *The Ten Commandments* (1956), *Paint Your Wagon* (1969), and *Monte Walsh* (1970). A member of the Stuntmen's Association, Escalante died after a battle with Alzheimer's Disease at the age of 86.

See: Oliver, Myrna. "Henry Escalante, 86, Movie Stuntman." *Los Angeles Times.* January 29, 2002.

CHAD EVANS (1941–)

Chad Evans was born William Holden in Smyrna, Georgia. A U.S. Navy veteran, he was working as a police officer in his hometown when he decided to re-enlist. He was stationed as a recruiter in California, where he landed a role in a commercial that led to work as a stunt extra on the TV shows *Bonanza, Guns of Will Sonnett,* and *High Chaparral.* He formed his own stunt team with a group of Navy buddies for live shows at Calico Ghost Town. They toured throughout the western United States as the Ghost Town Raiders.

The live shows led to appearances in John Wayne movies using the stage name Chad Evans. He also worked on *The Wild Bunch* (1969), *They Shoot Horses, Don't They?* (1969), *Tora! Tora! Tora!* (1970), and *Blazing Saddles* (1974) before he was forced to retire from stunt work after suffering a heart attack. Using the name Cowboy Bill Holden, he moved back to Georgia and put together the western theatrical stunt team Los Pistoleros. He continued to work on local films and TV shows.

See: Smith, Dwight. "Stunt Man: Cobb Man Boasts About Loss to Wayne." *Marietta Journal.* March 8, 1981; www.lospistoleros.net.

DOUGLAS FAIRBANKS (1883–1939)

Five-foot-eight, 150-pound Douglas Fairbanks was born Douglas Elton Thomas Ullman in Denver, Colorado. As a youth he attended Jarvis Military Academy and took an interest in acrobatics at Denver's East High. Film allowed him to showcase his fantastic athleticism that added to his movie star popularity. The graceful Fairbanks starred in several swashbuckling roles, among them *The Mark of Zorro* (1920), *The Three Musketeers* (1921), *Robin Hood* (1922), *The Thief of Bagdad* (1923), *The Black Pirate* (1926), and *The Gaucho* (1927). On *Thief* he leapfrogged from a series of giant jars containing hidden trampolines. Perhaps Fairbanks' greatest stunt was a one-handed handspring balanced on a short dagger on *The Three Musketeers.*

Fairbanks worked closely with stuntman Richard Talmadge so that he could perform the bulk of his own stunt work for the cameras. Still, there were a few stunts deemed too dangerous for the star to attempt, such as a leap onto a sloping roof in *The Mark of Zorro,* a jump from a cliff to a tree on *The Mollycoddle* (1920), and the dagger-ride down a sail on *The Black Pirate.* On *Robin Hood* Fairbanks tricked the filmmakers by masquerading as a stuntman brought in to double him for a leap onto a drawbridge. They didn't find out until after Fairbanks had completed his dangerous stunt. That film saw him slide down a balustrade and charge a chain of rising drawbridges. For the most part, Fairbanks performed every bit of daring. He had the studio rigged like a gymnasium with trampolines and ropes. In some instances, furniture or props were shortened to make Fairbanks' leaps seem more spectacular for the camera.

See: Vance, Jeffrey, & Tony Maietta. *Douglas Fairbanks.* Berkeley, California: Univ. of California Press, 2008.

RICHARD FARNSWORTH (1920–2000)

Two-time Oscar nominee Richard Diamond Farnsworth spent nearly forty years as one of the stunt profession's top men before transitioning his venerable presence into mainstream character actor recognition. Los Angeles–born Farnsworth worked at the Green Acres Polo Barn in Van Nuys, cleaning stalls and exercising the horses of Will Rogers and "Big Boy" Williams. He was recruited as a horseback extra for *The Adventures of Marco Polo* (1938), earning $7 a day and a box lunch. He was taught the business by Yakima Canutt and went on to appear in over 300 films as a stuntman. He initially earned $35 for a saddle fall and $75 for a horse fall.

In the early 1940s Farnsworth was a horse-back guide at Glacier National Park and traveled the rodeo circuit. In addition to his skills as a horseman and stage driver, he was the top archer in the film business. He could hit running targets and earned up to $200 per arrow fired. His stunt comrades trusted him so much they took live arrow hits into balsa wood protectors under their clothes. He had several trophies from archery competitions and hunting expeditions.

The 170-pound six-footer's most notable assignment came doubling Montgomery Clift for the cowboy action on *Red River* (1948). He doubled Henry Fonda on *Fort Apache* (1948) and *The Tin Star* (1957), Ronald Reagan on *Stallion Road* (1947), Robert Walker on *Vengeance Valley* (1951), Kirk Douglas on *Man Without a Star* (1955), *The Indian Fighter* (1955), and *Spartacus* (1960), and Troy Donahue on *A Distant Trumpet* (1964). He also subbed for Gary Cooper, Roy Rogers, Jimmy Wakely, Spade Cooley, and Wild Bill Elliott. On TV he doubled Guy Madison on *Wild Bill Hickok* (1951–58), Dennis Weaver on *Gunsmoke* (1955–64), and Steve McQueen on the pilot to *Wanted—Dead or Alive.*

He worked on *A Day at the Races* (1937), *Wells Fargo* (1937), *Gunga Din* (1939), *Gone with the Wind* (1939), *The Outlaw* (1943), *Five Graves to Cairo* (1943), *Duel in the Sun* (1946), *Angel and the Badman* (1947), *The Man from Colorado* (1948), *Silver River* (1948), *Mighty Joe Young* (1949), *Texans Never Cry* (1951), *Whirlwind* (1951), *Horizons West* (1952), *The Lusty Men* (1952), *The Cimarron Kid* (1952), *The Lawless Breed* (1952), *Law and Order* (1953), *Arrowhead* (1953), *The Man from the Alamo* (1953), *Pony Express* (1953), *War Arrow* (1953), *The Wild One* (1953), *The Desert Song* (1953), *The Caine Mutiny* (1954), *The Violent Men* (1955), *Chief Crazy Horse* (1955), *A Lawless Street* (1955), *The Conqueror* (1956), *Pardners* (1956), *The Ten Commandments* (1956), *Raw Edge* (1956), *Red Sundown* (1956), *The Hard Man* (1957), *How the West Was Won* (1962), *Six Black Horses* (1962), *Kings of the Sun* (1963), *Major Dundee* (1965), *The War Lord* (1965), *The Great Race* (1965), *Cat Ballou* (1965), *Duel at Diablo* (1966), *The Professionals* (1966), *Texas Across the River* (1966), *Camelot* (1967), *The War Wagon* (1967), *The Stalking Moon* (1969), *Butch Cassidy and the Sundance Kid* (1969), *Paint Your Wagon* (1969), *The Good Guys and the Bad Guys* (1969), *Monte Walsh* (1970), *The Omega Man* (1971), *Shoot Out* (1971),

Jerry Summers and Richard Farnsworth double Tony Curtis and Kirk Douglas in a *Spartacus* (1960) sword battle.

Skin Game (1971), *Ulzana's Raid* (1972), *The Cowboys* (1972), *Life and Times of Judge Roy Bean* (1972), *Papillon* (1973), *High Plains Drifter* (1973), *Soul of Nigger Charley* (1973), *Blazing Saddles* (1974), *The Front Page* (1974), *The Master Gunfighter* (1975), *Duchess and the Dirtwater Fox* (1976), and *The Outlaw Josey Wales* (1976). Other TV credits include *Kit Carson, Texas John Slaughter, Laramie, The Big Valley, Cimarron Strip, High Chaparral,* and *Bonanza.*

Farnsworth was chosen for a character role on *Comes a Horseman* (1978) due to his weathered look, silver hair, piercing blue eyes, and folksy manner. He scored a surprising Oscar nomination for his first significant acting role and launched a new career. For *The Grey Fox* (1983) he won the Canadian Genie, that country's equivalent of the Oscar. He was nominated as Best Actor for *The Straight Story* (1999). Farnsworth's son Diamond Hill Farnsworth became a noted stuntman. A founding member of the Stuntmen's Association, an inductee of the Stuntmen's Hall of Fame, and a Golden Boot Award honoree, Farnsworth died in 2000 at the age of 79 from a self-inflicted gunshot wound following a terminal bone cancer diagnosis.

See: Miller, Ron. "Horseman Parlays Stunt Work into Successful Acting Career." September 15, 1989; *Ocala Star-Banner.* Thomas, Bob. "After 46 Years in the Movies, Richard Farnsworth Is a Star." *Spokesman Review.* August 9, 1983; Welkos, Robert. "Farewell to a True Good Guy." *Los Angeles Times.* October 13, 2000.

LEE FAULKNER (1943–)

Lee Elmer Faulkner graduated from Tuscaloosa High in Alabama. He entered the U.S. Army Special Forces and became a Green Beret during the early days of the Vietnam War. After his discharge, Faulkner took a ski vacation to Heavenly Valley and by chance stumbled onto the movie *Wild Wild Winter* (1966). He found work as a ski extra and attracted the attention of stunt gaffer Roy Sickner. Faulkner began performing stunt work while attending UCLA and studying karate with Joe Lewis. His highest profile assignments were doubling Robert Blake on *In Cold Blood* (1967) and Dustin Hoffman on *The Graduate* (1967). On *Paint Your Wagon* (1969) he was launched out a second story window in a bed and broke his collarbone.

The 5'7" Faulkner also worked on *Viva Las Vegas* (1964), *Tobruk* (1967), *Camelot* (1967), *Thoroughly Modern Millie* (1967), *Don't Make Waves* (1967), *Riot on Sunset Strip* (1967), *Counterpoint* (1968), and *Ice Station Zebra* (1968). On TV he made the rounds of the popular shows *Batman, The Man from U.N.C.L.E., Mission: Impossible, Mannix,* and *The FBI.* His stunt career was short-lived as he began promoting martial arts tournaments and producing television commercials. He worked extensively in Japan and is credited with introducing kickboxing to the United States.

See: "Faulkner Seen in Movie Stunts." *Tuscaloosa News.* August 24, 1969; MacLaughlin, Bob. "Americanization of Kickboxing." *Black Belt.* February 1972; Teague, Archie. "Fall Guy." *Los Angeles Times.* October 9, 1966.

RALPH FAULKNER (1891–1987)

Born in San Antonio, Texas, swordfight choreographer Ralph Faulkner was initially a stuntman in Hollywood but injured his knee when he slipped off a log in a river scene on *Man from Glengarry* (1922). Part of his rehabilitation involved the sport of fencing, and it became a passion. He won the World Amateur Sabre Championship in 1928 and competed in the Olympics in fencing in both 1928 and 1932. His expertise and growing reputation in Hollywood saw him cast as the villainous Jussac on *The Three Musketeers* (1935), a film on which he performed stunt work and served as the fencing choreographer.

Faulkner choreographed the swordfighting between Errol Flynn and Basil Rathbone on *Captain Blood* (1935) and *The Adventures of Robin Hood* (1938). He continued in that capacity on a number of swashbuckling adventures, including *Zorro's Fighting Legion* (1939), *The Thief of Bagdad* (1940), *The Corsican Brothers* (1941), *The Court Jester* (1956), and *Jason and the Argonauts* (1963). He served as a double as well, most notably for Ronald Colman on *The Prisoner of Zenda* (1937) and Henry Daniell on *The Sea Hawk* (1940). He worked on over 100 films and taught at his Hollywood fencing studio into his nineties. He was a member of the Stuntmen's Hall of Fame, Faulkner died at the age of 95.

See: Folkart, Burt A. "Actor, Fencing Teacher: Ralph B. Faulkner, 95, Film Swordsman Dies." *Los Angeles Times.* January 31, 1987; www.fencersquarterly.com.

JIMMY FAWCETT (1906–1942)

San Francisco–born James Fawcett was a former baseball player for the Ogden Gunners and boxer for Westminster before turning circus and vaudeville acrobat. He was married to stuntwoman Helen Thurston, his partner in a stage act with Ken Terrell. On film Fawcett became known for taking wild high falls into nets and onto tables, throwing his body around in fight scenes on Republic serials such as *Zorro's Fighting Legion* (1939), *King of the Royal Mounted* (1940), *Drums of Fu Manchu* (1940), *King of the Texas Rangers* (1941), *King of the Mounties* (1942), and *Spy Smasher* (1942). On *Daredevils of the Red Circle* (1939) Fawcett actually doubled lead actor Dave Sharpe, one of the greatest stuntmen ever. Fawcett doubled Bert Lahr on *The Wizard of Oz* (1939) and performed stunts on *The Hunchback of Notre Dame* (1939) and *Seven Sinners* (1940), where he went off a balcony with Sharpe. Fawcett died at the age of 35 in a motorcycle accident after shooting *King of the Mounties* (1942). He and his fellow stuntmen were leaving a restaurant and the driver of a car failed to see him on his bike.

JIM FEAZELL (1928–)

James Lloyd Feazell was born in West Monroe, Louisiana, and grew up working on a Texas ranch. He served with the Army Air Corps of Engineers, was a Merchant Marine and deep seadiver, and spent a season playing minor league baseball for the New York Yankees organization. Active on the rodeo circuit as a saddle bronc rider, he entered Hollywood in the early 1950s. His specialty became horse falls, specifically off the back of a horse in what he termed a rump roll. Feazell doubled Lee Marvin on *Paint Your Wagon* (1969) and *Monte Walsh* (1970) and Jeremy Slate being shot off a bike on *Born Losers* (1967). He was bothered by a back injury suffered making a fall at Corriganville and moved away from stunts in the early 1970s to begin his own production company.

He worked on *Man of the West* (1958), *Ride Lonesome* (1959), *The Horse Soldiers* (1959), *Rio Bravo* (1959), *The Magnificent Seven* (1960), *Cimarron* (1960), *The Comancheros* (1961), *Blood on the Arrow* (1964), *The Sons of Katie Elder* (1965), *El Dorado* (1967), *The War Wagon* (1967), *Hells Angels on Wheels* (1967), *The Undefeated* (1969), *The Wild Bunch* (1969), *Butch Cassidy and the Sundance Kid* (1969), and *Chisum* (1970). TV credits include *Gunsmoke, Bonanza, Maverick, The Virginian,* and *The Wild Wild West.*

See: Feazell, Jim. *Feathers.* Indianapolis, IN: Iuniverse, 2011; www.jimfeazell.com.

EVELYN FINLEY (1916–1989)

Five-foot-three horse riding specialist Evelyn Finley was born in Douglas, Arizona, and grew up on a ranch. She was a Physical Education major at the University of New Mexico when she was declared winner of the Miss Albuquerque contest. The title helped secure her first doubling assignment for Jean Parker on *Texas Rangers* (1936). More doubling followed, as did female leads opposite Tex Ritter on *Arizona Frontier* (1940) and the Range Busters on *Trail Riders* (1942). Finley doubled Loretta Young on *Along Came Jones* (1945), Julie Adams on *The Man from the Alamo* (1953), Donna Reed on *Gun Fury* (1953), and Jean Peters on *Apache* (1954) in addition to Olivia de Havilland, Judy Garland, Elizabeth Taylor, Kim Novak, Barbara Hale, and Gale Storm.

She worked on *Mule Train* (1950), *Across the Wide Missouri* (1951), *Scaramouche* (1952), *Stranger on Horseback* (1955), *The Guns of Fort Petticoat* (1957), *Swiss Family Robinson* (1960), and *Hush...Hush Sweet Charlotte* (1964). TV credits include *The Lone Ranger, Wagon Train,* and *The Virginian.* An inductee of the Stuntmen's Hall of Fame, Finley died from a heart attack at the age of 73.

See: "Evelyn Finley." *Variety.* May 12, 1989; "Filmed in These Here Hills." *Western Clippings.* #81, January-February 2008; Othman, Frederick.

"Due to War Makers of Western Movies Are Substituting Heroines for Heroes." *Telegraph-Herald.* September 18, 1942; Taylor, Barbara. "Taylor Talks." *Albuquerque Tribune.* February 2, 1967.

LILA FINN (1909–1996)

Lila Finn was born Lila Shanley in Los Angeles. Her first film was high-profile, handling the swimming and diving for Dorothy Lamour on *The Hurricane* (1937). She followed that up doubling Vivien Leigh on *Gone with the Wind* (1939), Paulette Goddard on *Reap the Wild Wind* (1942) and *Unconquered* (1947), Donna Reed on *It's a Wonderful Life* (1946), Betty Hutton on *The Perils of Pauline* (1947), and Sandra Dee on *A Summer Place* (1959). She also doubled Jane Powell, Olivia de Havilland, Ida Lupino, Veronica Lake, Joan Fontaine, Frances Dee, and Sonja Henie. Finn became a competitive volleyball player and played for the U.S. Women's team from 1955 to 1960. She won a silver medal in the 1959 Pan-American Games in Chicago at the age of fifty.

She worked on *Typhoon* (1940), *Frenchman's Creek* (1944), *Scarlet Angel* (1952), *To Catch a Thief* (1955), *Guys and Dolls* (1955), *The Ten Commandments* (1956), *The Court Jester* (1956), *Spartacus* (1960), The *Spiral Road* (1962), *The Poseidon Adventure* (1972), *Blazing Saddles* (1974), *The Towering Inferno* (1974), and *Earthquake* (1974). A charter member of the Stuntwomen's Association and an inductee into the Stuntmen's Hall of Fame, she received a Lifetime Achievement Award from Women in Film. Finn died from heart failure at the age of 86.

See: Hays, Richard E. "Suffers for Art Without Acclaim." *Seattle Daily Times.* March 17, 1946; "Lila Shanley, Veteran Stuntwoman." *Los Angeles Times.* November 20, 1996.

JOE FINNEGAN

Joe Finnegan was born Joe Yrigoyen, Jr., the son of the veteran stuntman. A product of the rodeo team at Pierce College, Finnegan was one of the best horse teamsters in the business. However, he was hurt (a compound fracture of his leg) in a wagon turnover doubling Donald Pleasence on *Soldier Blue* (1970). He eventually returned to stunt work, often working with his brother-in-law Mickey Gilbert. Finnegan was one of the stuntmen escaping the exploding helicopter on *Apocalypse Now* (1979).

The 5'7", 150-pound stunter also worked on *Young Fury* (1965), *Alvarez Kelly* (1966), *Duel at Diablo* (1966), *Camelot* (1967), *The Green Berets* (1968), *The Wild Bunch* (1969), *Che!* (1969), *The Good Guys and the Bad Guys* (1969), *The Great Bank Robbery* (1969), *Butch Cassidy and the Sundance Kid* (1969), *Little Big Man* (1970), *Dirty Harry* (1971), *The Don Is Dead* (1973), *Mame* (1974), *The Fury* (1978), *Mountain Men* (1980), *Heaven's Gate* (1980), and *Smokey and the Bandit 2* (1980). His TV credits include *The Girl from U.N.C.L.E.*. A member of the Stuntmen's Association, he developed an air ram for stunt work.

GEORGE FISHER (1937–)

Six-foot-two, 195-pound George Jury Fisher started his acting and stunt career on the East Coast before moving to Hollywood in the mid–1970s. He was a double for Gene Hackman on *The French Connection* (1971), *The Domino Principle* (1977), and *Superman* (1978). In 1979 Fisher donned actor George Reeves' original Superman outfit to recreate stunts for a TV special entitled *Superman—Superstar*. Over the years Fisher's name has become associated with the original series as a double for George Reeves. This is incorrect.

Fisher was a familiar stunt heavy who could handle dialogue and is the main antagonist in the bar fight with Clint Eastwood and William Smith on *Any Which Way You Can* (1980). He also worked on *The Boston Strangler* (1968), *Night of Dark Shadows* (1970), *Lady Liberty* (1971), *Blacula* (1972), *Melinda* (1972), *Unholy Rollers* (1972), *Girls Are for Loving* (1973), *Badlands* (1973), *The Don Is Dead* (1973), *Blazing Saddles* (1974), *The Master Gunfighter* (1975), *Mr. Ricco* (1975), *Hawmps!* (1976), *Movie, Movie* (1978), and *The Big Brawl* (1980). On TV he appeared on episodes of *Mannix, Mission: Impossible, The Rockford Files,* and *The Six Million Dollar Man*. Fisher is a member of the Stuntmen's Association.

HARPER FLAHERTY (1920–1993)

Ohio-born Harper Anthony Flaherty was raised in California and served with the U.S. Navy during World War II. As a professional ice skater he performed at Madison Square Garden with the Hollywood Ice Revue. Flaherty was the longtime stand-in and double for Doug McClure on the TV series *Overland Trail* (1960), *The Virginian* (1962–70), *Men from Shiloh* (1970–71), and *Search* (1972–73) as well as the films *The Lively Set* (1964), *Beau Geste* (1966), *The King's Pirate* (1967), and *Nobody's Perfect* (1968). Flaherty additionally had a running role as ranch hand Harper on the later seasons of *The Virginian*. He worked on *Psycho* (1960) and the TV westerns *Laredo, Lancer,* and *Alias Smith and Jones*.

ERROL FLYNN (1909–1959)

Popular myth would have audiences believe dashing rogue Errol Flynn performed all of his own swashbuckling stunts. In his autobiography Flynn himself alluded to the notion that it was he doing his "Fearless Flynn" screen action, at least in his earliest films. While Flynn was a fine athlete, he was in fact doubled often on screen by a number of stuntmen. Yet Flynn's films were crammed with so much leaping, swinging, and dueling that he did inevitably perform more in the way of stunts than many of his contemporaries. His sword duels with Basil Rathbone on *Captain Blood* (1935) and *The Adventures of Robin Hood* (1938) are considered classics, as is the all-out action on *The Charge of the Light Brigade* (1936) and *They Died with Their Boots On* (1941). Flynn jumped a horse over a cannon with lance in hand for *Light Brigade* and performed much of his own boxing for *Gentleman Jim* (1942).

Six-foot-two, 190-pound Errol Leslie Thomson Flynn was born in Hobart, Tasmania, and raised in Australia. He lived a life of high adventure. Flynn laid claim to amateur success in the sports of swimming, diving, and boxing and set to sea as a young shipmaster. For a brief time he was a police constable in Papua New Guinea and a mercenary soldier of fortune before finding his way as an actor. Taking regular weight and boxing workouts at the Hollywood Athletic Club, Flynn was one of the top tennis players in Hollywood and a man who would stand up to anyone and everyone with his fists if need be. The hard-living excesses eventually caught up with Flynn, who died from a heart attack at age 50. His daughter Deirdre became a stuntwoman in the 1970s.

See: Flynn, Errol. *My Wicked, Wicked Ways.* New York: G.P. Putnam, 1959.

Errol Flynn (left) duels Basil Rathbone on *Captain Blood* (1935).

BOB FOLKERSON (1918–1976)

Utah-born Robert J. Folkerson was a rodeo champion and horseback specialist. His biggest assignment came on *Johnny Guitar* (1954) where he doubled Scott Brady, Mercedes McCambridge, and Ben Cooper. He also doubled James Cagney on *Run for Cover* (1955) and Moe Howard on *Snow White and the Three Stooges* (1961). His credits also include *Melody Ranch* (1939), *Bad Day at Black Rock* (1955), *Around the World in Eighty Days* (1956), *Westward Ho, the Wagons!* (1956), *Flaming Star* (1960), *Will Penny* (1968), and the TV series *Cimarron Strip, Police Woman,* and *Oregon Trail.* He is the father of stuntwoman Cindy Folkerson.

GLENN FORD (1916–2006)

Versatile leading man Glenn Ford was one of Hollywood's finest horsemen and was named so by the Rodeo Cowboys Association. At Columbia Pictures he was good friends with Dave Sharpe and liked doing his own riding and fighting on films such as *Texas* (1941), *The Desperados* (1943), *Cowboy* (1958), and *Cimarron* (1960). Unfortunately, on *The Man from the Alamo* (1953) Ford was doing his own hard riding and his horse ran him into a tree. Ford broke three ribs; production was shut down for a month. Ford was also a fast draw, having trained with Arvo Ojala and Rodd Redwing for *The Fastest Gun Alive* (1956).

Gwyllyn Samuel Newton Ford was born in Quebec, Canada, and raised in Santa Monica, California. He was a stable boy for Will Rogers, who taught him trick riding and cowboy stunts. The 5'10", 165-pound Ford served with the Coast Guard and the U.S. Marine Corps during World War II. He played polo competitively and competed in rodeo events. He was still game for doing some of his own stunts as late as the TV series *Cade's County* (1971–72) where he jumped out of a moving Jeep. An honorary member of the Stuntmen's Association, Ford died following a series of strokes at the age of 90.

See: Ford, Peter. *Glenn Ford: A Life.* University of Wisconsin, 2011; "Glenn Ford: Using a Stuntman Is Cheating." *Kentucky New Era.* March 14, 1973.

VICTOR FRENCH (1934–1989)

The son of veteran B-western stuntman Ted French, Santa Barbara, California–born Victor Edwin French got his start in the business as a stuntman on TV's *Gunsmoke.* The rough-hewn French was a talented actor and began playing cruel heavies on *Gunsmoke* and other TV westerns such as *Daniel Boone* and *Bonanza.* His best fight with *Gunsmoke* star James Arness came on the 1970 episode "Kiowa." He brawled with Anthony Quinn on *Flap* (1970) and did a partial fire burn on *Rio Lobo* (1970) playing the main bad guy opposite John Wayne. The 6'1" French found his greatest success as the bearded character Isaiah Edwards on the long-running TV series *Little House on the Prairie* (1974–83) with his good friend Michael Landon. A boxing aficionado and collector of B-western memorabilia, French died from lung cancer at the age of 54.

See: Buck, Jerry. "Victor French Says Landon Was Answer to His Prayers." *Daily News.* July 19, 1985; Folkart, Burt. "Victor French; Actor, Director on *Highway to Heaven, Little House.*" *Los Angeles Times.* June 16, 1989.

HARRY FROBOESS (1899–1985)

Harry Arias Froboess was born in Dresden, Germany, or Bern, Switzerland, according to varying sources. The ex–Olympic diving and gymnastic champ was the performer of incredible high falls into bodies of water. His greatest leap was claimed to be 110 meters into Lake Constance off the Graf Zeppelin airship in 1936, a Guinness Record that skeptics doubt ever actually occurred since Froboess lived to tell about it. At the age of 70 he attempted a leap from a helicopter into the lake of Zurich from forty meters. Despite the fact he authored an autobiography in 1953, details of his film work in Hollywood are spotty, and there is curiously little mainstream fanfare or recognition. In the United States he toured carnivals and circuses with a swaying-pole act and authored the book *The Official Guide to Diving.* Some suspect the circus performer stretched the truth with claims of doubling Harold Lloyd, Buster Keaton, and Stan Laurel in Hollywood.

In the silent days Froboess worked on *The Cabinet of Dr. Caligari* (1920) and the German Harry Hill films. He transferred from a balloon to a plane on *Harry Hill—der Herr der Welt* (1923) and made a sixty-meter fall with a horse off a bridge for *Harry Hills Jagd auf den Tod* (1925). In Hollywood he doubled Greta Garbo on *Queen Christina* (1933) and Marlene Dietrich on *Destry Rides Again* (1939). He also worked on *Christopher Columbus* (1923), *The Sea Hawk* (1940), *The Bride Came C.O.D.* (1941), *Against All Flags* (1952), *River of No Return* (1954), *The Man from Laramie* (1955), *The Alamo* (1960), and *The Hallelujah Trail* (1965). Froboess died at the age of 85.

See: Froboess, Harry. *The Reminiscing Champ: A World Famous Stunt Man Tells His Story.* New York: Pageant, 1953; www.cyranos.ch/froboe-e.htm.

CLEM FULLER (1908–1961)

Los Angeles–born Clement D. Fuller was discovered bronc-busting and sharpshooting in a rodeo by Will Rogers and put to work in Hollywood. In his thirty-year movie career, Fuller worked with Gary Cooper and was best known as the original bartender on TV's *Gunsmoke* (1958–61). He received a Purple Heart during World War II and suffered a compound fracture of his leg doing a fall over a horse's head on *Saskatchewan* (1954). Other credits include *Gunga Din* (1939), *Colorado Sunset* (1939), *Canadian Pacific* (1949), *Sundowners* (1950), *The Kid from Texas* (1950), *High Lonesome* (1950), *Warpath* (1951), *Westward the Women* (1951), *Cavalry Scout* (1951), *Bend of the River* (1952), *The Duel at Silver Creek* (1952), *Gunsmoke* (1953), *The Great Sioux Uprising* (1953), *Column South* (1953), *Calamity Jane* (1953), *Tumbleweed* (1953), *Riding Shotgun* (1954), *Walk the Proud Land* (1956), *Night Passage* (1957), and *They Came to Cordura* (1959). A member of the Stuntmen's Hall of Fame, Fuller died from cancer at the age of 52.

See: "Clem Fuller." *Variety.* August 31, 1961;

ROBERT FULLER (1933–)

Popular TV western star Robert Fuller captivated audiences with thrilling fisticuffs and horsemanship throughout the runs of *Laramie* (1959–63) and *Wagon Train* (1963–65). His characters Jess Harper and Coop Smith are two-fisted cowboy legends. The highlight of any episode was the fight scenes, which Fuller enthusiastically did without a double. However, he had to lobby producers heavily to do his own stunts. Hal Needham was Fuller's favored fight partner and doubled the show's guests. Needham was on a 1964 *Wagon Train* episode titled "The Santiago Quesada Story" that featured a saloon brawl in which Fuller was hurt for real. Pressed for time at the end of the day, they made the mistake of not checking all the props before doing the fight a second time for the cameras. Fuller was flipped onto a breakaway table, and one of the chairs turned out to be real. Fuller broke his leg and ankle in three places and was forced to miss three months of work, to the studio's great displeasure. The accident reinforced the reason why studios are reluctant to have stars do their own stunts.

The 5'11", 175-pound Fuller was born Leonard Leroy "Buddy" Lee in Troy, New York. He was taught dancing by his parents, as well as calisthenics, falls, and gymnastic flips. He graduated from the Miami Military Academy and moved to Hollywood where his parents opened a dance studio. He began in films as a dance extra and stuntman on *Above and Beyond* (1952), *I Love Melvin* (1953), *Latin Lovers* (1953), and *Gentlemen Prefer Blondes* (1953). After a two-year stint with the U.S. Army's 24th Infantry during the Korean War, he picked up stunt assignments doubling Steve McQueen on TV's *West Point Story* and Jerry Lewis on *The Delicate Delinquent* (1957). During the first season of *Laramie* Fuller moonlighted with a beard and no credit as a stuntman on *Spartacus* (1960). He ran through a fight with Red West for the cameras during a massive battle.

Fuller loved making westerns and for a long time turned down anything that was not a cowboy show. He patterned his fighting style after *The Range Rider*'s Jock Mahoney, who became a close personal friend. His best pal was Chuck Courtney, who helped break him into acting by staging a fight scene for the director of *Teenage Thunder* (1957). On his TV shows Fuller was known to sneak in with the stunt extras for horse charges when he wasn't on camera. He starred with Yul Brynner on *Return of the Seven* (1966) and headlined the underrated biker film *Hard Ride* (1971).

Fuller is a recipient of the Golden Boot Award and an inductee of the Hall of Great Western Performers.

See: "A Former Stuntman with a Broken Leg." *St. Petersburg Times.* January 20, 1964; Lousararian, Ed. "Robert Fuller: Cowboy King of Cool." *Wildest Westerns.* #3, 2001; www.robert fuller.info.

FRED GABOURIE, JR. (1922–)

Senaca Indian Fred W. Gabourie, Jr., hailed from the Six Nations Reserve in Ontario, and was raised in Hollywood. He was the son of Buster Keaton's technical director. After World War II service, Gabourie became a stuntman doubling James Mason, Thomas Gomez, Richard Conte, Dane Clark, Frank DeKova, and Elisha Cook. A strong swimmer, he worked on *20,000 Leagues Under the Sea* (1954), *The Killing* (1956), *Yaqui Drums* (1956), and *It's a Mad, Mad, Mad, Mad World* (1963). His TV credits include *Wild Bill Hickok* and *The Untouchables*. In 1965 he performed in the live action play *Teddy Roosevelt Rides Again*, staged in the Burning Hills Amphitheatre in the Badlands of North Dakota.

Gabourie worked for the Motion Picture Factory that supplied breakaway furniture props to the studios. He would fill the studio order and proceed to break his own merchandise in staged barroom brawls for TV cameras. He put himself through law school at Southwestern University by doing stunts. He began practicing law in 1965 and the amount of stunt work dropped considerably. His highest profile law work came negotiating a settlement at Wounded Knee, South Dakota, in 1973. By the mid–1970s he became a municipal judge in the Los Angeles court system. Gabourie was a member of the Stuntmen's Association and an inductee of the Stuntmen's Hall of Fame.

See: Lieber, Leslie. "TV's Big Boom in Brawls." *Los Angeles Times.* March 15, 1959; Meagher, Ed. "New Role for Indian." *Los Angeles Times.* February 2, 1976.

JACK GALLAGHER

Expert horseman Jack Gallagher entered motion pictures from the professional rodeo ranks. In silent films he doubled Ramon Novarro and wrecked chariots on *Ben-Hur* (1925) and rode a steed for Rudolph Valentino on *Son of the Sheik*

(1926). He fell from a buckboard on *The Painted Desert* (1931), was a sailor on *King Kong* (1933), doubled Joe Sawyer on *The Westerner* (1934), and was shot off a roof on *Billy the Kid* (1941). Gallagher totaled more than 1,000 screen deaths during a long career, including over fifteen years at MGM. He coordinated action with over eighty horses and riders on *The North Star* (1943) and later became a wrangler.

See: Hughes, Elinor. "Theater and Screen." *Boston Herald.* July 1, 1944; "Veteran Stunt Man Has Role in *Billy the Kid.*" *Register-Republic.* July 28, 1941.

TOMMY GARLAND (1920–2001)

Thomas Leonard Garland fought as a middleweight and light-heavyweight from 1939 to 1948, amassing a professional record of 45–13–5 even during service with the Coast Guard during World War II. The 5'10", Canadian-born Garland was a ring double for Robert Montgomery on *Here Comes Mr. Jordan* (1941) and worked as his stand-in on *Mr. and Mrs. Smith* (1941). Garland parlayed this experience into more boxing movies and stunt assignments. He worked on *Golden Boy* (1939), *Golden Gloves* (1940), *When the Redskins Rode* (1950), *Soldiers Three* (1951), *City Beneath the Sea* (1953), *The Harder They Fall* (1956), and *Somebody Up There Likes Me* (1956).

JAMES GARNER (1928–)

TV and movie star James Garner's laid-back screen persona does not immediately conjure up the image of a Hollywood stuntman, but Garner performed a majority of his own stunts. He starred in the groundbreaking automotive film *Grand Prix* (1966) and did his own Formula One racing. He even performed a fire stunt gone awry that saw Lloyds of London cancel his insurance policy. The thrill led Garner to take an interest in speed, and he competed in the Baja 1000 off-road race several times. While visiting a friend on the Texas location of the Steve McQueen film *The Getaway* (1972), Garner drove one of the stunt cars in a chase scene. (That's Garner behind the wheel of the orange Volkswagen Beetle.) Director Sam Peckinpah paid him a token dollar bill for his impromptu stunt work. Garner also did the majority of the Pontiac Firebird driving on the TV series *The Rockford Files* (1974–80).

A recurring theme throughout Garner's career was as a reluctant man of action who often found himself outnumbered in fisticuffs. When the odds were even, he could handle himself in a scrap. However, the odds were rarely even in Garner's career save for a memorable brawl opposite a young Clint Eastwood on a 1957 episode of the TV western *Maverick*. Garner did the bulk of a nifty fight with three stuntmen on *Duel at Diablo* (1966), and outsmarted martial artist Bruce Lee during a *Marlowe* (1969) confrontation. Usually it was Garner who ended up beaten into the pavement by an army of stunt thugs on every episode of *Rockford*. The repeated falls required Garner to have annual knee surgery throughout the course of the show. Garner's stuntman was his friend Roydon Clark, and it was a testament to both that they were able to involve Garner in so much believable screen action.

The 6'2", 210-pound Garner was born James Scott Bumgarner in Norman, Oklahoma. He played high school football both there and for Hollywood High in California in between time with the Merchant Marine. His prowess as a kicker had USC showing interest in him for a scholarship, but Army service during the Korean War and two Purple Hearts intervened. He was working as a carpet layer when he decided to look up an old acquaintance who had advanced as an agent in the picture business. Best Actor Oscar nominee Garner is a recipient of a Golden Boot for his western roles.

See: Garner, James, & Jon Winokur. *The Garner Files: A Memoir.* New York: Simon & Schuster, 2011.

DONNA GARRETT (1942–)

Five-foot-seven Donna Garrett was born in Santa Ana, California. A gymnast and diver, she majored in Physical Education at Los Angeles Valley Junior College. She doubled Raquel Welch on *Fantastic Voyage* (1966), *Bandolero!* (1968), *100 Rifles* (1969), *Flare Up* (1969), and *Kansas City Bomber* (1972. She is best known for being credited as Bambi on *Diamonds Are Forever* (1971) despite the fact that Lola Larson ended up playing the role. It is likely Garrett was the stuntwoman for the fight with Sean Connery and the acting credit was an error.

Garrett doubled Jacqueline Bisset on *Airport* (1970), Ali McGraw on *The Getaway* (1972), Karen Black on *Portnoy's Complaint* (1972), Barbra Streisand on *What's Up, Doc?* (1972), and Susan St. James on *Outlaw Blues* (1977). On TV she doubled June Lockhart on *Lost in Space* (1965–68), Angie Dickinson on *Police Woman* (1974–78), and Kate Jackson on *Charlie's Angels* (1976–79). On *Shadow of the Hawk* (1976) she went over a gorge on a rickety drawbridge for Marilyn Hassett.

She also worked on *Soldier Blue* (1970), *Star Spangled Girl* (1971), *The Poseidon Adventure* (1972), *Earthquake* (1974), *The Drowning Pool* (1975), *Drum* (1976), *Logan's Run* (1976), and *Comes a Horseman* (1978). TV credits include *Star Trek*, *Mission: Impossible*, *The Rockford Files*, and *Wonder Woman* as a double for guest star Lynda Day George. The wife of stuntman Ralph Garrett, Donna is a charter member of the Stuntwomen's Association and an inductee of the Stuntmen's Hall of Fame.

See: Boorstin, Paul. "A Hollywood Stunt Pair Enjoys Many Happy Landings—So Far." *People*. December 23, 1974; Silden, Isobel. "Stunt Women." *Australian Women's Weekly*. February 17, 1982; Wetherby, Terry. *Conversations: Working Women Talk About Doing a "Man's Job."* Les Femmes, 1977.

RALPH GARRETT (1938–)

At age thirteen Ralph Leland Garrett became a professional acrobat in his father's troupe, Homer Garrett's Why-Knot Twirlers. After service with the U.S. Army, the 6'1", 190-pound Garrett became a stuntman in 1961. His highest profile assignment came doubling Jon Voight wrecking a canoe in the rapids and climbing up the side of a cliff on *Deliverance* (1972). Garrett also doubled Lee Majors, Ryan O'Neal, Chad Everett, and Leonard Nimoy, the latter on *Star Trek*. He also worked on *Some Kind of a Nut* (1969), *Soylent Green* (1973), *Earthquake* (1974), *Rollercoaster* (1977), *One Man Jury* (1978), and *The Electric Horseman* (1979). TV credits include *Voyage to the Bottom of the Sea*, *Land of the Giants*, and *The Rockford Files*. The husband of stuntwoman Donna Garrett, he is a member of the Stuntmen's Association.

See: Boorstin, Paul. "A Hollywood Stunt Pair Enjoys Many Happy Landings—So Far." *People*. December 23, 1974.

JERRY GATLIN (1933–)

Five-foot-eleven, 165 pound Jerry Joe Gatlin was born in Springfield, Colorado. He worked as a hunt guide and competed in rodeos, winning a scholarship to New Mexico A&M College. He turned professional in 1953 when he joined the Rodeo Cowboys Association. While serving in the U.S. Army's Mountain Ski Troop, Gatlin set a Fort Carson record for their Mountain and Cold Weather Training Squad by climbing the Devil's Tower in one hour and 36 minutes. After his Army service he returned to the professional rodeo circuit. Gatlin took top money in bronc riding at the 1954 Rice Springs Roundup in Texas and was named the All-Around Champion of the Colorado Cowboy's Association in 1956.

In the winter he traveled to Tucson, Arizona, to work as a wrangler, but ended up as a stuntman doing horse falls. When he found out the money he could make falling off a horse as opposed to staying on one, he decided to give the picture business a try. In Hollywood he got a job in horse trainer Ralph McCutcheon's barn as he broke into films. Gatlin began working for stunt coordinators Chuck Hayward and Henry Wills, making a name for himself doubling Horst Buchholz, Eli Wallach, Charles Bronson, and Robert Vaughn on *The Magnificent Seven* (1960). One of his first regular stuntman gigs was on the TV series *Have Gun—Will Travel*. His falling horse was named Trader.

Gatlin doubled Tab Hunter on *Gunman's Walk* (1958), Earl Holliman on *Last Train from Gun Hill* (1959) and the TV series *Hotel de Paree* (1959–60) and *The Wide Country* (1962–63), Roddy McDowall on *5 Card Stud* (1968), and Ernest Borgnine for the classic fight with Lee Marvin on *Emperor of the North* (1973). He was a ubiquitous presence in the films of John Wayne, appearing on *The Comancheros* (1961), *Donovan's Reef* (1963), *McLintock!* (1963), *The Sons of Katie Elder* (1965), *The War Wagon* (1967), *The Undefeated* (1969), *Rio Lobo* (1970), *Big Jake* (1971), *The Cowboys* (1972), *Cahill, U.S. Marshal* (1973), *The Train Robbers* (1973), and *Rooster Cogburn* (1975).

He also worked on *Posse from Hell* (1961), *Kings of the Sun* (1963), *Cheyenne Autumn* (1964), *The Greatest Story Ever Told* (1965), *Major Dundee* (1965), *The Hallelujah Trail* (1965), *The Rounders* (1965), *Nevada Smith* (1966), *Will Penny* (1968), *Bandolero!* (1968),

The Devil's Brigade (1968), Little Big Man (1970), Support Your Local Gunfighter (1971), Ulzana's Raid (1972), The Culpepper Cattle Co. (1972), Legend of Nigger Charley (1972), Pat Garrett and Billy the Kid (1973), The Don Is Dead (1973), Blazing Saddles (1974), Bite the Bullet (1975), The Master Gunfighter (1975), The Great Scout and Cathouse Thursday (1976), The Outlaw Josey Wales (1976), F.I.S.T. (1978), Convoy (1978), and Mountain Men (1980). TV credits include Gunsmoke, Bonanza, Hondo, High Chaparral, The FBI, and Little House on the Prairie. A member of the Stuntmen's Association and an inductee of the Stuntmen's Hall of Fame, Gatlin was once married to stuntwoman Polly Burson. His daughter Joie Gatlin became a show jumping champ.

See: Bacon, James. "Gatlin Achieves Stardom, But No One May Know It." Boca Raton News. September 23, 1973; Lilley, Tim. Campfire Conversations Complete. Akron, OH: Big Trail, 2010.

JAMES W. GAVIN (1935–2005)

Helicopter and airplane pilot James W. Gavin was born in Denver, Colorado. He flew evac chopper missions in Korea and was later a pilot for the U.S. Forest Service. This led to his being recruited to fly the camera on The Misfits (1961). Gavin became the top chopper pilot in Hollywood, his smooth aviating enabling cameramen to get shots that, with a lesser pilot at the controls, would be too shaky. He was sometimes given a line or two of dialogue, for which he would flip his name and be listed in the credits as Gavin James.

Some of his best helicopter stunts came during the chase scenes on Dirty Mary, Crazy Larry (1974). The six-foot, 185-pound Gavin was so good that he was able to touch his skids onto the roof of a car at high speeds. The Towering Inferno (1974) saw him negotiating around the burning skyscrapers. On Airport '75 (1974) Gavin was the coordinator and pilot for the stunt that saw Joe Canutt lowered from a helicopter to transfer into the ripped-open cockpit of a 747. He was also behind the controls of the chopper that pursues Clint Eastwood on a motorcycle in The Gauntlet (1977).

He also worked on Coogan's Bluff (1968), Dirty Harry (1971), Vanishing Point (1971), Skyjacked (1972), Hickey and Boggs (1972), Earth-

quake (1974), Breakout (1975), Black Sunday (1977), Airport '77 (1977), Rollercoaster (1977), Domino Principle (1977), Mr. Billion (1977), The Cat from Outer Space (1978), and The Nude Bomb (1980). He was especially active on TV shows such as Mannix, McCloud, Police Story, Emergency, The Rockford Files, and Baa Baa Black Sheep. He was a member of the Stuntmen's Association and the founder of the Motion Picture Pilot's Association.

See: Stump, Al. "Whirlybird Catches the Crook." TV Guide. October 30, 1976.

BUD GEARY (1898–1946)

Bud Geary was born Sigsby Maine Geary in Salt Lake City, Utah. The 6'1" World War I veteran played Will Scarlett opposite Douglas Fairbanks on Robin Hood (1922). He continued with athletic roles throughout the 1920s, eventually portraying villainous henchmen in any number of Saturday afternoon matinee movies. He was especially valued as a colorful tough guy at Republic during the 1940s where his stunt skills were put to use for any number of fight scenes opposite Allan Lane on King of the Royal Mounted (1940), Don "Red" Barry on Adventures of Red Ryder (1940), Kane Richmond on Haunted Harbor (1944), and Sunset Carson on Santa Fe Saddlemates (1945). Geary doubled Warren Hull on the serial The Spider's Web (1938).

He also worked on The Miracle Rider (1935), San Francisco (1936), Trail of the Lonesome Pine (1936), Big City (1937), Dick Tracy's G-Men (1939), Zorro's Fighting Legion (1939), Flowing Gold (1940), Captain Caution (1940), Texas (1941), Adventures of Captain Marvel (1941), All Through the Night (1941), Perils of Nyoka (1942), Fall In (1942), Pittsburgh (1942), Two Yanks in Trinidad (1942), Five Graves to Cairo (1943), Bataan (1943), Lady Takes a Chance (1943), The Masked Marvel (1943), In Old Oklahoma (1943), The Fighting Seabees (1944), and Flame of Barbary Coast (1945). An honorary member of the Stuntmen's Association, Geary died as a result of injuries sustained in a car wreck at the age of 48.

RICHARD GEARY (1925–2000)

Born in Los Angeles, Richard Clark Geary was the son of character actor–stuntman Bud Geary. The younger Geary entered the stunt profession in the mid–1950s and was a co-founder of the Stuntmen's Association of Motion Pictures in 1961. He served as stunt coordinator for the TV series *Perry Mason* (1957–64), *The Man from U.N.C.L.E.* (1964–68), and *Delphi Bureau* (1972–73). On the *U.N.C.L.E.* series he was the main double for Robert Vaughn with his most difficult stunt being a jump from the hood of a Jaguar XKE onto the open ladder of a taxiing plane. He later doubled Ralph Waite of TV's *The Waltons*.

The 5'11", 160-pound Geary also worked on *The Silver Chalice* (1954), *Elmer Gantry* (1960), *Everything's Ducky* (1961), *It's a Mad, Mad, Mad, Mad World* (1963), *The Great Race* (1965), *What Did You Do in the War, Daddy?* (1966), *Bullitt* (1968), *The Love Bug* (1968), *Detroit 9000* (1973), *Friday Foster* (1975), and *Prisoner of Zenda* (1979). TV credits include *Sea Hunt*, *Whirlybirds*, *Twilight Zone*, *Star Trek*, *Mannix*, *Adam–12*, *Kolchak: The Night Stalker*, and *The Six Million Dollar Man*. He was a member of the Stuntmen's Association and an inductee of the Stuntmen's Hall of Fame.

See: "Live Bullets One of the Dangers for Robert and David." *TV Week*. July 1966.

LENNIE GEER (1914–1989)

Six-foot-one, 185-pound Leonard P. Geer was born in Chicago and entered stunts after military service in World War II. He is best known as the stable hand Ollie on the Walt Disney TV show *Adventures of Spin and Marty* (1955) and became an established character man on TV westerns where his bushy eyebrows often got him cast as villains. He doubled Robert Mitchum on *Man with the Gun* (1955) and George Montgomery on *Robbers' Roost* (1955). His best-known stunt work came on Alfred Hitchcock's *North by Northwest* (1959) and *The Birds* (1963); in the latter, he was the man attacked outside the phone booth.

Geer was important to the industry as a trainer of young stuntmen, among them Hal Needham, Dave Perna, Hank Calia, and Ronnie Rondell. He had a traveling road show that was known as the original Stunts Unlimited and was a top horse trainer. For many years Geer and his horses Rick and Skyrocket entertained audiences with his young stunt troupe. Geer, prone to calling everyone "Daddy-O," was known as the Be-Bop Cowboy.

He worked on *Flame of Calcutta* (1953),

Masterson of Kansas (1954), *White Feather* (1955), *The Rawhide Years* (1955), *A Lawless Street* (1955), *The Great Locomotive Chase* (1956), *The Proud Ones* (1956), *Canyon River* (1956), *The Oklahoman* (1957), *The Tall Stranger* (1957), *Man from God's Country* (1958), *Black Samson* (1974), *Freebie and the Bean* (1974), *Another Man, Another Chance* (1977), and *Lord of the Rings* (1978). TV credits include *Wild Bill Hickok*, *Annie Oakley*, *Wyatt Earp*, *Tales of Wells Fargo*, *Have Gun—Will Travel*, *Restless Gun*, *The Rifleman*, *Bat Masterson*, *The Westerner*, *Tall Men*, *Lassie*, *Laramie*, *Wagon Train*, *Gunsmoke*, *The Virginian*, *Daniel Boone*, *Laredo*, and *Starsky and Hutch*. A member of the Stuntmen's Association, an honorary member of Stunts Unlimited, and an inductee of the Stuntmen's Hall of Fame, Geer died of heart failure at the age of 74.

See: "Lean Lennie Daddy-O to Hipster Set." *Pasadena Independent*. January 5, 1956.

ALAN GIBBS (1940–1988)

Alan Gibbs did many signature stunts during the 1970s as a double for superstars Charles Bronson and Burt Reynolds. On *Little Big Man* (1970) he doubled Dustin Hoffman for a multiple horse transfer with Hal Needham. *Werewolves on Wheels* (1971) saw him execute a wild fire stunt on a bike. On *Life and Times of Judge Roy Bean* (1972) the 5'10", 165 pound Gibbs perfectly timed a two-story jump into a moving wagon. On *The Mechanic* (1972) he doubled Bronson on a motorcycle and bailed before a dummy-occupied bike flew off a cliff and exploded upon impact. The climax of *Electra Glide in Blue* (1973) saw Gibbs shot off a motorcycle in Monument Valley for Robert Blake in what would be an iconic image. His biggest stunt came on *Smokey and the Bandit* (1977) when he jumped Burt Reynolds' black Trans-Am over the Mulberry Bridge.

Florida-born Alan Robert Gibbs was a champion cross country motorcyclist but got into the stunt world by accident. He lived next door to stuntman Chuck Bail and became so intrigued by the men working out in Bail's backyard he asked if he could give it a try. Gibbs became a protégé of Hal Needham and quickly developed into one of the top stunt coordinators and second unit directors in the business. Initially a member of the Stuntmen's Association, Gibbs made the break to Stunts Unlimited. A decade later he left that organization and founded the International Stunt Association. Gibbs was the double for Jack Nicholson on many films, including *Chinatown* (1974) and *One Flew Over the Cuckoo's Nest* (1975).

He also worked on *Savage Seven* (1968), *The Green Berets* (1968), *Chubasco* (1968), *The Great Bank Robbery* (1969), *The Undefeated* (1969), *The Good Guys and the Bad Guys* (1969), *Beneath the Planet of the Apes* (1970), *Angel Unchained* (1970), *C.C. and Company* (1970), *Sometimes a Great Notion* (1970), *Ulzana's Raid* (1972), *Conquest of the Planet of the Apes* (1972), *The Man Who Loved Cat Dancing* (1973), *Scorpio* (1973), *The Stone Killer* (1973), *Midnight Man* (1974), *Three the Hard Way* (1974), *Death Wish* (1974), *Crazy Mama* (1975), *Mitchell* (1975), *Cannonball* (1976), *Nickelodeon* (1976), *Convoy* (1978), *Zero to Sixty* (1978), *Avalanche Express* (1979), *Heaven's Gate* (1980), and *Stunts Unlimited* (1980). TV credits include *Star Trek, Mannix, CHiPs,* and *Vega$.* An inductee of the Stuntmen's Hall of Fame, Gibbs died from cancer at the age of 47.

See: Conrad, Barnaby. "Hollywood's Sometimes Fatal Jobs." *True.* June 1972; "Stuntman Helps in Court Cases." *Leader-Post.* February 17, 1982.

HELEN GIBSON (1892–1977)

Generally regarded as the first professional stuntwoman, Helen Gibson was born Rose August Wenger in Cleveland, Ohio, and was raised in frontier towns. She had backgrounds in vaudeville and rodeo trick riding and was extremely athletic and daring. She doubled early serial star Helen Holmes for a horse-to-train transfer on *Hazards of Helen* (1914), then became a short and serial star herself. Some of her titles include *Danger Ahead!* (1915), *Wolves of the Range* (1918), and *Nine Points of the Law* (1922). Gibson's most acclaimed stunt came on a motorcycle for *Daughter of Daring* (1917). She crashed through a gate and rode the cycle through an open boxcar onto a moving train.

She was married to stuntman turned cowboy star Hoot Gibson until 1920 and remained active in stunt work doubling Marie Dressler, Marjorie Main, and Ethel Barrymore. She doubled Georgia Hale on *Lightning Warrior* (1931) while compiling stunts and bit parts on over 400 films. Other credits include *Stagecoach* (1939), *The Man from* *the Alamo* (1953), and *The Man Who Shot Liberty Valance* (1962), for which she drove a team of horses. An inductee in the Stuntmen's Hall of Fame, Gibson died from a heart attack at the age of 85.

See: "Hazards of Helen: Those Were the Days." *Herald Examiner.* September 9, 1962.

HOOT GIBSON (1892–1962)

Early silent movie cowboy star Hoot Gibson was born Edmund Richard Gibson in Tekameh, Nebraska. He grew up breaking broncos for Dick Stanley's Congress of Rough Riders and claimed he was the first stuntman in California. Weighing only 125 pounds when he began stunting in 1910, he could double women as well as men. His earliest stunts saw him doubling Alice Joyce, Carlyle Blackwell, George Medford, and Helen Holmes for horse-to-train transfers on *Hazards of Helen* (1914). Hoot specialized in horse work, but once rode a motorcycle off a drawbridge to a forty-foot drop. His favorite stunt was jumping horses off cliffs, for which he'd earn $25 a jump. He routinely made $5 a day as a riding extra on his wife Helen Gibson's early films. He began doubling Harry Carey and eventually top-lined his own films.

Throughout his early days Hoot continued to rodeo, winning the All-Around World Championship at Pendleton in 1912. The same year he was the World Champion Fancy Roper, so his skills were genuine. Hoot became one of the 1920s' most popular cowboy stars at which point he began to let his stunt crews take over the dangerous work. He was still interested in extracurricular pursuits such as airplane racing, cracking up his body in a plane crash during the National Air Races in 1932. Gibson died from cancer at the age of 70.

See: "Hoot Gibson, Film Cowboy Dies." *New York Times.* August 23, 1962; "Hoot Gibson: In His Own Words." *Western Clippings.* #38, November-December 2000.

FRANK GIFFORD (1930–)

The 6'1", 200-pound Francis Newton Gifford was an eight-time Pro Bowl halfback and Most Valuable Player of the NFL in 1956 for the New York Giants. The Santa Monica–born Gifford excelled as a quarterback at Bakersfield High and Bakersfield Junior College, where he was named Junior All-American. That got him out of the oil fields and landed him at USC, where he again attained All-American status. His popularity and location gained him employment at the movie studios in the off-season.

Gifford played football players on *Saturday's Hero* (1951) and *All-American* (1953), where he was also the technical advisor and taught Tony Curtis how to play. He doubled Jerry Lewis for football scenes on *That's My Boy* (1951) and was a full-fledged stuntman on *Sign of the Pagan* (1954), where he fell off walls, horses, and took a spear through the heart. He signed a Warner Bros. acting contract, but considered himself no more than a "talking stuntman" with small speaking roles on *Darby's Rangers* (1958) and *Up Periscope* (1959). In the former he dove in front of a tank for a $500 stunt adjustment and rolled down a hill to the tune of $250. On *Up Periscope* he was blown off a tower. Gifford is an inductee of the Pro Football Hall of Fame.

See: Frank, Stanley. "Pro Football's All-Around Man." *Saturday Evening Post*. #230, 1957; Gifford, Frank, & Harry Walters. *The Whole Ten Yards*. NY: Ivy, 1994; "Pro Football's MVP May Quit for Movies." *Lebanon Daily News*. January 31, 1957.

MICKEY GILBERT

Some claim Mickey Gilbert was the best athlete among stuntmen, high praise for any individual whose body's abilities fuel his trade. The six-foot, 165-pound Gilbert is best known for jumping off a cliff for Robert Redford on *Butch Cassidy and the Sundance Kid* (1969), a stirrup drag and horse fall during the opening shootout on *The Wild Bunch* (1969), doubling Gene Wilder going off the top of a train to a signal post on *Silver Streak* (1976), rolling a horse down a hill on *Return of a Man Called Horse* (1976), making a 187-foot car jump through a drive-in movie screen on *Our Winning Season* (1978), and taking a horse off a cliff into water for Wilder on *The Frisco Kid* (1979). He doubled Paul Newman, Steve McQueen, Charles Bronson, and Lee Majors, the latter on the TV series *The Fall Guy* (1981–86), where he hung underneath helicopters, crashed through windows, and made incredible truck jumps.

Early gymnastics training benefited

Hollywood-born R. Michael Gilbert in track and field and rodeo endeavors. He won championships in each sport. At age thirteen he entered a televised junior rodeo competition and took eleven first place finishes and two second place finishes. He turned rodeo professional at the age of sixteen and attended Pierce College, winning a National Championship in calf roping, bareback riding, and bulldogging. He was a horse wrangler on *Ben-Hur* (1959) and kept a careful eye on the stuntmen. Director Edward Dmytryk tabbed him as stunt double for Richard Widmark on *Warlock* (1959) and his career was off and running. Gilbert married stuntman Joe Yrigoyen's daughter and began to work regularly in the movie industry alongside his stepfather. One of his first big jobs was doubling Hugh O'Brian evading a rhinoceros on *Africa, Texas Style* (1967). This led to the interesting assignment of doubling 6'5" Chuck Connors on the TV series *Cowboy in Africa* (1967–68).

He worked on *Alvarez Kelly* (1966), *Beau Geste* (1966), *Camelot* (1967), *Cool Hand Luke* (1967), *The Devil's Brigade* (1968), *Hellfighters* (1968), *The Undefeated* (1969), *Ballad of Cable Hogue* (1970), *Little Big Man* (1970), *Beneath the Planet of the Apes* (1970), *Rio Lobo* (1970), *Sometimes a Great Notion* (1970), *Pocket Money* (1972), *Junior Bonner* (1972), *Joe Kidd* (1972), *When the Legends Die* (1972), *Cleopatra Jones* (1973), *The Don Is Dead* (1973), *Westworld* (1973), *The Sting* (1973), *Blazing Saddles* (1974), *Mame* (1974), *Mr. Majestyk* (1974), *The Towering Inferno* (1974), *Earthquake* (1974), *The Great Waldo Pepper* (1975), *The Wind and the Lion* (1975), *Rooster Cogburn* (1975), *Breakheart Pass* (1976), *The Gumball Rally* (1976), *Bound for Glory* (1976), *The World's Greatest Lover* (1977), *Every Which Way But Loose* (1978), *The Fury* (1978), *FM* (1978), *Hooper* (1978), *Who'll Stop the Rain* (1978), *Concorde, Airport '79* (1979), *Buck Rogers in the 25th Century* (1979), *The Electric Horseman* (1979), *Prisoner of Zenda* (1979), *Apple Dumpling Gang Rides Again* (1979), and *Stunts Unlimited* (1980). On TV he doubled Wayne Maunder on *Custer* (1967) and worked on *The Man from U.N.C.L.E.*, *Kolchak: The Night Stalker,* and *Vega$*. A member of Stunts Unlimited and an inductee of the Stuntmen's Hall of Fame, Gilbert received an ActionFest Lifetime Achievement Award. His sons Lance and Troy became top stuntmen.

See: Keller, Elizabeth. "Mickey Gilbert." *In-*

side Stunts. Summer, 2006; "Stuntmen Compete in Sports Spectacular." *Joplin Globe.* January 15, 1977; www.twitchfilm.com.

MATT GILMAN

Matt Gilman was a husky West Virginia–born oil field worker turned auto crack-up specialist. He doubled W.C. Fields on *If I Had a Million* (1932) and Wallace Beery on *The Mighty Barnum* (1934) and *Stand Up and Fight* (1939). He was Beery's brother-in-law and doubled him many times. He later managed Beery's Jackson Hole, Wyoming, ranch. Gilman doubled actress Marie Dressler falling off a motorboat on *Min and Bill* (1930) and worked on *Treasure Island* (1934), *High Tension* (1936), *Shadow of the Thin Man* (1941), and *Soldiers Three* (1951). He was featured on a segment of the 1938 radio show *Daredevils of Hollywood.*

SANDRA GIMPEL (1939–)

Los Angeles–born Sandra Lee Gimpel was a professional dancer at Pacific Ocean Park on the Santa Monica Pier. She was hired to dance on Walt Disney films and made the transition to stunt woman on the TV series *Lost in Space* (1965–68), where the 5'1" performer doubled child actor Billy Mumy. Gimpel stunted for Lindsay Wagner on *The Bionic Woman* (1976–78) in addition to Sally Fields Barbara Eden, Debbie Reynolds, Sissy Spacek, Kate Mulgrew, Sally Struthers, and Annie Potts. One of her highest profile jobs came as a brawling Girl Scout opposite Paula Marie Moody on *Airplane!* (1980).

She was one of the earliest female stunt co-ordinators accepted into the Directors Guild. A fourth degree black belt in tae kwon do, Gimpel released the 2008 exercise video *Sandy Gimpel's Stunt Blasters Workout.* She worked on *A Fine Madness* (1966), *Clambake* (1967), *The Gnome-Mobile* (1967), *Rafferty and the Gold Dust Twins* (1975), *The Pack* (1977), *Avalanche* (1978), *Battlestar Galactica* (1979), *Tourist Trap* (1979), and *Prophecy* (1979).

See: Goodale, Gloria. "Forty Years On Stuntwoman Sandy Gimpel Still Loves Her Occupational Hazards." *Christian Science Monitor.* November 16, 2007; Kuklenski, Valerie. "Healthy Stunt." *Daily News.* July 8, 2007; Silden, Isobel. "Trio Thrives on Thrill of Stunt Work." *Wisconsin State Journal.* August 17, 1986.

LEN GLASCOW

Len Glascow was born in St. Louis and raised in Los Angeles. At Polytechnic High he excelled at basketball, football, and baseball. He was a Green Beret and paratrooper in Vietnam and a Los Angeles Sheriff's Deputy. The 170-pound six-footer became the leader of a mock 10th Cavalry Buffalo Soldiers drill team that was featured in the movie *Hello, Dolly!* (1969) and became the focus of an episode of TV's *High Chaparral.* Glascow and his outfit were recruited by Eddie Smith to be the first members of the Black Stuntman's Association. He worked on *The Great White Hope* (1970), *Cleopatra Jones* (1973), *Uptown Saturday Night* (1974), *Two-Minute Warning* (1976), *Drum* (1976), *King Kong* (1976), *A Piece of the Action* (1977), *Telefon* (1977), *Hooper* (1978), *Meteor* (1979), and *The Black Hole* (1979). TV credits include *Mannix, Gunsmoke, Ironside, Police Story, Police Woman, BJ and the Bear,* and *The Dukes of Hazzard.*

BERT GOODRICH (1906–1991)

Bert M. Goodrich is known in bodybuilding circles as the first Mr. America, but at the time (1939) he was considered one of Hollywood's top stuntmen. At the age of fourteen the Tempe, Arizona–born Goodrich was a state champion flyweight boxer and diver. He built his 5'11", 195-pound physique up for football and gymnastics in high school and went on to be a superb sprinter for Arizona State University, excelling in track events such as the shot, javelin, and long jump. He boxed professionally at Madison Square Garden and was a trapeze artist and adagio performer with acrobatic partner George Redpath.

Goodrich doubled Red Grange on *Galloping Ghost* (1931), John Wayne on *Hurricane Express* (1932), and Buster Crabbe on *Tarzan the Fearless* (1933). He also doubled Victor McLaglen, Ken Maynard, Harry Carey, and Gene Autry. During World War II he served with the U.S. Navy as a Chief Athletic Specialist and later opened a famous gym on Hollywood Boulevard. An honorary member of the Stuntmen's Association, Goodrich died from complications of intestinal surgery at the age of 84.

See: "First Mr. America Flexes His Muscles for Valley Seniors." *Daily News.* April 30, 1986; Folkart, Burt. "Bert Goodrich, 84; Gym Owner,

First Mr. America." *Los Angeles Times.* December 11, 1991; Lamparski, Richard. *2nd Annual Lamparski's Whatever Became Of?* NY: Bantam, 1977.

ALINE GOODWIN (1889–1980)

Massachusetts-born horsewoman Aline Goodwin is best known for taking the tumble down the stairs for Vivien Leigh on *Gone with the Wind* (1939). Goodwin had other notable doubling assignments, standing in for Fay Wray on *King Kong* (1933), Claudette Colbert on *Under Two Flags* (1936), Marlene Dietrich on *The Garden of Allah* (1936), Frances Grant on *Oh, Susanna!* (1936), and Margaret Hamilton on *The Wizard of Oz* (1939). She was a leading lady herself on *Hellion* (1922) in which she engaged in a fight scene with Marin Sais.

SOL GORSS (1908–1966)

Sol Gorss made his name on *The Adventures of Robin Hood* (1938) when he allowed archer Howard Hill to fire arrows into a small shield he had hidden under his tunic. Each arrow cost the studio $150 and Gorss took more hits than anyone. The following year he was blown up in a luggage car on *Dodge City* (1939). On *The Boss* (1956) he was part of a tricky three-man stair fall with Harvey Parry and Paul Stader. His highest profile assignment came doubling Cary Grant atop Mount Rushmore on *North by Northwest* (1959). On TV he doubled George Reeves on *Superman* (1952–58), doing all the fight and flying action.

An expert fight man, high-fall specialist, and fencer, Gorss was employed on a number of swashbucklers and served as a sword-master and choreographer for the major studios. His most memorable duel came on *The Three Musketeers* (1948) with Gene Kelly. His best fistfight was on a freight-elevator against Humphrey Bogart on *All Through the Night* (1941). Gorss often doubled Errol Flynn, whom he taught to fence on *Captain Blood* (1935). Other actors he doubled were Randolph Scott, Robert Ryan, Gary Cooper, Clark

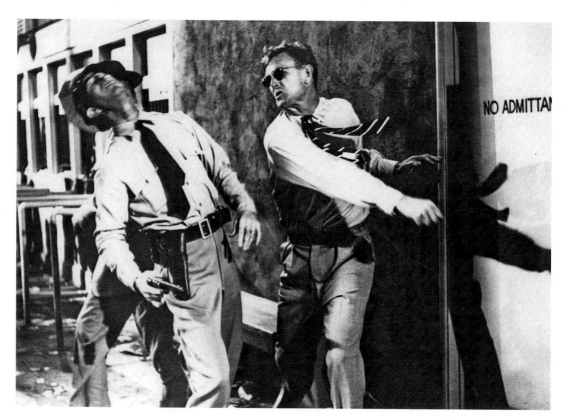

Sol Gorss takes a punch from Sterling Hayden on *The Killing* (1956).

Gable, George Montgomery, Victor Jory, Anthony Quinn, Gregory Peck, Stewart Granger, Stephen McNally, James Craig, Reed Hadley, and John Russell.

Six-foot-two, 185-pound Saul Michael Gorss was born in Cincinnati. Relocating to Los Angeles, he excelled in football and track at Roosevelt High. This athleticism won him an athletic scholarship to the University of Nevada to play fullback on the football squad. Gorss turned semi-pro in football and dabbled in boxing. An excellent golfer, he was an assistant pro at various courses. He served with the U.S. Marine Corps before embarking on a stunt career at Warner Brothers in the 1930s. In 1942 Gorss served with the Army Air Force but was discharged due to a bad leg, an unfortunate fate that befell many Hollywood stuntmen whose bodies were considered to be too banged up to serve their country. The injury didn't prevent him from resuming his duties in Hollywood.

He worked on *San Quentin* (1937), *God's Country and the Woman* (1937), *Valley of the Giants* (1938), *Heart of the North* (1938), *The Private Lives of Elizabeth and Essex* (1939), *Secret Service of the Air* (1939), *Flowing Gold* (1940), *Dive Bomber* (1941), *They Died with Their Boots On* (1941), *Sergeant York* (1941), *The Phantom* (1943), *Jeep Herders* (1945), *The Razor's Edge* (1946), *Monsieur Beaucaire* (1946), *The Farmer's Daughter* (1947), *The Exile* (1947), *Adventures of Don Juan* (1948), *South of St. Louis* (1949), *Dakota Lil* (1950), *The Secret Fury* (1950), *The Asphalt Jungle* (1950), *Fortunes of Captain Blood* (1950), *Only the Valiant* (1951), *The Thing from Another World* (1951), *His Kind of Woman* (1951), *Don Daredevil Rides Again* (1951), *Carson City* (1952), *The World in His Arms* (1952), *His Majesty O'Keefe* (1953), *Column South* (1953), *Prince Valiant* (1954), *The Egyptian* (1954), *It's Always Fair Weather* (1955), *Prince of Players* (1955), *Pirates of Tripoli* (1955), *Battle Cry* (1955), *The Killing* (1956), *Around the World in Eighty Days* (1956), *Yaqui Drums* (1956), *Designing Woman* (1957), *The Tijuana Story* (1957), *Baby Face Nelson* (1957), *The Buccaneer* (1958), *Warlock* (1959), *Spartacus* (1960), *North to Alaska* (1960), *Elmer Gantry* (1960), *Ice Palace* (1960), *The Honeymoon Machine* (1961), *How the West Was Won* (1962), *From Russia with Love* (1963), *The Birds* (1963), *It's a Mad, Mad, Mad, Mad World* (1963), *4 for Texas* (1963), *Quick Before It Melts* (1964),

The Great Race (1965), *Our Man Flint* (1966), *The Silencers* (1966), *Fantastic Voyage* (1966), and *Red Tomahawk* (1967). TV credits include *Cheyenne, Zane Grey, Richard Diamond, M Squad, Peter Gunn, Trackdown, Riverboat, Laramie, The Man from U.N.C.L.E.,* and *Perry Mason*. Gorss died of a heart attack at the age of 58 while on the Columbia Studios set of *Murderers' Row* (1966). A member of the Stuntmen's Association, he was inducted into the Stuntmen's Hall of Fame.

See: "Dodges Reaper for Six Years, Retires at 30." *Plain Dealer*. March 27, 1938; "Sol Gorss." *Variety*. September 21, 1966.

BERNIE GOZIER (1917–1979)

Born in Los Angeles, Bernard Kikume Gozier was the son of Hawaiian actor Al Kikume. His dark skin allowed Gozier to portray Pacific Islanders, Native Americans, and Mexicans. His best known screen moment came fighting Ben Chapman's Gill Man with a machete in *Creature from the Black Lagoon* (1954). On TV he portrayed King Moses on the syndicated series *Bold Venture* (1959). Gozier doubled Anthony Quinn.

He also worked on *Mask of the Avenger* (1951), *Viva Zapata!* (1952), *Hiawatha* (1952), *City Beneath the Sea* (1953), *The Nebraskan* (1953), *Sign of the Pagan* (1954), *Kiss of Fire* (1955), *The Conqueror* (1956), *The Ten Commandments* (1956), *Walk the Proud Land* (1956), *Around the World in Eighty Days* (1956), and *Fort Massacre* (1958). TV credits include *Jim Bowie, Wagon Train, Sea Hunt, Wanted—Dead or Alive, Hawaiian Eye, Adventures in Paradise,* and *The Man from U.N.C.L.E.*

DICK GRACE (1898–1965)

Minnesota-born stunt pilot Dick Grace referred to himself as a "crash engineer," as his specialty was sending airplanes plummeting into the ground on films such as *Wings* (1927), *Lilac Time* (1928), *Young Eagles* (1930), and *Lost Squadron* (1932). The World War I flyer had a special technique he used to minimize the severity of his eighty MPH wrecks, first snapping off the right wing on contact with the ground, but his walking away in one piece was always in question. He crashed into a barn on *Sky High* (1920) and broke his neck tempting fate on *Wings*. In the course of nearly fifty on-screen crashes, Grace broke eighty bones. The former barnstormer's air crashes were popular as evidenced by the fact he top-lined *Flying Fool* (1925) and *Wide Open* (1927).

Grace entered the business with twenty-three other thrill-seeking pilots, called the "Squadron of Death." After a few years, eighteen of them had died making pictures, and the remaining men outside of Grace were crippled. Grace was still able to work, although he was knocked unconscious by the majority of his spectacular plane crashes. He wore shock absorbers, emptied gas tanks, and always had a rescue crew on hand to pull him out of burning wreckage. He studied the physics of any crash beforehand and tried to perform stunts at the time of 11:45 a.m. to minimize being blinded by the sun. Grace left Hollywood to serve with the Army Air Corps in World War II as a combat pilot and later opened a charter service in South America. An honorary member of the Stuntmen's Association and an inductee of the Stuntmen's Hall of Fame, Grace died from emphysema at the age of 67.

See: Grace, Dick. "Crashing Planes for the Movies." *Modern Mechanics.* July 1930; Grace, Dick. "I Crash for a Living." *Chums Annual.* 1933–1934; Grace, Dick. *I Am Still Alive.* New York: Rand, McNally, 1931; Grace, Dick. *Squadron of Death: The True Adventures of a Movie Plane Crasher.* NY: Doubleday, 1929.

MARTIN GRACE (1942–2010)

Six-foot-two, 200-pound Martin Ryan Grace was born in Kilkenny, Ireland. Grace was a talented rugby hurler who played for Lisdowney in the 1955 championship. The next year he won the St. Kieran's School League title. He played for Kilkenny City College and could have gone professional, but he set his sights on a career in the movies. He moved to London and joined boxing, wrestling, and fencing clubs while working as a lifeguard. He was enamored with bodybuilding and won the Hertford-Shire weightlifting championship. In addition to live stunt shows, he landed a job at the Butlins by the Sea resort as a sports organizer. In the mid–1960s he became the Cadbury Milk Tray Man, doing James Bond–like stunts in a series of commercials. These attracted the attention of Bob Simmons, who hired Grace for the volcano ninja sequence on *You Only Live Twice* (1967). He was briefly the Arthur Rank gong beater.

Grace became Roger Moore's double on *The Spy Who Loved Me* (1977), beginning a decade-long association with both Moore and the Bond franchise as double and stunt coordinator. Highlights include the cable car fight with Richard Kiel on *Moonraker* (1979), a wild helicopter ride on *For Your Eyes Only* (1981), a train-top battle on *Octopussy* (1983), and fights at both the Eiffel Tower and the Golden Gate Bridge on *A View to a Kill* (1985). He doubled Oliver Reed on *Assassination Bureau* (1969), Kirk Douglas on *To Catch a Spy* (1971), Richard Burton and Richard Harris on *The Wild Geese* (1978), and Harrison Ford on *Raiders of the Lost Ark* (1981), *Indiana Jones and the Temple of Doom* (1984), and *Indiana Jones and the Lost Crusade* (1989). He fought Anthony Hopkins on *When Eight Bells Toll* (1971) and he made a 100-foot fall off the Minaret in Rhodes on *Escape to Athena* (1979).

His career was not without injury. Grace broke his neck doubling Albert Finney on *Scrooge* (1970) and suffered a serious, life-threatening injury making *Octopussy* while holding onto the side of the train. While capturing aerial shots, the complicated communication and logistics involved between all parties became bungled as Grace concentrated on the actual physical action. When the train passed under a bridge on uncharted track, Grace's hip was slammed into a wall built parallel to the track. Amazingly, he had the arm strength to hold on despite suffering a broken pelvis and a deep thigh laceration. Had he been unable to maintain his grip during the impact, he likely would have fallen under the train and died. Grace was laid up in the hospital for nearly a year but was back in action on the next Bond film. He also worked on *Dr. Who and the Daleks* (1965), *Mayerling* (1968), *Great Catherine* (1968), *Alfred the Great* (1969), *Moon Zero Two* (1969), *Cromwell* (1970), *Yellow Dog* (1976), *Superman* (1978), *Ffolkes* (1979), and *The Sea Wolves* (1980). TV credits include *The Protectors* and *Space 1999*. An inductee into the Stuntmen's Hall of Fame, Grace died at the age of 67 following a bicycle accident in Spain.

See: Autry, Jon. "Martin Grace: Local Hero." Retrieved on July 11, 2013, at www.issuu.com; Hayward, Anthony. "Martin Grace: Roger Moore's Stunt Double in the James Bond Films." *Independent.* February 12, 2010; Pirani, Adam. "Martin Grace: Bruising It Out with James Bond." *Starlog.* February 1986; Weiner, David Jon. *Burns, Falls, and Crashes.* Jefferson, NC: McFarland, 1996; www.roger-moore.com.

FRED GRAHAM (1908–1979)

Fred "Slugger" Graham was known as one of the best fight men in the business, having gained his reputation at Warner Brothers on *Dodge City* (1939) before moving on to Republic. Graham often played bit parts, saying a few lines before trading punches with the leads. On occasion he was the top dog heavy. Graham fought all the B-cowboy heroes, including Roy Rogers, Sunset Carson, Bill Elliott, Allan Lane, William Boyd, Monte Hale, Tim Holt, and Rex Allen. His best fights came against Victor McLaglen on *She Wore a Yellow Ribbon* (1949), Robert Preston on *Tulsa* (1949), Arthur Kennedy on *Rancho Notorious* (1952), Rod Cameron on *Fort Osage* (1952), and Jock Mahoney on *Overland Pacific* (1954). Graham served as John Wayne's double for the better part of a decade beginning with *In Old California*

(1942) and including *Tall in the Saddle* (1944) and *Sands of Iwo Jima* (1949).

Charles Frederick Graham was born in Springer, New Mexico. He played for the USC football squad and was a semi-pro baseball player, though there's little history on Graham's early years. Graham began working behind the scenes at the movie studios and was recruited to double Nat Pendleton as a baseball catcher on *Death on the Diamond* (1934). He doubled Basil Rathbone for the fall from the top of a wall on *The Adventures of Robin Hood* (1938), Charles Bickford on *The Storm* (1938) and *Valley of the Giants* (1938), Ward Bond for the classic brawl on *Canyon Passage* (1946), Albert Dekker for the donnybrook on *Wyoming* (1947), and Robert Preston on *Wild Harvest* (1947). He doubled Clark Gable on *Mutiny on the Bounty* (1935), as well as Gregory Peck, John Payne, Nelson Eddy, Roy Barcroft, Johnny Mack Brown, Barton MacLane, Joe Sawyer, Reed Hadley, and William Haade.

In the Republic western *Silver City Kid*

Fred Graham is knocked through a store window by actor Kirk Douglas on *20,000 Leagues Under the Sea* (1954).

(1944), Graham shows up early as Glenn Strange's double in a saloon brawl with star Allan Lane's double Tom Steele. Graham is next seen a few scenes later playing a henchman who fights Lane. Shortly after that, Lane fights Steele (who is playing another henchman), and Graham doubles Lane for this fight. By the film's end Lane fights dress heavy Harry Woods on a cliff's edge, and Woods is doubled by none other than Graham. On *Dakota* (1945) he was hired to double John Wayne, played a thug heavy, and wound up doubling Mike Mazurki when the pro wrestler suffered an injury.

The 200-pound six-footer also worked on *Heart of the North* (1938), *The Roaring Twenties* (1939), *Each Dawn I Die* (1939), *Seven Sinners* (1940), *Brother Orchid* (1940), *Flowing Gold* (1940), *Winners of the West* (1940), *Manpower* (1941), *Shadow of the Thin Man* (1941), *Reap the Wild Wind* (1942), *Pittsburgh* (1942), *In Old Oklahoma* (1943), *The Masked Marvel* (1943), *Murder My Sweet* (1944), *Captain America* (1944), *Haunted Harbor* (1944), *The Tiger Woman* (1944), *Zorro's Black Whip* (1944), *Passage to Marseille* (1944), *Buffalo Bill* (1944), *Manhunt of Mystery Island* (1945), *The Spanish Main* (1945), *Federal Operator 99* (1945), *The Razor's Edge* (1946), *Angel and the Badman* (1947), *Exposed* (1947), *Tycoon* (1947), *Jesse James Rides Again* (1947), *Son of Zorro* (1947), *The Man from Colorado* (1948), *Adventures of Frank and Jesse James* (1948), *Fort Apache* (1948), *Wake of the Red Witch* (1948), *The Fighting Kentuckian* (1949), *Samson and Delilah* (1949), *The Woman on Pier 13* (1950), *Mister 880* (1950), *Captain China* (1950), *The Asphalt Jungle* (1950), *Dallas* (1950), *Key to the City* (1950), *Lorna Doone* (1951), *Flying Leathernecks* (1951), *Across the Wide Missouri* (1951), *The San Francisco Story* (1952), *The Big Sky* (1952), *Kansas Pacific* (1952), *The World in His Arms* (1952), *Scarlet Angel* (1952), *The War of the Worlds* (1953), *Escape from Fort Bravo* (1953), *Demetrius and the Gladiators* (1954), *Rear Window* (1954), *20,000 Leagues Under the Sea* (1954), *The Killing* (1956), *The Conqueror* (1956), *Backlash* (1956), *The Last Hunt* (1956), *Seven Men from Now* (1956), *Thunder Over Arizona* (1956), *The Wings of Eagles* (1957), *Man in the Shadow* (1957), *Jet Pilot* (1957), *The Sheepman* (1958), *Vertigo* (1958), *Badman's Country* (1958), *Rio Bravo* (1959), *The Horse Soldiers* (1959), *The Alamo* (1960), *North to Alaska* (1960), *Seven Ways from Sundown* (1960), and *Arizona Raiders* (1965). TV credits include *Roy Rogers*, *Sgt. Preston*, *Wyatt Earp*, *Zane Grey*, *Broken Arrow*, *Restless Gun*, *Maverick*, *Gunsmoke*, *Tales of Wells Fargo*, *Have Gun—Will Travel*, *Law of the Plainsman*, *Yancy Derringer*, *The Rifleman*, *The Texan*, *Sugarfoot*, *Lawman*, *Laramie*, *Shotgun Slade*, *Surfside 6*, *Rawhide*, and *Perry Mason*. An honorary member of the Stuntmen's Association and an inductee of the Stuntmen's Hall of Fame, Graham retired to Arizona to head up the Department of Economic Planning and Development of Motion Pictures while fronting a small film studio in Carefree.

See: Andrews, Bart. "Super Stunt Man: Fred Graham." *Falling for Stars*. Vol. 1 #7 September/October 1965; "Fred Graham." *Variety*. November 7, 1979.

JOE GRAY (1912–1971)

Brooklyn-born Joe Gray was the brother of George Raft's long-time stand-in and gopher Mack Gray. Joe also stood in for Raft and doubled him for a fight on *Christmas Eve* (1947). A 170-pound middleweight, the six-foot-tall Joe Gray boxed professionally and portrayed pugilists on *A Star Is Born* (1937), *Golden Boy* (1939), *City for Conquest* (1940), *Body and Soul* (1947), and *Champion* (1949). He later became a technical advisor and fight choreographer. Gray was a stand-in and stuntman for Tony Curtis on *Some Like it Hot* (1959), and Elvis Presley on *Loving You* (1957), *Jailhouse Rock* (1957), *King Creole* (1958), *G.I. Blues* (1960), and *Kid Galahad* (1962). He was with Dean Martin on more than thirty films, including *Rio Bravo* (1959).

He worked on *Each Dawn I Die* (1939), *Beau Geste* (1939), *Mighty Joe Young* (1949), *The War of the Worlds* (1953), *The Buccaneer* (1958), *The Young Lions* (1958), *Some Came Running* (1958), *Ocean's Eleven* (1960), *The Comancheros* (1961), *The Manchurian Candidate* (1962), *Taras Bulba* (1962), *Sergeants Three* (1962), *4 for Texas* (1963), *Von Ryan's Express* (1965), *None But the Brave* (1965), *Our Man Flint* (1966), *The Silencers* (1966), *Murderers Row* (1966), *Rough Night in Jericho* (1967), *The Ambushers* (1967), *Bandolero!* (1968), *The Wrecking Crew* (1969), *Che!* (1969), and *Airport* (1970). Gray died from a heart attack in Mexico while working on *Something Big* (1971).

See: Wallace, Stone. *George Raft: The Man*

Who Would Be Bogart. Albany, GA: BearManor, 2008; Winslow, Kathryn. *Henry Miller: Full of Life.* NY: J.P. Tarcher, 1986.

RICHARD GRAYDON (1922–)

Five-foot-eight, 140-pound former jockey Richard Graydon is known for performing high work on the Bond films. His best moment came in a fight atop a cable car with Martin Grace on *Moonraker* (1979). He doubled George Lazenby on a cable for *On Her Majesty's Secret Service* (1969) and Roger Moore atop a train on *Octopussy* (1983). Other Bond films that Graydon worked include *From Russia with Love* (1963), *Goldfinger* (1964), *Thunderball* (1965), *You Only Live Twice* (1967), *The Spy Who Loved Me* (1977), *For Your Eyes Only* (1981), and *A View to a Kill* (1985).

Graydon began stunts after World War II service on *Robin Hood and His Merrie Men* (1952) and later worked on *Lawrence of Arabia* (1962), *Charge of the Light Brigade* (1968), *Where Eagles Dare* (1968), *The Last Valley* (1971), *When Eight Bells Toll* (1971), *Don't Look Now* (1973), *Royal Flash* (1975), *The Man Who Fell to Earth* (1976), *The Duelists* (1977), *Star Wars* (1977), *International Velvet* (1978), *Ffolkes* (1979), and *Raiders of the Lost Ark* (1981).

DUKE GREEN (1900–1984)

Duke Green was one of the best "high-men" in the stunt business, where he earned the nickname "Crazy Duke" for his spectacular falls. If someone is falling from a balcony during a fight from the 1920s to the 1940s there's a high probability that man is Duke Green. He was paid $800 to fight atop a power pole on *Manpower* (1941). On *Spy Smasher* (1942) he launched himself off a twenty-foot staircase onto Dave Sharpe, then fell another thirty feet onto a table. He was capable of brawling on terra firma as well and did many conventional fight scenes. He and fellow stuntman Chick Collins worked a memorable fight with James Cagney on *Something to Sing About* (1937). Green doubled John Barrymore on *The Sea Beast* (1926) and *Don Juan* (1926), Jack Oakie on *Call of the Wild* (1935), Edward G. Robinson on *Brother Orchid* (1940), Humphrey Bogart on *Action in the North Atlantic* (1943), and even big John Wayne swinging from a chandelier on *Seven Sinners* (1940). He also doubled Brian Donlevy,

Buck Jones, J. Carrol Naish, Akim Tamiroff, and Allan Lane.

William A. Green was born in Los Angeles and was a fancy diver, tumbler, and competitive swimmer. He worked as a lifeguard and telephone lineman while continuing as an exhibition diver. Green was one of the bedrock contributors of the Republic serial stunt aces, often essaying as many as a half dozen roles in a single serial such as *The Masked Marvel* (1943). On *The Flame and the Arrow* (1950) he suffered a serious injury. The stunt called for his foot to be trapped in a snare and for Green to be whipped off the ground. Unfortunately, the rigging broke and sent Green plummeting head first to the ground, breaking his neck. Covered only by Worker's Compensation, he endured several operations. He was reduced to extra work although he occasionally found himself throwing punches on the outskirts of large crowd brawls.

He worked on *Lucky Devils* (1932), *Fireman, Save My Child* (1932), *King Kong* (1933), *Footlight Parade* (1933), *High Tension* (1936), *Thank You, Jeeves* (1936), *Nancy Steele Is Missing* (1937), *Slave Ship* (1937), *The Lone Ranger* (1938), *Dick Tracy Returns* (1938), *Beau Geste* (1939), *Dodge City* (1939), *Man of Conquest* (1939), *Secret Service of the Air* (1939), *King of the Royal Mounted* (1940), *Drums of Fu Manchu* (1940), *King of the Texas Rangers* (1941), *Birth of the Blues* (1941), *Perils of Nyoka* (1942), *Wake Island* (1942), *Desperate Journey* (1942), *Daredevils of the West* (1943), *Haunted Harbor* (1944), *Saratoga Trunk* (1945), *Manhunt of Mystery Island* (1945), *The Spanish Main* (1945), *They Were Expendable* (1945), *Federal Operator 99* (1945), *Adventures of Frank and Jesse James* (1948), *G-Men Never Forget* (1948), *Mighty Joe Young* (1949), *The Stand at Apache River* (1953), *Blood Alley* (1955), *Donovan's Reef* (1963), and *The Great Race* (1965). He was an honorary member of the Stuntmen's Association and an inductee of the Stuntmen's Hall of Fame.

TURK GREENOUGH (1905–1995)

Thurkel James Greenough was born in Red Lodge, Montana, and grew up in a rodeo family. As a young man "Turk" performed in the Miller Bros. 101 Show and enjoyed great success as a bronc rider, becoming the first cowboy to capture titles at Calgary, Cheyenne, and Pendleton in the same year. Greenough worked on more than fifty films doubling Tex Ritter, Roy Rogers, Gene Autry, Randolph Scott, and Bruce Cabot. During World War II he served with the U.S. Cavalry. Upon retiring from films, he worked as a security guard in Las Vegas casinos.

The 5'10", 170-pound stunter's credits include *Billy the Kid* (1930), *The Crusades* (1935), *Phantom Empire* (1935), *Song of the Gringo* (1936), *Man from Texas* (1939), *Beau Geste* (1939), *Gone with the Wind* (1939), *Boom Town* (1940), *Prairie Pioneers* (1941), *The Outlaw* (1943), *Duel in the Sun* (1946), *Angel and the Badman* (1947), *Warpath* (1951), and *The Homesteaders* (1953). He was a member of the National Cowboy Hall of Fame.

See: Ringley, Tom. *When the Whistle Blows: The Turk Greenough Story.* Greybull, WY: Pronghorn, 2008; "Turk Greenough." *Lexington Herald Ledger.* June 4, 1995.

TED GROSSMAN (1931–)

Ted Grossman played basketball and football for Beverly Hills High and was a backup quarterback at the College of the Pacific. He toured Australia, New Zealand, and France on an American All-Star rugby team in the early 1950s despite the fact that none of the football players on the team had played rugby. He also played volleyball in the Maccabiah Games. The 5'10", 160-pound Grossman worked as a policeman as he began a stunt career. Early on he doubled Clark Gable and Alan Ladd. He is best known for being Roy Scheider's stuntman and the estuary victim on *Jaws* (1975). Grossman was a stuntman on several Steven Spielberg and George Lucas films such as *Return of the Jedi* (1983), *Indiana Jones and the Temple of Doom* (1984), and *Indiana Jones and the Last Crusade* (1989). He leaped off a capsizing van into mud on *The Sugarland Express* (1974) and portrayed the Peruvian Porter on *Raiders of the Lost Ark* (1981).

He worked on *John Goldfarb, Please Come Home* (1965), *Che!* (1969), *The Only Game in Town* (1970), *What's Up, Doc?* (1972), *Conquest of the Planet of the Apes* (1972), *The Thief Who Came to Dinner* (1973), *The Don Is Dead* (1973), *Magnum Force* (1973), *Sssssss* (1973), *The Godfather Part II* (1974), *Thunderbolt and Lightfoot* (1974), *Night Moves* (1975), *Swashbuckler* (1976), *Jaws 2* (1978), and *Last Embrace* (1979). TV credits include *Bearcats, Police Story,* and *Starsky and Hutch.*

See: Simers, T.J. "This Power Lunch Leads to Guy with Fishy Story." *Los Angeles Times.* September 30, 2003; Zimmerman, Paul. "Smartest Man in the NFL." *Sports Illustrated.* August 29, 1988.

DAN HAGGERTY (1941–)

Dan Haggerty is best known as the bearded star of the popular TV series *Grizzly Adams* (1977–79), based on the successful independent films *The Life and Times of Grizzly Adams* (1974) and *Adventures of Frontier Fremont* (1976). For a short time period, audiences couldn't get enough of the man and his bear, and the series remains a nostalgic favorite. Haggerty got the mountain man roles due to his reputation as an animal trainer-stuntman on the TV series *Tarzan* (1966–68) and *Daktari* (1967–69). As the star of *Tender Warrior* (1971) he wrestled every animal the script threw at him. Haggerty was also a motorcyclist and could not only handle the big bikes for the screen but custom-build them as well.

The 6'1", 195-pound Haggerty was born in Hollywood and played football at Burbank High. He worked construction and was cast as a bodybuilder on *Muscle Beach Party* (1963). During the filming of *Tarzan and the Great River* (1967), star Mike Henry was bit on the chin by a chimpanzee in Brazil. Haggerty stepped in to double Tarzan so the film wouldn't have to shut down. He also worked on *Tarzan and the Valley of Gold* (1966), *Lt. Robin Crusoe* (1966), *Monkeys, Go Home!* (1967), *Tarzan and the Jungle Boy* (1968), *Glory Stompers* (1967), *The Christmas Tree* (1969), *Angels Die Hard* (1970), *Wild Country* (1970), *Chrome and Hot Leather* (1971), *Hex* (1973) and *When the North Wind Blows* (1974).

See: Davidson, Bill. "Bozo and Dan Are an Item!" *TV Guide.* June 11, 1977; Scott, Vernon. "Grizzly Star is Real Animal Trainer." *Rome Tribune.* February 11, 1977; Pearson, Howard. "Stuntmen the Unsung Heroes." *Deseret News.* July 16, 1977.

JOHNNY HAGNER (1928–)

John G. Hagner was born in Baltimore and served with the U.S. Navy. Upon coming to California he landed a job as the double for Gardner McKay on the TV series *Adventures in Paradise* (1959–62). The 6'2" stunter doubled Walter Pid-

Actor-stuntman Dan Haggerty scales a mountain with a bear cub on his back on *The Life and Times of Grizzly Adams* (1974).

geon on *Voyage to the Bottom of the Sea* (1961) and Gregory Peck on *Captain Newman, M.D.* (1963), and was seen as a baker during the pie fight sequence in *The Great Race* (1965). He worked on *The Greatest Story Ever Told* (1965) and the TV series *Voyage to the Bottom of the Sea, Batman,* and *Felony Squad*. In 1965 he staged action for the play *Teddy Roosevelt Rides Again* at the Burning Hills Amphitheatre in the Badlands of North Dakota. Hagner was the founder of the Hollywood Stuntmen's Hall of Fame and wrote a number of self-published books on stuntmen featuring his original illustrations.

See: Hagner, John. *Inside Stunts.* "John Hagner's Hollywood Stuntmen's Hall of Fame." Summer, 2006.

FRANK HAGNEY (1884–1973)

Six-foot-two, 215-pound Frank Sidney Hagney was born in Sydney, New South Wales, Australia, and participated in athletics for Sydney College. The muscular Hagney distinguished himself as one of the best oarsmen in the world when he was crowned the Champion Professional Single Sculler of Australia 1912–1913. As late as 1927 he won the 24-mile Long Beach to Santa Catalina Island rowboat race. Not content having mastered this sport, Hagney competed as a bicycle racer and as a professional heavyweight boxer from 1910 to 1921. He won the Australian Heavyweight Championship and fought solid competition. He lost a six-round decision to Luis Firpo and served as heavyweight champion Jack Johnson's sparring partner from 1914 to 1917. Hagney even wrestled professionally and performed in vaudeville acts.

His boxing reputation landed him in Hollywood as the technical director for the fight scenes on *The Battler* (1919). Hagney worked for silent movie action star Charles Hutchinson on *Hurricane Hutch* (1921) and was paid $5 a stunt. Hagney opposed Fred Thomson on several westerns and boxing films such as *Two Gun Man* (1926), fought heavyweight champ Gene Tunney on *Fighting Marine* (1926), and stood out as the Mexican titlist who boxes Wallace Beery on *The Champ* (1931). By the end of his first decade of acting, Hagney had lost the heavyweight title twenty-nine times on the big screen. His thick build and features made him a fine choice to double Victor McLaglen. Hagney subsequently played

all kinds of thugs and mugs. He continued to perform physical roles into his eighties, making over 350 films.

He worked on *Captain Lash* (1929), *The Squaw Man* (1931), *Fighting Caravans* (1931), *Treasure Island* (1934), *The Informer* (1935), *Magnificent Brute* (1936), *Mysterious Mr. Moto* (1938), *The Adventures of Robin Hood* (1938), *Captain Fury* (1939), *Dark Command* (1940), *Seven Sinners* (1940), *Reap the Wild Wind* (1942), *Gentleman Jim* (1942), *Frenchman's Creek* (1944), *Saratoga Trunk* (1945), *Adventure* (1945), *Wild Harvest* (1947), *The Three Musketeers* (1948), *Joan of Arc* (1948), *Samson and Delilah* (1949), *Fortunes of Captain Blood* (1950), *Soldiers Three* (1951), *The Big Trees* (1952), *The Last Posse* (1953), *Demetrius and the Gladiators* (1954), *King Richard and the Crusaders* (1954), *The Silver Chalice* (1954), *The Ten Commandments* (1956), *Showdown at Abilene* (1956), *The Buccaneer* (1958), and *Donovan's Reef* (1963).

See: "Frank Hagney Is Film Specialist in Fast Scrapt." *Los Angeles Times.* July 20, 1924; "Safe Business." *Toledo Blade.* May 13, 1931.

DONNA HALL (1928–2002)

Rodeo trick rider Donna Hall was born in Los Angeles. Her father was jockey-stuntman Frank "Shorty" Hall, a silent film double for Mary Pickford and Marion Davies. Donna's first stunt involved racing a thoroughbred around a track at the age of eight on *Little Miss Adventure* (1938). She entered stunts full-time after graduating from Burbank High with Polly Burson serving as her mentor. Hall's specialty was horses, and she was capable of driving four-up and six-up teams as evidenced by her doubling of Susan Clark on *The Apple Dumpling Gang* (1975). She doubled Doris Day on *Calamity Jane* (1953), Barbara Stanwyck on *The Violent Men* (1955) and *The Maverick Queen* (1956), Debbie Reynolds on *How the West Was Won* (1962), and Jane Fonda on *Cat Ballou* (1965). She also stood in for Judy Garland, Shirley Temple, Joan Collins, and Ginger Rogers. On TV, Hall doubled Gail Davis on *Annie Oakley* (1954–57).

She worked on *Annie Get Your Gun* (1950), *Westward the Women* (1952), *The Big Country* (1958), *Spartacus* (1960), *Cheyenne Autumn* (1964), *The Great Race* (1965), *The Rare Breed* (1965), *The Reivers* (1969), *Little Big Man* (1970),

Black Sunday (1977), and *Hot Lead and Cold Feet* (1978). She was a charter member of the Stuntwomen's Association, an inductee of the Stuntmen's Hall of Fame, and a Golden Boot Award honoree. Married to horse wrangler Jay Fishburn, Hall died from pneumonia at the age of 74.

See: De Witt, Barbara. "Those Stunts Were No Act for Hollywood's Horse Women." *Chicago Tribune.* March 16, 1995; McLellan, Dennis. "Donna Hall Fishburn, 74; Veteran Stunt Double Worked on Westerns." *Los Angeles Times.* August 19, 2002; Thomas, Bob. "Hollywood's Angry." *Oakland Tribune.* June 13, 1976.

JACKIE HAMBLIN (1933–)

Jackie Hamblin from Kanab, Utah, was a local legend. She came from a family of wranglers who worked on films made in the area. At the age of six she was recruited for her first stunt on *Drums Along the Mohawk* (1939), portraying a child attacked by an Indian. Her next films were *Buffalo Bill* (1944) and *Green Grass of Wyoming* (1948). As an adult, Hamblin became a regular presence doubling female stars on area films, including Denise Darcel on *Westward the Women* (1951). She was a stand-in or double for Marie Windsor, Mamie Van Doren, Rita Moreno, Mona Freeman, and Peggie Castle.

She worked on *Red Canyon* (1949), *Calamity Jane and Sam Bass* (1949), *The Outriders* (1950), *Pony Express* (1953), *Yellow Tomahawk* (1954), *Fort Yuma* (1955), *Revolt at Fort Laramie* (1957), *War Drums* (1957), *Dragoon Wells Massacre* (1957), *Fort Bowie* (1958), *The Badlanders* (1958), and *Sergeants Three* (1962). In later years she worked at the Kanab Visitors Center. The Little Hollywood Museum in Kanab honored her with the exhibit "Jackie Hamblin: Hard Fighting Stuntwoman."

See: "Kanab's Walk of Fame to Laud 70 Year Old Utahn." *Deseret News.* May 25, 2004; "Utah Film Stunt Girl Starts Emcee Career" *Deseret News.* March 22, 1957.

CHUCK HAMILTON (1903–1978)

Charles Hamilton Pracht was born in Vallejo, California. Of rugged stature, he played soldiers, warriors, and pirates in the costume epics *The Ten Commandments* (1923), *Cleopatra* (1934),

The Crusades (1935), and *The Buccaneer* (1938). His career was lengthy and prolific enough that Hamilton worked in the same capacity on the Cecil B. DeMille remakes of *The Ten Commandments* (1956) and *The Buccaneer* (1958). He handled doubling assignments for actors such as Lyle Talbot and racked up credits on more than 300 films.

He worked on *Her Man* (1930), *The Plainsman* (1936), *Big Broadcast of 1936* (1936), *Gone with the Wind* (1939), *Union Pacific* (1939), *North West Mounted Police* (1940), *Winners of the West* (1940), *Holt of the Secret Service* (1941), *Reap the Wild Wind* (1942), *Pittsburgh* (1942), *Captain Midnight* (1942), *Desert Hawk* (1944), *The Spanish Main* (1945), *Unconquered* (1947), *Brute Force* (1947), *Wild Harvest* (1947), *Joan of Arc* (1948), *The Fuller Brush Man* (1948), *The Doolins of Oklahoma* (1949), *Samson and Delilah* (1949), *Flame of Araby* (1951), *The Greatest Show on Earth* (1952), *Against All Flags* (1952), *Lone Star* (1952), *Yankee Buccaneer* (1952), *Law and Order* (1953), *Prince Valiant* (1954), *Dawn at Socorro* (1954), *The Man from Bitter Ridge* (1955), *Around the World in Eighty Days* (1956), *The Tin Star* (1957), and *Slaughter on Tenth Avenue* (1957). He appeared as an extra on several later TV episodes. Hamilton died at the age of 75.

See: "Vets Go Modern in Radio Picture." *Evening Tribune.* January 28, 1936.

CHICK HANNAN (1901–1980)

Michigan-born Chester William Hannan went from being a rodeo champion to horse rider in B-westerns. He was small enough in stature to double females such as Tex Ritter's actress wife Dorothy Fay. He worked on *Melody Ranch* (1939), *In Old California* (1942), *Albuquerque* (1948), *Return of the Badmen* (1948), *The Plunderers* (1948), *The Paleface* (1948), *Warpath* (1951), *Flaming Feather* (1952), *The Lawless Breed* (1952), *The Man Behind the Gun* (1953), *Arrowhead* (1953), *Escape from Fort Bravo* (1953), *Column South* (1953), *Johnny Guitar* (1954), *Around the World in Eighty Days* (1956), and *Gun Duel in Durango* (1957). TV credits include *Hopalong Cassidy, Stories of the Century, Kit Carson,* and *Wagon Train.* He became a representative for the American Humane Association on *The Good Guys and the Bad Guys* (1969) and *Wild Country* (1970).

See: "Movie Animals Get Protector." *Miami News.* October 16, 1968.

DON HAPPY (1916–2006)

Don Happy from Lewiston, Idaho, was a successful high school athlete at Clarkson High. He played football and competed in track at Washington State. Happy was a champion in the Pendleton Rodeo as a bulldogger and saddle bronc rider and later specialized as a pickup man separating the riders and animals after a throw. A dislocated shoulder kept him from military service, but he did build a landing strip in Alaska as part of a construction crew. Happy worked as a stuntman on TV's *Gunsmoke* (1955–75) for all twenty years that the show was on the air. He doubled Steve Cochran on *The Lion and the Horse* (1951) as well as Robert Mitchum, Ronald Reagan, and Ken Curtis.

He worked on *Gunsmoke* (1953), *Column South* (1953), *Tumbleweed* (1953), *Westward Ho, the Wagons!* (1956), *Walk the Proud Land* (1956), *Ride a Crooked Trail* (1958), *The Sheepman* (1958), *Westbound* (1959), *Seven Ways from Sundown* (1960), *Spartacus* (1960), and *Flaming Star* (1960). TV credits include *Roy Rogers, The Big Valley,* and *Bonanza*. His wife Edith was a stuntwoman, and their children Bonnie and Clifford and daughter-in-law Marguerite all became stunt people.

See: Brinkerhoff, Mary. "Rodeo's Most Happy Family." *Dallas Morning News*. December 27, 1961; "Empty Saddles." *Western Clippings*. #72, July-August 2006; "Movie Stunt Couple Will Appear in Rodeo." *Los Angeles Times*. November 29, 1957.

BOB HARRIS (1923–)

Born in Long Beach, California, Robert Harris worked for Union Pacific Railroad and in shipyards before entering the U.S. Army. Postwar he earned a commercial pilot's license and had a chance meeting with actor Keenan Wynn. The two became friends and Wynn got Harris into the Screen Extras Guild. The 5'11", 170-pound Harris had an acting part in addition to performing stunt work on the TV series *Troubleshooters* (1959–60). He was the driving double for Elvis Presley on *Viva Las Vegas* (1964), *Spinout* (1966), and *Speedway* (1968). A vehicular specialist, he drove can-am race cars competitively for his actor friend Dan Blocker and was still racing motorcycles into his eighties.

He worked on *The Crowded Sky* (1960), *Bonnie and Clyde* (1967), *Bullitt* (1968), *Angels from Hell* (1968), *The Love Bug* (1968), *Hells Angels '69* (1969), *Dirty Harry* (1971), *Evel Knievel* (1971), *Diamonds Are Forever* (1971), *What's Up, Doc?* (1972), *Dillinger* (1973), *Magnum Force* (1973), *Thunderbolt and Lightfoot* (1974), *The Sugarland Express* (1974), *The Gumball Rally* (1976), *Family Plot* (1976), *Herbie Goes to Monte Carlo* (1977), *The Deer Hunter* (1978), *The Cat from Outer Space* (1978), and *The China Syndrome* (1979). TV credits include *Bonanza, Mannix,* and *Barnaby Jones*. Harris is a member of the Stuntmen's Association and an inductee of the Stuntmen's Hall of Fame.

See: McGuire, Barbara Sueko. "Memento Mori." *Sunday Salon*. February 2009.

BRAD HARRIS (1933–)

Five-foot-eleven, 185-pound Bradford Jan Harris was born in St. Anthony, Idaho. He was raised in California, where he was an excellent athlete at Burbank High in football, basketball, and track. Harris began lifting weights with William Smith in the latter's garage and received a scholarship to play football at UCLA as a fullback. He tore up his knee in his first season and rehabilitated through weight-lifting and martial arts. He took to the dedicated training, and rippling muscles exploded across his body. He sported 18" arms, a 49" chest, and a 31" waist. He never sought out any bodybuilding competition, but he became a fixture of the Muscle Beach scene with time out for service in the U.S. Army.

Harris doubled for Richard Jaeckel and appeared in war action for *The McConnell Story* (1955) and *Monkey on My Back* (1957). He was in the Mae West Revue, appeared as a muscleman on *Li'l Abner* (1959), and logged time as a stuntman on *Spartacus* (1960). While visiting the 1960 Olympic Games in Rome he accepted an offer to coordinate stunts and handle second unit chores on a European production and realized they had much to learn in the way of stunt work. He began training stunt crews there, and served as a stunt coordinator on many European films.

His presence in Europe coincided with the popularity of the Steve Reeves sword-and-sandal films. With his square jaw and handsome face, Harris was quickly recruited to top-line *Samson* (1961), *Fury of Hercules* (1961), and *Goliath*

Against the Giants (1961). When the peplum films died out, he was versatile enough to move into spy films and spaghetti westerns, enjoying great popularity as an international action star who always did his own wild stunts. Arnold Schwarzenegger was a fan and trained with Harris at Vince's Gym when he first came to America. Harris is an inductee of the Stuntmen's Hall of Fame.

See: Boller, Reiner. *Brad Harris: Ein Amerikanischer Bayer.* Munchen: Gryphon-Verlag, 2005; "Brad Harris." *MuscleMag International.* January 1983; Mozee, Gene. "Brad Harris: Very Alive at 75." *Iron Man.* October 2008; Tyler, Dick. *West Coast Bodybuilding Scene.* Santa Cruz, CA: On Target, 2004.

BILL HART (1934–)

Bill Hart was born as Bill Welch in Red Oak, Texas. A 180-pound six-footer, he was a fine athlete and excelled at football for Edinburgh High. A skull fracture prevented him from going further in that sport, but didn't keep him from spending four years with the U.S. Marines. He relocated to California and married stuntman Chuck Roberson's daughter. His first big film was *The Alamo* (1960), and it was John Wayne who wrote Hart's letter of recommendation for the Guild. Hart was a fight and horse specialist featuring a falling horse named Tadpole and a rearing-falling horse named Alamo.

Hart was stunt coordinator on the TV rodeo series *Stoney Burke* (1962–63) and also served as Jack Lord and Warren Oates' double for non-rodeo scenes. This was in addition to portraying the recurring character Red. Hart was one of the stuntmen blown off the bridge in the famous stunt scene on Sam Peckinpah's *The Wild Bunch* (1969). He became the double for Glenn Ford and continued with him for twenty-five years on *The Last Challenge* (1967), *Day of the Evil Gun* (1968), *Heaven with a Gun* (1969), *Santee* (1973), and the TV series *Cade's County* (1971–72).

He worked on *The Comancheros* (1961),

Bill Hart is jerked off a horse as Kevin Corcoran hits him with a rifle on *Savage Sam* (1963).

McLintock! (1963), *Savage Sam* (1963), *A Distant Trumpet* (1964), *Mail Order Bride* (1964), *The Rounders* (1965), *Duel at Diablo* (1966), *Hurry Sundown* (1967), *Firecreek* (1968), *There Was a Crooked Man...* (1970), *The Getaway* (1972), *Pat Garrett and Billy the Kid* (1973), *Drum* (1976), *Bound for Glory* (1976), *The Frisco Kid* (1979), *The Sacketts* (1979), *Tom Horn* (1980), *The Hunter* (1980), and *Heaven's Gate* (1980). TV credits include *Have Gun—Will Travel, Zane Grey, Wanted: Dead or Alive, Stagecoach West, The Outer Limits, Bonanza, Cimarron Strip,* and *Gunsmoke.* Hart was a charter member of the Stuntmen's Association and an inductee of the Stuntmen's Hall of Fame. His son Chuck Hart became a stuntman.

See: Lilley, Tim. *Campfire Conversations Complete.* Akron, Ohio: Big Trail, 2010; "Valley Stunt Man Hits TV Big Time." *San Antonio Express.* May 12, 1963.

JOHN HART (1917–2009)

Six-foot-two, 200-pound John Lewis Hart was born in Los Angeles. An excellent swimmer, skin diver, and surfer, he served as a lifeguard and worked on cattle ranches during summer breaks. At South Pasadena High he played football and basketball and went on to Pasadena Junior College until a leg injury forced him to give up football. He dabbled in amateur boxing, fighting fifteen bouts until a broken nose convinced him to quit. Hart landed a Paramount contract and played a pirate on *The Buccaneer* (1938). To supplement his acting income he worked for a private detective agency. During World War II Hart served with the U.S. Army's Coast Artillery and Air Service Command and was stationed in the Philippines at Subic Bay with the Signal Service Battalion of the First Air Force.

Hart found it difficult to resume his acting career and took a job doubling Jon Hall on *Last of the Redmen* (1947). This led to stunt assignments on Sam Katzman serials in addition to *Two Flags West* (1950) and *Warpath* (1951), where he doubled Forrest Tucker for a fight. One of his most interesting jobs came as the stunt double for stuntman Jock Mahoney on the serial *Gunfighters of the Northwest* (1954). Mahoney did all of his own stunts, but Hart wound up doubling co-star Clayton Moore for some horse work.

Hart landed starring roles on the serials *Jack Armstrong* (1947) and *Adventures of Captain Africa* (1955) and won the role of TV's the Lone Ranger in 1952 when Clayton Moore left during a contract dispute. Hart played the Masked Man for fifty-two episodes over a season and a half until Moore returned to the popular role, thus forever labeling Hart as "the other Lone Ranger." Hart next starred on the Canadian series *Hawkeye and the Last of the Mohicans* (1956–57). He took a recurring assignment as a nondescript drover on *Rawhide* for two seasons as his career wound down. He was very good at fight scenes and prided himself for his ability to make them look realistic. One of his best brawls came against Jim Davis in the little seen *Wolf Dog* (1958), a Canadian feature Hart filmed using the pseudonym B. Braithwaite (his wife's name) due to Canadian labor laws.

See: Jackson, Jr., Greg. *Serial World.* "An Interview with John Hart." #3, 1974; Weaver, Tom. *Eye on Science Fiction.* Jefferson, NC: McFarland, 2003.

ORWIN HARVEY (1926–1994)

Orwin C. Harvey, a 220-pound six-footer, was a circus high diver who often appeared as a stunt clown to amuse audiences. His career received a boost when he doubled Lorne Greene on TV's *Bonanza.* He doubled Leif Erickson on *High Chapparal* (1967–71), John Schuck on *McMillan & Wife* (1971–77), and Dan Haggerty on *Grizzly Adams* (1977–79). His specialty was high falls. He made a high dive from an oil rig on *Diamonds Are Forever* (1971), took a fall after hanging from an inverted table on *The Poseidon Adventure* (1972), and did a thirty-five-foot back-fall from a tree doubling Claude Akins on *Battle for the Planet of the Apes* (1973). As a publicity stunt he performed a hundred-foot fall on fire off the AVCO Theatre in Los Angeles to promote *Fire Sale* (1977).

He worked on *Beneath the Planet of the Apes* (1970), *99 and 44/100 percent Dead* (1974), *The Towering Inferno* (1974), *The Hindenburg* (1975), *The Eiger Sanction* (1975), *Swashbuckler* (1976), *Silent Movie* (1976), *The Last Remake of Beau Geste* (1977), *Every Which Way But Loose* (1978), *F.I.S.T.* (1978), *Prisoner of Zenda* (1979), *Stunt Seven* (1979), and *Any Which Way You Can* (1980). TV credits include *Lost in Space, The Time Tunnel, The Invaders, Daniel Boone, Young Rebels, Mannix, Here's Lucy, Kung Fu, Search,* and *The Six Million Dollar Man.* He was a member of the Stuntmen's Association and an inductee of the Stuntmen's Hall of Fame.

HAZEL HASH (1914–2008)

Hazel Hash from Harlowton, Montana, was a rodeo trick rider and horse trainer, initially settling in California where her family ran stables in Culver City. She was the horseback double for Vivien Leigh on *Gone with the Wind* (1939) and claimed to have done Leigh's fall down the stairs; a stunt also attributed to the more established Aline Goodwin. It's possible both did takes of the stunt. Other films include *Wuthering Heights* (1939), *National Velvet* (1944), and *Ben-Hur* (1959).

See: "Hazel Warp: Stunt Double for Vivien Leigh." *Los Angeles Times.* September 1, 2008; Ronnow, Karin. "Stuntwoman, Stand-In Hazel Warp Dies at 93." *Bozeman Chronicle.* August 28, 2008.

MARY ANN HAWKINS (1919–1993)

Top aquatic stuntwoman Mary Ann Hawkins was born in Pasadena, California, and began to win swimming, diving, surfing, and paddleboard contests while still in her teens. She was the 1934 National Junior Champion in the half mile and the AAU freestyle champ in the 100-yard and 500-meter events. She had an Olympic tryout in 1936 but found her energies focusing on surfing over swimming. She reigned as the Pacific Coast Women's Surf champ from 1938 to 1940. Hawkins doubled Dorothy Lamour and Esther Williams and logged several Tarzan and Jungle Jim films.

She broke her ankle doubling Shirley Jones jumping from a burning haystack on *Oklahoma* (1955). On *Giant* (1956) she doubled Elizabeth Taylor and Carroll Baker. Other credits include *Guys and Dolls* (1955), *The Prodigal* (1955), and *The Ten Commandments* (1956). On TV's *You Asked for It* she set a world record holding her breath underwater for two minutes and fifteen seconds. She sometimes went by her married names Mary Ann McGuire and Mary Ann Sears. In 1956 she relocated to Hawaii to open a Waikiki swimming school for infants. Hawkins died from cancer at the age of 73.

See: Warshaw, Matt. *The Encyclopedia of Surfing.* Orlando, Florida: Harcourt, 2005; www.legendarysurfers.com.

CHESTER HAYES (1913–2000)

Chester Anthony Hayes was born in Spring Valley, Illinois. He attended Sam Houston High in Texas where he excelled in football, track, baseball, and basketball. Hayes played football at Rice University, during which time he held AAU boxing and wrestling titles. He pursued the latter vocation and became a professional wrestler under the moniker Tarzan Hayes. A California base allowed him to pursue stunt work in the film business. He was proficient on a horse and worked several westerns and costume dramas.

Hayes was skilled at standing on stilts and did this on *The Big Circus* (1959) and *Hello, Dolly!* (1969). This excellence of balance got him cast in the cumbersome costume required to portray a tree monster on the sci-fi film *From Hell It Came* (1957). Hayes also essayed a caveman beast on *Valley of the Dragons* (1961) and took on a bear costume for *The Great Race* (1965). Hayes had a monkey named Fuzzy and played many organ grinders late in his career.

He also worked on *Jim Thorpe, All-American* (1951), *Million Dollar Mermaid* (1952), *Blackbeard the Pirate* (1952), *Botany Bay* (1953), *Julius Caesar* (1953), *All the Brothers Were Valiant* (1953), *The Veils of Bagdad* (1953), *The Prodigal* (1955), *Around the World in Eighty Days* (1956), and *The Wonderful Country* (1959). TV credits include *Wagon Train, Gunsmoke,* and *Bonanza.* Hayes died in a fire at the age of 86.

See: Parla, Paul. "And Now the Award for Best Wooden Performance—Tree Monster Chester Hayes Speaks." *Filmfax.* March 1996.

MICHAEL HAYNES (1939–)

Michael Allen Haynes was born in Haynesville, Louisiana. His first film was *The Long Hot Summer* (1958). The 180-pound six-footer played football at Louisiana State, dabbled in rodeo events, and took part in a high act in Las Vegas. He doubled James Darren on the TV series *The Time Tunnel* (1966–67) and Fabian on *Maryjane* (1968), *Devil's Eight* (1969), and *A Bullet for Pretty Boy* (1970). He worked on a number of motorcycle pictures prior to landing an endorsement contract as the Winchester Man of cigarette ads.

Taking advantage of his windfall, Haynes wrote, produced, and co-starred in the bike pic *Chrome and Hot Leather* (1971). He was a ski double for Roger Moore on *A View to a Kill* (1985).

He worked on *Hells Angels on Wheels* (1967), *Savage Seven* (1968), *Angel Unchained* (1970), *The Dunwich Horror* (1970), and *Wild Rovers* (1971). TV credits include *The Six Million Dollar Man, CHiPs,* and *The Fall Guy*. Haynes is a member of the International Stunt Association and head of the horseback group Michael Haynes Outriders.

See: Bacon, James. "Traveling with Mike Haynes Like Being with Redford or Newman." *Sarasota Journal*. October 7, 1974; Christy, Marion. "Winchester Man Is Anti-Hero." *Telegraph Herald*. August 26, 1973; Kleiner, Dick. "Michael Haynes Struggling Actor." *Waycross Journal Herald*. June 8, 1981.

KENT HAYS

Five-foot-eight, 155-pound Kent Hays was a rodeo cowboy before becoming a stuntman and horse wrangler. He served as a background drover on the TV series *Rawhide* (1959–66) and worked on *Young Fury* (1965), *Planet of the Apes* (1968), *The Good Guys and the Bad Guys* (1968), *The Great Bank Robbery* (1969), *Little Big Man* (1970), *Beneath the Planet of the Apes* (1970), *Skin Game* (1971), *The Cowboys* (1972), *The Villain* (1979), and *Butch and Sundance* (1979). He was a member of the Stuntmen's Association.

CHUCK HAYWARD (1920–1998)

Chuck Hayward was born in Alliance, Nebraska, and grew up on a horse ranch. He joined the Merchant Marines, then worked as a lineman until a fall from a pole broke two vertebrae. He moved on to work at the C.C. Gentry Ranch as a cowboy and competed in the rodeo arena before entertaining the idea of a movie stunt career. With his horse Twinkletoes, Hayward became one of the top stuntmen in the business. For many years he was the regular double for Yul Brynner beginning with *The Magnificent Seven* (1960) and extending to a fall out a window and tumble down a roof on *Westworld* (1973). On *Hondo* (1953) Hayward doubled John Wayne on a bucking horse. On *The Searchers* (1956) he doubled Jeffrey

Hunter. On *The Big Country* (1958) he did the Roman riding playing one of the Hannassey brothers.

Hayward, a 180-pound six-footer, and Chuck Roberson were fixtures on the films of director John Ford. By default Hayward was known as Good Chuck in light of his pal's reputation as a carouser. One of Hayward's best moments came when he rode his horse into the station on *The Horse Soldiers* (1959). Hayward was part of the fourteen-man horse fall on *The Alamo* (1960) and did the individual saddle fall where the Mexican rider is shot by Richard Widmark. Hayward eventually became a respected stunt coordinator and second unit director.

He worked on *The Fighting Kentuckian* (1949), *She Wore a Yellow Ribbon* (1949), *Brimstone* (1949), *Rock Island Trail* (1950), *Rio Grande* (1950), *Wagon Master* (1950), *Viva Zapata!* (1952), *The World in His Arms* (1952), *The Big Sky* (1952), *Fort Osage* (1952), *Arena* (1953), *San Antone* (1953), *The Rains of Ranchipur* (1955), *Showdown at Abilene* (1956), *Red Sundown* (1956), *Gun for a Coward* (1957), *The Wings of Eagles* (1957), *Designing Woman* (1957), *Run of the Arrow* (1957), *Legend of the Lost* (1957), *Forty Guns* (1957), *The Young Land* (1958), *Rio Bravo* (1959), *Pork Chop Hill* (1959), *Spartacus* (1960), *Sergeant Rutledge* (1960), *The Comancheros* (1961), *The Deadly Companions* (1961), *Two Rode Together* (1961), *Merrill's Marauders* (1962), *The Man Who Shot Liberty Valance* (1962), *How the West Was Won* (1962), *Taras Bulba* (1962), *The Great Escape* (1963), *It's a Mad, Mad, Mad, Mad World* (1963), *Kings of the Sun* (1963), *McLintock!* (1963), *Cheyenne Autumn* (1964), *Major Dundee* (1965), *The Sons of Katie Elder* (1965), *The Great Race* (1965), *The Rounders* (1965), *The Rare Breed* (1966), *7 Women* (1966), *Nevada Smith* (1966), *Beau Geste* (1966), *Return of the Seven* (1966), *El Dorado* (1967), *The War Wagon* (1967), *Blue* (1968), *5 Card Stud* (1968), *Villa Rides* (1968), *The Devil's Brigade* (1968), *True Grit* (1969), *The Good Guys and the Bad Guys* (1969), *Chisum* (1970), *Rio Lobo* (1970), *Big Jake* (1971), *The Horsemen* (1971), *Support Your Local Gunfighter* (1971), *Joe Kidd* (1972), *Buck and the Preacher* (1972), *High Plains Drifter* (1973), *The Train Robbers* (1973), *Emperor of the North* (1973), *Mame* (1974), *Blazing Saddles* (1974), *The Longest Yard* (1974), *Rooster Cogburn* (1975), *Airport '77* (1977), *March or Die* (1977), *Who'll Stop the Rain*

(1978), *The Swarm* (1978), *The Frisco Kid* (1979), and *Tom Horn* (1980). TV credits include *Have Gun—Will Travel, Zane Grey, Wagon Train, Johnny Ringo, Wanted—Dead or Alive, Gunsmoke, Bonanza, The Rat Patrol,* and *Kung Fu.* A member of the Stuntmen's Association and an inductee of the Stuntmen's Hall of Fame, Hayward died from Hodgkin's Disease at the age of 77.

See: "Empty Saddles." *Western Clippings.* #23, May-June 1998; Lilley, Tim. *Campfire Conversations.* Akron, OH: Big Trail, 2007.

CHARLES HEARD (1917–2005)

Charles MacDonald Heard was born in San Carlos, Arizona, on the Apache Indian reservation and raised in San Antonio, Texas. As a boy he was an Eagle Scout, shot on pistol and rifle teams, and was an arms curator for the Alamo. He was also an expert with a bow and arrow. Heard was an accomplished fencer who worked with Errol Flynn, Cornel Wilde, and Louis Hayward. On westerns he doubled James Stewart and worked as a technical advisor. He wrote a book on handguns and published articles debunking the so-called "fast draws" of Hollywood.

He worked on *Cyrano de Bergerac* (1950), *Rogues of Sherwood Forest* (1950), *Fortunes of Captain Blood* (1950), *Lady and the Bandit* (1951), *Captain Pirate* (1952), *Against All Flags* (1952), *Casanova's Big Night* (1954), *The Command* (1954), *Adventures of Hajji Baba* (1954), *Daniel Boone, Trailblazer* (1956), *Around the World in Eighty Days* (1956), *Hidden Guns* (1956), *Gunman's Walk* (1958), *The Buccaneer* (1958), and *The Young Land* (1959). TV credits include *Roy Rogers, Death Valley Days, Bat Masterson,* and *The Rebel.* Heard died from organ failure at the age of 88.

See: "Charles MacDonald Heard." *San Antonio Express.* December 18, 2005; Heard, Charles. "Truth About Hollywood Gunfighters." *Guns.* December 1957; Vasquez, Crystal. "Scriptwriter to Stuntman, Heard, 88, Filled Many Hollywood Roles." *San Antonio Express.* December 19, 2005.

JACK HENDRICKS (1903–1990)

Five-foot-nine, 190-pound B-western performer John T. Hendricks was a capable horseman and picture fighter. South Carolina-born, he played dozens of henchmen who chased and fought cowboy heroes throughout the 1930s and 1940s in more than 200 low-budget features. He doubled Fred Kohler, Jr., on *Pecos Kid* (1935) and Dana Andrews on *Kit Carson* (1940) and was still brawling on screen as late as *Guns of the Timberland* (1960). His most notable moment came fighting Buster Crabbe atop a stagecoach on *Law and Order* (1942). His TV credits include several episodes of *The Cisco Kid.* Hendricks, who served with the U.S. Army during World War II, occasionally went by the screen name Ray Henderson.

See: *Panama City News Herald.* October 25, 1942.

TOM HENNESY (1923–2011)

Six-foot-five, 235-pound Thomas Daniel Hennesy was born in La Canada, California, and played football for two USC Rose Bowl teams in 1943 and 1944. Hennesy boxed, served with the U.S. Navy during World War II, and worked as a forest ranger and police officer on Catalina Island. He doubled John Wayne, Randolph Scott, Charlton Heston, Rod Cameron, Rock Hudson, Jeff Chandler, Robert Francis, Van Johnson, Mickey Simpson, Walter Matthau, and professional boxer Buddy Baer, the latter as The Giant on *Jack and the Beanstalk* (1952). He was a stuntman for Clint Walker on the early episodes of *Cheyenne* and the river flooding on *Yellowstone Kelly* (1959). Hennesy specialized in fights, horse work, and water work. His greatest bit of notoriety came playing the Creature from the Black Lagoon on *Revenge of the Creature* (1955).

Hennesy was a regular in John Ford's stunt troupe and a sailing buddy of John Wayne. The Duke liked fighting Hennesy on his films since he was such a big guy. He is especially memorable as the Tennessean who challenges Wayne to a feather-balancing and punching competition on *The Alamo* (1960). Wayne kept encouraging Hennesy to get bigger. By the time they traded punches on *The Comancheros* (1961) Hennesy was weighing in at 285 pounds, over fifty pounds heavier than when he started in films. On *Big Jake* (1971) Hennesy has a brief comic fight with Wayne, who surprisingly doesn't land a single punch. The Duke does break a pool cue over Hennesy's head to no avail.

He worked on *Iron Man* (1951), *Trouble Along the Way* (1953), *The Robe* (1953), *The High*

Tom Hennesy takes a punch from John Wayne on *The War Wagon* (1967).

and the Mighty (1954), *The Caine Mutiny* (1954), *Blood Alley* (1955), *The Ten Commandments* (1956), *Giant* (1956), *The Wings of Eagles* (1957), *Onionhead* (1958), *The Buccaneer* (1958), *The Horse Soldiers* (1959), *North to Alaska* (1960), *The Man Who Shot Liberty Valance* (1962), *Donovan's Reef* (1963), *McLintock!* (1963), *Stagecoach* (1966), *The War Wagon* (1967), and *The Green Berets* (1968). TV credits include *Gunsmoke, Have Gun—Will Travel,* and *Thriller.*

See: Lilley, Tim. *Campfire Conversations Complete.* Akron, OH: Big Trail, 2010; Weaver, Tom. *It Came from Horrorwood: Interviews with Moviemakers in the Science Fiction and Horror Tradition.* Jefferson, NC: McFarland, 2004.

BUZZ HENRY (1931–1971)

Robert Dee Henry was born in Colorado and was competing in junior rodeos and tumbling in vaudeville acts while just a boy. He made it to Hollywood as child star Buzzy Henry; cowboy films that featured his expert riding include *Buzzy Rides the Range* (1940) and *Buzzy and the Phantom Pinto* (1941). His mother ran a riding stable and trained her son. In his teens he continued his acting and rodeo careers upon his horse Golden Pat. By the mid–1950s the six foot, 160-pound Henry was transitioning to full-fledged stuntman. He was stunt double for Glenn Ford on *Jubal* (1956), *3:10 to Yuma* (1957), *The Sheepman* (1958), *Cowboy* (1958), and *The Rounders* (1965). Henry's lean, wiry frame made him a fine double for Frank Sinatra on *The Manchurian Candidate* (1962), *4 for Texas* (1963), *Von Ryan's Express* (1965), and *Tony Rome* (1967). He was stunt coordinator for James Coburn's spy spoofs *Our Man Flint* (1966) and *In Like Flint* (1967).

He worked on *Against All Flags* (1952), *Westward Ho, the Wagons!* (1956), *The Canadians* (1961), *Taras Bulba* (1962), *McLintock!* (1963), *Captain Newman, M.D.* (1963), *Mail Order Bride*

(1964), *Major Dundee* (1965), *Shenandoah* (1965), *Texas Across the River* (1966), *El Dorado* (1967), *Camelot* (1967), *Waterhole #3* (1967), *Mackenna's Gold* (1969), *Macho Callahan* (1970), and *The Cowboys* (1972). He moved into second unit direction, highlighted by his work on *The Wild Bunch* (1969) for Sam Peckinpah. TV credits include *Wild Bill Hickok, Stories of the Century, Champion, Colt .45, The Outer Limits, The Rounders, Mannix,* and *Mission: Impossible.* A member of the Stuntmen's Association and an inductee of the Stuntmen's Hall of Fame, Henry died at the age of 40 in a car-motorcycle accident while drag racing near Forest Lawn Cemetery.

See: "Stuntman Killed in Cycle Drag Racing." *Los Angeles Times.* October 1, 1971.

CAROL HENRY (1918–1987)

Carol D. Henry was born in Oklahoma and raised in Shasta, California. He entered stunt work after a career as a steer wrestler in the rodeo. The 6'1" Henry specialized in playing B-western henchmen while doubling actors such as Russell Hayden and Richard Martin. He worked on a number of Gene Autry's later films. Credits include *Belle Starr's Daughter* (1948), *Ghost of Zorro* (1949), *Stampede* (1949), *Ambush* (1949), *Annie Get Your Gun* (1950), *Winchester '73* (1950), *Warpath* (1951), *Cattle Drive* (1951), *Apache Country* (1952), *The Lusty Men* (1952), *Fort Osage* (1952), *The Stranger Wore a Gun* (1953), *Riding Shotgun* (1954), *Walk the Proud Land* (1956), *A Thunder of Drums* (1961), *The Hallelujah Trail* (1965), and TV westerns such as *The Cisco Kid, Kit Carson, Sergeant Preston,* and *Daniel Boone.* Henry died of cardiovascular disease at the age of 69.

JEAN HEREMANS (1914–1970)

Belgium-born Jean Louis Joseph Heremans was the five-time national fencing champion of his country; he was a member of the Belgium Olympic team in 1936. During World War II he was with the French underground. After the war he came to America to teach fencing at USC and the Los Angeles Athletic Club. Many of his pupils were actors and actresses who needed training for the movies. Heremans began to work as a fencing choreographer and stuntman with standout work coming on *The Three Musketeers* (1948) and the eight-minute duel on *Scaramouche* (1952). He also worked on *Singin' in the Rain* (1952), *The Prisoner of Zenda* (1952), *Julius Caesar* (1953), *Demetrius and the Gladiators* (1954), *Prince Valiant* (1954), *Princess of the Nile* (1954), *Valley of the Kings* (1954), *The Silver Chalice* (1954), *The King's Thief* (1955), *The Swan* (1956), and *The Buccaneer* (1958).

See: MacPherson, Virginia. "Ladies Adore a Swordsman, Fencer Says." *Berkeley Daily Gazette.* February 27, 1948; Thomas, Bob. "Jean Heremans Bares Secrets of Dueling Scenes in Movies." *Reading Eagle.* June 7, 1952.

BOB HERRON (1924–)

Five-foot-ten, 200-pound Robert Dwayne Herron was born in Los Angeles but spent much of his youth in Hawaii. Herron's stepfather was stuntman-horse wrangler Ace Hudkins, a former pro boxer who taught the youngster how to box while he worked on the ranch. Herron boxed Golden Gloves and excelled at football and track. He had a track scholarship pending at USC when he entered the U.S. Navy in 1943 at the height of World War II. He was involved in the Pacific Theater aboard a sub chaser during the invasions of Saipan, Tinian, Guadalcanal, the Philippines, and Okinawa. He won a boxing championship in the Navy.

Returning home, he went to work as a horse wrangler. Eventually Herron made his film debut as a stuntman on *Rocky Mountain* (1950). He was a top fight man whose specialty was high falls (up to sixty feet) into cardboard boxes. His falling horse's name was BCNU. While working on the TV series *Hawaiian Eye* as a stunt double for Robert Conrad, Herron taught the young actor judo. Herron followed Conrad onto *The Wild Wild West,* but Conrad thought that Herron was too big to believably double him and he was intent on doing all his own fights anyway. Herron ended up doubling Ross Martin for the run of the show. He was the stunt double for Ernest Borgnine on *Chuka* (1967), *The Wild Bunch* (1969), *Convoy* (1978), and *The Black Hole* (1979). He also doubled Tony Curtis, Dean Martin, Cliff Robertson, Richard Burton, Robert Vaughn, and Robert Phillips. On TV he doubled Pernell Roberts on *Bonanza* (1959–65) and Jeffrey Hunter on the pilot to *Star Trek.* Herron's most challenging stunt was changing a trio of horses on bareback while doubling John Saxon on *The Unforgiven* (1960). He had a thrilling fight with Terence Hill on the edge of the Grand Canyon with no safety nets in sight on *Mr. Billion* (1977). On *Convoy* (1978) he drove a car 165 feet through a billboard and a barn. He was concussed and separated his sternum on that stunt.

He worked on *The Flame and the Arrow* (1950), *Winchester '73* (1950), *The Red Badge of Courage* (1951), *Ten Tall Men* (1951), *Battle at Apache Pass* (1952), *Red Ball Express* (1952), *Yankee Buccaneer* (1952), *Wings of the Hawk* (1953), *Invaders from Mars* (1953), *Column South* (1953), *The Charge at Feather River* (1953), *Gun Fury* (1953), *River of No Return* (1954), *Four Guns to the Border* (1954), *Saskatchewan* (1954), *The Man from Bitter Ridge* (1955), *Abbott and Costello Meet the Keystone Kops* (1955), *The Rawhide Years* (1955), *The Ten Commandments* (1956), *Away All Boats* (1956), *Walk the Proud Land* (1956), *The Mole People* (1956), *Pillars of the Sky* (1956), *The Burning Hills* (1956), *Man Afraid* (1957), *The Deep Six* (1958), *Ride a Crooked Trail* (1958), *Rio Bravo* (1959), *Westbound* (1959), *Spartacus* (1960), *Elmer Gantry* (1960), *Seven Ways from Sundown* (1960), *Lonely Are the Brave* (1962), *The Spiral Road* (1962), *The Chapman Report* (1962), *Six Black Horses* (1962), *Taras Bulba* (1962), *It's a Mad, Mad, Mad, Mad World* (1963), *Kings of the Sun* (1963), *A Distant Trumpet* (1964), *Bullet for a Badman* (1964), *Gunfight at Comanche Creek* (1963), *Major Dundee* (1965), *In Harm's Way* (1965), *Shenandoah* (1965), *The War Lord* (1965), *The Great Race* (1965), *The Rare Breed* (1966), *Not with My Wife You Don't* (1966), *What Did You Do in the War, Daddy?* (1966), *The Silencers* (1966), *Stagecoach* (1966), *Beau Geste* (1966), *Tobruk* (1967), *In Like Flint* (1967), *Hot Rods to Hell* (1967), *Ice Station Zebra* (1968), *Journey to Shiloh* (1968), *Mackenna's Gold* (1969), *The Great Bank Robbery* (1969), *Paint Your Wagon* (1969), *A Time for Dying* (1969), *There Was a Crooked Man...* (1970), *Shaft* (1971), *Diamonds Are Forever* (1971), *The Great Northfield Minnesota Raid* (1972), *Prime Cut* (1972), *Joe Kidd* (1972), *Soylent Green* (1973), *Oklahoma Crude* (1973), *Dillinger* (1973),

Bob Herron jumps a police car through the roof of a house on *Convoy* (1978).

The Don Is Dead (1973), American Graffiti (1973), Blazing Saddles (1974), 99 and 44/100 percent Dead (1974), Earthquake (1974), Doc Savage (1975), Lepke (1975), The Hindenburg (1975), Silent Movie (1976), Swashbuckler (1976), Rocky (1976), Silver Streak (1976), The Enforcer (1976), Rollercoaster (1977), Movie, Movie (1978), 1941 (1979), Stunt Seven (1979), and Any Which Way You Can (1980). TV credits include Cheyenne, Maverick, Bronco, Sugarfoot, Lawman, Peter Gunn, Route 66, Temple Houston, Laredo, I Spy, Batman, The Green Hornet, F Troop, Run for Your Life, Dundee and the Culhane, Guns of Will Sonnett, High Chaparral, Gunsmoke, Hawaii Five-O, Ironside, Mission: Impossible, Kung Fu, McCloud, Columbo, Banacek, McMillan & Wife, The Streets of San Francisco, The Rockford Files, The Six Million Dollar Man, Police Story, Petrocelli, Kojak, Wonder Woman, Logan's Run, Little House on the Prairie, Black Sheep Squadron, Barnaby Jones, Charlie's Angels, The Dukes of Hazzard, and Hart to Hart. Herron is a member of the Stuntmen's Association and an inductee of the Stuntmen's Hall of Fame.

See: Cason, Colleen. "T.O. Stuntman Gives Actor Ernest Borgnine Full Credit." Ventura County Star. July 21, 2012; Ivie, Mark, & John D. Ross. "Robert Herron: 80, Unbreakable ... And Still Going Strong!" Inside Stunts. Summer, 2004; Jauregui, Jannette. "Of War and Life: Sailor Went from Military to Hollywood Screen." Ventura County Star. October 7, 2011.

CHARLTON HESTON (1923–2008)

Major movie star Charlton Heston did all but the single most dangerous stunt during the legendary chariot race on Ben-Hur (1959). Heston worked diligently for several weeks with stunt legend Yakima Canutt to master the challenging task and the results were some of the most

Charlton Heston does his own chariot driving on Ben-Hur (1959). Yakima Canutt trained Heston and coordinated the classic action.

thrilling sequences ever committed to celluloid. Heston was renowned for his physical preparation and willingness to learn and master new abilities, be it sword fighting for the costume epic *El Cid* (1961), playing football for *Number One* (1969), or learning to fly a 747 for *Skyjacked* (1972). On the original *Planet of the Apes* (1968) Heston had one of the most physically demanding roles ever required of a leading man, and again he was not afraid to get down and dirty as he was dragged, beaten, hosed, and hung upside down in a net.

Heston performed the bulk of his own fights and had classic confrontations with Mike Mazurki on *Dark City* (1950), Jack Palance on *Arrowhead* (1953), Gregory Peck on *The Big Country* (1958), James Franciscus on *Beneath the Planet of the Apes* (1970), and Chuck Connors on *Soylent Green* (1973). Through the years he worked closely with stunt coordinator Joe Canutt to do as much of his own action as possible without endangering a production. Nevertheless, the 6'3", 205-pound actor often wound up dinged and battered by the end of his films.

John Charles Carter from Evanston, Illinois, wasn't the most coordinated of youths when he was playing football for New Trier High. He filled out his gangly frame and gained confidence in his strapping body while serving with the U.S. Army Air Force as an aerial gunner during World War II. Heston hit the ground running with his film career, starring in some of the most celebrated films of all time. He learned horsemanship from Frank Cordell and was adept and authentic in the saddle. Heston had a stellar reputation with the stunt personnel on his films (stunt ace Dave Sharpe named Heston an honorary "Stunt Cousin"). Heston served on the Board of Directors for the Hollywood Stuntmen's Hall of Fame. An honorary member of the Stuntmen's Association, Heston died from pneumonia after a battle with Alzheimer's Disease at the age of 84.

See: Heston, Charlton. *In the Arena.* New York: Simon and Schuster, 1995; Heston, Charlton. *The Actors Life: Journals 1955–1976.* New York: E.P. Dutton, 1978; "Stunts Earn New Nickname for Charlton Heston." *San Diego Union.* January 30, 1957.

EDDIE HICE (1931–)

Edward Louis Hice hails from Fort Wayne, Indiana. He is best known as the stunt double for Don Adams on TV's *Get Smart* (1965–69). During this period he also doubled Frank Gorshin on TV's *Batman* (1965–68) and Bruce Lee on *The Green Hornet* (1966–67). Later it was Charles Dierkop on *Police Woman* (1974–78). On film the 5'9", 150-pound Hice doubled Robert Duvall on *Countdown* (1968) and *MASH* (1970) and Dick Bakalyan on *Charley and the Angel* (1973). He was a founding member of the Viewfinders motorcycle adventure club and raced dirt bikes competitively. He was once married to stuntwoman Patty Elder; their son Fred Hice became a stuntman.

He worked on *Young Fury* (1965), *Bonnie and Clyde* (1967), *First to Fight* (1967), *Planet of the Apes* (1968), *Hell's Belles* (1969), *The Moonshine War* (1970), *Beneath the Planet of the Apes* (1970), *Conquest of the Planet of the Apes* (1972), *Soul of Nigger Charley* (1973), *Battle for the Planet of the Apes* (1973), *The Towering Inferno* (1974), *The Front Page* (1974), *Earthquake* (1974), *Corvette Summer* (1978), and *The Nude Bomb* (1980). TV credits include *The Texan, Gunsmoke, Star Trek,* and *S.W.A.T.* Hice is a member of the Stuntmen's Association.

See: www.ilovegetsmart.com/eddie_hice.html.

BILL HICKMAN (1921–1986)

Bill Hickman is best known as the man behind the wheel of the most white-knuckle exciting car chase scenes in film history due to his work on *Bullitt* (1968), *The French Connection* (1971), and *The Seven-Ups* (1973). In the landmark *Bullitt,* Hickman was the bad guy's hit man and drove the black Dodge Charger 440 Magnum. On *The French Connection,* he doubled for star Gene Hackman in a 1970 Pontiac speeding through the streets of Brooklyn at up to ninety miles per hour beneath the elevated train. On *The Seven-Ups,* which might be the best of the lot, he was once again the bad guy muscle behind the wheel of a Pontiac Grandville pursued by Roy Scheider. Onscreen, Hickman approached his thrilling stunt work with such a detached coolness and steely nerve that he developed a cult following of his own that exists to this day among speed aficionados.

William Hickman was born in Los Angeles and first appeared on screen at the age of six. He was a military veteran and race car driver prior to entering films as a stuntman for MGM. The 6'3",

Bill Hickman jumps a Charger over the streets of San Francisco on *Bullitt* (1968).

195-pound Hickman doubled Clark Gable on *To Please a Lady* (1950) and other films. Hickman didn't stick to car stunts exclusively, and his burly presence got him a lot of on-camera work playing stunt thugs. As an actor he was the guard who whips Elvis Presley on *Jailhouse Rock* (1957). Hickman worked the chicken run on *Rebel Without a Cause* (1955) and was a real-life pal of actor James Dean. He was the one who came upon the Porsche Spyder car wreck that killed the young actor, and Dean died in his arms.

He worked on *Salute to the Marines* (1943), *The Red Badge of Courage* (1951), *Fixed Bayonets* (1951), *The Wild One* (1953), *The Far Horizons* (1955), *Raintree County* (1957), *It's a Mad, Mad, Mad, Mad World* (1963), *The Great Race* (1965), *How to Stuff a Wild Bikini* (1965), *A Fine Madness* (1966), *Spinout* (1966), *El Dorado* (1967), *The Flim-Flam Man* (1967), *Point Blank* (1967), *The Love Bug* (1968), *The Wrecking Crew* (1969), *Flap* (1970), *Patton* (1970), *Vanishing Point* (1971), *Diamonds Are Forever* (1971), *Hickey and Boggs* (1972), *Rage* (1972), *What's Up, Doc?* (1972), *Electra Glide in Blue* (1973), *The Thief Who Came*

to *Dinner* (1974), *The Hindenburg* (1975), and *Capricorn One* (1978). TV credits include *Peter Gunn, Mr. Lucky, Lawless Years, Bonanza, Bat Masterson, Twilight Zone, The Outer Limits, The Fugitive, Branded, The Man from U.N.C.L.E., Honey West, Batman, Voyage to the Bottom of the Sea,* and *The FBI*. A member of the Stuntmen's Association and an inductee of the Stuntmen's Hall of Fame, Hickman died of cancer at the age of 65.

See: Beath, Warren. *The Death of James Dean*. Grove Press, 2007; "Stuntman Plays Havoc with Cars." *Augusta Chronicle*. January 1, 1967; www.curbsidecinema.com.

CHUCK HICKS (1927–)

Muscular fight specialist Chuck Hicks has had one of the longest active stunt careers in Hollywood, beginning in the early 1950s and continuing some sixty years later. He was the stunt coordinator for the famous fight on *Cool Hand Luke* (1967). He doubled Forrest Tucker for an epic battle with Max Baer, Jr., on *The Wild McCullochs*

(1975) and Walter Barnes for the climactic brawl with Clint Eastwood on *Every Which Way But Loose* (1978). Hicks was utilized as one of Eastwood's favorite punching bags on *Dirty Harry* (1971), *The Enforcer* (1976), and *Bronco Billy* (1980). He doubled Clint Walker on the TV western *Cheyenne* and was briefly featured as one of Eliot Ness' men on *The Untouchables* (1959–60). The 6'2", 220-pound Hicks also doubled Aldo Ray, Brian Keith, Tom Reese, Merlin Olsen, Brian Dennehy, and Paul Sorvino. He was cast as The Brow on *Dick Tracy* (1990).

Charles Hicks was born in Stockton, California. He was a star running back for Burbank High's football team in the mid–1940s. During World War II he did hitches in the Merchant Marine and the U.S. Navy, where he was the boxing champ of the Navy's 5th Fleet. He attended Loyola University on a football scholarship and became the university's heavyweight boxing champ. He was instrumental in introducing rugby to Southern California in the early 1950s and was inducted into Loyola's Athletes Hall of Fame. In professional football Hicks had tryouts with the Los Angeles Rams and the Washington Redskins but was cut at the end of the Rams' 1951 training camp. He ended up playing seven years of semi-pro football for the Eagle Rock Athletic Club, where he was the three-time MVP. Hicks boxed professionally under the name Chuck Daley. He fought eight pro fights, going 6–2 and winning five of those by a first round knock-out. When Hicks broke his hand, he decided to retire from boxing. He was a lifeguard at Pickwick Pool in Burbank when he decided to give the movies a shot. He was first cast as football players on 1952's *She's Working Her Way Through College* and *The Rose Bowl Story*.

He also worked on *Siren of Bagdad* (1953), *The Prodigal* (1955), *Battle Cry* (1955), *Around the World in Eighty Days* (1956), *Designing Woman* (1957), *Hell Is for Heroes* (1962), *Merrill's Marauders* (1962), *4 for Texas* (1963), *PT 109* (1963), *The Great Race* (1965), *Our Man Flint* (1966), *Not With My Wife, You Don't* (1966), *What Did You Do in the War, Daddy?* (1966), *Johnny Reno* (1966), *The Silencers* (1966), *Murderers Row* (1966), *Point Blank* (1967), *The Split* (1968), *Paint Your Wagon* (1969), *The Molly Maguires* (1970), *There Was a Crooked Man...* (1970), *Something Big* (1971), *Slaughter's Big Rip-Off* (1973), *Magnum Force* (1973), *The Trial of*

Billy Jack (1974), *Night Moves* (1975), *Hard Times* (1975), *F.I.S.T.* (1978), *Movie, Movie* (1978), and *Stunt Seven* (1979). He was a stunt heavy on episodes of *Maverick, Zane Grey, Trackdown, Lawman, Peter Gunn, The Rebel, The Man from U.N.C.L.E., Branded, Iron Horse, Custer, Batman, The Green Hornet, Mannix, Mission: Impossible, Kung Fu, Gunsmoke, The Streets of San Francisco, Cannon, The Rockford Files, Harry O, Little House on the Prairie, Kojak, Police Story, Bert D'Angelo, Starsky and Hutch, Wonder Woman, CHiPs, Vega$, Hart to Hart,* and *The Fall Guy*. A charter member of the Stuntmen's Association and an inductee of the Stuntmen's Hall of Fame, Hicks married stuntwoman Kaye Wade.

See: McCarthy, Dennis. "At 83, Actor Chuck Hicks Is Stepping Out of the Shadows." *Daily News.* January 26, 2011; www.chuckhicks.com.

BRYAN "SLIM" HIGHTOWER (1905–1978)

Texas-born Slim Hightower was reputed by actor Harry Carey, Jr., to be John Ford's favorite stuntman among his stock company. Ford named John Wayne's character after him on *Three Godfathers* (1948), a film in which Hightower worked as a stuntman. He was raised in New Mexico as a bull-riding rodeo cowboy and champion roper. A fine horseman, Hightower doubled Gary Cooper on *The Plainsman* (1936) and Sam Jaffe for the fall from the dome atop the temple on *Gunga Din* (1939).

He worked on *The Texans* (1938), *She Wore a Yellow Ribbon* (1949), *Mighty Joe Young* (1949), *Wagon Master* (1950), *Dakota Lil* (1950), *Warpath* (1951), *The Quiet Man* (1952), *Arrowhead* (1953), *Prince Valiant* (1954), *The Searchers* (1956), *The Horse Soldiers* (1959), *The Alamo* (1960), *The Unforgiven* (1960), *Two Rode Together* (1961), *The Man Who Shot Liberty Valance* (1962), and *Cheyenne Autumn* (1964).

See: Carey, Harry. *Company of Heroes: My Life as an Actor in the John Ford Stock Company.* Scarecrow, 1994.

BOB HINKLE (1930–)

Robert Hinkle was born in Brownfield, Texas, where he played football and learned to fly a Piper cub at the age of sixteen. "Texas Bob" joined the U.S. Air Force and participated in the

Berlin Airlift. Upon his discharge he was a commercial pilot, construction worker, carpenter, and rodeo cowboy. In Oregon, Budd Boetticher hired him as a stuntman for location filming on *Bronco Buster* (1952). Hinkle liked the pay and headed to Hollywood, where Boetticher gave him another break on *Wings of the Hawk* (1953). The 6'2" Hinkle doubled Richard Burton on *The Robe* (1953), Robert Mitchum on *River of No Return* (1954), John Wayne on *The Conqueror* (1956), Charlton Heston on *The Ten Commandments* (1956), Rock Hudson on *Giant* (1956), and Jim Davis on *Badge of Marshal Brennan* (1957). Hinkle set up the pig scramble scene on *Hud* (1963) as stunt coordinator and second unit director.

He also worked on *All-American* (1953), *The Charge at Feather River* (1953), *King of the Khyber Rifles* (1953), *Riding Shotgun* (1954), *Broken Lance* (1954), *Sign of the Pagan* (1954), *The Bamboo Prison* (1954), *Kismet* (1955), *White Feather* (1955), *Oklahoma!* (1955), *I Killed Wild Bill Hickok* (1956), and *The Misfits* (1961). TV credits include *Wyatt Earp, Wagon Train,* and *Bonanza.* Hinkle directed *Ole Rex* (1961) and *Guns of a Stranger* (1973). He made several short films at Paramount, among them *Dean Smith, Hollywood Stuntman.*

See: Hinkle, Robert. *Call Me Lucky: A Texan in Hollywood.* University of Oklahoma, 2009; www.roberthinkle.com.

PETER HOCK

Five-foot-nine, 150 pound Peter Hock was a former U.S. Marine and a karate devotee when he began performing stunts on the East Coast. Hock was best known as a commercial rep for Bull Durham cigarettes. He doubled Rock Hudson on *Blindfold* (1965) and James Garner on *Mister Buddwing* (1966) despite being much shorter. He also worked on *A Lovely Way to Die* (1968), *Lady in Cement* (1968), *Across 110th Street* (1972), *Prisoner of Second Avenue* (1975), and *God Told Me To* (1976). TV credits include *Hawk* and the soap operas *Love of Life, Ryan's Hope, The Edge of Night,* and *The Doctors.*

See: Lewis, Don. "Professional Stunter Says He Just Fell Into Show Business." *Milwaukee Journal.* July 5, 1967; "Stuntman Makes Trouble His Career." *Syracuse Herald Journal.* June 21, 1967.

HERBERT HOLCOMBE (1904–1970)

Bronx-born Herbert Holcombe first acted as a juvenile lead. Photos of his muscular physique helped him win a Mr. Apollo contest, and he captured the title of Strongest Man in New Jersey. A professional adagio dance act led him to Broadway and Hollywood. On *The Charge of the Light Brigade* (1936) Holcombe executed a ninety-foot fall from a bell tower into a net. He worked often with Errol Flynn, including on *Dodge City* (1939) and *They Died with Their Boots On* (1941). Holcombe doubled Ralph Graves on *Black Coin* (1936) and worked on *The Sign of the Cross* (1932), *She Done Him Wrong* (1933), *Boom Town* (1940), *The Seventh Cross* (1944), and *Kiss of Death* (1947). He relocated to New York City in the 1950s, working there on *The Hustler* (1961) and the TV series *Dark Shadows.* He was a veteran of more than 300 films and 200 TV shows.

See: Warren, James. "I Risk My Life!" *Wildest Westerns.* August 1961.

JACK HOLT (1888–1951)

Popular leading man Jack Holt got his start as a stuntman. Born in New York City as Charles John Holt, he was raised in Virginia and attended the Virginia Military Institute. The six-foot, 175-pound Holt spent time as an Alaskan gold miner, railroad worker, and cowboy before encountering a film crew near San Francisco. He volunteered to ride a horse off a fifteen-foot cliff into the Russian River for the film *Salomy Jane* (1914). This led him to Hollywood and more western stunt work. He once drove a motorcycle off an open drawbridge at Alameda.

Holt impressed Universal to the point where they elevated him to star status. He made many Zane Grey westerns at Paramount and later starred in action serials such as *Holt of the Secret Service* (1941) which featured his name in the title. Throughout his stardom Holt was known as one of the top polo players on the West Coast. During World War II he served as a horse buyer for the cavalry. His son Tim Holt became a popular B-movie cowboy star in the 1940s. Jack Holt died from a heart attack at the age of 62.

See: Holt, Jack. "My Greatest Thrill." *Oregonian.* August 6, 1922; "Jack Holt Was Stuntman in Earlier Films." *Daily Register.* March 7, 1924;

Lewis, Jack. "Hard Ridin' Holts." *Guns of the Old West.* Summer 2003.

LARRY HOLT

Five-foot-ten, 165-pound Larry E. Holt was born in Joplin, Missouri. He trained at Paul Stader's Santa Monica stuntman gym and worked on a number of Irwin Allen–produced TV shows such as *Voyage to the Bottom of the Sea, The Time Tunnel,* and *Land of the Giants.* He was run down by a car on *Flare-Up* (1969) and executed a spectacular cliff stunt on an episode of TV's *Kung Fu.* His career perked up when he doubled Roddy McDowall on *The Poseidon Adventure* (1972) and Paul Newman on *The Towering Inferno* (1974). Holt was one of the busiest stuntmen of the 1970s.

He also worked on *Beyond the Valley of the Dolls* (1970), *They Call Me Mister Tibbs* (1970), *Escape from the Planet of the Apes* (1971), *Legend of Nigger Charley* (1972), *Conquest of the Planet of the Apes* (1972), *Hit!* (1973), *Battle for the Planet of the Apes* (1973), *Earthquake* (1974), *99 and 44/100 percent Dead* (1974), *Doc Savage* (1975), *The Ultimate Warrior* (1975), *Lepke* (1975), *Lucky Lady* (1975), *Silent Movie* (1976), *Swashbuckler* (1976), *Black Sunday* (1977), *Domino Principle* (1977), *Mr. Billion* (1977), *Rollercoaster* (1977), *Every Which Way But Loose* (1978), *The Swarm* (1978), *The Norseman* (1978), *Prisoner of Zenda* (1979), *Butch and Sundance* (1979), *1941* (1979), *The Nude Bomb* (1980), and *Any Which Way You Can* (1980). TV credits include *The FBI, The Streets of San Francisco, Emergency, The Six Million Dollar Man, The Rockford Files,* and *Barnaby Jones.*

See: Brothers, Kit. "Larry Holt, Joplin Resident, Enjoys Life as Movie, TV Stuntman." *Joplin Globe.* January 18, 1975; "Former Joplin Man Doubling for Roddy McDowall in Movie." *Joplin Globe.* July 30, 1972.

BUDDY JOE HOOKER
(1942–)

Born in Vallejo, California, Buddy Joe Hooker was the son of stuntman Hugh Hooker. Buddy Joe, known as Joey Hooker or Buddy Hart in his early days, played Wally's friend Chester on the TV series *Leave It to Beaver* before becoming one of the top stuntmen of the 1970s. In 1977 and 1978 he won First Place as the All-Around Stunt Champ on the CBS Stunt Awards competitions. In 1979 he took Second Place to Stunt Champ

Buddy Joe Hooker makes a record car jump on *Hooper* (1978).

Bill Burton. Buddy Joe set a world record for a rocket car jump of 197 feet on *Hooper* (1978) and set records for rappelling, rolling a car, and a ramp-to-ramp motorcycle jump over a helicopter. He was the primary double for action star Jan-Michael Vincent and doubled for Al Pacino, Sam Shepard, and Kurt Russell. Five-foot-nine and 155 pounds, Hooker was a top man at car stunts, fire work, air rams, and high falls and the favored stunt coordinator of directors Francis Ford Coppola and William Friedkin.

On *Clay Pigeon* (1971) Hooker rolled an auto down a hill twenty-two times, gaining immediate respect within the industry. Doubling Perry King on *Search and Destroy* (1979), he tumbled down a hillside and fell into the gorge at Niagara Falls. On *First Blood* (1982) he performed a 100-foot high fall through trees doubling Sylvester Stallone's Rambo character. Hooker coordinated the action on *To Live and Die in L.A.* (1985), including a standout wrong way freeway chase. On a 1969 episode of TV's *The Dating Game* he staged a fight with stuntmen Paul Nuckles and Lance Rimmer while winning an excursion with Farrah Fawcett.

He worked on *What Did You Do in the War, Daddy?* (1966), *Tobruk* (1967), *Ice Station Zebra* (1968), *Harold and Maude* (1971), *The Omega Man* (1971), *Westworld* (1973), *White Lightning* (1973), *No Mercy Man* (1973), *Blazing Saddles* (1974), *Three the Hard Way* (1974), *The Conversation* (1974), *White Line Fever* (1975), *Posse* (1975), *Rafferty and the Gold Dust Twins* (1975), *Vigilante Force* (1976), *Bound for Glory* (1976), *Close Encounters of the Third Kind* (1977), *Game of Death* (1978), *Hot Lead and Cold Feet* (1978), and *The Odd Angry Shot* (1979). TV credits include *Mod Squad*, *The Wild Wild West*, *Mannix*, and *Mission: Impossible*. A member of Stunts Unlimited, Hooker is an inductee of the Stuntmen's Hall of Fame and has been awarded the Action-Fest Lifetime Achievement Award.

See: Souther, Justin. "Legend of the Fall." *Mountain Xpress.* April 5, 2011; "Stuntman Buddy Joe Hooker." *American Profile.* March 12, 2006; www.craveonline.com.

HUGH HOOKER (1919–1987)

Texas-born Hugh Milford Hooker made the trek to California in the 1940s and became a rancher in the San Fernando Valley. He bred horses for the motion picture industry and worked as a stuntman on westerns. Hooker doubled George O'Brien on *Gold Raiders* (1951) and subbed for Gene Autry, John Derek, and Richard Basehart. His work ranged from *King of the Bullwhip* (1950), *Cattle Drive* (1951), and *Fort Defiance* (1951) to *Hooper* (1978) and *Hot Lead and Cold Feet* (1978). TV credits include *The Man from U.N.C.L.E.* His sons Buddy Joe and Billy Hank both became stuntmen. Buddy starred under the name Buddy Hart on *The Littlest Hobo* (1958), a film his father produced.

WESLEY HOPPER (1904–1965)

Born in San Mateo, California, Wesley Irving Hopper doubled Randolph Scott on *High, Wide, and Handsome* (1937) and Joel McCrea on *Sullivan's Travels* (1941). He worked on *King Kong* (1933), *Valley of the Giants* (1938), *Joan of Arc* (1948), *Samson and Delilah* (1949), and *Soldiers Three* (1951). As an actor Hopper did a comic bit where he is attacked by Jane Withers' monkey and dogs, crashes into a vase, and takes a fall on *45 Fathers* (1937). Hopper was far more comfortable doing stunts than essaying acting roles; and his name and face never had a chance to register with audiences. During World War II Hopper served with the U.S. Navy as a petty officer. He was director John Ford's combat photographer for two years, most famously capturing images of the Battle of Midway. He was an honorary member of the Stuntmen's Association.

See: "Stunt Man Finds Acting Hazardous." *Ames Daily Tribune.* November 27, 1937.

CHARLES HORVATH (1920–1978)

Six-foot-three, 220-pound Charles Frank Horvath was born in Upper Macungie Township, Pennsylvania. Nicknamed "Moose," Horvath excelled at football and played fullback for Brown University prior to service with the Armed Forces. He was a sergeant with the U.S. Marines during World War II where he was an instructor in judo and karate. He was the service jiu jitsu champion and wrote the Marine Corps manual on hand-to-hand combat training. During the bulk of the war he was the personal bodyguard to General Eisenhower. He later taught judo to agents of the FBI. After the war, Horvath became one of the group who trained with Allen Pomeroy to become professional stuntmen.

Horvath doubled Burt Lancaster for a dive from the yardarms of a ship on *The Crimson Pirate* (1952). He also worked with Lancaster on *The Flame and the Arrow* (1950), *Jim Thorpe—All American* (1951), *His Majesty O'Keefe* (1954), *Vera Cruz* (1954), *The Kentuckian* (1955), and *Elmer Gantry* (1960). Horvath doubled Rock Hudson on *Scarlet Angel* (1952), *Seminole* (1953), *The Lawless Breed* (1953), *Back to God's Country* (1953), *Taza, Son of Cochise* (1954), *Twilight for the Gods* (1958), and *Blindfold* (1965), Vincent Price on *House of Wax* (1953), Jack Palance on *Sign of the Pagan* (1954) and *Kiss of Fire* (1955), and Jeff Chandler on *East of Sumatra* (1953), *Pillars of the Sky* (1956), *Drango* (1957), and *Man in the Shadow* (1957). Randolph Scott, Errol Flynn, and Mickey Simpson were others whose clothes Horvath wore. He was known for fight scenes, brawling with Gene Evans on *Park Row* (1952), George Montgomery on *Pawnee* (1957), Yul Brynner on *The Brothers Karamazov* (1958), Jim Brown on *Kenner* (1969), and Gene Hackman on *The Domino Principle* (1977). He doubled Leo Gordon on *Seventh Cavalry* (1956) and Tom Reese on *Flaming Star* (1960) in notable fight action.

He worked on *Adventures of Don Juan* (1948), *Silver River* (1948), *Colorado Territory* (1949), *Dallas* (1950), *His Kind of Woman* (1951), *Don Daredevil Rides Again* (1951), *The Man Behind the Gun* (1953), *Thunder Over the Plains* (1953), *Destry* (1954), *Seven Brides for Seven Brothers* (1954), *Border River* (1954), *Prince Valiant* (1954), *The Last Command* (1955), *Chief Crazy Horse* (1955), *Tall Man Riding* (1955), *Around the World in Eighty Days* (1956), *The Conqueror* (1956), *The First Texan* (1956), *The Guns of Fort Petticoat* (1957), *Designing Woman* (1957), *High School Confidential!* (1958), *The Gunfight at Dodge City* (1959), *Spartacus* (1960), *Seven Ways from Sundown* (1960), *Guns of the Timberland* (1960), *Posse from Hell* (1961), *Sergeants Three* (1962), *How the West Was Won* (1962), *McLintock!* (1963), *4 for Texas* (1963), *Showdown* (1963), *Advance to the Rear* (1964), *The Rounders* (1965), *Cat Ballou* (1965), *The Great Race* (1965), *Johnny Reno* (1966), and *Sometimes a Great Notion* (1970). He was a familiar and menacing character heavy on the TV shows *Cheyenne*, *Jim Bowie*, *Broken Arrow*, *Zorro*, *Mike Hammer*, *Richard Diamond*, *Yancy Derringer*, *Peter Gunn*, *The Westerner*, *Hong Kong*, *Bonanza*, *Adventures in Paradise*, *The Untouchables*, *Wagon Train*, *The Man from U.N.C.L.E.*, *Branded*, *I Spy*, *The Wild Wild West*, *Laredo*, *Get Smart*, *Batman*, *Voyage to the Bottom of the Sea*, *Lost in Space*, *Daniel Boone*, *The Big Valley*, *Cimarron Strip*, *High Chaparral*, and *Mannix*. In the late 1960s Horvath suffered a back injury that ended his stunt career. He tended bar at the Backstage, famous watering hole near CBS Studios (the old Republic Studios lot), where stuntmen would stage fights for their own entertainment. A member of the Stuntmen's Hall of Fame.

See: "Charles Horvath, Top TV Stuntman Risks Neck Often." *Van Nuys Valley News*. December 1, 1967.

LUCILLE HOUSE (1910–2008)

Lucille House is best known as the personal double for Maureen O'Hara. Their association lasted nearly thirty years, beginning at RKO in the early 1940s and including the films *Tripoli* (1950), *Flame of Araby* (1951), *Spencer's Mountain* (1963), and *McLintock!* (1963). A noted trick rider, the Ohio-born House came from a family of horse wranglers and livestock suppliers from the House Stables. She also worked on *The Great Gatsby* (1949), *Westward, the Women* (1951), and *Destry* (1954). House died after a battle with Alzheimer's.

See: Lilley, Tim. *Campfire Conversations*. Akron, OH: Big Trail, 2007.

FRANK HOWARD

British stuntman Frank Howard specialized in high falls and being killed on screen, suffering screen deaths on *Helen of Troy* (1955), *Zarak* (1956), *The Bridge on the River Kwai* (1957), *Solomon and Sheba* (1960), and *The Guns of Navarone* (1961). On *The Crimson Pirate* (1952) he was the underwater double for Nick Cravat. The Merchant Navy veteran entered the stunt profession after he was discovered performing in an adagio act. He was a member of Jock Easton's stunt team.

See: "Death Has No Sting for Stunt Man Howard." *Plain Dealer*. May 1, 1960.

CLYDE HOWDY (1921–1969)

Six-foot-three Clyde Woodard Houdeshell was a stand-in and double for his friend Clint

Walker on the TV series *Cheyenne* (1955–63). Ironically, he had to wear lifts on his boots when standing in for the 6'5" Walker. The Ohio-born rodeo and U.S. Navy veteran was a competitive motorcycle and off-road racer in addition to being a horseman. He garnered publicity as a member of the Freedom Riders in 1960 when a Pony Express team traveled to Washington. A wilderness enthusiast, he was one of the original members of the Viewfinders Motorcycle Club in 1966.

He worked on *Gun Duel in Durango* (1957), *Yellowstone Kelly* (1959), *The Jayhawkers!* (1959), *Westbound* (1959), *PT 109* (1963), *4 for Texas* (1963), *Send Me No Flowers* (1964), *A Distant Trumpet* (1964), *Bonnie and Clyde* (1967), *Coogan's Bluff* (1968), and *There Was a Crooked Man...* (1970). TV credits include *Gunsmoke, Lawman, Maverick, Bronco, Bonanza, Death Valley Days, The Virginian,* and *Laredo*. As an actor he portrayed forest ranger Hank Whitfield on TV's *Lassie* (1964–66).

See: "Tall, but Short." *Salt Lake Tribune.* August 22, 1959.

REED HOWES (1900–1964)

Hermon Reed Howes, a native of Washington, D.C., was an all-around athlete at the University of Utah where he participated in swimming, wrestling, basketball, and squash. A veteran of the U.S. Navy during World War I, Howes was the captain of the Pacific Fleet Swim Team. He initially came into prominence as a model for J.C. Leyendecker's popular Arrow Collar Shirt ads. This exposure attracted the attention of Hollywood. Six-foot, 200-pound Howes became a silent film action star on films like *Roughhouse Rosie* (1927). He was well known at the time for his thrilling stunt work. It's been said he was the first man to jump from the wing of an airplane into an open motorboat for the cameras on *Broken Violin* (1923). In 1924 he was named the Handsomest Man in Hollywood, and females of the day were ecstatic over his muscles.

Quite adept at fisticuffs, Howes' greatest bout was with the bottle. He also had trouble with the transition to sound. By the 1930s he was appearing in support in many westerns and working as an anonymous stuntman, earning $35 for a fight or a fall in films such as *Dodge City* (1939), *Virginia City* (1940), *The Desperadoes* (1943), *Ali Baba and the Forty Thieves* (1943), *Desert Hawk* (1944), *Belle of the Yukon* (1944), *River Lady* (1948), and *The Last Posse* (1953). In all, he made over 240 films, approximately 175 of them as a stuntman. His fight skills typed him as a henchman heavy, and his roles grew smaller until he was making blink-and-you-miss-him cameos. His best fights came opposite John Wayne on *Dawn Rider* (1935), Herman Brix on *Million to One* (1937), and Tex Fletcher on *Six Gun Law* (1938). Howes died of prostate cancer at the age of 64.

See: "Male of the Movies!" *Los Angeles Times.* March 6, 1927; "Reed Howes, Silent Star Tries for Film Comeback." *Lewiston Morning Times.* September 19, 1943; "Talks on Fights." *Repository.* October 12, 1925.

ROBERT HOY (1927–2010)

Bob Hoy was one of the few stuntmen who went on to a distinguished career as a character actor, beginning with his popular supporting work as ranch hand Joe Butler on the western series *High Chaparral* (1967–71). He became in-demand for acting parts on *Bite the Bullet* (1975), *The Outlaw Josey Wales* (1976), and *The Duchess and the Dirtwater Fox* (1976) even though he was still a capable stuntman. Clint Eastwood didn't forget his stunt abilities and punched him around on *The Enforcer* (1976) and *Bronco Billy* (1980).

Robert Francis Hoy was born in New York City, raised in the Adirondacks and worked at a dude ranch in the Catskill Mountains. Hoy attended New York Military Academy and was being groomed for West Point, but chose to join the U.S. Marines at the close of World War II. After serving in Okinawa, the 5'10", 165-pound he stayed active in the Marine Reserves. He found work as a cowboy on a Nevada ranch before migrating to Hollywood. When the Korean Conflict broke out, he tried to re-enlist with the Marines but was turned down because of a bad leg injury he had sustained doing stunt work.

Hoy apprenticed with Dave Sharpe and doubled Tony Curtis for the rapids work on *The Defiant Ones* (1958). He subbed for Curtis on *Spartacus* (1960) and *The Great Race* (1965). He doubled Charles Bronson diving down a rock ledge on *Drum Beat* (1954) and Telly Savalas for a backward fall on *Beau Geste* (1966). Other actors he took bumps for include Tyrone Power, Audie Murphy, Charles McGraw, Jay Silverheels, David Janssen, Stuart Whitman, Anthony Caruso,

Paul Picerni, and Robert Forster. On TV he doubled Robert Vaughn on *The Man from U.N.C.L.E.* On *Choke Canyon* (1986) Hoy fought Stephen Collins while hanging on a giant wrecking ball suspended beneath a helicopter. Hoy was lauded for his knowledge of horses and the measure of safety he brought to difficult stunts.

He worked on *Ambush* (1949), *The Lawless Breed* (1952), *War Arrow* (1952), *The Man from the Alamo* (1953), *Wings of the Hawk* (1953), *Border River* (1954), *Destry* (1954), *River of No Return* (1954), *Saskatchewan* (1954), *Four Guns to the Border* (1954), *Taza, Son of Cochise* (1954), *The Silver Chalice* (1954), *The Black Shield of Falworth* (1954), *Kiss of Fire* (1955), *The Long Gray Line* (1955), *One Desire* (1955), *Revenge of the Creature* (1955), *To Hell and Back* (1955), *The Rawhide Years* (1955), *Away All Boats* (1956), *Raw Edge* (1956), *Walk the Proud Land* (1956), *The Mole People* (1956), *Slim Carter* (1957), *Gun for a Coward* (1957), *No Time for Sergeants* (1958), *Twilight for the Gods* (1958), *Operation Petticoat* (1959), *The Spiral Road* (1962), *The Ugly American* (1963), *It's a Mad, Mad, Mad, Mad World* (1963), *Quick Before It Melts* (1964), *Tickle Me* (1965), *Cat Ballou* (1965), *Slender Thread* (1965), *Nevada Smith* (1966), *Assault on a Queen* (1966), *What Did You Do in the War, Daddy?* (1966), *First to Fight* (1967), *Tobruk* (1967), *Rogue's Gallery* (1968), *5 Card Stud* (1968), *The Love Bug* (1968), *Che!* (1969), *The Don Is Dead* (1973), *Scream, Blacula, Scream* (1973), *99 and 44/100 percent Dead* (1974), and *The Gauntlet* (1977). TV credits include *Zane Grey, Have Gun—Will Travel, Trackdown, Johnny Ringo, Whispering Smith, The Rifleman, Laramie, The Virginian, Combat, Branded, Laredo, The Wild Wild West, The Man from U.N.C.L.E., Mission: Impossible, Guns of Will Sonnett, The Green Hornet, The FBI, Mannix, Mod Squad, Cade's County, Kung Fu, The Six Million Dollar Man, The Rockford Files, Police Story, Cannon, Bronk, Police Woman, Switch, Hawaii Five-O, Wonder Woman, Vega$,* and *The Fall Guy.* He was a founding member of the Stuntmen's Association and an inductee of the Stuntmen's Hall of Fame, and received the final Golden Boot Award on his hospital death bed. Hoy died at the age of 82 from cancer.

See: Cutts, Terry. *Armchair Cowboy.* Canterbury, England: Parker, 2012; Pavillard, Dan. "*High Chaparral* Stuntmen Seek Renown, Security." *Tucson Daily Citizen.* January 18, 1968; www.bobhoy.com.

ACE HUDKINS (1905–1973)

Asa "Ace" Hudkins was a legendary boxer known for fighting bloodbaths throughout the ranks from bantam to light-heavyweight. The 5'8" Nebraska Wildcat was never knocked out, but his penchant for drinking undid a promising career. The California State champ was a top draw at L.A.'s Olympic Auditorium, and his fight against Sammy Baker was said to be the bloodiest ever seen. After a deluge of arrests in the early 1930s, he settled down to the family ranch to wrangle horses and do stunts for the movie business with his brother Clyde.

He worked on *San Antonio* (1945), *The Spanish Main* (1945), *Objective Burma!* (1945), *The Great John L* (1945), *Champion* (1949), *Prince Valiant* (1954), *Around the World in Eighty Days* (1956), *Westward Ho, the Wagons!* (1956), *Tonka* (1958), and *Batman* (1966). He doubled William Holden on *The Man from Colorado* (1948). An inductee of the World Boxing Hall of Fame, Hudkins died at the age of 67 after a battle with Parkinson's Disease.

See: "Ace Hudkins Dies at 67." *Spokane Daily Chronicle.* April 18, 1973; Becker, Bill. "Ex Fighter Herds Horses for Films." *New York Times.* March 9, 1962.

DICK HUDKINS (1925–1983)

Dick Hudkins was born in Lincoln, Nebraska. The 5'8", 160-pound cousin of Ace and Clyde Hudkins, Jr., he did stunts on *San Antonio* (1945), *The Younger Brothers* (1949), *Colt .45* (1950), *Ride a Crooked Trail* (1958), *The Hanging Tree* (1959), *Ocean's Eleven* (1960), *Stagecoach* (1966), *Welcome to Hard Times* (1967), *The Great Bank Robbery* (1969), *Paint Your Wagon* (1969), *The Good Guys and the Bad Guys* (1969), *Beneath the Planet of the Apes* (1970), *Sometimes a Great Notion* (1970), and *Skin Game* (1971). He was a member of the Stuntmen's Association.

JOHN HUDKINS (1918–1997)

John "Bear" Hudkins was far and away the most skilled and best known of the Hudkins stuntmen. The 5'11", 185-pound Hudkins was born in Lincoln, Nebraska, and learned to ride at a young age. He moved to California to play football and baseball on scholarship for UCLA. Unfortunately, his father passed away and the rest of the family in Nebraska was in desperate need of money. John gave up his athletic career to work on his uncles' ranch in California. He learned the rudiments of the stunt trade from Ace and Clyde Hudkins and Yakima Canutt.

He doubled Spencer Tracy and Arthur Kennedy several times, as well as James Cagney on *The Oklahoma Kid* (1939), Richard Widmark on *Pickup on South Street* (1953), William Holden on *The Horse Soldiers* (1959), Lee Marvin on *The Professionals* (1966), and George C. Scott on *Oklahoma Crude* (1973). His comic doubling of Jonathan Winters for the garage fight in *It's a Mad, Mad, Mad, Mad World* (1963) was especially memorable. As a wagon team driver and horse-fall specialist he was employed often by John Ford and John Wayne. On *Fort Apache* (1948) he broke his back doing a saddle drag and was laid up for a year. His return to full-time stunt work solidified his reputation. On his first day back he performed twenty-three horse falls. He did the majority of his falls on the horse Jerry Brown. On *The Alamo* (1960) he was bulldogged by Dean Smith and was in the mass horse fall.

He worked on *They Died with Their Boots On* (1941), *Angel and the Badman* (1947), *She Wore a Yellow Ribbon* (1949), *The Fighting Kentuckian* (1949), *Rio Grande* (1950), *Prince Valiant* (1954), *The Prodigal* (1955), *The Searchers* (1956), *Westward Ho, the Wagons!* (1956), *The Wings of Eagles* (1957), *Designing Woman* (1957), *Ride Out for Revenge* (1957), *Westbound* (1959), *Rio Bravo* (1959), *Pork Chop Hill* (1959), *The Hanging Tree* (1959), *The Man Who Shot Liberty Valance* (1962), *A Distant Trumpet* (1964), *The Great Race* (1965), *The Rounders* (1965), *Alvarez Kelly* (1966), *Stagecoach* (1966), *Point Blank* (1967), *Bandolero!* (1968), *The Devil's Brigade* (1968), *The Green Berets* (1968), *Paint Your Wagon* (1969), *The Undefeated* (1969), *Monte Walsh* (1970), *Rio Lobo* (1970), *Dirty Harry* (1971), *Bless the Beasts and the Children* (1971), *Prime Cut* (1972), *Life and Times of Judge Roy Bean* (1972), *High Plains Drifter* (1973), *The Stone Killer* (1973), *99 and 44/100 percent Dead* (1974), *Doc Savage* (1975), *The Outlaw Josey Wales* (1976), *Family Plot* (1976), *Hawmps!* (1976), *The Domino Principle* (1977), and *F.I.S.T.* (1978). TV credits include *The Lone Ranger, The Outer Limits, The Wild Wild West, Cimarron Strip,* and *Gunsmoke*. He was a member of the Stuntmen's Association and the Stuntmen's Hall of Fame.

See: Lilley, Tim. *Campfire Conversations Complete*. Akron, OH: Big Trail, 2010.

TOMMY J. HUFF (1943–2006)

Five-foot-ten, 150-pound Thomas J. Huff was born in Los Angeles and attended North Hollywood High. After service with the U.S. Army he found work as a carpenter while pursuing a career as a professional boxer. As a welterweight he attracted the attention of fight fan Robert Conrad, who put him to work on the final TV season of *The Wild Wild West* (1968–69). Huff doubled Jerry Reed on *Gator* (1976) and *Smokey and the Bandit* (1977) and Dan Aykroyd on *The Blues Brothers* (1980). One of his specialties was driving big rigs.

He worked on *Slaughter's Big Rip-Off* (1973), *Freebie and the Bean* (1974), *The Dion Brothers* (1974), *The Front Page* (1974), *Earthquake* (1974), *Big Bad Mama* (1974), *Day of the Locust* (1975), *Farewell, My Lovely* (1975), *Capone* (1975), *Mother, Jugs, and Speed* (1976), *Nickelodeon* (1976), *Gable and Lombard* (1976), *Two-Minute Warning* (1976), *Logan's Run* (1976), *Hooper* (1978), *Convoy* (1978), *Who'll Stop the Rain* (1978), *Hot Lead and Cold Feet* (1978), *Buck Rogers in the 25th Century* (1979), *The Warriors* (1979), *The Frisco Kid* (1979), and *Steel* (1979). TV credits include *Vega$*. He was a member of Stunts Unlimited and the Stuntmen's Hall of Fame.

WHITEY HUGHES (1920–2009)

Robert James "Whitey" Hughes was born in Arkoma, Oklahoma. He grew up on a farm, learning to break horses and operate machinery. When his family moved to Los Angeles, he worked on the docks and drove trucks. He briefly served with the U.S. Navy but was discharged due to an ear infection. The 5'6", 140-pound Hughes began in the movie business as a livestock teamster but got his SAG card in 1947 while driving a taxi cab. He had driven to a film location and watched a scene in progress where an actress couldn't accomplish a horse stunt. Whitey volunteered and was soon doing stunt work; his small size made him ideal to double women and children. He regularly stunted for Bobby Diamond on the TV series *Fury* (1955–60), Johnny Crawford on *The Rifle-*

Tommy Huff, doubling Jerry Reed, gets knocked around by Burt Reynolds on *Gator* (1976).

man (1958–63), and Jon Provost on *Lassie* (1957–64). He doubled for actresses Rita Hayworth, Lana Turner, Stefanie Powers, Virginia Mayo, and Anne Baxter, as well as actors Nick Adams, Dub Taylor, Sammy Davis, Jr., J. Carrol Naish, Edward G. Robinson, Spade Cooley, and Warren Oates.

Whitey's greatest claim to fame was as the stunt coordinator for the majority of the run of the TV series *The Wild Wild West* (1965–69), where he staged and participated in some of the greatest TV brawls seen on the small screen. Blessed with perfect timing, Whitey was an all-around stuntman who could do it all: fights, falls, cars, motorcycles, planes, trains, wagons, and especially horses. He performed a fifty-foot high fall between two ships docked seven feet apart in San Francisco Bay on *The Killer Elite* (1975) and drove a motorcycle into a pine tree, then fell fifty-five feet on *The Gumball Rally* (1976). He doubled actress Barbara Hershey for a fall off a rock into the ocean on *The Stunt Man* (1980).

He worked on *Along the Great Divide* (1951), *Son of the Renegade* (1953), *The Charge at Feather River* (1953), *The Wild One* (1953), *Sitting Bull* (1954), *Giant* (1956), *Westward Ho, the Wagons!* (1956), *Darby O'Gill and the Little People* (1959), *Geronimo* (1962), *Major Dundee* (1965), *The Glory Guys* (1965), *Planet of the Apes* (1968), *Guns for San Sebastian* (1968), *The Wild Bunch* (1969), *Beneath the Planet of the Apes* (1970), *The Omega Man* (1971), *Conquest of the Planet of the Apes* (1972), *The Getaway* (1972), *Dillinger* (1973), *Battle for the Planet of the Apes* (1973), *Pat Garrett and Billy the Kid* (1973), *Freebie and the Bean* (1974), *Bring Me the Head of Alfredo Garcia* (1974), *The Big Bus* (1976), *Logan's Run* (1976), *Convoy* (1978), and *The Nude Bomb* (1980). TV credits include *Gunsmoke, Wonder Woman,* and *The Fall Guy.* A member of the Stuntmen's Hall of Fame, Whitey was awarded a Golden Boot for his contributions to the western genre.

See: Cutts, Terry. *Armchair Cowboy.* Canter-

Whitey Hughes pilots a motorcycle through a billboard on *The Gumball Rally* **(1976).**

bury, England: Parker, 2012; Villanueva, Hollie. "So Long, Cowboy." *Yuma Sun.* August 15, 2009; "Whitey Hughes: A Country Boy from Oklahoma." *Bonanza Gold.* January-February-March 2006.

CHARLES HUTCHISON (1879–1949)

Charles Hutchison was born in Pittsburgh, Pennsylvania. As a boy he took dives into the Allegheny River and played on ship riggings. His athleticism and daring served him well as the star of early Pathe serials such as *Wolves of Culture* (1918). The 5'10", 160-pound Hutchison designed the stunt scenarios for his films and set out to prove that they could be done. Many involved trick motorcycle jumps. Unfortunately, he broke his body apart in his climb to stardom. On his later serials *Hurricane Hutch* (1922), *Speed* (1922),

and *Lightning Hutch* (1926) he was reluctant to perform his own action and had stuntmen Joe Cuny and Frank Hagney on hand as doubles. Pathe continued to claim he did his own stunt work, billing him as "The Thrill-a-Minute Stunt King." Hutchison eventually moved into work as a director. He was an inductee of the Stuntmen's Hall of Fame.

See: Weitzel, Edward Winfield. *Intimate Talks with Movie Stars, Volume 1.* Dale, 1921.

JOHN INDRISANO (1905–1968)

John Indrisano was born in Boston, Massachusetts. He began boxing as a youth and won the 1922 New England Amateur Boxing Championship as a welterweight. He had over 155 amateur fights before turning pro, originally under the name Johnny Andrews. The 5'9" pugilist later

John Indrisano coordinated an army of stuntmen battling one another on *4 for Texas* (1963).

fought as a middleweight, compiling a 64–9–4 professional record with thirteen knockouts. Indrisano defeated five world champs along the way but never claimed a title of his own. He was a bodyguard for Mae West and entered films under her guidance. He stayed in the fight game as a referee for more than a decade until he established himself as a boxing coordinator and trainer of such stars as John Garfield, Robert Taylor, Fred MacMurray, Ricardo Montalban, Mickey Rooney, Danny Kaye, Zachary Scott, and Robert Ryan. Indrisano played dozens of bit parts and worked as a stuntman for many years. During World War II he taught jiu jitsu to the Coast Guard and served in the U.S. Marines.

Indrisano revolutionized the way boxing was put on the screen. He would read the script to understand the character of each fighter and treated the action like a choreographed ballet for the movie cameras as opposed to having two men slugging away at one another's shoulders. He could often be seen as referees overseeing the ring action on films such as *Body and Soul* (1947). One of his greatest achievements came in the brilliantly choreographed ring action between Robert Ryan and Hal Baylor on *The Set-Up* (1949). Indrisano coordinated the fight between Ryan and Mike Mazurki on *Behind the Rising Sun* (1943), the famous battle between Spencer Tracy and Ernest Borgnine on *Bad Day at Black Rock* (1955), and the fight between Frank Sinatra and Henry Silva on *The Manchurian Candidate* (1962).

He worked on *Silk Hat Kid* (1935), *Reaching for the Moon* (1941), *Murder My Sweet* (1944), *Johnny Angel* (1945), *The Southerner* (1945), *The Great John L* (1945), *Wild Harvest* (1947), *Killer McCoy* (1947), *Lulu Belle* (1948), *Bodyguard* (1948), *Roadhouse* (1948), *Force of Evil* (1948), *Westward the Women* (1951), *Across the Wide Missouri* (1951), *Scaramouche* (1952), *99 River Street* (1953), *It's Always Fair Weather* (1955), *Guys and Dolls* (1955), *The Sea Chase* (1955), *Shack Out on 101* (1955), *Somebody Up There Likes Me* (1956), *The Harder They Fall* (1956), *Jailhouse Rock* (1957), *Chicago Confidential* (1957), *Ten North Frederick* (1958), *The Buccaneer* (1958), *Lafayette Escadrille* (1958), *King Creole* (1958), *Pillow Talk* (1959), *Ocean's 11* (1960), *It Happened at the World's Fair* (1962), *Hud* (1963), *4 for Texas* (1963), *In Harm's Way* (1965), *Situation Hopeless—But Not Serious* (1965), *The War Wagon* (1967), *The Ambushers* (1967), and *Skidoo* (1968).

TV credits include *Richard Diamond*, *Man with a Camera*, *Tightrope*, and *Peter Gunn*. An Honorary Member of the Stuntmen's Association, Indrisano was found dead of an apparent suicidal hanging at the age of 62.

See: "Indrisano, Coach of Film Fights." *Ring Magazine*. August 1963; Lindeman, Edith. "Johnny Indrisano's Fists Pay Off in Hollywood." *Richmond Times*. January 4, 1948; MacPherson, Virginia. "Film Boxers Look Like Pros When Indrisano Starts Work." *St. Petersburg Times*. July 27, 1945.

JACK INGRAM (1902–1969)

Prolific character actor Jack Ingram performed stunt work with horses, autos, four-ups, and six-ups during the early 1930s. Chicago-born John Samuel Ingram broke his arm, a wrist, and several ribs doubling Errol Flynn for a fantastic leap onto a man on a horse on *The Charge of the Light Brigade* (1936). This convinced him to move into acting over stunts. The World War I veteran worked often in B-westerns and serials because he could ride and fight as an action heavy, though he began to be doubled later in his career. One of his best fights came opposite Johnny Mack Brown and Tex Ritter on *Lone Star Trail* (1943). At one point publicity claimed he had been killed on screen more than any other actor. At the peak of his career, Ingram acquired the land that became the Ingram Ranch western set, where he lived and worked during the 1950s. Ingram died of a heart attack at the age of 66.

See: Jones, Ken. "Jack Ingram: A Nice Bad Man." *Western Film Collector*. July 1973.

LOREN JANES (1931–)

Stunt legend Loren Janes was known as One Take Janes due to his ability to nail a stunt perfectly on the first try. One of the best pure athletes in the profession, he pulled off amazing stunts for the cameras. For *Attack!* (1955) he took a face-first dead fall for Eddie Albert. On *Swiss Family Robinson* (1960) he wrestled a 400-pound python while doubling James MacArthur. On *How the West Was Won* (1962) he was shot off a moving train going thirty miles per hour and hit a cactus in flight. On *It's a Mad, Mad, Mad, Mad World* (1963) he doubled Eddie "Rochester" Anderson falling off a ladder onto a trampoline and being bounced up onto a nearby statue. On *Nevada Smith* (1966) he was in the center of a cattle stampede. On the TV series *The FBI* he made a twenty-three-foot broad jump across two cliffs. On *Bullitt* (1968) he dove between the wheels of a jet airplane. On *What's Up, Doc?* (1972) he leaped out of a convertible going seventy MPH off a pier. For *The Other Side of the Mountain* (1975) he did a sixty-foot high fall off a cliff on skis. On *The Drowning Pool* (1975) he was blasted

Loren Janes times a spectacular leap off a train onto a cactus on *How the West Was Won* (1962).

by a torrent of water escaping from a sealed chamber. *Good Guys Wear Black* (1978) saw him make a 187-foot ski jump followed by a 250-yard wipeout after being shot. On Steve McQueen's last film *The Hunter* (1980) he hung from a ladder extended off a Chicago rail car going fifty-five MPH.

Janes doubled Kirk Douglas on *Spartacus* (1960) and Steve McQueen on the TV series *Wanted—Dead or Alive* (1958–62). He befriended McQueen and stuck with him for the next twenty years on films such as *The Sand Pebbles* (1966). Among the other actors Janes doubled were Frank Sinatra, Yul Brynner, Paul Newman, Jack Nicholson, Charles Bronson, Robert Wagner, Tony Curtis, Jack Lemmon, and James Franciscus. On TV he doubled Efrem Zimbalist, Jr., on *The FBI*, Don Adams on *Get Smart*, William Shatner on *Star Trek*, and Michael Douglas on *The Streets of San Francisco*. He also doubled females, standing in for the likes of Debbie Reynolds and Shirley MacLaine. In all he appeared in over 500 films and 2100 TV shows.

Loren Janes was born in Sierra Madre, California. He worked on a dairy farm and spent a great deal of his youth riding horses bareback. Influenced by Tarzan books, he would arm himself with only a hunting knife and take off into the wild. Four times he hiked the 222-mile John Muir Trail. He was an excellent gymnast and a champion swimmer and diver, breaking a number of high school records. The 5'10", 160-pound Janes won the Junior National Swim Title and later competed in the Nationals. He excelled in water polo and was a certified lifeguard. Janes was a swimmer and diver at Cal Poly. He served as a U.S. Marine during the Korean War, breaking Corps records in the obstacle course and on the firing range.

He was teaching high school trigonometry when students recommended him to a film producer looking for someone to make an eighty-foot dive off a Catalina Island cliff on the film *Jupiter's Darling* (1955). Janes made the dive and the producers kept calling. His stunt training came courtesy of David Sharpe and Richard Talmadge. Janes never broke a bone in stunt work, a testament to his superb conditioning and safety measures. Twice he qualified for the U.S. Olympic trials in the Pentathlon, in 1956 and 1964, becoming the first non-military athlete to do so. He was a member of the Explorer's Club and a one-time president of the Adventurer's Club.

He worked on *The Ten Commandments* (1956), *Friendly Persuasion* (1956), *Walk the Proud Land* (1956), *The First Texan* (1956), *The Oklahoman* (1957), *The Tall Stranger* (1957), *The Buccaneer* (1958), *High School Confidential!* (1958), *Darby O'Gill and the Little People* (1959), *Thunder in the Sun* (1959), *The Magnificent Seven* (1960), *North to Alaska* (1960), *Flaming Star* (1960), *Everything's Ducky* (1961), *Hell Is for Heroes* (1962), *Taras Bulba* (1962), *Captain Newman, M.D.* (1963), *McLintock!* (1963), *Cheyenne Autumn* (1964), *The Greatest Story Ever Told* (1965), *In Harm's Way* (1965), *The Sons of Katie Elder* (1965), *Camelot* (1967), *The King's Pirate* (1967), *Planet of the Apes* (1968), *Coogan's Bluff* (1968), *Ice Station Zebra* (1968), *Paint Your Wagon* (1969), *The Good Guys and the Bad Guys* (1969), *Little Big Man* (1970), *Beneath the Planet of the Apes* (1970), *Support Your Local Gunfighter* (1971), *The Poseidon Adventure* (1972), *The Don Is Dead* (1973), *99 and 44/100 percent Dead* (1974), *Blazing Saddles* (1974), *Earthquake* (1974), *The Towering Inferno* (1974), *The Master Gunfighter* (1975), *The Ultimate Warrior* (1975), *Logan's Run* (1976), *Swashbuckler* (1976), *King Kong* (1976), *F.I.S.T.* (1978), *The Swarm* (1978), *1941* (1979), and *The Big Brawl* (1980). Janes was a founding member of the Stuntmen's Association and a recipient of the Golden Boot and the Silver Spur Awards. He is a Taurus Lifetime Achievement honoree and has been inducted into both the Stuntmen's Hall of Fame and the World Acrobatic Society Hall of Fame.

See: Ciarfalio, Carl. "Loren Janes: Living Life to Its Fullest." *Inside Stunts*. Winter, 2008; Hill, Graham. "Loren Janes: Falling for Hollywood." *Wildest Westerns*. #4, 2002; King, Susan. "Tribute to the Unknown Stuntmen." *Los Angeles Times*. June 1, 2002; Lilley, Tim. *Campfire Conversations Complete*. Akron, OH: Big Trail, 2010; Robison, Nancy. "Visit with a Hollywood Stuntman." *Christian Science Monitor*. July 22, 1964; Row, Erica. "Stuntman's Life on Display." *Valley Sun*. August 14, 2008; Wood, Daniel. "King of Stuntmen." *Christian Science Monitor*. January 20, 1989; www.lorenjanes.com.

ANDY JAUREGUI (1903–1990)

As a rodeo cowboy in the 1920s and 1930s, Santa Paulo, California–born Andy Jauregui was a successful saddle bronc rider and later a World

Champion Steer Roper, Calf Roper, and Team Roper. As a stuntman he doubled on horseback for Richard Dix and Bob Steele. Legend has it he made the controversial horse jump over Beale's Cut for Tom Mix on *Three Jumps Ahead* (1923). Brother Eddie was also a stuntman on a number of John Ford films and brother Bob was a movie wrangler. Andy was the head of the Jauregui Ranch in Placerita Canyon and provided livestock for motion pictures and rodeos for a number of years. He was inducted into the Cowboy Hall of Fame and Newhall, California's Walk of Western Stars. Jauregui died from Parkinson's Disease at the age of 87.

See: "Champion Cowboy Andy Jauregui, 87, Dies." *Los Angeles Times.* July 17, 1990.

ED JAUREGUI (1912–1980)

California-born Michael Edward Jauregui became perhaps the highest profile member of the Jauregui family, well known in Hollywood circles as top rodeo performers. Ed was cast as the Athenian charioteer on *Ben-Hur* (1959) and did stunts on *Spy Smasher* (1942), *Buffalo Bill* (1944), *Wagon Master* (1950), *Across the Wide Missouri* (1951), *Westward the Women* (1951), *Westward Ho, the Wagons!* (1956), *Cattle Empire* (1958), *The Alamo* (1960), *Two Rode Together* (1961), *The Man Who Shot Liberty Valance* (1962), *How the West Was Won* (1962), *Cheyenne Autumn* (1964), *Camelot* (1967), and *Earthquake* (1974).

ROY JENSON (1927–2007)

Burly Roy Jenson became one of the most familiar character players of the 1970s in films such as *Sometimes a Great Notion* (1970), *The Getaway* (1972), *Life and Times of Judge Roy Bean* (1972), *Soylent Green* (1973), *Dillinger* (1973), *Thunderbolt and Lightfoot* (1974), *Chinatown* (1974), *99 and 44/100 percent Dead* (1974), *The Wind and the Lion* (1975), *Breakheart Pass* (1976), *Duchess and the Dirtwater Fox* (1976), *Telefon* (1977), *The Gauntlet* (1977), *Every Which Way But Loose* (1978), *Tom Horn* (1980), and *Any Which Way You Can* (1980). Prior to that, he was a much in-demand stuntman whose reputation as a real-life tough guy was legendary. The Canadian-born Jenson worked construction jobs in California and in logging camps as a lumberjack prior to service with the U.S. Navy at the end of World War II.

He was a standout lineman for UCLA, which led to professional football stints with the Calgary Stampeders, the Montreal Alouettes, and the British Columbia Lions over a nine-year period. In 1954 the 6'2", 215-pound Jenson was selected as a Western All-Star in the Canadian Football League.

Jenson began working as a stuntman in the football off-season, getting his big break when he doubled Robert Mitchum for the dangerous rafting scenes on the Bow River rapids in *River of No Return* (1954). Jenson went on to double Victor Mature, Jack Palance, Aldo Ray, and Scott Brady. His most notable stunt was the longest stair-fall ever performed when he rolled down the length of the steps of a Mayan pyramid doubling Leo Gordon on the film *Kings of the Sun* (1963). Jenson was a strong swimmer, which served him well for any type of aquatic action, and he was capable with horses, motorcycles, and high falls. His true forte was fight scenes, with an excellent showcase coming as the double for Richard Egan on *These Thousand Hills* (1959). He can be spotted in the famous brawls on both *McLintock!* (1963) and *The Great Race* (1965). James Coburn karate chopped him on *Our Man Flint* (1966), Dean Martin knocked him into a beer vat on *The Ambushers* (1967), and Charlton Heston hit him over the head with a frying pan on *Will Penny* (1968). His fight opposite Joe Don Baker on *Framed* (1975) is regarded as one of the screen's most brutal and realistic. As an actor Jenson excelled at portraying cruel villains who often met justifiably violent deaths. His acting career gained momentum after he menaced Paul Newman on *Harper* (1966), throwing some of the most sadistic punches the screen had ever seen.

He worked on *Samson and Delilah* (1949), *Flame and the Arrow* (1950), *Westward the Women* (1951), *Anne of the Indies* (1951), *Demetrius and the Gladiators* (1954), *The Caine Mutiny* (1954), *Broken Lance* (1954), *Saskatchewan* (1954), *The Harder They Fall* (1956), *The Sharkfighters* (1956), *3:10 to Yuma* (1957), *The Buccaneer* (1958), *The Missouri Traveler* (1958), *Buchanan Rides Alone* (1958), *Ride Lonesome* (1959), *Warlock* (1959), *Career* (1959), *Never So Few* (1959), *The Rise and Fall of Legs Diamond* (1960), *North to Alaska* (1960), *Flaming Star* (1960), *The Fiercest Heart* (1961), *Atlantis the Lost Continent* (1961), *Marines, Let's Go* (1961), *Confessions of an Opium Eater* (1962), *How the West Was Won*

(1962), *The Great Escape* (1963), *4 for Texas* (1963), *Mail Order Bride* (1964), *Law of the Lawless* (1964), *Stage to Thunder Rock* (1964), *Baby, the Rain Must Fall* (1965), *Black Spurs* (1965), *The War Lord* (1965), *Morituri* (1965), *The Rounders* (1965), *Shenandoah* (1965), *Apache Uprising* (1965), *Blindfold* (1965), *The Fortune Cookie* (1966), *Red Tomahawk* (1967), *Hostile Guns* (1967), *Camelot* (1967), *The Thomas Crown Affair* (1968), and *Mountain Men* (1980). Jenson

Roy Jenson (left) fights actor James Coburn on *Our Man Flint* (1966).

was a frequent television guest, fighting nearly all the heroes of the small screen on everything from *Star Trek* to *Kung Fu*. He appeared on *Yancy Derringer, Peter Gunn, Hong Kong, Bonanza, Wagon Train, Rawhide, The Outer Limits, The Fugitive, Daniel Boone, Honey West, Batman, The Big Valley, Hondo, Tarzan, Voyage to the Bottom of the Sea, Gunsmoke, I Spy, The Man from U.N.C.L.E., Mission: Impossible, Mannix, High Chaparral, Outcasts, Lancer, Search, Chase, Toma, The Streets of San Francisco, Barnaby Jones, Manhunter, Baretta, Kojak, The Rockford Files, Charlie's Angels, How the West Was Won, Vega$,* and *The Dukes of Hazzard*. He drifted away from performing stunt work for others, but many of his own roles still required him to take falls or punches. He did so with charismatic aplomb. Jenson died from cancer at the age of 80.

See: Crumley, James. *The Muddy Fork & Other Things*. Livingston, Mont: Clark City, 1991; "Empty Saddles." *Western Clippings*. #78, July-August 2007; McCoy, Heath. "Jenson Dove into Hollywood." *Calgary-Herald*. May 16, 2007; Roesler, Bob. "Sports Scene." *Times-Picayune*. July 6, 1972; "Roy Jenson, 80." *Los Angeles Times*. May 4, 2007.

BEN JOHNSON (1918–1996)

Expert horseman Ben Johnson attracted the attention of director John Ford when he stopped a real-life runaway wagon on the set of *Fort Apache* (1948). He had been hired to double John Wayne, John Agar, and Henry Fonda and thought his heroism might lead to more doubling work. Ford not only put him in his stock company but rewarded him with leading roles on *Mighty Joe Young* (1949) and *Wagon Master* (1950). One of the classic movie images is Johnson galloping hell bent for leather across Monument Valley for Ford's appreciative camera on *She Wore a Yellow Ribbon* (1949). On *Rio Grande* (1950) Ford showcased Johnson and Harry Carey, Jr. doing Roman riding standing astride two mounts.

Johnson settled into character roles, providing an excellent antagonist for Alan Ladd to fight on *Shane* (1953) and a grizzled outlaw on Sam Peckinpah's *The Wild Bunch* (1969). Johnson won an Academy Award as Best Supporting Actor for *The Last Picture Show* (1971), the first full-fledged stuntman to receive the honor. He lent dignity and class to any number of character roles after that.

Six-foot-three, 210-pound Ben Johnson was born in Foraker, Oklahoma, as Francis Benjamin Johnson, Jr. He was the son of legendary rodeo champion Ben Johnson. By the age of eleven he was a working cowboy at the Chapman Barnard Ranch, riding fence, herding cattle, and breaking horses. He began competing in the rodeo arena, specializing in trick riding, calf-roping, bulldogging, and bronco-busting. Johnson enlisted in the U.S. Army when he became of age but was discharged due to their concerns over a badly broken arm (an injury suffered in his youth). He traveled to Hollywood in the late 1930s to provide livestock for the Howard Hughes film *The Outlaw* (1943). Johnson stuck around as a horse wrangler and began to pick up work as a stuntman.

He quickly became regarded as the best horseman in Hollywood and had a knack for performing in fight scenes as evidenced by his work for Wild Bill Elliot on the Republic western *Wyoming* (1947). Johnson was a solid double for John Wayne on *Tall in the Saddle* (1944), *Angel and the Badman* (1947), and *Three Godfathers* (1948), Robert Mitchum on *Nevada* (1944), Randolph Scott on *Badman's Territory* (1946), Fred MacMurray on *Smoky* (1946), and Joel McCrea on *Ramrod* (1947). He even doubled Tarzan Johnny Weissmuller for a leap onto a horse on *Tarzan's Desert Mystery* (1943) and Frank Sinatra for riding scenes on *The Kissing Bandit* (1948). Johnson also doubled Gary Cooper and Jimmy Stewart and stepped in to take over B-western action scenes for Tom Tyler, Charles Starrett, Ken Maynard, Tex Ritter, Rod Cameron, Sunset Carson, Monte Hale, and Russell Hayden.

In 1953 Johnson decided to return to the rodeo circuit and won the World Steer Roping Championship. The prized silver buckle became his proudest possession. He was lured back to motion pictures by the money to be made. As he was getting his acting career back in order, he doubled Rod Steiger for the runaway wagon sequence on *Oklahoma!* (1955) and John Payne on *Rebel in Town* (1956). Leading roles in several minor westerns followed, and Johnson never had to double anyone else again. By the 1960s he was a western icon and living legend, appearing on the John Wayne films *The Undefeated* (1969), *Chisum* (1970), and *The Train Robbers* (1973). He was a personal favorite of Wayne, who respected Johnson's authentic cowboy naturalism and honesty. Johnson was still capable of smooth action, as ev-

Ben Johnson takes a series of squib shots on *The Wild Bunch* (1969).

idenced by the scene in *Hang 'Em High* (1968) where he gallops down and cuts the rope around Clint Eastwood's neck. Johnson had stand-out fight scenes with Richard Boone and James Arness on the TV shows *Have Gun—Will Travel* and *Gunsmoke*, respectively.

Johnson was an honorary member of the Stuntmen's Association, an inductee of the Stuntmen's Hall of Fame and the Cowboy Hall of Fame, and a winner of a Golden Boot Award and a Western Heritage Award. None of those awards compared to the pride he had in that silver rodeo buckle. Johnson died of a heart attack at the age of 77.

See: http://benjohnsonscreencaps.shutter fly.com/; Jensen, Richard D. *The Nicest Fella*. Iuniverse, 2010; McLellan, Dennis. "True Grit: It's the Cowboy Way." *Los Angeles Times*. June 3, 1994; Van Gelder, Lawrence. "Ben Johnson, 75; Won Oscar for *Picture Show*." *New York Times*. April 9, 1996.

GRAY JOHNSON (1939–)

Gray Johnson received his professional start as a Corriganville western street performer. In those days he went by his real name Gary Cooper. To avoid confusion with the famous movie star, he went by the nickname Rusty. At some point he changed his name to Gary Johnson, only to find there was already a Gary Johnson registered with SAG. So he became Gray Johnson. He was a stuntman on the 20th Century–Fox and Universal Studios tours in the early 1970s.

Johnson is best known for doubling Steve Railsback on *The Stunt Man* (1980) where he made several impressive leaps and a pinpoint landing falling through a roof. Johnson also made a great leap between two ships for Alan Arkin on the TV movie *The Defection of Simas Kudirka* (1978). He worked on *The Last Movie* (1971), *The Hired Hand* (1971), *Werewolves on Wheels* (1971), *Freebie and the Bean* (1974), *Black Samson* (1974), *The Ultimate Warrior* (1975), *The Killer Elite* (1975), *Rafferty and the Gold Dust Twins* (1975),

Gray Johnson performs a great leap for Steve Railsback atop the Del Coronado hotel on *The Stunt Man* (1980).

Rocky (1976), *The Gumball Rally* (1976), *The Bees* (1978), *Love at First Bite* (1979), and *The In-Laws* (1979).

JULIE ANN JOHNSON
(1939–)

Born in Los Angeles 5'7" Julie Ann Johnson was the granddaughter of Hall of Fame baseball player Sam Crawford. Her dad was a junior high coach, and Julie Ann grew up a prize-winning athlete at Fullerton High. She excelled at basketball, softball, volleyball, swimming, field hockey, and golf. Johnson doubled for Doris Day, most notably hanging from a helicopter over Mammoth Mountain on *Caprice* (1967). On TV she doubled Stefanie Powers for karate fights on *The Girl from U.N.C.L.E.* (1966–67), Lynda Day George on *Mission: Impossible* (1971–73), and Susan Saint James on *McMillan & Wife* (1971–76). She was a

stunt coordinator on *Charlie's Angels* (1976–81), in addition to doubling all the leads. She also doubled Jane Fonda, Kim Hunter, Jeanette Nolan, Ida Lupino, Juliet Prowse, Kathleen Nolan, Vera Miles, Jean Simmons, Celeste Yarnell and Joyce Jillson.

Johnson doubled Carol Burnett on *Pete 'n' Tillie* (1972) and coordinated an extended comic fight between Burnett and Geraldine Page. Her best known stunt came doubling Jessica Walter on *Play Misty for Me* (1971): She attacks star Clint Eastwood and is knocked through a glass door and over a balcony railing. She doubled Ava Gardner on *Earthquake* (1974), falling into a flash flood. In the 1980s she sued for discrimination, alleging that she was blackballed from the industry after complaining about safety issues and drug use on the set of *Charlie's Angels*. She won the case, but her stunt career was over. Johnson wrote a book about the ordeal.

She also worked on *The St. Valentine's Day Massacre* (1967), *Dr. Dolittle* (1967), *Some Kind of a Nut* (1969), *Little Big Man* (1970), *Dirty Harry* (1971), *Magnum Force* (1973), *The Don Is Dead* (1973), *Blazing Saddles* (1974), *Nickelodeon* (1976), *Drum* (1976), *The Cat from Outer Space* (1978), and *Hot Lead and Cold Feet* (1978). TV credits include *The Man from U.N.C.L.E., Star Trek,* and *Mannix.*

See: Blanchard, Nina. *How to Break into Motion Pictures, Television, Commercials, & Modeling.* NY: Doubleday, 1978; Kosman, Bill. *Park City Daily News.* "Julie Ann Johnson Takes Her Chances." July 20, 1970; Robb, David, & Julie Ann Johnson. *The Stuntwoman: The True Story of a Hollywood Heroine.* Xlibiris, 2012; Witbeck, Charles. *Toledo Blade.* "Julie's a Fall Girl for TV, Movie Stars." July 15, 1967.

LEROY JOHNSON (1922–1995)

Leroy Johnson was born in Dixon, Wyoming. An expert horseman, cattleman, and rodeo champ, the 6'1", 170-pound Johnson served with the U.S. Army during World War II. His sister Faye was a trick rider and stuntwoman, better known as Faye Blessing after her marriage to rodeo champ–stuntman Wag Blessing. Johnson doubled for Barry Sullivan on films such as *Forty Guns* (1957) and subbed for Yul Brynner on *The Magnificent Seven* (1960). He was a capable four-up driver who specialized in rolling over wagons and blind driving (where the man with the reins is hidden from view). He did the tricky wagon driving on *How the West Was Won* (1962) and worked often on the TV series *Wagon Train* (1957–65).

He also appeared in *The Kid from Texas* (1950), *Colt .45* (1950), *The Cimarron Kid* (1951), *The Lusty Men* (1952), *Gunsmoke* (1953), *Pony Express* (1953), *Column South* (1953), *Arrowhead* (1953), *The Far Horizons* (1955), *Friendly Persuasion* (1956), *Westward Ho, the Wagons!* (1956), *Badman's Country* (1958), *The Alamo* (1960), *Seven Ways from Sundown* (1960), *Major Dundee* (1965), *Shenandoah* (1965), *The Rare Breed* (1966), *Duel at Diablo* (1966), *Beau Geste* (1966), *Camelot* (1967), *Buckskin* (1968), *The Good Guys and the Bad Guys* (1969), *Monte Walsh* (1970), and *Heaven's Gate* (1980). TV credits include *Tales of Wells Fargo, Tall Men,* and *Bonanza.* He was a member of the Stuntmen's Association and an inductee of the Stuntmen's Hall of Fame.

See: "Leroy Johnson." *Redding Record Searchlight.* October 27, 1995.

ROSEMARY JOHNSTON

Rosemary Johnston appeared as a stunt-woman for Victoria Shaw on *Edge of Eternity* (1959), dangling from an ore car over the Grand Canyon. On *Heller in Pink Tights* (1960) she walked a tightrope thirty feet above a western street. The 5'4" Johnston doubled Anne Bancroft on *Gorilla at Large* (1954) and worked on *The Last Hunt* (1956), *The Don Is Dead* (1973), *Blazing Saddles* (1974), *The Hindenburg* (1975), *Logan's Run* (1976), and *Rollercoaster* (1977). Johnston was a charter member of the Stunt-women's Association and an inductee of the Stuntmen's Hall of Fame.

See: "No Stand-In." *State Times Advocate.* July 23, 1959.

ALF JOINT (1927–2005)

British stuntman Alf Joint's highest profile assignment came on *Goldfinger* (1964) as Capungo, the assassin who fights Sean Connery and is subsequently electrocuted in a bathtub. He also doubled Connery jumping from a wall in the pre-title sequence. His greatest stunt work came doubling Richard Burton during the alpine ski lift cable car fight on *Where Eagles Dare* (1968). On that film Joint leapt from one moving car to another some 1500 feet above the ground, a stunt that earned him the title "Britain's most famous stuntman."

The 6'1", 190-pound Alfred Charles R. Joint was born in Hertfordshire, England. He became a champion swimmer and graduated to high dives, representing his country in the Olympics. In the Army he was a physical fitness trainer. Joint entered films in the early 1960s as an apprentice of Bob Simmons, gaining notice for an impressive high dive on *The Long Ships* (1963). He became proficient in the British Stunt Registry's six sport skill sets including martial arts, swimming, trampoline, and high diving, and was known as an expert fencer and fight arranger. He stayed in shape with weight training and judo.

In the early 1970s Joint achieved infamy as the Milk Tray Man in a series of secret agent commercials in which he would perform spectacular stunts while delivering chocolates. For one of these commercials he performed a record-setting 163-foot fall into the Mediterranean. He broke his back on the second try but was soon back doing stunts. Along with Vic Armstrong, Doug Robinson, and Paul Weston, Joint started Stunts Incorporated in the late 1970s. He was a regular double for Richard Burton and also subbed for Clint Eastwood, Kirk Douglas, and Anthony Hopkins.

He worked on *Heroes of Telemark* (1965), *The Sorcerers* (1967), *Witchfinder General* (1968), *Oedipus the King* (1968), *Great Catherine* (1968), *On Her Majesty's Secret Service* (1969), *Kelly's Heroes* (1970), *Villain* (1971), *Macbeth* (1971), *Brannigan* (1975), *The Omen* (1976), *A Bridge Too Far* (1977), *Superman* (1978), *Les Miserables* (1978), *Bear Island* (1979), and *Superman II* (1980). TV credits include *Danger Man, The Prisoner, The Avengers, The Persuaders, The Adventurer,* and *Space 1999.* Joint died from cancer at the age of 77.

See: Peterson, Derek. "Man of Danger." *Photoplay.* May 1971; www.thestage.co.uk.

BILLY JONES (1912–1975)

Small-statured, 140-pound Billy Jones was a favorite of director John Ford, who used him as comedy relief on his films. He was also a highly accomplished stunt performer, once dubbed "Hollywood's greatest." Dublin-born Jones jumped from a truck just before a train plowed into it on *Dude Ranch* (1931). On *House of Frankenstein* (1944) he doubled J. Carrol Naish for a fall from a rooftop. Due to his size, Jones often doubled women. On *The Perils of Pauline* (1947) he doubled Betty Hutton but broke his arm in three places swinging from a curtain. His specialties were turning over cars and water stunts.

He also worked on *Hot News* (1928), *Heritage of the Desert* (1932), *King Kong* (1933), *King Solomon of Broadway* (1935), *The Glass Key* (1935), *Nancy Steele Is Missing* (1937), *Daughter of Shanghai* (1937), *Mysterious Mr. Moto* (1938), *The Hunchback of Notre Dame* (1939), *The Real Glory* (1939), *Santa Fe Marshal* (1940), *The Desperadoes* (1943), *The Spanish Main* (1945), *The Fuller Brush Man* (1948), *She Wore a Yellow Ribbon* (1949), *Two Flags West* (1950), *Wagon Master* (1950), *Soldiers Three* (1951), *The Quiet Man* (1952), and *Prince Valiant* (1954). He was an inductee of the Stuntmen's Hall of Fame.

See: Coons, Robbin. "In Hollywood." *North Adams Transcript.* December 20, 1935; O'Donnell, Jack. "Thrill Makers." *Elks.* #37, 1932.

BUCK JONES (1891–1942)

Buck Jones was born Charles Frederick Gebhart in Vincennes, Indiana. At the age of sixteen he joined the U.S. Cavalry, seeing action along the Mexican border and in the Philippines where he was wounded in the leg during the Moro Insurrection. Returning to Indiana he tested race cars and fought a handful of professional boxing bouts. In 1910 he rejoined the U.S. Army and wound up in the Chicago stockyards, breaking horses for the British and French armies. He traveled to Oklahoma to test the rodeo circuit and was hired by the Miller Brothers 101 Ranch. His superb horsemanship led to a job with the Julie Allen Wild West Show. He married fellow performer Odille "Dell" Osborne and joined the Ringling Brothers Circus for a tour in 1917.

Checking out the Hollywood scene, the 5'10", 175-pound Jones was signed as a bit player and stuntman by Universal Studios in 1917. He later moved to Fox Studios where he made $40 a week as a stuntman and double for Tom Mix, William Farnum, and William S. Hart. Fox recruited the rugged performer as a potential backup to Mix and gave him his first starring role on *Last Straw* (1920) as Charles "Buck" Jones. He gained many admirers among audience members and colleagues alike for doing much of his own riding and fighting on screen. At one time he was the most popular cowboy star in the world. He was able to break away from Fox as an independent star at the advent of the sound era.

On November 28, 1942, Jones was in Boston on a war bond promotion when tragedy struck: He was one of 492 people who perished in the Cocoanut Grove nightclub blaze, at a function that was ironically being held in his honor. Legend has it that Jones succumbed to the flames after repeatedly pulling others to safety, but the truth is he was likely trapped in the crowded basement club by the flash fire like everyone else. He died two days later from his burns at the age of 51.

See: Rainey, Buck. *The Life and Films of Buck Jones: The Silent Era.* World of Yesterday, 1988; Rainey, Buck. *The Life and Films of Buck Jones: The Sound Era.* World of Yesterday, 1991.

DICK JONES (1927–)

Richard Percy Jones was born in Snyder, Texas, and became known as the world's youngest trick rider. This led to work in Hollywood as a child stunt performer and actor. That's Dickie Jones on wires flying around as an angel on *Wonder Bar* (1934) and later falling off a wagon on *Virginia City* (1940). After service with the U.S. Army, the 5'7", 150-pound Jones garnered attention doing his own horse work on *Rocky Mountain* (1950), specifically firing a gun from underneath his horse's neck as he hung from its side. That trick was repeated from several camera angles and Jones received a stunt adjustment each time they shot it. On *The Old West* (1952) he had a big comic fight with Gene Autry. These assignments led to his hiring as Jock Mahoney's sidekick on *The Range Rider* (1950–53) and his own starring role as *Buffalo Bill, Jr.* (1955–56).

Jones did all of his own stunt work on these popular TV shows, and the tandem fights and horseback mounts that he performed with Mahoney are some of the best the screen has ever seen. On one *The Range Rider* episode, the handy Jones doubled guest star Rodd Redwing for a big fight atop a fallen red wood tree with Jocko. Jones is an honorary member of the Stuntmen's Association and an inductee of the Stuntmen's Hall of Fame. He has been presented Golden Boot and Silver Spur Awards.

See: Copeland, Bobby. "Dick Jones: From Child Star to Buffalo Bill, Jr." *Under Western Skies.* #50, 1997; Cutts, Terry. *Armchair Cowboy.* Canterbury, England: Parker, 2012.

JACK JONES (1906–1995)

Jack Jones was born Ferris John Jones in Bingham Canyon, Utah, and boxed professionally before landing in Hollywood. "The Pocatello Kid" worked primarily on 1930s B-westerns as an expert horseman for $100 a week plus stunt adjustments. He doubled John Wayne falling off a horse on *Texas Terror* (1935) and did stunts for Hal Taliaferro a.k.a. Wally Wales. On *Phantom Empire* (1935) he was one of the masked riders. Jones suffered a badly broken leg when he was thrown off a wagon and run over by the rear wheel on *Dawn Rider* (1935), ending his stunt career. A member of the Riding Actors Association, Jones died from a stroke at the age of 89.

JAY JONES (1943–)

Five-foot-eleven Jimmy Jay Jones from Dallas, Texas, came to Hollywood via the rodeo circuit. He worked as a stunt double for Robert Vaughn on *The Man from U.N.C.L.E.* (1964–66) and James Doohan and DeForest Kelley on the original *Star Trek* (1966–69). Jones doubled Slim Pickens for the brutal whip fight on *Rough Night in Jericho* (1967). He again showcased his bullwhip skills fighting Dan Blocker on the 1971 *Bonanza* TV episode "Kingdom of Fear." TV credits include *Mannix, Mission: Impossible, High Chaparral, Kung Fu,* and *Griff.* He left stunt work to pursue his interest in racquetball, winning the national amateur title in 1975 and competing for the professional championship.

See: Heitland, Jon. *The Man from U.N.C.L.E. Book.* Macmillan, 1987; Phillips, Mark, & Frank Garcia. *Science Fiction Television Series.* Jefferson, NC: McFarland, 1996; "Racquetball Star Just Hums Along." *Tucson Daily Citizen.* January 22, 1977; "Sober Mr. Martin Plays Film Heavy." *Lima News.* October 30, 1966.

PEACHES JONES (1951–1986)

Peaches Jones was born in Pasadena, California. When her father Sam Jones became a member of the newly formed Black Stuntmen's Association, Peaches showed interest in what he was doing and began attending stunt workouts with him. Peaches already had an impressive background in gymnastics, track, basketball, cheerleading, and the Junior Olympics while a student at John Muir High. As one of the very first black stuntwomen, Peaches received mention in the media and appeared on *The Tonight Show* in 1972.

She doubled Ruby Dee on *Buck and the Preacher* (1972) and worked on *Halls of Anger* (1970), *Strawberry Statement* (1970), *Melinda* (1972), *Coffy* (1973), *Foxy Brown* (1974), *Black Samson* (1974), *Freebie and the Bean* (1974), and *Earthquake* (1974). On TV she worked on *Mod Squad, The FBI, The Rookies,* and *Shaft.* She doubled Teresa Graves on *Get Christie Love* (1974–75) until an injury sidelined her. Peaches' last role was an acting part on *Human Tornado* (1976). Jones died from a drug overdose at the age of 34.

See: Avery, Sue. "Stuntwoman Made of Guts, Grace." *Los Angeles Times.* June 2, 1974; Burrell, Walter Price. "Hollywood Stunt Girl." *Ebony.* December 1971; "Peaches Jones." *Variety*. July 23, 1986.

SONNY JONES (1930–1990)

Sonny Jones was born John J. Jones in Shreveport, Louisiana. He and his brother Al Jones were raised on a ranch and became professional musicians. They played with Johnny Horton and Hank Williams, the husbands (at different times) of the Jones boys' sister Billie Jean. A proficient horseman, Sonny was trained for stunt work by Hal Needham and Tony Epper. He specialized in western stunts, fights, and high falls. He doubled Roddy McDowall on *Planet of the Apes* (1968), Charles Bronson on *From Noon Til Three* (1976), and John Saxon on *The Bees* (1978). On TV he worked on *Bonanza, The Wild Wild West, Here Come the Brides,* and *Mod Squad.* Jones died from lung disease at the age of 60.

See: "Sonny Jones." *Los Angeles Times*. June 30, 1990.

SID JORDAN (1889–1970)

Oklahoma-born Sid Jordan was a stunt double for Tom Mix and George O'Brien on B-westerns from silent films up to 1940. In addition to doubling them, he often paired up with them for fight scenes either as a heavy or as the double for the main bad guy.

An excellent horseman and sharpshooter, Jordan had received his education at the Cherokee Indian School in Vinita. Jordan befriended a young Tom Mix while working on the Miller 101 Ranch Show and the two were deputy sheriff lawmen together in Dewey, Oklahoma. In 1913 Jordan ventured west to reconnect with Mix, who put him to work immediately. Whenever a live round needed to be fired, Jordan was the only man Mix trusted to do it. On *Bear of a Story* (1916) Mix and Jordan roped a live bear on film and struggled to rein him in. The men remained close friends until Mix's 1940 death in an Arizona car accident. On *The Ox-Bow Incident* (1943), Jordan gave star Henry Fonda Mix's old saddle to use for the film. With advancing age he began to move away from stunts and work as a horse wrangler and livestock supervisor.

See: Jensen, Richard. *The Amazing Tom Mix: The Most Famous Cowboy of the Movies.* Iuniverse, 2005.

REMY JULIENNE (1930–)

French car specialist Remy Julienne was born in Cepot, Loiret. A Rallycross and French Motocross champion, his stunt career took off after he handled the Mini-Cooper action on *The Italian Job* (1969). His greatest feat was jumping the tiny cars sixty feet between two rooftops at seventy miles per hour. The Flying Frenchman followed with hard-driving action on *Stuntman* (1968), *Cold Sweat* (1970), *The Burglar* (1971), *The French Connection II* (1975), and *Strange Shadows in an Empty Room* (1976). He did a number of eye-opening commercials for Renault and Citroen, one in which he drove a Fiat over a waterfall.

At this point he was accepted into the James Bond franchise and began to double Roger Moore behind the wheel and handle all of the automotive action on *For Your Eyes Only* (1981), *Octopussy* (1983), *A View to a Kill* (1985), *The Living Daylights* (1987), and *Licence to Kill* (1989). Julienne's car stunts were noted for their exact precision and pre-calculation. His sons Michel and Dominic followed him into the business as part of the stunt company Remy Julienne's L'Equipe.

KIM KAHANA (1930–)

Hawaiian-born Kim Kahana made a name for himself as Chongo on the Saturday morning live-action series *Danger Island* (1968–69). For one episode he executed a 350-foot slide down a jungle embankment. During this period Kahana was allegedly the highest paid stuntman in the business due to his weekly feats of athleticism. The 5'7", 150-pound Kahana doubled Charles Bronson for over twenty years on movies such as *Mr. Majestyk* (1974) and *Breakout* (1975). He even doubled Stefanie Powers on TV's *The Girl from U.N.C.L.E.* (1966–67) and Sally Field on *The Flying Nun* (1967–69).

As a young man Kahana found employment as a knife and fire dancer for a stage show called the Samoan Warriors. A much-decorated paratrooper in the Korean War, he was awarded a Silver Star, a Bronze Star, and two Purple Hearts. Kahana studied martial arts in Japan, attaining six different black belts in disciplines including shotokan karate, aikido, and jiu jitsu. Kahana made his first film as one of the motorcycle riders on *The Wild One* (1953) and learned stunts from

Yakima Canutt. He began his own karate dojo and entered movies for good in the early 1960s between stints as a professional bodyguard. During this period he belonged to the Stuntmen's Association. In the 1970s Kahana opened a stunt school in Chatsworth, California, eventually relocating to Central Florida. His three sons and daughter Debbie have all worked in the film business.

He also worked on *Cool Hand Luke* (1967), *Planet of the Apes* (1968), *Che!* (1969), *Patton* (1970), *The Omega Man* (1971), *Joe Kidd* (1972), *Soylent Green* (1973), *Castaway Cowboy* (1974), *Earthquake* (1974), *Airport '75* (1974), *Judge Dee and the Monastery Murders* (1974), *Doc Savage* (1975), *The Killer Elite* (1975), *The Apple Dumpling Gang* (1975), *MacArthur* (1977), *Smokey and the Bandit* (1977), *Good Guys Wear Black* (1978), *Buck Rogers in the 25th Century* (1979), *Samurai* (1979), and *Smokey and the Bandit 2* (1980). TV credits include *Adventures in Paradise, The Time Tunnel, High Chaparral, Then Came Bronson, Mission: Impossible, The Brady Bunch, Kung Fu, Ironside, The Six Million Dollar Man, Quincy, Fantasy Island, Vega$,* and *Charlie's Angels.*

See: Campbell, Ramsey. "School of Hard Knocks." *Orlando Sentinel.* December 1, 1991; Frizzelle, Nancy. "So You Want to Be a Stuntperson?" *Fighting Stars.* October 1978; Lelis, Ludmilla. "Hollywood Stuntman Kim Kahana Going Strong at 83 with Lake County Stunt School." *Orlando Sentinel.* December 12, 2012; Martinez, Al. "He Found Success Despite Bad Breaks." *Los Angeles Times.* February 4, 1982; Richiusa, Gordon. "Falls in the Family." *Fighting Stars.* February 1983; Zappia, Rocco. "And in the Center Ring." *Fighting Stars.* October 1974.

LUCKY KARGO

New York–based stuntman and dancer Lucky Kargo was popular for his athletic bodybuilder physique. He appeared on Broadway in *Kismet* and *Li'l Abner* and was at one time the national jitterbug and Harvest Moon Ball Dance Champion. Skilled in acrobatics, boxing, and karate, the 6'2", 195-pound Kargo gained some infamy for appearing as an actor in several soft-core adult films in the 1960s, most notably *Sex Club International* (1967) and *Two Girls for a Madman* (1968). In his later years he became a dance instructor, cruise ship host, and ballroom dance companion in Florida to adoring senior citizen females.

He worked on *The West Point Story* (1950), *Somebody Up There Likes Me* (1956), *Baby Doll* (1956), *The Wrong Man* (1956), *Beau James* (1957), *Slaughter on Tenth Avenue* (1957), *Edge of the City* (1957), *How to Murder Your Wife* (1965), *A Lovely Way to Die* (1968), and *The Projectionist* (1971) in addition to a number of New York–based TV shows such as *Big Story, Danger, Janet Dean, U.S. Steel Hour, Studio One, Omnibus, Colgate Hour,* and *Captain Video.*

See: Orlick, Ron. "Lucky Kargo: Movie Stuntman Trains with Weights. *Muscle Training Illustrated.* July-August 1967.; Walker, Louann. "Getting Lucky." *Independent.* May 27, 1995.

JOHNNY KASCIER (1889–1974)

Five-foot-two Johnny Kascier doubled Peter Lorre on Mr. Moto films such as *Think Fast, Mr. Moto* (1937) and Charles Chaplin on *Monsieur Verdoux* (1947). In the 1940s he was the oldest active stuntman in Hollywood, yet still able to execute a thirty-foot dive on *Destroyer* (1943). The Minnesota-born Kascier served as Moe Howard's stand-in and double on many Three Stooges shorts at Columbia. On those he was often cast as a pratfall victim of the Stooges' bumbling. He also worked on *Escape to Glory* (1940), *The Shadow* (1940), *The Green Archer* (1940), *Holt of the Secret Service* (1941), *Two Yanks in Trinidad* (1942), *Gallant Journey* (1946), and *Kill the Umpire* (1950). An older Kascier served as the stand-in for teenager Ricky Nelson on the TV show *Adventures of Ozzie and Harriet.*

See: "*Destroyer* Has Veteran Stunt Actor." *Seattle Daily Times.* September 5, 1943; "Ricky's Stand-In Must Wear Lifts." *Racine Journal Times.* March 6, 1955.

BUSTER KEATON (1895–1966)

Buster Keaton was an influential stone-faced comic actor with a body of rubber. He was also known for his abilities as a writer, director, stunt performer, and editor. To this day many consider him a genius. The 5'6", 140-pound Keaton performed one of the greatest bits of daring ever captured on film: For *Steamboat Bill, Jr.* (1928) he allowed the frame of a house to fall on top of him during a cyclone. His body was positioned perfectly so that an opening for a window landed in the spot where he was standing. A miscalculation of mere inches would have resulted in serious injury or death as the house frame weighed 2000 pounds.

At his peak Keaton almost always refused the use of a double, allowing only USC pole vault athlete Lee Barnes to do specific action for him on the film *College* (1927) because Keaton didn't feel he had the time necessary to master that act. He performed other ingenious stunts that were triumphs of timing and execution. His high-speed chases on *Cops* (1922) and *Seven Chances* (1925) are marvels for the day and age. *The General* (1926) contains great bits of comic action involving a train. On *Our Hospitality* (1923) he hung upside down beneath the torrents of a waterfall. His boxing scenes on *Battling Butler* (1926) were

said to have influenced Martin Scorsese's filming of the ring action on *Raging Bull* (1980).

Joseph Frank Keaton was born in Piqua, Kansas, and gained the nickname Buster as a toddler after tumbling down a flight of stairs without injury. His parents were struggling vaudevillians who devised an act around Buster's ability to be tossed around a stage minus harm. He was called "The Little Boy Who Can't Be Damaged." Despite protests of child abuse, Buster was a star of the stage from the age of five. He had a love for playing sandlot baseball but most of his youth was spent on the road. He entered films as a young man in the short comedies of Fatty Arbuckle, and even after tremendous success he still opted to do a stunt as an Indian being shot off a horse on Arbuckle's *The Round Up* (1920).

On his films, Keaton often doubled for other actors who needed to take a fall, although this was against the studio bosses' wishes. A million dollar

Buster Keaton takes a train ride on *The General* (1926).

life insurance policy was put into place for Keaton, who once fractured his neck falling from a train for the cameras. On a whim he served as a stunt double for actor Lew Cody, taking a stair fall on *Baby Cyclone* (1928). This too earned him a chastising from the studio. As late as *A Funny Thing Happened on the Way to the Forum* (1967) Keaton was still smashing himself into a tree. An honorary inductee into the Stuntmen's Hall of Fame, Keaton died from lung cancer at the age of 70.

See: Brownlow, Kevin. *The Parade's Gone By.* Berkeley, Ca: Univ. of California, 1968; Meade, Marion. *Buster Keaton: Cut to the Chase.* New York: Harper Collins, 1995.

BRIAN KEITH (1921–1997)

Rough-hewn character lead Brian Keith got his start as a stunt double for Victor Mature on *Cry of the City* (1948). Keith was asked to fall down an escalator for the star but didn't realize that he would be required to do multiple takes of the stunt. That experience put an end to his stunt career, though not his two-fisted portrayals that ranged from tough detective Mike Hammer in a failed TV pilot to Sam Peckinpah's quintessential cowboy loner on the cult TV series *The Westerner* (1960). Keith took part in an early judo fight on *5 Against the House* (1955) and had notable screen brawls with James Stewart on *The Rare Breed* (1966) and Dean Martin on *Something Big* (1971). Keith was asked to play stunt legend Jocko Doyle (based on Jock Mahoney) on the popular stuntman film *Hooper* (1978).

Brian Keith was born Robert Allen Keith in Bayonne, New Jersey. After time at the Merchant Marine Academy, he served with the Marines as an aerial gunner during World War II. The 6'1, 195-pound Keith tackled a variety of jobs such as longshoreman, aircraft riveter, and mechanic. He was a longtime proponent of pumping iron at Vince's Gym and was still showing off his impressive biceps in tight T-shirts as late as the 1980s TV series *Hardcastle and McCormick*. Keith died from a self-inflicted gunshot wound at the age of 75. He was suffering from emphysema and lung cancer, and had recently endured the death of his daughter.

See: *Hooper* (1978) press kit; Van Gelder, Lawrence. "Brian Keith, Hardy Actor, 75; Played Dads and Desperadoes." *New York Times.* June 25, 1997.

PETE KELLETT (1922–1982)

Pete Kellett was born in West Plains, Missouri, as George Foster Kellett and starred in football at Hollywood High. A fencing specialist, the 6'1" Kellett doubled Sterling Hayden on *Johnny Guitar* (1954) and Peter Boyle on *Swashbuckler* (1976). As a stuntman and bit player, he worked on *Black Arrow* (1948), *Canadian Pacific* (1949), *Bright Leaf* (1950), *The Enforcer* (1951), *Prince Valiant* (1954), *Westward Ho the Wagons!* (1956), *Spartacus* (1960), *Birdman of Alcatraz* (1962), *Law of the Lawless* (1964), *Finian's Rainbow* (1968), *A Walk in the Spring Rain* (1970), and *Prisoner of Zenda* (1979). TV credits include *Gunsmoke, Wyatt Earp, Mike Hammer, Rawhide, The Virginian, Bonanza, Branded, The Man from U.N.C.L.E., The Wild Wild West, Star Trek, Mannix, Mission: Impossible, The Big Valley,* and *Land of the Giants.*

FRED KENNEDY (1909–1958)

Five-foot-nine, 200-pound Frederick O. Kennedy was born in Ainsworth, Nebraska. The former professional fighter was a veteran of the John Ford films *She Wore a Yellow Ribbon* (1949), *Rio Grande* (1950), *Wagon Master* (1950), *The Quiet Man* (1952), and *The Searchers* (1956). On the latter he doubled an Indian maiden who is trampled. Behind the scenes he trained falling horses named Trixie, Dixie, and Shanghai and designed a safety wagon. It came equipped with a padded coffin he could duck into when called to stage a wreck. He was the mentor of stuntman Chuck Roberson.

He worked on *The Adventures of Robin Hood* (1938), *Valley of the Sun* (1942), *Buffalo Bill* (1944), *The Spanish Main* (1945), *Jeep Herders* (1945), *Red River* (1948), *Mighty Joe Young* (1949), *South of St. Louis* (1949), *Two Flags West* (1950), *Across the Wide Missouri* (1951), *The Charge at Feather River* (1953), *Hondo* (1953), and *Prince Valiant* (1954). He died in Louisiana making the Ford film *The Horse Soldiers* (1959): While doubling William Holden, the 48-year-old Kennedy executed a saddle fall and broke his neck. He was a member of the Stuntmen's Hall of Fame.

See: Carey, Harry. *Company of Heroes: My Life as an Actor in the John Ford Stock Company.* Scarecrow, 1994; "Second Broken Neck Fatal to Kennedy." *Variety.* December 10, 1958.

GARY KENT (1933–)

Gary Kent was born on a ranch in Walla Walla, Washington. He excelled in track and football at Renton High and attended the University of Washington as a pole vault athlete and football player. During the Korean War the six-foot, 170-pound Kent joined the U.S. Navy and served with the Naval Air Corps. Kent found work as a construction worker, bar bouncer, private detective and movie studio electrician while breaking into films in the late 1950s. He dabbled as an amateur rodeo cowboy and realized his best chance at finding work was doing stunts. He often worked on low-budget independent films, sometimes using a pseudonym for non-union work and often times using his varied talents to serve as a set builder, special effects technician, or production manager.

Kent talked his way into a job doubling Cameron Mitchell and a then unknown Jack Nicholson on the cult westerns *Ride in the Whirlwind* (1965) and *The Shooting* (1966). This led to an assignment doubling Nicholson on the biker film *Hells Angels on Wheels* (1967) and an association with director Richard Rush that included stunt work on *Savage Seven* (1968), *Psych-Out* (1968), and *Freebie and the Bean* (1974). Kent doubled Paul Mantee on *A Man Called Dagger* (1967) and for a brief period in 1966 served as Robert Vaughn's stunt double on the TV series *The Man from U.N.C.L.E.*. Kent also performed stunts on the TV series *Daniel Boone* and *The Green Hornet*.

His greatest notoriety came as the male lead in Al Adamson's violent biker film *Satan's Sadists* (1969). Kent plays a former U.S. Marine who takes on the gang and beats them at their own game of death. Kent got to showcase his skill as a "fight man" in a battle with fellow low-budget stuntman John "Bud" Cardos in the rocky desert near Palm Springs. Kent eventually began to write and direct his own films, winning critical kudos for *Rainy Day Friends* (1985).

See: Albright, Brian. *Wild Beyond Belief.* Jefferson, NC: McFarland, 2008; Fultz, Lawrence. "Gary Kent: On the Edge of Hollywood." *Filmfax.* December 2008; "He Found His Direction in Movies." *Seattle Times.* April 30, 1986; Kent, Gary. *Shadows and Light: Journeys with Outlaws in Revolutionary Hollywood.* Austin, TX: Dalton, 2009; Plante, Robert. "Gary Kent." *Psychotronic Video.* #31, 1999.

HUBIE KERNS (1920–1999)

Hubie Kerns is best known as the double for Adam West on the *Batman* TV series (1965–68) and as a distinguished collegiate athlete. Los Angeles-born Hubert Jay Kerns was a USC football halfback and an All-American track star after a standout career at Manual Arts High. Kerns set a national record in the 4:40 and twice qualified for the Olympics but was unable to compete due to World War II. Kerns served in the U.S. Army and set a service track record. The 6'1", 180-pound Kerns was most notably cast opposite Burt Lancaster as a rival athlete on *Jim Thorpe—All American* (1951). He doubled Jerry Lewis on *The Sad Sack* (1957) and *Don't Give Up the Ship* (1959). Son Hubie, Jr., and daughter Desiree Ayers Kerns became stunt performers.

He worked on *Spirit of West Point* (1947), *Fort Apache* (1948), *Dark City* (1950), *All the Brothers Were Valiant* (1953), *Sign of the Pagan* (1954), *Them!* (1954), *The Ten Commandments* (1956), *The Young Lions* (1958), *The Buccaneer* (1958), *Spartacus* (1960), *Hell Is for Heroes* (1962), *Batman* (1966), *Paradise, Hawaiian Style* (1966), *Skidoo* (1968), *Hello, Dolly!* (1969), *The Big Bounce* (1969), *Beneath the Planet of the Apes* (1970), *Conquest of the Planet of the Apes* (1972), and *Battle for the Planet of the Apes* (1973). TV work includes *The Californians, The Rebel, Gunsmoke, Perry Mason, Voyage to the Bottom of the Sea, Cimarron Strip, Ironside,* and *The Rockford Files.* An inductee of the Stuntmen's Hall of Fame, Kerns died from cancer at the age of 78.

See: Ayres, Desiree. *Beyond the Flame.* Creation House, 2012; Kraychir, Hank. *USC Athletic Stories Volume III.* Create Space, 2009.

BILLY KILROY (1927–2011)

Billy Kilroy was born William C. Ramoth in Passaic, New Jersey. He fought with great success in the Golden Gloves as an amateur. In the U.S. Navy he was All-Service Middleweight Champion. Turning professional, he was undefeated in his first twenty-four fights. Once ranked as the thirteenth middleweight in the world, Kilroy began having doubts about boxing after paralyzing a fellow fighter, and his ring record suffered. He retired at the age of twenty-two with a 35–7 record and twenty-one knockouts.

He became a policeman in Clifton, New Jersey, and was discovered by director Elia Kazan while visiting a fellow boxer on the set of *On the Waterfront* (1954). Kazan thought he resembled the film's star and hired him to double Marlon Brando for the movie's fight scenes. Kilroy later doubled Paul Newman on *Somebody Up There Likes Me* (1956) and *The Hustler* (1961) and served as a technical director for boxing scenes. His other films include *A Face in the Crowd* (1957), *Pretty Boy Floyd* (1960), and *Murder, Inc.* (1960). He made a dozen films before retiring from stunts to become a Deputy U.S. Marshal. An inductee of the New Jersey Boxing Hall of Fame, Kilory died at the age of 84.

See: Becker, George. "Ex-Boxer, Movie Actor Writes Poems." *Cumberland News.* December 6, 1973; Schwartz, Jordan. "Kilroy Was Here: The Story of Boxer and Stuntman Billy 'Kilroy' Ramoth." *Bleacher Report.* February 23, 2009; Weathersby, Jeff. "Marshal Ramoth Pools Ring, Movie Past in His Poetry." *Trenton Evening Times.* November 14, 1976.

WAYNE KING

Wayne A. King was a pioneer in the stunt industry, although he is not as well known as some of his contemporaries. He was a member of the Black Stuntmen's Association prior to becoming one of the first black members of the Stuntmen's Association. King was behind STOPS (Stunt Talent Opposing Paint Downs), a coalition designed to end the practice of white performers taking work away from minorities. His activism likely kept him from attaining higher footing within the industry. The 6'3", 185-pound King doubled Sidney Poitier, Robert Hooks, Bernie Casey, Rockne Tarkington, and Lincoln Kilpatrick.

He worked on *The Omega Man* (1971), *Trouble Man* (1972), *Cleopatra Jones* (1973), *Scream, Blacula, Scream* (1973), *Black Samson* (1974), *Doc Savage* (1975), *Death Journey* (1976), *Dr. Black, Mr. Hyde* (1976), and *The Domino Principle* (1977). On TV he worked on *High Chaparral* and doubled Otis Young on the western *Outcasts* (1968–69). His son Wayne King, Jr., became a stuntman.

HENRY KINGI (1943–)

Masao Henry Kingi was born in Los Angeles of Cherokee, African-American, and European ancestry. He is noted for his long hair and his acting role on the comedy hit *Car Wash* (1976). One of his earliest doubling assignments was for actress Tamara Dobson on *Cleopatra Jones* (1973). An original member of the Black Stuntman's Association, the 6'4", 195-pound Kingi was recruited from the Buffalo Soldiers 10th Cavalry Unit. Kingi garnered media attention when he married TV's Bionic Woman Lindsay Wagner in 1981. Kingi had been a stuntman and coordinator on her 1970s show. Kingi was best known for his driving skills. On TV he regularly performed car jumps on *The Dukes of Hazzard* (1979–85). He became one of those ubiquitous stunt performers seen on big action films of the 1980s and 1990s who were always recognizable for the brief instant before they are killed on screen.

He worked on *Halls of Anger* (1970), *R.P.M.* (1970), *There Was a Crooked Man...* (1970), *The Omega Man* (1971), *Smoke in the Wind* (1971), *Buck and the Preacher* (1972), *Conquest of the Planet of the Apes* (1972), *Melinda* (1972), *Black Gunn* (1972), *Battle for the Planet of the Apes* (1973), *Black Belt Jones* (1974), *Uptown Saturday Night* (1974), *Truck Turner* (1974), *Earthquake* (1974), *The Ultimate Warrior* (1975), *Let's Do It Again* (1975), *Swashbuckler* (1976), *Dr. Black, Mr. Hyde* (1976), *Drum* (1976), *A Piece of the Action* (1977), *Mr. Billion* (1977), *Delta Fox* (1978), and *Zero to Sixty* (1978). TV credits include *Daniel Boone, Kung Fu, Get Christie Love, The Six Million Dollar Man, Gemini Man, The Quest,* and *B.J. and the Bear.* Sons Henry Kingi, Jr., and Dorian Kingi are also stuntmen. A member of Stunts Unlimited, Kingi is an inductee of the Stuntmen's Hall of Fame.

See: "Black Stunt Men." *Ebony.* December 1969; Fischer, Mary A. "While Lindsay Wagner Romps with Son Dorian, Her Third Marriage Heads for a Fall." *People.* January 30, 1984; Longwell, Todd. "Henry Kingi." *Emmy.* #24, 2002; Ortiz, Sergio. "Black Stuntmen Shatter Filmdom's Race Barrier." *Fighting Stars.* February 1974.

JACK KIRK (1895–1948)

Jack Kirk was born in Nickerson, Kansas, as John Asbury Kirkhuff. Of heavy build, "Pappy" Kirk doubled character players Max Terhune and Smiley Burnette on B-westerns in addition to playing a host of henchmen and other characters. He was capable of handling the reins of stage and wagon teams and made more than 350 films, among them *Under Two*

Flags (1936), *Gunsmoke Ranch* (1937), *The Lone Ranger* (1938), *Dark Command* (1940), *In Old California* (1942), *Angel and the Badman* (1947), and *Adventures of Frank and Jesse James* (1948). He left Hollywood in 1948 to work on a fishing boat in Alaska, dying from a heart attack suffered while loading supplies at the age of 53.

MAX KLEVEN (1933–)

Born in Norway, Max J. Kleven had boxing and competitive skiing backgrounds when he began his Hollywood stunt career while still in his teens. His first job was a beer commercial for which he made a ski jump and earned SAG status. He opened the Viking Ski Shop on Ventura Boulevard and set out to learn the stunt trade by practicing horse and saddle falls in dry river beds. An early break was doubling Peter Graves on *The Long Gray Line* (1955). The 6'2", 190-pound Kleven became a noted second unit director and helmed first unit on several minor films.

He was one of the top stuntmen working on TV in the early 1960s as the double for Paul Burke on *Naked City* (1958–63) and Martin Milner on *Route 66* (1960–64). Nicknamed One-Take Max, he moved to film work where he doubled Robert Mitchum on *Going Home* (1971), Gene Hackman on *Zandy's Bride* (1974), and Paul Newman on *Silent Movie* (1976). Kleven was stunt coordinator on the action classics *Dillinger* (1973), *Hard Times* (1975) and *Rollerball* (1975).

He also worked on *Around the World in Eighty Days* (1956), *Billy the Kid Versus Dracula* (1966), *Our Man Flint* (1966), *Murderers' Row* (1966), *The Perils of Pauline* (1967), *Who's Minding the Mint?* (1967), *A Covenant with Death* (1967), *Never a Dull Moment* (1968), *The Good Guys and the Bad Guys* (1969), *Cotton Comes to Harlem* (1970), *Come Back, Charleston Blue* (1972), *Slither* (1973), *Book of Numbers* (1973), *Slaughter's Big Rip-Off* (1973), *Frasier, the Sensuous Lion* (1973), *Tough Guys* (1974), *99 and 44/100 percent Dead* (1974), *The Other Side of the Mountain* (1975), *St. Ives* (1976), *F.I.S.T.* (1978), and *Damien: Omen II* (1978). TV credits include *Rin Tin Tin, Tallahassee 7000, Combat, Mission: Impossible, Batman, The Invaders, Star Trek, Mannix,* and *The Streets of San Francisco.* He is a member of the Stuntmen's Association.

See: Dunne, John Gregory. *Quintana & Friends.* New York: Washington Square, 1978;

Silden, Isobel. "Stuntmen are Daring Heroes, Unsung and Unknown." *Milwaukee Journal.* September 11, 1973.

MEL KOONTZ (1910–1992)

Big cat animal trainer Melvin L. Koontz was a farm boy from Fort Scott, Kansas. He moved to California in his teens and worked at the Selig Zoo. Koontz became an animal handler, working most famously with the MGM lion Jackie and the tiger Satan. He performed at the 1940 World's Fair and based his motion picture services out of the wild animal park Jungleland. He trained all kinds of animals for films, including elephants and camels. Koontz or his protégé Pat Anthony performed the specialized on-screen animal action for the stars. Koontz doubled Elmo Lincoln being pounced on by a lion on *King of the Jungle* (1927), Clark Gable battling a tiger on *Red Dust* (1932), Mae West sticking her head in a lion's mouth on *I'm No Angel* (1933), Victor Mature versus lions and tigers on *Samson and Delilah* (1949) and *Demetrius and the Gladiators* (1954), and Richard Conte falling into a pit of tigers on *Slaves of Babylon* (1953). His only injury came on *Rose Marie* (1954) when he was attacked by a lion.

He worked on more than 600 films, approximately 300 of them before the cameras as a stuntman, including *The Sign of the Cross* (1932), *Cat People* (1942), *The Sin of Harold Diddlebock* (1947), *Africa Screams* (1948), *Mighty Joe Young* (1949), *The Greatest Show on Earth* (1952), *Androcles and the Lion* (1952), *Fearless Fagan* (1952), *The Lion and the Horse* (1952), *Kismet* (1955), *The Rains of Ranchipur* (1955), *The Conqueror* (1956), *The Ten Commandments* (1956), *Merry Andrew* (1958), and *Rampage* (1963). His TV credits include *Circus Boy.*

See: Brann, Jim. "Mel Koontz Made 600 Pictures Never a Star." *News Chronicle.* May 11, 1969; Kerr, Carson. "Mel Koontz Twists Tiger's Tails." *Popular Mechanics.* March 1954; Reese, John. "Secrets of a Lion Tamer." *Saturday Evening Post.* July 11, 1959.

IRVIN "ZABO" KOSZEWSKI (1924–2009)

Five-foot-ten, 185-pound Irvin "Zabo" Koszewski of Camden, New Jersey, excelled as an amateur athlete at Collingswood High. He was

All-State in football and won letters in track, swimming, and wrestling. Zabo served with the U.S. Army in World War II and was involved in three combat landings. After the war he turned to professional wrestling as Jungle Boy, the valet to Buddy "Nature Boy" Rogers. He became interested in bodybuilding and won the 1948 Mr. New Jersey contest. Relocating to California, Zabo became one of the most popular of the Muscle Beach bodybuilders. He won the 1953 Mr. Los Angeles, the 1953 Mr. Pacific Coast, and the 1953 and 1954 Mr. California contests and was awarded the Best Abdominals Award in the Mr. America contest.

Zabo appeared as musclemen in *Athena* (1954) and *Li'l Abner* (1959) in the Mae West chorus line. This led to stunt work on *Spartacus* (1960), *El Cid* (1961), *John Goldfarb, Please Come Home* (1965), and *Planet of the Apes* (1968). Zabo doubled Kirk Douglas, Charles Bronson, Richard Jaeckel, and Cheech Marin. He worked on TV's *Combat* and *Star Trek,* and was a Marlboro Man for print ads. In later years he was a manager for

Gold's Gym and World Gym. Koszewski died from pneumonia at the age of 84.

See: Hise, Bob. "Fabulous Zabo Koszewski." *Strength and Health*. August 1967; Thurber, Jon. "Irvin 'Zabo' Koszewski Dies at 84; Bodybuilder Renowned for His Abs." *Los Angeles Times*. May 2, 2009; "Zabo Koszewski: Mr. Pacific Coast." *Strength and Health*. June, 1954; www.ironage. com.

FRED KRONE (1930–2010)

Fred Krone earned the nickname "Krunch" because of how hard he hit the ground in fights and falls. One of the best stuntmen of his era, he worked great fight scenes with Jock Mahoney and Dick Jones on TV's *The Range Rider* (1950–53) and *Buffalo Bill, Jr.* (1955–56). For *Kiss Me Deadly* (1955) Krone took what was at the time the longest stair fall in film history, beginning at Bunker Hill and ending up on Third Street in Los Angeles. On TV Krone doubled Guy Madison on

Fred Krone (left) fights Jock Mahoney on *California* (1963).

Wild Bill Hickok, Steve McQueen on *Wanted—Dead or Alive,* Russell Johnson on *Black Saddle,* and Steven Hill on *Mission: Impossible.* Others doubled include David Janssen, Robert Taylor, Dick Powell, Ronald Reagan, George Nader, John Smith, Stanley Baker, Don Durant, Lawrence Tierney, Richard Denning, Paul Richards, Michael Dante, and Audie Murphy.

Six-foot, 175-pound Fredrick A. Krone was born in Kentucky and did a little stunt work while attending Hollywood High. He lost a thumb and a finger on his left hand in a 1946 bottle rocket accident, but managed to be active in the rodeo arena as a bronc and bull rider and rodeo photographer. He re-entered films in 1951 under the mentoring of Jock Mahoney and quickly established himself as a top fight and high fall man. Krone retired in the mid–1970s to operate a clock repair business. Had he remained active, it is likely his name would have become better known as the stunt industry then began to unveil itself to the public.

He worked on *Hondo* (1953), *Last of the Pony Riders* (1953), *Battle of Rogue River* (1954), *The First Texan* (1956), *Reprisal!* (1956), *Badman's Country* (1958), *Apache Territory* (1958), *The Man from God's Country* (1958), *Three Blondes in His Life* (1961), *California* (1963), *The Quick Gun* (1964), *Apache Rifles* (1964), *Arizona Raiders* (1965), *Young Fury* (1965), *The Rare Breed* (1966), *Not With My Wife, You Don't* (1966), *Forty Guns to Apache Pass* (1967), *The Devil's Brigade* (1968), *The Mini-Skirt Mob* (1968), *The Love Bug* (1968), *The Undefeated* (1969), *The Great Bank Robbery* (1969), *Hell's Belles* (1969), *Support Your Local Gunfighter* (1971), *Life and Times of Judge Roy Bean* (1972), and *Westworld* (1973). TV credits include *Boots and Saddles, The Rifleman, Johnny Ringo, Maverick, Peter Gunn, The Westerner, Stoney Burke, Laredo, The Virginian, Get Smart, The Green Hornet, Lost in Space, Mannix,* and *The FBI.* A member of the Stuntmen's Association and an inductee of the Stuntmen's Hall of Fame, Krone died from cancer at the age of 79.

See: Magers, Boyd. "Stuntman Extrordinaire Fred 'Krunch' Krone." *Western Clippings.* #100, March 2011.

STUBBY KRUGER (1897–1965)

Born in Honolulu, Harold "Stubby" Kruger won the 1919 Hawaiian Freestyle Championship and defeated island legend Duke Kahanamoku in a one-mile swimming race. At the 1920 and 1924 Olympics he made his name in the backstroke and played on the water polo team. He was a National Water Polo Champion at St. Mary's College and a member of six national champion relay teams. In 1923 Kruger became the Central AAU champion in the freestyle, backstroke, and medley, earning himself the title of Swimmer of the Year. The media called him "the Apollo of Mermen" due to his fine physique. Kruger was also an accomplished diver, touring with Johnny Weissmuller and portraying a water clown in Billy Rose's Aquacade.

The 5'11" Kruger doubled Douglas Fairbanks on *The Black Pirate* (1926), Johnny Weissmuller on *Tarzan the Ape Man* (1932), and Spencer Tracy on *The Old Man and the Sea* (1958). He doubled Tracy for many years and also worked on *The Spanish Main* (1945), *Wild Harvest* (1947), *Soldiers Three* (1951), *Blackbeard, the Pirate* (1952), *20,000 Leagues Under the Sea* (1954), *Prince Valiant* (1954), *The Egyptian* (1954), *Abbott and Costello Meet the Keystone Kops* (1955), *Blood Alley* (1955), and *Spartacus* (1960). An honorary member of the Stuntmen's Association and an inductee of the Stuntmen's Hall of Fame, Kruger died from a heart attack at the age of 68.

See: "Former Olympic Ace, Stubby Kruger Dies." *Los Angeles Times.* October 8, 1965; Warden, Al. "Career Closes for Famed Hawaii Swim Star and Olympic Champion." *Ogden Standard Examiner.* October 13, 1965.

VINCENT LA DUKE (1929–1992)

Chippewa Indian Vincent La Duke from the White Earth Reservation in Minnesota later adopted the name Sun Bear and became a writer of New Age spirituality. During the late 1950s and 1960s he was a Hollywood stuntman specializing in horse falls on *Spartacus* (1960), *Comanche Station* (1960), *Taras Bulba* (1962), *The Greatest Story Ever Told* (1965), and *What Did You Do in the War, Daddy?* (1966). TV credits include *Brave Eagle, Broken Arrow, Cheyenne, Maverick, Wagon Train, The Rifleman, Bonanza,* and *Daniel Boone.* La Duke died from cancer at the age of 62.

See: "New Age Author Sun Bear Dies." *St. Paul Pioneer Press.* June 24, 1992; Sun Bear. *Sun Bear: The Path of Power.* Touchstone, 1992.

ETHAN LAIDLAW (1899–1963)

Ethan Allen Laidlaw was born in Butte, Montana, and labored as a copper miner, mechanic, bus driver, steam fitter, and policeman prior to entering motion pictures in the 1920s. The 6'1", 180-pound U.S. Navy veteran appeared in countless westerns as a mustached henchman, hired not only due to his menacing appearance but for his ability to ride and fight. He was a stuntman or rider on *The Virginian* (1929), *Cimarron* (1931), *King Kong* (1933), *Last of the Mohicans* (1936), *Conquest* (1937), *Man of Conquest* (1939), *When the Daltons Rode* (1940), *Virginia City* (1940), *Give Us Wings* (1940), *Captain Caution* (1940), *The Sea Wolf* (1941), *Road to Utopia* (1946), *Fortunes of Captain Blood* (1950), and *Warpath* (1951).

See: "Always a Villain and Dies 200 Times." *San Diego Union.* May 22, 1936.

MONTY LAIRD (1929–2004)

Monty Laird was a top bullwhip and gun expert who won many championships in fast draw competition. 5'11" and 160 pounds, he doubled numerous actors for hand insert shots of a fast draw. At Corriganville he played the parts of Wyatt Earp, Doc Holliday, and Bat Masterson, serving as the stunt instructor in the early to mid–1960s. He was the favored fight partner of Ray Corrigan when they put on live shows. Military veteran Laird stunted on the TV series *The Virginian* and was hired for *Alias Smith and Jones* (1971–72) as the double for Ben Murphy, Pete Duel, and later Roger Davis. He worked with Murphy again on the TV series *Griff* (1973) and *Gemini Man* (1976). Other credits include *There Was a Crooked Man...* (1970), *Hearts of the West* (1975), *Another Man, Another Chance* (1977), *Apple Dumpling Gang Rides Again* (1979), *Legend of the Golden Gun* (1979), *Stunts Unlimited* (1980), and the TV shows *Mod Squad* and *The Incredible Hulk.* He was a member of the Calico Ghost Town Hall of Fame.

See: Schneider, Jerry L. *Corriganville: The Story of Ray 'Crash' Corrigan and His Movie Ranch.* Rialto, California: Corriganville Press, 2005; www.asjcollection.com.

MIKE LALLY (1900–1985)

Manhattan-born Michael Edward Lally grew up a tough Irish kid fighting on the streets of Brooklyn. He worked in Hollywood as an assistant director, stand-in, extra, stuntman, and jack of all trades, integral to the formation of the Screen Actor Guild. He doubled Robert Armstrong on *King Kong* (1933) and stood in or doubled for James Cagney, Pat O'Brien, and John Garfield. Lally doubled Claude Rains on *Casablanca* (1942), Brian Donlevy on *Wake Island* (1942), and Paul Muni on *Commandos Strike at Dawn* (1942).

He also worked on *Suicide Fleet* (1931), "G" *Men* (1935), *Ceiling Zero* (1936), *Submarine D-1* (1937), *Each Dawn I Die* (1939), *The Roaring Twenties* (1939), *Gunga Din* (1939), *Seven Sinners* (1940), *Castle on the Hudson* (1940), *All Through the Night* (1941), *Call Out the Marines* (1942), *The Navy Comes Through* (1942), *Two Yanks in Trinidad* (1942), *Lady Takes a Chance* (1943), *Bombardier* (1943), *In Old Oklahoma* (1943), *The Hairy Ape* (1944), *Unconquered* (1947), *Wild Harvest* (1947), *Mighty Joe Young* (1949), *His Kind of Woman* (1951), *The Man Behind the Gun* (1953), *A Lawless Street* (1955), *Guns of the Timberland* (1960), and *Elmer Gantry* (1960). He was Peter Falk's stand-in throughout the television run of *Columbo* (1972–76). His son Michael had some stunt credits in the 1970s.

See: "Filmdom's Old-Timers Track Detectives." *Valley News.* December 23, 1977; www.columbo-site.freeuk.

ARCHIE FIRE LAME DEER (1935–2001)

Lakota Sioux Indian Archie Fire Lame Deer was born in Corn Creek, South Dakota. His father John Fire Lame Deer was a rancher and rodeo cowboy and Archie followed in his footsteps. He was a horseback extra on *Tomahawk* (1951), *Across the Wide Missouri* (1951), *The Savage* (1952), and *Battles of Chief Pontiac* (1952). He served with the U.S. Army during the Korean War, exterminated rattlesnakes, and performed stunts on *Chief Crazy Horse* (1955), *Stagecoach* (1966), and *Return of a Man Called Horse* (1976). His best known assignment came doubling Elvis Presley for bull-riding scenes on *Stay Away, Joe* (1968).

See: Lame Deer, Archie Fire & Richard Erdoes. *Gift of Power: The Life and Teachings of a Lakota Medicine Man.* Bear, 1992.

BURT LANCASTER
(1913–1994)

Director John Frankenheimer declared Burt Lancaster the greatest stuntman in movies, high praise for the multi-talented movie star. While that might have been a stretch, there was no doubt that Lancaster was one of the most agile, energetic actors in Hollywood. Born in New York City, Burton Stephen Lancaster had been a professional acrobat with the Kay Brothers Circus before reaching movie stardom. The 6'1", 180-pound Lancaster led DeWitt Clinton to the Bronx Championship in high school basketball and received an athletic scholarship to New York University prior to service with the U.S. Army's special services. His rise to Hollywood fame was meteoric.

Lancaster initially built his career playing tough guys in film noir. What he desired was to make films like his boyhood hero Douglas Fairbanks. Lancaster showcased his gymnastic talents in the swashbucklers *The Flame and the Arrow* (1950) and *The Crimson Pirate* (1952) to great fanfare. It was important for Lancaster that he performed all his own stunts on these, and studio publicity played up that fact. On *Flame* the stunt crew signed affidavits that were released to the media stating that Lancaster had done his own stunts on the picture, including a back-flip from a tree, sliding down a high tapestry, walking along a long pole, and doing a horizontal bar routine twenty feet above the ground. With his former acrobatic partner Nick Cravat, Lancaster did a flagpole perch for the film. Nevertheless an extra named Jules Garrison attempted to sue Warner Bros. and collect a $1,000,000 bounty the studio was offering to anyone who could prove it wasn't Lancaster on the screen. Garrison claimed he witnessed stuntman Don Turner double Lancaster on the film, but the studio won the suit when it was revealed that Turner was only around for rehearsals and non-dangerous stunts.

Burt Lancaster does his own stunt work on *The Crimson Pirate* (1952).

After these fun films, Lancaster allowed stuntmen to perform some of his on-screen action, knowing that an injury to the star could jeopardize an entire production. On *The Flame and the Arrow* the studio had taken out a $750,000 life insurance policy on him. Lancaster was still game for performing his own action when it enhanced the film. He trained in football and track to play the title role on *Jim Thorpe—All-American* (1951) and did much of his own aerial work on *Trapeze* (1956). On *The Train* (1965) he jumped from a moving train. Fight scenes of note came on *The Kentuckian* (1955) and *The Scalphunters* (1968). Lancaster died from a heart attack at the age of 80.

See: Buford, Kate. *Burt Lancaster: An American Life*. Maine: Thorndyke, 2000; Clary, Patricia. "Lancaster Does Own Acrobatic Stunts on Movie." *State Times Advocate*. August 25, 1950; Krebs, Albin. "Burt Lancaster, Rugged Circus Acrobat Turned Hollywood Star, Is Dead at 80." *New York Times*. October 22, 1994; Liademen, Edith. "Burt Lancaster Does His Own Stunting for Film." *Richmond Times Dispatch*. July 16, 1950; "Million Dollar Suit Denies Star's Stunts." *Omaha World Herald*. July 22, 1953.

MICHAEL LANDON
(1936–1991)

Bonanza TV star Michael Landon enthusiastically performed his own fight scenes on the show, so much so that stunt coordinator Bob Miles began to think of him along the lines of another stuntman. Miles was coordinating a low-budget A.C. Lyles western at Paramount titled *Town Tamer* (1965) and Landon began to lobby to double his friend DeForest Kelley in a fight scene. *Bonanza* producer David Dortort approved Landon's involvement and the star worked the short fight with Dana Andrews' stuntman Dale Van Sickel. The fight attracted a large audience of crew members from both shows. When it was over, Landon gave his stunt check to the studio's Christmas party fund.

The 5'8", 160-pound actor was born Eugene Maurice Orowitz in Queens, New York. Despite his small stature, he was a standout track athlete at Collingswood High in New Jersey and threw the javelin for USC until a shoulder injury quelled Olympic aspirations. Landon found his niche as Little Joe on the popular *Bonanza* (1959–73),

where he had fine fisticuffs with guest stars Charles Bronson, James Coburn, and Roy Jenson. On film he had a solid fight on *Legend of Tom Dooley* (1959). An honorary member of the Stuntmen's Association, Landon died from pancreatic cancer at the age of 54.

See: Daly, Marsha. *Michael Landon*. New York: St. Martin's, 1987; Rioux, Terry Lee. *From Sawdust to Stardust: The Biography of DeForest Kelley*. New York: Simon and Schuster, 2005.

WALT LA RUE
(1918–2010)

Five-foot-eight and 155 pounds Walt La Rue was born in Fall River, Massachusetts although some references report he was born in Canada. He was an amateur boxer and learned to break horses before he hit his teens. He worked as a packer and guide in Glacier National Park and Yosemite and spent twelve years on the rodeo circuit. La Rue entered films as a horseback specialist, doubling Gabby Hayes at Republic and later stunting on the Audie Murphy movies *Walk the Proud Land* (1956), *Hell Bent for Leather* (1960), *The Quick Gun* (1964), *Arizona Raiders* (1965), *Gunpoint* (1966), and *A Time for Dying* (1969). He was a cowboy singer and a splendid western artist.

He also worked on *Five Graves to Cairo* (1943), *The Tiger Woman* (1944), *Fort Apache* (1948), *Ambush* (1949), *Cow Town* (1950), *Wyoming Mail* (1950), *Texans Never Cry* (1951), *The Desert Song* (1953), *Man with the Steel Whip* (1954), *Cowboy* (1958), *Gunman's Walk* (1958), *They Came to Cordura* (1959), *It's a Mad, Mad, Mad, Mad World* (1963), *Savage Sam* (1963), *A Distant Trumpet* (1964), *Major Dundee* (1965), *El Dorado* (1967), *Never a Dull Moment* (1968), *More Dead Than Alive* (1969), *Paint Your Wagon* (1969), *The Good Guys and the Bad Guys* (1969), *Jeremiah Johnson* (1972), *The Cowboys* (1972), *Slither* (1973), *99 and 44/100 percent Dead* (1974), *Blazing Saddles* (1974), *Mame* (1974), *F.I.S.T.* (1978), and *1941* (1979). TV credits include *The Lone Ranger, Bat Masterson, Cimarron Strip,* and *High Chaparral*. He was a member of the Stuntmen's Association and a Golden Boot Award honoree.

See: "Art and Ways of Walt La Rue." *Ranch and Reata*. August 2011.

HAROLD "BEECH" LASWELL (1927–1992)

California-born Harold Beecher Laswell served with the U.S. Navy before entering stunt work in the late 1950s. "Beech" was a stunt coordinator for the 1960s Universal Studio tour and later worked in that capacity for Disneyworld and Epcot Center in Florida. He doubled Lee Marvin on *Paint Your Wagon* (1969) and James Coburn on *Pat Garrett and Billy the Kid* (1973). He also worked the TV shows *Wagon Train, The Virginian,* and *Laredo.* He claimed that his life was the model for the Burt Reynolds stuntman character on *Hooper* (1978). Laswell died of heart failure at the age of 65.

See: "Harrold Laswell." *Variety.* October 16, 1992.

BERT LeBARON (1901–1956)

Bert LeBaron was born Bert Krieger in Wisconsin. He was a platform high diver, swimmer, and street fighter skilled in judo and the French martial art savate. In Philadelphia he was an enforcer for local criminal types. Moving to Hollywood, he played polo and handball competitively at the Hollywood YMCA. LeBaron's stunt career dates back to the 1920s. He made a leap from a coal car to a machine-gun placement on *Brute Force* (1947), dueled Gene Kelly on *The Three Musketeers* (1948), and had a 200-pound flaming candelabra fall on him on *Adventures of Don Juan* (1948). LeBaron served with the Merchant Marine in World War II and doubled character types Lionel Atwill and Raymond Burr.

He worked on *The Adventures of Robin Hood* (1938), *Daredevils of the Red Circle* (1939), *Dick Tracy's G-Men* (1939), *Footlight Fever* (1941), *Spy Smasher* (1942), *Captain America* (1944), *The Tiger Woman* (1944), *Monsieur Beaucaire* (1946), *Jesse James Rides Again* (1947), *The Inspector General* (1949), *King of the Rocket Men* (1949), *The Kid from Texas* (1950), *Across the Wide Missouri* (1951), *Don Daredevil Rides Again* (1951), *Scarlet Angel* (1952), *Scaramouche* (1952), *The Egyptian* (1954), *Prince Valiant* (1954), *Battle Cry* (1955), *The Conqueror* (1956), and *Around the World in Eighty Days* (1956). A member of the Stuntmen's Hall of Fame, LeBaron died on the handball court at the age of 54.

See: http://bootslebaronsworld.wordpress.com.

GENE LeBELL (1932–)

Legendary fight specialist "Judo" Gene LeBell has rightfully been called "the toughest man alive." Ironically, he endured fifty-plus years in Hollywood and claimed he never won a screen fight. He was beaten up by everyone from Elvis Presley on *Blue Hawaii* (1961) and *Paradise, Hawaiian Style* (1966) to Joe Don Baker on *Walking Tall* (1973) to Steve Martin on *The Jerk* (1979). Clint Eastwood got in his licks on *Every Which Way But Loose* (1978) and Robert Stack flipped him on *Airplane!* (1980). One of LeBell's best fights came against Jim Brown on *Slaughter's Big Rip-Off* (1973). On TV LeBell fought Bruce Lee on *The Green Hornet*, Robert Conrad on *The Wild Wild West,* David Carradine on *Kung Fu,* James Garner on *The Rockford Files,* and Lee Majors on *The Fall Guy.* As a stunt double he filled in for Jack Warden, James Whitmore, Darren McGavin, Van Johnson, Rod Steiger, Pat Hingle, Nicholas Worth, Lionel Stander, and Ken Swofford.

Five-foot-eleven, 215-pound Ivan LeBell was born in Los Angeles. His mother Aileen Eaton was the owner of the Olympic Auditorium, so LeBell had access to professional wrestlers and boxers. He learned wrestling holds from Ed "Strangler" Lewis and the legendary Lou Thesz, and took a shine to the emerging Japanese art of judo. He had formative training with Jack Sergil at Van Rose's Gym. After joining the Coast Guard Reserves he won the AAU California State Judo Championship in 1953 at a body weight of 170 pounds. He went on to win the AAU National Judo Championship in both 1954 and 1955 and traveled with the U.S. Judo team to tour Japan. In all he won more than 2,000 judo matches and only lost once in his early teens.

LeBell knew that if he wanted to make a career out of his athleticism, professional wrestling was where the money was at. Much to the dismay of the judo community, LeBell turned pro wrestler. He made his mark in the Texas territory as a heel wrestler in the mid–1950s and won the NWA World Heavyweight Title in 1960. Other individual titles include the NWA World Junior Heavyweight Title, the WWA World Junior Heavyweight Title, the NWA Texas Brass Knuckles Title, the Central States Mid America Title, and the Hawaiian Championship. As a masked wrestler known as The Hangman, he wrestled with a tag team partner and captured the Pacific Northwest Tag Team Title, the AWA World Tag Team Title, the MWCA World Tag Team Title, and the WWA World Tag Team Title.

LeBell began working in Hollywood in 1955 on the TV show *Adventures of Ozzie and Harriet*, where he was knocked around by singer Ricky Nelson. In the late 1950s he went on a promotional tour with TV's Superman, George Reeves, and became his friend and judo instructor. When he wasn't wrestling, LeBell worked for a private detective agency, taught judo at Los Angeles City College, or found employment at the movie studios taking falls for numerous actors on TV and film.

In 1963 he fought in a heavily promoted mixed martial arts match pitting him against feared light-heavyweight boxer Milo Savage. LeBell put Savage to sleep with a rear-single lapel tourniquet choke and won the bout. He later served as the referee for the 1976 match between Muhammad Ali and Antonio Inoki in Japan. One of LeBell's greatest claims to fame was

Gene LeBell (top) fights Jim Brown on *Slaughter's Big Rip-Off* (1973).

his Hollywood dojo, where many serious fighters went to train with the master himself. Some of his students include Ed Parker, Chuck Norris, Benny "The Jet" Urquidez, Hayward Nishioka, Bill "Superfoot" Wallace, Gokor Chivichyan, and wrestler Rowdy Roddy Piper.

He worked on *4 for Texas* (1963), *Love and Kisses* (1965), *Seven Women* (1966), *Three on a Couch* (1966), *What Did You Do in the War, Daddy?* (1966), *Planet of the Apes* (1968), *P.J.* (1968), *The Split* (1968), *Marlowe* (1969), *There Was a Crooked Man...* (1970), *Beneath the Planet of the Apes* (1970), *Blacula* (1972), *Conquest of the Planet of the Apes* (1972), *Hammer* (1972), *Melinda* (1972), *Slither* (1973), *Battle for the Planet of the Apes* (1973), *Hell Up in Harlem* (1973), *Cleopatra Jones* (1973), *Black Samson* (1974), *Freebie and the Bean* (1974), *Busting* (1974), *99 and 44/100 percent Dead* (1974), *The Towering Inferno* (1974), *Earthquake* (1974), *The*

Killer Elite (1975), *Day of the Locust* (1975), *Let's Do It Again* (1975), *The Big Bus* (1976), *King Kong* (1976), *Rocky* (1976), *Black Sunday* (1977), *F.I.S.T.* (1978), *The One and Only* (1978), *The Prizefighter* (1979), *Stunt Seven* (1979), *The Big Brawl* (1980), *Bronco Billy* (1980), and *Any Which Way You Can* (1980). TV credits include *Maverick*, *Bat Masterson*, *Burke's Law*, *The Munsters*, *Honey West*, *I Spy*, *Batman*, *The Beverly Hillbillies*, *Bonanza*, *The Big Valley*, *Land of the Giants*, *The Invaders*, *Mannix*, *Ironside*, *The FBI*, *Cade's County*, *Kolchak: The Night Stalker*, *Get Christie Love*, *Manhunter*, *Joe Forrester*, *Police Story*, *Gemini Man*, *Starsky and Hutch*, *Baretta*, *The Bionic Woman*, *Little House on the Prairie*, *Charlie's Angels*, *Man from Atlantis*, *The Incredible Hulk*, *CHiPs*, *Battlestar Galactica*, *Buck Rogers*, and *The Dukes of Hazzard*. An inductee of the Stuntmen's Hall of Fame, LeBell was a long time member of the Stuntmen's Association who switched late in his career to Stunts Unlimited. His son Dave became a stuntman.

See: Foon, George. "Gene LeBell: Real to Reel." *Inside Stunts.* Spring, 2006; LeBell, Gene. *The Godfather of Grappling.* Los Angeles: Gene LeBell, 2005; LeBell, Gene. *The Toughest Man Alive.* Health 'n' Life, 2004; Nilsson, Thomas. "A Conversation with the Toughest Man Alive." *Black Belt.* April 1994; www.genelebell.com.

CHRISTOPHER LEE (1922–)

Christopher Frank Carandini Lee was one of the most popular and prolific character actors working in films. Born in Belgrave, London, he served with the Royal Air Force during World War II and was active in British Intelligence. In some of his first movie assignments he was a stand-in for Stewart Granger, Chips Rafferty, and Burt Lancaster. On the sets, 6'5" Lee found himself hanging out with the stuntmen. He had a boxing background and was a capable fencer trained by Paddy Crean. Lee found abundant work on swashbucklers and costume dramas and performed his own swordplay and stunts. On *That Lady* (1955) Lee was contracted to play "Captain of the Guard and other parts." This involved all manner of stunt work as he played masked assassins and Arab horsemen for the cameras. On *Dark Avenger* (1955) he fought Errol Flynn with broad swords.

When he became a star portraying Dracula and the Mummy in Hammer horror films, stuntman Eddie Powell doubled Lee. Even then he was still capable of action, taking part in memorable sword duels on *The Three Musketeers* (1973) and *The Four Musketeers* (1974). He played the title Bond villain on *The Man with the Golden Gun* (1974), and on *Airport '77* (1977) performed his own underwater stunts for which he was awarded an honorary belt buckle from the Stuntmen's Association. Lee was a member of three stuntmen's unions.

See: Lee, Christopher. *Lord of Misrule.* London, England: Orion, 2004.

GEORGE LEECH (1921–2012)

Born in London, George Leech excelled at boxing, diving, swimming, and gymnastics. He was a Butlins Redcoat dance performer and took part in high-diving shows. After service in World War II, Leech made his film debut doubling James Mason on *Odd Man Out* (1947) and joined Jock Easton's Stunt Team. He became the professional partner of Bob Simmons and worked on many of the James Bond films, doubling the Joseph Wiseman title character on *Dr. No* (1962), Sean Connery driving the Aston Martin on *Goldfinger* (1964), and Roger Moore driving the Lotus on *The Spy Who Loved Me* (1977). He was set to double George Lazenby for *On Her Majesty's Secret Service* (1969) but dislocated his shoulder practicing pull-ups on the cable car line. He was the stunt coordinator on that Bond film. He doubled Dick Van Dyke on *Chitty Chitty Bang Bang* (1968).

He also worked on *Ivanhoe* (1952), *Helen of Troy* (1955), *Quentin Durward* (1956), *The Guns of Navarone* (1961), *Thunderball* (1965), *Casino Royale* (1967), *You Only Live Twice* (1967), *Kelly's Heroes* (1970), *Diamonds Are Forever* (1971), *The Pink Panther Strikes Again* (1976), *A Bridge Too Far* (1977), *The Wild Geese* (1978), *Revenge of the Pink Panther* (1978), *Superman* (1978), *For Your Eyes Only* (1981), *Octopussy* (1983), *Never Say Never Again* (1983), and *A View to a Kill* (1985). His daughter Wendy Leech followed him into the industry and married stuntman Vic Armstrong. He was an inductee of the Hollywood Stuntmen's Hall of Fame.

See: www.vicarmstrong.com.

LANCE LeGAULT (1935–2012)

Born in Chicago, six-foot, 175-pound William Lance LeGault spent part of his youth in Louisiana and Kansas City. In Chicago he attended Chillicothe Township High, where he was a star quarterback on the football team and earned a full athletic scholarship to Wichita State. He made a name for himself as a rhythm and blues performer and was given his first film work by John Wayne on *The Horse Soldiers* (1959). LeGault befriended Elvis Presley and doubled the singer throughout the 1960s on *Girls! Girls! Girls!* (1962), *Roustabout* (1964), *Viva Las Vegas* (1964), *Kissin' Cousins* (1964), and others. By the 1970s he emerged as a valued character actor, noted for his deep voice and commanding presence on TV shows such as *Magnum P.I.* and *The A-Team.* LeGault died from heart failure at the age of 75.

See: "Funeral Services Pending Character Actor Lance LeGault." *Beverly Hills Courier.* September 11, 2012; Gillespie, Marianne. "Lance LeGault: LeGault Leaves Legacy in Field." *Chillicothe Times-Bulletin*. September 19, 2012; Kleiner, Dick. "Lance LeGault: A Good Heavy." *Altoona Mirror*. March 13, 1978.

TERRY LEONARD (1940–)

One of the toughest, most resilient stuntmen to come down the pike, Terry Leonard earned his legendary status the hard way. Few big men flew through the air or pounded the ground as hard and for as long. He performed some of the biggest stunts the movies have ever known, tackling assignments that left viewers and peers in awe. He was known for his ability to rebound from all kinds of physical punishment and carry on through the pain. That "Teflon Terry" was still working stunts through six decades is both a testament to his athletic skill and an uncommon toughness of body and mind.

Leonard doubled Sean Connery and coordinated the spectacular action for *The Wind and the Lion* (1975), including a horse fall through a window that broke his back. He knocked himself out with his knee doing a record eighty-foot high fall off the Wilshire Hyatt building into cardboard boxes for *Cover Me, Babe* (1970) and nearly died doing another high fall on *Black Samson* (1974) when his boxes gave way and he landed on the pavement. Leonard was one of the men blown up in the helicopter on *Apocalypse Now* (1979), another magnificent action film he coordinated. On *Legend of the Lone Ranger* (1981) he attempted a repeat of Yakima Canutt's famous *Stagecoach* stunt but was run over by the coach's wheels, tearing up an already bad leg. Leonard's most famous action was a variation on that stunt, doubling Harrison Ford for a horse transfer and then a drag underneath a truck on *Raiders of the Lost Ark* (1981). He also famously doubled Michael Douglas as he goes over a waterfall in a Jeep for *Romancing the Stone* (1984).

Six-foot-one, 210-pound Terry J. Leonard was born in West Allis, Wisconsin. Growing up on a farm he became accustomed to baling hay, working with livestock, and the operation of heavy machinery. As an athlete he excelled in football and track at West Allis Central, setting a state record in the pole vault and winning state championships in the broad jump and the low hurdles. He attended the University of Wisconsin on an

athletic scholarship, playing football and track. He was invited to the 1960 Olympic trials in Rome as a decathlete, participating in the high jump, pole vault, hurdles, and rings. Leonard returned to the Tokyo Olympic trials in 1964 as a representative of the University of Arizona. In football at U of A he broke his ankle. In Tokyo he sprained the same ankle in the third event, an injury that prevented him from accepting an invitation to play professional football for the Los Angeles Rams. Leonard caught on in the Canadian Football League as a punter and strong safety for the British Columbia Lions, and he spent three seasons with them. A bulging disc in his back ended his pro career in 1966.

In 1962 Leonard was working as a lifeguard at the Tucson Ramada Inn, where the crew of *McLintock!* (1963) was staying. He befriended some of the stuntmen and received work as a stunt extra. Chuck Roberson told him to look him up if he was interested in a stunt career. When football ended for Leonard, he gave Roberson a call. Roberson let him stay at his California house and schooled him in the ways of a Hollywood stuntman. Leonard got his first official stunt gig working on *El Dorado* (1967) with John Wayne. Leonard doubled many tough guy actors, including Richard Boone on *Hombre* (1967), *Big Jake* (1971), and the TV series *Hec Ramsey* (1972–73), Telly Savalas on *Mackenna's Gold* (1969), Jim Brown on *100 Rifles* (1969), John Wayne and Jorge Rivero on *Rio Lobo* (1970), Richard Harris on *A Man Called Horse* (1970), *The Deadly Trackers* (1973), *99 and 44/100 percent Dead* (1974), and *Return of a Man Called Horse* (1976), Robert Mitchum on *Wrath of God* (1972), Rock Hudson on the TV series *McMillan & Wife* (1971), Nick Nolte on *Return to Macon County* (1975) and *48 HRS.* (1982), and Arnold Schwarzenegger on *Conan the Barbarian* (1982).

When the Western died out, he was savvy enough to begin race car driving so as not to be pigeonholed as merely a Professional Rodeo Cowboys Association horseman. Leonard was one of the first personal students of karate champion Joe Lewis, anticipating another shift in genre action. Richard Boone helped Leonard's career when he let him direct second unit on his TV series. Director John Milius had Leonard stage and shoot action for all his films. In later years Leonard was the stunt coordinator and second unit director on *The Fugitive* (1993) and *Tombstone* (1993). His

son Matt was a defensive tackle for Stanford University, while son Malosi was a wide receiver for the University of Arizona. Both performed movie stunts.

He worked on *Planet of the Apes* (1968), *Hard Contract* (1969), *Che!* (1969), *Barquero* (1970), *Skullduggery* (1970), *Beneath the Planet of the Apes* (1970), *Soldier Blue* (1970), *Sometimes a Great Notion* (1970), *Life and Times of Judge Roy Bean* (1972), *The Train Robbers* (1973), *Cleopatra Jones* (1973), *Dillinger* (1973), *Slaughter's Big Rip-Off* (1973), *Mr. Majestyk* (1974), *Blazing Saddles* (1974), *Earthquake* (1974), *Nightmare Honeymoon* (1974), *Night Moves* (1975), *Breakheart Pass* (1976), *The Shootist* (1976), *Death Journey* (1976), *The Norseman* (1978), *Big Wednesday* (1978), *FM* (1978), *Lord of the Rings* (1978), *Circle of Iron* (1979), *Firepower* (1979), *1941* (1979), *Highpoint* (1979), *Mountain Men* (1980), and *The Long Riders* (1980). TV credits include *The Wild Wild West, Daniel Boone, Ironside, Search, The Rockford Files, The Six Million Dollar Man, The Quest, The Fall Guy,* and the TV mini-series *Centennial* (1978). A member of the Stuntmen's Association, Leonard was an inductee of the Stuntmen's Hall of Fame and a recipient of a Golden Boot and a World Taurus Lifetime Achievement stunt award.

See: Conley, Kevin. *The Full Burn.* Bloomsbury, 2008; Heffernan, Harold. "Stuntman Lives Like There's No Tomorrow." *Sarasota Journal.* December 9, 1970; Ivie, Mark. "Terry Leonard." *Inside Stunts.* Summer, 2004; Premako, Josh. "Accidental Stuntman: A Local Reflects on His Career in Movies." *Santa Clarita Valley News.* April 25, 2009; Redfern, Gary. "He Takes Hard Knocks for a Hollywood Living." *Milwaukee Journal.* February 13, 1985.

(1974). He was a bare-knuckle fighter who lasts one punch against Charles Bronson on *Hard Times* (1975). Six-foot-one, 185-pound Lerner doubled Lou Antonio on the TV series *Snoop Sisters* (1973–74) and Jack Lord for the final season of *Hawaii Five-O* (1979–80). He was stunt coordinator for the last episodes of *Gunsmoke* (1974–75).

He also worked on *They Came to Cordura* (1959), *The President's Analyst* (1967), *Planet of the Apes* (1968), *Butch Cassidy and the Sundance Kid* (1969), *Che!* (1969), *Little Big Man* (1970), *Flap* (1970), *Soldier Blue* (1970), *Sometimes a Great Notion* (1970), *Dirty Harry* (1971), *Skin Game* (1971), *Conquest of the Planet of the Apes* (1972), *Jeremiah Johnson* (1972), *Battle for the Planet of the Apes* (1973), *Soul of Nigger Charley* (1973), *99 and 44/100 percent Dead* (1974), *Young Frankenstein* (1974), *The Towering Inferno* (1974), *Earthquake* (1974), *The Master Gunfighter* (1975), *Bound for Glory* (1976), *Smokey and the Bandit* (1977), *Black Oak Conspiracy* (1977), *Stunt Seven* (1979), and *The Nude Bomb* (1980). TV credits include *A Man Called Shenandoah, The Man from U.N.C.L.E., Cimarron Strip, Land of the Giants, The Immortal, Kung Fu, Planet of the Apes, Manhunter, The Rockford Files, The Six Million Dollar Man, Wonder Woman, Charlie's Angels, Spiderman, Vega$,* and *The Fall Guy.* His son Allen Michael became a stuntman. A member of the Stuntmen's Association, Lerner died from lung cancer at the age of 74.

See: "Empty Saddles." *Western Clippings.* #91, September-October 2009; "Stuntman." *Senior Scholastic.* September 28, 1970; "Want to Earn a Hundred Dollars a Day?" *Independent Star.* January 9, 1966.

FRED LERNER (1935–2009)

Frederick Marshall Lerner was born in Los Angeles but raised on a Nevada cattle ranch. He had a rodeo background prior to appearing on TV's *Rawhide* and began studying karate in the 1960s to aid him in fight scenes. For a cowboy he transitioned well into urban action. By the early 1970s he established himself as a stunt heavy, with memorable turns opposite Steve McQueen on *Papillon* (1973) and Pam Grier on *Foxy Brown*

JACK LEWIS (1924–2009)

A writer of varied interests and a career U.S. Marine, Iowa-born Jack Lewis dabbled in the stunt business as he did several trades. At any given time he was a steel worker, private eye, or cowboy. Lewis was a machine gunner in World War II and won a Bronze Star for bravery in the Korean War. Between wars he was on the swim team at the University of Iowa and pursuing a career as a screenwriter while stationed at Camp

Opposite: **Terry Leonard performs a record-setting eighty-foot fall into boxes on *Cover Me, Babe* (aka *Run, Shadow, Run*) (1970).**

Pendleton near San Diego. It was there that Lewis was an assistant technical advisor during the making of *Sands of Iwo Jima* (1949). While stationed in Hawaii he served as a liaison to Hollywood providing Marine Corps extras for several early 1950s films. In this capacity he did stunt work on *Mister Roberts* (1955), making dives off a ship and riding a motorcycle off a pier. His $700 payment for the latter stunt was confiscated by his military superiors, although director John Ford opened a tab for him at a local bar.

In Hollywood, Lewis trained with Jock Mahoney and landed a handful of stunt assignments. He made a $40 saddle fall on *Buffalo Bill in Tomahawk Territory* (1952), rolled down an embankment for Rick Vallin on *Naked Gun* (1956), fell from rocks on *Dakota Incident* (1956), and took another saddle fall on *Sergeant Rutledge* (1960). He was a wrangler on *The Horse Soldiers* (1959). In the early 1960s Lewis became the publisher of *Gun World* and *Horse and Horseman* magazines. He wrote many screenplays and fictional books, including a number featuring a Mescolero Indian stuntman named Charlie Cougar. Lewis died from lung cancer at the age of 84.

See: Lewis, C. Jack. *White Horse, Black Hat: A Quarter Century on Hollywood's Poverty Row.* Lanham, MD: Scarecrow, 2002; Perry, Tony. "Jack Lewis Dies at 84; Marine, Novelist, and Movie Writer." *Los Angeles Times.* June 11, 2009.

JACK LILLEY (1933–)

Texas-born Jack Lilley grew up in California and wrangled at the Hudkins Ranch. In his teens he worked as a horseback extra on the Durango Kid films before serving with the U.S. Navy during the Korean War. His first stunt was a saddle fall on *Omar Khayyam* (1957). The burly Lilley doubled Brian Keith on *Scandalous John* (1971) and *Mountain Men* (1980). On TV he doubled Victor French on *Little House on the Prairie* (1974–83). He later provided livestock for the industry. His sons Clay and Clint became stuntmen.

He worked on *The Big Fisherman* (1959), *One-Eyed Jacks* (1961), *Cat Ballou* (1965), *The Rounders* (1965), *Johnny Reno* (1966), *Rough Night in Jericho* (1967), *Support Your Local Sheriff* (1969), *Blazing Saddles* (1974), and *Meteor* (1979). TV credits include *Cheyenne, Zorro, Wanted—Dead or Alive, Have Gun—Will Travel, Rawhide, The Virginian, Bonanza, The Big Valley,* *The Wild Wild West, High Chaparral,* and *Gunsmoke.* Lilley has been honored on the Newhall Walk of Western Stars.

See: Brown, J.P.S. "A Double Life." *American Cowboy.* June 2004; "Hollywood Wrangler Riding High." *Daily News.* August 13, 1991; Jonas, Karen. "Hoofed into Hollywood." *Santa Clarita Valley Signal.* July 23, 2012; Michael, Martha. "Lilleys of the Valley." *Canyon County Magazine.* February 2009; www.petticoatsandpistols.com.

GARY LITTLEJOHN (1946–)

Vermont-born motorcycle specialist Gary Littlejohn came to California to study metallurgical engineering at Pierce College and worked as a welder in the aerospace industry. On the side he customized hot rods and choppers, which brought him to the attention of Hollywood. Littlejohn provided motorcycles for *Wild Angels* (1966) and received a small part in the follow-up *Devil's Angels* (1967). From there he took off with acting and motorcycle stunts on *Hells Angels on Wheels* (1967), *Savage Seven* (1968), *Cycle Savages* (1969), *Angels Die Hard* (1970), *C.C. and Company* (1970), and *Angels Hard as They Come* (1971).

When the biker genre died out, Littlejohn was able to stick around in stunts, having the foresight to train as an all-around athlete. He was stunt coordinator on *Badlands* (1973) and doubled Martin Sheen. The 6'1", 185-pound Littlejohn also doubled Gene Hackman, David Carradine, and Joe Namath, and did long motorcycle jumps for William Smith on *Hollywood Man* (1976). In all, he worked on more than 300 films. He was the designer of the Littlejohn sidehack, for which he is in the BMX Hall of Fame, and has been honored by the Stuntmen's Hall of Fame.

See: Albright, Brian. *Wild Beyond Belief.* Jefferson, NC: McFarland, 2008; Lim, Fifi. "Seeing Double." *New Straits Times.* July 16, 1987; Masker, Mark. "Renaissance Man." *Street Chopper.* October 2010.

EDDIE LITTLE SKY (1926–1997)

Six-foot-two, 205-pound Ogala Sioux and Cheyenne Native American Eddie Little Sky was born in Pine Ridge, South Dakota, as Edsel Wallace Little. A Navy veteran of World War II service, Little Sky was an oil field wildcat and active on the rodeo circuit as a bull rider and bareback bronco rider. With Vincent St. Cyr he created a dance troupe known as the Roadrunners prior to entering films as a stuntman in the early 1950s. He was hired to ride a horse at Disneyland for the Painted Desert attraction and was soon playing character roles in western fare. He is best known as the prisoner who tangles with Woody Strode in the opening moments of *The Professionals* (1966).

He also worked on *Last Frontier* (1955), *Westward Ho, the Wagons!* (1956), *Hell Bent for Leather* (1960), *Cimarron* (1960), *Sergeants Three* (1962), *The Hallelujah Trail* (1965), *Duel at Diablo* (1966), *The Way West* (1967), *Paint Your Wagon* (1969), *A Man Called Horse* (1970), *Journey Through Rosebud* (1972), and *Breakheart Pass* (1976). He was technical advisor on *Soldier Blue* (1970). TV credits include *Cheyenne, Sugarfoot, Bronco, The Rebel, The Rifleman, Maverick, Have Gun—Will Travel, Bat Masterson, The Travels of Jamie McPheeters, Wagon Train, Branded, Daniel Boone, The Virginian, Laredo, Death Valley Days, High Chaparral,* and *Gunsmoke.*

See: "Ogala Sioux Star Back in State for Picture Filming." *Aberdeen Daily News.* July 28, 1971.

BOB LIVINGSTON (1904–1988)

Bob Livingston was born Robert Edgar Randall in Quincy, Illinois. In California he attended Westlake Military School and excelled in track as a pole vaulter. He learned to ride as a dude ranch cowboy, garnering work as a stunt rider on *Man-Woman-Marriage* (1921) and *Queen of Sheba* (1921). At Glendale High he injured his leg quarterbacking the football team, putting an end to that sport. He toiled as a lumberjack, merchant seaman, ditch digger, and construction worker, getting back into films by putting on a fight scene for *Brown of Harvard* (1926). The next few years he was a swimming and baseball extra while doubling William Haines, John Gilbert, George J. Lewis, Eddie Phillips, and Colin Clive. For the 180-pound six-footer, his most notable assignment came performing the track scenes for Richard Dix on *Redskin* (1929).

Livingston played the masked heroes The Lone Ranger and Zorro on screen. As hot-headed but charming Stony Brook, one of Republic's popular Three Mesquiteers, he did many of his own

stunts and virtually all his fight scenes. His fight with Yakima Canutt on *Heart of the Rockies* (1937) is considered to be one of the best of the B-western genre. While making *Trigger Trio* (1937) Livingston fractured his skull when he struck a rock performing a dive into the Kern River. Honored by the Stuntmen's Hall of Fame and the Golden Boot Awards, Livingston died of emphysema at the age of 83.

See: McCord, Merrill. *Brothers of the West: The Life and Films of Robert Livingston and Jack Randall.* Bethesda, Maryland: Alhambra, 2003.

HAROLD LLOYD (1893–1971)

Harold Clayton Lloyd was born in Burchard, Nebraska, and boxed as an amateur. The physical comedian starred in popular thrill comedy shorts where his bespectacled character would be placed in peril. His most famous stunt was hanging from a clock on *Safety Last* (1923) in the days before back projection. The ingenious camera angles gave the appearance that Lloyd was dangling several stories above the sidewalk. In actuality a set was built on the roof of the building, with mattresses underneath Lloyd. The angle of the camera made it look as if he had nothing beneath him. Lloyd was the one directly responsible for these innovative and pioneering film techniques.

Lloyd followed this up with a wild streetcar chase on *Girl Shy* (1924), a thrilling double-decker bus ride on *For Heaven's Sake* (1926) and another skyscraper climb on *Feet First* (1930). Harvey Parry actually did the *Feet First* long shots but was under contract not to reveal his participation until after Lloyd had passed away. Lloyd and the studio wanted audiences to believe he was doing all of his own death-defying stunts. Stuntmen Richard Talmadge and Dave Sharpe also worked with Lloyd under the same arrangement.

The 5'10", 150-pound Lloyd got his start working for Hal Roach and taking bumps in Keystone comedies. In 1919 he was posing for a publicity photograph holding a small prop bomb that turned out to be live. When Lloyd lit the bomb, it exploded in his hand. He was temporarily blinded and lost a significant portion of the right hand. He was eventually fitted with a glove to hide his disfigurement for the cameras. In light of this permanent injury, his later building climbs are deemed all the more impressive.

See: Brownlow, Kevin. *The Parade's Gone By.*

Harold Lloyd hangs from the hands of a clock on *Safety Last* (1923).

Berkeley, Ca: University of California, 1968; Dardis, Tom. *Harold Lloyd: The Man on the Clock*. Viking, 1983; www.haroldlloyd.com.

ORMER "OMAR" LOCKLEAR (1891–1920)

Greenville, Texas–born Ormer Leslie Locklear was a famed wing-walker and barnstorming pilot who today is largely forgotten. The former Army Air Corps flight instructor was the first man to jump from plane to plane. He also enacted plane-to-train and plane-to-car transfers and performed handstands on the wings. Audiences made his debut film *The Great Air Robbery* (1919) a hit and the dashing Locklear seemed on the brink of major movie stardom had he not perished on his second film *Skywayman* (1920). He died in a plane crash executing a descending spin for the cameras. Theories suggest he either blacked out or was blinded by the motion picture lights. Locklear was 28 years old.

See: "Omar Lockleer." *Variety*. August 6, 1920; Ronnie, Art. *Locklear: The Man Who Walked on Wings*. Cranbury, NJ: A.S. Barnes, 1973.

GARY LOCKWOOD (1937–)

Best known as the star of Stanley Kubrick's *2001 A Space Odyssey* (1968), Gary Lockwood got his start doubling John Wayne's son Patrick on *The Young Land* (1958) and Anthony Perkins during basketball scenes on *Tall Story* (1960). Lockwood was born in Van Nuys, California, as John Gary Yurosek. He was a star football player and track athlete at William S. Hart High and played linebacker for UCLA. Lockwood did stunts on *Spartacus* (1960) and numerous TV westerns.

By the early 1960s the six-foot, 180-pound Lockwood was a rising star, twice sharing the screen with Elvis Presley and engaging in fight scenes on *Wild in the Country* (1961) and *It Happened at the World's Fair* (1962). A martial art fight of interest came against Leslie Nielsen on the Filipino-made *Project: Kill* (1976). On the TV series *The Lieutenant* (1963–64) Lockwood insisted on doing many of his own stunts. He was most proud of smashing through a wooden porch for a death scene on *Firecreek* (1968).

See: "Actor Has Producers in Flutter." *Trenton Evening Times.* October 13, 1963; Lockwood, Gary, & R.A. Jones. *2001 Memories: An Actor's Odyssey.* Cowboy Press, 2001; Roberts, Jeremy. "Two Tough Guys: Actor Gary Lockwood Pulls No Punches with Steve McQueen." *Examiner.* September 13, 2012.

JIMMY LODGE

British horse master Jimmy Lodge doubled David Niven on *The Guns of Navarone* (1961) and *Casino Royale* (1967) and Gregory Peck on *Arabesque* (1966). A veteran of several James Bond films, he recruited stunt legend Vic Armstrong for his first job. Lodge also worked on *Lawrence of Arabia* (1962), *From Russia with Love* (1963), *Goldfinger* (1964), *The Long Duel* (1967), *You Only Live Twice* (1967), *Where Eagles Dare* (1968), *Alfred the Great* (1969), *Figures in a Landscape* (1970), *Kelly's Heroes* (1970), *Diamonds Are Forever* (1971), *Catlow* (1971), *Live and Let Die* (1973), *The Spy Who Loved Me* (1977), *Never Say Never Again* (1983), *Octopussy* (1983), and *A View to a Kill* (1985).

See: Armstrong, Vic, & Robert Sellers. *The True Adventures of the World's Greatest Stuntman.* London: Titan, 2012.

CAREY LOFTIN (1914–1997)

A legendary car and motorcycle specialist, Carey Loftin was the number one man for vehicular action for the better part of five decades. He contributed heavily as a driver and coordinator to the famous car stunts and chase scenes for *Rebel Without a Cause* (1955), *Thunder Road* (1958), *On the Beach* (1959), *Grand Prix* (1966), *Bullitt* (1968), *The French Connection* (1971), and *Vanishing Point* (1971). He was the mysterious truck driver who menaces Dennis Weaver on the TV movie *Duel* (1971) and did the bulk of the driving on *It's a Mad, Mad, Mad, Mad World* (1963),

earning a then record fee of $100,000. Loftin was noted for his meticulous planning, precision, and superb execution. On *Thunder Road* he skidded and rolled a Ford Tudor 150 feet and stopped within eighteen inches of his mark as a pair of power transformers were rigged to explode. On *White Line Fever* (1975) he jumped a semi through a billboard.

William Carey Loftin was born in Blountstown, Florida, and raised in Alabama and Mississippi. He first rode a motorcycle at the age of ten and soon purchased a 37 cubic inch single-cylinder Indian motorcycle for $10. He refined his mechanic skills, installing a filed-down car piston that suddenly made his bike the fastest in town. The athletic Loftin did acrobatics on his motorcycle, attracting attention from barnstormer Skip Fordyce. After witnessing Loftin perform a back-flip off the bike in which he caught the seat with his hands and still managed to control the speeding bike, Fordyce was hooked. At the age of 19 Loftin became part of the Fordyce show. He performed in thrill shows and raced competitively in the Catalina Grand Prix, the Big Bear Run, and the Greenhorn Enduro. He served with the U.S. Marines.

He began doing movies in 1936, with his car and motorcycle work on the W.C. Fields film *The Bank Dick* (1940) putting him on the map as a member of the famed "Stunt Cousins." He could do stunts outside of his specialty, most notably doubling Spencer Tracy for the judo scene on *Bad Day at Black Rock* (1955). The 180-pound six-footer showed up in large-scale brawls on *Seven Sinners* (1940), *Soldiers Three* (1951), *Spartacus* (1960), and *The Great Race* (1965) but rarely worked westerns as he distrusted horses. In fifty-plus years of high-speed stunts, his only injuries were a Ferrari crack-up on *Viva Las Vegas* (1963) and minor burns on *Red Line 7000* (1965). He co-starred on the short-lived action series *Troubleshooters* (1959–60), doubling series star Keenan Wynn. Others doubled include Robert Mitchum, Lee Marvin, Bud Abbott, Boris Karloff, Robert Lowery, Onslow Stevens, House Peters, Jr., and Huntz Hall. Even nearing the age of seventy he remained the go-to man to double James Woods in a Ferrari for a high speed racing game through heavy traffic on *Against All Odds* (1984).

He worked on *Dick Tracy's G-Men* (1939), *Perils of Nyoka* (1942), *The Masked Marvel* (1943), *Haunted Harbor* (1944), *Zorro's Black*

Automotive expert Carey Loftin handled the exciting car and truck action on *White Line Fever* (1975).

Whip (1944), *The Tiger Woman* (1944), *The Body Snatcher* (1945), *What Next, Corporal Hargrove?* (1945), *The Crimson Ghost* (1946), *Jesse James Rides Again* (1947), *Dangers of the Canadian Mounted* (1948), *G-Men Never Forget* (1948), *Adventures of Frank and Jesse James* (1948), *Joan of Arc* (1948), *Raw Deal* (1948), *Mighty Joe Young* (1949), *Trouble Makers* (1949), *Side Street* (1949), *King of the Rocket Men* (1949), *Armored Car Robbery* (1950), *The Racket* (1951), *Sealed Cargo* (1951), *Don Daredevil Rides Again* (1951), *Fearless Fagan* (1952), *Radar Men from the Moon* (1952), *Code Two* (1953), *Jalopy* (1953), *The Wild One* (1953), *20,000 Leagues Under the Sea* (1954), *A Star Is Born* (1954), *Abbott and Costello Meet the Keystone Kops* (1955), *Walk the Proud Land* (1956), *The Perfect Furlough* (1958), *The Big Operator* (1959), *The Rebel Set* (1959), *Thunder in Carolina* (1960), *Hatari* (1962), *The Great Escape* (1963), *The Killers* (1964), *Dr. Goldfoot and the Bikini Machine* (1965), *Munster, Go Home!* (1966), *The Silencers* (1966), *Spinout* (1966), *Bonnie and Clyde* (1967), *Wait Until Dark* (1967), *The Love Bug* (1968), *Speedway* (1968), *The Wrecking Crew* (1969), *The Great Bank Robbery* (1969), *Patton* (1970), *Which Way to the Front?* (1970), *Slaughterhouse Five* (1972), *The New Centurions* (1972), *Come Back, Charleston Blue* (1972), *The Getaway* (1972), *The Hot Rock* (1972), *Fear Is the Key* (1973), *Walking Tall* (1973), *Magnum Force* (1973), *The Don Is Dead* (1973), *The Sugarland Express* (1974), *The Front Page* (1974), *Thunderbolt and Lightfoot* (1974), *Killdozer* (1974), *Night Moves* (1975), *Framed* (1975), *The Eiger Sanction* (1975), *Part Two, Walking Tall* (1975), *Special Delivery* (1976), *Viva Knievel!* (1977), *Herbie Goes to Monte Carlo* (1977), *Outlaw Blues* (1977), *The Deer Hunter* (1978), *Stingray* (1978), and *The China Syndrome* (1979). TV credits include *Richard Diamond, Peter Gunn, Yancy Derringer, Whirlybirds, The Fugitive, The Man from U.N.C.L.E., Laredo, Star Trek,* and *Mission: Impossible.* A member of the Stuntmen's Association and an inductee of the Stuntmen's

Hall of Fame and the Motorcycle Hall of Fame, Loftin died of natural causes at the age of 83.

See: Bowden, Robert. "Carey Loftin's Success Is No Accident." *St. Petersburg Times.* March 20, 1979; Crosse, Jesse. *The Greatest Movie Car Chases of All Time.* St. Paul, MN: Motorbooks, 2006; Johnson, Erskine. "Daredevil Stuntman a Very Cautious Guy." *Springfield Union.* January 21, 1958; Weaver, Tom. "An Interview with Carey Loftin." *Western Clippings.* #17, May-June 1997.

DEL LORD (1894–1970)

Canadian-born circus acrobat Delbert Edward Lord went from set builder to stuntman in Mack Sennett's Keystone Cop and Fire Brigade series. He was the driver of the Keystone wagon, speeding it through traffic, ahead of trains, and into a multitude of precarious situations with expert timing. He drove vehicles off cliffs and piers and once jumped in front of a streetcar. In addition to driving in the chases, Lord was the thrower for pie-in-the-face comedy action. Sennett promoted him to assistant director to help design the comedy gags, while comedy greats such as Charlie Chaplin, a regular tennis partner, extolled his virtues. He eventually became a full-fledged director, handling the majority of the action on the Three Stooges shorts. Lord died at the age of 75.

See: Brownlow, Kevin. *The Parade's Gone By.* Berkeley, California: Univ. of California, 1968; Foster, Charles. *Stardust and Shadows: Canadians in Early Hollywood.* Toronto: Dundurn, 2000.

SHARON LUCAS (1928–2006)

Oklahoma-born Sharon Elise Lucas got her start as a popular trick rider touring the rodeo circuit with her sister Shirley. They would perform acrobatic side stands, back shoulder stands, and cartwheels on their horses Pie, Pistol Pete, and Cotton Eyed Joe. Five-foot-seven Sharon doubled Jane Russell on *The Paleface* (1948), *Son of Paleface* (1952), and *The Tall Men* (1955), Marie Windsor on *Hellfire* (1949), Rosalind Russell on *Woman of Distinction* (1950), Esther Williams on *Jupiter's Darling* (1955), Audrey Hepburn on *The Unforgiven* (1960), Juliet Prowse on *The Fiercest Heart* (1961), and Carol Lynley on *Once You Kiss a Stranger* (1969). On TV she was the main double for Anne Francis on the judo-heavy action series *Honey West* (1965–66).

She also worked on *Annie Get Your Gun* (1950), *Westward the Women* (1951), *The Story of Will Rogers* (1952), *Blood Alley* (1955), *The Guns of Fort Petticoat* (1957), *The FBI Story* (1959), *How the West Was Won* (1962), *The Great Race* (1965), *The Rare Breed* (1966), and *Paint Your Wagon* (1969). Her back and neck were injured performing a fall on the last film and she subsequently retired from stunt work. TV credits include *The Cisco Kid* and *Twilight Zone*. She was a charter member of the Stuntwomen's Association.

See: Lucas Jauregui, Shirley. *It Takes a Good Horse.* Pilot Peak, 2011; "Sharon Lucas." *Union.* January 27, 2006; www.thelucassisters.com.

SHIRLEY LUCAS (1924–)

The older sister of Sharon Lucas, Oklahoma-born Shirley Lucas grew up swimming at the local YMCA and taking dance and gymnastic classes. She was a cheerleader for Bartlesville High. As the sisters' trick riding act grew in popularity on the rodeo circuit, they were recruited by Hollywood. Shirley doubled Betty Hutton on *Annie Get Your Gun* (1950), Marilyn Monroe on *Monkey Business* (1952), Esther Williams on *Texas Carnival* (1951), Eleanor Parker on *Valley of the Kings* (1954), Lana Turner on *The Prodigal* (1955), Shirley Jones on *Oklahoma!* (1955), Elizabeth Montgomery on *The Court Martial of Billy Mitchell* (1955), Lauren Bacall on *Blood Alley* (1955), and Diane Varsi on *Ten North Frederick* (1958). On TV she doubled Lucille Ball on *I Love Lucy.*

She also worked on *Westward the Women* (1951), *The Story of Will Rogers* (1952), and *The FBI Story* (1959). On the 1955 TV show *So This Is Hollywood* she doubled Mitzi Green playing a stuntwoman jumping from a saloon balcony. Her stunt was covered in the pages of *TV Guide.* Other TV credits include *The Cisco Kid* and *Gilligan's Island.* Shirley married Bob Jauregui and semi-retired from stunt work in the late 1950s.

See: "A Stunt Girl's Stunt Girl." *TV Guide.* May 1955; Lucas Jauregui, Shirley. *It Takes a Good Horse.* Pilot Peak, 2011; "This Pretty Girl Loves Falling Down Stairs." *Spokesman Review.* March 8, 1958; www.thelucassisters.com.

TOM LUPO (1943–)

Six-foot-one, 205-pound Thomas Lee Lupo is best known as the double for Tom Selleck on

TV's *Magnum P.I.* (1982–88) and several films. He also filled in for Robert Urich on the first season of *Vega$* (1978–79). Lupo was born in Baltimore and raised in California's San Fernando Valley. He was an All-American quarterback and track star at Birmingham High. In college he played defensive end, fullback, and kicker for the 1962 USC National Champions and became a Rose Bowl hero when he converted a record six extra points. Lupo was forced to sit out a year due to a knee injury, playing pro football briefly in Montreal. Ranch work and competitive archery helped him gain a foothold in the stunt profession after several years of extra work.

Lupo worked on *Tobruk* (1967), *Swashbuckler* (1976), *Bound for Glory* (1976), *Convoy* (1978), *Hooper* (1978), *One Man Jury* (1978), *Avalanche Express* (1978), *Buck Rogers in the 25th Century* (1979), and the TV mini-series *Greatest Heroes of the Bible* (1978). Other TV credits include *Star Trek, The Streets of San Francisco, Barbary Coast, Bronk, Baretta, Kojak, Serpico, Starsky and Hutch, Wonder Woman, Grizzly Adams, Charlie's Angels, CHiPs,* and *Fantasy Island.* He was a member of Stunts Unlimited; his children Diana, Curtis, and Khristian have all done stunts.

See: Block, Bill. *Trojans 1962: John McKay's First National Championship.* IUniverse, 2012; Katsilometes, John. "Fall Guy: Tom Lupo a Seasoned Stuntman." *Redding Record Searchlight.* January 19, 1992.

PIERCE LYDEN (1908–1998)

Veteran character actor Pierce Lyden was a ubiquitous black-hat presence in 1940s B-westerns due to his ability to do his own horseback stunts and fistfights. He often played second fiddle villains, which unfortunately kept him from attaining bigger roles in better productions. Nonetheless, Lyden was greatly appreciated by film festival fans who recalled him punching it out with the likes of Lash LaRue on *Dead Man's Gold* (1948) and Johnny Mack Brown on *Whistling Hills* (1951). He did stunts on serials such as *Holt of the Secret Service* (1941) and *The Phantom* (1943). Lyden shared many of his valuable memories of friends and co-workers from his more than 300 films through a series of self-published books.

The Nebraska-born Lyden grew up on a ranch and was competing in small rodeos as a young man. He came to Hollywood a theatrical veteran, but due to the Great Depression took what jobs came his way. Much of it was stunt-related car work in gangster pictures and horse riding in westerns where he'd earn a little extra for a fall. With the death of the B-western, Lyden moved into TV shows such as *The Cisco Kid* and *The Range Rider.* He was still asked to do his own stunts, but this time for free. Lyden opted to retire and went to work for Disneyland. An inductee of the Cowboy Hall of Fame and a Golden Boot Award honoree, Lyden died from cancer at the age of 90.

See: Fagen, Herb. *White Hats and Silver Spurs.* Jefferson, NC: McFarland, 1996; Lyden, Pierce, & Mario De Marco. *Pierce Lyden: The Movie Bad Man.* Self, 1985; McLellan, Dennis. "Pierce Lyden, Movie Bad Guy, Dies; Wore His Boots Proudly." *Los Angeles Times.* October 13, 1998; "Pierce Lyden Made a Career as Villain." *Orange County Register.* October 13, 1998.

CLIFF LYONS (1901–1974)

Clifford William Lyons was born in Clarno Township, South Dakota. Farm-raised, he began entering rodeos and formed a Wild West show touring Nebraska and Kansas. The husky (six feet, 185 pounds) cowboy found his way to Hollywood and worked as a stunt rider on *Ben-Hur* (1925) and *Beau Geste* (1927). He starred in a few silent westerns as Tex Lyons. As talkies came in, Lyons became one of the top stuntmen in the business, specializing in horse stunts. He doubled Johnny Mack Brown, Buck Jones, Ken Maynard, George O'Brien, William Boyd, Tom Mix, John Wayne, Errol Flynn, Henry Fonda, Tyrone Power, Anthony Quinn, Gene Autry, Bill Elliott, Richard Dix, and Ronald Reagan.

Lyons was known for a 75-foot jump on a horse into white water doubling Tyrone Power and Henry Fonda on *Jesse James* (1939). This is often regarded as one of the industry's greatest stunts. Lyons was paid $2,350 for performing the stunt twice. Both horses used reportedly perished, bringing the American Humane Association out against the film and insuring that horses would not be jumped under those conditions again. Lyons did a similar stunt the following year, taking a wagon off a cliff on *Dark Command* (1940). He often worked alongside Yakima Canutt, and the two emerged as the go-to men for the studios.

Cliff Lyons holds onto John Wayne as Mike Mazurki watches Fred Graham about to deliver a punch on *Dakota* (1945).

John Ford used him as the stunt ramrod and second unit director on many of his films, among them *Three Godfathers* (1948), *She Wore a Yellow Ribbon* (1949), *Wagon Master* (1950), *Rio Grande* (1950), *The Searchers* (1956), *The Horse Soldiers* (1959), *Sergeant Rutledge* (1960), *Two Rode Together* (1961), *Cheyenne Autumn* (1964), and *Seven Women* (1966). Stuntmen were unanimous in describing Lyons as a driven taskmaster, but he was able to put great action onto the screen on *The Conqueror* (1956) and *The Alamo* (1960). Canutt used him as the Lubian charioteer in *Ben-Hur* (1959).

He also worked on *Stingaree* (1934), *In Old Chicago* (1937), *The Painted Stallion* (1937), *Valley of the Giants* (1938), *Dodge City* (1939), *Man of Conquest* (1939), *Winners of the West* (1940), *They Died with Their Boots On* (1941), *Valley of the Sun* (1942), *Lady Takes a Chance* (1943), *In Old Oklahoma* (1943), *Saratoga Trunk* (1945), *Dakota* (1945), *San Antonio* (1945), *Red River* (1948), *The Fighting Kentuckian* (1949), *Stampede* (1949), *The Red Badge of Courage* (1951), *Bend of the River* (1952), *Lone Star* (1952), *Hondo* (1953), *The Man Behind the Gun* (1953), *Drums Across the River* (1954), *The Prodigal* (1955), *The Rains of Ranchipur* (1955), *Westward Ho, the Wagons!* (1956), *Seven Men from Now* (1956), *The Wings of Eagles* (1957), *The Missouri Traveler* (1958), *Spartacus* (1960), *The Comancheros* (1961), *How the West Was Won* (1962), *Taras Bulba* (1962), *Donovan's Reef* (1963), *McLintock!* (1963), *Mail Order Bride* (1964), *The Long Ships* (1964), *Major Dundee* (1965), *Genghis Khan* (1965), *The War Wagon* (1967), *The Green Berets* (1968), *The Great Bank Robbery* (1969), *Chisum* (1970), *Big Jake* (1971), and *The Train Robbers* (1973). He was an honorary member of the Stuntmen's Association and an inductee of the Stuntmen's Hall of Fame.

See: Snuggs, Ann. *Uncredited*. Crosby, Texas: Painted Word Studios, 2008.

GEORGE MAGRILL
(1900–1952)

Brooklyn-born George Magrill sported an imposing physique at six feet and 190 pounds. He was an expert swimmer, boxer, and horseman who spent two years with the Sam Rice Wild West shows. In the U.S. Navy he was the light-heavyweight boxing champion. Magrill was advertised as "the stunt king of the movies" when he had a starring role on *Paradise Hole* (1924). He was most often employed as a menace to cowboy star Fred Thomson. Magrill specialized in fight scenes, most notably exchanging blows with Jack Holt on *Wild Horse Mesa* (1925). As a stuntman he doubled Bela Lugosi.

Magrill worked on more than 300 films, among them *King Kong* (1933), *Dante's Inferno* (1935), *Barbary Coast* (1935), *Phantom Empire* (1935), *San Francisco* (1936), *Union Pacific* (1939), *North West Mounted Police* (1940), *Winners of the West* (1940), *The Sea Wolf* (1941), *Call Out the Marines* (1942), *Reap the Wild Wind* (1942), *Commandos Strike at Dawn* (1942), *Two Yanks in Trinidad* (1942), *Sudan* (1945), *The Crimson Ghost* (1946), *Monsieur Beaucaire* (1946), *Pirates of Monterey* (1947), *Joan of Arc* (1948), *River Lady* (1948), *G-Men Never Forget* (1948), *Samson and Delilah* (1949), *Short Grass* (1950), *Don Daredevil Rides Again* (1951), *Lone Star* (1952), and *Denver and Rio Grande* (1952). Magrill died from a heart attack at the age of 52.

See: "George Magrill." *Variety*. June 4, 1952.

FRANK MAHER (1929–2007)

London-born Francis James Maher is best known as the double for Patrick McGoohan on the TV shows *Danger Man* (1960–61), *Secret Agent* (1964–67), and *The Prisoner* (1967–68). He also doubled for Roger Moore on *The Saint*. Maher was a champion boxer in school and served with the British Army's parachute regiment in World War II. He was wounded in action in the Battle of Arnhem. Maher was recruited to be a Roman centurion extra on *Caesar and Cleopatra* (1946), earning extra money when he and his pal drew blood on one another fake-fighting. A stunt career was born.

Maher doubled Burt Lancaster sliding down a sail on *The Crimson Pirate* (1952) and later for riding stunts on *The Devil's Disciple* (1959). He doubled Errol Flynn on *Master of Ballantrae* (1953) and worked on *Ivanhoe* (1952), *Bandit of Zhobe* (1959), *Children of the Damned* (1964), *The Italian Job* (1969), *Innocent Bystanders* (1973), and *Ffolkes* (1979). TV credits include *The Avengers, Man in a Suitcase, Champions, Space 1999*, and *Blake's 7*. Maher died from emphysema at the age of 78.

See: *Independent*. "Obituary: Frank Maher." July 20, 2007; www.theunmutual.co.uk/interview smaher.htm.

JOCK MAHONEY (1919–1989)

Jock Mahoney is considered by many to be the greatest all-around stuntman the screen has ever seen. He routinely performed jaw-dropping stunts that combined amazing courage and incredible athletic ability. The 6′4″, 200-pound Mahoney, known as Jocko to his many friends, had a fantastic leaping ability and a charismatic personality that led him to be one of the first and only stuntmen to make the transition to screen stardom as a leading man. He was a popular TV cowboy on *The Range Rider* (1950–53) and the screen's oldest Tarzan in the 1960s, braving real jungles that nearly killed him for the sake of authenticity. Even as a star he insisted on performing his own stunts because no one could do it better. On *Slim Carter* (1957) he made a fifty-foot dive into less than six feet of water that had nervous Universal Studio executives biting their nails. On the TV series *Yancy Derringer* (1958–59) he swung seventy feet from an opera box to a stage to knock out a villain, then returned by rope to deliver his dialogue to the leading lady in a single take.

Mahoney was a standout football and basketball player at Davenport High and the University of Iowa. He also won numerous awards for his gymnastics, swimming, and diving abilities. He was a state champion diver and set a national record in the 40-yard freestyle. He was training for the Olympics when World War II intervened and he became a Marine fighter pilot and survival instructor. After the war he found himself in Hollywood as the double for Charles Starrett on the Durango Kid western series. Mahoney quickly raised eyebrows with his ability to dive off high balconies and leap over three horses and land in the saddle of the fourth.

Mahoney doubled Errol Flynn for a fantastic

leap down a staircase on *Adventures of Don Juan* (1948) and went on to perform stunts for Gregory Peck, Randolph Scott, John Wayne, Gary Cooper, Joel McCrea, George Montgomery, Rod Cameron, Stewart Granger, and Gene Autry. He was quickly acknowledged as a top fight man, an expert fencer, and one of the best horsemen in the business; he could mount and dismount with unique agility. His fight scenes opposite Gene Autry on *Rim of the Canyon* (1949) and Randolph Scott on *Santa Fe* (1951) are considered classics. Mahoney performed stunt work on approximately 175 films over a five-year period, but by the 1950s was a star in his own right.

Mahoney and his *The Range Rider* co-star Dick Jones toured the United States with popular rodeo shows in which they showcased extensive fight routines and did saddle falls for thrilled audiences. Mahoney's *The Range Rider* fights are some of the most innovative and energetic the

screen has ever seen. Mahoney had expert timing and camera awareness, often taking on multiple opponents coming at him from different angles without ever cutting the action. Mahoney's work on *The Range Rider* was the catalyst for many impressionable youngsters growing up to enter the ranks of professional stuntmen.

Mahoney played the bad guy opposite Gordon Scott on *Tarzan the Magnificent* (1960), and the two put on one of the screen's greatest fight scenes on location in Kenya, Africa. The producer was so impressed that he cast the 42-year-old Mahoney as the Ape Man in both *Tarzan Goes to India* (1962) and *Tarzan's Three Challenges* (1963). Mahoney was determined to play Tarzan as an educated man and do all of his own jungle action. On the second film he contracted amoebic dysentery, pneumonia, and dengue fever swimming in the polluted Klong River during an action scene. He became so sick that he lost forty pounds

Ron Ely dodges a Jock Mahoney kick on *Tarzan's Deadly Silence* (1970).

but continued shooting until the final exciting fight scene with Woody Strode was in the can. The part almost killed him and it took a significant amount of time to recover. Many felt he was never quite the same, but Mahoney was soon in the jungle again to play bad guys opposite Ron Ely on TV's *Tarzan* and coordinate stunts for that late 1960s show.

In the early 1970s Mahoney suffered a stroke on the set of a *Kung Fu* TV episode, but kept it hidden until his scenes were finished. He recovered enough to resume his acting career and even performed a stunt falling off a bridge in a wheelchair for the Burt Reynolds film *The End* (1978). Reynolds was a Jocko fan, and the character Brian Keith played in the film *Hooper* (1978) is based on Mahoney. In the twilight of his career, Mahoney received every award a stuntman could, including membership in the Stuntmen's Hall of Fame, the Yakima Canutt Award for Stunt Excellence, and Lifetime Achievement recognition from the Stuntmen's Association of Motion Pictures.

Prior to becoming a leading man, he worked on *Slave Girl* (1947), *The Swordsman* (1948), *To the Ends of the Earth* (1948), *Prince of Thieves* (1948), *Black Arrow* (1948), *Untamed Breed* (1948), *Adventures in Silverado* (1948), *Coroner Creek* (1948), *Silver River* (1948), *Yellow Sky* (1948), *Wake of the Red Witch* (1948), *The Plunderers* (1948), *You Gotta Stay Happy* (1948), *Return of the Bad Men* (1948), *Lust for Gold* (1949), *The Doolins of Oklahoma* (1949), *Colorado Territory* (1949), *The Gal Who Took the West* (1949), *The Walking Hills* (1949), *The Fighting Kentuckian* (1949), *Canadian Pacific* (1949), *Montana* (1950), *Short Grass* (1950), *Kim* (1950), *Rogues of Sherwood Forest* (1950), *Dallas* (1950), *Cariboo Trail* (1950), *The Tougher They Come* (1950), *Cow Town* (1950), *The Nevadan* (1950), *Lady and the Bandit* (1951), *Only the Valiant* (1951), *Texas Rangers* (1951), *Whirlwind* (1951), *The Barefoot Mailman* (1952), *Against All Flags* (1952), *The World in His Arms* (1952), and *The Prisoner of Zenda* (1952). An honorary member of the Stuntmen's Association, Mahoney died in 1989 at the age of 70 when he crashed his car after suffering another stroke.

See: Freese, Gene. *Jock Mahoney: The Life and Films of a Hollywood Stuntman*. Jefferson, NC: McFarland, 2013; Hagner, John. *Kangeroo Legs*. Self-Published, 1994; "Jock Mahoney, Stunt-

man Made a Career of Action." *Los Angeles Times*. December 16, 1989; members.shaw.ca/mahoney 13/jm1.html.

PAUL MALVERN (1902–1993)

Paul William Malvern was born in Portland, Oregon. A child acrobat with his family's vaudeville troupe, he was billed as "the greatest child acrobat on the American stage." He later performed for the Ringling Brothers Circus and entered stunt work in the early 1920s. His first stunt came doubling Mary Pickford. He is best known for doubling Eileen Sedgwick on *Beasts of Paradise* (1923) and John Barrymore for the catapult shots on *Beloved Rogue* (1927). Malvern survived a river stunt on *The Trail of '98* (1928) that saw others perish. After a seventy-foot fall from the mast of a ship, injuries forced him to give up stunts and move into assistant directing. He became a producer for Monogram and Universal, helming many of John Wayne's earliest B-westerns. Even then he was known to physically show the stuntmen how he wanted stunts performed.

See: "Paul Malvern Is Dead; Former Stunt Man, 91." *New York Times*. June 4, 1993.

TEDDY MANGEAN (1901–1964)

Raymond Frederick Mangean was born in Elmhurst, California. A professional wire walker who toured Cuba and South America, Mangean was a regular stunt double for Larry Fine of the Three Stooges. On film Mangean doubled Peter Coe on *The Mummy's Curse* (1944) and Robert Cornthwaite on *The Thing from Another World* (1951), where he also appeared as the mid–sized incarnation of the alien. Due to his modest height, Mangean was often cast as pages, bellboys, and messengers. He was part of a short-lived early stunt organization, the Studio Chase Troupe.

He worked on *Hypnotized* (1932), *Thirteen Women* (1932), *The Mighty Barnum* (1934), *Three on a Honeymoon* (1934), *The Nitwits* (1935), *Professional Soldier* (1935), *The Shadow* (1937), *Bringing Up Baby* (1938), *Hollywood Cavalcade* (1939), *Cargo to Capetown* (1950), *Abbott and Costello Meet Dr. Jekyll and Mr. Hyde* (1953), *Jalopy* (1953), *The Egyptian* (1954), and *Abbott and Costello Meet the Keystone Kops* (1955). He was an honorary member of the Stuntmen's Association.

HANK MANN (1887–1971)

Walrus-mustached Hank Mann was born David William Lieberman in New York City. A steeplejack turned flying trapeze acrobat, he was known as the toughest of the stuntmen in Mack Sennett's Keystone Cop comedies. On *Tale of Twenty Stories* (1915) he balanced on a rooftop. On *City Lights* (1931) he played the prizefighter who boxed Charlie Chaplin. Mann worked as an extra, bit player, or bump man on over 400 films, among them *Scarface* (1932), *Hollywood Cavalcade* (1939), *The Perils of Pauline* (1947), and *Abbott and Costello Meet the Keystone Kops* (1955).

See: "Hank Mann." *Variety.* December 12, 1971.

PAUL MANTZ (1903–1965)

Flying ace Paul Mantz died at the age of 61 while working as a double for James Stewart on *The Flight of the Phoenix* (1965). He was flying over sand dunes outside of Yuma, Arizona, in a specially built P-1 when he touched down and the cobbled-together plane busted apart, killing him instantly as his cockpit nosedived. Passenger Bobby Rose was injured but survived. The crash footage remains in the film. A veteran of nearly 300 films, Mantz was the pilot of the Boeing B-17 that bellylands on *Twelve O'Clock High* (1949) and was in charge of the flying sequences on *It's a Mad, Mad, Mad, Mad World* (1963).

Born Albert Paul Mantz in Alameda, California, he began flying while still in his teens. As an Army Air Cadet, Mantz was not allowed to graduate due to his penchant for pulling dangerous stunts in the air. That type of flying was fine for the movies as Mantz was hired to fly through a canyon on *Galloping Ghost* (1932) and negotiate a hangar with minimal clearance on *Air Mail* (1932). During World War II Mantz flew with the First Motion Picture Unit. At the conclusion of the war he bought a fleet of planes for use in motion pictures through his Paul Mantz Air Services. As a competitive air racer, Mantz won the Bendix Speed Trophy three years in a row (1946 to 1948) in a converted P-51. He joined forces with pilot Frank Tallman to form TallMantz Aviation, gaining a monopoly on Hollywood's flying stunts.

He worked on *Hell's Angels* (1930), *Here Comes the Navy* (1934), *Ceiling Zero* (1936), *Men with Wings* (1938), *Test Pilot* (1938), *Only Angels Have Wings* (1939), *Coast Guard* (1939), *Flight Command* (1940), *Flying Cadets* (1941), *A Yank in the RAF* (1941), *The Bride Came C.O.D.* (1941), *Captain of the Clouds* (1942), *Flying Tigers* (1942), *Thunderbirds* (1942), *For Whom the Bell Tolls* (1943), *Air Force* (1943), *The Desert Fox* (1951), *Flying Leathernecks* (1951), *Around the World in Eighty Days* (1956), *Jet Pilot* (1957), *The Spirit of St. Louis* (1957), *Zero Hour* (1957), *The Wings of Eagles* (1957), *The Crowded Sky* (1960), *A Gathering of Eagles* (1962), and *How the West Was Won* (1962). TV credits include *Sky King* (1952). Mantz was an honorary member of the Stuntmen's Association and an inductee of the Stuntmen's Hall of Fame.

See: Dwiggins, Don. *Hollywood Pilot: The Biography of Paul Mantz.* Garden City, NY: Doubleday, 1967; "Mantz Once Had World's Seventh Biggest Air Force." *Yuma Daily Sun.* July 9, 1965; "Paul Mantz." *Variety.* July 4, 1965.

TED MAPES (1901–1984)

Six-foot-three, 185-pound Ted Mapes was born John Tylor Mapes in St. Edwards, Nebraska. He grew up on a wheat farm familiar with livestock. In Los Angeles he drove oil trucks and moving vans. After he began working as a studio grip, the tall, lanky Mapes was noticed by director Joseph Kane. Footage of Mapes was shot to show to the studios as a potential cowboy star. Columbia liked Mapes but asked if he would serve as Charles Starrett's double. He agreed and learned the rudiments of being a stuntman. Starrett went on to become one of the most prolific cowboy actors as the star of the Durango Kid series. Those in the know began to appreciate his action double Mapes as well. Mapes doubled Starrett for over a decade until Jock Mahoney took over.

Mapes is best known as the chief double for Gary Cooper, whom he strongly resembled. Their association lasted through seventeen pictures, including *North West Mounted Police* (1940), *Sergeant York* (1941), *Saratoga Trunk* (1945), *Along Came Jones* (1945), *Unconquered* (1947), *Springfield Rifle* (1952), and *Man of the West* (1958). In 1950 he began doubling James Stewart, continuing in that capacity on more than thirty films, among them *Winchester '73* (1950), *Broken Arrow*

(1950), *Bend of the River* (1952), *The Naked Spur* (1953), *Thunder Bay* (1953), *Rear Window* (1954), *The Far Country* (1955), *The Man from Laramie* (1955), *The Man Who Knew Too Much* (1956), *Night Passage* (1957), *Vertigo* (1958), *Two Rode Together* (1961), *The Man Who Shot Liberty Valance* (1962), *How the West Was Won* (1962), *Shenandoah* (1965), *Flight of the Phoenix* (1965), *The Rare Breed* (1966), *Firecreek* (1968), and *Bandolero!* (1968). He doubled Joel McCrea on *Union Pacific* (1939) and *Foreign Correspondent* (1940), John Wayne on *Lady from Louisiana* (1941) and *Dakota* (1945), Ben Johnson on *Mighty Joe Young* (1949), Forrest Tucker on *Rock Island Trail* (1950), Raymond Massey on *Barricade* (1950), and Gregory Peck on *The Gunfighter* (1950), in addition to Bill Elliott, Russell Hayden, Smith Ballew, and Herman Brix (aka Bruce Bennett) on B-films.

Mapes also worked on *Hawk of the Wilderness* (1938), *Zorro's Fighting Legion* (1939), *Daredevils of the Red Circle* (1939), *King of the Royal Mounted* (1940), *Captain Midnight* (1942), *The Outlaw* (1943), *Desert Hawk* (1944), *Monster and the Ape* (1945), *Gunfighters* (1947), *Jesse James Rides Again* (1947), *The Paleface* (1948), *Fort Apache* (1948), *Samson and Delilah* (1949), *Brimstone* (1949), *Fort Worth* (1951), *Calamity Jane* (1953), *Man from God's Country* (1958), *Cheyenne Autumn* (1964) and the TV shows *Hopalong Cassidy, Kit Carson, The Cisco Kid, Wagon Train, Tales of Wells Fargo, The Virginian,* and *Gunsmoke.* When his career wound down, he went behind the cameras monitoring animal activity on film sets for the American Humane Association. He was an inductee of the Hollywood Stuntmen's Hall of Fame.

See: "Ted Mapes." *Variety.* September 19, 1984.

LEE MARVIN (1924–1987)

Tough guy movie legend Lee Marvin, star of *The Professionals* (1966) and *The Dirty Dozen* (1967), handled weapons as well as anyone in Hollywood and was nearly as good at fight scenes. The loose-limbed Marvin was involved in several noteworthy screen fights where he did the majority of the action, including *The Missouri Traveler* (1958), *Donovan's Reef* (1963), *Emperor of the North* (1973), and *Shout at the Devil* (1976). One of his best fights came on *Point Blank* (1967) with stuntmen Ted White and Jerry Catron. They were

so impressed with Marvin that at the end of the film the star was presented a stuntman's check. Marvin had a long history with stuntmen. In 1961 he was an original sponsor of the Stuntmen's Association of Motion Pictures, of which he became an Honorary Member. In 1977 he hosted the TV special *Super Stunt.*

The 6'3", 185-pound Marvin was born in New York City and was a track star at St. Leo Prep in Florida. He served with the U.S. Marines as a sniper in World War II, receiving a Purple Heart after being injured at the battle of Saipan. Marvin became a premier character villain as the motorcycle gang leader Chino on *The Wild One* (1953) and achieved name recognition with audiences as a TV star on the cop drama *M-Squad* (1957–60), where he did his own judo fights. Hard-living Lee Marvin died from heart failure at the age of 63.

See: Epstein, Dwayne. *Lee Marvin: Point Blank.* Tucson, AZ: Schaffner, 2013; "Lee Marvin Gets Paid for Stuntman Chores." *Ottawa Citizen.* November 3, 1967; Zec, Donald. *Marvin: The Story of Lee Marvin.* New York: St. Martin's, 1980.

BUDDY MASON (1902–1975)

Pennsylvania-born Bruce Cameron Mason got his start as a vaudeville acrobat and became one of the top stuntmen during the silent era. Nicknamed Suicide Mason, he was fearless jumping from autos, leaping off bridges, and balancing on the edge of skyscrapers. Mason was the regular double for Fred Thomson and Jack Holt in the 1920s. He subbed for Robert Armstrong on *King Kong* (1933) and Errol Flynn on *The Charge of the Light Brigade* (1936). He was one of the top stuntmen on *Lucky Devils* (1932) and worked on *Gunga Din* (1939). In the early 1930s he was part of one of the first stunt organizations, known as the Studio Chase Troupe.

Mason was known for his motorcycle work, although it was a bike jump that ended his career. He was badly broken up jumping a motorcycle onto a moving train (he missed his mattress on the train). He continued working on films as an extra and stand-in, but his stunting days were through. An honorary member of the Stuntmen's Association and an inductee of the Stuntmen's Hall of Fame, Mason died at the age of 72.

See: "Well Known Double in Keaton Picture." *Boston Herald.* October 16, 1927; Hagner, John. *Falling for Stars.* El Jon, 1964;

MIKE MASTERS (1929–2003)

Five-foot-eleven, 195-pound Mike Masters was born Michael A. Shanto in Chicago, Illinois. He was an AAU wrestling champion at Mt. Carmel High and wrestled for Iowa State while studying to be a veterinarian. After service with the U.S. Army in Europe he worked as a dog trainer, lumberjack, lifeguard, and dance instructor. The muscular actor felt no role was too small and from the 1950s on appeared in over 300 film and TV productions. He was an excellent horseman, and his ability to do his own stunts saw him cast in many physical roles.

One of his earliest credits is stunt work on *Spartacus* (1960), and he can be spotted engaging in a short catwalk fight with James Coburn on *Our Man Flint* (1966). Masters is best known for many appearances as a stunt heavy fighting Robert Conrad on TV's *The Wild Wild West* (1965–69). He did stunts on *Combat* (1962–67) and *The Rat Patrol* (1966–68) while appearing numerous times on episodes of *Sea Hunt, The Rebel, Branded, The Man from U.N.C.L.E., Mission: Impossible, Mannix,* and *The Six Million Dollar Man.* By the 1970s he concentrated solely on acting parts over stunt assignments. Masters died from cancer at the age of 74.

CARL MATHEWS (1899–1959)

Oklahoma-born Carl Davis Matthews occasionally went by the stage name Duke Mathews, working on more than 150 B-westerns as a henchman. Nicknamed Cherokee due to his Native American ancestry, he doubled cowboy stars Ray "Crash" Corrigan, Fred Scott, and Johnny Mack Brown. He worked on *North West Mounted Police* (1940), *Reap the Wild Wind* (1942), *Law of the Lash* (1947), *Unconquered* (1947), *Return of the Lash* (1947), *Escape to Burma* (1955), and *Westward Ho, the Wagons!* (1956). TV credits include *The Cisco Kid.*

See: Conley, Robert J. *A Cherokee Encyclopedia.* University of New Mexico, 2007.

FRANK MATTS (1920–1990)

Born in San Luis Obispo, California, the wiry rodeo champion Frank Matts was a skilled horseman and driver of wagons and coaches who gave riding lessons to U.S. Army officers. He doubled Gregg Barton on Gene Autry films, portrayed villains on TV's *The Cisco Kid,* and toured with Duncan Renaldo as the character Black Jack Matts. His other credits include *Red River* (1948), *Thunder Over the Plains* (1953), *Escape from Fort Bravo* (1954), and the serials *Cody of the Pony Express* (1950) and *Roar of the Iron Horse* (1951). He retired from stunt work to run ranches and rent horses out to the motion picture studios. Matts died from pneumonia at the age of 70.

See: "Frank Matts, Actor, Rancher." *Los Angeles Times.* November 17, 1990.

DENVER MATTSON (1937–2005)

5'10", 180 pound Denver Mattson was born in Selfridge, North Dakota, and raised in Washington. He began boxing at the age of nine and was a paratrooper in the U.S. Army. In Los Angeles he worked construction jobs and trained at Paul Stader's gym. He worked for Stader on the disaster epics *The Poseidon Adventure* (1972) and *The Towering Inferno* (1974), but is best known for doubling Luke Askew in a fire stunt on *Flare-Up* (1969) and George C. Scott on *Movie, Movie* (1978).

He also worked on *Sidehackers* (1969), *Lost Flight* (1970), *Support Your Local Gunfighter* (1971), *Conquest of the Planet of the Apes* (1972), *Cleopatra Jones* (1973), *Battle for the Planet of the Apes* (1973), *Earthquake* (1974), *The Hindenburg* (1975), *The Master Gunfighter* (1975), *Death Game* (1976), *Mr. Billion* (1977), *The Domino Principle* (1977), *Texas Detour* (1978), *One Man Jury* (1978), *The Main Event* (1979), *1941* (1979), and *Stunt Seven* (1979). TV credits include *Voyage to the Bottom of the Sea, I Spy, Laredo, The Wild Wild West, The Time Tunnel, Star Trek, Land of the Giants,* and *The Rockford Files.* A member of the Stuntmen's Association, Mattson died from kidney failure at the age of 68.

See: Carinci, Justin. "Final Salute: Stuntman Honed Skills in Orchards." *Columbian.* October 8, 2005; McNamara, Miles. "All Fired Up: Stuntman Will Take Any Risk." *Milwaukee Journal.* May 23, 1978.

BOB MAY (1939–2009)

Bob May is best known as the small man inside the Robot on the TV series *Lost in Space*

(1965–68). Robert M. May was born in New York City to a family of entertainers, first appearing on stage at the age of two. After service in the U.S. Navy, he danced in early Elvis Presley films such as *Jailhouse Rock* (1957) and worked on nine films with Jerry Lewis beginning with *The Nutty Professor* (1963). He did stunt work on *Palm Springs Weekend* (1963), *Quick Before It Melts* (1964), *Beach Blanket Bingo* (1965), and *Stagecoach* (1966), in the latter as Red Buttons' double. TV credits include *Cheyenne, The Roaring Twenties, Hawaiian Eye, Surfside 6, 77 Sunset Strip,* and *Laredo.* May died from congestive heart failure at the age of 69.

See: Clark, Mike, & Bill Cotter. "Bob May: Life Inside the Robot." *Starlog.* April 1982; "*Lost in Space* Actor Bob May Dies at 69." *Los Angeles Times.* January 18, 2009; Weaver, Tom. "Man in the Bubble Headed Mask." *Starlog.* April 1994; www.robot-b9.com.

KERMIT MAYNARD
(1897–1971)

The brother of cowboy star Ken Maynard, Kermit Maynard was born in Vevay, Indiana. He excelled as a multi-sport athlete at Columbus North and Garfield High. For Indiana University he lettered in baseball, basketball and track, and was an All-Western Conference halfback for the football team. Kermit played semi-pro baseball and basketball in the Minnesota area. By the mid–1920s his brother had found success in Hollywood and urged Kermit to work as a stuntman. Kermit did just that, brushing up on his riding skills at Fat Jones' stables. He made his debut as a football player and double on *Wild Bull of the Campus* (1925).

In 1927 Kermit got his own series of films for Rayart where he was billed as Tex Maynard. When those finished, he went back to being a double for the likes of his brother as well as Tom Tyler, George O'Brien, Victor McLaglen, Jack Hoxie, Tom Keene, and Rex Bell. Fox Studios considered him their main stuntman. Kermit also tried his hand at the National Competition Rodeo in Salinas and was crowned the World Champion Trick Rider and Fancy Roper in 1931 and 1933. He got another chance at Ambassador Films in 1934 in a series of Northwest Mounted Police films. In these, Kermit won many admirers for his trick riding astride his dapple gray horse Rocky. One of his best screen fights was an acrobatic barroom brawl on *Song of the Trail* (1936). He settled into playing B-Western bad guys on dozens of films but the 180-pound six-footer never ceased taking stunt assignments.

He worked on *Winners of the West* (1940), *Texas* (1941), *The Phantom* (1943), *Buffalo Bill* (1944), *Desert Hawk* (1944), *The Spanish Main* (1945), *Along Came Jones* (1945), *Duel in the Sun* (1946), *My Darling Clementine* (1946), *Wild Harvest* (1947), *Mighty Joe Young* (1949), *Fighting Man of the Plains* (1949), *The Doolins of Oklahoma* (1949), *Stampede* (1949), *Canadian Pacific* (1949), *Short Grass* (1950), *Fort Worth* (1951), *The Great Sioux Uprising* (1953), *Law and Order* (1953), *The Charge at Feather River* (1953), *War Arrow* (1953), *Wichita* (1955), *The Oklahoman* (1957), *Man from God's Country* (1958), *Westbound* (1959), *North to Alaska* (1960), *Hell Bent for Leather* (1960), and *Taras Bulba* (1962). In later years he doubled James Craig on *Northwest Stampede* (1948) and Steve Cochran on *The Lion and the Horse* (1952). Upon retirement, he became the head of the Screen Extras Guild. An inductee of the Stuntmen's Hall of Fame, Maynard passed away from a heart attack at the age of 73.

See: Anderson, Chuck. "Saga of Kermit Maynard." *Favorite Westerns.* #5 & #6, 1982.

MICKEY McCARDLE
(1922–1997)

College football star Mickey McCardle was born Leon Vincent McCardle in Los Angeles. After a stellar career at Manual Arts High, the 5'11", 170-pound USC halfback was drafted by the Green Bay Packers in 1944 but opted for the U.S. Marines instead. Following the war he returned to USC and was named All-Coast in both 1946 and 1947. He worked as a stuntman on *Spirit of West Point* (1947), *The Fighting Kentuckian* (1949), *Sands of Iwo Jima* (1949), *The Flame and the Arrow* (1950), and *At Sword's Point* (1952). He was a football technical advisor on *Father Was a Fullback* (1949), *That's My Boy* (1951), and *Saturday's Hero* (1951).

McCardle's stunt career was short-lived as he became an assistant director and second unit director on *North by Northwest* (1959), *What Did You Do in the War, Daddy?* (1966), *Sometimes a Great Notion* (1970), and *Life and Times of Judge Roy Bean* (1972). He worked often with director

Blake Edwards. On *The Great Race* (1965) McCardle put on a cowboy outfit and got into the stunt action during the big barroom brawl. His daughter Susan was a stuntwoman in the 1970s. An honorary member of the Stuntmen's Association, McCardle died at the age of 74.

See: "Ex-Gridder McCardle Still Tough in Films." *Oregonian*. September 17, 1950.

FRANK McCARROLL (1892–1954)

Frank Leo McCarroll was born in Morris, Minnesota and drifted to North Dakota and Montana as a young cowboy. Of stout physique, he had careers as a wrestler and boxer in Idaho. In 1912 he tried steer wrestling for the rodeo and became a two-time steer wrestling champion at Pendleton. He set a world record in the bulldogging event and won championships in Chicago and Madison Square Garden. McCarroll broke into films as a stuntman and worked as a B-western henchman on more than 100 films. He was most often used for fight scenes and doubled character players Smiley Burnette, Dub Taylor, and Fuzzy Knight.

He worked on *The Storm* (1938), *Destry Rides Again* (1939), *Melody Ranch* (1939), *The Kansan* (1943), *In Old Oklahoma* (1943), *Buffalo Bill* (1944), *Desert Hawk* (1944), *Flame of Barbary Coast* (1945), *Bells of Rosarita* (1945) *Along Came Jones* (1945), *Jeep Herders* (1945), *Silver River* (1948), *Cow Town* (1950), and *Dallas* (1950). An inductee of the Pendleton Rodeo Hall of Fame, McCarroll died from a coronary and subsequent fall from a ladder at the age of 61.

See: "Stunt Man Dies in Fall." *San Diego Union*. March 11, 1954; www.pendletonhalloffame.

KENT McCORD (1942–)

Six-foot-two, 185-pound Kent McCord starred as Officer Jim Reed on the popular police show *Adam–12* (1968–75). He was born Kent Franklin McWhirter in Los Angeles and was a football lineman at Baldwin High and Citrus Junior College. He played for the University of Utah and transferred to USC as a Physical Education major. At the time he weighed 230 pounds and competed in arm-wrestling events. He was friends with actor-singer Rick Nelson and often appeared on the TV series *Adventures of Ozzie and Harriet*. On weekends they played touch football against a team captained by Elvis Presley. This led to McCord doing minor stunt work, most notably as a football player on *John Goldfarb, Please Come Home* (1965) and in a fight scene for the Elvis movie *Girl Happy* (1965).

See: "Grid Game Led to Acting." *San Antonio Light*. December 29, 1968; www.kentmccord.com.

JOEL McCREA (1905–1990)

Joel Albert McCrea was born in South Pasadena, California, and sat in the saddle as well as anyone in the business. He had been a stable boy at Los Angeles riding schools and a hand for the King Cattle Company in the Tehachapi Mountains. He loved roping and was an excellent horseman, keeping his own profitable ranches even after he became a star. As a young man the 6'3", 200-pound McCrea stood out in track and field at Hollywood High and continued to throw the disc at Pomona College. He spent ample time playing volleyball, swimming, and surfing the waves at the Santa Monica Beach Club.

McCrea entered films as a stuntman on *Penrod and Sam* (1923) and *Self Made Failure* (1923). He served rather improbably as a riding double for actresses Greta Garbo on *The Torrent* (1926) and Marion Davies on *Fair Co-Ed* (1927) and stunted on a Ruth Roland serial while graduating from USC. McCrea nabbed an early lead with a standout fight scene on *Silver Horde* (1930) and had a long career as a western star. He proved quite adept at fights and had a solid reputation with stuntmen. His son Jody broke into the business doing stunts. McCrea died of pulmonary complications at the age of 84.

See: "McCrea Started in Movies as Stunt Double." *Wichita Eagle*. January 26, 1992; Thomas, Tony. *Joel McCrea: Riding the High Country*. Burbank: Riverwood, 1991.

RUSS McCUBBIN (1935–)

Julian Russell McCubbin worked as Clint Walker's stunt double on the early '60s TV seasons of *Cheyenne* and doubled him on *Send Me No Flowers* (1964) and *Night of the Grizzly* (1966). The 6'5", 225-pound McCubbin worked stunts for Fess Parker on TV's *Daniel Boone* and filled the stunt ranks of *Waco* (1966) and *Camelot* (1967). By the latter part of the '60s he began to focus his career as an actor, working guest shots on a number of TV shows. McCubbin's best known fight came against Clint Eastwood on *Sudden Impact* (1983). Eastwood had earlier blown him through a saloon window on *High Plains Drifter* (1973). The West Virginia–born McCubbin had been a star football player and track athlete at the Hargrave Military Academy and attended Virginia Tech on a football scholarship prior to service with the U.S. Army.

See: Anderson, Bob. "Russ McCubbin: The Cheyenne Show." *Trail Dust.* Vol. 2, #1, Spring 1994; www.russmccubbin.com.

FRANK McGRATH (1903–1967)

Frank McGrath's friendship with actor Ward Bond led to his casting as grizzled cook Charlie Wooster on the TV series *Wagon Train* (1957–65) in a perfect match of personality and character. Benjamin Franklin McGrath was born in Mound City, Missouri, and started his career as a jockey. Legend has it he jumped off a train and landed on a film set, entering the business in the early 1920s. He'd had some rodeo experience and was an excellent all-around horseman. The 5'7", 150-pound McGrath worked on *Ben-Hur* (1925) and doubled Warner Baxter as the Cisco Kid on *In Old Arizona* (1929). He subbed for Stan Laurel, Buster Keaton, J. Carrol Naish, Pedro Armendariz, Jr., Walter Huston, and Charles McGraw in addition to actress Gene Tierney. On *The Three Musketeers* (1948) he doubled Gene Kelly for riding scenes. A Navy veteran of World War II, McGrath and his falling horse Baldy became a fixture in John Ford's stock company, working on *Three Godfathers* (1948), *Fort Apache* (1948), *She Wore a Yellow Ribbon* (1949), *Rio Grande* (1950), and *The Searchers* (1956).

He also worked on *Perils of the Yukon* (1922), *Out of the Silent North* (1923), *Mystery Ranch* (1932), *Elinor Norton* (1934), *Western Union* (1941), *The Ox-Bow Incident* (1943), *Mighty Joe Young* (1949), *Side Street* (1949), *Broken Arrow* (1950), *Devil's Doorway* (1950), *The Red Badge of Courage* (1951), *Across the Wide Missouri* (1951), *Soldiers Three* (1951), *Westward, the Women* (1951), *Pony Soldier* (1952), *Apache War Smoke* (1952), *Hondo* (1953), *The Naked Spur* (1953), *20,000 Leagues Under the Sea* (1954), *The Tin Star* (1957), *The Wings of Eagles* (1957), and *The Young Land* (1958). He was featured on the radio program *Daredevils of Hollywood.* An honorary member of the Stuntmen's Association and an inductee of the Stuntmen's Hall of Fame, McGrath died from a heart attack at the age of 64.

See: Grant, Hank. "Frank McGrath Is Actor After Long Stunt Period." *Advocate.* November 19, 1963; Witbeck, Charles. "Train Role Suits McGrath." *Charleston Gazette.* March 7, 1962.

JOE McGUINN (1904–1971)

Brooklyn-born Joseph Ford McGuinn attended Clason Point Military Academy. He was recruited off the handball court at the Hollywood YMCA for stunt work, standing in and doubling John Boles on *Wild Gold* (1934), *Redheads on Parade* (1935), and *Orchids to You* (1935) and Gilbert Roland on *Mystery Woman* (1935). He also worked on *3 on a Honeymoon* (1934), *Gunga Din* (1939), *Zorro's Fighting Legion* (1939), *Daredevils of the Red Circle* (1939), *Dick Tracy's G-Men* (1939), *Calling All Marines* (1939), *Dark Command* (1940), and *In Old California* (1942). A veteran of many serials and B-westerns, McGuinn died of a heart attack at the age of 67.

WAYNE McLAREN (1940–1992)

Louisiana-born Wayne McLaren was a gifted pianist who played at Carnegie Hall at the age of nine. That promising career ended when he was shot in the left hand in a hunting accident. He began riding rodeo in his teens and did so competitively for McNeese State College before turning professional as a bronc and bull rider. In 1963, that career was also cut short by injury when a bull stepped on his knee. Fellow rodeo cowboys helped him get started falling off horses in Hollywood. McLaren worked on *Paint Your Wagon* (1969), *Butch Cassidy and the Sundance Kid* (1969), *The Honkers* (1972), and *Junior Bonner* (1972), as well as the TV series *Gunsmoke, Cannon, Mod Squad, The FBI, The Streets of San Francisco,* and *Mission: Impossible.*

In 1976 McLaren was a co-founder of the National Rodeo League, a short-lived attempt to set up a dozen rodeo team franchises throughout the western states. That same year he did print advertisements as a Marlboro Man, which came to light when he developed lung cancer at a young age and spoke out publicly against cigarettes. McLaren died at the age of 51.

See: Donnelly, Suzanne. "Stunt Man Eyes Acting Career." *Oregonian.* September 1, 1968; Hernandez, Greg. "Bedridden Actor Still Fighting War on Smoking." *Los Angeles Times.* July 14, 1992; Lait, Matt. "Ex–Marlboro Man, Doctor Settle." *Los Angeles Times.* September 26, 1991; Marchese, John. "Life, Death of Marlboro Cowboy." *Plain-Dealer.* September 29, 1992.

GARY McLARTY (1940–)

Five-foot-nine, 165-pound Gary Raymond McLarty was known in Hollywood circles as "Whiz Kid" for his all-around stunt skills. He did the first cannon roll on *McQ* (1974), going nearly eighty miles per hour when he rolled a Chevy Impala on Washington's Pacific Beach four times.

A former bronc rider in rodeos, McLarty entered the business as a protégé of Hal Needham and was memorably thrown into a saloon mirror on *The War Wagon* (1967). McLarty was a competitive dirt-bike racer and performed long motorcycle jumps onto a moving flat car on *Run,*

Angel, Run (1969) and over a hut on *The Losers* (1970). He was the stunt coordinator on *Animal House* (1978), negotiating a Harley Davidson up a stairwell and taking a fall off a ladder for John Belushi. He doubled Kris Kristofferson on *Convoy* (1978) and coordinated the incredible car chases and crashes on *The Blues Brothers* (1980).

Controversy dogged McLarty throughout his career. In 1971 he was injured on a sixty-eight-foot Jeep jump on *Cade's County* that incapacitated Roy Sickner. He was the stunt coordinator during the helicopter accident on *Twilight Zone: The Movie* (1983) that killed actor Vic Morrow and two children. Many critics thought McLarty should have been doubling Morrow for the scene but director John Landis wanted Morrow in the shot. On TV's *Baretta*, McLarty doubled Robert Blake, who later allegedly propositioned McLarty to kill his (Blake's) wife. His testimony at Blake's murder trial revealed a number of skeletons in McLarty's closet. McLarty was a member of Stunts Unlimited and an inductee of the Stuntmen's Hall of Fame. His son Cole has done stunt work.

He worked on *Beau Geste* (1966), *The Way West* (1967), *Ice Station Zebra* (1968), *Chubasco*

Gary McLarty does a cannon roll on the beach on the John Wayne action film *McQ* (1974).

(1968), *Bandolero!* (1968), *Blue* (1968), *Hellfighters* (1968), *Bridge at Remagen* (1969), *The Wild Bunch* (1969), *The Good Guys and the Bad Guys* (1969), *The Undefeated* (1969), *Hell's Angels '69* (1969), *Beneath the Planet of the Apes* (1970), *Little Big Man* (1970), *C.C. & Company* (1970), *Chisum* (1970), *Sometimes a Great Notion* (1970), *Chrome and Hot Leather* (1971), *The Stone Killer* (1973), *The Front Page* (1974), *The Dion Brothers* (1974), *Dirty Mary, Crazy Larry* (1974), *The Longest Yard* (1974), *Posse* (1975), *Rafferty and the Gold Dust Twins* (1975), *Rooster Cogburn* (1975), *A Boy and His Dog* (1975), *Crazy Mama* (1975), *Mitchell* (1975), *Return of a Man Called Horse* (1976), *Vigilante Force* (1976), *Hooper* (1978), and *Apple Dumpling Gang Rides Again* (1979). TV credits include *Combat, The Girl from U.N.C.L.E., Bearcats, Kung Fu, McCloud,* and *The Bionic Woman.*

See: Baker, Dean. "Rough Stuff Enriches Stuntman." *Eugene Register-Guard.* October 26, 1977; Lilley, Tim. *Campfire Conversations.* Akron, OH: Big Trail, 2007; "Stuntmen Compete in Sports Spectacular." *Joplin Globe.* January 15, 1977.

"BIG" JOHN McLAUGHLIN (1927–)

Born in Charleston, South Carolina, John McLaughlin has made a professional living in the water. He became a certified diver at the age of twelve and worked as a lifeguard prior to joining the Navy in World War II where he was a demolition instructor and deep water salvage expert. Upon his discharge he worked on oil rigs in the Gulf Coast and became an instructor for the Divers Training Academy in Miami. In Florida he came to the attention of the makers of the TV series *Sea Hunt.* Along with Courtney Brown, McLaughlin began doubling star Lloyd Bridges. There was already a John McLaughlin in the union so he became "Big John."

McLaughlin worked as a water stuntman and underwater cinematographer, logging diving action on several James Bond films. He doubled Adolfo Celi on *Thunderball* (1965) and Sean Connery on *Never Say Never Again* (1983). McLaughlin worked on *Goldfinger* (1964), *Lady in Cement* (1968), *Day of the Dolphin* (1973), *Live a Little, Steal a Lot* (1975), *Lucky Lady* (1975), *Mako, the Jaws of Death* (1976), and *The Spy Who Loved Me* (1977). TV credits include *Flipper,* *Gentle Ben,* and *The Six Million Dollar Man.* McLaughlin was a member of the Stuntmen's Association.

See: Cogswell, Cathleen. "Diver Profits from Underwater Treasure." *Register Star.* October 29, 1979; www.bobwirt.com; www.internationallegendsofdiving.com.

LEO McMAHON (1913–1995)

Born in Sonora, California, Leo J. McMahon was lured into film work when the Hopalong Cassidy film *Heart of the West* (1936) was shot at his family's ranch. Utilizing his riding skill, he journeyed to Hollywood and began working on *The Charge of the Light Brigade* (1936) and *They Died with Their Boots On* (1941). He was one of the doubles for Clark Gable on *Gone with the Wind* (1939). During World War II McMahon served with the Army Air Corps as a bombardier and earned a Purple Heart for his valor.

He also worked on *Station West* (1948), *Joan of Arc* (1948), *Samson and Delilah* (1949), *Canadian Pacific* (1949), *Dakota Lil* (1950), *Colt .45* (1950), *Warpath* (1951), *Fort Worth* (1951), *Denver and Rio Grande* (1952), *Son of Paleface* (1952), and *Walk the Proud Land* (1956). He became known as "the man who dies a thousand deaths" for his penchant for suffering screen fatalities. McMahon suffered a real injury when a runaway horse team ran his wagon into a tree. The accident ended his stunt career. He turned to writing screenplays, selling *Madron* (1970). He was an honorary member of the Stuntmen's Association.

See: "Leo McMahon in Moving Pictures." *Union Democrat.* November 6, 1936.

STEVE McQUEEN (1930–1980)

Terence Steven McQueen was born in Beech Grove, Indiana. The son of a stunt pilot, he was raised in Missouri on his uncle's farm. At the age of seventeen he joined the Marines and was assigned to the tank division. After the Marine Corps, McQueen worked a variety of jobs, from mechanic to truck driver before landing in Hollywood. He became a television star as western bounty hunter Josh Randall on the series *Wanted—Dead or Alive* (1958–61) and a genuine film star on *The Magnificent Seven* (1960). As his acting career took off, the 5'10", 165-pound McQueen became synonymous with speed, particularly after a famous motorcycle jump (actually his friend Bud Ekins didn't) on *The Great Escape* (1963) and a wild car chase on the streets of San Francisco on *Bullitt* (1968). McQueen did a great deal of his own driving in the film, but was doubled for the more dangerous bits by Ekins and Loren Janes.

His forays into motorcycling, off-road, and Formula One racing became well-publicized. In a Porsche racecar he managed wins at Del Mar and

Steve McQueen throws a punch at stuntman Henry Wills on *Nevada Smith* (1966).

Santa Barbara and set a course lap record in Phoenix. He had respectable showings in the Las Vegas Mint 400, the Greenhorn Enduro, the Baja 1000, and the Lake Elsinore Grand Prix. In 1964 he and Ekins represented the United States in the International Six-Day Trials on 650-cc Triumphs. For filming of *Le Mans* (1971), McQueen entered a twelve-hour race and finished second to Mario Andretti. As a motorcyclist McQueen was very good, gaining a posthumous membership in the Motorcycle Hall of Fame. He actually doubled as a German soldier chasing himself on *The Great Escape* (1963) and worked anonymously as a dirt-bike stuntman on the low-budget *Dixie Dynamite* (1976) for stunt coordinator Ekins.

McQueen was enamored with the martial arts and trained with Ed Parker, Bruce Lee, Chuck Norris, Bob Wall, and Pat Johnson. His best screen fight was a classic barroom brawl on *Soldier in the Rain* (1963). An Honorary Member of the Stuntmen's Association and an inductee into the Stuntmen's Hall of Fame, McQueen died of lung cancer at the age of 50. Former Apacheland Movie Studio stuntman Jody McQueen surfaced after his death claiming to be his brother and put on live stunt shows where he was billed as "The Bounty Hunter."

See: "Star Performs His Own Stunts." *Times-Picayune.* June 16, 1968; Terrill, Marshall. *Steve McQueen: Portrait of an American Rebel.* Dutton, 1994.

PAUL McWILLIAMS (1919–)

Paul McWilliams was the son of Warner Brothers studio medic Paul McWilliams, himself a former stuntman. The younger McWilliams appeared in his first movie at the age of three months old with Douglas Fairbanks and later befriended Errol Flynn with whom he worked on *Captain Blood* (1935), *The Adventures of Robin Hood* (1938), *Dodge City* (1939), *Virginia City* (1940), and *Objective, Burma!* (1945). He served as Flynn's stand-in and stunt double for the last five years of Flynn's life on films such as *Too Much, Too Soon* (1958).

After Flynn's death the six-foot McWilliams worked in the same capacity with Efrem Zimbalist, Jr., on the TV series *77 Sunset Strip* (1958–64) and *The FBI* (1965–74). An expert with a bow and arrow, McWilliams was an instructor for the Pasadena Roving Archer's Club and did archery stunts on TV's *Kung Fu.* He also worked on *Task Force* (1949), *The Story of Will Rogers* (1952), *Hell on Devil's Island* (1957), and *The Unearthly* (1957).

See: Goodking, Mark. "Filling in for Stars Thrill in Itself." *Toledo Blade.* May 8, 1977; "Paul MacWilliams." *Archery.* #44, April 1972.

TROY MELTON (1921–1995)

Six-foot, 170-pound Troy Melton was born in Jackson, Tennessee, and raised in Southern California. He entered films after service with the Army Air Corps during World War II, working most often with fellow stuntman Bill Catching. On TV, Melton doubled Duncan Renaldo on *The Cisco Kid* (1950–55), Kent Taylor on *Boston Blackie* (1951–52) and *Rough Riders* (1958–59), and Martin Landau on *Mission: Impossible.* He also subbed for James Coburn, Richard Webb, Gregory Walcott, and Don Collier. Melton bought the Playboy Restaurant outside of Paramount Studios and owned it for over twenty-five years.

He also worked on *Giant* (1956), *Mohawk* (1956), *How the West Was Won* (1962), *It Happened at the World's Fair* (1963), *Dr. Goldfoot and the Bikini Machine* (1965), *The Great Race* (1965), *The Rounders* (1965), *Coogan's Bluff* (1968), *The Great Bank Robbery* (1969), *Dirty Harry* (1971), *Conquest of the Planet of the Apes* (1972), *Scorpio* (1973), *Magnum Force* (1973), *Battle for the Planet of the Apes* (1973), *Blazing Saddles* (1974), *Earthquake* (1974), *Zero to Sixty* (1978), *Every Which Way But Loose* (1978), and *The Deer Hunter* (1978). Other TV credits include *The Lone Ranger, The Range Rider, Gene Autry, Roy Rogers, Kit Carson, Annie Oakley, Jim Bowie, Wyatt Earp, Highway Patrol, Cheyenne, Maverick, Gunsmoke, Tombstone Territory, Zane Grey, The Rifleman, Wanted—Dead or Alive, Peter Gunn, Sea Hunt, Have Gun—Will Travel, Whispering Smith, Klondike, Bat Masterson, Bonanza, Rawhide, Wagon Train, The Virginian, The Big Valley, Laredo, The Wild Wild West, Star Trek, Batman, The Green Hornet, The Invaders, Mannix, Mod Squad, The Six Million Dollar Man, Little House on the Prairie,* and *The Dukes of Hazzard.* A member of the Stuntmen's Association and an inductee of the Stuntmen's Hall of Fame, Melton died from cancer at the age of 74.

See: Nevins, Francis M. *The Films of the Cisco Kid.* 1998.

FRANK MERRILL (1893–1966)

When Joe Bonomo broke his leg prior to the start of production on the serial *Tarzan the Mighty* (1928), the call went out for a replacement to play Tarzan. Muscular Frank Merrill, the stunt double for Elmo Lincoln on *Tarzan of the Apes* (1918) and *Adventures of Tarzan* (1921) as well as Kamuela Searle on *Son of Tarzan* (1920), was called into service to portray the ape man when Bonomo went down. Merrill devised the vine-swinging stunts which became a staple in the Tarzan pictures. He continued in the part for a second serial, *Tarzan the Tiger* (1929), but with the emergence of sound was deemed replaceable. He subsequently retired from the screen and became a gym instructor for children.

Born in New Jersey as Otto Pell, the six-foot, 185-pound former mounted policeman distinguished himself as a champion gymnast in Southern California and was a national champ in the Roman rings from 1916 to 1918. He also won awards in boxing, wrestling, swimming, and track and field. After winning a "World's Most Perfect Man" competition, he went to work in Hollywood as a boxing trainer to the stars and worked as a stuntman with Buck Jones. Known as "Hercules of the Screen," he had starring roles on *Reckless Speed* (1924), *Battling Mason* (1924), and *Perils of the Jungle* (1927).

See: Brooks, Doug Elmo. "Frank Merrill: The Hercules of the Screen." *Jasoomian.* 1973; Essoe, Gabe. *Tarzan of the Movies.* New York: Cadillac, 1968.

OTTO METZETTI (1890–1949)

Otto Metzetti was the brother of stunt ace Richard Talmadge and a member of their vaudeville act The Flying Metzettis. He worked on the majority of his brother's films, specializing in falls and fights. Otto spent a year in the hospital following a failed stunt on a Douglas Fairbanks film: He was to dive off a balcony into a net six stories below, but his toes caught the railing's edge and sent him off course into one of the net's support poles. He worked on *Pirate Treasure* (1934), *Trail of the Lonesome Pine* (1936), *Nancy Steele Is Missing* (1937), *Slave Ship* (1937), *Beau Geste* (1939), *Gunga Din* (1939), *Captain Caution* (1940), *Frenchman's Creek* (1944), and *The Spanish Main* (1945). He was a member of the Stuntmen's Hall of Fame.

See: "Stunt Men Sub for Stars." *Trenton Evening Times.* March 2, 1944.

VICTOR METZETTI (1895–1949)

German-born Victor Metzetti was another brother of Richard Talmadge and veteran of their acrobatic troupe. He sometimes went by the professional name of Victor Metz or Victor Stanford. He worked more with automobiles and motorcycles. Victor once did a high fall through a series of awnings designed to break his fall. There was no safety pad at the bottom, but Metzetti emerged unscathed. He worked on *Pirate Treasure* (1934), *Professional Soldier* (1935), *Trail of the Lonesome Pine* (1936), *Nancy Steele Is Missing* (1937), *The Hunchback of Notre Dame* (1939), *Gunga Din* (1939), *Captain Caution* (1940), *Passage to Marseille* (1944), *The Spanish Main* (1945), and *Jeep Herders* (1945). A member of the Stuntmen's Hall of Fame, Metzetti died of pneumonia at the age of 53.

See: "Stunt Men Sub for Stars." *Trenton Evening Times.* March 2, 1944.

TED V. MIKELS (1929–)

Low-budget film director Ted V. Mikels, the man behind *Astro Zombies* (1968), *The Corpse Grinders* (1970), *Blood Orgy of the She Devils* (1973), and *The Doll Squad* (1974), got his start as a muscular stuntman on westerns made in his native Oregon. As a horseman, Theodore Vincent Mikacevich worked on *The Indian Fighter* (1955), *Oregon Passage* (1957), and *Tonka* (1958). On some of these, the archery expert shot flaming arrows for the camera. He is the subject of the documentary *The Wild World of Ted V. Mikels* (2010).

See: www.tedvmikels.com.

MIKE MIKLER (1933–2008)

Florida-born stunt actor Michael Theodore Mikler was a favorite of director Sam Peckinpah beginning with several appearances on TV's *The Westerner* (1960) and including a fight scene on *Ride the High Country* (1962). Mikler got his start as a stuntman on the TV series *Johnny Ringo* (1959–60) and appeared on several episodes of *Zane Grey, Bonanza,* and *Gunsmoke.* He had a starring role on the low-budget western *War Party*

(1965) and acted in support on *Ice Station Zebra* (1968), *Pat Garrett and Billy the Kid* (1973), and *Westworld* (1973) before disappearing from the screen.

BETTY MILES (1910–1992)

Low-budget western actress Betty Miles got her start in films as a horsewoman on *Nothing Sacred* (1937). She doubled Linda Darnell and Dorothy Lamour on *Chad Hanna* (1940), Louise Currie on *The Masked Marvel* (1943), and Carole Mathews and Rosemary Lane on *Sing Me a Song of Texas* (1945). She is best known for her action heroine leads at Monogram opposite Tex Ritter, Bill Elliott, Ken Maynard, and Hoot Gibson. Her credits include *Ridin' the Cherokee Trail* (1941), *Return of Daniel Boone* (1941), *Wild Horse Stampede* (1943), and *Sonora Stagecoach* (1944).

Born Elizabeth Harriet Henninger in Santa Monica, California, she learned to ride on her father's cattle ranch. Monogram publicity claimed she had been a rodeo champion at Saugus. Upon leaving Hollywood she toured with the S.L. Cronin Circus, the Al Dean Circus, and the C.R. Montgomery Wild Animal Circus. She was typically showcased with her movie horse Sonny.

BOB MILES (1927–2007)

Robert Jennings Miles, Jr., was born in Hollywood and raised in Utah. He was the son of motion picture stuntman Robert Miles and stuntwoman Frances Miles. He began in the business as a child stunt performer, doubling other kids on horseback. At the tail end of World War II he was stationed at Fort Lewis in the state of Washington. Miles began working as a stuntman at RKO Studios, where he was hired to be the driver for studio mogul Howard Hughes.

The 5'11", 160-pound Miles was married to actress Vera Miles. After five years working for Hughes, he re-entered the stunt profession. Miles was long associated with Paramount Studios and the TV series *Bonanza* (1958–72) where he coordinated stunts and served as stunt double for Michael Landon and David Canary. He doubled Robert Hutton on *The Slime People* (1963) and worked on *Gunsmoke* (1953), *Ride Clear of Diablo* (1954), *Spartacus* (1960), *Young Fury* (1965), *The Great Bank Robbery* (1969), and *Dirty Harry* (1971). TV credits include *Gunsmoke, The Wild West,* and *Star Trek,* where he doubled DeForest Kelley. A member of the Stuntmen's Association and an inductee of the Stuntmen's Hall of Fame, Miles died from emphysema at the age of 79.

JACK MILES (1928–)

Born in Philadelphia, John "Jack" Miles was a sickly, undersized child who needed weekly blood transfusions due to a malfunctioning spleen. He became determined to overcome his maladies through athletics, excelling at Germantown High in track, diving, soccer, and gymnastics. He was named the school's most outstanding athlete and earned a gymnastics scholarship to Florida State University. It was there that he won the first of four national championships on the still rings, where he came up with a move he called "the whippet." Miles won Gold at the Pan-American Games in 1955 and competed in the 1956 Olympics.

In the late 1950s the 5'6" Miles moved to New York City and worked as a stuntman on the TV shows *Car 54, Where Are You?* and *The Defenders.* He doubled Bing Crosby, Andy Williams, Ray Bolger, and Jamie Farr. Returning to Florida he worked on the TV series *Flipper* and *Gentle Ben* and served as a double for Frank Sinatra on *Tony Rome* (1967) and *Lady in Cement* (1968), where he got to swim with forty sharks and get thrown through a car window by Dan Blocker. He doubled Tony Randall on *Hello, Down There* (1969) and William Shatner for a two-story jump on *Impulse* (1974). Miles worked for Florida State University and the Fort Lauderdale Recreation Department, launching a gymnastics program for youngsters. He was inducted into the International Gymnastics Hall of Fame.

See: Adams, Damon. "Jack-of-All-Trades Teaches Motivational Skills." *Sun-Sentinel.* September 6, 1989; Heeren, Dave. "Was Gymnastics Miles' Greatest Sport?" *Sun-Sentinel.* November 13, 1986; Milian, Jorge: Lord of the Rings." *Sun-Sentinel.* May 7, 1993; www.fsugymnastics.org.

BOB MINOR (1944–)

Robert Lee Minor was born in Birmingham, Alabama, and raised in Los Angeles. He was a stand-out athlete at Manual Arts High in football, basketball, baseball, and track, receiving a schol-

Bob Minor (upper left) is one of several stunt performers braving the onrushing waters of a flooded storm drain on *Earthquake* (1974).

arship to Pepperdine University. Minor's specialty was the 120-yard high hurdles, though he ran a 9.7 100-yard dash, high jumped 6'1", and long jumped 23'9". He became a competitive bodybuilder and won a handful of contests, including the 1969 Mr. Los Angeles competition, Mr. Southern California, and Mr. Venice Beach. Minor's intention at the time was to join the Los Angeles Police Department.

Minor was lifting weights at Bud Mucci's Olympic Health Club when he encountered professional stuntmen. Knowing of his athletic background, they suggested Minor could make a lot of money as there were no established black stuntmen in the business. They took him to Paul Stader's Gym, and he began toning down his 18" arms and 50" chest to train as a stuntman. His first assignment came doubling James Iglehart for a fight on *Beyond the Valley of the Dolls* (1970). The newly formed Black Stuntmen's Association wanted Minor as a member, but he determined he could learn more from those who were more experienced. He worked in the Universal Studios tour cracking a bullwhip and concentrated on his cowboy skills. The 6'2", 220-pound Minor made his name on *Come Back, Charleston Blue* (1972) on which he doubled ten characters, including jumping forty feet down an elevator shaft and crashing a car into a brick wall. Minor became the first black member of the Stuntmen's Association in 1972, and within a few years was one of the highest paid stuntmen in the business.

He doubled Jim Brown on *Black Gunn* (1972), Fred Williamson on *Legend of Nigger Charley* (1972), *That Man Bolt* (1973), and *Black Eye* (1974), and William Marshall on *Blacula* (1972) and *Scream, Blacula, Scream* (1973). He was stunt coordinator and double for Roger E. Mosley throughout the run of the TV series *Magnum P.I.* (1980–88). He also doubled James Earl Jones, Bill Cosby, Yaphet Kotto, Richard Roundtree, Carl Weathers, and Hal Williams. Minor was stunt coordinator on the Pam Grier exploitation classics *Coffy* (1973) and *Foxy Brown* (1974). He proved to be a cool, charismatic, and engaging actor, often showing up with supporting parts on films like *Rollerball* (1975) and *The Driver* (1978).

Minor had notable screen fights with heavyweight boxer Ken Norton on *Drum* (1976) and Nick Nolte on an open cliff-side elevator on *The Deep* (1977). A fight with Charles Bronson on

Hard Times (1975) did not make the film's final cut, although Minor received screen credit and appeared in publicity photos for the film. He performed an eighty-foot high fall off the Watts Tower on *Dr. Black, Mr. Hyde* (1976). On *Let's Do it Again* (1975) he made a nineteen-foot jump for Sidney Poitier between two thirteen-story buildings.

He also worked on *Ben* (1972), *Black Caesar* (1972), *Cleopatra Jones* (1973), *Live and Let Die* (1973), *Hit!* (1973), *Soul of Nigger Charley* (1973), *Detroit 9000* (1973), *Black Eye* (1974), *Uptown Saturday Night* (1974), *Black Samson* (1974), *Dirty Mary, Crazy Larry* (1974), *Earthquake* (1974), *Switchblade Sisters* (1975), *Swashbuckler* (1976), *The Next Man* (1976), *A Piece of the Action* (1977), *Mr. Billion* (1977), *Black Sunday* (1977), *MacArthur* (1977), *The Choirboys* (1977), *The Driver* (1978), *Norma Rae* (1979), *Stunt Seven* (1979), and *Smokey and the Bandit 2* (1980). TV credits include *Search, McCloud, The Six Million Dollar Man, McCoy, Kojak, Man from Atlantis, Baretta, Starsky and Hutch, Quincy, Wonder Woman, Spiderman, Buck Rogers,* and *The Fall Guy*. Minor is a member of the Stuntmen's Hall of Fame.

See: Flora, Doris. "Stuntman Landing Acting Roles." *Tuscaloosa News.* June 2, 1978; Gryphon, A.W. "Bob Minor: A Stunt/Miracle Man Breaking Down Barriers On and Off the Set." *Examiner.* September 27, 2010; Konow, David. "#1 Bad-Ass." *Shock Cinema.* #28, 2005; Martinez, Al. "Breakthrough for a Stuntman." *New York Post.* April 28, 1977; "Meet Bob Minor: Major Stunt Man." *Chicago Metro News.* April 7, 1973; Steinberg, Jay, & Pat Salvo. "Incredible Hollywood Stuntman." *Sepia.* November 1978; Williams, Cresandra. "Call to Glory." *Tuscaloosa News.* January 10, 1990.

TOM MIX (1880–1940)

Legendary cowboy star Tom Mix was famous for doing his own flashy stunt work, ensuring that he was the most popular cowboy star of his era. Showman Mix was an excellent horseman and roper, though studio publicity and Mix himself created a mind-boggling back history that severely stretched the truth of his accomplishments. The 5'10", 175-pound Mix had served in the Army, was a cowboy on the Miller Brothers 101 Ranch, and did work as a peace officer for labor camps and as an Oklahoma deputy. However, tales of him being a Texas Ranger, a frontier marshal, chasing Pancho Villa, and fighting in wars in China, Africa, and the Philippines were as tall as the day is long. He only rode with President Teddy Roosevelt in a parade, not as one of his Rough Riders at San Juan Hill.

Once one gets past the fabrications involving Mix, they are left with his cinema record. Thomas Hezikiah Mix from Mix Run, Pennsylvania, was the All-Around Cowboy Champ at the 101 Ranch when he was recruited to appear in *Ranch Life in the Great Southwest* (1909). This led to stunt work and one-reel action with the Selig Polyscope Company and a quick ascension to starring roles at Fox Studios. A fine example of a Mix stunt came on *Mr. Logan, USA* (1918) when he made a daring ride down a 200-foot embankment. On *The Cyclone* (1920) he rode his stunt horse Buster up a flight of stairs that collapsed behind him. Due to

his reputation as a stuntman, Mix was asked to supervise the chariot action on *Queen of Sheba* (1921).

It remains debatable if Mix's most famous stunt ever occurred, let alone if he was the one who did it. That is the infamous horse leap over the canyon at Beale's Cut for *Three Jumps Ahead* (1923). The names Richard Talmadge, Earl Simpson, and Andy Jauregui have surfaced as those responsible for the jump. However, the existing photo of the stunt shows the horse and rider out of proportion with the surroundings, leading some to believe it was a case of Hollywood camera trickery. Legend has it Mix himself and his horse Tony made the jump.

Mix continued into the sound era but was hurt when his horse fell on *Terror Trail* (1933). After starring in the serial *The Miracle Rider* (1935) Mix called it quits, his battered body incapable of performing stunt action to his past high

Tom Mix and his horse Tony.

standards. In between circus appearances, he pursued other interests such as airplane racing and fast cars. Mix was killed at the age of 60 when his 1937 Cord Sportster ran off the road outside of Florence, Arizona, and a suitcase flew from the backseat and struck him in the head.

See: Jensen, Richard. *The Amazing Tom Mix: The Most Famous Cowboy of the Movies.* Lincoln, NE: IUniverse, 2005; Mix, Paul. *Tom Mix: A Heavily Illustrated Biography of the Western Star.* Jefferson, NC: McFarland, 1995; "Tom Mix First to Perform New Stunts." *Victoria Advocate.* March 31, 1920; "Tom Mix Is Badly Hurt." *San Jose News.* October 22, 1932; www.elsemerecanyon.com.

KANSAS MOEHRING (1897–1968)

Kansas Moehring was born Carl L. Moehring in St. Mary's, Ohio. He was raised in Kansas and learned to rope and ride for the rodeo, where he became a champion at Pendleton. After service with the military in World War I, "Kansas" began doubling Hoot Gibson. His biggest stunt for "Hooter" was taking a horse off a cliff into water. He doubled Frank Fay on *Under a Texas Moon* (1930) and became a familiar henchman during the golden age of B-westerns. Other credits include *Captain Blood* (1935), *Heart of the North* (1938), *Virginia City* (1940), *San Antonio* (1945), *The Man from Colorado* (1948), *Fighting Man of the Plains* (1949), *Cariboo Trail* (1950), *Colt .45* (1950), *The Stranger Wore a Gun* (1953), *The Man Behind the Gun* (1953), and *North to Alaska* (1960). On TV he worked on *The Lone Ranger* and *The Cisco Kid.* Featured on the 1938 radio program *Daredevils of Hollywood,* Moehring died at the age of 71.

See: Russell, Bill. "Hoot Gibson Stock Company." *Western Clippings.* #96. July-August 2010.

JOHN MOIO (1939–)

John Angelo Moio was raised in Clairton, Pennsylvania. He found work as a dance instructor at the Arthur Murray Studios and landed a job entertaining at the New Orleans Mardi Gras. A member of the Stuntmen's Association, Moio doubled Tony Curtis on *The Manitou* (1978) and David Janssen on TV's *Harry O* (1974–76). On *Coma* (1978) the 5'10", 175-pound Moio performed a forty-foot fall down concrete steps for Lance LeGault.

He worked on *The Hallelujah Trail* (1965), *The Satan Bug* (1965), *The Great Race* (1965), *The Cincinnati Kid* (1965), *The Russians Are Coming, The Russians Are Coming* (1966), *Hawaii* (1966), *What Did You Do in the War, Daddy?* (1966), *In the Heat of the Night* (1967), *The Thomas Crown Affair* (1968), *Ice Station Zebra* (1968), *What's Up, Doc?* (1972), *The Poseidon Adventure* (1972), *The Sting* (1973), *The Towering Inferno* (1974), *The Great Waldo Pepper* (1975), *Night Moves* (1975), *Pete's Dragon* (1977), *Black Sunday* (1977), *The Car* (1977), *The Swarm* (1978), *Prisoner of Zenda* (1979), *Meteor* (1979), and *The In-Laws* (1979). His TV credits include *The Streets of San Francisco* and *Barnaby Jones.*

See: "Donorans at Farewell Event in Clairton." *Monessen Valley Independent.* March 12, 1962.

MONTE MONTAGUE (1891–1959)

Veteran small part actor Walter H. Montague was born in Somerset, Kentucky, and got his start as an acrobat with the Ringling Brothers Circus. He doubled Tarzan star Elmo Lincoln on *Elmo the Fearless* (1920), *Flaming Disc* (1920), and *The New Adventures of Tarzan* (1921). He starred in the B-western *One Man Trail* (1926) which melded Montague with stock footage of Buck Jones. He went back to bits and stunts, doubling Boris Karloff on *The Raven* (1935). His best moment came as a henchman who engages George O'Brien in a two-minute fight on *Legion of the Lawless* (1940). He also worked on *Bride of Frankenstein* (1935), *Flash Gordon* (1936), *The Buccaneer* (1938), *The Storm* (1938), *Dick Tracy's G-Men* (1939), *Virginia City* (1940), and *Billy the Kid* (1941).

MONTIE MONTANA (1910–1998)

Montana-born Owen Harlan Mickel became a popular trick rider and roper headlining rodeos, circuses, and parades for decades. As Montie Montana he had a starring role in the B-western *Circle of Death* (1935) but mostly stayed behind the scenes in Hollywood. He was a polo-riding double for Dennis O'Keefe on *Kid from Texas* (1939), doubled Will Rogers, Jr., on *The Story of Will Rogers* (1952), and worked stunts on *Two Rode Together* (1961) and *Cheyenne Autumn* (1964). On *The Man Who Shot Liberty Valance* (1962) he memorably rode his horse up a staircase and lassoed a man. In real life he lassoed President Eisenhower at his inauguration. His wife Lucille also performed movie stunts. A member of the Pro Rodeo Hall of Fame, Montana died from complications of a stroke at the age of 87.

See: Montana, Montie. *Montie Montana: Not Without My Horse!* Agua Dulce, CA: Double M, 1993.

GEORGE MONTGOMERY (1916–2000)

Six-foot-two, 195-pound George Montgomery Letz was born in Brady, Montana, and learned horsemanship on the family ranch. He excelled in baseball, football, and track at Great Falls High. At the University of Montana he boxed and was the Northwest Heavyweight Champion. His first film work came as a stunt rider on *Singing Vagabond* (1935). As a stuntman on more than twenty films at Republic Studios he doubled John Wayne as one of the Three Mesquiteers, Preston Foster on *Army Girl* (1938), Herman Brix on *Hawk of the Wilderness* (1938), and John Payne on *Star Dust* (1940). His biggest picture at the studio was *Man of Conquest* (1939). He appeared in the 1938 serial *The Lone Ranger* as one of a group of men suspected of being the masked hero, which gained him notice and a professional name change.

Montgomery served with the Army Air Corps in World War II, and his subsequent marriage to Dinah Shore made him a celebrity. One of his best roles was as Raymond Chandler's private eye Philip Marlowe on *The Brasher Doubloon* (1946), though he seemed more at home playing frontiersmen Davy Crockett and Hawkeye. With his stunt background, the handsome Montgomery made a capable action hero and handled the majority of his own fights. His best brawls came on *Lulu Belle* (1947) and *Cripple Creek* (1952), and he had big battles against Rod Cameron on *Belle Starr's Daughter* (1948) and *Dakota Lil* (1950). Montgomery died of heart failure at the age of 84.

See: "Empty Saddles." *Western Clippings.* #39, January-February 2001; Montgomery, George. *The Years of George Montgomery.* Los Angeles: Sagebrush, 1981.

JACK MONTGOMERY (1891–1962)

John Travers Montgomery was born in Omaha, Nebraska, and became an expert horseman working as a cowboy from Canada to Arizona. He did his first horse fall on a Broncho Billy Anderson western shooting in Tucson. He traveled to Hollywood with the influx of real cowboys who hung around Gower Gulch looking for movie work. Montgomery was luckier than most background riders, doubling Tom Mix for $7.50 a day in 1920, Ronald Colman on *The Winning of Barbara Worth* (1925), and Walter Pidgeon on *Dark Command* (1940) during a thirty-year career. There were occasional gaps where he worked at a dude ranch, ran his own spread, or managed his daughter's career. (He was the father of Baby Peggy, the 1920s silent screen child actress.)

He also worked on *The Ten Commandments* (1923), *King of Kings* (1927), *The Crusades* (1935), *The Charge of the Light Brigade* (1936), *Melody Ranch* (1939), *Northwest Passage* (1940), *My Darling Clementine* (1946), *Unconquered* (1947), *Angel and the Badman* (1947), *Red River* (1948), *Three Godfathers* (1948), *Denver and Rio Grande* (1952), *The Man Behind the Gun* (1953), and *Johnny Guitar* (1954). In the early days of the Disneyland resort he handled mule pack teams.

See: Cary, Diana Serra. *The Hollywood Posse.* Boston: Houghton Mifflin, 1975; King, Susan. "Highs and Lows of Child Star Baby Peggy." *Los Angeles Times.* March 19, 2011.

HARRY MONTY (1904–1999)

Standing 4'5" and weighing 80 pounds, Harry Monty will forever be known as the flying monkey on *The Wizard of Oz* (1939). He was born Hymie Liechtenstein in Dallas, Texas. He had a vaudeville background and spent many years in Hollywood doubling children such as Johnny Sheffield on *Tarzan Finds a Son!* (1939), Tommy Rettig during the river rapid scenes on *River of No Return* (1954), and Clint Howard on the TV series *Gentle Ben* (1967–69). He doubled Jerry Austin on *Saratoga Trunk* (1945) and Margaret O'Brien on *Bad Bascomb* (1946).

Other stunt credits include *Invaders from Mars* (1953), *The Conqueror* (1956), *How the West Was Won* (1962), *Our Man Flint* (1966), *Planet of the Apes* (1968), *Papillon* (1973), and *Earthquake* (1974). On TV he worked on *Lost in Space* (1965–68) and played various characters on the children's show *H.R. Pufnstuf* (1969–70). In the early 1950s he toured as a professional wrestler with Billy Curtis in an act known as The Mighty Midgets. Monty died at the age of 95.

See: Oliver, Myrna. "Harry Monty: Munchkin in *Wizard of Oz*." *Los Angeles Times*. December 31, 1999.

CLAYTON MOORE (1914–1999)

Six-foot-one, 185-pound Clayton Moore was born Jack Carlton Moore in Chicago, Illinois. His grade school playground had ring and bars, and Moore enjoyed working out on this equipment. At the Illinois Athletic Club he won the Club Championship in a 100-yard dash swim. His skill on the trampoline and at gymnastics led him to join an acrobatic circus troupe, performing as an aerialist for the Flying Behrs. He worked the 1934 Chicago World's Fair, but a knee injury suffered on the trapeze led him to seek something else.

In Hollywood he worked as a bit player under the name Jack Carlton. His earliest appearances were as a cowboy riding extra on *Forlorn River* (1937) and *Thunder Trail* (1937). He was schooled for stunts by Tom Steele and Dave Sharpe at Republic Studios. After serving with the Army Air Force during World War II, he fought throughout serials and B-westerns. In 1949 Moore was cast as the Lone Ranger on TV and achieved stardom rearing his horse Silver, an action that garnered him an extra stunt pay adjustment. At one point in the early 1950s Moore was replaced as the Lone Ranger, with John Hart taking over the role. Unconfirmed legend has it that he worked the famous saloon brawl in *Shane* (1953) as a stuntman under the name Rex Moore. A member of the Stuntmen's Hall of Fame and a Golden Boot honoree, Moore died of a heart attack at the age of 85.

See: Moore, Clayton, & Frank Thompson. *I Was That Masked Man*. Dallas, TX: Taylor, 1998.

BOB MORGAN (1916–1999)

One of the most in-demand stunt performers of the 1950s was six-foot-four, 210-pound Bob Morgan. He moved exceptionally well for a big man and practically every leading man in town clamored to have Morgan contracted to make them look good. On *Apache* (1954) he dove beneath the wheels of a moving wagon for Burt Lancaster. On *The Alamo* (1960) he doubled John Wayne and played the soldier who spears "The Duke" during the battle. On *North to Alaska* (1960) Morgan leaped off a wagon going down a steep hill and landed in mud. A top fight man, he had classic fisticuffs doubling Jeff Chandler on *The Spoilers* (1955) and Charlton Heston on *The Big Country* (1958).

The husband of actress Yvonne De Carlo, Morgan is best remembered for the stunt assignment that almost killed him. He was doubling George Peppard hanging from logs piled onto a flatcar for the climactic gunfight on *How the West Was Won* (1962). Between takes the hydraulics were reset and Morgan was accidentally knocked from a prop log and run over on the rails. His body was mangled and he ended up losing a leg and an eye to the mishap. The injuries would certainly have killed a lesser man. After a long recovery, Morgan returned to motion pictures to play small character roles on *Alvarez Kelly* (1966), *Chisum* (1970), *Skin Game* (1971), *The Culpepper Cattle Co.* (1972), and *Swashbuckler* (1976). He even distinguished himself as a golfing champion despite his handicap.

Robert Drew Morgan was born in Mt. Carmel, Illinois, and attended Menlo Junior College and the University of Wyoming on basketball and swimming scholarships. He was a professional swimmer with Billy Rose's Aquacade. During World War II he served with the Naval Air Transport Command as a naval aviator. Upon his discharge he trained with Allen Pomeroy and doubled Errol Flynn, Bruce Bennett, Sonny Tufts, and Robert Ryan. Morgan doubled Rod Cameron on *Panhandle* (1948), *Belle Starr's Daughter* (1948), *Brimstone* (1949), *Dakota Lil* (1950), and *San Antone* (1953), Joel McCrea on *South of St. Louis* (1949), *Saddle Tramp* (1950), *The San Francisco Story* (1952), *Border River* (1954), *Black Horse Canyon* (1954), and *The First Texan* (1956), Forrest Tucker on *The Nevadan* (1950), Randolph Scott on *Cariboo Trail* (1950), *Santa Fe* (1951),

Bob Morgan doubles George Peppard on *How the West Was Won* **(1962). Morgan was seriously injured** *after* **doing his stunt.**

Man in the Saddle (1951), and *Shootout at Medicine Bend* (1957), Wayne Morris on *The Big Gusher* (1951), Lee Marvin on *Hangman's Knot* (1952), Scott Brady on *Untamed Frontier* (1952), Sterling Hayden on *Flaming Feather* (1952), *The Golden Hawk* (1952), *Denver and Rio Grande* (1952), *Shotgun* (1955), and *The Killing* (1956), Stewart Granger on *All the Brothers Were Valiant* (1953), Jack Palance on *Second Chance* (1953), Jack Lambert on *99 River Street* (1953), Phil Carey on *Gun Fury* (1953), Bob Wilke on *The Lone Ranger* (1956), Fred MacMurray on *Good Day for a Hanging* (1959), and Willard Parker on *Walk Tall* (1960). On TV, Morgan doubled John Russell on *Soldiers of Fortune* (1955–56), Rod Cameron on *State Trooper* (1956–59), and James Arness on *Gunsmoke*. He was there for Jock Mahoney on *Yancy Derringer,* but Jocko ended up doing everything once the cameras rolled.

He also worked on *Dark Passage* (1947), *Pirates of Monterey* (1947), *Tripoli* (1950), *The Thing from Another World* (1951), *Ten Tall Men* (1951), *Sealed Cargo* (1951), *Don Daredevil Rides Again* (1951), *The Quiet Man* (1952), *Carson City* (1952), *Cripple Creek* (1952), *Blackbeard the Pirate* (1952), *The War of the Worlds* (1953), *Vera Cruz* (1954), *The Conqueror* (1956), *Tension at Table Rock* (1956), *Star in the Dust* (1956), *The Boss* (1956), *The Ten Commandments* (1956), *The Wings of Eagles* (1957), *Designing Woman* (1957), *Slim Carter* (1957), *The Hanging Tree* (1959), *Timbuktu* (1959), *Spartacus* (1960), *The Comancheros* (1961), and *The Man Who Shot Liberty Valance* (1962). He was an honorary member of the Stuntmen's Association and an inductee of the Stuntmen's Hall of Fame.

See: "Bob Morgan Likes Dangerous Career." *San Diego Union.* September 19, 1948; Carroll, Harrison. "Gets Chance to See a Dangerous Stunt." *Boston Daily Record.* June 4, 1958; Lilley, Tim. *Campfire Conversations.* Akron, OH: Big Trail, 2007; Thomas, Bob. "Stunt Man Is Recovering from Near Death Accident." *Ocala Star-Banner.* October 26, 1962.

BOYD "RED" MORGAN (1915–1988)

Born in Oklahoma, Boyd Franklin Morgan won a football scholarship to USC and was recruited to play football players on *Touchdown* (1935) and *Rose Bowl* (1936). Drafted by the Washington Redskins in 1939, he played two seasons as a fullback and appeared in the 1940 NFL Championship Game. He later ran in the Pacific Coast League for the Hollywood Bears and the Birmingham Generals. At the outset of World War II Morgan joined the Navy and graduated from the Naval Academy. He was sent to St. Mary's Pre-Flight Training Center and became a military officer in the Navy's V-5 training and aviation prep program. After the war he coached football and baseball at Polytechnic High in Long Beach and taught Phys Ed before giving the movies another shot.

Six-foot-one, 200-pound Morgan was an expert horseman who made over 1,000 horse falls for the cameras on films such as *The Conqueror* (1956), *The Alamo* (1960), and *The Comancheros* (1961). His horse's name was Hot Rod, and they were one of the best pairs in the business. Morgan doubled John Wayne, James Arness, Randolph Scott, Brian Keith, Leo Gordon, Jim Davis, Scott Brady, Peter Graves, Jack Lambert, Willard Parker, Chill Wills, Robert Horton, and Gene Evans. He was a capable actor and essayed heavies opposite Charles Starrett, Bill Elliott, Allan Lane, Gene Autry, and Rex Allen. A top screen brawler, he can be spotted throwing or taking punches on the John Wayne films *North to Alaska* (1960), *Donovan's Reef* (1963), *McLintock!* (1963), and *The War Wagon* (1967). He had a memorable fight with Michael Pate on *The Revolt of Mamie Stover* (1955). Brother Stacy Morgan followed him into stunts.

He also worked on *The Flame and the Arrow* (1950), *Texas Rangers* (1951), *Cripple Creek* (1952), *The Great Sioux Uprising* (1953), *Law and Order* (1953), *Column South* (1953), *Thunder Over the Plains* (1953), *Gun Belt* (1953), *Riding Shotgun* (1954), *Lone Gun* (1954), *Sign of the Pagan* (1954), *The Last Command* (1955), *The Rawhide Years* (1955), *Ten Wanted Men* (1955), *Westward Ho, the Wagons!* (1956), *The Ten Commandments* (1956), *Around the World in Eighty Days* (1956), *The Broken Star* (1956), *Designing Woman* (1957), *Black Patch* (1957), *Gun Duel in Durango* (1957), *The Defiant Ones* (1958), *The Left Handed Gun* (1958), *Ride Lonesome* (1959), *The Jayhawkers!* (1959), *Spartacus* (1960), *Two Rode Together* (1961), *Sergeants Three* (1962), *How the West Was Won* (1962), *A Distant Trumpet* (1964), *The Quick Gun* (1964), *Apache Rifles* (1964), *The Sons of Katie Elder* (1965), *The Great Race* (1965), *Cat Ballou* (1965), *The Rounders* (1965), *Arizona Raiders* (1965), *Nevada Smith* (1966), *Our Man Flint* (1966), *Waco* (1966), *Duel at Diablo* (1966), *Camelot* (1967), *5 Card Stud* (1968), *True Grit* (1969), *Support Your Local Sheriff* (1969), *The Stalking Moon* (1969), *The Cheyenne Social Club* (1970), *Rio Lobo* (1970), *Kelly's Heroes* (1970), *Wild Rovers* (1971), *Dirty Harry* (1971), *Magnum Force* (1973), *Dillinger* (1973), and *Blazing Saddles* (1974). He was on all the TV westerns, among them *Roy Rogers, Maverick, Zane Grey, The Texan, Wagon Train, The Westerner, The Virginian, Bonanza, Gunsmoke, Cimarron Strip,* and *Kung Fu.* At one point he modeled for the Mr. Clean commercials. A member of the Stuntmen's Association and an inductee of the Stuntmen's Hall of Fame, Morgan died of heart failure at the age of 72.

See: "Boyd F. Morgan, Stuntman, 72." *New York Times.* January 20, 1988; Lilley, Tim. *Campfire Conversations.* Akron, OH: Big Trail, 2007; Silden, Isobel. "Stuntmen are Daring Heroes, Unsung and Unknown." *Milwaukee Journal.* September 11, 1973.

CHICK MORRISON (1878–1924)

Chick Morrison was known as one of the best horsemen and trainers in early Hollywood. Born Charles Pacific Morrison in Morrison, Colorado, he got his start as a rodeo cowboy. He was recruited for stunt work on *Best Man Wins* (1909) by the Selig film company when they came to Colorado to make Broncho Billy Anderson films. Morrison relocated to Hollywood and doubled Broncho Billy for several years. He doubled other actors and began starring in his own films such as *Black Beauty* (1921) and *White Eagle* (1922). Morrison was killed on a Hal Roach movie at the age of 46 when his horse Young Steamboat fell backward on top of him before the cameras. His younger brother Pete Morrison became a popular actor in the silent era.

STEVIE MYERS (1929–1991)

Born in Amarillo, Texas, and raised in California, Stevie Lee Myers' career dates back to the 1930s as a stuntwoman, wrangler, and horse trainer. Her father Roy Myers provided horses for the movies and young Stevie doubled for Shirley Temple. As an adult the former president of the Stuntwomen's Association was a double for Barbara Stanwyck. As a horse trainer, she was the owner of James Stewart's long-time screen mount Pie, trainer of John Wayne's horse Dollor for *True Grit* (1969), and riding teacher for Dustin Hoffman on *Little Big Man* (1970). She worked on *The Women* (1939), *Winchester '73* (1950), *Westward the Women* (1951), *The Far Country* (1955), *Around the World in Eighty Days* (1956), *Molly and Lawless John* (1972), *Earthquake* (1974), *The Ultimate Warrior* (1975), *Nickelodeon* (1976), *The Villain* (1979), and *The Black Hole* (1979).

See: Seaman, Debbie. "'It's Not Just Any Bull in a China Shop: It's Merrill, Trained by Joan Edwards and Stevie Myers." *People.* January 11, 1982.

DON NAGEL (1926–1996)

Donald Francis Nagel was born in Hollywood and began working as an extra while still a child. As an adult, post–World War II service, he moved into stunt work. Nagel starred in a western short for the infamous Ed Wood, Jr. titled *Streets of Laredo* (1949) and subsequently was called in to help Wood as an actor and assistant director on a number of his low-budget productions. On *Bride of the Monster* (1955) Nagel doubled Paul Marco rolling down a hill. He also worked on *She Wore a Yellow Ribbon* (1949), *Sands of Iwo Jima* (1949), *Tumbleweed* (1953), *Saskatchewan* (1954), *Rails into Laramie* (1954), *Dawn at Socorro* (1954), and *Airport* (1970). TV credits include *M Squad, Columbo, Barnaby Jones,* and *The Rockford Files.* As a sideline Nagel was a knife-maker to the stars with Cooper Knives. In later years he was co-chairman of the Screen Actors Guild Stunt and Safety Committee.

See: Parla, Paul & Donna. "Wood Worker." *Filmfax.* #63–64 October-November 1998.

ERWIN NEAL (1930–1986)

Erwin Neal is best known as the double for William Holden on *Alvarez Kelly* (1966) and the western action classic *The Wild Bunch* (1969). The Arizona-born bronc rider was a member of the Pierce Junior College rodeo team and captured the National All-Around Cowboy Championship at the Cow Palace in 1959. He doubled Jack Lord for rodeo scenes on the TV series *Stoney Burke* (1962–63). He worked on *The Rains of Ranchipur* (1955), *The Long Gray Line* (1955), *The Last Wagon* (1956), *The True Story of Jesse James* (1957), *3:10 to Yuma* (1957), *Born Reckless* (1958), *From Hell to Texas* (1958), *The Badlanders* (1958), *Last Train from Gun Hill* (1959), *Lonely Are the Brave* (1962), *A Distant Trumpet* (1964), *A Covenant with Death* (1967), *Kona Coast* (1968), and *Showdown* (1973). TV credits include *Tales of Wells Fargo, Lost in Space,* and *Cimarron Strip.*

HAL NEEDHAM (1931–2013)

Perhaps the highest profile stuntman of all time, Hal Needham was a man possessed of nerves of steel and guts to spare. He attempted and pulled off some of the most amazing stunts the screen has seen. He became the highest paid stuntman in the industry in the 1960s and invented or perfected many industry standards such as the airbag for high falls and the cannon-ram for car rolls. Needham claimed to have broken fifty-six bones, including his back twice. He fell from a balcony onto a table for Charles Bronson on *4 For Texas* (1963), lit himself on fire for *The War Lord* (1965), leapt onto an overturning wagon on *The Rare Breed* (1966), was blown off a bridge on *Bridge at Remagen* (1969), jumped horse to horse on a six-up team on *Little Big Man* (1970), crashed a motorcycle into an exploding car on *C.C. and Company* (1970), and leaped from a second story window for George Peppard on *One More Train to Rob* (1971).

The stunts he performed or worked out for his buddy Burt Reynolds' action films made him famous. He jumped a car onto a barge for *White Lightning* (1973), drove a Citroen Maserati in reverse off a rising drawbridge on *The Longest Yard* (1974), jumped a speedboat a record 138 feet on *Gator* (1976) and leaped off a flying truck on that same film. His long association with Reynolds allowed him the opportunity to direct *Smokey and the Bandit* (1977), and its success led Needham to abandon his stunt career for full-time status as a director of such action-heavy Reynolds comedies as *Hooper* (1978) and *Cannonball Run* (1981).

Hal Needham throws a punch during the famous mud pit brawl on *McLintock!* (1963).

Six foot, 180-pound Hal Brett Needham was born in Memphis, Tennessee. After employment as a tree-topper, he joined the Army and served as a paratrooper with the 82nd Airborne. After his discharge he worked as a logger and cleaned swimming pools in California. By chance he met stuntman Cliff Rose and found work as a wing-walker on *The Spirit of St. Louis* (1957). On the TV show *You Asked for It* he bulldogged Rose off a horse from the wing of an airplane. Needham supported himself as a model for Viceroy Cigarettes until he gained steadier employment. He was an extra on the TV series *Have Gun—Will Travel* when his experience as a tree-climber was needed. Star Richard Boone, impressed, took Needham under his wing and made him his double and the show's stunt coordinator. Needham performed a tremendous high fall from a tree in the episode "Tax Gatherer." Another Needham mentor was stunt veteran Chuck Roberson, who used him on the John Wayne films *Donovan's Reef* (1963) and *McLintock!* (1963). Director Andrew McLaglen had Needham coordinate all of his films begin-

ning with *Little Shepherd of Kingdom Come* (1961).

In addition to Reynolds and Boone, Needham doubled Dean Martin, Clint Walker, Peter Breck, Peter Brown, Henry Silva, James Farentino, Gary Lockwood, and Christopher George. In 1970 he broke away from the Stuntmen's Association and formed Stunts Unlimited with fellow stuntmen Ronnie Rondell and Glenn Wilder. Eventually he moved into second unit directing. Needham worked on more than 300 feature films and appeared in 4500 TV episodes.

He worked on *The Big Country* (1958), *Timbuktu* (1959), *Thunder in the Sun* (1959), *Pork Chop Hill* (1959), *Thunder of Drums* (1961), *The Man Who Shot Liberty Valance* (1962), *How the West Was Won* (1962), *Captain Newman, M.D.* (1963), *Advance to the Rear* (1964), *Mail Order Bride* (1964), *Major Dundee* (1965), *Shenandoah* (1965), *In Harm's Way* (1965), *The Great Race* (1965), *Our Man Flint* (1966), *Stagecoach* (1966), *Beau Geste* (1966), *Alvarez Kelly* (1966), *The War Wagon* (1967), *The Way West* (1967), *Tobruk*

(1967), *Camelot* (1967), *The Devil's Brigade* (1968), *Bandolero!* (1968), *Chubasco* (1968), *Hellfighters* (1968), *100 Rifles* (1969), *Che!* (1969), *The Undefeated* (1969), *The Great Bank Robbery* (1969), *Chisum* (1970), *Sometimes a Great Notion* (1970), *Something Big* (1971), *Culpepper Cattle Co.* (1972), *Life and Times of Judge Roy Bean* (1972), *The Man Who Loved Cat Dancing* (1973), *McQ* (1974), *Blazing Saddles* (1974), *Chinatown* (1974), *Take a Hard Ride* (1975), *The French Connection II* (1975), *Lucky Lady* (1975), *Nickelodeon* (1976), and *Stunts Unlimited* (1980). TV credits include *Riverboat, Black Saddle, Rawhide, Laramie, Wagon Train, Gunsmoke, The Virginian, The Wild Wild West, Laredo, Star Trek, Custer,* and *Baretta*. Needham is a member of the Stuntmen's Hall of Fame, a Golden Boot winner, and a Lifetime Achievement honoree from the Taurus World Stunt Awards. In 2012 he became the second stuntman in history to receive an Honorary Oscar. Needham died from cancer at the age of 82.

See: Lilley, Tim. *Campfire Conversations.* Akron, OH: Big Trail, 2007; Needham, Hal. *Stuntman! My Car-Crashing, Plane-Jumping, Bone-Breaking, Death-Defying Hollywood Life.* Little, Brown, 2011; Ross, John. "Hal Needham." *Inside Stunts.* Fall, 2004; Scott, Vernon. "Burt's Boost in Right Direction." *San Diego Union.* December 24, 1981; Shivey, Rick. "Stunts? Any Old Wing Walker Can Do Them." *Fighting Stars.* February 1974; Thomas, Bob. "Toughest Stunt Was First Break." *San Diego Union.* October 9, 1977.

ED NELSON (1928–)

Respected character actor Ed Nelson got his start doing all kinds of behind-the-scenes stunt work on low-budget Roger Corman films. He wrestled an alligator on *Swamp Women* (1956), swam across San Pedro Harbor on *She Gods of Shark Reef* (1958), and was besieged by dogs on *Teenage Cave Man* (1958). On *Attack of the Crab Monsters* (1957) Nelson scuba dived for Richard Garland and Pamela Duncan in addition to donning a crab outfit to play the title creature. Outside of his films with Corman, Nelson doubled Kevin McCarthy sitting atop a window sill eleven stories above the ground on *Nightmare* (1956).

Six-foot Edwin Stafford Nelson was born in New Orleans and raised in North Carolina. He attended Edwards Military Institute and played football and basketball for Camp Lejeune High before a tour with the U.S. Navy. Once he became established as an actor, Nelson still enjoyed doing the majority of his own fight scenes. He took part in one of the best opposite Steve McQueen and Jackie Gleason on *Soldier in the Rain* (1963). A long-running role on TV's *Peyton Place* led to more sedate roles.

See: Nelson, Ed, & Alvin M. Cotlar. *Beyond Peyton Place.* Tarentum, PN: Word Association, 2008; Weaver, Tom. *Attack of the Monster Movie Makers.* Jefferson, NC: McFarland, 1994.

HERBIE NELSON (1927–1983)

London-born Herbie Nelson Purches followed family tradition and worked as a clown with Chipperfield's Circus. In the British Special Service he was a physical instructor and held the rank of sergeant in the SAS, mastering the self-defense art of judo. After being wounded in Korea, he was recruited by Jock Easton for stunt work. Nelson made over 300 films, doubling Errol Flynn, David Niven, and Gregory Peck on titles such as *The Guns of Navarone* (1961) and *55 Days at Peking* (1963). On the early days of the TV series *The Avengers* he taught Honor Blackman judo moves. In 1963 Nelson made a permanent move to Australia and became the leading stuntman on that continent. He was profiled on the TV special *The Stuntmen* (1973) and the films *Dare Devils* (1973) and *Death Cheaters* (1976). Nelson and his stuntwoman wife Margaret Nelson ran the Herb Nelson Stunt School in Seven Hills NSW.

He worked on *Knights of the Round Table* (1953), *Red Beret* (1953), *Moby Dick* (1956), *Hell Drivers* (1957), *Zarak* (1957), *Steel Bayonet* (1957), *Fire Down Below* (1957), *Bridge on the River Kwai* (1957), *A Night to Remember* (1958), *Sheriff of Fractured Jaw* (1958), *The Key* (1958), *Devil's Disciple* (1959), *Wreck of the Mary Deare* (1959), *Corridors of Blood* (1962), *Pirates of Blood River* (1962), *The Longest Day* (1962), *Cleopatra* (1963), *The Great Escape* (1963), *Cars That Ate Paris* (1974), *Stone* (1974), and *Man from Hong Kong* (1975). TV credits include *Ivanhoe, Sir Francis Drake, The Avengers, The Saint, The Baron, Danger Man, Contrabandits, Battlers, Riptide,* and *The Spoiler*. Nelson died of a heart attack at the age of 57.

See: "Farewelling a Man of Style." *Hawkesbury Gazette.* November 17, 1983; Kusko, Julie.

"Daredevils of the Screen." *Australian Women's Weekly*. July 4, 1973.

JIM NICKERSON (1949–)

Six-foot-one, 190-pound Jim Nickerson was born in Pittsburgh, Pennsylvania. He grew up amidst California horse country, befriending stuntmen and rodeo riders who lived in the area. Nickerson made his rodeo debut at the age of fifteen and amassed a 16–1 amateur boxing record. He excelled as a defensive back on the football field at Sylmar and San Fernando Valley High schools, earning All-Valley honors. He had scholarship offers until an ulnar nerve injury ended his football career. Nickerson attempted to join the U.S. Army at the height of the Vietnam escalation but failed a physical due to his injury. He attended Pierce Junior College before gaining entry to the film world via stuntman contacts.

Nickerson was the preferred double for James Caan on *Freebie and the Bean* (1974), *The Killer Elite* (1975), and *Rollerball* (1975). His car jump between two moving freights on *Freebie* was especially noteworthy. As he grew in size he doubled Gene Hackman on *Bite the Bullet* (1975) and Nick Nolte on *The Deep* (1977). On TV he doubled Ben Murphy on *Alias Smith and Jones* (1971–73), James Coleman on *S.W.A.T.* (1975–76), and Lee Horsley on *Matt Houston* (1982–85). One of his best stunts came on the 1980s TV series *Mike Hammer* doubling Stacy Keach being dragged over a cliff by a thirty-foot ladder hanging from a helicopter.

Nickerson is known as a fight choreographer for boxing films going back to his work on the original *Rocky* (1976). Having studied all the old fight films, Nickerson understood that much of the success of the action stemmed from the speed of the camera and the positioning of the combatants. He reasoned that no contact needed to be made at all, but that the action could look good with proper preparation. He emphasized dramatic moments in the action, setting about with actors Sylvester Stallone and Carl Weathers to make the bout one of the screen's most memorable. He topped himself with *Rocky 2* (1979), although that film didn't have the same emotional pull the original did. Finally, he reached perfection with the ring action on *Raging Bull* (1980).

He also worked on *Topaz* (1969), *MASH* (1970), *Kansas City Bomber* (1972), *Hammer* (1972), *Slither* (1973), *99 and 44/100 percent Dead* (1974), *Earthquake* (1974), *The Gambler* (1974), *Hard Times* (1975), *The Hindenburg* (1975), *Harry and Walter Go to New York* (1976), *The Outlaw Josey Wales* (1976), *MacArthur* (1977), *The White Buffalo* (1977), *Another Man, Another Woman* (1977), *Movie, Movie* (1978), *Paradise Alley* (1978), *The Main Event* (1979), and *The Long Riders* (1980). TV credits include *Lancer, Shaft, Charlie's Angels, Fantasy Island,* and *Hart to Hart.* A member of Stunts Unlimited, he was inducted into the Stuntmen's Hall of Fame.

See: Bess, Lisa Twyman. "In the Rocky Realm of Filmic Fisticuffs." *Sports Illustrated*. November 18, 1991; Corcoran, John. "Jimmy Nickerson: Hollywood's Fight Film Genius." *Martial Arts Movies*. May 1982; Honeycutt, Kurt. "Stuntmen Are More Than Falling Off a Horse." *Evening Independent*. May 12, 1986; Mahany, Barbara. "Fall Guy." *Chicago Tribune*. March 19, 1991.

RON NIX (1943–)

Arizona-born Ron Nix played baseball and football and wrestled at St. Mary's and Carl Hayden High. He worked construction jobs but longed to be a western stuntman. In 1966 Nix began doing live stunt shows at Apacheland outside of Phoenix. Stunt work came on locally filmed TV episodes of *Death Valley Days, Dundee and the Culhane, Bonanza,* and *High Chaparral.* On film Nix worked on *A Time for Dying* (1969), *Charro* (1969), *The Great White Hope* (1970), *Dirty Dingus Magee* (1970), *Wild Rovers* (1971), *Man and Boy* (1972), *The Trial of Billy Jack* (1974), and *White Line Fever* (1975), where he had a significant part as a crooked deputy harassing trucker Jan-Michael Vincent. On the western *Guns of a Stranger* (1973) he doubled singer Marty Robbins.

Nix supplemented his film work with live stunt shows at Legend City and landed in the Guinness Book of World Records for a ninety-foot fall into flaming cardboard boxes. In the mid–1970s he built his own western town outside of Phoenix and held annual events known as "A Day in the West" with Jock Mahoney judging stunt competitions. He trained prospective stunt people at what became known as Cowtown and hosted crews for films, TV, and commercial production. Nix received the Rex Allen Western Legends Award and has been inducted into the Apacheland Stuntman Hall of Fame.

See: Conley, Jr., John. *The Heart of a Cowboy.* CreateSpace, 2010; Heider, Harvey. *Ron Nix's Cowtown.* Phoenix, AZ: Day in the West, 1987; "Nix Brings Stunt Show for Area Performances." *Prescott-Courier.* October 18, 1973; www.apachelanddays.com.

FRANK NOEL (1941–)

Franklin LeRoy Noel, Jr. was born in Wichita, Kansas. Noel became a cowboy stunt performer at Kansas' Frontier Village in 1961 before moving on to Old Tucson Studios in 1964. The 5'11", 190-pound Noel got his first movie break on the Audie Murphy western *Arizona Raiders* (1965). He also worked on *Devil's Angels* (1967), *The Great White Hope* (1970), *C.C. and Company* (1970), *Man and Boy* (1972), *The Bravos* (1972), *Dirty Little Billy* (1972), *Duchess and the Dirtwater Fox* (1976), and the TV mini-series *Centennial* (1978) and *The Chisholms* (1979). His other TV credits include *Wagon Train* and *The New Dick Van Dyke Show,* filmed in Carefree, Arizona. A former firefighter, Noel is a member of the Old Western Cowboys Association and has worked as a period advisor.

See: "Old Tucson Gunfighters Reunion." *Arizona Daily Star.* March 9, 2013.

LEO NOMIS (1889–1932)

Iowa-born Leo C. Nomis (aka Noomis) had a circus acrobat background prior to entering motion picture stunt work for D.W. Griffith on *Birth of a Nation* (1915). Nomis performed high falls into a net on *Intolerance* (1916) and Cecil B. De-Mille's *Joan the Woman* (1916). He doubled Milton Sills being thrown off a train on *Honor System* (1925), and filled in for Jack Mower speeding a motorcycle into a car on *Manslaughter* (1922), a stunt on which Nomis was badly broken up.

A veteran of the air service in World War I, he began to concentrate on aerial stunt work, flying for *Wings* (1927), *Lilac Time* (1928), *Hell's Angels* (1930), *Dawn Patrol* (1930), and *Lost Squadron* (1932). He injured his back doing car work on *The Crowd Roars* (1932). An inductee of the Stuntmen's Hall of Fame, Nomis died at the age of 42 in a plane crash while performing a thousand-foot spin for *Sky Bride* (1932).

See: "Aerial Daredevil Plunges to Death." *Springfield Republic.* February 6, 1932; Brownlow,

Kevin. *The Parade's Gone By.* Berkeley, Ca: Univ. of California, 1968; "Saved By Movie Training." *Moving Picture News.* September 4, 1918; "Stunt Flyer Killed." *Variety.* February 9, 1932.

PAUL NUCKLES (1939–)

Paul Nuckles' stunt specialty was wrecking motorcycles and autos. He worked on TV's *The Rat Patrol* (1966–68) and attracted attention flying through catty-corner windows on *The Grissom Gang* (1971). He was best known for his cannon rolls on *Race with the Devil* (1975) and staging the weekly vehicular crashes on the TV series *CHiPs* (1977–83). Nuckles worked often with director Jack Starrett and action actor William Smith on low-budget films such as *The Losers* (1970) and *Hollywood Man* (1976). Nuckles doubled Pat Renella on *Bullitt* (1968), Joe Namath on *C.C. and Company* (1970), Bruce Glover on *Black Gunn* (1972), and John Travolta on *Saturday Night Fever* (1977).

Six-foot-one, 180-pound William Paul Nuckles was born in Johnson City, Tennessee. After military service he set out to be an actor. His first stunt was performed on *Sniper's Ridge* (1961) when the film's lone stuntman went down with an injury. Nuckles parked cars on the Sunset Strip and ironically began doubling Edd "Kookie" Byrnes on the TV series *77 Sunset Strip*. Nuckles became a member of Stunts Unlimited as he graduated to coordinating and second unit direction. On an episode of *The Dating Game* he engaged in a staged fight with fellow stuntmen Lance Rimmer and Buddy Joe Hooker while courting Farrah Fawcett.

He worked on *Chubasco* (1968), *The Undefeated* (1969), *There Was a Crooked Man...* (1970), *Cleopatra Jones* (1973), *Earthquake* (1974), *The Front Page* (1974), *The Dion Brothers* (1974), *The Taking of Pelham One Two Three* (1974), *Mitchell* (1975), *A Small Town in Texas* (1976), *Futureworld* (1976), *Scorchy* (1976), *Final Chapter—Walking Tall* (1977), *Stunts* (1977), *Speedtrap* (1977), and *Texas Detour* (1978). TV credits include *Gunsmoke, Mission: Impossible, The FBI,* and *Emergency.* In the 1980s he was the stunt coordinator for the popular TV series *Miami Vice.* Nuckles is a member of the Stuntmen's Hall of Fame.

See: Cauthen, Linda. "Behind the Scenes of *CHiPs.*" *Action Films.* March 1983; "Stunt Driver's

Career an Accident." *Spokesman Review.* June 1, 1978.

DAVE O'BRIEN (1912–1969)

B-western actor Dave O'Brien was born David Poole Fronabarger in Big Springs, Texas.

He broke into films dancing in studio choruses. As a stuntman he doubled Don Terry, Warren Hull, and Donald Woods on the serials *Secret of Treasure Island* (1938), *Spider's Web* (1938), and *Sky Raiders* (1941). As O'Brien progressed up the credit ladder he found leading roles in the serial *Captain Midnight* (1942) and the Texas Rangers

Paul Nuckles coordinates a skiing car-to-helicopter transfer by Gary Davis on *Stunts* (1977).

series at PRC. He appeared as Buster Crabbe's sidekick on four Billy the Kid films. O'Brien was popular due to his fighting ability and the riding he performed on his horse King.

Beginning in the 1940s O'Brien made several Pete Smith shorts for MGM which featured humorous pratfalls, culminating with a highlight reel entitled *Fall Guy* (1955). He became a stuntman and Emmy-winning writer (under the name Dave Barclay) for the popular TV series *The Red Skelton Show*. O'Brien died of a heart attack at the age of 57 immediately following a Marina Del Rey to Catalina Island boat race he won. He was posthumously inducted into the Stuntmen's Hall of Fame.

See: "Dave O'Brien: Actor, Writer, and Director." *Los Angeles Times*. November 10, 1969.

GEORGE O'BRIEN (1899–1985)

George Joseph O'Brien was born in San Francisco, California. At Polytechnic High he participated in football, baseball, basketball, track, boxing, and swimming. He became a standout athlete at Santa Clara College. While in the Navy in World War I, O'Brien was crowned the Pacific Fleet's Light-Heavyweight Boxing Champ. He later transferred to the U.S. Marines and won five decorations for bravery under fire as a stretcher-bearer. The muscular six-foot, 198-pound O'Brien went to work in Hollywood as a lifeguard and entered motion pictures as an assistant cameraman and stuntman.

One of O'Brien's first stunts was to portray a shark, requiring him to swim in the ocean while holding up a dorsal fin. Another early film, *Moran of the Lady Letty* (1922), had Rudolph Valentino knocking him off the rigging of a ship over seventy feet into the sea. O'Brien worked on several Tom Mix westerns and doubled Buck Jones before being tapped by John Ford as a new star. Part of his audition for Ford's *Iron Horse* (1924) involved performing a fight scene with Fred Kohler. A year later Ford goaded O'Brien and Victor McLaglen into fighting for real before the cameras on *Fighting Heart* (1925).

O'Brien was a popular cowboy action star from the silent days into the talkies and often performed his own stunts when the studio would allow it. He was especially adept at hard riding, transfers, and bulldogs, actions showcased on films such as *Last of the Duanes* (1930) and *Riders of the Purple Sage* (1931). Most of his films had fistfights where his athleticism pleased the fans. On *Stage to Chino* (1940) he took on a half-dozen real ex-boxers for the cameras. When World War II broke out he re-enlisted in the Navy and became highly decorated. O'Brien died from a stroke at the age of 86.

See: Menefee, David W. *George O'Brien: A Man's Man in Hollywood*. Albany, GA: Bear Manor, 2009.

MAUREEN O'HARA (1920–)

Feisty 5'8" Maureen O'Hara was popular with stunt crews who referred to her as their "little Irish stunt girl." Although she was a star, she was game for action and enjoyed doing a great deal of her own stunt work. On *The Hunchback of Notre Dame* (1939) she worked closely with stuntmen Sailor Vincent and Dick Crockett, who swung and balanced her in the air. On *The Quiet Man* (1952) John Wayne dragged her across a field. On *The Parent Trap* (1961) she punched Brian Keith. O'Hara was the first to go down the mud slide on *McLintock!* (1963), shaming the reluctant stuntmen who were trying to get stunt adjustments. On that film she also jumped into a hay wagon and fell off a ladder into a water trough.

Born Maureen FitzSimons in Dublin, Ireland, O'Hara was capable of fencing, horseback riding, judo, and cracking a bullwhip. She starred in several swashbuckling adventure films, including *The Black Swan* (1942), *The Spanish Main* (1945), *Sinbad the Sailor* (1947), *Against All Flags* (1952), and *At Sword's Point* (1952). She did as much action as was allowable by the insurance companies, although Lucille House did the majority of her horseback riding.

See: Lilley, Tim. *Campfire Conversations*. Akron, OH: Big Trail, 2007; Magers, Boyd, & Michael G. Fitzgerald. *Westerns Women*. Jefferson, NC: McFarland, 2004; O'Hara, Maureen, & John Nicoletti. *'Tis Herself: An Autobiography*. New York: Simon & Schuster, 2005.

ARVO OJALA (1920–2005)

Fast-draw expert Arvo Ojala is best known as the gunman shot by James Arness during the opening credits of the early seasons of TV's *Gunsmoke* (1955–64). In reality, Ojala taught Arness his quick draw and even designed the patented holster he was drawing from. Ojala's rig incorporated a small piece of metal between the leather to facilitate a smooth pulling action of the Single Action Colt. Legend has it that Ojala could draw in a sixth of a second and repeatedly hit his target.

Raised on a Yakima Valley ranch in the state of Washington, Ojala honed his skill shooting at rattlesnakes. He moved to Los Angeles in 1950 and began working construction jobs while making the studio rounds as a prospective stuntman. Once on set, he was seen handling a gun and drawing in the blink of an eye. He was promptly recruited to coach numerous actors such as Kirk Douglas, Frank Sinatra, Paul Newman, Audie Murphy, Rory Calhoun, John Payne, Richard Boone, Hugh O'Brian, Dale Robertson, Sammy Davis, Jr., Jerry Lewis, and all the Warner Brothers TV stars from James Garner to Clint Walker. If they couldn't clear leather convincingly enough for the camera, inserts of Ojala drawing were spliced in.

He worked on *The Kid from Texas* (1950), *Gunsmoke* (1953), *River of No Return* (1954), *The Return of Jack Slade* (1955), *To Hell and Back* (1955), *The McConnell Story* (1955), *Two Gun Lady* (1955), *Johnny Concho* (1956), *Friendly Persuasion* (1956), *The Burning Hills* (1956), *Flesh and the Spur* (1957), *The Tin Star* (1957), *The Left Handed Gun* (1958), *The Big Country* (1958), *Rio Bravo* (1959), *The Oregon Trail* (1959), *The War Wagon* (1967), *Firecreek* (1968), *More Dead Than Alive* (1969), *Butch Cassidy and the Sundance Kid* (1969), *Chisum* (1970), and *Zachariah* (1971). TV credits include *Wyatt Earp, Restless Gun, Tales of Wells Fargo, Maverick, Cheyenne, Bronco, Sugarfoot, Lawman, Colt .45, Have Gun—Will Travel, Bonanza,* and *Lancer.* He made a tidy fortune selling his buscadero gun belts and training manuals and still worked sporadically up through films like *Silverado* (1985). Ojala died from natural causes at the age of 85.

See: Degnon, Dick. "*Gunsmoke* Villain Is TV's Noted Gun Tutor." *Los Angeles Times.* April 19, 1959; Irwin, Ben. "Arvo Ojala: The Man Who Teaches Hollywood to Shoot." *Guns.* July 1956; McLellan, Dennis. "Arvo Ojala, 85: Quick Draw Expert Coached Actors in TV Westerns." *Los Angeles Times.* July 20, 2005; Shearer, Lloyd. "He's the Fastest Gun in the West." *St. Petersburg Times.* September 29, 1957; www.arvoojalaholster company.biz.

DENNIS O'KEEFE (1908–1968)

Athletic 1940s leading man Dennis O'Keefe climbed his way up the Hollywood ranks from extra to stuntman to star. When he began in films as a dance extra, Edward Vance Flanagan was known as Bud Flannigan. He spent seven years doing every kind of film bit imaginable until Clark Gable took a shine to him on the set of *Saratoga* (1937). When he recommended the 6'3" Fort Madison, Iowa, native to his MGM bosses as a potential action lead, "Dennis O'Keefe" was placed under contract. As a tough guy leading man, his best fight scene came against John Ireland on the film noir *Raw Deal* (1948). O'Keefe died from cancer at the age of 60.

See: "Dennis O'Keefe, Actor Is Dead." *New York Times.* September 2, 1968.

GERRY OKUNEFF (1932–)

Five-foot-eleven, 210-pound Gerald Okuneff played linebacker and fullback at UCLA, participating in the 1954 Rose Bowl for the National Champs. He was in training camp with the Washington Redskins and played football for the Naval Training Center. Stunt work being nailed to a cross on *Spartacus* (1960) led him to keep that profession as a side vocation while taking jobs as an assistant football coach at UCLA, Washington State, and Cal State. He was a scout for the Los Angeles Rams and personnel director for the Southern California Sun of the World Football League.

On *Day of the Locust* (1975) Okuneff fell over twenty feet from a collapsing stage in a stunt that went wrong. He was knocked out while several other stuntmen suffered broken bones. He worked on seventy-five films, including *Birdman from Alcatraz* (1962), *John Goldfarb, Please Come Home* (1965), *In Cold Blood* (1967), *The Shakiest Gun in the West* (1968), *MASH* (1970), *There Was a Crooked Man...* (1970), and *Two-Minute Warning* (1976).

See: Guskey, Earl. "Suns Executioner Pares Team Down to Size." *Los Angeles Times.* July 3, 1974; Nack, William. "A Little Bit of Heaven." *Sports Illustrated.* July 15, 1991.

ALAN OLINEY (1945–)

Alan W. Oliney was a gymnast at UCLA when he was recruited to double Clarence Williams III for the duration of the TV series *Mod Squad*

(1968–73). Originally a member of the Black Stuntmen's Association, the 6'0, 170-pound Oliney joined up with Stunts Unlimited in the 1970s. He doubled karate expert Jim Kelly on *Black Belt Jones* (1974), Richard Pryor on *Which Way is Up?* (1977), and Eddie Murphy on *Beverly Hills Cop* (1984).

He also worked on *Che!* (1969), *Cotton Comes to Harlem* (1970), *Westworld* (1973), *Mandingo* (1975), *Drum* (1976), *Gray Lady Down* (1978), *Hooper* (1978), *Convoy* (1978), *Delta Fox* (1978), *The Black Hole* (1979), and *Buck Rogers in the 25th Century* (1979). TV credits include *The Immortal, The Rookies, Police Story, Gemini Man, Vega$,* and the mini-series *Roots* (1977). His brother Ron Oliney also did stunts.

RYAN O'NEAL (1941–)

TV and film star Ryan O'Neal got his start in the business as a teenage stuntman on the German-made TV series *Tales of the Vikings* (1959–60). His parents, an actor and a screenwriter, were living abroad and helped Munich American high school student O'Neal get extra work to keep him occupied. On the set O'Neal was taken under the wing of European stuntman John Sullivan and trained to take part in the action on the Jerome Courtland show doing fights, falls, and duels.

Los Angeles–born Charles Patrick Ryan O'Neal had a Golden Gloves boxing background at University High and was comfortable throwing punches for the cameras. Early TV success on *Peyton Place* (1964–69) guaranteed that the six foot, 170-pound O'Neal would never have to work in Hollywood as a stuntman. As a film star he had notable fights with Pat Roach on *Barry Lyndon* (1975) and Burt Reynolds on *Nickelodeon* (1976). He showed a gift for slapstick physical comedy on *What's Up, Doc?* (1972) and the steely nerve needed to portray the title character in the high-octane *The Driver* (1978). As proof of his athleticism, he won the Los Angeles Silver Annual Handball Tournament in 1970.

See: "Stunt Man Glad to Leave N.Y." *Sarasota Herald Tribune.* February 15, 1963; Thompson, Ruth. "Young Star Got Break in Germany." *Kittaning Simpson Leader Times.* March 30, 1963.

BOB ORAN (1916–1996)

Stocky New York–based stuntman Bob Oransky was a former boxer and barnstorming professional wrestler. Oran wrestled as the Cowboy and the Masked Marvel. The World War II veteran performed in Wild West shows as Black Bob. Among his varied careers, Oran was a Brahma bull rider and a private investigator, but became known in the film industry as a masseur to the stars. He worked as a stuntman on films from *Saratoga Trunk* (1945) to *A Lovely Way to Die* (1968) and on East Coast TV shows such as *NYPD* and *Coronet Blue.* He achieved a small degree of notoriety for appearing as an actor in Doris Wishman soft-core films of the late 1960s. Oran died at the age of 79.

See: McCarthy, Dennis. "Toughs Find Out That More Than Two Can Tango." *Daily News.* March 29, 1990.

BOB ORRISON (1930–)

Robert P. Orrison from Bakersfield, California, was a steer wrestler and bulldogger in the rodeo. The brother of stuntman George Orrison and brother-in-law of Walter Wyatt, he doubled Dean Martin on *5 Card Stud* (1968). On TV he doubled Leonard Nimoy and DeForest Kelley on *Star Trek* (1966–69), James Best on *The Dukes of Hazzard* (1979–85), and George Peppard on *The A-Team* (1983–86). His career as a cowboy stuntman went in a different direction after he performed driving stunts on *Smokey and the Bandit* (1977).

The 6'1", 170-pound Orrison also worked on *Bandolero!* (1968), *The Wild Bunch* (1969), *The Great Bank Robbery* (1969), *The Undefeated* (1969), *Chisum* (1970), *Culpepper Cattle Co.* (1972), *Molly and Lawless John* (1972), *Mitchell* (1975), *A Boy and His Dog* (1975), *Return of a Man Called Horse* (1976), *Bound for Glory* (1976), *Zero to Sixty* (1978), *Hooper* (1978), *Convoy* (1978), *Tom Horn* (1980), and *Smokey and the Bandit II* (1980). TV credits include *Mannix.* A member of Stunts Unlimited and an inductee of the Stuntmen's Hall of Fame, Orrison is the father of stuntmen Brad and Mark Orrison.

GEORGE ORRISON (1929–2001)

George Orrison began doubling Clint Eastwood in the 1970s, and the association lasted twenty years through such films as *Joe Kidd* (1972), *High Plains Drifter* (1973), and *Pale Rider*

(1985). He also doubled Lee Marvin on *Cat Ballou* (1965), Leslie Nielsen on *The Plainsman* (1966), and Richard Harris on *Camelot* (1967). The 6'1", 185-pound Orrison was born in Los Angeles and raised in Bakersfield, California. He joined the U.S. Army and built the Alcan Highway in Alaska with the Army Corps of Engineers. Orrison met stuntmen on the rodeo circuit and landed a steady TV job as the double for John Smith on *Laramie* (1960–63). He also doubled William Smith on *Laredo* (1965–67), Kevin Tighe on *Emergency* (1972–77), and Charles Napier on *Oregon Trail* (1977).

He worked on *4 for Texas* (1963), *The War Lord* (1965), *Texas Across the River* (1966), *Flap* (1970), *There Was a Crooked Man...* (1970), *Wild Country* (1971), *Bless the Beasts and Children* (1972), *Blazing Saddles* (1974), *The Gauntlet* (1977), *Every Which Way But Loose* (1978), *Bronco Billy* (1980), *Heaven's Gate* (1980), and *Any Which Way You Can* (1980). TV credits include *Tall Men, Wide Country, Gunsmoke, Bonanza, Wagon Train, The Virginian, Run for Your Life, Road West, Guns of Will Sonnett, Custer, Mannix, It Takes a Thief, Outcasts, Here Come the Brides, Name of the Game, Young Rebels,* and *Little House on the Prairie*. Orrison died from lung cancer at the age of 71.

ERNIE ORSATTI (1940–)

Ernie Orsatti gained cult status as the boyfriend of Pamela Sue Martin on the disaster epic *The Poseidon Adventure* (1972), in particular when he undertook a thirty-two–foot back fall into a glass skylight. The camera was trained on Orsatti, who audiences thought was nothing more than an actor. Ironically, Orsatti thought that he *had* been signed as an actor only for the film.

The 5'11", 175-pound Orsatti was born in Beverly Hills, the son of former pro baseball player and occasional stuntman Ernest Orsatti. His brother Frank Orsatti was a stuntman as well. A champion swimmer and male model for Foster Grant sunglasses, he acted under the humorous pseudonym Brick Wahl on the low-budget *Acid Eaters* (1968).

He also worked on *The Green Berets* (1968), *Star Spangled Girl* (1971), *The Mechanic* (1972), *Battle for the Planet of the Apes* (1973), *The Last American Hero* (1973), *The Stone Killer* (1973), *The Towering Inferno* (1974), *Death Wish* (1974),

Night Moves (1975), *Sky Riders* (1976), *The Big Bus* (1976), *Viva Knievel* (1977), *The Car* (1977), and *The Swarm* (1978). TV credits include *Columbo, Police Story, Wonder Woman,* and *The Incredible Hulk*. He is the father of stuntmen Noon Orsatti and Rowbie Orsatti and the subject of the *Poseidon Adventure* short *Falling Up with Ernie*.

See: Chernin, Donna. "Stars Came on Days Off to Watch Orsatti Fall." *Plain Dealer*. December 31, 1972.

FRANK ORSATTI (1942–2004)

Five-foot-ten, 190-pound Frank Orsatti was born in Los Angeles, the son of Buster Keaton stuntman Ernest Orsatti. Like his father, Frank played minor league baseball for the St. Louis Cardinals, but a shoulder injury ended his career. He was a merchant marine prior to taking on stunt work full time in the late 1960s. He made his name with a jump off the Golden Gate Bridge on *B.S. I Love You* (1971), a bicycle chase on the pilot for the TV series *McMillan & Wife* (1971), and the fire burn for James Hampton on *The Longest Yard* (1974). The muscular Orsatti doubled Burt Reynolds for several years, as well as Sylvester Stallone on *First Blood* (1982) and Arnold Schwarzenegger on *The Terminator* (1984). On TV Orsatti doubled Bill Bixby on *The Magician* (1973–74) and *The Incredible Hulk* (1977–81), James Naughton on *Planet of the Apes* (1974), and David Birney on *Serpico* (1976).

He worked on *Planet of the Apes* (1968), *Bullitt* (1968), *Rosemary's Baby* (1968), *Paint Your Wagon* (1969), *Che!* (1969), *The Arrangement* (1969), *Star Spangled Girl* (1971), *The Jesus Trip* (1971), *The Poseidon Adventure* (1972), *Fuzz* (1972), *The Mechanic* (1972), *The Stone Killer* (1973), *The Towering Inferno* (1974), *Freebie and the Bean* (1974), *Black Samson* (1974), *Midnight Man* (1974), *Rancho Deluxe* (1975), *Street People* (1975), *Cleopatra Jones and the Casino of Gold* (1975), *Marathon Man* (1976), *Moonshine County Express* (1977), and *Blue Collar* (1978). His TV credits include *Daniel Boone, Mission: Impossible, The Immortal, The FBI, Mod Squad, Dan August, Cannon, The Streets of San Francisco, Barnaby Jones, Man Hunter, Barbary Coast,* and *Starsky and Hutch*. A member of Stunts Unlimited, Orsatti died from lung disease at the age of 62.

See: Fox, Charles. "Falls, Fractures, & Fortunes." *True.* January 1971; "Frank Orsatti." *Variety.* January 7, 2005; "Frank Orsatti, Star Stuntman Sherman Oaks Resident Worked in Films and Television." *Daily News.* January 9, 2005.

ARTIE ORTEGO (1890–1960)

Arthur Andrew Ortego was born in San Jose, California, and grew up on the family ranch. His mother was a member of the Digger Indian tribe while his father was Mexican and Irish. Ortego's earliest jobs came breaking horses, and he was considered an equine specialist upon journeying to Hollywood in the early days of motion pictures. He doubled Ramon Novarro on *The Barbarian* (1933) and worked on *Captain Blood* (1935) and *Stagecoach* (1939) in addition to many bit parts as Indians and western henchmen. He drove mini-stagecoaches in the early days of Disneyland until a wild team tipped one over, badly injuring him.

See: Cary, Diana Serra. *The Hollywood Posse.* Boston: Houghton Mifflin, 1975.

BUD OSBORNE (1884–1964)

Prolific B-western performer Lennie B. Osborne was one of the top drivers of four-up and six-up horse teams in the business. When he wasn't playing a henchman, he was behind the reins of wagons and stagecoaches on dozens of horse operas. Raised on a ranch in Indian Territory in Oklahoma, Osborne joined the Miller Brothers 101 Wild West Show and came to Hollywood in 1912 to make the first of over 600 films. A highlight was a knife fight with Tim McCoy on *The Indians Are Coming* (1930).

He worked on *The Plainsman* (1936), *Dodge City* (1939), *Virginia City* (1940), *Winners of the West* (1940), *Silver River* (1948), *Blood on the Moon* (1948), *Return of the Bad Men* (1948), *Winchester '73* (1950), *Fort Worth* (1951), *Gun Belt* (1953), and *The Hanging Tree* (1959). TV credits include *Cisco Kid, The Lone Ranger, The Range Rider, Hopalong Cassidy, Annie Oakley, Wild Bill Hickok, Wyatt Earp, Maverick, The Rifleman,* and *Have Gun—Will Travel.* Osborne died from a heart attack at the age of 79.

JACK O'SHEA (1906–1967)

Western henchman Black Jack O'Shea was born in San Francisco as John Rellaford. He worked on shipping docks, performed in vaudeville, and competed in dance contests. This background led the short, stocky O'Shea into stunt work as a double for Lou Costello, Leo Carrillo, and Orson Welles. A popular cowboy player in more than a hundred B-westerns, he toured with Bob Steele and Lash LaRue putting on fights for live audiences. He broke both his ankles jumping off a stagecoach in 1949, ending his stunt career. He worked on *Melody Ranch* (1939), *Stage to Chino* (1940), *Perils of Nyoka* (1942), *Lady Takes a Chance* (1943), *Desert Hawk* (1944), *Angel and the Badman* (1947), and *The Fighting Kentuckian* (1949). O'Shea died at the age of 61 of heart failure.

See: Copeland, Bobby. "Man You Love to Hate." *Western Clippings.* #32, November-December 1999.

JACK PADJAN (aka JACK DUANE) (1887–1960)

Blackfoot Indian Jack Padjan was born in Silver Bow, Montana, and entered Hollywood alongside Tom Mix. He played Wild Bill Hickok on *Iron Horse* (1924) and had a brief shot at cowboy stardom with *Land of the Lawless* (1928) and *Crashing Through* (1928) using the name Jack Duane. He doubled Victor McLaglen on *Under Two Flags* (1936) and was the stunt ramrod on *The Big Trail* (1930), giving young star John Wayne pointers on horsemanship.

He worked on *The Ten Commandments* (1923), *The Covered Wagon* (1923), *King of Kings* (1927), *The Painted Stallion* (1937), and *Gunsmoke Ranch* (1937). Injured performing a high fall on *The Lives of a Bengal Lancer* (1935), he eventually moved out of stunt work to become a ranch foreman in Chatsworth, California.

See: Russell, Bill. "Jack Padjan." *Western Clippings.* #49, September-October 2002; "Silent Movie Actor Dies." *Hollywood Citizen News.* February 3, 1960; Wyatt, Ed. "Jack Padjan, A Real Cowboy, First and Last." *Films of the Golden Age.* Fall 1997.

JOE PALMA (1905–1994)

Joe Palma was born Joseph Provenzano in New York City. He is best known as Shemp Howard's regular double on Three Stooges shorts. When Howard died in 1955, Palma who stood in for him for remaining scenes to be filmed. Observant Stooge fans took to calling Palma "the Fake Shemp." Palma played many pratfalling waiters and cab drivers and did stunt work on *Johnny O'Clock* (1947), *The Lady from Shanghai* (1947), *Law of the Canyon* (1948), *The Doolins of Oklahoma* (1949), *Cargo to Capetown* (1950), and *The Out-of-Towners* (1970). He worked as Jack Lemmon's stand-in on *Some Like it Hot* (1959), *The Notorious Landlady* (1962), and *The Great Race* (1965).

See: "Stand-Ins." *Advocate.* April 29, 1962.

POST PARK (1899–1955)

Missouri-born Custer B. Park was one of the top six-up stagecoach and wagon drivers in Hollywood, seemingly able to lead a team of horses down trails that were deemed unable to be navigated while stopping precisely in front of the camera. He worked on *The Adventures of Robin Hood* (1938), *Gone with the Wind* (1939), *Melody Ranch* (1939), *Adventures of Red Ryder* (1940), *Ghost of Zorro* (1949), *Hangman's Knot* (1952), *Gun Fury* (1953), *Dawn at Socorro* (1954), *Santa Fe Passage* (1955), and TV shows like *Roy Rogers*. In the early 1930s he was part of the Studio Chase Troupe, one of the first stunt organizations. He dislocated a shoulder in a 1955 wagon turnover on the TV series *Stories of the Century*; it was his last stunt. Park died at the age of 55.

See: Carey, Harry. *Company of Heroes: My Life as an Actor in the John Ford Stock Company.* Scarecrow, 1994.

EARL PARKER (1927–2002)

Earl Parker from Eveleth, Minnesota, is best known as Vic Morrow's double on the World War II TV series *Combat* (1962–67). A high school acrobat, Parker proved a handy extra and was able to graduate to stunt work as a double for Anthony Steel on *Valerie* (1957) and Craig Hill on the TV series *Whirlybirds* (1957–60). After *Combat,* Parker was a stunt coordinator and double for Ron Harper on *Garrison's Gorillas* (1967–68).

He worked on *Fury at Gunsight Pass* (1956), *Project X* (1968), *Target: Harry* (1968), *How to Make It* (1969), *A Man Called Sledge* (1970), and *River of Mystery* (1970). TV credits include *Wyatt Earp, Boots and Saddles, Gunsmoke, Have Gun—Will Travel, Rawhide, The Rebel, Tall Men, Outlaws, Death Valley Days, The Untouchables, The FBI,* and *Emergency.* Parker died at the age of 74.

See: Davidsmeyer, Jo. *Combat! A Viewer's Companion to the WWII Series.* Strange New Worlds, 2008.

EDDIE PARKER (1900–1960)

Edwin Parker is affectionately known as Universal Studio's "Monster Man": He reportedly doubled for the likes of Lon Chaney, Jr., Boris Karloff, and Bela Lugosi as Frankenstein, The Wolf Man, Dracula, and The Mummy. His most notable assignment in that genre came in the fight scene in *Frankenstein Meets the Wolf Man* (1943). Some debate has been generated in recent years over how many monsters Parker portrayed as his work went without credit and it has surfaced that other stuntman may have been involved in some cases. There is not debate that outside of the horror genre, Parker specialized in screen brawls, serving as John Wayne's double for the classic fights with Randolph Scott on *The Spoilers* (1942) and *Pittsburgh* (1942). Two of his best fights came against Wayne on *Star Packer* (1934) and Robert Mitchum on *The Racket* (1951).

A former vaudeville dancer and weightlifter, the 6'4", 200-pound Parker was born in Waukegan, Illinois, and raised in Minnesota. He doubled Ray Corrigan on *Undersea Kingdom* (1936) and *The Three Mesquiteers* (1936), Buster Crabbe on *Flash Gordon* (1936), *Red Barry* (1938), *Flash Gordon's Trip to Mars* (1938), *Buck Rogers* (1939), and *Flash Gordon Conquers the Universe* (1940), Lloyd Bridges on *Secret Agent X-9* (1946), and Gary Cooper on *Cloak and Dagger* (1946). Gaining weight, he doubled Dick Foran, Roy Barcroft, Dick Curtis, Grant Withers, Bob Wilke, Roy Roberts, David Brian, and Barton MacLane. Parker played many henchmen fighting off Johnny Mack Brown, Eddie Dean, Rod Cameron, Allan Lane, Charles Starrett, Roy Rogers, and Gene Autry. He was a ubiquitous serial presence, essaying half a dozen roles in both *Ace Drummond* (1936) and *The Tiger Woman* (1944). As a "Stunt Cousin," Parker continued to amass a staggering number of credits throughout the 1950s.

He worked on *Professional Soldier* (1935), *Fighting Marines* (1935), *San Quentin* (1937), *Heart of the North* (1938), *When the Daltons Rode* (1940), *Virginia City* (1940), *Seven Sinners* (1940), *Northwest Passage* (1940), *Winners of the*

West (1940), *They Died with Their Boots On* (1941), *The Ghost of Frankenstein* (1942), *Fall In* (1942), *The Mummy's Tomb* (1942), *Lone Star Trail* (1943), *Batman* (1943), *In Old Oklahoma* (1943), *Daredevils of the West* (1943), *The Phantom* (1943), *Desert Hawk* (1944), *Haunted Harbor* (1944), *Monster and the Ape* (1945), *Flame of Barbary Coast* (1945), *House of Dracula* (1945), *Manhunt of Mystery Island* (1945), *Sudan* (1945), *Detour to Danger* (1946), *The Crimson Ghost* (1946), *Daughter of Don Q* (1946), *Angel and the Badman* (1947), *Jesse James Rides Again* (1947), *Dangers of the Canadian Mounted* (1948), *Adventures in Silverado* (1948), *Adventures of Frank and Jesse James* (1948), *Superman* (1948), *Silver River* (1948), *Abbott and Costello Meet Frankenstein* (1948), *Adventures of Sir Galahad* (1949), *Ghost of Zorro* (1949), *Mighty Joe Young* (1949), *Batman and Robin* (1949), *King of the Rocket Men* (1949), *Santa Fe* (1951), *Texas Rangers* (1951), *Don Daredevil Rides Again* (1951), *Cripple Creek* (1952), *Scarlet Angel* (1952), *Horizons West* (1952), *The Cimarron Kid* (1952), *The Lawless Breed* (1952), *Law and Order* (1953), *The Man from the Alamo* (1953), *Abbott and Costello Meet Dr. Jekyll and Mr. Hyde* (1953), *Lone Hand* (1953), *Rear Window* (1954), *20,000 Leagues Under the Sea* (1954), *Ride Clear of Diablo* (1954), *Dawn at Socorro* (1954), *Yankee Pasha* (1954), *Abbott and Costello Meet the Mummy* (1955), *Battle Cry* (1955), *Tarantula* (1955), *The Far Country* (1955), *The Rawhide Years* (1955), *The Mole People* (1956), *Around the World in Eighty Days* (1956), and *Spartacus* (1960). TV credits include *The Cisco Kid*, *Kit Carson*, and *Tales of the Texas Rangers*. Parker died of a heart attack at the age of 59 after a short fight with Ken Terrell on TV's *The Jack Benny Show*. He was posthumously honored with membership in the Stuntmen's Hall of Fame.

See: Glut, Donald. *The Frankenstein Archive.* Jefferson, NC: McFarland, 2002; Grant, Donald F. "Monster Man for All Occasions." *Modern Monsters.*#3, August 1966.

CLIFF PARKINSON (1899–1950)

Clifford Emmitt Parkinson was born in Kansas and grew up competing on the rodeo circuit. In Hollywood he portrayed henchmen and did stunts primarily on B-westerns although he did double for Joel McCrea on *Buffalo Bill* (1944)

and *Ramrod* (1947). Parkinson gave horse riding pointers to Robert Mitchum on his first films, *Hoppy Serves a Writ* (1943) and *Border Patrol* (1943). He worked on *Rough Ridin' Rhythm* (1937), *Rawhide* (1938), *Tombstone—The Town Too Tough to Die* (1942), *The Kansan* (1943), *Riders of the Deadline* (1943), and *Zorro's Black Whip* (1944). Parkinson died from cancer at the age of 51.

See: Roberts, Jerry. *Mitchum: In His Own Words.* NY: Limelight, 2000.

HARVEY PARRY (1900–1985)

The Dean of Stuntmen Harvey Parry served many years as James Cagney's chief double, claiming he worked on all of the star's films from *The Public Enemy* (1931) through *Ragtime* (1981). That would include standout Cagney fights on *Frisco Kid* (1935), *The Oklahoma Kid* (1939), and *Blood on the Sun* (1945). Parry doubled Peter Lorre on the *Mr. Moto* films and worked with Humphrey Bogart on *High Sierra* (1941), *Casablanca* (1942), and *The Treasure of the Sierra Madre* (1948) while running stunts at Warner Brothers. Parry doubled George Raft for a notable brawl on *The Bowery* (1933) and became one of the industry's top automotive men, expert at turning over speeding cars.

Movie fans thought Harold Lloyd was doing all his own stunts on *Never Weaken* (1921) and *Safety Last* (1923), but it was Parry doing the long shots. He was contractually sworn to secrecy for years until Lloyd passed. On *Play Safe* (1923) Parry was stretched between a car and a train with another train approaching. Doubling Edmond O'Brien on *Denver and Rio Grande* (1952), Parry jumped 195 feet off a railroad trestle into a boulder-filled canyon. Alongside Paul Stader and Saul Gorss, he executed a tricky three-man handcuffed stair fall on *The Boss* (1956). One of his greatest stunts was a fiery crash for *On the Beach* (1959). On *How the West Was Won* (1962) he jumped off a 50-foot water tower into a buffalo stampede. Parry appeared semi-regularly as the stumbling drunk on the comedy western *F Troop* (1965–67).

Five-foot-six, 150-pound Harvey G. Parry was born in San Francisco. He learned tumbling at an early age and swam the length of the Golden Gate Bridge across San Francisco Bay. He won two national diving championships, dove at the 1915

Harvey Parry rolls a fiery car on *On the Beach* (1959).

World's Fair in San Francisco, and toured with carnivals, circuses, and knockabout vaudeville acts as an acrobatic clown diver. Parry was a champion boxer, taking both the bantam and featherweight national titles in the same year. He won medals in boxing and diving at the Pan Am Games and narrowly missed qualifying for the Stockholm Olympics. He won the Pacific Coast Championship and fought forty-five amateur and professional bouts.

Parry entered films in 1919 as a prop man, but his athleticism, driving skill, and fearlessness in the face of heights soon had him in front of the cameras as a stunt double for Harold Lloyd. In the early silents he doubled Dustin Farnum, Ben Turpin, Ramon Novarro, John Gilbert, Tom Mix, and Buck Jones. When talkies came in he doubled Edward G. Robinson, Spencer Tracy, Brian Donlevy, John Garfield, and James MacArthur. Due to his small stature he could also fill in for actresses

Mary Pickford, Carole Lombard, Anne Baxter, and Shirley Temple, the latter on *Heidi* (1937). His boxing skill landed him work as a trainer to Cagney and Clark Gable. Forty-puls years later he gave pointers to Robert DeNiro on *Raging Bull* (1980).

He worked on *The Hunchback of Notre Dame* (1923), *The Trail of '98* (1928), *The Big Trail* (1930), *Lucky Devils* (1932), *King Kong* (1933), *Footlight Parade* (1933), *Dante's Inferno* (1935), *Call of the Wild* (1935), *Mutiny on the Bounty* (1935), *Professional Soldier* (1935), *High Tension* (1936), *Thank You, Jeeves* (1936), *Nancy Steele Is Missing* (1937), *Slave Ship* (1937), *San Quentin* (1937), *Mysterious Mr. Moto* (1938), *Suez* (1938), *Angels with Dirty Faces* (1938), *Each Dawn I Die* (1939), *The Roaring Twenties* (1939), *Dodge City* (1939), *Johnny Apollo* (1940), *They Drive By Night* (1940), *Seven Sinners* (1940), *Flowing Gold* (1940), *Desperate Journey* (1942),

Action in the North Atlantic (1943), *Lady Takes a Chance* (1943), *Passage to Marseille* (1944), *Saratoga Trunk* (1945), *The Spanish Main* (1945), *Detour to Danger* (1946), *Prince Valiant* (1954), *20,000 Leagues Under the Sea* (1954), *Blood Alley* (1955), *The Rains of Ranchipur* (1955), *The Killing* (1956), *A Killer Is Loose* (1956), *Light in the Forest* (1958), *No Time for Sergeants* (1958), *The Last Hurrah* (1958), *Spartacus* (1960), *North to Alaska* (1960), *It's a Mad, Mad, Mad, Mad World* (1963), *McLintock!* (1963), *4 for Texas* (1963), *The Comedy of Terrors* (1963), *Viva Las Vegas* (1964), *The Great Race* (1965), *Harper* (1966), *The St. Valentine's Day Massacre* (1967), *Bonnie and Clyde* (1967), *Hang 'Em High* (1968), *Paint Your Wagon* (1969), *Oklahoma Crude* (1973), *99 and 44/100 percent Dead* (1973), *Blazing Saddles* (1974), *Earthquake* (1974), and *Silent Movie* (1976). TV credits include *Superman, Maverick, The Californians, Laredo, The Green Hornet, Baretta, Starsky and Hutch, Fantasy Island,* and *CHiPs.* In all he appeared in well over 600 films. A member of the Stuntmen's Association and the Stuntmen's Hall of Fame, Parry died from a heart attack at the age of 85.

See: Bies, Frank. "Harvey Parry." *TV Guide.* 1983; "Harvey Parry, Dean of Stuntmen Dies." *Los Angeles Times.* September 20, 1985; Kahn, Alexander. "Movie Stunt Man Reveals Job Is Easy." *Pittsburgh Press.* February 20, 1944; Keavy, Hubbard. "Two Foot Fall Injures Stuntman for Films." *St. Petersburg Times.* April 7, 1935; Scott, Vernon. "Stuntman Still Tumbling Strong." *Milwaukee Journal.* March 4, 1971; Thomas, Bob. "Stuntman, 74, Still Takes Tumbles." *Omaha World Herald.* August 7, 1974.

ZALE PARRY

Zale Perry was born Rosalia Perry in Milwaukee, Wisconsin. A female scuba specialist, she was a pioneer in that field, setting a depth record of 209 feet for the TV series *Kingdom of the Sea.* The former UCLA swim champion regularly worked on TV's *Sea Hunt* (1958–61) doubling female guest stars underwater. Five-foot-two Parry was the mermaid on *Underwater Warrior* (1958) and a diving double for Sophia Loren on *Boy on a Dolphin* (1957). She performed stunts on both the *Voyage to the Bottom of the Sea* in 1961 and the later TV series. Parry was inducted into the Scuba Hall of Fame.

See: Sonne, Ann. "World Champion Skin Diver Gets Into Hollywood Swim." *Los Angeles Times.* September 8, 1957; Wertheim, L. Jon. *Sports Illustrated.* "Zale Perry, Diver." May 23, 1955.

REG PARTON (1917–1996)

Regis A. Parton was born in Cambria, Pennsylvania. He swam with the Navy's Southern Cross Swimming Club and once requested to swim the Panama Canal from the Atlantic to the Pacific Ocean. The planned swim was vetoed by the naval commander. Parton was a Santa Monica lifeguard and made brief film appearances while winning several Pacific Coast swimming championships. The 6'1", 180-pound Parton doubled Howard Keel on *Callaway Went Thataway* (1951), Tyrone Power on *Rawhide* (1951) and *Pony Soldier* (1952), Gary Cooper on *High Noon* (1952), Victor Mature on *Chief Crazy Horse* (1955), and Milton Berle on *It's a Mad, Mad, Mad, Mad World* (1963). He was best known as the long-time double for Rory Calhoun on films and the TV series *The Texan* (1958–60) and as the Metaluna Mutant on *This Island Earth* (1955). He coordinated the action on a series of A.C. Lyles westerns in the 1960s.

He worked on *Anne of the Indies* (1951), *All the Brothers Were Valiant* (1953), *Destry* (1954), *Valley of the Kings* (1954), *Four Guns to the Border* (1954), *The Man from Bitter Ridge* (1955), *Battle Cry* (1955), *The Last Frontier* (1955), *Blood Alley* (1955), *Backlash* (1956), *Walk the Proud Land* (1956), *A Day of Fury* (1956), *The Mole People* (1956), *Man Afraid* (1957), *The Hired Gun* (1957), *Night Passage* (1957), *Ride Out for Revenge* (1957), *High School Confidential!* (1958), *Ride a Crooked Trail* (1958), *The Saga of Hemp Brown* (1958), *Apache Territory* (1958), *Spartacus* (1960), *Gun Hawk* (1963), *Law of the Lawless* (1964), *Stage to Thunder Rock* (1964), *Young Fury* (1965), *Black Spurs* (1965), *Apache Uprising* (1965), *The Great Race* (1965), *Johnny Reno* (1966), *Waco* (1966), *What Did You Do in the War, Daddy?* (1966), *Red Tomahawk* (1967), *Hostile Guns* (1967), *Camelot* (1967), *Fort Utah* (1967), *Arizona Bushwhackers* (1968), *Buckskin* (1968), *The Split* (1968), *The Love Bug* (1968), *The Molly Maguires* (1970), *Skin Game* (1971), *Freebie and the Bean* (1974), *Blazing Saddles* (1974), *Earthquake* (1974), *The Ultimate Warrior* (1975), *Her-*

bie Goes to Monte Carlo (1977), *Hooper* (1978), *Butch and Sundance* (1979), and *The Stunt Man* (1980). TV credits include *Yancy Derringer, The Rifleman, Rawhide, The Man from U.N.C.L.E., Branded, Daniel Boone, Batman, The Green Hornet, Cimarron Strip, Mannix, The Streets of San Francisco,* and *The Rockford Files.* A member of the Stuntmen's Association and the Stuntmen's Hall of Fame, Parton died of a heart attack at the age of 79.

REGINA PARTON (1945–)

Born in California, Regina Lucia Parton was the daughter of stuntman Reg Parton. In 1965 she left a job as a dental assistant to take up her dad's profession. Her first stunt was a thirty-foot fall on the TV series *T.H.E. Cat.* Specializing in car chases and rollovers, she became president of the Stuntwomen's Association. She doubled Cloris Leachman on *Crazy Mama* (1975) and Jenny Agutter on *Logan's Run* (1976). On TV Parton doubled Jaclyn Smith on *Charlie's Angels* (1976–81) and Stefanie Powers on *Hart to Hart* (1979–84).

She also worked on *The Love Bug* (1968), *The Reivers* (1969), *Dirty Harry* (1971), *Conquest of the Planet of the Apes* (1972), *Battle for the Planet of the Apes* (1973), *Freebie and the Bean* (1974), *The Trial of Billy Jack* (1974), *The Towering Inferno* (1974), *Blazing Saddles* (1974), *The Hindenburg* (1975), *Hooper* (1978), *Convoy* (1978), *The Black Hole* (1979), *The Villain* (1979), *1941* (1979), and *Stunt Seven* (1979). TV credits include *The FBI, Mod Squad, Adam–12, Emergency, Kolchak: The Night Stalker, The Rockford Files,* and *Wonder Woman.*

See: Hobson, Dick. "I Am Totally Feminine." *TV Guide.* May 16, 1970; Willson, Karen E. "Invisible Superheroes of Hollywood." *Starlog.* January 1980.

VICTOR PAUL (1927–2011)

Five-foot-nine, 155-pound Victor Paul was the double for Burt Ward on the TV series *Batman* (1965–68) and the stunt coordinator on *The Untouchables* (1959–63). Born Philip Paul Romano in Los Angeles, he was a fan of Errol Flynn's *Robin Hood* and became a fencing specialist. He was Pacific Coast Champ in three weapons, a Greco Award honoree, and in later years a Senior Olympic Sabre Champion. Paul worked with Flynn on *Adventures of Don Juan* (1948) and *Against All Flags* (1952) and served as the stunt coordinator on the Flynn TV bio *My Wicked, Wicked Ways* (1985). He was the preferred fencing partner of Tony Curtis on *The Prince Who Was a Thief* (1951), *Son of Ali Baba* (1952), and *The Black Shield of Falworth* (1954). Outside of his sword work, Paul performed high falls on *The Poseidon Adventure* (1972) and *The Towering Inferno* (1974). He was the father of stuntmen John Phillip and Philip Romano.

He worked on *Battleground* (1949), *Mask of the Avenger* (1951), *Blackbeard the Pirate* (1952), *Around the World in Eighty Days* (1956), *The Buccaneer* (1958), *Spartacus* (1960), *Batman* (1966), *The Boston Strangler* (1968), *Skidoo* (1968), *Che!* (1969), *The Big Bounce* (1969), *Hello, Dolly!* (1969), *WUSA* (1970), *Skin Game* (1971), *Dirty Harry* (1971), *Diamonds Are Forever* (1971), *Star Spangled Girl* (1971), *What's Up, Doc?* (1972), *Conquest of the Planet of the Apes* (1972), *The Don Is Dead* (1973), *Magnum Force* (1973), *Battle for the Planet of the Apes* (1973), *Cleopatra Jones* (1973), *Night Moves* (1975), *The Master Gunfighter* (1975), *The Gumball Rally* (1976), *Swashbuckler* (1976), *The Great Smokey Roadblock* (1977), *One Man Jury* (1978), and *Prisoner of Zenda* (1979). TV credits include *Zorro, Cimarron Strip, Mission: Impossible, Star Trek,* and *Banyon.* He was a member of the Stuntmen's Association and an inductee of the Stuntmen's Hall of Fame.

See: Dooley, Gerry. *The Zorro Television Companion.* Jefferson, NC: McFarland, 2005.

GENE PERKINS (1901–1922)

Considered to be one of the most athletic of the silent film stuntmen, Gene Edward Perkins was known for high wire work, dives into nets, and early fire stunts. He doubled for Eddie Polo, Ruth Roland, William Desmond, and Helen Holmes on *Hazards of Helen* (1914), earning $75 a week for his daring. He tempted fate on a regular basis, falling forty feet onto his head off a rooftop and catching a rope prior to going over a waterfall.

Perkins was killed in Riverside, California, doubling Fred Thomson on a plane-to-train transfer for *Eagle's Talons* (1923). An inexperienced pilot brought Perkins in at the wrong angle and slammed him into the side of the train. Perkins was unable to hang on and dropped from his rope ladder to the ground. The exact film and date have changed depending on the source, but the basic details of his death remain the same. Perkins was posthumously inducted into the Hollywood Stuntmen's Hall of Fame.

See: Brownlow, Kevin. *The Parade's Gone By.* Berkeley, Ca: Univ. of California, 1968.

GIL PERKINS (1907–1999)

Gil Perkins was one of the top men in his profession for the better part of four decades, performing in over 1500 productions. Gilbert Vincent Perkins was born in Melbourne, Victoria, Australia, and was riding horses bareback while still a boy. He was a champion track athlete and skilled at his country's style of football, where he learned to tumble and take falls with minimal damage to his body. He practiced high dives into the local river, all skills that would aid his stunt career. He left home as a deckhand on a Norwegian freighter and entered moving pictures in the late 1920s.

The balding, fair-haired Perkins doubled William Boyd on early Hopalong Cassidy films and Red Skelton throughout his career on the slapstick comedies *Whistling in the Dark* (1943) and *The Fuller Brush Man* (1948). The six foot, 185-pound Perkins filled in for Rod LaRocque on *Delightful Rogue* (1929), Bruce Cabot on *King Kong* (1933), Spencer Tracy on *Captains Courageous* (1937), *Northwest Passage* (1940), and *Dr. Jekyll and Mr. Hyde* (1941), Eddie Albert on *The Fuller Brush Girl* (1950), Danny Kaye on *Hans Christian Andersen* (1952), Kirk Douglas on *20,000 Leagues Under the Sea* (1954), and Peter

Gil Perkins leaps over a railing on the serial *Adventures of Sir Galahad* (1947).

Boyle on *Young Frankenstein* (1974). He also doubled Clark Gable, Robert Taylor, Yul Brynner, and Gene Hackman. Action director Phil Karlson used Perkins on almost all of his films, among them *Hell to Eternity* (1960), *Walking Tall* (1973), and *Framed* (1975).

All-around stuntman Perkins was a staple in the outstanding serial action at Republic during the 1940s and worked for all the other studios too. Career highlights include a fall for Randolph Scott during the famous fight on *The Spoilers* (1942), a fifty-five–foot dive off a dam for William Boyd on *Riders of the Timberline* (1943), and a sequence where Perkins became a human torch on *The Prodigal* (1955). He worked famous brawls on *Dodge City* (1939), *Seven Sinners* (1940), and *The Great Race* (1965). One of his best stunts came doubling Will Geer for a dangerous battle with Dave Sharpe along rocky Arizona cliffs on *Lust for Gold* (1949). He donned the green Monster makeup to double Bela Lugosi during the climactic battle against Eddie Parker on *Frankenstein Meets the Wolf Man* (1943). Over a decade later he was the title creature on *Teenage Monster* (1958). On *City of Bad Men* (1953) Perkins played real-life boxer Bob Fitzsimmons.

He worked on *Seven Days Leave* (1930), *The Sea Wolf* (1930), *Suicide Fleet* (1931), *Dante's Inferno* (1935), *Mutiny on the Bounty* (1935), *Captain Blood* (1935), *The Informer* (1935), *God's Country and the Woman* (1937), *Valley of the Giants* (1938), *The Adventures of Robin Hood* (1938), *Virginia City* (1940), *They Died with Their Boots On* (1941), *High Sierra* (1941), *Reap the Wild Wind* (1942), *Pittsburgh* (1942), *Desert Hawk* (1944), *Adventure* (1945), *The Spanish Main* (1945), *Cloak and Dagger* (1946), *The Killers* (1946), *My Darling Clementine* (1946), *Jesse James Rides Again* (1947), *Wake of the Red Witch* (1948), *The Three Musketeers* (1948), *Fort Apache* (1948), *G-Men Never Forget* (1948), *Adventures of Sir Galahad* (1949), *She Wore a Yellow Ribbon* (1949), *Wagon Master* (1950), *His Kind of Woman* (1951), *Lone Star* (1952), *Demetrius and the Gladiators* (1954), *Prince Valiant* (1954), *The Sea Chase* (1955), *Guys and Dolls* (1955), *The Conqueror* (156), *The Killing* (1956), *Moby Dick* (1956), *Around the World in Eighty Days* (1956), *Jailhouse Rock* (1957), *The Tijuana Story* (1957), *Baby Face Nelson* (1957), *The Buccaneer* (1958), *Spartacus* (1960), *The Alamo* (1960), *How the West Was Won* (1962), *It's a Mad, Mad, Mad, Mad World* (1963), *4 for Texas* (1963), *A Distant Trumpet* (1964), *The Greatest Story Ever Told* (1965), *Batman* (1966), *The Sand Pebbles* (1966), *Hawaii* (1966), *Bonnie and Clyde* (1967), *Tobruk* (1967), *The Wrecking Crew* (1969), *The Undefeated* (1969), *The Molly Maguires* (1970), *Flap* (1970), *The Poseidon Adventure* (1972), *What's Up, Doc?* (1972), *The Towering Inferno* (1974), and *Prisoner of Zenda* (1979). TV credits include *Wyatt Earp*, *Cheyenne*, *Bronco*, *Gunsmoke*, *Trackdown*, *Mike Hammer*, *Richard Diamond*, *Peter Gunn*, *Wanted—Dead or Alive*, *Wagon Train*, *The Virginian*, *Laredo*, *Bonanza*, *Batman*, *Star Trek*, *The Man from U.N.C.L.E.*, *Mission: Impossible*, and *Mannix*. He was a founding member of the Stuntmen's Association and an inductee of the Stuntmen's Hall of Fame. Perkins died of natural causes at the age of 91.

See: Barker, Nicholas. "Gil Perkins." *Independent.* April 30, 1999; Lilley, Tim. *Campfire Conversations.* Akron, OH: Big Trail, 2007; Parla, Paul & Donna. "I Was a Teenage Monster." *Filmfax.* August 1998; Rosenberg, Bernard, & Harry Silverstein. *The Real Tinsel.* New York: MacMillan, 1970; Weaver, Tom. "Legend of the Falls." *Starlog.* September 1995.

JACK PERKINS (1921–1998)

Earl John Perkins was born in Medford, Wisconsin. He was a Master Sergeant in the Marine Corps and a combat veteran of World War II. Upon his discharge he played football for Eau Claire State Teachers College as a fullback, where he emitted a lion's roar to intimidate opponents or entertain teammates. He played semi-pro for the Chicago Rockets of the All-America League. When his playing days were done, he became a pro wrestler. He landed in Hollywood in the mid–1950s as a stuntman. Perkins' specialty was brawling, as he doubled Barry Kelley on *The Tall Stranger* (1957), Ernest Borgnine on *The Badlanders* (1958), and Dan Blocker on TV's *Bonanza*.

Six-foot-one and 240 pounds, the burly, bug-eyed Perkins was showcased on the 1968 *High Chaparral* TV episode "Shadow of the Wind" as a drunk who wanders through a big brawl and comically manages to get hit by most of the participants. He showed up often on *Gunsmoke*. In the episode "Lavery" he is a drunken trapper who demands a drink and chokes bartender Glenn

John Wayne punches Jack Perkins as bartender Cliff Lyons watches on *North to Alaska* (1960).

Strange to get it. James Arness arrives and punches Perkins into the street. As he aged, Perkins became a familiar face on TV sitcoms for his ability to convincingly play staggering drunks on shows such as *Happy Days*.

He worked on *Spartacus* (1960), *North to Alaska* (1960), *The Plunderers* (1960), *Confessions of an Opium Eater* (1962), *It's a Mad, Mad, Mad, Mad World* (1963), *4 for Texas* (1963), *The Great Race* (1965), *Cat Ballou* (1965), *The Glory Guys* (1965), *Bullitt* (1968), *A Man Called Gannon* (1969), *The Great Bank Robbery* (1969), *The Good Guys and the Bad Guys* (1969), *Paint Your Wagon* (1969), *There Was a Crooked Man...* (1970), *Skin Game* (1971), *What's Up, Doc?* (1972), *Oklahoma Crude* (1973), *Slither* (1973), *Magnum Force* (1973), and *Blazing Saddles* (1974). TV credits include *Peter Gunn*, *The Man from U.N.C.L.E.*, *Get Smart*, *Batman*, and *The Green Hornet*. He was a member of the Stuntmen's Association and the Stuntmen's Hall of Fame.

DAVE PERNA (1935–2004)

Born in Chicago, David L. Perna attended riding academies, served in the Boy Scouts, and played football for J. Sterling Morton East High. In Hollywood he trained under Lennie Geer, putting on live shows under the show name Stunts Unlimited. On TV the 190-pound six-footer doubled Gene Barry on *Bat Masterson* (1958–61) and *Name of the Game* (1968–71) and Leonard Nimoy and DeForest Kelley on *Star Trek* (1966–69). He worked on *Hell Is for Heroes* (1962), *Hour of the Gun* (1967), *The St. Valentine's Day Massacre* (1967), *A Man Called Gannon* (1969), *Che!* (1969), and *The Don Is Dead* (1973). TV credits include *Rawhide*, *Have Gun—Will Travel*, *Riverboat*, *Wagon Train*, *The Virginian*, *Laredo*, *The Outer Limits*, *The Green Hornet*, *Dundee and the Culhane*, *Mission: Impossible*, *S.W.A.T.*, and *Charlie's Angels*. He was an honorary member of the Stuntmen's Association, Perna died at the age of 69.

See: *State-Journal Register.* "David L. Perna." November 6, 2004.

PRESTON "PETE" PETERSON (1913–1983)

Francis Preston Peterson was born in Rockport, Texas, and raised in Santa Monica, California. He was a famed Santa Monica Beach lifeguard, creating much of that group's innovative lifesaving equipment. Six-foot-two, 200-pound Peterson competed with great success as a swimmer, paddle-boarder, and surfer. He twice won the Pacific Coast Guard Championship and was the four-time winner of the Pacific Coast Surf Riding Championship and the All-Around Waterman Title. He was the first man to paddle from Catalina Island to the mainland, and in 1932 was one of the first Californians to begin chasing waves in Hawaii. Peterson was still winning world championship tandem surfing competitions into the 1960s.

From the 1950s on, Peterson worked as a deep-sea diving salvage expert off the Santa Monica pier while maintaining a side vocation as a Hollywood stuntman, often working alongside Paul Stader. He worked on *Blood Alley* (1955), *The Ten Commandments* (1956), *The Buccaneer* (1958), *Spartacus* (1960), *Confessions of an Opium Eater* (1962), *The Poseidon Adventure* (1972), *99 and 44/100 percent Dead* (1974), *The Towering Inferno* (1974), *Lucky Lady* (1975), and *Beyond the Poseidon Adventure* (1972). A member of the Stuntmen's Association and an inductee of the International *Surfing Magazine's* Hall of Fame, Peterson died from a heart attack at the age of 70.

See: Lockwood, Craig. *Surfer's Journal.* "Waterman Preston 'Pete' Peterson." December-January 2005–2006; Warshaw, Matt. *The Encyclopedia of Surfing.* Orlando, Florida: Harcourt, 2005.

CHARLIE PICERNI (1935–)

Born in Queens, New York, Charles Picerni drove a construction truck and worked on high-rise girders. His character actor brother Paul convinced him to come to Hollywood in 1961 and work as his stand-in on the TV series *The Untouchables.* Charlie learned stunts on the set and began doubling his brother. On TV the 5'11", 180-pound Charlie doubled Harry Guardino on *The Reporter* (1964), James Darren on *The Time Tunnel* (1966–67), Mike Connors on *Mannix* (1967–75), Tony Franciosa on *The Name of the Game*

(1968–71) and *Matt Helm* (1975–76), Christopher George on *The Immortal* (1970–71), Telly Savalas on *Kojak* (1973–78), Paul Michael Glaser on *Starsky and Hutch* (1975–79), and Bill Bixby on *The Incredible Hulk* (1978–79). He often served as these series' stunt coordinator and second unit director.

He doubled Henry Silva on *Johnny Cool* (1963), Robert Forster on *The Don Is Dead* (1973), Richard Benjamin on *Westworld* (1973), and Burt Reynolds on *Shamus* (1973). He was the main sailor on fire during the Pearl Harbor attack on *Tora! Tora! Tora!* (1970). Picerni became an original member of Stunts Unlimited in 1970 and emerged as one of the top fight men and coordinators in the business. His work for producer Aaron Spelling on *Charlie's Angels* and *Fantasy Island* led to directing assignments on several TV shows. He handled the action on some of the industry's biggest action films of the late 1980s for producer Joel Silver, including *Die Hard* (1988).

He worked on *4 for Texas* (1963), *What Did You Do in the War, Daddy?* (1966), *Batman* (1966), *In Like Flint* (1967), *Tobruk* (1967), *The Boston Strangler* (1968), *Che!* (1969), *Flap* (1970), *Star Spangled Girl* (1971), *Blacula* (1972), *Enter the Dragon* (1973), *The Man Who Loved Cat Dancing* (1973), *American Graffiti* (1973), *The Outfit* (1973), *Black Samson* (1974), *Busting* (1974), *Three the Hard Way* (1974), *Big Bad Mama* (1974), *Earthquake* (1974), *Capone* (1975), *Midway* (1976), *The Gumball Rally* (1976), *Swashbuckler* (1976), *Smash-Up on Interstate 5* (1976), *One Man Jury* (1978), *The Prizefighter* (1979), and *Stunts Unlimited* (1980). TV credits include *The Man from U.N.C.L.E.*, *Mission: Impossible, Batman, The Green Hornet, The Wild Wild West, The Rat Patrol, Star Trek, Mod Squad, Bearcats, Search, The Streets of San Francisco, Cannon, Toma, Shaft, Gunsmoke, Kolchak: The Night Stalker, The Rookies, McCloud, S.W.A.T., Emergency, Police Story, The Bionic Woman, The Rockford Files,* and *Vega$.* His sons Chuck and Steve are stuntmen.

See: Medley, Tony. "One-On-One with Charlie Picerni." *Tolucan Times.* May 27, 2009; Picerni, Paul, and Tom Weaver. *Steps to Stardom: My Story.* Albany, GA: Bear Manor, 2007; Scott, Vernon. "Charles Picerni: Stuntman Choreographs Wrecks for TV." *Palm Beach Post.* December 11, 1976; www.charliepicerni.com.

Charlie Picerni does a fire burn on *Tora! Tora! Tora!* (1970).

SLIM PICKENS (1919–1983)

Slim Pickens' appearance as atom bomb–riding Major King Kong in *Dr. Strangelove* (1964) cemented his career as a much-loved character actor who could serve as either drawling comic relief or rough-hewn, threatening menace with equal skill. It was no coincidence that he was playing a cowboy in that film because that's what Slim Pickens was to the bone. He had a stunt background and lent authenticity to westerns such as *The Last Command* (1955) and *Major Dundee* (1965) with his riding ability. His elegiac death scene on Sam Peckinpah's *Pat Garrett and Billy the Kid* (1973) is one of the most memorable ever put on film.

Six-foot-three, 230-pound Pickens was born Louis Bert Lindley, Jr., in Kingsberg, California. He entered his first rodeo at the age of twelve without his father's consent. When he told the promoter he couldn't use his real name, the man suggested "Slim Pickens" since that was his chance of making any money that day. He became a successful horseman and bull wrangler in the rodeo arena, ultimately wrestling over 3,000 Brahma bulls and breaking nearly every bone in his body. At one event he took a third place finish with a fractured skull. The Army turned him down when he tried to enlist as a paratrooper during World War II due to his broken body. He was finally accepted into the Army Air Corps and assigned as a radio man, a humorous mistake since the Army misread his vast "rodeo" experience as "radio" experience. On an off-duty weekend he was thrown from a horse and broke his back, effectively ending his military career.

Pickens worked in a Wild West Show before beginning a career as a rodeo clown, a job at which he excelled to the point of being inducted into the Rodeo Hall of Fame. He first worked stunts on *Smoky* (1946), for which he was paid $25 to ride a bronc. The action footage looked so good it was used again in the 1966 remake. Pickens co-starred in the Errol Flynn western *Rocky Mountain* (1950) and became a sidekick to Rex Allen at Republic, where he was noted for his horsemanship. Pickens continued to pick up stunt assignments with his blue roan Appaloosa named Dear John. That's Pickens doing the bronc-busting scenes on *The Big Country* (1958) without credit. He was often cast as stagecoach drivers for his ability to handle a six-up team, most notably on the remake of *Stagecoach* (1966). Pickens handled the majority of his fight scenes on *One-Eyed Jacks* (1961), *Rough Night in Jericho* (1967), *Blazing Saddles* (1974), and *Mr. Billion* (1977). Pickens died of a brain tumor at the age of 64.

See: Lewis, Jack. "Slim Pickens: The Man from Wind River." *Guns of the Old West.* Summer 2003; Mitchum, Petrina Day, & Audrey Paiva. *Hollywood Hoofbeats.* BowTie, 2005; Scott, Vernon. "Pickin's Not Slim for Slim Pickens." *Cedar Rapids Gazette.* October 6, 1979; "Slim Pickens Still Known for Drawl, Availability for Very Tough Roles." *Colorado Springs Gazette.* December 17, 1975.

BILL PINCKARD (1929–)

Six-foot-three, 210-pound William Payton Pinckard was born in Rockford, Illinois, and became a legendary minor league baseball player. He spent twelve seasons in the Boston, Cleveland, Pittsburgh, St. Louis, and Cincinnati systems as a slugging outfielder without ever reaching the big leagues. It wasn't for lack of production. In 1950 the Los Angeles High athlete slugged thirty homeruns and hit .300 for Billings of the Pioneer League. In 1952 he knocked thirty-five tape-measure homeruns for Denver and again batted .300, capturing the minor league home run crown. Army service during the Korean War interrupted his rise to the majors. After his discharge he was one of the first Caucasians to play in Japan, where he was nicknamed Marco Polo. A bad back bothered Pinckard, and his off-season vocation as a Hollywood stuntman didn't help his body heal.

Pinckard subbed for Charlton Heston on *The Big Country* (1958), *Ben-Hur* (1959), and *Wreck of the Mary Deare* (1959). On the latter he

Slim Pickens on the receiving end of punch from Terence Hill on *Mr. Billion* (1977).

also stood in for Gary Cooper. He worked on the TV shows *Maverick, Cheyenne,* and *77 Sunset Strip,* but by the 1960s his Hollywood career was over. In 1963 Pinckard designed a new baseball made from cowhide rather than horsehide and began marketing it to schools and colleges. When that venture became successful and was eventually adopted by the professional leagues, he turned to making baseball gloves.

See: "Did Anyone See the Movie Star?" *Winnipeg Free Press.* August 26, 1959; www.pinckardbaseballgloves.com.

ALLEN PINSON (1916–2006)

Allen Dodd Pinson was born in Muskogee, Oklahoma. A veteran of the U.S. Army, Pinson was a fencing expert who worked with Stewart Granger, John Derek, Richard Greene, Errol Flynn, Burt Lancaster, Louis Hayward, Tony Curtis, Danny Kaye, and Basil Rathbone in the golden age of swashbucklers from *The Three Musketeers*

(1948) to *The Court Jester* (1956). On TV the versatile 175-pound six-footer doubled Clayton Moore on *The Lone Ranger* (1955–57), Robert Culp on *I Spy* (1965–68), Martin Landau on *Mission: Impossible ,* and Leonard Nimoy on *Star Trek.* Pinson doubled Montgomery Clift for fights on *From Here to Eternity* (1953), took a plunge into the Kern River on *The Burning Hills* (1956), received a boot to the face from Clint Eastwood during the pool hall brawl on *Coogan's Bluff* (1968), and doubled Al Lettieri being shot through a window on *Mr. Majestyk* (1974).

He also worked on *Frenchman's Creek* (1944), *Joan of Arc* (1948), *In a Lonely Place* (1950), *Lorna Doone* (1951), *Texas Rangers* (1951), *Singin' in the Rain* (1952), *Bandits of Corsica* (1953), *Thunder Bay* (1953), *Tumbleweed* (1953), *Prince Valiant* (1954), *Sign of the Pagan* (1954), *Ride Clear of Diablo* (1954), *The Rains of Ranchipur* (1955), *The Last Frontier* (1955), *Lady Godiva* (1955), *Around the World in Eighty Days* (1956), *Hell on Devil's Island* (1957), *Gunman's*

Allen Pinson takes a boot from Clint Eastwood on *Coogan's Bluff* (1968).

Walk (1958), *Timbuktu* (1959), *The Crimson Kimono* (1959), *Platinum High School* (1960), *Advance to the Rear* (1964), *Once Before I Die* (1965), *The Wrecking Crew* (1969), *The Great Bank Robbery* (1969), *Conquest of the Planet of the Apes* (1972), *The Poseidon Adventure* (1972), *Melinda* (1972), *Live and Let Die* (1973), *Battle for the Planet of the Apes* (1973), and *Deliver Us from Evil* (1973). His TV credits include *The Cisco Kid, Zane Grey, Tales of Wells Fargo, Peter Gunn, Yancy Derringer, Stoney Burke, The Outer Limits,* and *Mod Squad.* He was a member of the Stuntmen's Association and an inductee of the Stuntmen's Hall of Fame.

See: "Allen Pinson: His Final Stunt." *Kaweah Commonwealth.* February 3, 2006; "Ex-Stuntman Says He Fell into the Job." *Fresno Bee.* September 22, 1997.

CARL PITTI (1916–2003)

Born in Des Moines, Iowa, and raised in Culver City, California, six foot, 175-pound Carl C. Pitti was the son of rancher-stuntman Ben Pitti. He made his film debut in a Ruth Roland serial at the age of two. His father worked for Will Rogers and his son did the same before getting a job as a Yosemite Park guide and touring Wild West shows as a trick rider. After service with the U.S. Army in World War II, Pitti began stunts under the stage name Cal Perry. He was a solid rider astride his horse Warrior and became well known as a gun, rope, archery, and knife expert. He taught Glenn Ford fast draw for *The Fastest Gun Alive* (1956) and tutored actors and actresses such as Robert Taylor, Barbara Stanwyck, Stewart Granger, Rock Hudson, Joel McCrea, and Joan Crawford. He doubled Bob Hope on *Boy, Did I Get a Wrong Number* (1966) and Henry Darrow on TV's *High Chaparral* (1967–71).

He worked on *Of Mice and Men* (1939), *Billy the Kid* (1941), *The Kissing Bandit* (1949), *Bandit Queen* (1950), *A Ticket to Tomahawk* (1950), *Stars in My Crown* (1950), *The Story of Will Rogers* (1952), *The Lawless Breed* (1952), *The Duel at Silver Creek* (1952), *Gunsmoke* (1953), *Escape from Fort Bravo* (1953), *Column South* (1953), *Johnny Guitar* (1954), *The Command* (1954), *The Marauders* (1955), *Tribute to a Bad Man* (1956), *Gun Glory* (1957), *The Law and Jake Wade* (1958), *How the West Was Won* (1962), *Sergeants Three* (1962), *Major Dundee* (1965), *The Hallelujah*

Trail (1965), and *High Plains Drifter* (1973). TV credits include *Gunsmoke, Zorro, Bonanza,* and *Little House on the Prairie,* where he stood in for Michael Landon and drove wagons. He was a member of the Stuntmen's Hall of Fame.

See: "Actor, Stuntman, Western Tutor Carl Pitti Dies at 86." *Napa Valley Register.* August 16, 2003; Johnson, Erskine. "Romance Detective Johnson Gets No Clue from Hutton." *Trenton Evening Times.* April 20, 1950; "Old Gunfighters Slow Compared to Modern." *Augusta Chronicle.* July 15, 1956.

ALEX PLASSCHAERT (1932–2007)

Born in Los Angeles, Alexander Edward Plasschaert played football at Huntington Park High, tumbled, and won swimming and diving championships. As a professional dancer he worked on *The Unsinkable Molly Brown* (1962), *My Fair Lady* (1964), *Mary Poppins* (1964), and *Hello, Dolly* (1969). As a stuntman the 5'8", 145-pound Plasschaert doubled Roddy McDowall on *Adventures of Bullwhip Griffin* (1967) and Don Knotts on *No Deposit, No Return* (1976). He coordinated live *Miami Vice* stunt shows at Universal Studios, owned the dance studio Action Unlimited, and founded the stunt group Plasschaert and Associates.

He worked on *The Absent Minded Professor* (1961), *Five Weeks in a Balloon* (1962), *Not with My Wife You Don't* (1966), *Murderers' Row* (1966), *Riot on Sunset Strip* (1967), *King Kong* (1976), *The Shaggy D.A.* (1976), *Logan's Run* (1976), and *Pete's Dragon* (1977). TV credits include *Red Skelton, Laugh-In, Jerry Lewis, Here's Lucy, Ironside,* and *Emergency.* A member of the Stuntmen's Association, Plasschaert died from a stroke at the age of 75.

See: "Alex Edward Plasschaert." *Los Angeles Times.* March 29, 2007; www.entertainmentriskandsafety.com.

GEORGE PLUES (1895–1953)

Born in Irwin, Pennsylvania, George Edward Plues was a cowboy henchman and stage driving specialist in dozens of B-westerns of the 1930s and 1940s. He customarily came in to handle the reins when scenes called for fast action chases or nifty maneuvering. He doubled Fuzzy Knight and performed stunts on *Zorro's Fighting Legion* (1939), *Winners of the West* (1940), *Western Union* (1941), *Perils of Nyoka* (1942), *The Ox-Bow Incident* (1943), and *Along Came Jones* (1945).

EDDIE POLO (1875–1961)

Eddie Polo was born Edward W. Wyman in San Francisco to a family of circus performers. Some reports say his birthplace is Vienna, Austria, but many of the mystery of his early life stem from Polo's own embellishments. Polo spent time with various circuses including Barnum and Bailey as an acrobat, strongman, tightrope walker, aerialist, and stunt rider. He entered films as a stuntman in 1913 in Broncho Billy westerns and Slippery Sam comedies. In 1915 he was given a featured role on *Broken Coin* and opened filmmakers' eyes with a thrilling plane-to-boat transfer. At his insistence he began starring in motion pictures due to his athletic abilities and penchant for attaining publicity. He was a star for Universal on silent action serials such as *Gray Ghost* (1917), *Bull's Eye* (1917), *Lure of the Circus* (1918), *Vanishing Dagger* (1920), *King of the Circus* (1920), and *Do or Die* (1921).

Known as the "Hercules of the Screen" because of his physique, the 5'9", 175-pound Polo was renowned for doing his own stunts. In 1915 he was the first man to parachute off the Eiffel Tower and set a record for the highest altitude parachute jump at 4,280 feet. His popularity with audiences was a direct result of his daring, although his body took a tremendous beating. He endured horse trampling, lion attacks, and hard falls onto the ground. By the early 1920s he yielded some of his action to doubles.

Polo was badly injured on *Dangerous Hour* (1921) when his horse stepped in a gopher hole. Doctors told him his career was over, but Polo went to Europe and proved them wrong. Upon returning to the States he was unable to secure anything more than bit parts. He was erroneously reported dead in 1949 when a high-wire artist using his name fell to his death. A member of the Stuntmen's Hall of Fame, Polo died from a heart attack at the age of 86.

See: "Ed Polo Dies, Early Stuntman." *Racine Journal Times.* June 15, 1961; Harrison, Paul. "In Hollywood." *Trenton Evening Times.* March 27, 1940; Russell, Bill. "Eddie Polo." *Western Clippings.* #73, September-October 2006.

ALLEN POMEROY (1900–1976)

The name Allen Pomeroy is not well known, but he was an early and influential pioneer in the world of stunts. Alongside John Wayne and Yakima Canutt, Pomeroy helped devise the "Pass System" for fight scenes in the early 1930s on films such as *'Neath Arizona Skies* (1934). The "Pass System" involved throwing punches that did not connect, but gave the appearance of doing so due to strategic camera placement and editing. Prior to this, stuntmen merely pounded away at one another's arms and shoulders for extended takes. Pomeroy also negotiated with the studios to set standard prices for stunt work and provide guaranteed insurance policies.

The Connecticut-born Pomeroy headed up the stunt units at Republic Studios in the 1930s and Warner Brothers throughout the 1940s. This put him in charge of hiring the stunt personnel and coordinating the stunts that made it to the screen. After World War II he was instrumental in training many ex-soldiers for stunt work. Some of these stuntmen became top performers in the field. Pomeroy had been one of the chariot drivers in the original *Ben-Hur* (1925), experience which led him to travel to Europe in the 1950s to train stuntmen for epic films such as *Helen of Troy* (1955).

Pomeroy played football and was an intercollegiate boxing champion for Columbia University. Standing 6'1" and weighing in at 200 pounds, former Marine Pomeroy boxed professionally and played semi-pro football. He gained national notoriety when he set a speed record for a cross-country motorcycle trip. This landed him in Hollywood, where he became a motorcycle and automotive specialist. He was also a top fight man, having worked as Randolph Scott's double in the famous fight scene with John Wayne on *The Spoilers* (1942), which is often acknowledged as being one of the all-time great screen brawls. Pomeroy also doubled George Bancroft, Rod LaRocque, Preston Foster, William Bendix, Wayne Morris, and Joel McCrea. For *Manpower* (1941) he was paid $800 for a fight atop a power pole. He was known for an exemplary safety record and was not afraid to turn down stunts he felt were unsafe. In over thirty years in the industry, Pomeroy was never injured and never taken to the hospital.

He worked on *Seven Days Leave* (1930), *Thirteen Women* (1932), *King Kong* (1933),

Allen Pomeroy and Eddie Parker (lying across the bar) double Randolph Scott and John Wayne in the famous fight on *The Spoilers* (1942).

Mutiny on the Bounty (1935), *Professional Soldier* (1935), *Cain and Mabel* (1936), *San Quentin* (1937), *Mysterious Mr. Moto* (1938), *Dodge City* (1939), *Flowing Gold* (1940), *Road to Singapore* (1940), *The Strawberry Blonde* (1941), *Sullivan's Travels* (1941), *Wake Island* (1942), *Desperate Journey* (1942), *Pittsburgh* (1942), *Daredevils of the West* (1943), *Guadalcanal Diary* (1943), *Lady Takes a Chance* (1943), *Tall in the Saddle* (1944), *Saratoga Trunk* (1945), *Objective, Burma!* (1945), *San Antonio* (1945), *Adventures of Don Juan* (1948), *Silver River* (1948), *Key Largo* (1948), *The Flame and the Arrow* (1950), *The Crimson Pirate* (1952), *Master of Ballantrae* (1953), *Blowing Wild* (1953), and *The Conqueror* (1956). He was a member of the Stuntmen's Hall of Fame and an honorary member of the Stuntmen's Association.

See: "Allen Pomeroy." *Catholic Digest.* November 1947; Berg, Louis. "How to Drop Dead." *Plain Dealer.* February 27, 1955; Pomeroy, Allen.

"Movie Stunts Well Planned." *Omaha World Herald.* September 26, 1948; "Want to Be a Film Stuntman? All It Takes Is Salesmanship." *Trenton Evening Times.* December 29, 1940.

DINNY POWELL (1932–)

London-born Dennis "Dinny" Powell got his start as a teenager, ditching school to hang around the studios doing odd jobs before becoming a professional heavyweight boxer. As a stuntman Dinny doubled Sean Connery and Roger Moore on Bond films. A fight specialist and horse master, he is the brother of stuntman Nosher Powell. He worked on *Dr. No* (1962), *From Russia with Love* (1963), *You Only Live Twice* (1967), *Casino Royale* (1967), *You Can't Win 'Em All* (1970), *The Pink Panther Strikes Again* (1976), *The Spy Who Loved Me* (1977), *Revenge of the Pink Panther* (1978), *Moonraker* (1979), *Ffolkes*

(1979), *Never Say Never Again* (1983), and *A View to a Kill* (1985). TV credits include *The Avengers, The Prisoner, Doctor Who,* and *The Persuaders.*

EDDIE POWELL (1927–2000)

London-born Eddie Powell, brother of stuntman Joe Powell, was a dispatch rider with the first battalion grenadier guards. He was the regular double for Christopher Lee and Gregory Peck whenever he worked overseas on films ranging from *The Guns of Navarone* (1961) to *The Omen* (1976). Doubling Peck on *The Sea Wolves* (1980), Powell ruptured his spleen doing a sixty-foot backfall. He doubled Clint Eastwood atop the cable car on *Where Eagles Dare* (1968) and worked on *Kelly's Heroes* (1970). Powell was inside the costume of the title creature on *Alien* (1979).

He also worked on *The Vikings* (1958), *Jason and the Argonauts* (1963), *From Russia with Love* (1963), *You Only Live Twice* (1967), *Diamonds Are Forever* (1971), *Live and Let Die* (1973), *Man with the Golden Gun* (1974), *The Spy Who Loved Me* (1977), *For Your Eyes Only* (1981), *Octopussy* (1983), *Never Say Never Again* (1983), and *A View to a Kill* (1985). Powell died at the age of 73.

See: Parla, Paul. "Never a Dull Moment for Hollywood Stuntman Eddie Powell." *Scary Monsters.* January 1998; Powell, Joe. *The Life and Times of a Fall Guy.* Book Guild, 2007.

JOE POWELL (1922–)

Joe Powell can lay claim to one of the all-time great movie stunts, a 100-foot fall off a rope bridge for Sean Connery on *The Man Who Would Be King* (1975). Powell had to land precisely on a small cardboard box catcher built onto the side of a cliff. Had he missed his target, he would have fallen to a certain death. The film's director John Huston thought it was the best stunt he had ever seen, and to this day it remains top-drawer. High falls such as one on *A Night to Remember* (1958) were a Powell specialty. He did a ninety-foot plunge into the sea on *The Guns of Navarone* (1961) and a sixty-foot fall with ineffective wings on *Those Magnificent Men in Their Flying Machines* (1965).

The London-born Powell joined the Grenadier Guards at seventeen. While in the service he began boxing as a heavyweight. As a member of Number Four Special Service commando unit he was involved in the D-Day landing and several reconnaissance missions into Holland and France. Powell became a film extra after the war. Upon meeting fellow commando Jock Easton, they started Jock Easton's Stunt Team.

Powell impressed many when he crashed a motorcycle into a tree at forty miles per hour for *The Small Voice* (1948), but walking away from that stunt was mostly luck. Powell and his cohorts eventually became highly skilled, proving their mettle on the American-produced *Captain Horatio Hornblower* (1951). Powell was hired as the underwater double for Burt Lancaster on *The Crimson Pirate* (1952) and doubled Anthony Quinn on *The Guns of Navarone* (1961), Jack Hawkins on *Zulu* (1964), Nigel Green on *Africa, Texas Style* (1967), and Telly Savalas on *On Her Majesty's Secret Service* (1969).

He worked on *Master of Ballantrae* (1953), *Knights of the Round Table* (1953), *Quentin Durward* (1955), *Helen of Troy* (1955), *Alexander the Great* (1956), *Moby Dick* (1956), *Zarak* (1956), *Steel Bayonet* (1957), *Exodus* (1960), *Lawrence of Arabia* (1962), *Billy Budd* (1962), *The Longest Day* (1962), *Cleopatra* (1963), *Heroes of Telemark* (1965), *High Wind in Jamaica* (1965), *Cast a Giant Shadow* (1966), *Khartoum* (1966), *The Dirty Dozen* (1967), *You Only Live Twice* (1967), *Casino Royale* (1967), *Where Eagles Dare* (1968), *Murphy's War* (1971), *The Last Valley* (1971), *Young Winston* (1972), *The Odessa File* (1974), *Land That Time Forgot* (1975), *Pink Panther Strikes Again* (1976), *At the Earth's Core* (1976), *Ffolkes* (1979), and *A View to a Kill* (1985).

See: Powell, Joe. *The Life and Times of a Fall Guy.* Sussex, England: Book Guild, 2007.

NOSHER POWELL (1928–2013)

Six-foot-four, 240-pound George Frederick Bernard Powell was born in Camberwell, South London. Nosher ran track in school before discovering that his talent lay in his fists. He joined the Air Training Corps, entering the squared circle of their boxing club. He built his strength by carrying around a heavy mace. At seventeen he was asked to spar at Jack Solomon's Gym with heavyweight champion Joe Louis, who was fighting exhibitions. Nosher sparred with the Brown Bomber for an entire month, experience that greatly aided his own ring savvy. He subsequently entered the Army as a physical training instructor and was sent to Egypt, where he became both the United and Imperial Services Heavyweight Champion.

He turned professional, amassing a record of 34–16–2 with eleven knockouts. At one time he was the third-ranked heavyweight in Britain. Nosher was sparring partner for Archie Moore, Sugar Ray Robinson, Jersey Joe Walcott, Ingmar Johannson, Nino Valdez, and Muhammad Ali. Working as a nightclub bouncer, he crossed paths with such London criminal types as the Krays and John Bindon. Nosher's reputation as a heavy hitter got him bodyguard work for Frank Sinatra, Sammy Davis, Jr., and J. Paul Getty. He was picking up film work as far back as *Henry V* (1944) and *Caesar and Cleopatra* (1945).

His biggest stunt job was doubling Gert Frobe on *Those Magnificent Men in Their Flying Machines* (1965). Nosher was an excellent horseman, at home in period pictures, particularly knights in shining armor. He worked a number of Bond films, though his best screen moment came in the comedy *Eat the Rich* (1986) where he plays a bruising British Home Secretary who punches out terrorists himself. On TV he doubled comedian Benny Hill and performed stunt heavies on *Danger Man, The Saint, The Avengers,* and *The Persuaders.* His brother Dinny was a stuntman, as were sons Greg and Gary.

He worked on *Master of Ballantrae* (1953), *The Robe* (1953), *Demetrius and the Gladiators* (1954), *Hell Below Zero* (1954), *Dark Avenger* (1955), *Bridge on the River Kwai* (1957), *Horror of Dracula* (1958), *Ben-Hur* (1959), *Exodus* (1960), *Guns of Navarone* (1961), *Lawrence of Arabia* (1962), *Cleopatra* (1962), *The Longest Day* (1962), *From Russia with Love* (1963), *The Pink Panther* (1963), *Zulu* (1964), *Goldfinger* (1964), *A Fistful of Dollars* (1964), *Battle of the Bulge* (1965), *Thunderball* (1965), *Khartoum* (1966), *For a Few Dollars More* (1967), *The Dirty Dozen* (1967), *You Only Live Twice* (1967), *Casino Royale* (1967), *Charge of the Light Brigade* (1968), *Where Eagles Dare* (1968), *On Her Majesty's Secret Service* (1969), *The Italian Job* (1969), *Cromwell* (1970), *You Can't Win 'Em All* (1970), *Diamonds Are Forever* (1971), *The Last Valley* (1971), *Live and Let Die* (1973), *The Mackintosh Man* (1974), *Man with the Golden Gun* (1974), *Brannigan* (1975), *Star Wars* (1977), *The Spy Who Loved Me* (1976), *Superman* (1978), *Moonraker* (1979), *For Your Eyes Only* (1981), *Octopussy* (1983), and *A View to a Kill* (1985). He was an inductee of the Hollywood Stuntmen's Hall of Fame.

See: Morton, James. "Nosher Powell." *Guardian.* April 26, 2013; Powell, Nosher, & William Hall. *Nosher.* Blake,1999.

REG PRINCE (1936–)

Reg Prince served as the notorious Oliver Reed's stand-in, double, and bodyguard from the early 1960s until the late 1980s when the two had a falling out (literally): Prince's back was broken when Reed pushed him over a banister onto a coral reef. Prince was a match for the notorious hellraiser when it came to drinking and carousing. His background was cloaked in mystery, much of it fueled by his own short and cryptic answers. He was said to be a karate expert and former boxing champion with a background in an elite Army regiment active in British Intelligence in the Far East. Reed and Prince were bar-brawling buddies, egging one another on into ever more outlandish behavior. When they couldn't find someone to fight, they would end up arm-wrestling or roughhousing with one another.

Prince worked on all Reed's films from *The Party's Over* (1965) to *Castaway* (1986), often doubling men that Reed was supposed to fight. Among the more than sixty films they did together were *The Devils* (1971), *Sitting Target* (1972), *The Three Musketeers* (1973), *The Four Musketeers* (1974), *The Great Scout and Cathouse Thursday* (1976), and *Crossed Swords* (1978). Prince also appeared as stunt heavies on TV's *Champions* and films such as *Inspector Clouseau* (1968). Prince lost a well-publicized lawsuit against Reed, with the judge determining the injury to Prince's back was merely the hazard of being in business with Reed.

See: "Oliver Reed Fractured Stand-in's Spine." *Independent.* December 14, 1993; Prince, Reg. *Photoplay Film Monthly.* "My Wild Days and Nights with Ollie." February 1976.

JANOS PROHASKA (1919–1974)

Janos Prohaska was born in Budapest, Hungary, and began acrobatics at a young age. This led to a professional act that brought him to the United States and entrance into the stunt profession in the mid–1950s. Prohaska doubled Peter Falk for falls and Arnold Stang for the fight on *It's a Mad, Mad, Mad, World* (1963). He is best known for portraying gorillas and the hungry bear

"Cookie" on *The Andy Williams Show*. The 5'4", 140-pound actor owned twenty-five handmade animal suits which kept him in regular employment throughout the 1960s on movies, TV, and variety shows.

He worked on *Billy Rose's Jumbo* (1962), *Advance to the Rear* (1964), *Bikini Beach* (1964), *Camelot* (1967), *Hang 'Em High* (1968), and *Escape from the Planet of the Apes* (1971). TV credits include *Man and the Challenge, Riverboat, Sea Hunt, The Outer Limits, Perry Mason, The Munsters, Lost in Space, Honey West, Gilligan's Island, Voyage to the Bottom of the Sea, Star Trek, Land of the Giants,* and *Here's Lucy*. He, his stuntman son Robert Prohaska and many others died in a plane crash in Bishop, California, while returning from making the TV show *Primal Man*. A member of the Stuntmen's Association and an inductee of the Stuntmen's Hall of Fame, Prohaska was 54 years old.

See: Hagner, John. "In Memory." *Falling for Stars*. #1, 1974; "Cookie Begging Bear Gets Heavy Fan Mail." *Palm Beach Daily News*. April 24, 1970.

JOE PRONTO

Fight specialist Joe Pronto fought Kirk Douglas on *A Lovely Way to Die* (1968) and doubled Michael Pataki for the slam-bang battle on the low-budget *Grave of the Vampire* (1972). On that film he was flung wall to wall by William Smith with a chain around his neck. This came on the heels of participating in the car chase on *The French Connection* (1971) and executing a tricky fall down a stairwell on *Shaft* (1971). Based on the success of these assignments, Pronto appeared on *The Tonight Show* with Johnny Carson in 1972 to show the TV host how to be "killed" on screen.

The 5'7" New York–born Pronto was a cow-

Kirk Douglas (left) throws a punch at Joe Pronto on *A Lovely Way to Die* (1968).

boy for live stunt shows at Dodge City, New Jersey, and Wild West City in Netcong. A fight opposite Hugh O'Brian on the TV special *The Secret World of Eddie Hodges* gained him notice and resulted in his casting as a brawling miner on the Broadway show *The Unsinkable Molly Brown*. In California, Pronto performed live western shows at Universal and was a quick-draw specialist. He doubled character types Jack Kruschen, Edmond O'Brien, Sebastian Cabot, Conrad Bain, Jacques Marin, Joe Santos, Herschel Bernardi, Philip Ahn, Phil Roth, and Ron Carey. On TV he doubled Gerald S. O'Loughlin on *The Rookies* (1972–76), Art Metrano on *Amy Prentiss* (1974–75), and George Savalas on *Kojak* (1974–78). On one occasion he doubled Telly Savalas.

He worked on *It's a Mad, Mad, Mad, Mad World* (1963), *Harper* (1966), *The King's Pirate* (1967), *What's So Bad About Feeling Good?* (1968), *Sidehackers* (1969), *Too Late the Hero* (1970), *Dream No Evil* (1970), *Night of Dark Shadows* (1971), *The Gang That Couldn't Shoot Straight* (1971), *Who Killed Mary What's 'Er Name?* (1971), *Clay Pigeon* (1971), *What's Up, Doc?* (1972), *Blacula* (1972), *The Sting* (1973), *Blazing Saddles* (1974), *Island at the Top of the World* (1974), *Hearts of the West* (1975), *Day of the Locust* (1975), *Silent Movie* (1976), *King Kong* (1976), *The White Buffalo* (1977), and *Herbie Goes to Monte Carlo* (1977). TV credits include *Diagnosis Unknown, Red Skelton, Wagon Train, Gunsmoke, The Virginian, Laredo, The Girl from U.N.C.L.E., Mannix, N.Y.P.D., Dark Shadows, Nichols, Kung Fu, Police Woman, Police Story*, and *How the West Was Won*. Pronto later became a cowboy guitarist on the Grand Canyon Railway.

See: www.prescottfilmfestival.com.

DON PULFORD (1936–)

Five-foot-eleven, 170-pound Donald Bert Pulford was born in Burbank, California, the son of former professional baseball pitcher Don Pulford. He was All-State in football at John Burroughs High and played on the league championship basketball squad. He spent several years as a minor league baseball shortstop in the Pittsburgh Pirates organization. His best season came for the Douglas Copper Kings of the Arizona/Mexican League when he hit .320 and swatted twelve homeruns. Pulford worked extra on *Around the World in Eighty Days* (1956) and

A Distant Trumpet (1964) and by the 1970s was a full-time stuntman doubling William Shatner and Nick Nolte. He worked on *Capone* (1975), *Vigilante Force* (1976), *Texas Detour* (1978), *The Black Hole* (1979), *Disaster on the Coastliner* (1979), *The Stunt Man* (1980), and the TV shows *Gunsmoke, The Streets of San Francisco, Emergency*, and *The Six Million Dollar Man*. An inductee of the Burroughs High Hall of Fame, he was the husband of stuntwoman Lee Pulford.

See: Oppenheimer, Cris. "Reality for the Stuntmen Is Skill, Trust in Colleagues." *The Day*. July 19, 1979; www.burbanknbeyond.com.

STEVE RAINES (1916–1996)

Cowboy Steve Raines was cast as cattle drover Jim Quince on *Rawhide* (1959–66), lending authenticity to the cast. Born in Grants Pass, Oregon, Raines was a bulldogger and bronco rider in rodeo events across the United States and into South America. He'd win some but lose more, usually making only enough to pay expenses. Times were once so tough he was forced to compete while wearing a cast. He made additional money as a hunting guide and Hollywood stuntman between serving his country during World War II. Raines doubled Alan Ladd on horseback in *Shane* (1953).

He worked on *Broken Lance* (1954), *Drums Across the River* (1954), and *Cattle Empire* (1958). Raines could drive a stagecoach and appeared on a number of TV westerns such as *Roy Rogers, Gene Autry, Kit Carson, Sgt. Preston, Brave Eagle, Daniel Boone, The Virginian, Laredo, The Wild Wild West, Bonanza, High Chaparral*, and *Gunsmoke*. Raines died from a stroke at the age of 79.

See: *Fresno Bee*. "Rawhide Regular Finds TV is Cowboy's Paradise." August 22, 1965;

BILL RAISCH (1905–1984)

New Jersey-born Carl William Raisch was a construction worker, adagio performer, Ziegfeld dancer, bodybuilder, and amateur boxer. He served with the Merchant Marine in World War II, losing his right arm at the elbow in a ship's fire. He worked in films as an extra, stand-in, and occasional stuntman on *Around the World in Eighty Days* (1956) and *Spartacus* (1960), playing a soldier who gets a fake arm cut off in battle. At 5'9" he stood four inches shorter than Burt Lancaster but worked as the star's stand-in for many years.

Kirk Douglas cast him as a bullying saloon tough that engages in a classic fight on *Lonely Are the Brave* (1962). Raisch gained additional notoriety as the "one-armed man" on TV's *The Fugitive* (1963–67). Struggling with David Janssen he employed the same vicious fighting tactics he used against Douglas, culminating on the show's finale with a battle atop a water tower. Raisch died of lung cancer at the age of 79.

See: "Dr. Kimble's Elusive One-Armed Man Does Exist." *Trenton Evening Times.* January 26, 1964; Heffernan, Harold. "Kirk Douglas and One-Armed Actor Wage Barroom Brawl for New Movie." *Oregonian.* February 3, 1962; Scott, Vernon. "Bill Raisch Enjoys Fame." *Seattle Daily Times.* July 3, 1966.

GLENN RANDALL, JR. (1941–)

Five-foot-ten, 170 pound Glenn H. Randall Jr. from Bakersfield, California, distinguished himself as the stunt coordinator on the action blockbusters *Raiders of the Lost Ark* (1981), *Return of the Jedi* (1983), and *Indiana Jones and the Temple of Doom* (1984). On *Raiders* he was the driver for Terry Leonard's famous stunt crawl underneath the truck. Randall was the son of the long-time Hollywood wrangler and stuntman who trained Roy Rogers' Palomino horse Trigger and worked on *Ben-Hur* (1959). Glenn Jr. and his brother Corky worked alongside their dad on the back lots and entertained in rodeos at Madison Square Garden and the Cow Palace. Glenn Jr. wanted to be a professional football player but lacked the size, so he became a fulltime stuntman in the 1960s with his top horse Rocket.

He worked on *It's a Mad, Mad, Mad, Mad World* (1963), *Duel at Diablo* (1966), *Camelot* (1967), *Planet of the Apes* (1968), *The Good Guys and the Bad Guys* (1969), *Che!* (1969), *Little Big Man* (1970), *Soldier Blue* (1970), *Diamonds Are Forever* (1971), *Skin Game* (1971), *The Omega Man* (1971), *The Great Northfield Minnesota Raid* (1972), *The Cowboys* (1972), *What's Up, Doc?* (1972), *The Don is Dead* (1973), *99 and 44/100 percent Dead* (1974), *Blazing Saddles* (1974), *Earthquake* (1974), *Mame* (1974), *Firepower* (1979), *The Black Stallion* (1979), and *Never Say Never Again* (1983). TV credits include *Gunsmoke, The Wild Wild West, Cimarron Strip,* and *Hondo.* A member of the Stuntmen's Association,

Randall set up the original Indiana Jones live stunt show at Florida's Disney-MGM Studios Theme Park.

See: "Glenn Randall, Jr." *American Cinematographer.* #62, 1981; Morgan, Patty. "It Takes Guts, Practice to Pull a Stunt Like That." *Star News.* November 29, 1983.

JERRY RANDALL (1942–1974)

Six-foot, 170 pound Gerald R. Randall was a military veteran who joined the Stuntmen's Association before moving to Stunts Unlimited. On *Clay Pigeon* (1971) Randall was in a truck with Buddy Joe Hooker that rolled over twenty-two times, gaining immediate notice within the industry. Randall doubled Buck Taylor on TV's *Gunsmoke* and performed motorcycles stunts on *Hells Angels '69* (1969), *Angel Unchained* (1970), *Harold and Maude* (1971), and the TV series *Then Came Bronson.* Credits include *Camelot* (1967), *Moonrunners* (1974), and the TV show *The Beverly Hillbillies* where Randall portrayed a female wrestler. Randall died at the age of 31 in a hang-gliding accident. His son Chad Randall became a stuntman.

PHIL RAWLINS (1930–2009)

Phil Rawlins was best known as a director on TV westerns such as *F Troop* and *High Chaparral,* but he had a background as a stuntman. Rawlins was born in Glendale, California and attended Pierce College. Traveling the rodeo circuit, he attained stunt work on *Fort Defiance* (1951), *Gun Fury* (1953), *The Last Wagon* (1956), and TV's *Gunsmoke.* Rawlins doubled Don Murray on *Bus Stop* (1956) and Clint Eastwood on TV's *Rawhide.* He also doubled Robert Ryan and Randolph Scott. He moved into second unit and production manager work, first on TV then on *The Wild Bunch* (1969), *The Man Who Loved Cat Dancing* (1973), and *Wind and the Lion* (1975). Rawlins died at the age of 79.

See: "Phil Rawlins Dies at 79." *Variety.* June 7, 2009; Premako, Josh. "Movie Stuntman Lives Life with His Boots On." *Signal.* April 29, 2007.

BILL RAYMOND

Los Angeles-raised Bill Raymond was a veteran of live stunt shows at Corriganville, Old Tucson, Knott's Berry Farm, and Universal Studios. Inspired by lion tamer Mel Koontz, he worked with wild animals at Africa USA in Soledad Canyon. This led to stunt jobs on *Rampage* (1963) and the TV series *Daktari* (1967–69) and *Cowboy in Africa* (1967–68). He worked on *El Dorado* (1967), as well as the TV westerns *The Virginian, Big Valley, Outcasts,* and *Alias Smith and Jones.*

See: Beck. Ken. *The Encyclopedia of TV Pets: A Complete History of Television's Greatest Animal Stars.* Thomas Nelson, 2002.

RODD REDWING (1904–1971)

Chickasaw Indian Rodd Redwing was renowned in Hollywood as one of the top gun coaches and fast-draw experts, able to draw a Colt .45 in four-tenths of a second and hit a target. He did some horse stunt work but was most often used as a hand double for quick insert shots for stars such as Alan Ladd on *Shane* (1953). He built his reputation working with pupils Burt Lancaster on *Vera Cruz* (1954) and Glenn Ford on *Fastest Gun Alive* (1956), teaching them how to be both fancy and quick for the camera. He also handled rifles, tutoring Chuck Connors on his Winchester for TV's *The Rifleman* (1958–63). Redwing was an expert with knives, tomahawks, bow and arrow, and whips, able to throw and hit or shoot any on-screen target. He was employed as a technical director whenever these skills were needed.

Redwing was born in New York City and excelled on the football field at Harron High and New York University. He came to Hollywood for *Squaw Man* (1931) and his only time off came for military service during World War II. He became popular for his live shows enacting a trick where he could throw a knife, draw and shoot his Colt, and have the knife stick in the hole made by the speeding bullet. Some of his personal appearances featured stuntman-turned-cowboy-star Jock Mahoney, who would hold up targets Redwing would hit with live ammunition. When he wasn't filming Paramount Studios gun coach Redwing was a gunsmith at Steambridge Gun Rentals.

He worked on *Gunga Din* (1939), *The Outlaw* (1943), *Objective Burma* (1945), *Duel in the Sun* (1946), *Unconquered* (1947), *Samson and Delilah* (1949), *The Gunfighter* (1950), *High Noon* (1952), *Gunfighters of the Northwest* (1954), *Cattle Queen of Montana* (1954), *Pardners* (1956), *Gun-fight at the O.K. Corral* (1957), *The Buccaneer* (1958), *From Hell to Texas* (1958), *Warlock* (1959), *Last Train from Gun Hill* (1959), *Flaming Star* (1960), *Walk Like a Dragon* (1960), *Heller in Pink Tights* (1960), *One-Eyed Jacks* (1961), *Sergeants Three* (1962), *Four for Texas* (1963), *Invitation to a Gunfighter* (1964), *Nevada Smith* (1966), *El Dorado* (1967), *Shalako* (1968), *Charro!* (1969), and *The McMasters* (1970). TV credits included *The Range Rider, Wild Bill Hickok, Kit Carson, Wyatt Earp, Gunsmoke, Bonanza, Wagon Train, Rawhide, The Virginian,* and *Mannix.* Redwing died from a heart attack at the age of 66 while returning home from Spain after working on *Red Sun* (1971).

See: Arganbright, Bob. "Rodd Redwing: Hollywood's Indian Gunfighter." *Guns of the Old West.* #30, 2002; Redwing, Rodd. "TV's Big Man: Fast Rifle." *Guns.* May 1960; Willett, Bob. "Hollywood's Shooting Star." *American Legion Magazine.* #72, 1962.

IONE REED (1910–1995)

Born in Hanford, California, early stuntwoman Ione Reed was an excellent horseback rider and acrobat. She was a leading lady in b-westerns opposite stuntman Cliff Lyons before transitioning into sound era stunt work where she doubled Claire Trevor on *Elinor Norton* (1934), Mary Maguire on *Mysterious Mr. Moto* (1938), and Maureen O'Hara on *Hunchback of Notre Dame* (1939). Reed worked on major films like *The Buccaneer* (1938) and did all kinds of stunts with lions, bears, and elephants. She specialized in auto to train transfers and runaway buckboard stunts.

Reed attained some publicity for her profession when she advertised Camel cigarettes in print ads and was featured on the radio program *Daredevils of Hollywood.* Her Hollywood life was fictionalized in a 1940 novel she co-wrote with Rose Gordon entitled *Stunt Girl,* but she was soon out of the business due to a bad reaction to movie makeup. She became a safety engineer for the Lewyt Corporation. Reed died at the age of 85.

See: Gordon, Rose & Ione Reed. *Stunt Girl.* Hollywood: G.P. Putnam, 1940; "Stunt Girl Now Teaches Safety to War Workers." *Manitowoc Herald.* May 28, 1945; "Three Seconds from Death." *Modern Mechanix.* November 1938.

MARSHALL REED (1917–1980)

Marshall Jewel Reed was born in Englewood, Colorado and spent summers wrangling horses. Upon arriving in Hollywood in 1942 he became a stuntman for Republic Studios. His biggest assignment came doubling Kane Richmond on the serial *Spy Smasher* (1942). After only a few months Reed injured his ankle taking a wagon off a cliff, causing him to rethink the profession. After time with the U.S. Navy during World War II, Reed opted not to return to full-time stunt work. His handsome profile and strapping 6'1" physique quickly elevated him to featured roles.

Despite his heroic look, Reed played many b-western heavies, working often because he could perform his own riding, fighting, and bullwhip work. He had exciting fights against cowboy hero Johnny Mack Brown on *Trailin' Danger* (1947) and *Oklahoma Justice* (1951) and brawled memorably with Lash LaRue on *Mark of the Lash* (1948). On TV he had big fights with Jock Mahoney on *The Range Rider*. He landed a starring role on the serial *Riding with Buffalo Bill* (1954), but it didn't do much for his career. Reed died at age 62 following complications from a brain tumor.

See: Jackson, Jr., Greg. "An Interview with Marshall Reed." *Serial World.* #9, 1976; Lewis, C. Jack. "Marshall Reed: Not Always the Bad Guy." *Guns of the Old West.* Spring 2009; "Marshall Reed." *Variety.* October 1, 1980.

CHARLES REGAN (1904–1977)

New York born Charles Regan boxed professionally while still in his teens and moved to the West Coast for more than seventy fights. It's likely these were fought under a different name. He was a bodyguard for actor Robert Montgomery, doubled Gregory Peck, and found employment on several Robert Mitchum RKO films. Regan worked on *The Storm* (1938), *Dick Tracy's G-Men* (1939), *Adventure* (1945), *Out of the Past* (1947), *Wild Harvest* (1947), *Mighty Joe Young* (1949), *The Thing* (1951), *Fearless Fagan* (1952), *Lone Hand* (1953), *Prince Valiant* (1954), *The Egyptian* (1954), and *20,000 Leagues Under the Sea* (1954). An honorary member of the Stuntmen's Association and an inductee of the Stuntmen's Hall of Fame, Regan died at the age of 74.

See: "Ex-Boxers Play Part in Movie." *San Diego Union.* August 3, 1947.

MIKE REID (1940–2007)

London-born Mike Reid was best known as a British TV comedian on the BBC's *EastEnders*, but he got his start as an extra and stuntman known for his driving skill on *Those Magnificent Men in Their Flying Machines* (1965), *The Dirty Dozen* (1967), *Casino Royale* (1967), *The Devil Rides Out* (1968), *Chitty Chitty Bang Bang* (1968) and the TV shows *Dr. Who, The Avengers, The Baron, The Champions,* and *The Saint,* where he doubled Roger Moore. The 6'2" former amateur boxer, coalman, and Merchant Navy veteran died of a heart attack at the age of 67. He is the subject of the documentary *The Unforgettable Mike Reid* (2010).

See: Barker, Dennis. "Mike Reid." *Guardian.* July 30, 2007; Reid, Mike. *T'rific.* London: Bantam, 1999.

JIMMY RENO (1933–)

Corriganville stuntman Jimmy Reno was born James Charles Sargeant in Corvallis, Oregon. Raised in California, the Long Beach track star doubled James Coburn on *The Magnificent Seven* (1960) and was the bandit rider taken off his horse by a noose on that film. On TV Reno doubled Earl Holliman on *Hotel De Paree* (1959–60). Between live performances he worked on the TV shows *Gunsmoke, Bonanza, Lawman, Rawhide, Wanted—Dead or Alive,* and *Tombstone Territory.* He was injured with a collapsed lung doing a saddle fall for Richard Boone on *Have Gun—Will Travel* and was unable to resume stunting.

See: Sergeant, James & Gary Thomas. *Alias Jimmy Reno: Exploits of a Western Stuntman.* Denver, CO: Outskirts, 2013.

BURT REYNOLDS (1936–)

Five-foot-nine, 175 pound Burton Leon Reynolds, Jr. was born in Waycross, Georgia, and raised in Florida. He was an excellent football player at Palm Beach High and was named All-State and All-Southern as a fullback. He played two seasons at Florida State where he was awarded All-Star Southern Conference Freshman honors. The Baltimore Colts sent a letter of interest, but Reynolds tore cartilage in his knee and was sidelined his sophomore season. Shortly after that he was involved in a car accident in which he broke

Burt Reynolds leaps onto bags of cement on *Shamus* (1973).

four ribs, punctured his kidneys and spleen, and further damaged both knees. This ended his football career.

Reynolds left Florida for New York City where he found work as a bar bouncer, truck driver, and dockworker. He worked on live TV as a stuntman, crashing through windows, falling down stairs, and getting lit on fire for the camera. For years he said he did all his own stunts as a leading man, but Hal Needham or Stan Barrett had always been on hand for the dangerous gigs. Burt did do a great deal of physical action that few actors would attempt, especially one who had reached superstar status with such popular films as *Smokey and the Bandit* (1977). He rode the rapids on *Deliverance* (1972), dove all over the screen on *Shamus* (1973), and took hits from real football players on *The Longest Yard* (1974). He demanded to be able to do his own stunts on the TV detective series *Hawk* (1966) and *Dan August* (1970–71).

The macho Reynolds excelled at movie fights with notable brawls on *Armored Command* (1961), *Operation CIA* (1965), *100 Rifles* (1969),

The Man Who Loved Cat Dancing (1973), *Nickelodeon* (1976), *Hooper* (1978), and *Sharky's Machine* (1981). On *City Heat* (1984) his jaw was broken when he was hit with a chair during a fight, leading to years of medical problems involving TMJ. Reynolds was inducted into the Stuntmen's Hall of Fame and was given a Taurus World Stunt Lifetime Achievement Award for his support of the stunt industry. His brother Jim worked as a stuntman.

See: "Burt Reynolds Stuntman Rests While Star Enjoys Taking Risks." *Joplin Globe.* July 16, 1972; Etter, Jonathan. *Quinn Martin, Producer.* Jefferson, NC: McFarland, 2008; Pack, Harvey. "Ex-Stuntman Star in Adventure Show." *Winona Daily News.* October 2, 1966; Reynolds, Burt. *My Life.* NY: Hyperion, 1994.

LOREN RIEBE (1910–1956)

North Dakota-born Loren Riebe was raised in Seattle, Washington, and took part in gymnastics at Roosevelt High. He became a vaudeville acrobat with The Three Cachalots and a trapeze artist in the circus. For the movies he enacted precision jumps and dives. He dove off a cliff into the ocean for Ray Mala on *Robinson Crusoe of Clipper Island* (1936) and jumped out a third story window to land on a canvas-topped truck for George Raft on *Each Dawn I Die* (1939). That stunt netted him $500. He doubled Bob Livingston and Jack Randall at Republic and worked as a stunt pilot on *High and the Mighty* (1954).

Credits include *Painted Stallion* (1937), *Dick Tracy* (1937), *S.O.S. Coast Guard* (1937), *Zorro Rides Again* (1937), *Gunsmoke Ranch* (1937), *Dick Tracy Returns* (1938), *The Lone Ranger* (1938), *Hawk of the Wilderness* (1938), *Daredevils of the Red Circle* (1939), *Seven Sinners* (1940), *King of the Royal Mounted* (1940), *Footlight Fever* (1941), *King of the Texas Rangers* (1941), *Adventures of Captain Marvel* (1941), *Perils of Nyoka* (1942), *Spy Smasher* (1942), *Crimson Ghost* (1946), *Angel and the Badman* (1947), *Jesse James Rides Again* (1947), *Sands of Iwo Jima* (1949), and *South Sea Sinner* (1950). An inductee of the Stuntmen's Hall of Fame, "Stunt Cousin" Riebe died in a plane crash during a Lancaster, California air show at the age of 45.

See: "A Stunter Manufactures a Movie Thrill." *Oregonian.* August 27, 1939; "Seattle Boys in Featured Act at the Orpheum." *Seattle Daily Times.* November 19, 1934; Witney, William. *In a Door, Into a Fight, Out a Door, Into a Chase.* Jefferson, NC: McFarland, 1996.

RUDY ROBBINS (1933–2011)

Rudy Robbins was born in Evergreen, Louisiana, and raised in Texas. He was a top javelin thrower in the U.S. Army and became head wrangler at the Dixie Dude Ranch in Bandera, Texas. He was originally hired as an extra on *The Alamo* (1960), but John Wayne bumped him up to a small running part as one of Davy Crockett's Tennesseans and allowed him to do horse stunts. Robbins' continued uttering of the line, "It do," made him stick in the memory of both audiences and the Duke. Robbins worked for a year as a stuntman in live shows at Bracketville's Alamo Village before obtaining more movie work on the John Ford film *Two Rode Together* (1961). This prompted Robbins to move to California and train with stuntman Lennie Geer.

He worked on *McLintock!* (1963), *Cheyenne Autumn* (1964), *The Rounders* (1965), *Adventures*

of *Bullwhip Griffin* (1967), *The Green Berets* (1968), *Rio Lobo* (1970), and *The Sugarland Express* (1974). In the mid–1960s he briefly served as the double for James Arness on TV's *Gunsmoke.* He later toured the world as the main character in the Buffalo Bill Wild West Show. Settling back in Texas he created the Rudy Robbins Western Variety Show. He was awarded a plaque of excellence from the Texas Stuntmen's Association, an organization run by his cousin Dean Dawson. Robbins died from cancer at age the age of 77.

See: Hankins, Robert. "Old West Travels to Southeast Texas." *Orange Leader.* April 4, 2002; Lilley, Tim. *Campfire Conversations Complete.* Akron, OH: Big Trail, 2010; Pannebaker, Judith. "Saying Adios to Bandera's Rudy Robbins." *Bandera Courier.* February 24, 2011.

CHUCK ROBERSON (1919–1988)

Chuck Roberson served as John Wayne's primary double for over twenty-five years, from *The Fighting Kentuckian* (1949) to *The Shootist* (1976). In that period Roberson also proved his worth as a stuntman on several of John Ford's classic films such as *The Searchers* (1956) and was often called upon to say a line or two of dialogue. He was one of Ford's favorites, christened as "Bad Chuck" due to his penchant for drinking, fighting, and womanizing. The 6'4", 225-pound Roberson was in constant demand as a horse fall specialist when westerns were at their peak. Roberson's horse Cocaine was one of the best in the business, trained to fall on a dime at Roberson's command. On *Chisum* (1970) Roberson and Cocaine memorably jumped through a plate glass window.

Charles Hugh Roberson was born in Texas and raised as a cowhand on a New Mexico ranch where he developed expert horseback skills. When he wasn't working as a cowboy, Roberson spent time as an oilfield roughneck. He served with the U.S. Army during World War II, earning a Purple Heart when he was injured in Okinawa during a kamikaze attack. Roberson happened into stunt work by chance: He was employed as a policeman in California when he encountered stuntman Fred Kennedy during a strike at Warner Brothers. Kennedy noted Roberson's resemblance to actor John Carroll and suggested he look into doubling the actor at Republic Studios. Roberson did just

Chuck Roberson and Bob Morgan double Gregory Peck and Charlton Heston for the famous fight on *The Big Country* (1958).

that, learning the ropes from Kennedy, Ben Johnson, and Allen Pomeroy. Chuck's brother Lou soon followed him into the business.

In addition to doubling John Wayne, Roberson doubled Gregory Peck on *The Big Country* (1958) and *How the West Was Won* (1962), Robert Mitchum on *The Wonderful Country* (1959), and Clark Gable on *The Misfits* (1961). He took falls for Gary Cooper, Rock Hudson, Jeff Chandler, Rory Calhoun, Burt Lancaster, Charlton Heston, Randolph Scott, Joel McCrea, Ronald Reagan, Stewart Granger, Fred MacMurray, Macdonald Carey, Van Heflin, and Robert Ryan. Roberson doubled John Payne for a unique stunt on *The Eagle and the Hawk* (1950) where he was tied between two galloping horses running the length of an open field. On *Rio Conchos* (1964) he was dragged behind a horse for Richard Boone. In addition to his skill with horses, Roberson was a solid fight man, working notable brawls with fellow stuntman Bob Morgan on *The Spoilers* (1955) and *The Big Country* (1958). Roberson played a supporting part on Sam Fuller's *Shock Corridor* (1963) and engaged star Peter Breck in a lengthy battle throughout a mental ward. On *The Sons of Katie Elder* (1965) he doubled George Kennedy and took a John Wayne axe handle to the face.

One of the true "ground-pounders" in the business, Roberson suffered a few significant injuries: He broke both of his arms in a wagon wreck on *The Baron of Arizona* (1950) and his ankle on *Hondo* (1953), and fractured his back doing a forty-foot fall from a palm tree for *Merrill's Marauders* (1962). Roberson had a flair for coordinating stunts and directing second unit action as evidenced by his work on *100 Rifles* (1969). He was also instrumental in bringing two young stuntmen into the business, Hal Needham and Terry Leonard. Both went on to become stunt legends. In 1979 Roberson published his autobiography *The Fall Guy*, detailing many behind-the-scenes stories of his work with John Wayne and John Ford.

He also worked on *Jesse James Rides Again* (1947), *Albuquerque* (1948), *The Three Musketeers* (1948), *Wake of the Red Witch* (1948), *Stampede* (1949), *Winchester '73* (1950), *Rio Grande* (1950), *The Kid from Texas* (1950), *Across the Wide Missouri* (1951), *Cattle Drive* (1951), *Battle at Apache Pass* (1952), *Lone Star* (1952), *The Lusty Men* (1952), *Way of a Gaucho* (1952), *The Naked Spur* (1953), *Gun Belt* (1953), *City of Bad Men* (1953), *The Far Country* (1955), *Sign of the Pagan* (1954), *Lone Gun* (1954), *The Prodigal* (1955), *The Tall Men* (1955), *The Rawhide Years* (1955), *Ten Wanted Men* (1955), *The Conqueror* (1956), *Seven Men from Now* (1956), *The King and Four Queens* (1956), *Red Sundown* (1956), *Thunder Over Arizona* (1956), *The Wings of Eagles* (1957), *Run of the Arrow* (1957), *Night Passage* (1957), *Forty Guns* (1957), *The Hired Gun* (1957), *Man of the West* (1958), *Fort Massacre* (1958), *Pork Chop Hill* (1959), *Timbuktu* (1959), *Rio Bravo* (1959), *Spartacus* (1960), *The Alamo* (1960), *Two Rode Together* (1961), *The Comancheros* (1961), *The Last Sunset* (1961), *The Man Who Shot Liberty Valance* (1962), *Taras Bulba* (1962), *Captain Newman, M.D.* (1963), *Savage Sam* (1963), *Donovan's Reef* (1963), *McLintock!* (1963), *Mail Order Bride* (1964), *Advance to the Rear* (1964), *Cheyenne Autumn* (1964), *Black Spurs* (1965), *The War Lord* (1965), *Cat Ballou* (1965), *The Rounders* (1965), *Nevada Smith* (1966), *El Dorado* (1967), *The War Wagon* (1967), *Camelot* (1967), *The Green Berets* (1968), *The Scalphunters* (1968), *The Undefeated* (1969), *Rio Lobo* (1970), *A Man Called Horse* (1970), *Big Jake* (1971), *The Train Robbers* (1973), *The Stone Killer* (1973), *Cahill—U.S. Marshal* (1973), *McQ* (1974), and *99 and 44/100 percent Dead* (1974). TV credits include *The Lone Ranger, Gene Autry, Roy Rogers, Have Gun—Will Travel, Wagon Train, Death Valley Days, Yancy Derringer, Rawhide, Laramie, Gunsmoke, Stoney Burke, Daniel Boone, Laredo, Lost in Space, The Big Valley,* and *Lancer.* A member of the Stuntmen's Hall of Fame, Roberson died from cancer at the age of 69.

See: "Fall Guy of Yesterday." *Sacramento Bee.* September 2, 1985; Lilley, Tim. *Campfire Conversations.* Akron, OH: Big Trail, 2007; Martin, Bryce. "Daring Rider Doubled for Movie's Duke." *Bakersfield Californian.* April 13, 1975; Roberson, Chuck, & Bodie Thoene. *The Fall Guy.* North Vancouver, BC: Hancock House, 1980; "TV Notebook." *Independent Press.* September 22, 1968; "Venturan Has Role on *Have Gun.*" *Oxnard Press Courier.* December 10, 1960.

GERALD ROBERTS (1919–2005)

Legendary rodeo cowboy Gerald Roberts hailed from Council Grove, Kansas, and joined the Clyde Miller Wild West Show at the age of thirteen. He became the two-time All-Around World Champion Cowboy in 1942 and 1948 and the North American Calgary All-Around Champion in 1950. He won sixty-seven championships over a thirty-year period, riding bulls and saddle broncs. Roberts had a side career as a Hollywood stuntman, most notably doubling Arthur Kennedy on *The Lusty Men* (1952) and Glenn Ford and Jack Lemmon on *Cowboy* (1958). He also worked on *Jubal* (1956), *Born Reckless* (1958), *Westbound* (1959), and the TV shows *Gunsmoke, Maverick,* and *Have Gun—Will Travel.* He was a member of the Pro Rodeo Hall of Fame and the Cowboy Hall of Fame, Roberts died at the age of 85.

See: "Gerald Roberts, 85, Longtime Rodeo Star." *New York Times.* January 16, 2005; "Gerald Roberts Is Movie Stunt Man and Rodeo Star." *Tucson Daily Citizen.* February 14, 1953; www.geraldroberts.com.

J.N. ROBERTS (1942–)

James Nelson Roberts was a legendary desert racer as a three-time winner of the Mint 400 and four-time champion of the Barstow to Vegas Run on his Husky. He won the Baja 500 and the Baja 1000 twice each. He represented the United States in the International Six Day Trial and was featured in the dirt bike documentary *On Any Sunday* (1971). Ironically Roberts first worked in the film industry as a carpenter and never climbed aboard a motorcycle until he was twenty-three years old.

Roberts turned heads with a cycle jump on *Suppose They Gave a War and Nobody Came* (1970) and doubled Paul Newman for motorcycle scenes on *Sometimes a Great Notion* (1970). His best known stunt work came as the pursued during chases on the Charles Bronson films *The Mechanic* (1972) and *The Stone Killer* (1973). Roberts was involved in the motorcycle chase on *Electra Glide in Blue* (1973) and was thrown into a fire on that film. Branching out from motorcycle work, Roberts became an expert at rolling over cars.

He also worked on *A Time for Dying* (1969), *Hells Angels '69* (1969), *The Undefeated* (1969), *Little Big Man* (1970), *Smokey and the Bandit* (1977), and *Hooper* (1978). TV credits include

J.N. Roberts makes a motorcycle jump on *The Mechanic* (1972).

The Dukes of Hazzard. His son Jimmy N. Roberts became a stuntman. Roberts was a member of Stunts Unlimited and an inductee of the Stuntmen's Hall of Fame, the AMA Motorcycle Hall of Fame, and the Off-Road Motorsports Hall of Fame.

See: "At 66, Motorbiker Still Racing." *Billings Gazette.* July 19, 2008.

ANN ROBINSON (1929–)

This Hollywood-born leading lady of the sci-fi classic *The War of the Worlds* (1953) got her start in Hollywood as a stuntwoman under the name Ann Robin. Although she grew up riding horses, she had to exaggerate her handiness to double June Havoc climbing over a barbed wire fence on *The Story of Molly X* (1949). She was more in her element riding for Lyn Thomas on *Black Midnight* (1949) and did all manner of stunts doubling Shelley Winters on *Frenchie* (1950). It would be the last of her stunt roles as her acting career took off at Paramount. She quit acting upon marrying matador Jaime Bravo.

See: Weaver, Tom. "Ann Robinson Remembers Johnny Carpenter." *Western Clippings.* #74, November-December 2006; Weaver, Tom. "In Martian Combat." *Starlog.* #195, 1993.

DAR ROBINSON (1947–1986)

Stunt legend Dar Allen Robinson emerged as the greatest of the new breed of stuntmen in the 1970s, uncharacteristically pushing the anonymous job of stuntman into celebrity status. Repetition of tried-and-true stunts for the camera did not interest him. He strived to challenge himself with stunts the world had never seen. Dar was an all-around athlete, but his forte was high work. With the emergence of airbags he was able to jump from heights not previously attempted, possessing an uncanny ability to control his body in the air. In the 1980s the design of a decelerator allowed him to slow his descent speed and do away with the airbag, taking his jumps even further. A supreme combination of meticulous preparation and physical skill, his stunts were showcased on

Doubling David Soul, Dar Robinson jumps a motorcycle off a ship on *Magnum Force* (1973).

the popular TV shows *Super Stunt* and *That's Incredible.*

His stunt work for the movies is most impressive beginning with a hundred-foot cliff jump into rugged surf at Keanae, Hawaii, for Steve McQueen on *Papillon* (1973). The same year saw him double David Soul driving a motorcycle forty-five feet off an aircraft carrier at thirty-five miles per hour on *Magnum Force* (1973). On *Highpoint* (1979) he jumped 1,100 feet off the CN Tower in Toronto for Christopher Plummer, opening his parachute at the last possible moment. The following year he went off the tower again without a chute to prove his decelerator could handle such a leap. He fell off a cable car for Rutger Hauer on *Nighthawks* (1981), made a 150-foot jump doubling Henry Silva on *Sharky's Machine* (1981), took a twenty-two–story fall while emptying a gun at Burt Reynolds on *Stick* (1985), jumped off a bridge for William Peterson on *To Live and Die in L.A.* (1985), and made a two-man high jump on *Lethal Weapon* (1987).

Five-foot-eleven, 170-pound Dar Allen Robinson was born in Los Angeles. His dad Jess Robinson owned a trampoline center in Burbank that was frequented by top gymnasts and stuntmen. At a young age Dar began training with stuntmen Bob Yerkes and Loren Janes, who gave him his first professional job. In addition to being a champion gymnast, Dar was a high school football star and scuba expert who owned a salvage diving business. He set several world records and created amazing stunts such as jumping on a trampoline suspended from a helicopter 400 feet above the earth, driving a car out of a cargo plane, transferring from one airplane to another in a freefall dive, and driving a car off the Grand Canyon.

Robinson, who never broke a bone doing stunt work, died from a lacerated liver following a freak accident on *Million Dollar Mystery* (1987). He was doing a routine motorcycle pass by the camera and somehow lost control in a turn and flew off the road into rugged terrain. The remote location near Page, Arizona, prevented him from getting emergency treatment and he died on the way to the nearest medical facility.

He also worked on *Star!* (1968), *Paint Your Wagon* (1969), *The Towering Inferno* (1974), *Rollerball* (1975), *Doc Savage* (1975), *Burnt Offerings* (1976), *St. Ives* (1976), *Silent Movie* (1976), *Logan's Run* (1976), *Stunts* (1977), *Airport '77* (1977), *F.I.S.T.* (1978), *The Manitou* (1978), *Paradise Alley* (1978), *Concorde, Airport '79* (1979), and *Stunt Seven* (1979). TV credits include *The FBI, Columbo, Harry O, The Rockford Files, CHiPs,* and the TV movie *Smile Jenny, You're Dead* (1974) where he made a twelve-story leap off a building for Zalman King. He was a member of the Stuntmen's Association and an inductee of the Stuntmen's Hall of Fame and the World Acrobatic Hall of Fame. His sons Troy and Shawn became stuntmen. He is the subject of the documentary *The Ultimate Stuntman* (1987).

See: "Dar Robinson." *Variety.* November 26, 1986; Gorney, Cynthia. "Death of an Illusion." *Milwaukee Journal.* March 28, 1987; Grogan, David. "Death Cheats the King of Movie Daredevils, Dar Robinson." *People.* December 15, 1986; Hagner, John. "Dar Robinson." *Falling for Stars.* July-August 1974; Henry, George. "Dar Robinson: The Ultimate Stuntman." *Inside Stunts.* Spring, 2007; Williams, Tom. "Just Drop in Sometime." *Dallas Morning News.* May 1, 1976.

DOUG ROBINSON (1930–)

Douglas Bowbank Robinson was born in Newcastle, England, and raised in South Africa. He and his older brother Joe were trained in grappling and judo. Doug took on the physique of a bodybuilder while performing professionally in the wrestling ring. After a stint in the Army, he began appearing in films and working as a martial arts instructor. He gained acclaim with his brother as fight coordinators on the popular TV series *The Avengers* (1961–69). They co-authored *Honor Blackman's Book of Self Defence.*

Robinson acted in *Jason and the Argonauts* (1963) but never tackled leads like his brother. He was more content to wreck a motorcycle on *Where Eagles Dare* (1968). He doubled Kirk Douglas on *Catch a Spy* (1971), Doug McClure on *Land That Time Forgot* (1975), Robert Mitchum on *The Big Sleep* (1978), and Telly Savalas on *Escape to Athena* (1979). He appeared with regularity in the James Bond series, working on *Casino Royale* (1967), *You Only Live Twice* (1967), *Diamonds Are Forever* (1971), *Live and Let Die* (1973), *Man with the Golden Gun* (1974), *The Spy Who Loved Me* (1977), *For Your Eyes Only* (1981), *Never Say Never Again* (1983), and *A View to a Kill* (1985), where he executed a stair fall.

He also worked on *Ben-Hur* (1959), *Girl Hunters* (1963), *Deadlier Than the Male* (1966),

Attack on the Iron Coast (1968), *Cromwell* (1970), *The Mackintosh Man* (1973), *Callan* (1974), *Brannigan* (1975), *A Bridge Too Far* (1977), *Superman* (1978), *Revenge of the Pink Panther* (1978), *Zulu Dawn* (1979), *The Empire Strikes Back* (1980), *Superman II* (1980), and *Indiana Jones and the Temple of Doom* (1984). His TV credits include *The Persuaders* and *Space 1999.*

See: Fort, Hugh. "From Hollywood to Bracknell Stuntman Reveals All." *Get Bracknell.* May 4, 2012; www.bondpix.com.

ERNEST ROBINSON (1941–)

Ernie Robinson lettered in basketball, baseball, football, track, and gymnastics at high school in Indianapolis. In the late 1960s he left a job in the aerospace industry to become a member and eventual president of the Black Stuntmen's Association. It was a fortuitous move given the deluge of black action films that soon flooded cinemas. Robinson's best known assignment was as one of the bank robbers shot by Clint Eastwood in the beginning of *Dirty Harry* (1971). He doubled Billy Dee Williams on *Lady Sings the Blues* (1972).

He also worked on *Hello, Dolly!* (1969), *Halls of Anger* (1970), *Skin Game* (1971), *Blacula* (1972), *What's Up, Doc?* (1972), *Cleopatra Jones* (1973), *The Spook Who Sat By the Door* (1973), *Black Samson* (1974), *Earthquake* (1974), *The Killer Elite* (1975), *The Gumball Rally* (1976), *Drum* (1976), *Dr. Black, Mr. Hyde* (1976), *Swashbuckler* (1976), *Thank God It's Friday* (1978), and *The Dark* (1979). While doubling Philip Michael Thomas on TV's *Miami Vice*, Robinson was injured by an explosion on the show, ending his stunt career.

See: "Black Stunt Men." *Ebony.* December 1969; "Movie Stuntmen Like Life Rough." *Augusta Chronicle.* June 13, 1971; Ortiz, Sergio. "Black Stuntmen Shatter Filmdom's Race Barrier." *Fighting Stars.* February 1974.

WALT ROBLES (1938–)

Walter P. Robles was born in New York City. After serving in the Air Force, he intended to become a commercial pilot. A chance meeting led to stunt work at Corriganville in the late 1950s, a wrangling job at the Spahn Ranch, and participation in rodeo events with the Cavalcade of Wheels Wild West Show. The six-foot, 185-pound Robles

worked as a grip, electrician, special effects man, and stunt performer on the independent productions *Born Losers* (1967), *Hells Angels on Wheels* (1967), *Savage Seven* (1968), and *Fabulous Bastard from Chicago* (1969), eventually sustaining himself as a stuntman. His biggest stunt involved jumping into the Colorado River off a wrecking ball suspended by a helicopter on *Choke Canyon* (1986). He doubled King Moody for Ronald McDonald commercials in the 1970s and Christopher Lloyd on *Butch and Sundance* (1979).

He also worked on *The Towering Inferno* (1974), *Apple Dumpling Gang* (1975), *Crazy Mama* (1975), *Two-Minute Warning* (1976), *Logan's Run* (1976), *Airport '77* (1977), *MacArthur* (1977), *Capricorn One* (1978), *The Cat from Outer Space* (1978), *Lord of the Rings* (1978), *Delta Fox* (1978), *1941* (1979), *The Last Word* (1979), *Concorde, Airport '79* (1979), *Stunt Seven* (1979), *The Stunt Man* (1980), *Heaven's Gate* (1980), and *Any Which Way You Can* (1980). TV credits include *The Six Million Dollar Man, Happy Days,* and *Hawaii Five-O.* Robles is a member of the Stuntmen's Association.

See: Kent, Gary. *Shadows and Light: Journeys with Outlaws in Revolutionary Hollywood.* Austin, Texas: Dalton, 2009; Sacks, Janine. "Stunt Man, 30 Year Veteran Says Simplest-Looking Actions Are the Hardest." *Daily News.* July 27, 1988.

GEORGE ROBOTHAM (1921–2007)

Six-foot-two, 190-pound George Robotham was born in Sacramento, California. After a storied high school career at Redwood City's Sequoia High, he became a star football player for San Mateo Junior College. He transferred to UCLA and participated in the 1942 Rose Bowl. During World War II Robotham served with the Marines. He opened his own salvage diving business and returned to the gridiron representing UCLA at the 1946 East-West Shrine All-Star Game as an end. The Philadelphia Eagles drafted him but he began working as a stuntman through diving student Paul Stader. Robotham did play semi-pro football for the Los Angeles Bulldogs, winners of the 1947 Pacific Coast Title.

Robotham was best known for fight scenes, doubling Clark Gable on *Lone Star* (1952), Robert Mitchum on *Second Chance* (1953) and *Cape Fear* (1962), Anthony Quinn on *City Beneath the Sea*

(1953), and Stewart Granger on *North to Alaska* (1960). He performed a high fall into a fire pit on *The Prodigal* (1955), doubled Dick Shawn on *It's a Mad, Mad, Mad, Mad World* (1963), drove a Cadillac convertible off a pier on *What's Up, Doc?* (1972), and subbed for John Wayne on *Rooster Cogburn* (1975). Robotham doubled Kirk Alyn as the caped crusader on *Atom Man vs. Superman* (1950) and Denny Miller as the King of the Jungle on *Tarzan, the Ape Man* (1959). On TV he doubled Craig Stevens on *Peter Gunn* (1958–61), David Hedison on *Voyage to the Bottom of the Sea* (1964–68), and Rock Hudson on *McMillan & Wife* (1971–77). He was Hudson's chief stuntman for over twenty-five years and also doubled Rory Calhoun, Steve Cochran, and Kent Taylor. He had a starring role on the exploitation film *Mermaids of Tiburon* (1962) using the pseudonym George Rowe. His son John is a stuntman.

He also worked on *Batman* (1943), *Joan of Arc* (1948), *Adventures of Sir Galahad* (1949), *The Robe* (1953), *Seven Brides for Seven Brothers* (1954), *20,000 Leagues Under the Sea* (1954), *Prince Valiant* (1954), *The Egyptian* (1954), *Many Rivers to Cross* (1955), *Guys and Dolls* (1955), *The Ten Commandments* (1956), *The Mole People* (1956), *The Great Locomotive Chase* (1956), *The Deerslayer* (1957), *The Garment Jungle* (1957), *Twilight for the Gods* (1958), *Warlock* (1959), *Spartacus* (1960), *The Last Sunset* (1961), *The Spiral Road* (1962), *Confessions of an Opium Eater* (1962), *The Ugly American* (1963), *The Great Race* (1965), *The Glory Guys* (1965), *Blindfold* (1965), *Gunn* (1967), *Tobruk* (1967), *5 Card Stud* (1968), *The Split* (1968), *The Undefeated* (1969), *Hornet's Nest* (1970), *Darling Lili* (1970), *Diamonds Are Forever* (1971), *The Poseidon Adventure* (1972), *Charley Varrick* (1973), *The Don Is Dead* (1973), *Showdown* (1973), *Magnum Force* (1973), *Cleopatra Jones* (1973), *The Towering Inferno* (1974), *99 and 44/100 percent Dead* (1974), *The Manitou* (1978), *Meteor* (1979), *1941* (1979), and *Prisoner of Zenda* (1979). TV credits include *Zane Grey, Northwest Passage, Sea Hunt, Mr. Lucky, The Rifleman, Surfside 6, The Outer Limits, Laredo, Daniel Boone, Batman, The Green Hornet, Land of the Giants, The Time Tunnel, The Invaders, Felony Squad, It Takes a Thief, Mannix, Alias Smith and Jones, Planet of the Apes, The Rockford Files,* and *Wonder Woman.* A member of the Stuntmen's Association and the Stuntmen's

Hall of Fame, Robotham died of complications from Alzheimer's Disease at the age of 86.

See: Hagner, John. *Falling for Stars.* El Jon, 1964; Scott, Vernon. "Double Finds Little Danger in Stunt Work." *Herald Examiner.* July 28, 1972; Silden, Isobel. "Stuntmen Are Daring Heroes, Unsung and Unknown." *Milwaukee Journal.* September 11, 1973; Thomas, Bob. "Film Stunt Men Claim Business Not Up to Par." *Kerrville Daily Times.* May 1, 1952.

RONNIE RONDELL, JR.
(1937–)

Ronnie Rondell, Jr., earned a reputation as one of the top all-around stuntmen in the business. He was born in Los Angeles; his father was an assistant director and former stuntman. The young Rondell played all the major sports at North Hollywood High, excelling in gymnastics and on the swim team as a three-meter diver. Upon graduation Rondell entered the Navy, where he specialized in mine force demolition and the new sport of scuba diving. When he got out of the Navy he worked in construction.

While working as an extra the 5'10", 170-pound Rondell was performing gymnastic tumbles on the set of a western and impressed Lennie Geer, who began training him in fights, falls, and horseback riding. He got his big break when Paul Baxley hired him to double Paul Picerni for a fight on *The Deep Six* (1958). Another early assignment came doubling David Janssen on the TV series *Richard Diamond* (1957–59). Rondell threw his body around with such gusto that stuntmen began to hire him with regularity. He worked often at Universal Studios with Hal Needham. Rondell doubled Robert Horton on *Wagon Train*, Burt Reynolds on *Riverboat*, Robert Fuller on *Laramie*, Doug McClure on *The Virginian*, and Neville Brand on *Laredo*. He doubled Michael Cole on *Mod Squad* (1968–73) and subsequently worked as the stunt coordinator on all of producer Aaron Spelling's shows, including *The Rookies, S.W.A.T., Charlie's Angels, Fantasy Island, Vega$,* and *Hart to Hart.* He spent three years doubling Robert Blake on *Baretta* (1975–78).

Rondell added many wrinkles to traditional stunts with the precise coordination of his body in the air. He became a high fall artist after working on *Kings of the Sun* (1963) in Mexico. On that he performed what many rank one of the greatest

Ronnie Rondell balances atop a fiery pole prior to taking a high fall on *Kings of the Sun* (1963).

stunts ever, a leap off a fiery forty-five–foot pole into a thatched hut that becomes engulfed in flame. He was one of the first to add mini-trampolines, enabling him to vault from the ground and twist his body during battle scene explosions. He did a flying front flip with a half twist over a cannon on *Shenandoah* (1965). He helped perfect fire suits and did full burns on *The War Lord* (1965) and *Ice Station Zebra* (1968). In the 1970s he coordinated the first cannon roll on *McQ* (1974). In 1970 he broke away from the Stuntmen's Association and created Stunts Unlimited with Hal Needham and Glenn Wilder. His sons Reid and R.A. followed him into the industry. Reid died in the early 1980s in a helicopter crash while working on the TV series *Airwolf*.

He worked on *The Wings of Eagles* (1957), *The Enemy Below* (1957), *The Naked and the Dead* (1958), *Pork Chop Hill* (1959), *Spartacus* (1960), *Captain Newman, M.D.* (1963), *4 for Texas* (1963), *The Great Race* (1965), *Dr. Goldfoot and the Bikini Machine* (1965), *The Rare Breed* (1965),

The Glory Guys (1965), *Grand Prix* (1966), *What Did You Do in the War, Daddy?* (1966), *Tobruk* (1967), *The King's Pirate* (1967), *Counterpoint* (1968), *The Mini-Skirt Mob* (1968), *Hellfighters* (1968), *The Love Bug* (1968), *Che!* (1969), *Diamonds Are Forever* (1971), *Black Gunn* (1972), *Electra Glide in Blue* (1973), *The Front Page* (1974), *Busting* (1974), *Blazing Saddles* (1974), *Night Moves* (1975), *Hooper* (1978), and *Delta Fox* (1978). TV credits include *Mission: Impossible, Dragnet, Adam–12, Young Rebels, The Immortal,* and *Kolchak: The Night Stalker*. Rondell has been inducted into the Stuntmen's Hall of Fame and received a World Taurus Lifetime Achievement Award.

See: Conley, Kevin. *The Full Burn*. Bloomsbury, 2008; Fox, Charles. "Falls, Fractures, & Fortunes." *True*. January 1971; Libby, Bill. "Dying ... It's a Living." *Argosy*. 1967; Lilley, Tim. *Campfire Conversations Complete*. Akron, OH: Big Trail, 2010; Ross, John. *Inside Stunts*. "Ronnie Rondell: I Wanna Be a Stuntman." Summer, 2005.

BUDDY ROOSEVELT (1898–1973)

Colorado-born Kent Sanderson honed his horseback skills in rodeos and the C.B. Irwin Wild West show. According to publicity he spent time as a miner, ranch hand, and lumberjack. He doubled William S. Hart for $22 a week on *Hell's Hinges* (1916) before serving with the Navy at the end of World War I, where he survived the sinking of the U.S.S. *Norfolk*. Upon returning to Hollywood he doubled Rudolph Valentino on *The Sheik* (1921) and William Desmond on *Beasts of Paradise* (1923). These assignments led to a name change and over two dozen starring roles as cowboy star Buddy Roosevelt beginning with *Rough Ridin'* (1924).

He was replaced by Warner Baxter as the Cisco Kid for *In Old Arizona* (1929) after Roosevelt injured his leg and was forced to return to doubling for Marion Davies' riding scenes on *Operator 13* (1933). He became a longtime stand-in for Ronald Colman and took many bits and horseback assignments. After Coast Guard service during World War II, he worked on a number of Randolph Scott films during the 1940s and 1950s, suggesting that Scott was using the former star as a riding double or stand-in. He worked on *Stagecoach* (1939), *Abilene Town* (1946), *Colt .45* (1950), and *Fort Worth* (1951).

See: Rainey, Buck. *Heroes of the Range.* World of Yesterday, 1987; Russell, Bill. "Buddy Roosevelt." *Western Clippings.* #29, May-June 1999.

BOBBY ROSE (1901–1993)

Bobby Rose was born in Tennessee and raised in Texas. He was working as a jockey when he was discovered by Eddie Polo and put into films. Rose doubled Ruth Roland in a serial at age fourteen and was soon racing motorcycles and performing high dives. Five-foot-seven, 140 pound Rose doubled Tom Mix, Buck Jones, Harry Houdini, Eddie Cantor, William Gargan, Ben Turpin, Chico Marx, Mary Pickford, Maureen O'Sullivan, Fay Wray, and Buster Keaton in a stunt career that spanned six decades. He performed the first transfers to a plane off motorcycles, autos, boats, and horses and also walked on the wings of planes in flight. Rose wrote the story and was featured in the film *Lucky Devils* (1932), about the lives of stuntmen.

Known as a top all-around stuntman, Rose survived an era that saw many of his brethren perish attempting death-defying feats. Rose was one of the only stuntmen who didn't perish in the icy rapids of the Copper River when filming *The Trail of '98* (1928). On *Strike Me Pink* (1936) he jumped off a rollercoaster. Rose was badly injured in a deadly plane crash with Paul Mantz on *Flight of the Phoenix* (1965). Three months later he returned to the set and completed the stunt successfully. Later that year he was doubling Larry Fine of the Three Stooges on *The Outlaws Is Coming* (1965).

He also worked on *King Kong* (1933), *She* (1935), *Thank You, Jeeves* (1936), *The Hurricane* (1937), *Slave Ship* (1937), *Ali Baba Goes to Town* (1937), *Mysterious Mr. Moto* (1938), *The Rains Came* (1939), *Seven Sinners* (1940), *Saratoga Trunk* (1945), *Fort Apache* (1948), *She Wore a Yellow Ribbon* (1949), *Rio Grande* (1950), *The Quiet Man* (1952), *Attack* (1956), *The Alamo* (1960), *Guns of the Timberland* (1960), and *The Great Race* (1965). Rose was featured on the 1938 radio program *Daredevils of Hollywood.* He was a founding member of the Stuntmen's Association and an inductee of the Stuntmen's Hall of Fame.

See: Hagner, John. *Bob Rose: The Nerviest Stuntman Ever.* Self, 1994; Lilley, Tim. *Campfire Conversations Complete.* Akron, OH: Big Trail, 2010; Rawles, Wallace N. "Hollywood's Daring Stunt Man Tells of Fight in Air Which Gave Him His Biggest Thrill." *Tyrone Daily Herald.* December 14, 1932.

WALLY ROSE (1911–2000)

Five-foot-ten, 145-pound Wally Rose was born in New York City. The wiry pugilist worked on over 600 films, often cast as comic relief on Columbia comedy shorts. Somewhat limited in his abilities, he avoided western work altogether. He doubled Robert Shayne as the monster on *The Neanderthal Man* (1953), and on the side worked as a boxing trainer, promoter, and ringside cutman. Rose was erroneously reported to be injured in the plane crash that killed Paul Mantz on *Flight of the Phoenix* (1965), but it was Bobby Rose. In the twilight of his career he had plans to be listed in the Guinness Book of Records as the oldest working stuntman.

Credits include *Hawk of the Wilderness* (1938), *Brute Force* (1947), *The Killing* (1956),

Zombies of Mora Tau (1957), *The Tijuana Story* (1957), *Spartacus* (1960), *It's a Mad, Mad, Mad, Mad World* (1963), *Donovan's Reef* (1963), *The Comedy of Terrors* (1963), *The Great Race* (1965), *Batman* (1966), *Not with My Wife You Don't* (1966), *Camelot* (1967), *The Wrecking Crew* (1969), *The Undefeated* (1969), *Che!* (1969), *Flap* (1970), *Diamonds Are Forever* (1971), *Conquest of the Planet of the Apes* (1972), *What's Up, Doc?* (1972), *The Poseidon Adventure* (1972), *Battle for the Planet of the Apes* (1973), *Cleopatra Jones* (1973), *The Don Is Dead* (1973), *The Front Page* (1974), *Blazing Saddles* (1974), *Day of the Locust* (1975), and *Zero to Sixty* (1978). He was stunt coordinator on the TV series *The Californians* (1957–59). A founding member of the Stuntmen's Association and an inductee of the Stuntmen's Hall of Fame, Rose died from cancer at the age of 88.

See: "Empty Saddles." *Western Clippings.* #35, May-June 2000.

RONNIE C. ROSS (1936–2009)

Born in Halifax, Nova Scotia, and raised in Hollywood, Ronald Clark Ross began a 100-film stunt career in the late 1960s. He was known for his car crashes on Roger Corman films such as the action-packed *Eat My Dust* (1976). He owned that film's Camaro and rented stunt vehicles out to the film industry. He doubled William Shatner on the *Star Trek* TV series and worked on *The Green Berets* (1968), *The Losers* (1970), *Cleopatra Jones* (1973), *Gone in Sixty Seconds* (1974), *Earthquake* (1974), *Death Race 2000* (1975), *Joyride to Nowhere* (1977), *Zero to Sixty* (1978), and *Smokey and the Bandit 2* (1980). TV action included *The Rat Patrol, The FBI,* and *The Rockford Files.* Ross died from lung cancer at the age of 73.

See: Barnes, Mike. "Veteran Stuntman Ronald Ross Dies." *Hollywood Reporter.* September 18, 2009; Hinnan, Catherine. "Shooting on a Shoe String." *Orlando Sentinel.* July 23, 1989; Hotz, Amy. "Ross Helped Blaze Local Film Trail." *Star News.* September 30, 2009.

REX ROSSI (1919–2007)

Kentucky-born Rex Rossi, son of rodeo cowboy Joe Rossi, began performing at age four, eventually working with the Clyde Beatty Circus and the Tom Mix Wild West Show. A world champion in trick roping and riding, he became Bob Steele's riding double in 1938 and worked on all of his B-westerns. He also doubled for Roy Rogers, Hoot Gibson, and Dennis Morgan. Among his 300 films, Rossi worked on *Gone with the Wind* (1939), *The Mark of Zorro* (1940), and *The Three Musketeers* (1948). TV credits include *Bonanza* and *Rawhide.* He continued to perform at venues such as Madison Square Garden and the Boston Garden with his wife Wanda, a former stunt girl. He was an inductee of the Stuntmen's Hall of Fame.

See: Watson, Becky. "Stunt Rider." *Ocala Star-Banner.* November 22, 1982.

MATTY ROUBERT (1907–1973)

New York City-born Matty Roubert went from being the much heralded "Universal Boy" child star to anonymous B-western stuntman during the course of his nearly forty-year career. The pint-sized Roubert played henchies named Pee Wee and doubled for Don "Red" Barry, Bob Steele, Lash LaRue, Smiley Burnette, and Dub Taylor on horseback stunts. He worked on *Adventures of Red Ryder* (1940), *Texas* (1941), *Law of the Lash* (1947), *The Dalton Gang* (1949), and *I Shot Billy the Kid* (1950).

FROSTY ROYCE (1910–1965)

Oklahoma-born Forest Lee Royse is best known as the double for William Boyd on the later Hopalong Cassidy films. He accumulated nearly 1000 stunts during a career that lasted just shy of thirty years, including doubling Kirk Douglas for a horse fall on *Along the Great Divide* (1951). He trained falling horses and performed stunts on *Colorado Territory* (1949), *Texas Rangers* (1951), *Desert Legion* (1953), *Column South* (1953), *Broken Lance* (1954), *Riding Shotgun* (1954), *The Man from Laramie* (1955), *Around the World in Eighty Days* (1956), *Spartacus* (1960), the TV series *The Cisco Kid,* and many B-westerns. Royce died from a heart attack at the age of 54.

See: "Forest Royce." *Variety.* May 26, 1965.

LORETTA RUSH (1906–1972)

Chicago-born Loretta Rush won the junior national breast stroke championship and captured many aquatic titles living in the Panama Canal region where her father worked construction. She became a champion long-distance swimmer and diver for the Ambassador Club of Los Angeles and was first recruited by Hollywood to be shot through a submarine tube for $15. Diving stunts became her specialty; she charged $1 a foot. Rush was an expert on skates as evidenced by her work for Virginia Bruce on *There Goes My Heart* (1938) and even cracked a whip on skates for Irene Dunne on *Joy of Living* (1938).

Rush dove a hundred feet off a mountain into river rapids for Ann Little on *Eagle's Talons* (1923) and dove into flaming oil for Anna Q. Nilsson on *Flowing Gold* (1924). She doubled Shirley Mason on *Eleventh Hour* (1923), Fay Wray on *King Kong* (1933), and Jean Harlow on *China Seas* (1935). She also doubled Mary Pickford and worked on *Call of the Wild* (1935). Rush was injured in a car rollover with Gordon Carveth on *Footloose Heiress* (1937); fellow stuntwoman Marcella Arnold was killed with a broken neck.

See: "Doubles Risk Lives Daily for Pictures." *Morning Star.* July 2, 1925; "Filmland's Fatalists." *Oakland Tribune.* August 9, 1936; King, Walter. "Hollywood Is Full of People Who Earn Livings in Many Goofy Ways." *Ogden Standard Examiner.* August 18, 1947.

PADDY RYAN (1904–1990)

English stuntman Paddy Ryan performed one of the industry's best known stunts, a spectacular high fall off a castle into an eight-foot-deep moat on *Ivanhoe* (1952). On *Prize of Gold* (1955) he made another great dive into the Pool of London. Throughout the 1960s Ryan was the head stuntman at Britain's MGM studios. The 5'8" Ryan was born Frank Ryan McCree Singletary and began doing stunts in the late 1920s. During World War II he served in the Desert Rats. Considered the father of English stuntmen, Ryan created the British Stunt Register.

He also worked on *Captain Boycott* (1947), *Sword and the Rose* (1953), *Rob Roy* (1953), *Red Beret* (1953), *Hell Below Zero* (1954), *Helen of Troy* (1955), *Ben-Hur* (1959), *Sword of Sherwood Forest* (1960), and *You Only Live Twice* (1967). TV credits include *Adventures of Robin Hood, Richard the Lionheart, The Avengers,* and *The Persuaders.*

BILL RYUSAKI (1937–)

Bill Mutsoto Ryusaki was born in Kamuela, Hawaii, of Japanese descent. A black belt in judo, shotokan karate, aikido, and kajukenbo kenpo, Ryusaki began teaching fighting arts at Oregon State University. He taught hand-to-hand combat with the U.S. Army and formed the Ryu-dojo school of self-defense. As a stuntman he toured live western stunt shows portraying an Indian. He worked on *The Naked and the Dead* (1958), *Pork Chop Hill* (1959), *Taras Bulba* (1962), *The President's Analyst* (1967), *Planet of the Apes* (1968), *The Wrecking Crew* (1969), *Marooned* (1969), and *Golden Needles* (1974). TV credits include *77 Sunset Strip, Hawaiian Eye, Surfside 6, The Wild Wild West, The Green Hornet, Hawaii Five-O, Mannix,* and *Kung Fu.*

See: Shepherd, Dan. "Lights, Camera, Spinning Wheel Kick." *Fighting Stars.* August 1974;

EDDIE SAENZ (1927–1971)

Edwin Matthew Saenz grew up amidst a family of Culver City, California, boxers but distinguished himself in football. He was a well-known halfback at Loyola and USC. In 1943 he had an eighty-six–yard run from scrimmage and was the star of the 1944 Rose Bowl. Saenz served in the Navy during World War II and played pro football for the Washington Redskins. He was considered the most dangerous return man in the league until injuries cut his career short. As a stuntman the 5'11", 170-pound Saenz doubled Charles Bronson on the TV series *Man with a Camera* (1958–60). On film he doubled Tyrone Power, Steve Cochran, and Anthony Quinn.

He worked on *Saturday's Hero* (1951), *Prince Valiant* (1954), *Guys and Dolls* (1955), *The Killing* (1956), *The Buccaneer* (1958), *Tarzan's Fight for Life* (1958), *Pork Chop Hill* (1959), and *The St. Valentine's Day Massacre* (1967). TV credits include *Mike Hammer, Peter Gunn,* and *Batman.* He was the chief stuntman on the TV series *Sheriff of Cochise* (1956–58) and *U.S. Marshal* (1958–60). Star John Bromfield worked the show's fight scenes with Saenz, doubling guest stars since they had been football teammates at Venice High. He was an inductee of the Stuntmen's Hall of Fame.

See: Longoria, Mario. *Athlete's Remembered: Mexican/Latino Professional Football Players.* Tempe, AZ: Bilingual, 1997. Wilson, Earl. "No

One Doubles for Bromfield." *Plain Dealer.* January 25, 1959.

AL ST. JOHN (1892–1963)

Wiry acrobat Alfred St. John was born in Santa Ana, California. He started at Mack Sennett's studios as a rubber-limbed stuntman, appearing in the Keystone Cops series and opposite Fatty Arbuckle in comedy shorts. St. John was known for his ability on unicycles and bicycles and for agile leaps. He later became a bearded B-western sidekick under the name Fuzzy St. John, appearing often with Bob Steele and Buster Crabbe and still performing pratfalls and comic fights into the 1950s. In all he made over 300 films. St. John died from a heart attack at the age of 70.

BILL SAITO (1936–2012)

Japanese-American William Hiroshi Saito was born in Oklahoma City, Oklahoma. A veteran of the U.S. Army Reserve, he was a wrestling and judo champion while attending UCLA and became a martial arts sensei. As a stuntman and character actor, Saito took part in screen fights with Steve McQueen on *The Sand Pebbles* (1966), Dean Martin on *The Wrecking Crew* (1969), and Robert Mitchum on *The Yakuza* (1975). He was the truck driver who demolishes Jackie Gleason's car door on *Smokey and the Bandit* (1977).

He worked on *The Crimson Kimono* (1959), *Battle of the Coral Sea* (1959), *Green Mansions* (1959), *War Hunt* (1962), *The President's Analyst* (1967), *Too Late the Hero* (1970), *That Man Bolt* (1973), *Airport '75* (1974), *Midway* (1976), and *Rollercoaster* (1977). TV credits include *Hawaiian Eye, Mission: Impossible, Get Smart, Hawaii Five-O, Kung Fu, The Six Million Dollar Man,* and *A Man Called Sloane.* Saito died at the age of 75.

PAUL SALATA (1926–)

Paul Thomas Salata was born in Los Angeles. After a distinguished All-City amateur career as a football player and track athlete at Benjamin Franklin High, he became a solid football end at USC. Salata served with the Army Air Corps in World War II and played professionally with the Los Angeles Bulldogs, the San Francisco 49ers, the Baltimore Colts, and the Pittsburgh Steelers. In the Canadian Football League he played for the Calgary Stampeders and Ottawa Rough Riders, receiving CFL All-Star recognition in 1952.

During off-seasons the 6'2", 190-pound Salata worked on *Father Was a Fullback* (1949), *Angels in the Outfield* (1951), *Singin' in the Rain* (1952), *All the Brothers Were Valiant* (1953), *The Egyptian* (1954), *The Ten Commandments* (1956), *Omar Khayyam* (1957), *The Joker Is Wild* (1957), and *The Buccaneer* (1958). Salata gained national acclaim for handing out the Mr. Irrelevant Award yearly to the last player taken in the NFL draft.

See: Virgen, Steve. "Salata's Wonderful Life." *Los Angeles Times.* June 14, 2011.

SANDY SANDERS (1919–2002)

Sandy Sanders was born Grover S. Sanders in Hereford, Texas. After serving in World War II, he attracted Hollywood attention riding a golden palomino named Sunlight in rodeos and horse shows. He showed a flair for fight scenes as well as horse work and proved to be able to handle dialogue. Subbing for Gene Autry at Columbia, Sanders had memorable fights with heavy Jock Mahoney on *Rim of the Canyon* (1949) and *Cow Town* (1950). He was one of the leads on the sci-fi serial *Flying Disc Man from Mars* (1951). As a henchman, Sanders fought Clayton Moore on *The Lone Ranger,* Jock Mahoney on *The Range Rider,* and Gene Autry and Roy Rogers on their TV shows.

Sanders doubled Clayton Moore on *The Lone Ranger* and worked on several B-westerns and serials including *Don Daredevil Rides Again* (1951), *Cripple Creek* (1952), *Masterson of Kansas* (1954) and *Westward Ho, the Wagons!* (1956). He later taught riding and roping and owned a stable, a fallback to advancing age in the stunt business. After a fifteen-year professional hiatus he was credited with stunt work on *The Norseman* (1978). Sanders died at the age of 82.

HAROLD SANDERSON

Burly English stuntman Harold Sanderson started in the business with Jock Easton's Stunt Team and landed solid doubling jobs for American stars Victor Mature and Robert Mitchum on *Safari* (1956), *Zarak* (1956), *Hannibal* (1959), *The Angry Hills* (1959), *Night Fighters* (1959),

Man in the Middle (1963), *Ryan's Daughter* (1970), and *The Big Sleep* (1978). On the Bond film *Thunderball* (1965) he fought Sean Connery on the hydrofoil and served as Connery's double for the fight with stunt coordinator Bob Simmons. TV credits include *The Persuaders*.

DANNY SANDS (1914–1998)

Danny Sands was born in Carlsbad, New Mexico. He was discovered by film director Howard Hawks breaking horses at the race track and entered the stunt business as a horse specialist. His jumping horse was named Louie and his falling horse Chesterfield. Sands served with the Army during World War II, then doubled James Cagney on *Run for Cover* (1955) and *Tribute to a Bad Man* (1956). His best known stunts came doubling Ingrid Bergman for a turret fall on *Joan of Arc* (1948) and Cantinflas on a wagon tongue on *Around the World in Eighty Days* (1956). He also doubled Dane Clark, Lloyd Nolan, Henry Morgan, and Barbara Stanwyck.

He worked on *Arizona* (1940), *Red River* (1948), *Fort Apache* (1948), *Cavalry Scout* (1951), *Shane* (1953), *The Robe* (1953), *Bad Day at Black Rock* (1955), *The Tall Stranger* (1957), *How the West Was Won* (1962), *The Hallelujah Trail* (1965), *El Dorado* (1967), *Camelot* (1967), *Hombre* (1967), *The Undefeated* (1969), *The Wild Bunch* (1969), *Butch Cassidy and the Sundance Kid* (1969), and *Rio Lobo* (1970). He was a member of the Stuntmen's Hall of Fame.

See: Lilley, Tim. *Campfire Conversations Complete*. Akron, OH: Big Trail, 2010.

LUKE SAUCIER (1934–2008)

Mississippi-born alligator and reptile handler Luke Vardaman Saucier doubled Mike Connors on the locally shot *Swamp Women* (1956), prompting a move to California. He ran a "monster" show at the Long Beach amusement park and became a stand-in for Jock Mahoney on *Yancy Derringer* (1958–59). He is best known as the stand-in and riding double for Chuck Connors on *Ride Beyond Vengeance* (1966) and the TV shows *The Rifleman* (1958–63), *Branded* (1965–66), and *Cowboy in Africa* (1967–68). He worked for MGM, Paramount, and Warner Brothers handling reptiles.

See: Griffith, Evelyn Reid. "Giddayap, Mr. Gator." *Times Picayune*. Oct 27, 1957; www.eccentricneworleans.com.

AUDREY SAUNDERS

Five-foot-two Audrey Saunders was a dancer, swimmer, and acrobatic member of the Six DeWaynes circus outfit. As a stuntwoman she doubled Yvonne Craig on TV's *Batman* (1967–68) and Julie Andrews for a somersault on *Star!* (1968). She also worked on *Variety Girl* (1947), *The Night Has a Thousand Eyes* (1948), *Singin' in the Rain* (1952), *Million Dollar Mermaid* (1952), *Around the World in Eighty Days* (1956), *The Fastest Gun Alive* (1956), *The Big Circus* (1959), *Bonnie and Clyde* (1967), *Double Trouble* (1967), *Earthquake* (1974), *Freebie and the Bean* (1974), and *The Great Waldo Pepper* (1975). Saunders was a charter member of the Stuntwomen's Association and an inductee of the Stuntmen's Hall of Fame.

See: "Batgirl Has Become Her Own Stunt Girl." *Sandusky Register*. January 11, 1968.

RAY SAUNDERS (1922–2000)

Born in New York, Ray Saunders was the brother of stunt ace Russ Saunders and an acrobatic member of the Six DeWaynes. He and his brother were familiar figures at Muscle Beach in Santa Monica, California, performing gymnastic routines in the sand. When not touring circuses, the 5'9", 160-pound Saunders performed his tumbling as a stunt professional. He worked on *Variety Girl* (1947), *Julia Misbehaves* (1948), *The Night Has a Thousand Eyes* (1948), *Joan of Arc* (1948), *Rogues of Sherwood Forest* (1950), *Million Dollar Mermaid* (1952), *The Veils of Bagdad* (1953), *Take the High Ground* (1953), *Hell and High Water* (1954), *Dragnet* (1954), *The Fastest Gun Alive* (1956), *Around the World in Eighty Days* (1956), *The Buccaneer* (1958), *The Flying Fontaines* (1959), *Camelot* (1967), *Double Trouble* (1967), *Thoroughly Modern Millie* (1967), *Star!* (1968), *Darling Lili* (1970), and *Earthquake* (1974). He was a member of the Stuntmen's Association and an inductee of the Stuntmen's Hall of Fame.

RUSS SAUNDERS (1919–2001)

Russell Maurice Saunders was born in Winnipeg, Canada. Young Russ attended Sir Isaac

Newton School and became the Canadian National Diving and Gymnastics Champion. He was an excellent downhill skier and developed a front somersault while on one ski. Saunders traveled to California to explore diving scholarships to either USC or UCLA and fell in love with the California lifestyle. He became a legendary fixture of Santa Monica's Muscle Beach where he put on acrobatic displays. He performed with Bing Crosby's Aquacade and began working in movies as a stuntman on *The Mark of Zorro* (1940) and *Saboteur* (1942), where he made a sixty-foot jump for Robert Cummings and swam with handcuffs on.

During World War II the 5'9", 160-pound Saunders volunteered as a paratrooper with the U.S. Army but wound up assigned to the Armed Forces Aquacade in England. He officially became a U.S. citizen at the U.S. Embassy in London in 1944 and was decorated by President Truman for his work as a war correspondent in England and France. He was one of the first soldiers into Berlin. In the states he toured with an acrobatic troupe he put together with his brother Ray and resumed working in Hollywood, especially at MGM. In 1950 Saunders was chosen by artist Salvador Dali to pose for his photo "Christ of St. John" due to his perfect body proportions.

Saunders worked on over 500 pictures doubling Alan Ladd, Kirk Douglas, Burt Lancaster, Tyrone Power, Gene Kelly, Danny Kaye, Red Buttons, Lloyd Bridges, Gilbert Roland, Charles Boyer, Humphrey Bogart, and Steve McQueen. On *The Three Musketeers* (1948) he jumped across a series of roofs before swinging into a window on a ripped flag. He doubled Ladd for the famous fight on *Shane* (1953). Saunders received a badly broken arm doing a fifty-foot jump off a cliff for Richard Widmark on *Broken Lance* (1954). He could never fully straighten his arm, but that didn't stop him from continuing his gymnastics activities and teaching young students. Saunders taught judo and fencing at the Los Angeles Athletic Club. In later years he was the celebrity trainer for *Circus of the Stars*. His acrobatic partner was Paula Dell-Boelsems.

He worked on *The Great Profile* (1940), *Joan of Arc* (1948), *The Pirate* (1948), *Adventures of Don Juan* (1948), *Samson and Delilah* (1949), *The Thing from Another World* (1951), *The Greatest Show on Earth* (1952), *Singin' in the Rain* (1952), *Seven Brides for Seven Brothers* (1954), *The Rains of Ranchipur* (1955), *Around the World in Eighty Days* (1956), *The Ten Commandments* (1956), *The Buster Keaton Story* (1957), *North by Northwest* (1959), *Spartacus* (1960), *Platinum High School* (1960), *Guns of the Timberland* (1960), *Camelot* (1967), *The Poseidon Adventure* (1972), *The Towering Inferno* (1974), *Earthquake* (1974), *The Hindenburg* (1975), *Logan's Run* (1976), and *Rollercoaster* (1977). He was a member of the Stuntmen's Association and an inductee into the Stuntmen's Hall of Fame.

See: Burton, Ron. "Actor Kirk Douglas Is Film Colony's Top Judo Expert." *Terra Haute Tribune.* November 4, 1956; Campbell, Donald. "One Tough Guy." *Winnipeg Free Press.* July 28, 1989; Oliver, Myrna. "Russell Saunders; Muscle Beach Acrobat, Stunt Double." *Los Angeles Times.* June 6, 2001.

GEORGE SAWAYA (1923–2003)

Five-foot-eleven, 170-pound George C. Sawaya was born in Los Angeles and served with the Army during World War II. He entered films as a stand-in and double for character actor Charles McGraw on *The Narrow Margin* (1952). On TV he handled the same duties for Jack Webb on *Dragnet* (1952–57). Sawaya doubled Paul Mantee on *Robinson Crusoe on Mars* (1964), Warren Beatty on *Bonnie and Clyde* (1967), and Ernest Borgnine on numerous projects. Sawaya was memorable as a deformed sailor on *The Black Sleep* (1956) and as an Arab heavy on *Drums of Africa* (1963). His son Rick became a stuntman.

He also worked on *One Minute to Zero* (1952), *Desert Legion* (1953), *The Desert Song* (1953), *The Prodigal* (1955), *Everything's Ducky* (1961), *Five Weeks in a Balloon* (1962), *Batman* (1966), *The Green Berets* (1968), *The Boston Strangler* (1968), *Hello, Dolly!* (1969), *More Dead Than Alive* (1969), *Che!* (1969), *Tora! Tora! Tora!* (1970), *Beneath the Planet of the Apes* (1970), *Dirty Harry* (1971), *The Poseidon Adventure* (1972), *Magnum Force* (1973), *The Don Is Dead* (1973), *99 and 44/100 percent Dead* (1974), *Blazing Saddles* (1974), *The Four Deuces* (1975), *The Master Gunfighter* (1975), *St. Ives* (1976), *Domino Principle* (1977), and *Concorde, Airport '79* (1979). TV credits include *Restless Gun, Broken Arrow, Peter Gunn, The Rebel, Bonanza, The Man from U.N.C.L.E., Combat, Star Trek, The Wild Wild West, I Spy, Mission: Impossible, Get Smart, Batman, Mannix, The FBI, It Takes a Thief, The*

Name of the Game, Adam–12, Bearcats, Columbo, Cannon, The Streets of San Francisco, Barnaby Jones, Emergency, McMillan & Wife, The Rockford Files, Quincy, and *BJ and the Bear.* He was a member of the Stuntmen's Association and an inductee of the Stuntmen's Hall of Fame.

CARL SAXE (1910–1999)

Born in Cleveland, Ohio, Carl Saxe prepped at University School and was a star track athlete at Colgate University. He competed for the Cleveland Athletic Club and was an Olympic hopeful. He finished third in the U.S. Decathlon in 1932. Saxe doubled Jon Hall on *The Hurricane* (1937), Ralph Meeker on *Kiss Me Deadly* (1955), and Sid Caesar for a fall down a stairwell on *It's a Mad, Mad, Mad, Mad World* (1963). On TV he doubled Raymond Burr on *Ironside* (1967–75). The 6'1", 190-pound Saxe served with the Army Air Corps in World War II and specialized in fighting and swimming stunts.

He also worked on *Cleopatra* (1934), *Salute to the Marines* (1943), *O.S.S.* (1946), *Unconquered* (1947), *The Three Musketeers* (1948), *A Southern Yankee* (1948), *Samson and Delilah* (1949), *Battleground* (1949), *Armored Car Robbery* (1950), *Jim Thorpe—All American* (1951), *Operation Pacific* (1951), *Scarlet Angel* (1952), *Against All Flags* (1952), *Jalopy* (1953), *The Ten Commandments* (1956), *Omar Khayyam* (1957), *The Buccaneer* (1958), *Last Train from Gun Hill* (1959), *Night of the Quarter Moon* (1959), *Ladies Man* (1961), *Hud* (1963), *Seconds* (1966), *Wait Until Dark* (1967), *Skidoo* (1968), *The Split* (1968), *The Great Bank Robbery* (1969), *The Molly Maguires* (1970), *There Was a Crooked Man...* (1970), *Which Way to the Front?* (1970), and *What's Up, Doc?* (1972). TV credits include *Superman, Soldiers of Fortune, State Trooper, Mr. Lucky, Peter Gunn, Have Gun—Will Travel, The Rebel, T.H.E. Cat, Land of the Giants,* and *Star Trek.* He was a member of the Stuntmen's Association and an inductee of the Stuntmen's Hall of Fame.

ROY SCAMMELL (1932–)

Roy Scammell took part in gymnastics and ice hockey in his youth, turning professional skater with ice shows where he did a barrel jumping act. The former lifeguard turned high-fall specialist nightly did a twenty-foot fall onto a ban-

quet table for the 1967 play *The Four Musketeers.* He doubled Kirk Douglas on *Cast a Giant Shadow* (1965), Deborah Kerr on *Casino Royale* (1967), Michael Caine on *The Italian Job* (1969), Malcolm McDowell on *A Clockwork Orange* (1971), and Ryan O'Neal on *Barry Lyndon* (1975). He was director Stanley Kubrick's favored stunt arranger.

The 5'10", 160-pound Scammell also worked on *Psycho-Circus* (1966), *The Dirty Dozen* (1967), *Those Daring Young Men in Their Jaunty Jalopies* (1969), *Monte Carlo or Bust* (1969), *Death Wheelers* (1973), *Rollerball* (1975), *The Spy Who Loved Me* (1977), *Midnight Express* (1978), *Alien* (1979), *For Your Eyes Only* (1981), and the TV series *Doctor Who* and *Space 1999.* He is the subject of the 2013 documentary *Roy Scammell: My Life as a Stuntman.*

See: Moorhead, Rosy. "Stuntman Extraordinaire." *St. Alban's Review.* February 27, 2013.

CHARLES "RUBE" SCHAEFFER (1905–1981)

Charles Schaeffer was born in Reading, Pennsylvania, and competed as an amateur wrestler and boxer for the Los Angeles Athletic Club. He worked as a circus strongman before pursuing co-existing careers as a professional wrestler and Hollywood stuntman. The burly Schaeffer doubled Spencer Tracy on *Captains Courageous* (1937), Harry Cording on *Marshal of Mesa City* (1939), and Lee J. Cobb on *Miami Expose* (1956).

He also worked on *Cleopatra* (1934), *Mutiny on the Bounty* (1935), *Undersea Kingdom* (1936), *The Hunchback of Notre Dame* (1939), *Gunga Din* (1939), *Frenchman's Creek* (1944), *Superman* (1948), *Fortunes of Captain Blood* (1950), *The Tall Men* (1951), *Blackbeard the Pirate* (1952), *Prince Valiant* (1954), *Hell and High Water* (1954), *Pirates of Tripoli* (1955), *Around the World in Eighty Days* (1956), *The Tijuana Story* (1957), *Zombies of Mora Tau* (1957), and *Spartacus* (1960). TV credits include *Kit Carson* and *Wild Bill Hickok.*

See: Harrison, Paul. "Movie Stuntmen Get Fun Out of Misfortunes and Narrow Escapes." *Milwaukee Journal.* August 28, 1940.

FRED SCHEIWILLER (aka FRED SHAW) (1922–2001)

Fred Irving Scheiwiller was born in West New York, New Jersey. A Navy veteran, Scheiwiller was a light-heavyweight boxer prior to World War II. He showed up as a fighter on *The Harder They Fall* (1956) and became more visible on screen as he grew older and craggier. The 6'1", 200-pound Scheiwiller doubled for Jack Warden on *The Champ* (1979) and *Beyond the Poseidon Adventure* (1979) and Lionel Stander on *1941* (1979) and the TV series *Hart to Hart* (1979–84).

He also worked on *Around the World in Eighty Days* (1956), *Night of the Quarter Moon* (1959), *Psycho* (1960), *The Fiercest Heart* (1961), *It's a Mad, Mad, Mad, Mad World* (1963), *The Good Guys and the Bad Guys* (1969), *The Great Bank Robbery* (1969), *Flap* (1970), *Suppose They Gave a War and Nobody Came?* (1970), *Diamonds Are Forever* (1971), *Conquest of the Planet of the Apes* (1972), *What's Up, Doc?* (1972), *The Poseidon Adventure* (1972), *Magnum Force* (1973), *Charley Varrick* (1973), *Battle for the Planet of the Apes* (1973), *Black Samson* (1974), *Blazing Saddles* (1974), *The Towering Inferno* (1974), *Earthquake* (1974), *Mr. Majestyk* (1974), *Day of the Locust* (1975), *Black Sunday* (1977), *Hooper* (1978), *Zero to Sixty* (1978), and *Movie, Movie* (1978). TV credits include *The Man from U.N.C.L.E.*, *Laredo*, *Mod Squad*, *Harry O*, and *The Dukes of Hazzard*. He was a member of the Stuntmen's Association.

PHIL SCHUMACHER (1909–1975)

Six-foot-one, 200-plus–pound Phillip L. Schumacher was born in Rose, Minnesota. The burly military veteran doubled Broderick Crawford on *Lone Star* (1952) and Roy Barcroft on TV. He also worked on *Bataan* (1943), *Salute to the Marines* (1943), *Buffalo Bill* (1944), *They Were Expendable* (1945), *Slave Girl* (1947), *Fort Apache* (1948), *Coroner Creek* (1948), *Red Canyon* (1949), *Ambush* (1949), *Comanche Territory* (1950), *Santa Fe* (1951), *The World in His Arms* (1952), *The Lawless Breed* (1952), *Column South* (1953), *Escape from Fort Bravo* (1953), *Riding Shotgun* (1954), *Lone Gun* (1954), *The Marauders* (1955), *Around the World in Eighty Days* (1956), *The Deerslayer* (1957), *Ride Out for Revenge* (1957), *The Comancheros* (1961), *How the West Was Won* (1962), and *Duel at Diablo* (1966). TV credits include *Wyatt Earp*, *Broken Arrow*, *Zorro*, *Have*

Gun—Will Travel, *Outlaws*, *Gunsmoke*, and *The Rifleman*.

AUDREY SCOTT (1914–1973)

Missouri-born horse specialist Audrey Scott, a top-rated polo player, won the Governor's Cup of California in 1937. She doubled Greta Garbo on *Queen Christina* (1933), Marlene Dietrich on *The Scarlet Empress* (1934), Carole Lombard on *Lady by Choice* (1934), Joan Crawford on *Chained* (1934), Dolores Del Rio on *In Caliente* (1935), Jeanette MacDonald on *Rose Marie* (1936), *San Francisco* (1936), and *Bitter Sweet* (1940), Alice Brady on *In Old Chicago* (1937) and *Maryland* (1940), Bette Davis on *Jezebel* (1938), *Dark Victory* (1939), *The Bride Came C.O.D.* (1941), and *Now, Voyager* (1942), Norma Shearer on *The Women* (1939), Virginia Bruce on *The Virginian* (1946), Judith Anderson on *Pursued* (1947), Virginia Mayo on *White Heat* (1949), Gail Russell on *The Great Dan Patch* (1949), and Rosalind Russell on *Auntie Mame* (1958).

She also doubled Billie Dove, Clara Bow, Marion Davies, Binnie Barnes, Ida Lupino, and Barbara Stanwyck. Other credits include *Hangman's House* (1928), *The Furies* (1930), *The Squaw Man* (1931), *Thirteen Women* (1932), *Suez* (1938) *The Moon Is Down* (1941), *Buffalo Bill* (1944), *Murder, He Says* (1945), *Black Beauty* (1946), *Frontier Gal* (1946), *The Foxes of Harrow* (1947), *Stallion Road* (1947), *South of St. Louis* (1949), and *The Man from the Alamo* (1953). She published her autobiography in 1969. She was a member of the Stuntmen's Hall of Fame.

See: Scott, Audrey. *I Was a Hollywood Stunt Girl*. Philadelphia, PN: Dorrance,1969.

WALTER SCOTT (1940–)

Walter Edward Scott was born in Blythe, California. He won four junior rodeos and was an excellent football player at Palo Verde High, earning recognition as a Riverside County All-Star. In Hollywood the 6'3", 200-pound Scott found work as an extra on TV's *Rawhide* and eventually doubled Clint Eastwood. Scott made his name doing the hanging scene for Eastwood on *Hang 'Em High* (1968), doubling Lee Marvin for the train fight on *Emperor of the North* (1973), jumping onto a horse from a second story balcony for Jeff Bridges on *Hearts of the West* (1975), and doubling

Gene Hackman and James Coburn on *Bite the Bullet* (1975). Scott doubled Wayne Rogers on the TV series *City of Angels* (1976).

Scott survived death rumors as wire services erroneously reported he perished performing a stunt during *Ulzana's Raid* (1972). He did break his back doing a horse fall for Terence Hill on *Mr. Billion* (1977), necessitating a move into stunt co-ordination. Scott was a close friend of actor James Caan, and they competed together in rodeos. His younger brothers Ben and John-Clay Scott also became stuntmen.

He worked on *The Glory Guys* (1965), *More Dead Than Alive* (1969), *The Good Guys and the Bad Guys* (1969), *Beneath the Planet of the Apes* (1970), *Dirty Harry* (1971), *The Cowboys* (1972), *Buck and the Preacher* (1972), *Joe Kidd* (1972), *The Culpepper Cattle Co.* (1972), *Pat Garrett and Billy the Kid* (1973), *The Don Is Dead* (1973), *Soylent Green* (1973), *Soul of Nigger Charley* (1973), *99 and 44/100 percent Dead* (1974), *Night Moves* (1975), *The Master Gunfighter* (1975), *Hard Times* (1975), *Rollerball* (1975), *The Killer Elite* (1975), *The Outlaw Josey Wales* (1976), *Comes a Horseman* (1978), *Tom Horn* (1980), *Mountain Men* (1980), *Heaven's Gate* (1980), and *Any Which Way You Can* (1980). TV credits include *Daniel Boone, Hondo, Star Trek, High Chaparral, Gunsmoke, Mod Squad, Bearcats, Archer, Starsky and Hutch,* and *Vega$.*

See: Hendrickson, Paula. "Family Business." *Emmy.* December 2003; Silden, Isobel. "Stuntmen Are Daring Heroes, Unsung and Unknown." *Milwaukee Journal.* September 11, 1973.

JIM SEARS (1931–2002)

USC star halfback Jim Sears attracted attention as an All-American and Rose Bowl star in 1952. He began working in Hollywood as a stuntman during the football off-seasons while playing professionally for the Chicago Cardinals, the Los Angeles Chargers, and the Denver Broncos as a punt returner and defensive safety. A product of Inglewood High and El Camino Junior College, the 5'9", 185-pound Sears worked on *All-American* (1953), *The Long Gray Line* (1955), *Rally Round the Flag Boys* (1959), *The Big Operator* (1959), *Spartacus* (1960), *Son of Flubber* (1962), and the TV series *The Rifleman.*

See: "USC All-American Footballer Jim Sears Dies." *Los Angeles Times.* January 7, 2002.

ROCKY SHAHAN (1919–1981)

Best known as cattle drover Joe Scarlett on TV's *Rawhide* (1959–66), Robert Ray Shahan was born on a cattle ranch in Corinth, Texas. He followed the rodeo circuit with time out to serve as an instructor with the U.S. Cavalry at Fort Riley, Kansas, during World War II. He was a stunt double for Ward Bond on *Wagonmaster* (1950). As a horseback specialist he worked on *Across the Wide Missouri* (1951), *Johnny Guitar* (1954), *Run for Cover* (1955), *Westward Ho, the Wagons!* (1956), *Ride Out for Revenge* (1957), and *Cattle Empire* (1958).

DICK SHANE (1932–)

Dick Shane was raised Richard Lee Cheshire in Oregon and is best known as the double for James Drury on TV's *The Virginian* (1962–70) and *Men from Shiloh* (1970–71). He also doubled Fabian, Fernando Lamas, Clu Gulager, and Stewart Granger. The Navy veteran got his start at Corriganville before moving on to Universal Studio stunt shows. He put on live performances at Knotts Berry Farm, Six Flags Magic Mountain, and Las Vegas. In 1969 he traveled to Glasgow, Scotland, to headline appearances with Rory Calhoun. The 6'2" Shane was excellent with a bullwhip and Bowie knife and coached many stars in gun handling. He developed three stunt training centers and worked on *Young Warriors* (1967) and *Gone with the West* (1975). TV credits include *Highway Patrol* and *Iron Horse.* Shane is a lifetime member of the Appaloosa Horse Association.

See: Donaldson, Charles. "Stuntmen: They Die to Make Their Living." *Los Angeles Times.* November 26, 1967; Green, Paul. *A History of Television's* The Virginian *1962–1971.* Jefferson, NC: McFarland, 2009.

BILL SHANNON (1934–1981)

William Robert Shannon was born in Oklahoma and raised in Kansas. In addition to being a rodeo cowboy, he was a tumbler and judo expert. The 5'8", 160-pound Shannon gained attention for a series of comic falls on TV's *Spike Jones Show.* He doubled Sterling Holloway on *It's a Mad, Mad, Mad, Mad World* (1963), Joey Bishop on *Texas Across the River* (1966), Rod Taylor on *Chuka* (1967), and Mel Brooks on *Silent Movie*

(1976). His most famous stunt was being blown off a bridge on *The Wild Bunch* (1969).

He also worked on *The Rains of Ranchipur* (1955), *Pork Chop Hill* (1959), *Spartacus* (1960), *The Alamo* (1960), *This Rebel Breed* (1960), *Kings of the Sun* (1963), *Mail Order Bride* (1964), *The War Lord* (1965), *Harper* (1966), *Camelot* (1967), *The Green Berets* (1968), *Blue* (1968), *Little Big Man* (1970), *Buck and the Preacher* (1972), *Magnum Force* (1973), *Freebie and the Bean* (1974), *Blazing Saddles* (1974), *Black Samson* (1974), *The Master Gunfighter* (1975), *Rollercoaster* (1977), and *F.I.S.T.* (1978). TV credits include *77 Sunset Strip*, *The Wild Wild West*, *Bonanza*, *Felony Squad*, *High Chaparral*, *The Cowboys*, and *Little House on the Prairie*. A member of the Stuntmen's Association and an inductee of the Stuntmen's Hall of Fame, Shannon died from a heart attack after a bout with pneumonia at the age of 46.

See: May, E. Lawson. "People Speak on Television." *Hutchinson News.* August 12, 1961; "William Robert Shannon." *Variety.* July 15, 1981.

JACK SHANNON (1892–1968)

Ohio-born rodeo veteran Jack Tyler Shannon doubled popular cowboy stars Tom Mix, Hoot Gibson, William S. Hart, and William Boyd on westerns. Credits include *Colorado Sunset* (1939), *American Empire* (1942), *Buffalo Bill* (1944), and *Around the World in Eighty Days* (1956). In the latter portion of his career, Shannon worked as a wrangler and horse trainer. In the 1960s he joined the American Humane Association to monitor the treatment of horses on film and television.

See: *Beaver County Times.* "Horses Love Their Protector." October 30, 1964; "J. Shannon; Ex-Stuntman in Movies." *Los Angeles Times.* December 30, 1968.

ALEX SHARP (1921–2008)

Nebraska-born Alex Sharp is best known for the long-running TV series *Bonanza* (1959–73), where he befriended series star Michael Landon while working as a utility stuntman. Landon was instrumental in passing Sharp's comedic scripts along to the right people, and *Bonanza* produced seven of Sharp's teleplays. Sharp also had two screenplays produced for the western series *High Chaparral*. Fights were Sharp's specialty and he

and Landon did at least a half dozen with one another on *Bonanza* with Sharp doubling guests George Kennedy and Leif Erickson.

The 6'4", 200-pound Sharp was raised in Washington and Colorado, where he learned to break horses. He was with the U.S. Cavalry at Fort Riley and spent time with the Air Force as a gunner on a South Pacific bomber during World War II. One of his earliest assignments was doubling Scott Forbes on *Rocky Mountain* (1950). He continued with Forbes on the series *Adventures of Jim Bowie* (1956–58) and doubled James Arness on *Gunsmoke* (1955–75) and Richard Coogan on *The Californians* (1957–59). Sharp was hired to be Jock Mahoney's double on *Yancy Derringer* (1958–59), but Mahoney did all the action himself after Sharp rehearsed the stunts. In 1959 he worked a live show with Bill Couch and Chuck Bail at Radio City Music Hall in New York City to promote a Disney film.

He worked on *Horizons West* (1952), *Yankee Buccaneer* (1952), *Seminole* (1953), *Wichita* (1955), *Showdown at Abilene* (1956), *Red Sundown* (1956), *The Horse Soldiers* (1959), *Spartacus* (1960), *How the West Was Won* (1962), *It's a Mad, Mad, Mad, Mad World* (1963), *Law of the Lawless* (1964), *The Great Race* (1965), *El Dorado* (1967), *Planet of the Apes* (1968), *Bullitt* (1968), *The Wild Bunch* (1969), *The Great Bank Robbery* (1969), *Catch-22* (1970), *Flap* (1970), *Dirty Harry* (1971), *Diamonds Are Forever* (1971), *What's Up, Doc?* (1972), *Conquest of the Planet of the Apes* (1972), *Battle for the Planet of the Apes* (1973), *Mr. Majestyk* (1974), *Hearts of the West* (1975), *Bound for Glory* (1976), *Zero to Sixty* (1978), and *The Champ* (1979). TV work includes *The Lone Ranger*, *The Cisco Kid*, *Cheyenne*, *Have Gun—Will Travel*, *The Virginian*, *Branded*, *Batman*, *Mission: Impossible*, *The Rockford Files*, and *Little House on the Prairie*. A member of the Stuntmen's Association and an inductee of the Stuntmen's Hall of Fame, Sharp died from stroke-related ailments at the age of 86.

See: "Empty Saddles." *Western Clippings.* #83, May-June 2008.

DAVE SHARPE (1910–1980)

David Hardin Sharpe was born in St. Louis, Missouri. He has been called the "Crown Prince" and the greatest all-around stuntman in film history as he was highly skilled in every facet of film daredevilry, from judo fights to high falls.

In Los Angeles young Davey was a handball champion and became an exceptional acrobat touring with an adagio balancing act. He was discovered at age eight by Douglas Fairbanks at the Los Angeles Athletic Club and first appeared on *Robin Hood* (1922) and *The Thief of Bagdad* (1924). Thirty years later he estimated he had appeared in an incredible 4,500 films. At times he was doing stunts on as many as five movies a day. As a gymnast at Glendale High he won the National AAU Tumbling Championship in both 1925 and 1926.

In the 1930s the 5'8", 165-pound Sharpe starred in several minor films, and he was a Range Buster in the early 1940s, but stunt work for stars like Harold Lloyd paid better. This was illustrated clearly when he starred in the serial *Daredevils of the Red Circle* (1939) and his double Jimmy Fawcett brought home a bigger check. As a member of the "Stunt Cousins" he became ramrod for the Republic Studios stunt team from the late 1930s

until he entered the service as a fighter pilot in 1942; he oversaw several great action serials and doubled heroes Tom Tyler, Kane Richmond, and Clayton Moore. His action participation on *Dick Tracy Returns* (1938), *Dick Tracy's G-Men* (1939), *Drums of Fu Manchu* (1940), *Adventures of Red Ryder* (1940), *King of the Royal Mounted* (1940), *Mysterious Doctor Satan* (1940), *King of the Texas Rangers* (1941), *Adventures of Captain Marvel* (1941), *Dick Tracy vs. Crime, Inc.* (1941), *King of the Mounties* (1942), *Spy Smasher* (1942), and *Perils of Nyoka* (1942) is legend as he provides some of the most thrilling stunts the screen has ever seen.

After the war he picked up where he left off, specializing in swashbucklers as he doubled Douglas Fairbanks, Jr., on *The Exile* (1947), *Sinbad the Sailor* (1947), and *The Fighting O'Flynn* (1949), Gene Kelly on *The Three Musketeers* (1948), John Derek on *Rogues of Sherwood Forest* (1950), and Tony Curtis on *The Prince Who Was a Thief* (1951), *The Black Shield of Falworth*

Dave Sharpe makes a fantastic leap on the Republic serial *Dick Tracy vs. Crime Inc.* (1941).

(1954), and *The Vikings* (1958). He also doubled Alan Ladd, Tyrone Power, Glenn Ford, William Holden, Bob Steele, Richard Dix, Audie Murphy, and Marlon Brando. On TV Sharpe doubled Duncan Renaldo on *The Cisco Kid* (1950–56), Guy Madison on *Wild Bill Hickok* (1951–58), and James Darren on *The Time Tunnel* (1966–67). He was the little old lady who took stunt falls on *The Red Skelton Show* (1965–69).

The fantastically coordinated Sharpe first attracted wide acclaim for his high falls on *Gunga Din* (1939) and a two-man balcony drop onto tables with Jimmy Fawcett on *Seven Sinners* (1940). His high work remained unprecedented for years as he fought all over a rugged cliff on *Lust for Gold* (1949) and leaped from the top of a staircase for Tony Curtis on *The Great Race* (1965). On that film he executed a high fall out a castle window and through a rowboat into a shallow moat for Ross Martin, a stunt considered by his peers to be one of the best ever. Sharpe was a superb fight man, and had notable fisticuffs with Eddie Dean on *Colorado Serenade* (1946), Roy Rogers on *Bells of San Angelo* (1947), and Charlton Heston on *Touch of Evil* (1958). He was Tim Holt's double for the cantina fight on *The Treasure of the Sierra Madre* (1948). Sharpe was an exceptional quick-draw artist, gun trick master, and lariat roper. Nobody in the business was better at leaping, sliding, or jumping over bodies and furniture, and due to meticulous preparation Sharpe was never injured. He could still perform back flips at the age of 65 and once did a handstand on top of the Leaning Tower of Pisa. On *Blazing Saddles* (1974) he performed a saddle drag with a nifty special flip at the end. Sharpe liked to run through stunt rehearsals with a cigar stuck in his mouth so that film of him couldn't be used without his knowledge.

He also worked on *The Storm* (1938), *The Lone Ranger Rides Again* (1939), *Stagecoach* (1939), *Six Gun Rhythm* (1939), *The Hunchback of Notre Dame* (1939), *The Bank Dick* (1940), *They Died with Their Boots On* (1941), *Jungle Girl* (1941), *The Corsican Brothers* (1941), *Saboteur* (1942), *The Magnificent Ambersons* (1942), *Buckskin Frontier* (1943), *Ali Baba and the Forty Thieves* (1944), *Slave Girl* (1947), *To the Ends of the Earth* (1948), *The Fuller Brush Man* (1948), *A Southern Yankee* (1948), *Adventures of Frank and Jesse James* (1948), *G-Men Never Forget* (1948), *The Fighting Kentuckian* (1949), *Mighty Joe Young* (1949), *King of the Rocket Men* (1949),

Two Flags West (1950), *The Invisible Monster* (1950), *Cargo to Capetown* (1950), *Wyoming Mail* (1950), *Flying Disc Man from Mars* (1951), *Sealed Cargo* (1951), *Tomahawk* (1951), *Westward the Women* (1951), *Don Daredevil Rides Again* (1951), *The Cimarron Kid* (1952), *Radar Men from the Moon* (1952), *Singin' in the Rain* (1952), *Scarlet Angel* (1952), *Thief of Damascus* (1952), *Son of Ali Baba* (1952), *Yankee Buccaneer* (1952), *The Mississippi Gambler* (1953), *The Stand at Apache River* (1953), *Seminole* (1953), *Prince of Pirates* (1953), *All-American* (1953), *Forbidden* (1953), *Tumbleweed* (1953), *The Man from the Alamo* (1953), *Wings of the Hawk* (1953), *The War of the Worlds* (1953), *Column South* (1953), *The Wild One* (1953), *Desert Legion* (1953), *The Veils of Bagdad* (1953), *Siege at Red River* (1954), *Drums Across the River* (1954), *Prince Valiant* (1954), *The Violent Men* (1955), *Smoke Signal* (1955), *The Rawhide Years* (1955), *Three Violent People* (1956), *Designing Woman* (1957), *Slaughter on Tenth Avenue* (1957), *From Hell to Texas* (1958), *The Spiral Road* (1962), *Six Black Horses* (1962), *The Third Day* (1965), *Dr. Goldfoot and the Bikini Machine* (1965), *Torn Curtain* (1965), *What Did You Do in the War, Daddy?* (1966), *Not With My Wife You Don't* (1966), *Paint Your Wagon* (1969), *Life and Times of Judge Roy Bean* (1972), *The Poseidon Adventure* (1972), *Conquest of the Planet of the Apes* (1972), *The Towering Inferno* (1974), *The Master Gunfighter* (1975), and *Heaven Can Wait* (1978). TV credits include *The Lone Ranger, Riverboat, Zorro, Bob Hope, The FBI, I Spy, Batman, The Wild Wild West, Bonanza, The Girl from U.N.C.L.E., Star Trek,* and *High Chaparral*. A founding member of the Stuntmen's Association, an inductee of the Stuntmen's Hall of Fame, and a recipient of the Yakima Canutt Award, Sharpe died of Lou Gehrig's Disease at the age of 70.

See: "Ace of Stuntmen." *Screen Thrills Illustrated.* Vol. 2, #2. October 1963; Cook, Ben. "Makes Living Being Fall Guy in Hollywood." *Hartford Courant.* September 6, 1953; Hagner, John. *Dave Sharpe and Me.* Self, 1985; Hagner, John, & Scott Rhodes. "Dave Sharpe." *Filmfax.* February-March 1999; Law, Ken. "Dave Sharpe; Crown Prince of Daredevils." *Classic Images.* #109, July 1984; Lewis, C. Jack. "David Hardin Sharpe." *Guns of the Old West.* Spring 2011; Terrell, Ken. "Dave Sharpe." *Strength & Health.* June 1950; "Veteran Film Stuntman Dies." *Los Angeles Times.* March 31, 1980.

JIM SHEPPARD (1937–1977)

James Sheppard was born in Dallas and raised in Oregon. This rodeo cowboy was a good match for Audie Murphy, the former World War II hero turned sagebrush star. The 5'11", 155-pound Sheppard doubled Murphy on stunt-heavy westerns such as *Wild and the Innocent* (1959), *Seven Ways from Sundown* (1960), *Posse from Hell* (1961), *Six Black Horses* (1962), *Showdown* (1963), *Bullet for a Badman* (1964), *Apache Rifles* (1964), *Arizona Raiders* (1965), *Gunpoint* (1966), *40 Guns to Apache Pass* (1967), and *A Time for Dying* (1969). He was Deputy Jim on Murphy's short-lived series *Whispering Smith* (1960). After Murphy died in a plane crash, Sheppard doubled comedian Marty Feldman on *Silent Movie* (1976) and *The Last Remake of Beau Geste* (1977).

He also worked on *The Birds* (1963), *Major Dundee* (1965), *The War Lord* (1965), *Hour of the Gun* (1967), *Camelot* (1967), *Planet of the Apes* (1968), *The Wind and the Lion* (1975), *The Master Gunfighter* (1975), and *Silver Streak* (1976). He was one of the stuntmen blown off the bridge on *The Wild Bunch* (1969). TV credits include *Gunsmoke, The Big Valley, Hondo,* and *Star Trek.* Sheppard died in Colorado performing a horse drag stunt for Jason Robards on *Comes a Horseman* (1978) when his head hit a fence post. The scene remains in the film. Sheppard was a member of the Stuntmen's Association and an inductee of the Stuntmen's Hall of Fame.

See: Larkins, Bob, & Boyd Magers. *The Films of Audie Murphy.* Jefferson, NC: McFarland, 2004; Payne, William A. "Movie Stunt Record Set By *Dundee* Fall." *Dallas Morning News.* April 16, 1964.

ROY N. SICKNER (1928–2001)

Roy Sickner was born in Arizona and raised in Los Angeles, playing football for Santa Monica High. He was one of the original Marlboro Men and the best known during the era. A former ski

Jim Sheppard does a saddle fall as Walt La Rue follows behind him on *Gunpoint* (1966).

pro, Sickner doubled Richard Harris, Marlon Brando, Rod Taylor, and Yul Brynner. Sickner conceived the original story for *The Wild Bunch* (1969) as a starring role for pal Lee Marvin. He wound up with a co-producer credit on the groundbreaking Sam Peckinpah film and helped coordinate some of the stunts. In 1971 Sickner was severely injured in an open Jeep accident on the TV series *Cade's County*. He suffered cranial injuries and never worked again.

He worked on *Warlock* (1959), *King of the Wild Stallions* (1959), *The Great Escape* (1963), *McLintock!* (1963), *Major Dundee* (1965), *Morituri* (1965), *Winter A-Go-Go* (1965), *Nevada Smith* (1966), *Wild Wild Winter* (1966), *Chuka* (1967), *Planet of the Apes* (1968), and *The Omega Man* (1971). TV credits include *Hong Kong, Twilight Zone, The Wild Wild West, Batman, Voyage to the Bottom of the Sea, The Man from U.N.C.L.E., Mission: Impossible, Hondo,* and *Star Trek.* He was an honorary member of the Stuntmen's Association.

See: Prince, Stephen. *Sam Peckinpah's* The Wild Bunch. NY: Cambridge, 1999; "3 Stuntmen Hurt When Jeep Flips." *Press-Courier.* November 16, 1971.

FELIX SILLA (1937–)

Three-foot-eleven, 70-pound Felix Silla was born outside of Rome and came to the United States in the 1950s to tour in the Ringling Brothers and Barnum and Bailey Circus as an acrobat and bareback rider. He is best known for portraying Cousin Itt on the TV series *The Addams Family* (1964–66) and was the robot Twiki on the series *Buck Rogers in the 25th Century* (1979–81). He had acting roles on *Little Cigars* (1973) and *The Black Bird* (1975), but his small size let him double children and portray creatures. He was an Ewok on *Return of the Jedi* (1983) and doubled Jonathan Ke Quan's character Short Round on *Indiana Jones and the Temple of Doom* (1984).

He also worked on *A Ticklish Affair* (1963), *The Russians Are Coming, The Russians Are Coming* (1966), *Planet of the Apes* (1968), *Sssssss* (1973), *Don't Be Afraid of the Dark* (1973), *The Towering Inferno* (1974), *Earthquake* (1974), *The Kentucky Fried Movie* (1977), *Demon Seed* (1977), and *The Brood* (1979). TV credits include *Bonanza, H.R. Pufnstuf,* and *Battlestar Galactica.*

See: "Profile: Felix Silla." *Daily News.* May 29, 1980; www.felixsilla.com.

JAY SILVERHEELS (1912–1980)

Jay Silverheels was born Harold J. Smith in the Six Nations Reservation in Ontario, Canada. He was a successful Golden Gloves boxer, a champion amateur wrestler, and a standout player for Canada's national lacrosse team. A competition in Los Angeles brought him to the attention of Hollywood, and his first film involved stunt riding on *Make a Wish* (1937). He stunted on *The Sea Hawk* (1940), *Valley of the Sun* (1942), *Passage to Marseille* (1944), the Republic serial *Perils of Nyoka* (1942) and the Columbia serial *The Phantom* (1943). Silverheels served with the military during World War II.

He portrayed Apache warrior Geronimo in *Broken Arrow* (1950), but it was the role of Tonto on the popular TV series *The Lone Ranger* (1949–57) that became his signature. The six-foot Silverheels was noted for his smooth mounts onto his horse Scout. Silverheels had stuntmen doubling him after a heart attack took him out of commission. In later years he became involved in harness racing and teaching Native Americans to act and perform stunts at the Indian Actors Workshop. Silverheels died from a stroke at the age of 67.

BOB SIMMONS (1922–1988)

Bob Simmons was born in Fulham, England. He was light-heavyweight champion of the British Army and served as a gym instructor for the troops at Sandhurst Military Academy. Simmons' athleticism led him into stunts for Mickey Woods' Tough Guys Limited, and he quickly rose through the ranks as a stuntman and coordinator. The 5'11", 185-pound Simmons doubled Robert Taylor on *Ivanhoe* (1952), Alan Ladd on *The Red Beret* (1953) and *The Black Knight* (1954), Robert Mitchum on *Fire Down Below* (1957), Peter Sellers on *Tom Thumb* (1958), and Richard Burton on *The Wild Geese* (1978).

Simmons specialized in fights and highwork, executing a 120-foot dive off a cliff for *The Guns of Navarone* (1961) while doubling Gregory Peck. On *Scent of Mystery* (1960) he rode an umbrella 150 yards down a zip line for Denholm Elliott. *When Eight Bells Toll* (1971) had him hanging from a helicopter's skids for Anthony Hopkins. On *The Offence* (1973) he performed a sixty-foot fall into a concealed catcher and landed at Sean Connery's feet. For *The Spy Who Loved*

Bob Simmons, in drag, struggles with Sean Connery on *Thunderball* (1965).

Me (1977) he smashed through a train window doubling Richard Kiel.

Although he was a few inches shorter than Connery, Simmons began doubling the Bond star with *Dr. No* (1962). In the first three Bond films it's actually Simmons who does the famous silhouetted gun barrel opening. In *Dr. No* he was the chauffeur Bond fights; it's also Simmons that the tarantula crawls on. Simmons was a fixture on the spy series for two decades, including memorable fights on *From Russia with Love* (1963), *Goldfinger* (1964), *You Only Live Twice* (1967), and *Diamonds Are Forever* (1971). On *Thunderball* (1965) he appeared as Jacques Bouvier, fighting in drag against Connery in the film's opening sequence. When Connery left the series, Simmons resumed coordinating duties with Roger Moore on *Live and Let Die* (1973), *Man with the Golden Gun* (1974), *Moonraker* (1979), *For Your Eyes Only* (1981), *Octopussy* (1983), and *A View to a Kill* (1985).

Simmons also worked on *Zarak* (1956), *Action of the Tiger* (1957), *Naked Edge* (1961), *Hellions* (1961), *Fury at Smuggler's Bay* (1961), *Night Creatures* (1962), *Pirates of Blood River* (1962), *The Long Ships* (1964), *Genghis Khan* (1965), *Shalako* (1968), *Charge of the Light Brigade* (1968), *The Adventurers* (1970), *Catlow* (1971), *Murphy's War* (1971), *The Wilby Conspiracy* (1975), *The Man Who Would be King* (1975), *The Next Man* (1976), *Zulu Dawn* (1979), and *The Sea Wolves* (1980). He was a member of the Stuntmen's Hall of Fame.

See: McGregor, Don. "Bob Simmons: Trading Punches with James Bond." *Starlog*. February 1986; Simmons, Bob. *Nobody Does It Better*. NY: Javelin, 1987.

BARLOW SIMPSON (1906–1970)

Utah-born jack of all trades Barlow Simpson performed stunts on *Gunga Din* (1939), *Fort Apache* (1948), *Rio Grande* (1950), and *The Con-*

queror (1956). He doubled Russell Simpson on *My Darling Clementine* (1946) and James Cagney on *Run for Cover* (1955). He wrangled horses, elephants, and guns on everything from *She Wore a Yellow Ribbon* (1949) to *The Greatest Show on Earth* (1952). He later worked at Corriganville portraying one of the Indians attacking the stagecoach.

JOHNNY SINCLAIR (1900–1945)

Johnny Sinclair was born in Memphis, Tennessee, as John St. Clair, the name he went by in early 1920s physical comedies. He doubled W.C. Fields, Ken Maynard, Billy Sullivan, William Harrigan, and Reed Howes, and was known for designing gags for Fields. Sinclair took a memorable stair fall on a bicycle for the Fields short *The Barbershop* (1933). He was part of Jimmy Dundee's Suicide Squad. Credits include *Seven Days Leave* (1930), *King Kong* (1933), *The Glass Key* (1935), *Slave Ship* (1937), *Secret Service of the Air* (1939), *Hollywood Cavalcade* (1939), *Sullivan's Travels* (1941), and *All Through the Night* (1941). Sinclair died from cirrhosis of the liver at the age of 45.

DEAN SMITH (1932–)

Dean Smith entered the stunt business after winning Olympic Gold and could run, jump, and fight as well as anyone in the business. He put his skills to great use in the western genre, most notably doing scissor vaults for Frankie Avalon on *The Alamo* (1960) and Ben Johnson on *Cheyenne Autumn* (1964). Smith doubled Dale Robertson on the TV series *Tales of Wells Fargo* (1957–62) and *Iron Horse* (1966–67), Stuart Whitman on *The Comancheros* (1961) and *Rio Conchos* (1964), and Robert Redford on *Jeremiah Johnson* (1972), *The Sting* (1973), *The Great Waldo Pepper* (1975), and *Three Days of the Condor* (1975). Smith's greatest achievement was recreating Yakima Canutt's famous horse team stunt for Alex Cord on *Stagecoach* (1966). He earned $1,500 for the stunt. On *McLintock!* (1963) he doubled both Strother Martin and Maureen O'Hara for falls down stairs and on the street. On *Viva Knievel* (1977) he jumped over Gary Davis speeding at him on a motorcycle.

Smith was a capable actor, handling roles such as the gunman who falls from the bell tower

on *Big Jake* (1971) and the newscaster who is run off the road on *The Sugarland Express* (1974). On *Ulzana's Raid* (1972) he is the trooper who has his horse shot out from under him and takes surprising action when descended upon by the Apaches. He had a leading role as frontiersman Kit Carson on *Seven Alone* (1975). One of his best fights came doubling Gary Graham on *Hardcore* (1979) in a bruising battle with star George C. Scott.

Smith doubled Robert Forster on *The Stalking Moon* (1969), Jorge Rivero and Christopher Mitchum on *Rio Lobo* (1970), Paul Newman on *The Drowning Pool* (1975), and Bruce Dern on *Black Sunday* (1977). On TV he doubled Robert Culp at the outset of *I Spy* (1965–66), Don Murray on *Outcasts* (1968–69), and Michael Douglas on *The Streets of San Francisco* (1971–74). He also doubled for the stars of the series *Riverboat, The Big Valley, Laramie, Wagon Train, Bonanza, The Virginian,* and *The Fall Guy.* On the latter he doubled cowboy legend Roy Rogers, a treasured assignment. He had previously doubled Rogers on the film *Mackintosh and T.J.* (1975).

Six-foot, 165-pound Finis Dean Smith was born in Breckinridge, Texas, and began winning rodeo events while in his teens. He was an All-State football halfback and track standout for the Graham High Steers, winning the state title in the 100-yard dash. Smith played both sports at the University of Texas, winning a national AAU title in the 100 meters. He earned a Gold Medal at the Olympic Games in Helinske in 1952 as part of the 400-meter relay team. After service with the Army, Smith was signed by the Los Angeles Rams for the 1957 football season as a wide receiver. They ultimately decided he was plenty fast but too small for the sport. They wanted to trade him to the Pittsburgh Steelers, but Smith balked. He stayed in Los Angeles to pursue his dream of being a cowboy stuntman through a connection he made with James Garner at Warner Brothers. Garner introduced him to the right people, and Smith's natural, talents took over from there. Throughout his career he utilized rearing horses Crawdad and Sox and the falling horse Choya.

He worked on *The Law and Jake Wade* (1958), *Cat on a Hot Tin Roof* (1958), *They Came to Cordura* (1959), *Rio Bravo* (1959), *Darby O'Gill and the Little People* (1959), *Pork Chop Hill* (1959), *The Alamo* (1960), *Seven Ways from Sundown* (1960), *Two Rode Together* (1961), *How the West*

Was Won (1962), *Kings of the Sun* (1963), *PT 109* (1963), *The Birds* (1963), *Blood on the Arrow* (1964), *A Distant Trumpet* (1964), *In Harm's Way* (1965), *The Great Race* (1965), *What Did You Do in the War, Daddy?* (1966), *The War Wagon* (1967), *El Dorado* (1967), *Camelot* (1967), *Hurry Sundown* (1967), *The Scalphunters* (1968), *Charro!* (1969), *True Grit* (1969), *Butch Cassidy and the* *Sundance Kid* (1969), *Stiletto* (1969), *Little Big Man* (1970), *Airport* (1970), *The Cheyenne Social Club* (1970), *Sometimes a Great Notion* (1971), *Life and Times of Judge Roy Bean* (1972), *Hickey and Boggs* (1972), *Legend of Nigger Charley* (1972), *Westworld* (1973), *The Towering Inferno* (1974), *Earthquake* (1974), *Airport '75* (1974), *Hearts of the West* (1975), *Concorde, Airport '79*

Dean Smith hangs from the Goodyear blimp on *Black Sunday* (1977). Actor Robert Shaw is in the foreground.

(1979), and *1941* (1979). On TV he was a stunt coordinator on *How the West Was Won* (1978) and *Young Maverick* (1979). A member of the Stuntmen's Association and an inductee of the Stuntmen's Hall of Fame, Smith received both a Golden Boot and a Silver Spur Award. In Texas he was inducted into the Sports Hall of Fame, the University of Texas Hall of Fame, the Cowboy Hall of Fame, and the Texas Rodeo Cowboy Hall of Fame. He received a Lifetime Achievement Award from the National Cowboy and Western Heritage Museum.

See: Cartwright, Gary. "Man on the Run." *Dallas Morning News.* October 12, 1965; Lilley, Tim. *Campfire Conversations.* Akron, OH: Big Trail, 2007; Shearer, Lloyd. "Stuntman Dean Smith: He Falls for the Stars." *Oregonian.* January 9, 1966; Smith, Dean, & Mike Cox. *Cowboy Stuntman.* Austin, TX: Univ. of Texas, 2013; Stowers, Charles. "Dean Smith: In Search of Millions or Just Scale?" *Dallas Morning News.* February 3, 1980.

EDDIE SMITH (1924–2005)

Eddie Smith is best known for flying out of the water at 60 miles per hour and crashing into a wedding cake with a CV-19 speedboat on the Bond film *Live and Let Die* (1973). He was born in St. Louis and worked in Hollywood as an extra while freelancing as a TV news cameraman. While working background on *It's a Mad, Mad, Mad, Mad World* (1963) he was upset to see white stuntman Loren Janes being made up to double Eddie "Rochester" Anderson. He confronted director Stanley Kramer and was told there were no qualified black stuntmen. Smith went about finding and organizing these men, and in 1967 he cofounded the Black Stuntman's Association.

He worked on *Halls of Anger* (1970), *MASH* (1970), *Beneath the Planet of the Apes* (1970), *Dirty Harry* (1971), *Conquest of the Planet of the Apes* (1972), *Across 110th Street* (1972), *Unholy Rollers* (1972), *Battle for the Planet of the Apes* (1973), *Cleopatra Jones* (1973), *Trader Horn* (1973), *Truck Turner* (1974), *Black Belt Jones* (1974), *Dirty Mary, Crazy Larry* (1974), *Blazing Saddles* (1974), *Earthquake* (1974), *Dr. Black, Mr. Hyde* (1976), and *Drum* (1976). Smith was stunt coordinator on the epic TV mini-series *Roots* (1977) and appeared on TV's *Daktari* and *Cowboy in Africa*.

See: "Black Stunt Men." *Ebony.* December 1969; "Edward Smith, 81, Fought for Black Stuntmen." *Los Angeles Times.* July 9, 2005.

J. LEWIS "LEW" SMITH (1906–1964)

Lew Smith was born in Ohio and spent time as an amateur boxer in the Colorado Springs area. He met Clark Gable while playing polo and was invited by the star to be his stand-in and occasional stunt double, an occupation Smith held for twenty-five years, from *Mutiny on the Bounty* (1935) to *The Misfits* (1961). He missed only one Gable film while serving in the Navy during World War II. The 5'11", 185-pound Smith played the title robot character in *Tobor the Great* (1954) and performed stunts on *Gone with the Wind* (1939), *Around the World in Eighty Days* (1956), and *Pork Chop Hill* (1959). He died at the age of 58 after being shot outside the Retake Room near MGM.

See: Handseker, Gene. "Movie Stand-Ins." *Portsmouth Times.* October 22, 1949.

MILAN SMITH (1923–2001)

Sioux Indian Milan Smith was born in South Dakota. After World War II service in the Pacific, horseback specialist Smith began working on TV westerns. He doubled Clint Eastwood on *Rawhide* and Michael Landon on *Bonanza* and also logged time on *Wyatt Earp, Wagon Train, Rifleman, Wanted—Dead or Alive,* and *The Big Valley* during his nearly twenty years in Hollywood. Film credits include *Escape from Fort Bravo* (1953) and *Masterson of Kansas* (1954). He befriended Jay Silverheels while on *The Lone Ranger* and later became a trainer of champion harness race horses. His top race horse was named Hi-Ho Silverheels after his late friend.

See: Milbert, Neil. "Tonto's Pacer Ever Faithful." *Chicago Tribune.* November 17, 1994; "New Hit Role for Stunt Man." *San Mateo Times.* December 30, 1970; Schuelein, Steve. "Hi Ho Silverheels Tries to Gain Identity as a Winning Pacer." *Los Angeles Times.* March 3, 1995.

WILLIAM SMITH (1933–)

William Emmett Smith II was born on a cattle ranch in Columbia, Missouri. As a California-raised youth, Smith trained horses and cleaned mentor Jock Mahoney's stables. He played football at Burbank High and took up bodybuilding, developing a tremendous athleticism working out on the gymnastic rings at Muscle Beach in Santa Monica. While playing football at Glendale Junior College he was recruited to portray a footballer in *Saturday's Hero* (1951).

During the Korean War the 6'2", 210-pound Smith won Air Force weightlifting and boxing championships and played semi-pro football for the Wiesbaden Flyers as an end. He was discharged in France and worked on the French Riviera as a lifeguard. He was hired off the beach to double former Tarzan Lex Barker on *Strange Awakening* (1958). His stunt was to jump out of a car and tumble down a cliff. MGM tried casting Smith as Tarzan, but he wanted to be a serious actor and turned the role down. Smith's phenomenally chiseled 18 1/2" arms were the envy of most

bodybuilders of the day, and he made a name with his natural strength and athletic feats. He could reverse-curl his bodyweight, and twice won the 200-pound Arm-Wrestling Championship of the World at Petaluma.

Smith learned fancy horse mounts from Mahoney for the TV Western *Laredo* (1965–67) and was able to do all his own screen fights. He and Rod Taylor put on a legendary brawl on *Darker Than Amber* (1970) for which both were made honorary members of the Stuntmen's Association. Smith later did the longest two-man fight without doubles with Clint Eastwood on *Any Which Way You Can* (1980). TV fights against James Arness on *Gunsmoke*, David Carradine on *Kung Fu*, and Nick Nolte on the TV mini-series *Rich Man, Poor Man* were equally memorable.

Smith was an expert motorcyclist who could handle big bikes. This led to his casting on a num-

William Smith and Clint Eastwood work an epic fight without doubles on *Any Which Way You Can* (1980).

ber of cycle films where he did his own riding except for longer jumps. On *C.C. and Company* (1970) he served as one of the stunt riders for a dirt track race. On *Scorchy* (1976) he performed motorcycle and car work for an extended chase through the streets of Seattle. Smith received an award from the Stuntmen's Association for his physical acting and has also received a Golden Boot, a Silver Spur, induction into the Muscle Beach Hall of Fame, and a Lifetime Achievement Award from the Academy of Bodybuilding and Fitness. His son William became a stuntman.

See: Garmon, Ron. "King of the Bikers: William Smith." *Worldly Remains.* #4, 2001; Teymur. T. "William Smith: My Fight with Clint Eastwood Was the Longest Two-Man Fight on Screen." *BZ Film.* April 1, 2010; Stout, Jerry. "What Do You Say to a Naked Lady?" *Fighting Stars.* June 1974; www.williamsmith.org.

BOBBY SOMERS (1932–1982)

Five-foot-three, 140-pound Robert David Sommers was born in Los Angeles. In addition to horse stunts he was a professional dancer. His small size enabled him to double women and children. He worked on *Hondo* (1953), *Apache* (1954), *The Comancheros* (1961), *Rio Conchos* (1964), *The Professionals* (1966), *Duel at Diablo* (1966), *Bandolero!* (1968), and *Blazing Saddles* (1974). TV credits include *Cheyenne, Maverick, Bronco, Sugarfoot, Wagon Train, Laramie, The Rifleman, Rawhide, 77 Sunset Strip, Gunsmoke, Bonanza, Combat, Voyage to the Bottom of the Sea, The Virginian, Laredo, F Troop, Get Smart,* and *Hawaii Five-O.* Somers died from cancer at the age of 49.

FRED "CAP" SOMERS (1893–1970)

Born in Atlantic City, New Jersey, 6'3" Fredrick Grant Somers was a lifeguard who excelled in football, basketball, and baseball at Somers Point. In 1914 he played pro baseball with the New York Giants. Somers was a captain in the Marine Corps during World War I, earning his nickname. He became a movie stunt brawler and was called "The Bravest Man in Hollywood" when he let archer Howard Hill shoot an apple atop his head at fifty feet for the short *Follow the Arrow.* He worked on *Flash Gordon* (1936), *Fall*

In (1942), *Angel and the Badman* (1947), *A Perilous Journey* (1953), and *Around the World in Eighty Days* (1956). Somers died from a heart attack at the age of 77.

See: "Cap Somers Brave Man!" *Pittsburgh Press.* July 17, 1938.

GEORGE SOWARDS (1888–1975)

George Albert Sowards was a burly Missouri-born horse wrangler and stage driver who got his start on early silent films. He worked on several Hopalong Cassidy films alongside his stuntman brother Lem Sowards. His credits include *The Squaw Man* (1931), *Under Two Flags* (1936), *Santa Fe Marshal* (1940), *The Desperadoes* (1943), *The Kid from Texas* (1950), *Wyoming Mail* (1950), *The Cimarron Kid* (1952), *Thunder Over the Plains* (1953), *Gun Belt* (1953), *Tall Man Riding* (1955), *Seven Men from Now* (1956), *Gun Duel in Durango* (1957), and the TV shows *The Cisco Kid, Wild Bill Hickok,* and *Kit Carson.*

SPIKE SPACKMAN (1893–1981)

Spike Spackman was born Donald Leland Spackman in Fullerton, Nebraska. A broncbusting rodeo performer and trick roper, the Army veteran doubled Bing Crosby on *Rhythm on the Range* (1936) and Melvyn Douglas on *A Woman's Face* (1941). He also doubled Tom Mix. In later years he was employed as a ranch foreman for his friend Crosby. He worked on *Ben-Hur* (1925), *Fighting Caravans* (1931), *The Crusades* (1935), *The Charge of the Light Brigade* (1936), *The Plainsman* (1936), *Arizona Raiders* (1936), and *Under Two Flags* (1936). He wrote books of cowboy poetry and an autobiography.

See: Spackman, Spike. *Don't Fence Me In.* Carleton, 1963; Spackman, Spike. *Western Sage.* Self, 1971.

RAY SPIKER (1902–1964)

Ray Spiker was born in Wisconsin as Ray Faust, but took his mother's last name. He served two hitches in the Marines and built an impressive amateur boxing record with a string of knockouts. His heavyweight pro record was undistinguished. Fight specialist Spiker was a stuntman for Bing Crosby and Bob Hope at Paramount and is best

Paul Stader is behind the wheel as Larry Holt eludes him on *Flare-Up* (1969).

known for being hit over the head with a stool by Errol Flynn on *Adventures of Don Juan* (1948). He worked on *The Storm* (1938), *The Sea Wolf* (1941), *Reap the Wild Wind* (1942), *San Antonio* (1945), *The Spanish Main* (1945), *Cloak and Dagger* (1946), *Unconquered* (1947), *Silver River* (1948), *River Lady* (1948), *South of St. Louis* (1949), *Anne of the Indies* (1951), *Shane* (1953), *The Man Behind the Gun* (1953), *Demetrius and the Gladiators* (1954), *Prince Valiant* (1954), *The Conqueror* (1956), and *Around the World in Eighty Days* (1956).

See: "Ray Spiker." *Variety.* March 11, 1964.

PAUL STADER (1911–1991)

Paul Stader was born in Neosha, Missouri. Known by his nickname "Manny" Stader, he honed his multi-sport athletic skill at Liberty High and earned a scholarship to the University of Kansas where he played football and swam. He came to California to train for the 1932 Olympic Games. He didn't make the swim team, but he forged friendships with Johnny Weissmuller and Buster Crabbe. Stader became a lifeguard at Santa Monica Beach and was discovered there surfing and performing high dives. He was recruited to double Jon Hall for a seventy-foot cliff dive and a hundred-foot dive from the mast of a ship on *The Hurricane* (1937), stunts that created instant buzz throughout the industry. He later performed a ninety-foot dive at Fox Ranch doubling James Coburn on *Our Man Flint* (1966), a stunt that ran weekly on the opening credits to the TV series *The Fall Guy.*

The 6'2", 190-pound Stader doubled Weissmuller on all his Tarzan and Jungle Jim films. He did the same for Lex Barker when he took over the Ape Man role and doubled Kirk Alyn as *Superman* (1948). Stader doubled Lloyd Bridges on TV's *Sea Hunt* (1958–61) and was known as one of the best water men in the business. He expanded his skills to become a top fight man and fencer, working the epic duel on *Scaramouche* (1952) and parrying with Richard Burton on *Prince of Players* (1954). He doubled Rock Hudson for the famous diner fight on *Giant* (1956) and Cary Grant for the rooftop battle on *Charade* (1963). He also doubled Grant on *To Catch a Thief* (1955) and *North by Northwest* (1959). He did a three-man stair fall in handcuffs on *The Boss* (1956), but his toughest stunt was driving a Volkswagen off a pier on *What's Up, Doc?* (1972) because the windshield collapsed and trapped him inside for three minutes.

An accomplished boxing choreographer, Stader trained Robert Ryan for *The Set-Up* (1949). Years later he taught Carl Weathers for the original *Rocky* (1976). Stader doubled John Wayne on *Reap the Wild Wind* (1942) and *Wake of the Red Witch* (1948), Errol Flynn on *Gentleman Jim* (1942), Tyrone Power on *The Black Swan* (1942) and *King of the Khyber Rifles* (1954), Robert Ryan on *Return of the Badmen* (1948), *Horizons West* (1952), *Inferno* (1953), and *City Beneath the Sea* (1953), Robert Mitchum on *His Kind of Woman* (1951), *Macao* (1952), *Second Chance* (1953), and *Bandido* (1956), Gregory Peck on *Moby Dick* (1956), Gene Hackman on *The Poseidon Adventure* (1972), and Michael Caine on *Beyond the Poseidon Adventure* (1979). He also doubled Randolph Scott, Paul Henreid, Ray Milland, Buster Crabbe, Jim Bannon, Bill Elliott, John Ireland, Scott Brady, Tom Tyler, and Rod Cameron. On TV he doubled John Russell on *Soldiers of Fortune* (1955–57).

Stader was stunt coordinator on *I Spy* (1965–68) and ran all of Irwin Allen's sci-fi TV shows such as *Lost in Space, Voyage to the Bottom of the Sea,* and *Land of the Giants.* He was stunt coordinator for the Allen disaster epics *The Poseidon Adventure* (1972) and *The Towering Inferno* (1974), orchestrating impressive high-fall fire stunts. Stader had his own stunt school in Santa Monica where he trained prospective stuntmen. Many top stuntmen of the 1970s and 80s learned their trade at Stader's gym. His wife Marilyn Moe and his son Peter were involved in stunt work.

He worked on *One Million B.C.* (1940), *Talk of the Town* (1942), *Casablanca* (1942), *Frenchman's Creek* (1944), *Adventure* (1945), *Forever Amber* (1947), *River Lady* (1948), *Mighty Joe Young* (1949), *Two Flags West* (1950), *Vengeance Valley* (1951), *At Sword's Point* (1952), *Against All Flags* (1952), *The Lawless Breed* (1952), *Yankee Buccaneer* (1952), *House of Wax* (1953), *Demetrius and the Gladiators* (1954), *Prince Valiant* (1954), *Hell's Outpost* (1954), *The Wings of Eagles* (1957),

Last of the Badmen (1957), *Spoilers of the Forest* (1957), *The Missouri Traveler* (1958), *No Time for Sergeants* (1958), *Swiss Family Robinson* (1960), *Confessions of an Opium Eater* (1962), *It's a Mad, Mad, Mad, Mad World* (1963), *McLintock!* (1963), *4 for Texas* (1963), *The Great Race* (1965), *The Glory Guys* (1965), *Blindfold* (1965), *Tobruk* (1967), *Where Eagles Dare* (1968), *Alfred the Great* (1969), *Beneath the Planet of the Apes* (1970), *When Eight Bells Toll* (1971), *The Andromeda Strain* (1971), *Conquest of the Planet of the Apes* (1972), *Battle for the Planet of the Apes* (1973), *99 and 44/100 percent Dead* (1974), *Blazing Saddles* (1974), *The Great Waldo Pepper* (1975), *Lucky Lady* (1975), *Black Sunday* (1977), and *The Swarm* (1978). TV credits include *The Lone Ranger, Jungle Jim, Zane Grey, Trackdown, Wagon Train, Yancy Derringer, Wanted—Dead or Alive, The Westerner, Coronado 9, The Outer Limits, Daniel Boone, Star Trek, Planet of the Apes,* and *Man from Atlantis.* He was a member of the Stuntmen's Association and the Stuntmen's Hall of Fame.

See: Perry, James A. "Real Fall Guy." *Times Picayune.* June 26, 1982; Weiner, David Jon. *Burns, Falls, and Crashes.* Jefferson, NC: McFarland, 1996.

GINGER STANLEY (1931–)

Georgia-born Ginger Stanley began her career as an underwater mermaid at Weeki Wachee, Florida. While working as a photographers' model at Silver Springs, she was recruited to double Julie Adams for swimming scenes on *Creature from the Black Lagoon* (1954). She doubled Lori Nelson the following year on *Revenge of the Creature* (1955) and Esther Williams on *Jupiter's Darling* (1955). She worked on TV's *Sea Hunt* (1958–61) and served as an underwater weather girl for a New York TV broadcast with Dick Van Dyke.

See: Dickinson, Joy Wallace. "Swimming Belle Became Smiling Face of Florida." *Orlando Sentinel.* August 5, 2007; Paula, Paul, & Charles Mitchell. "Gill-Man's Underwater Mate." *Filmfax.* June-July 1999.

BARBARA STANWYCK (1907–1990)

Classic leading lady Barbara Stanwyck (born Ruby Catherine Stevens in Brooklyn) was as gutsy as they come. She enjoyed doing her own physical action and described herself as a frustrated stunt-woman. The former 5'4" Ziegfeld Girl and Broad-way dancer played the title role in *Annie Oakley* (1935) and insisted on doing many of her own stunts jumping on and off trains on *Union Pacific* (1939). She again refused a double for a railway crash on *No Man of Her Own* (1950). Jock Mahoney taught her horse stunts for *Cattle Queen of Montana* (1954) and she did her own drag behind a horse on *Forty Guns* (1957) after a stuntwoman turned it down. Even approaching the age of sixty, she was still doing a great deal of her own action on the TV series *The Big Valley* (1965–69), for which she was awarded a posthumous Golden Boot. Stanwyck died from congestive heart failure at the age of 82.

See: Callahan, Dan. *Barbara Stanwyck: The Miracle Woman.* Jackson, MS: University Press, 2012; Smith, Ella. *Starring Miss Barbara Stanwyck.* NY: Crown, 1973; "Stunt Girl." *St. Petersburg Times.* April 20, 1950; "Taking on Rough Scenes Just Fine with Barbara." *Victoria Advocate.* September 28, 1958.

MARY STATLER (1937–)

Five-foot-four rodeo trick rider Mary Statler was a charter member of the Stuntwomen's Association. On the Jerry Lewis comedy *Who's Minding the Store?* (1963) she was crushed by a throng of shoppers and run over by a vacuum cleaner. She doubled Carol Lynley on *Once You Kiss a Stranger* (1969) and Sharon Tate on *The Wrecking Crew* (1969). On TV she doubled Joan Collins getting hit by a truck on *Star Trek*. She worked on *Cheyenne Autumn* (1964), *The Great Race* (1965), *Bonnie and Clyde* (1967), *Paint Your Wagon* (1969), and TV's *Perry Mason*.

See: "Young Woman Does Stunts for Movies." *Star-News.* July 4, 1963.

FREDDIE STEELE (1912–1984)

Frederick Earl Burgett from Tacoma, Washington, became the Middleweight Champion of the World as Freddie Steele. 5'10" and 160 pounds, he doubled Errol Flynn for boxing scenes on *Gentleman Jim* (1942) and served as a stunt fighter on *Saratoga Trunk* (1945), *The Great John L* (1945), and *Gentleman Joe Palooka* (1946). He was noted for his acting roles as tough soldiers in *Hail the Conquering Hero* (1944) and *The Story*

of *G.I. Joe* (1945), but opted not to stay in Hollywood.

See: *Youngstown Vindicator.* "Freddie Steele Clicks in Movies." July 26, 1945.

TOM STEELE (1909–1990)

Stunt legend Tom Steele was born Thomas Skeoch in Scotland. The lanky youngster was raised in San Francisco where he worked in steel mills and played polo competitively. He attended Stanford University on a football scholarship, but took an interest in the film business. His first acting assignment was a fight scene with George O'Brien on *Lone Star Ranger* (1930). On his next role in *Their Own Desire* (1930) he played a polo player and performed his own stunts. When he saw how much stuntmen were making, he determined that was the career he wanted. Veteran stuntman George DeNormand taught him the ropes. The 6'1", 180-pound Steele was one of the first stuntmen to use pads to minimize the bumps and bruises. At first he had to hide them from his macho brethren, who were apt to show off their scars like trophies.

Steele began at Universal, became a "Stunt Cousin," and was soon heading up Republic's action unit when Dave Sharpe went off to war in 1942. Many of Republic's leading men were cast due to their resemblance to Steele, and he himself portrayed the title character in *The Masked Marvel* (1943). At Republic he doubled Allan Lane, Bill Elliott, Sunset Carson, Roy Rogers, Monte Hale, Clayton Moore, James Warren, and Rex Allen. On bigger films he covered for Henry Fonda, James Stewart, Randolph Scott, Gary Cooper, George Montgomery, Mike Connors, Joseph Cotten, and Hugh O'Brian. Steele doubled Robert Mitchum on *Lone Star Trail* (1943), Rod Cameron on *G-Men vs. the Black Dragon* (1943), *Secret Service in Darkest Africa* (1943), *Salome Where She Danced* (1945), *Brimstone* (1949), *Hell's Outpost* (1954), and *Santa Fe Passage* (1955), Ben Johnson on *Wild Stallion* (1951), James Arness on fire as *The Thing from Another World* (1951), and Lee Marvin on *The Wild One* (1953). One of his best fights was against Mike Connors on *Flesh and the Spur* (1957). Steele was known for his smooth, fluid fighting style. He glided across the screen with the footwork of a boxer.

He also worked on *Captain Blood* (1935), *The Charge of the Light Brigade* (1936), *Flash Gor-*

Ken Terrell tries to harpoon Tom Steele on the serial *The Masked Marvel* (1943).

don (1936), *Undersea Kingdom* (1936), *The Storm* (1938), *Dick Tracy Returns* (1938), *The Spider's Web* (1938), *Red Barry* (1938), *Flash Gordon's Trip to Mars* (1938), *Buck Rogers* (1939), *Gunga Din* (1939), *Dick Tracy's G-Men* (1939), *Seven Sinners* (1940), *Santa Fe Trail* (1940), *Flash Gordon Conquers the Universe* (1940), *Mysterious Doctor Satan* (1940), *King of the Texas Rangers* (1941), *Citizen Kane* (1941), *Holt of the Secret Service* (1941), *Spy Smasher* (1942), *Perils of Nyoka* (1942), *Pittsburgh* (1942), *Daredevils of the West* (1943), *In Old Oklahoma* (1943), *Captain America* (1944), *The Tiger Woman* (1944), *Haunted Harbor* (1944), *Zorro's Black Whip* (1944), *The Fighting Seabees* (1944), *Sudan* (1945), *The Purple Monster Strikes* (1945), *Manhunt of Mystery Island* (1945), *Federal Operator 99* (1945), *Jeep Herders* (1945), *The Big Sleep* (1946), *The Crimson Ghost* (1946), *Daughter of Don Q* (1946), *Wyoming* (1947), *Brute Force* (1947), *Jesse James Rides Again* (1947), *Gallant* *Legion* (1948), *Adventures of Frank and Jesse James* (1948), *Dangers of the Canadian Mounted* (1948), *G-Men Never Forget* (1948), *Ghost of Zorro* (1949), *Mighty Joe Young* (1949), *Radar Patrol vs. Spy King* (1949), *King of the Rocket Men* (1949), *Federal Agents vs. Underworld Inc.* (1950), *The Invisible Monster* (1950), *Flying Disc Man from Mars* (1951), *Soldiers Three* (1951), *Sealed Cargo* (1951), *Don Daredevil Rides Again* (1951), *Cripple Creek* (1952), *Radar Men from the Moon* (1952), *Montana Belle* (1952), *Law and Order* (1953), *All the Brothers Were Valiant* (1953), *Thunder Bay* (1953), *Seven Brides for Seven Brothers* (1954), *Cattle Queen of Montana* (1954), *Man with the Steel Whip* (1954), *The Prodigal* (1955), *Ten Wanted Men* (1955), *Day the World Ended* (1955), *The Rawhide Years* (1955), *Showdown at Abilene* (1956), *Tension at Table Rock* (1956), *The Wings of Eagles* (1957), *No Time for Sergeants* (1958), *These Thousand Hills* (1959), *Spartacus* (1960),

The Honeymoon Machine (1961), *The Spiral Road* (1962), *Donovan's Reef* (1963), *It's a Mad, Mad, Mad, Mad World* (1963), *McLintock!* (1963), *4 for Texas* (1963), *The Comedy of Terrors* (1963), *Cattle King* (1963), *Quick Before It Melts* (1964), *The Great Race* (1965), *Cat Ballou* (1965), *Our Man Flint* (1966), *The Silencers* (1966), *Harper* (1966), *Welcome to Hard Times* (1967), *Bullitt* (1968), *The Love Bug* (1968), *Skin Game* (1971), *Diamonds Are Forever* (1971), *The Poseidon Adventure* (1972), *Conquest of the Planet of the Apes* (1972), *The New Centurions* (1972), *Freebie and the Bean* (1974), *Blazing Saddles* (1974), *The Front Page* (1974), *Earthquake* (1974), *The Towering Inferno* (1974), and *Bound for Glory* (1976). TV credits include *The Lone Ranger, Wild Bill Hickok, Kit Carson, Wyatt Earp, Soldiers of Fortune, State Trooper, Have Gun—Will Travel, Zane Grey, Peter Gunn, Trackdown, Black Saddle, Yancy Derringer, Wanted—Dead or Alive, Mr. Lucky, Bat Masterson, The Westerner, Laramie, Wagon Train, Iron Horse, Star Trek, Hondo, Mod Squad,* and *Mission: Impossible.* He was a member of the Stuntmen's Association and the Stuntmen's Hall of Fame.

See: Copeland, Bobby. "Remembering Tom Steele." *Under Western Skies.* #40, 1991; Mallory, Michael. *Filmfax.* "Tom Steele." April-May 1992; Mallory, Michael. "Tom Steele: King of the Cliffhangers." *Starlog.* #137, December 1988.

RON STEIN

Ronald Gary Stein began his career as a crewman on the TV series *Voyage to the Bottom of the Sea* (1965–68). He continued performing action on *The Rat Patrol* (1966–68) and *Young Rebels* (1970–71) as the double for Alex Hentelhoff. Due to his husky physique (5'9", 200 pounds), Stein played stunt gorillas on the TV series *Planet of the Apes* (1974) in addition to doubling James Naughton. Stein was a top boxing coordinator, responsible for the Sugar Ray Robinson fights on *Raging Bull* (1980) and the ring action on *Rocky 3* (1982). He was the president of Stunts Unlimited.

He worked on *The Love-Ins* (1967), *Stay Away, Joe* (1968), *Charro* (1969), *A Dream of Kings* (1969), *The Illustrated Man* (1969), *MASH* (1970), *There Was a Crooked Man...* (1970), *The Magnificent Seven Ride* (1972), *The Poseidon Adventure* (1972), *Bound for Glory* (1976), *Nickelodeon* (1976), *A Star Is Born* (1976), *The Great*

Texas Dynamite Chase (1976), and *The Hills Have Eyes* (1977). TV credits include *The FBI, Firehouse, Kolchak: The Night Stalker, Barbary Coast, Charlie's Angels, Wonder Woman, Buck Rogers,* and *Fantasy Island.*

See: "It's Double Trouble." *Greensboro Daily News.* November 1, 1970.

JACK STERLING (1899–1978)

Jack Sterling was born in Russia as Jacob David Sterlin. The former Santa Monica lifeguard was a longtime stuntman for MGM and served with the Army Air Corps as a pilot during World War II. He worked on *Mutiny on the Bounty* (1935), *Captains Courageous* (1937), *Reap the Wild Wind* (1942), *Adventure* (1945), *O.S.S.* (1946), *Romance of Rosy Ridge* (1947), *Task Force* (1949), *Across the Wide Missouri* (1951), *Shane* (1953), *20,000 Leagues Under the Sea* (1954), *Dragnet* (1954), *Blood Alley* (1955), and *Friendly Persuasion* (1956).

ALEX STEVENS (1936–)

Connecticut-born Alex Poulos got his start as a cowboy stuntman with Joe Pronto at Wild West City in Netcong, New Jersey. He performed stunts on Broadway while tending bar through the lean times. Taking the professional name Alex Stevens, he was the werewolf on the cult TV series *Dark Shadows* (1968–70) and the cake baker who takes a stair fall on the long-running kids show *Sesame Street.* Stevens landed his big break as a double for Frank Sinatra on *Lady in Cement* (1968) and *The Detective* (1968). His most famous stunt involved being shot by Gene Hackman and tumbling down a flight of stairs on *The French Connection* (1971).

He also worked on *A Lovely Way to Die* (1968), *Hercules in New York* (1970), *House of Dark Shadows* (1970), *The Projectionist* (1971), *Night of Dark Shadows* (1971), *Who Killed Mary What's 'Er Name?* (1971), *Lady Liberty* (1972), *Shaft's Big Score* (1972), *Super Fly* (1972), *Shamus* (1972), *The Dion Brothers* (1974), *Claudine* (1974), *God Told Me To* (1976), *Eyes of Laura Mars* (1978), and *Superman* (1978). TV credits include *Kojak* and *Ryan's Hope.* He was president of the East Coast Stuntman's Association.

See: "Stuntman Likes Fistfights and High Falls." *Salina Journal.* October 7, 1973.

CHARLES STEVENS (1893–1964)

Studio publicity claimed Arizona-born Charles George Stevens was the grandson of Geronimo. He performed with the 101 Ranch Wild West Show and landed in Hollywood during the early days of picture-making on *Birth of a Nation* (1915). The 5'10", 150-pound Stevens became a regular horseman and stunt performer on the films of Douglas Fairbanks, often taking on the riskiest stunts. Fairbanks found Stevens to be good luck and rewarded him with larger roles in *Robin Hood* (1922) and *The Gaucho* (1928). When sound came in, Stevens became adept at playing wiry, back-stabbing Mexicans and Indians on dozens of films.

BOYD STOCKMAN (1916–1998)

Ira D. Boyd Stockman was born in Redrock, New Mexico. He grew up on a California cattle ranch and competed on the rodeo circuit as a calf roper and steer wrestler. He was an excellent horseman and regarded as one of the best teamsters, recruited as a chariot driver on *Ben-Hur* (1959). Stockman doubled Jimmy Wakely, Johnny Mack Brown, and Gene Autry on B-westerns. On TV he doubled Neville Brand on *Laredo* (1965–67). An able fight man, he battled Johnny Mack Brown on *Gun Talk* (1947) and Rod Cameron on *Stampede* (1949). Stockman played one of the title creatures on *The Alligator People* (1959).

He also worked on *Cow Town* (1950), *Stage to Tucson* (1950), *Texans Never Cry* (1951), *Whirlwind* (1951), *The Duel at Silver Creek* (1952), *Column South* (1953), *Gun Belt* (1953), *The Man from Laramie* (1955), *Ten Wanted Men* (1955), *Westward Ho, the Wagons!* (1956), *Night Passage* (1957), *3:10 to Yuma* (1957), *The Hanging Tree* (1959), *Ride Lonesome* (1959), *The Gambler Wore a Gun* (1961), and *Gone with the West* (1975). TV credits include *The Lone Ranger*, *The Range Rider*, *Gene Autry*, *Kit Carson*, *Buffalo Bill, Jr.*, *Soldiers of Fortune*, *Gunsmoke*, *Tales of Wells Fargo*, *Laramie*, and *The Virginian*.

JACK STONEY (1897–1978)

John J. Stoney was born in Chester, Pennsylvania. A former boxer and baseball player, he was known for his accurate arm. Whenever objects needed to be thrown on the screen, Stoney was the go-to man. He hit George Raft with a turnip on *The Bowery* (1933) and pelted Wallace Beery with tomatoes on *The Mighty Barnum* (1934). Stoney got his start on Keystone and Christie comedies and was regarded as a top fight man, doubling Charles Bickford on *The Farmer Takes a Wife* (1935) and George Sanders on *Son of Fury* (1942).

He also worked on *Thief of Baghdad* (1924), *Call of the Wild* (1935), *White Fang* (1936), *Slave Ship* (1937), *Hollywood Cavalcade* (1939), *Dodge City* (1939), *Santa Fe Marshal* (1940), *Reap the Wild Wind* (1942), *Fall In* (1942), *Lady Takes a Chance* (1943), *The Kansan* (1943), *Passage to Marseille* (1944), *They Were Expendable* (1945), *The Spanish Main* (1945), *Angel and the Badman* (1947), *The Three Musketeers* (1948), *Soldiers Three* (1951), *Cripple Creek* (1952), *Law and Order* (1953), *The Man Behind the Gun* (1953), *The War of the Worlds* (1953), *Prince Valiant* (1954), *The Egyptian* (1954), *20,000 Leagues Under the Sea* (1954), *Border River* (1954), *Abbott and Costello Meet the Keystone Kops* (1955), *The Boss* (1956), *Around the World in Eighty Days* (1956), *Red Sundown* (1956), and *Elmer Gantry* (1960). He finished off his career working as a TV extra. He was an honorary member of the Stuntmen's Association and an inductee of the Stuntmen's Hall of Fame.

See: "Behind the Scenes of Hollywood." *Tyrone Daily Herald*. October 13, 1934.

BLACKIE STORM (1926–2009)

Blackie Storm was born Kenneth Stephens in Piedmont, Alabama. He was raised in Texas and worked on a ranch prior to Navy service in World War II. Touring the rodeo circuit he was hired as a stunt rider on *The Lusty Men* (1952), paid $100 for each bucking bronc he rode. Stunt performances at Corriganville showcased his quick draw and bullwhip skills. He later formed a group of stuntmen he called the Storm Riders in the Houston area. He worked on *The Alamo* (1960) and *El Dorado* (1967), and was the black-shirted gunman shot down by James Arness during the opening credits of color *Gunsmoke* episodes. A famous outtake saw him shoot Marshal Dillon down. TV credits include *Have Gun—Will Travel*, *Rin Tin Tin*, *Rawhide*, *Wyatt Earp*, *Bat Masterson,* and *Wagon Train.*

Jack Stoney takes a punch from John Wayne on *The Lady Takes a Chance* (1943). Fred Graham is in the background between them and Richard Talmadge is over Wayne's shoulder.

See: Gidlund, Carl. "Cowboy Classic." *Spokesman-Review.* July 28, 2007; Toohey, Mark. "Ex-Rodeo Star Hit the Big Time." *Victoria Advocate.* December 13, 1984.

GLENN STRANGE (1899–1973)

Six-foot-five, 220-pound George Glenn Strange was born in Weed, New Mexico, and grew up to be a cowboy and sheriff's deputy. He competed in rodeo events, wrestling, and boxing. Strange entered the film industry in the early 1930s as a stuntman, doubling John Wayne on *Ride Him Cowboy* (1932), and was soon showing up as henchmen heavies due to his imposing size. He was hired often as he was a good actor and producers knew he could do his own riding and fights. Two of his best brawls came against Ray Corrigan on *The Kid's Last Ride* (1941) and *Fugitive Valley* (1941).

Because of his height, Strange was given out-of-the-ordinary assignments. He played a dragon in the serial *Flash Gordon* (1936) and the Frankenstein Monster on *House of Frankenstein* (1944), *House of Dracula* (1945), and *Abbott and Costello Meet Frankenstein* (1948). He was part of large-scale brawls on *Dodge City* (1939), *The Desperadoes* (1943), and *Saratoga Trunk* (1945). Strange broke a leg in a late 1940s stage wreck, putting an end to his stunt work, but found a home as Sam the bartender on TV's *Gunsmoke* (1961–73). Strange died of lung cancer at the age of 74.

See: Burns, Bob, & Tom Weaver. "Glenn Strange: One of a Kind." *Films of the Golden Age.* Fall 2003.

WOODY STRODE (1914–1994)

Woody Strode was one of the greatest physical specimens to ever walk across a movie screen. Strode became a track star at UCLA and played end on the school's 1939 Coast Conference co-champion football team. He trained for the 1940 Olympics as a decathlete but saw the games cancelled due to the pending World War. Strode played semi-pro football for the Hollywood Bears then enlisted with the Air Force. In 1946 he and Kenny Washington broke the color barrier in the NFL when they signed contracts with the Cleveland Rams. 6'4", 210-pound Strode played one year in the NFL before he joined the Canadian Football League's Calgary Stampeders and led them to

Woody Strode performs his own stunts leaping about a junkyard on *The Italian Connection* (1973).

a 1948 Grey Cup win. In his off-seasons he worked as a professional wrestler.

Many of his earliest 1950s assignments were spear-carrier roles in jungle adventure films. Johnny Weissmuller recruited him to do a fight on the TV series *Jungle Jim,* and Strode came away impressed by his stunt adjustment pay for taking a fall. He donned a lion costume for *Androcles and the Lion* (1952), when no other stuntman wanted to take that assignment. This was followed by stunt bits on *Demetrius and the Gladiators* (1954) and *The Silver Chalice* (1954), but his fortunes began to change after Cecil B. DeMille cast him in two parts on *The Ten Commandments* (1956).

Strode is best known as the noble opponent of Kirk Douglas in the gladiatorial arena on *Spartacus* (1960). Although the film had an army of stuntmen, none could believably double a stripped-down Woody Strode. He did all of his own fighting, as well as the leap into the box seats. When they needed to hang his body upside down, Strode did that too. He followed this with another memorable battle, balancing on bamboo netting against Jock Mahoney on *Tarzan's Three Challenges* (1963). Strode had a tense TV fight with Clint Eastwood on *Rawhide.* Neither actor employed a double. He was still doing his own stunts well into his fifties, running down a six-team stagecoach on *The Last Rebel* (1971). He received credit as a stunt archer on *The Gatling Gun* (1973), as did his son Kalai. An honoree of the Stuntmen's Hall of Fame, Strode died of lung cancer at the age of 80.

See: Epstein, Dwayne. "Woody Strode: With the Best." *Filmfax.* February-March 1999; Strode, Woody, & Sam Young. *Goal Dust.* Madison, 1990; "Woody Strode's Success: From Football to Westerns." *The Leader Post.* January 24, 1975.

FRED STROMSOE (1930–1994)

Fred Ferdinand Stromsoe was born in Denver, Colorado. At the age of twelve he was signed to a contract by Warner Bros. and put into a talent program. He was such a good athlete that he began to lean toward stunt work. He took time out for military service during the Korean War. A charter member of the Stuntmen's Association, Stromsoe doubled Martin Milner and Glenn Corbett on the TV series *Route 66* (1960–64). He had a running part as Officer Woods on *Adam–*

12 (1972–75) and worked all four years on *The Wild Wild West* (1965–69), taking part in many classic TV fights with Robert Conrad. Stromsoe doubled Tab Hunter, John Agar, Edd Byrnes, Sean McClory, Efrem Zimbalist, Jr., Barry Newman, and David Janssen.

The 165-pound six-footer worked on *The Sea Chase* (1955), *The McConnell Story* (1955), *Lafayette Escadrille* (1958), *The Deep Six* (1958), *Westbound* (1959), *The Slime People* (1963), *Dr. Goldfoot and the Bikini Machine* (1965), *Coogan's Bluff* (1968), *The Love Bug* (1968), *The Good Guys and the Bad Guys* (1969), *The Wrecking Crew* (1969), *Dirty Harry* (1971), *What's Up, Doc?* (1972), *Charley Varrick* (1973), *Cleopatra Jones* (1973), *The Don Is Dead* (1973), and *Blazing Saddles* (1974). TV credits include *The Fugitive, Batman, The Man from U.N.C.L.E., I Spy, Dundee and the Culhane, Gunsmoke, Bearcats, Shaft, Petrocelli, Logan's Run,* and *Dallas.* Stromsoe died at the age of 64 from emphysema.

DON STROUD (1943–)

Six-foot-two, 200-pound Don Stroud excelled at playing half-crazed tough guy villains on everything from *Hawaii Five-O* to *The Fall Guy.* He was born Donald Lee Stroud in Honolulu and stood out as a haole surfing champion. He won the 1960 Makaha Junior Surfing Championship and placed fourth overall in the Duke Kahanamoku International event. At age sixteen he earned a black belt in kajukenbo karate. Stroud was working on the Kahala Hilton beach as a lifeguard when the producers of the TV series *Hawaiian Eye* hired him to double Troy Donahue for surfing sequences. He later came to Los Angeles and served as Donahue's fight double and bodyguard. Stroud was the bouncer at the Whiskey A-Go-Go as his acting career took off playing heavies opposite Clint Eastwood on *Coogan's Bluff* (1968) and *Joe Kidd* (1972). The first film had a memorable motorcycle chase, and bike aficionado Stroud was able to do some of his own riding for the screen.

Stroud and Robert Conrad did a good deal of their own speedboat action for a memorable chase through the waterways of Fort Lauderdale on *Live a Little, Steal a Little* (aka *Murph the Surf*) (1975). The two also had a standout martial arts battle on *Sudden Death* (1975). Stroud excelled at fights and had another memorable karate fight with Park Jong Soo next to Niagara Falls on *Search and Destroy* (1979). On the World War I film *Von Richtofen and Brown* (1971) Stroud and stunt pilot Lynn Garrison were returning from aerial dogfight action in an open biplane when Garrison was knocked unconscious by a bird. The plane immediately crashed into Ireland's large Liffey River. Stroud was able to rescue the unconscious pilot and tread water for nearly an hour until rescue crews found them.

Billed as "Stuntman Don Stroud," he posed nude for *Playgirl* in 1973. He played a stuntman

Don Stroud reacts to a rifle butt to the face from Clint Eastwood on *Joe Kidd* (1972).

on the action film *Hollywood Man* (1976). In the early 1980s Stroud won a celebrity surfing championship and was still doing his own board work playing surf legend Kahuna on the TV series *The New Gidget*. A member of the Black Belt Hall of Fame, Stroud retired to the Hawaiian islands with his wife.

See: Buck, Jerry. "He Rode Ocean Waves into World of Showbiz." *Times-Picayune.* July 27, 1984; Ryan, Tim. "Stroud Returns Home to Isles." *Honolulu Star Bulletin.* July 7, 2005; "Stunt Airplane Crashes in River." *Mobile Register.* September 17, 1970.

CHARLES SULLIVAN (1899–1972)

Beefy, sleepy-eyed Charles B. Sullivan was born in Monroe, Louisiana, and served with the U.S. Navy. He had a professional boxing background as Charlie "Kid" Sullivan and later played fighters, referees, or corner-men in everything from *Kid Galahad* (1937) to *Champion* (1949). Sullivan was a prolific presence in 1930s gangster pictures as gun-toting henchmen in *Scarface* (1932) and *Angels with Dirty Faces* (1938). He was a menacing heavy opposite Harold Lloyd and Laurel and Hardy and doubled Robert Armstrong on *King Kong* (1933).

He also worked on *Her Man* (1930), *Suicide Fleet* (1931), *Dante's Inferno* (1935), *San Francisco* (1936), *The Storm* (1938), *Too Hot to Handle* (1938), *Army Girl* (1938), *Each Dawn I Die* (1939), *The Roaring Twenties* (1939), *Flowing Gold* (1940), *The Bank Dick* (1940), *The Sea Wolf* (1941), *Manpower* (1941), *All Through the Night* (1941), *Captain Midnight* (1942), *In Old Oklahoma* (1943), *The Fighting Seabees* (1944), *Flame of Barbary Coast* (1945), *Unconquered* (1947), *Wild Harvest* (1947), *River Lady* (1948), and *Dawn at Socorro* (1954). Sullivan moved into bits and extra work, although he doubled Gene Sheldon on the TV series *Zorro*. In all he appeared in nearly 500 films.

JOHN SULLIVAN (1925–1997)

London-born Irishman John Edward Sullivan was at one brief moment tagged by the press as the greatest stuntman in the industry, due not only to his athletic skill but to the high-profile assignments he was landing. A former World War II commando, Sullivan moved into stunt work in the early 1950s. He worked on *The Crimson Pirate* (1952), *Ivanhoe* (1952), *Knights of the Round Table* (1953), *Helen of Troy* (1955), *Moby Dick* (1956), and *Zarak* (1956).

Sullivan most famously served as the double for Kirk Douglas on *The Vikings* (1958), where he made a fourteen-foot leap across an eighty-foot high chasm and grasped hold of axe handles protruding from a vertical wooden drawbridge. Sullivan doubled Richard Burton on *Alexander the Great* (1956) and *Cleopatra* (1963), Peter O'Toole on *Lawrence of Arabia* (1962), and Michael Caine on *Zulu* (1964) and *The Last Valley* (1971).

Sullivan was the stunt coordinator for the TV series *Tales of the Vikings* (1959–60). Other top credits include *Exodus* (1960), *Tarzan the Magnificent* (1960), and *The Longest Day* (1962). He moved away from stunts to become a second unit director on *Lord Jim* (1965). He ran the stunts on *The Pink Panther Strikes Again* (1975) and worked on *Barry Lyndon* (1975). Sullivan died from bronchial pneumonia at the age of 72.

See: Williams, Elmo. *A Hollywood Memoir.* Jefferson, NC: McFarland, 2006.

JERRY SUMMERS (1931–2006)

Jerry Summers was born in New York and raised in Los Angeles. He was a track and gymnastic star and dabbled in the rodeo. He doubled Tony Curtis on *Spartacus* (1960) and drove for Roy Scheider on *The Seven-Ups* (1973), a chase scene so spectacular that 20th Century–Fox sent Summers on a publicity tour even though he wasn't credited for the film. On *Dirty Mary, Crazy Larry* (1974) he skidded a car backwards and flipped it into a canal. At one time the 5'8", 150-pound Summers held the record for the highest paid stunt in film history on *Darling Lili* (1970), because perfectionist director David Lean required so many retakes. Summers doubled Sal Mineo, Frank Sinatra, Robert Conrad, and Red Buttons. On TV he doubled Christopher Jones on *Legend of Jesse James* (1965–66) and Walter Koenig on *Star Trek* (1966–69). As an actor he spent one season playing Ira Bean on TV's *High Chaparral* (1967–68).

A veteran of 300 films, Summers suffered a badly broken ankle doubling Peter Falk on TV's *Columbo* doing a simple hanging drop. It affected the rest of his stunt career, causing him to turn to driving stunts. In that area he was one of the best at performing car jumps while working on TV's *The Dukes of Hazzard* (1979–85). Summers drove the roadster for racing scenes on TV's *The Munsters* and was on the first and last episodes of *Gunsmoke*.

He worked on *Little Shepherd of Kingdom Come* (1961), *Five Weeks in a Balloon* (1962), *Captain Newman, M.D.* (1963), *Surf Party* (1964), *The Great Race* (1965), *Harper* (1966), *First to Fight* (1967), *The Green Berets* (1968), *Coogan's Bluff* (1968), *Che!* (1969), *The Great Bank Robbery* (1969), *Flap* (1970), *The Phynx* (1970), *Big Jake* (1971), *Diamonds Are Forever* (1971), *The French Connection* (1971), *The Great Northfield Minnesota Raid* (1972), *What's Up, Doc?* (1972), *Hickey and Boggs* (1972), *The Poseidon Adventure* (1972), *Dillinger* (1973), *Charley Varrick* (1973), *Magnum Force* (1973), *The Front Page* (1974), *99 and 44/100 percent Dead* (1974), *Blazing Saddles* (1974), *Airport '75* (1974), *Rooster Cogburn* (1975), *Marathon Man* (1976), *Avalanche* (1978), *The In-Laws* (1979), *10* (1979), and *Lady in Red* (1979). TV credits include *Have Gun—Will Travel, Tales of Wells Fargo, Laramie, The Virginian, The Man from U.N.C.L.E., The Wild Wild West, Mission: Impossible, I Spy, It Takes a Thief, The FBI, Mod Squad, Barnaby Jones, Emergency, Manhunter, The Rockford Files,* and *Police Woman.* A member of the Stuntmen's Association and an inductee of the Stuntmen's Hall of Fame, Summers died from lung cancer at the age of 74.

See: Funk, Nancy. "Stunts Are No Tricks for Jerry Summers." *Salt Lake Tribune.* December 19, 1973; Pavillard, Dan. "*High Chaparral* Stuntmen Seek Renown, Security." *Tucson Daily Citizen.* January 18, 1968; Silden, Isabel. "Hollywood's Unheralded Heroes: The Stuntmen." *Des Moines Register.* November 26, 1973.

NEIL SUMMERS (1944–)

Neil Summers was born in London, England, but raised in Phoenix, Arizona. While at Camelback High he traveled to Tucson as a stunt extra for the famous mud pit brawl on *McLintock!* (1963). This began a pilgrimage throughout the remainder of the 1960s as the 5'9", 150-pound Summers followed productions throughout Arizona, Utah, and Colorado, seeking what riding extra work he could obtain on films such as *Cheyenne Autumn* (1964) and *The Greatest Story*

Ever Told (1965). He earned his SAG card doing a stair fall on the Audie Murphy film *Arizona Raiders* (1965), with Murphy himself sponsoring him.

Summers doubled Warren Oates, Roddy McDowall, Michael Anderson, Jr., and Michael J. Pollard. Wire services erroneously reported his death after a horse crushed him falling down a hill on *My Name Is Nobody* (1973). Summers was busted up but recovered quickly. He was capable of playing character parts, most notably the hilarious drunk gunfighter Snake River Rufus Krile who ill-advisedly shoots a photo of Lily Langtree on *Life and Times of Judge Roy Bean* (1972). He played a bad deputy harassing Jan-Michael Vincent throughout *White Line Fever* (1975). Summers was a western aficionado and authored several books on TV cowboys and stuntmen.

He worked on *A Distant Trumpet* (1964), *Shenandoah* (1965), *The Hallelujah Trail* (1965), *The Rounders* (1965), *Ride in the Whirlwind* (1965), *The Shooting* (1966), *Duel at Diablo* (1966), *The Plainsman* (1966), *El Dorado* (1967), *Rough Night in Jericho* (1967), *Mackenna's Gold* (1969), *True Grit* (1969), *Heaven with a Gun* (1969), *A Time for Dying* (1969), *Rio Lobo* (1970), *Shoot Out* (1971), *Dirty Little Billy* (1972), *Legend of Nigger Charley* (1972), *Guns of a Stranger* (1973), *Adios Amigo* (1975), *The Outlaw Josey Wales* (1976), *The Last Hard Men* (1976), *Hawmps!* (1976), and *Mr. Billion* (1977). He appeared on the mini-series westerns *Centennial* (1978) and *How the West Was Won* (1978–79). Other TV credits include *Death Valley Days, High Chaparral, Daniel Boone, Gunsmoke, Barnaby Jones, Petrocelli, Grizzly Adams,* and *The Fall Guy.*

See: Brunner, Dixie. "Hollywood Stuntman Is Fall Guy." *American Profile.* April 21, 2002; Ferrier, David. *Wildest Westerns.* "Neil Summers: Stuntman and Character Actor Par Excellence." #5, 2003.; Lilley, Tim. *Campfire Conversations.* Big Trail, 2007; Mayfield, Don. "Western Stuntman, Actor Gets Back on the Horse in N.M." *Albuquerque Journal.* September 26, 2008.

TOM SUTTON (1938–)

Rodeo veteran Tom Sutton entered films as a horse wrangler. He doubled Stuart Whitman on *Cimarron Strip* (1967–68) and married series co-star Jill Townsend. In 1968 he was badly injured in a steer-roping contest when his horse stumbled.

Sutton suffered a skull fracture and a broken ankle but recovered to work for Disney Studios in the 1970s. The 180-pound six-footer's other credits include *Young Fury* (1965), *Apple Dumpling Gang* (1975), *Strange Shadows in an Empty Room* (1976), *Run for the Roses* (1977), and TV's *Gunsmoke*. Sutton was a member of the Stuntmen's Association.

See: "Stuntman Badly Hurt While Roping Cow." *Press Telegram*. July 16, 1968.

GEORGE SUZANNE (1905–1951)

Paris-born Georges Suzanne was one of the top high-fall specialists in Hollywood. He was a stage acrobat who had a background as both a high-wire and circus trapeze artist. Suzanne built his screen rep taking impressive high falls on *Beau Geste* (1939), *The Real Glory* (1939), and *The Hunchback of Notre Dame* (1939). He set a record when he fell forty feet without a net onto a mattress for the film *God Is My Co-Pilot* (1944). He was paid $500 for that fall. Another of his impressive high bumps came on the western *San Antonio* (1945) when he was shot off a balcony and crashed through a saloon table. He doubled Humphrey Bogart on *Casablanca* (1942) and *To Have and Have Not* (1945). Other credits include *Drums of Fu Manchu* (1940), *Captain Caution* (1940), *Adventures of Captain Marvel* (1941), *Perils of Nyoka* (1942), *The Masked Marvel* (1943), *The Spanish Main* (1945), *Adventure* (1945), *Joan of Arc* (1948), and *Rogues of Sherwood Forest* (1950).

See: "Fall of Forty Feet Is All in Day's Work for Georges." *Winnipeg Free Press*. October 7, 1944.

TOM SWEET (1932–1967)

Rodeo bronc rider Thomas Alfred Sweet was born in Los Angeles. He did live shows with Don Durant to promote the TV show *Johnny Ringo* (1959–60) and gained notice as the White Knight of Ajax commercial fame. The popular ad ran over five years, enabling Sweet to buy a horse ranch. He was the owner of the horse Geronimo seen on *The Misfits* (1961). Sweet doubled Elvis Presley on *Flaming Star* (1960) and Tony Young on *Taggart* (1964). He also worked on *Alvarez Kelly* (1966), *The Silencers* (1966), *Stay Away, Joe* (1968),

The Scalphunters (1968), and the TV shows *Have Gun—Will Travel, Wagon Train,* and *Cimarron Strip*. A member of the Stuntmen's Association, Sweet died at the age of 35 in a private plane crash when he hit a 7,000-foot peak near China Lake. His ten-year-old daughter perished with him.

See: "Plane Crash Kills 2 of 4 in Family." *Van Nuys Valley News*. November 23, 1967; "TV's White Knight Says It Beats Bronc Busting." *Tuscaloosa News*. October 10, 1966; "White Knight Ad Runs Many Years." *Findlay Republican*. March 16, 1967.

JAY "SLIM" TALBOT (1895–1973)

Six-foot-three, 170-pound Jay Talbot was born Joseph Bovelle Talbot in Hamilton, Illinois. He was raised as a Montana cowboy and successfully took part in the rodeo circuit as a bronc rider and bulldogger. "Slim" Talbot entered the picture business for $10 a day alongside fellow cowboy Frank Cooper. When his pal became Gary Cooper and rose to stardom Slim was guaranteed a lifetime of employment as Cooper's stand-in and double, mostly doing horse work. In the beginning Cooper was paid $75 a week to play leading roles while Talbot earned up to $80 a week doubling him. Thirty years later Coop was making $150,000 a week while Talbot was earning $500, well above what a stand-in earned in that era.

One of Talbot's most notable stunts came taking a horse off a cliff on *The Adventures of Marco Polo* (1938). His piano safety wire snapped, but Talbot was able to bail out in time. He doubled Slim Summerville, and in *They Just Had to Get Married* (1932) Talbot jumped into a lake while wearing a suit of armor. He nearly drowned when he became stuck in the muddy bottom. Talbot had been a pilot in World War I and between pictures went on barnstorming tours or picked up money as a soldier of fortune. He was featured in the late 1930s radio program *Daredevils of Hollywood*. In the 1940s he temporarily left Hollywood to become the foreman of a ranch in Eugene, Oregon, but was back in the business by the close of the decade.

He worked on *The Lives of a Bengal Lancer* (1935), *The Texans* (1938), *Beau Geste* (1939), *Sergeant York* (1941), *Ball of Fire* (1942), *Saratoga Trunk* (1945), *Dallas* (1950), *Winchester '73* (1950), *Across the Wide Missouri* (1951), *Distant*

Drums (1951), *Springfield Rifle* (1952), *High Noon* (1952), *Vera Cruz* (1954), *Friendly Persuasion* (1956), *Giant* (1956), *The Big Country* (1958), *The Hanging Tree* (1959), and *The Man Who Shot Liberty Valance* (1962). Talbot died from cancer at the age of 77.

See: Finn, Dick. "Gary Cooper's Stand-In Got Star First Job." *Oxnard Press-Courier.* April 5, 1970; "Gary Cooper's Stand-In Back in Movie Again." *Advocate.* October 16, 1961; "Got a Revolution? Cooper's Stand-In Is Tired of Love." *San Diego Union.* June 30, 1938.

FRANK TALLMAN (1919–1978)

New Jersey–born flying ace Frank Gifford Tallman III flew a Beechcraft plane through a balsa wood billboard on *It's a Mad, Mad, Mad, Mad World* (1963), and nearly didn't make it back to the airport when the engine jammed up.

The 6'1", 170-pound Tallman, a former Pensacola Naval flight instructor, began collecting all manner of aircraft after World War II. He partnered with veteran flyer Paul Mantz in Tallmantz Aviation, but had to drop out of the filming of *Flight of the Phoenix* (1965) due to a leg injury. Mantz was killed on the film and Tallman ended up losing his leg to infection. He taught himself to fly with one leg and resumed his career with great success, performing several memorable flying sequences.

He worked on *The Spirit of St. Louis* (1957), *Lafayette Escadrille* (1958), *The Carpetbaggers* (1964), *The Wrecking Crew* (1969), *Catch–22* (1970), *Murphy's War* (1971), *Charley Varrick* (1973), *The Great Waldo Pepper* (1975), *Lucky Lady* (1975), *The Cat from Outer Space* (1978), and *Capricorn One* (1978). TV credits include *Spencer's Pilots* and *Black Sheep Squadron*. A member of the Stuntmen's Association and an in-

Frank Tallman doubles Walter Matthau piloting a biplane on *Charley Varrick* (1973).

ductee of the Stuntmen's Hall of Fame, Tallman died in a private plane crash in the Santa Ana Mountains at the age of 58.

See: "Frank Tallman." *Variety*. April 19, 1978.

RICHARD TALMADGE
(1892–1981)

Richard Talmadge was born in Munich as Sylvester Metzetti. He found success with his brothers Otto and Victor in an acrobatic act that headlined the Barnum and Bailey Circus. A quadruple somersault off a seesaw onto his brother's shoulders got him noticed by the picture business. In 1917 he was doubling Slim Summerville for $3 a day, and then a seventy-foot leap into a ravine led to starring offers. He changed his name to Richard Talmadge and became a silent

Stunt ace Richard Talmadge starred in *Yankee Don* (1931).

film star on *Wildcat Jordan* (1922), *Lucky Dan* (1922), *Speed King* (1923), and *Prince of Pep* (1925). It was his amazing athletic grace and stunting ability that garnered him lasting fame as the double for swashbuckling star Douglas Fairbanks. Talmadge customarily came up with the stunts and perfected them for Fairbanks to do before the cameras. Talmadge did double Fairbanks for a leap onto a roof on *The Mark of Zorro* (1920), a leap from a tree on *The Mollycoddle* (1920), and the dagger ride down the sail on *The Black Pirate* (1926). Talmadge also designed stunts and performed them under the cloak of secrecy for comedian Harold Lloyd. To his dying day Talmadge would not confirm or deny his doubling of Tom Mix leaping Beale's Cut on *Three Jumps Ahead* (1923). He did double George Raft on *Spawn of the North* (1938).

The 5'7", 150-pound Talmadge became renowned for his fearless high falls and precision timing, wowing audiences to the extent that he continued to headline his own films such as *Pirate Treasure* (1934) even as his doubling career was at its peak. His best fight scenes came against George Walsh on *The Live Wire* (1935) and *Step On It* (1936). By the time Yakima Canutt arrived on the scene, Talmadge was winding down his own physical activity. He had broken his neck and back, fractured his right ankle (five times), both arms and legs, and suffered two dozen fractured ribs doing movie stunts. He began to train others as he coordinated stunts and directed second unit action on *The Real Glory* (1939) and *Beau Geste* (1939). He worked with director Henry Hathaway in this capacity for over three decades.

He worked on *Million Dollar Mystery* (1913), *The Three Musketeers* (1921), *Robin Hood* (1922), *The Gaucho* (1927), *Devil Horse* (1932), *The Phantom Empire* (1935), *Trail of the Lonesome Pine* (1936), *Seven Sinners* (1940), *Captain Caution* (1940), *Santa Fe*

Marshal (1940), *Lady Takes a Chance* (1943), *The Desperadoes* (1943), *Frenchman's Creek* (1944), *The Spanish Main* (1945), *Detour to Danger* (1946), *Samson and Delilah* (1949), *Two Flags West* (1950), *Fortunes of Captain Blood* (1950), *Diplomatic Courier* (1952), *Prince Valiant* (1954), *The Egyptian* (1954), *From Hell to Texas* (1958), *Flaming Star* (1960), *North to Alaska* (1960), *300 Spartans* (1962), *How the West Was Won* (1962), *Circus World* (1964), *The Greatest Story Ever Told* (1965), and *Casino Royale* (1967). A member of the Stuntmen's Hall of Fame and an honorary member of the Stuntmen's Association, Talmadge died from cancer at the age of 88.

See: Gregory, Malcolm. "Fall Guy." *Fighting Stars.* February 1979; Hagner, John. *Richard Talmadge: Thrill Seeker.* Self, 1985; Katchmer, George. *Eighty Silent Film Stars.* Jefferson, NC: McFarland, 1991.

DUKE TAYLOR (1907–1982)

Duke Taylor was born Ruel Fenton Taylor III in Oklahoma. He excelled in football, boxing, track, and swimming at the University of Oklahoma. Taylor played professionally for the Chicago Bears, where he earned the nickname "Duke" for his casual disregard of team rules. In Hollywood, Taylor subbed for Bob Livingston, Gene Autry, Roy Rogers, Ray Corrigan, Allan Lane, Ralph Byrd, Grant Withers, Dan Duryea, and Rex Allen. He was expert at horse falls and a solid fight man.

The 180-pound six-footer appeared as the occasional henchman but rarely ended up performing dialogue. He was almost always uncredited. Because of this, he remains significantly less well known than some of his peers. Taylor was long associated with Republic Studios as one of their top stuntmen. During World War II he served with the Marines. In 1945 he made news reports when he and fiancée Lorna Gray were arrested for marijuana possession, a couple of years before Robert Mitchum's notorious bust. Until the heat died down, Taylor went by the name Ruel Fenton, though his appearances at Republic were usually unbilled anyway. After doubling Bill Williams on the TV series *Kit Carson* (1951–55), Taylor retired from stunt work.

He worked on *The Painted Stallion* (1937), *SOS Coast Guard* (1937), *Zorro Rides Again* (1937), *Gunsmoke Ranch* (1937), *Heart of the Rockies* (1938), *Man of Conquest* (1939), *Daredevils of the Red Circle* (1939), *King of the Royal Mounted* (1940), *Mysterious Doctor Satan* (1940), *King of the Texas Rangers* (1941), *Adventures of Captain Marvel* (1941), *Dick Tracy vs. Crime, Inc.* (1941), *Jungle Girl* (1941), *Two Yanks in Trinidad* (1942), *Spy Smasher* (1942), *Perils of Nyoka* (1942), *G-Men vs. the Black Dragon* (1943), *Zorro's Black Whip* (1944), *Manhunt of Mystery Island* (1945), *The Crimson Ghost* (1946), *The Phantom Rider* (1946), *Jesse James Rides Again* (1947), *Gallant Legion* (1948), *River Lady* (1948), *Adventures of Frank and Jesse James* (1948), *Whirlwind* (1951), *The Thing from Another World* (1951), *The Man from the Alamo* (1953), and *City Beneath the Sea* (1953). One of his more interesting assignments came when Bob Livingston took on a dual role and fought himself (Taylor) in *Outlaws of Sonora* (1938). An honorary member of the Stuntmen's Association and an inductee of the Stuntmen's Hall of Fame, Taylor died of a coronary thrombosis at the age of 74.

See: McCord, Merrill. *Brothers of the West: The Life and Films of Robert Livingston and Jack Randall.* Bethesda, Maryland: Alhambra, 2003; Thomas, Bob. "Stunt Men Say Their Business Not Up to Par." *San Mateo Times.* May 1, 1952.

LARRY TAYLOR (1918–2003)

Laurence Taylor was born in Peterborough, England. After World War II he joined Jock Easton's Stunt Team and specialized in fight scenes. Taylor played many swarthy character types, tangling with Mickey Spillane on *Girl Hunters* (1963) and Rod Taylor on *Young Cassidy* (1965). He doubled Mario Adorf on *Ten Little Indians* (1965) and Lee Marvin on *Shout at the Devil* (1976) for notable fights. The father of stuntman Rocky Taylor, he worked on *Alexander the Great* (1956), *Swiss Family Robinson* (1960), *Lawrence of Arabia* (1962), *Zulu* (1964), *The Last Valley* (1971), and *Zulu Dawn* (1979). TV credits include *The Saint, Danger Man, The Prisoner, The Avengers,* and *The Persuaders.* Taylor died from a heart attack at the age of 85.

NORM TAYLOR (1910–1993)

Norm Taylor was born in Salt Lake City, Utah, of Lakota Sioux and Irish heritage. He was also known as Spencer Taylor and Norman Spotted Horse. A horse specialist and wrangler, Taylor was a top level polo player. The 6'3" Taylor doubled Johnny Weissmuller on *Tarzan the Ape Man* (1932) and *Tarzan Escapes* (1936) and Jay Silverheels on *One Little Indian* (1973). He also worked on *Billy the Kid* (1941), *She Wore a Yellow Ribbon* (1949), *Rio Grande* (1950), *Yellow Tomahawk* (1954), *The Indian Fighter* (1955), *The Tall Men* (1955), *The Conqueror* (1956), *The Last Wagon* (1956), *Fort Dobbs* (1958), *Apache Rifles* (1964), *The Greatest Story Ever Told* (1965), *Rough Night in Jericho* (1967), and *Bandolero!* (1968).

ROCKY TAYLOR (1946–)

Laurie "Rocky" Taylor was born in Weybridge, Surrey, England. The son of stuntman Larry Taylor, Rocky began working on films while still in his teens. His film debut was a judo fight on *The Young Ones* (1961). He worked on *Raiders of the Lost Ark* (1981) and every James Bond film from *Dr. No* (1962) up to *Die Another Day* (2002), creating a legendary name within the industry. He jumped from a train for Roger Moore on *Octopussy* (1983) and doubled Sean Connery on *Never Say Never Again* (1983) and *Indiana Jones and the Last Crusade* (1989). He also doubled George C. Scott on *The Last Run* (1971) and Patrick Macnee on TV's *The Avengers*.

The 6'1", 200-pound Taylor was highly skilled, winning the 1982 Stuntman Challenge on Thames TV and taking second place in both 1983 and 1984. He toured the United States and Australia in a live jousting show entitled "Tournament of the Knight." He broke his back and pelvis jumping fifty feet from a burning building making *Death Wish III* (1985). His vision was apparently impaired by the heavy smoke and he missed his airbag. Surgeons implanted metal rods in his pelvis and a bolt in his knee, and he was in the hospital for a full year. This accounted for a shift to stunt coordination and second unit direction. Twenty-six years after his stunt gone wrong, Taylor performed it successfully for charity.

He worked on *From Russia with Love* (1963), *Goldfinger* (1964), *Those Magnificent Men in Their Flying Machines* (1965), *The Dirty Dozen* (1967), *Casino Royale* (1967), *You Only Live Twice* (1967), *Cromwell* (1970), *The Last Valley* (1971), *Man with the Golden Gun* (1974), *The Spy Who Loved Me* (1977), *A Bridge Too Far* (1977), *Force*

10 from Navarone (1978), *The Wild Geese* (1978), and *Superman* (1978). TV credits include *Danger Man*, *The Saint*, *Man in a Suitcase*, *The Baron*, *The Persuaders*, *The Professionals*, and *The Sweeney*.

See: "Britain's Oldest Stuntman Survives 40 Foot Plunge from Burning Building." *Daily Mail.* August 3, 2011; www.actionstuntsrockytaylor. com.

ROD TAYLOR (1930–)

Rugged, two-fisted Aussie Rod Taylor tackled a number of the 1960s' toughest screen assignments and was insistent on doing much of his own screen action. Alfred Hitchcock cast him as the leading man on *The Birds* (1963) because he knew Taylor could withstand being attacked by flying crows. Taylor fans treasure his action films where he engaged in standout fights: *Chuka* (1967), *Dark of the Sun* (1968), and *Darker Than Amber* (1970). The latter is legendary for Taylor and co-star William Smith deviating from the planned choreography into a wild close-quarter free-for-all that saw many of their punches land and cause damage. They both walked away with honorary memberships in the Stuntmen's Association for the memorable brawl.

Five-foot-ten, 185-pound Rodney Sturt Taylor was born in Sydney, Australia. At Parramatta High he was a track athlete and swim champion. Taylor was a lifeguard and captain of the Mona Vale Surf Club, but his greatest athletic success came in the boxing ring where the brawny lad packed a powerful punch. His first role in the United States saw him cast in a fight scene with Alan Ladd for *Hell on Frisco Bay* (1955). In those days Taylor lived on the beach in Malibu and worked out with Paul Stader and George Robotham. When he was cast as the star of the short-lived action series *Hong Kong* (1960–61), Taylor set out to do all his own stunts and deservedly earned his tough guy reputation. Stuntman Louie Elias commented, "Rod could do a fight scene as good as any stuntman."

See: McDaniel, Marlene. *Mr. Louie Elias: A Tribute.* Self, 2010; Scott, Vernon. "Gory Movie Fight for Real." *Seattle Daily Times.* April 26, 1970; Vagg, Stephen. *Rod Taylor: An Aussie in Hollywood.* Duncan, Oklahoma: Bear Manor, 2010.

William Smith and Rod Taylor during their legendary fight on *Darker Than Amber* (1970).

GUY TEAGUE (1913–1970)

Born in Mt. Vernon, Texas, Guy Teague doubled John Wayne, Randolph Scott, Phil Carey, and Rod Cameron. He was Eric Fleming's double on *Rawhide* (1959–66) and portrayed one of the drovers throughout the duration of the show. The 6'4" Teague helped co-star Clint Eastwood become comfortable in the saddle, and his children Brian and Melissa occasionally performed stunts.

He also worked on *Gone with the Wind* (1939), *Adventures of Frank and Jesse James* (1948), *Panhandle* (1948), *Batman and Robin* (1949), *The Gal Who Took the West* (1949), *Texas Rangers* (1951), *Don Daredevil Rides Again* (1951), *The Stranger Wore a Gun* (1953), *Arrowhead* (1953), *The Nebraskan* (1953), *Siege at Red River* (1954), *Man with the Steel Whip* (1954), *A Lawless Street* (1955), *Giant* (1956), *3:10 to Yuma* (1957), and *Guns of the Timberland* (1960). TV credits include *Kit Carson, Wild Bill Hickok, Zane Grey, Maverick,* and *Gunsmoke*. He was a member of the Stuntmen's Hall of Fame.

BOB TERHUNE (1928–)

Six-foot-two, 225-pound Robert Max Terhune was born in Dayton, Ohio, and raised in Indiana. The family moved to California in 1936 so his father Max could enter the motion picture business as comic relief on the Three Mesquiteers films. He played football for Burbank High and spent two years in the Armed Forces and six years on the rodeo circuit as a champion steer wrestler and bulldogger.

"Terrible Terhune" doubled big men such as Lon Chaney, Jr., Alan Hale, Jr., Forrest Tucker, and Gene Evans. He was George Kennedy's double for a number of years including *The Good Guys and the Bad Guys* (1969), *Guns of the Magnificent Seven* (1969), *Cahill, U.S. Marshal* (1973), and *Thunderbolt and Lightfoot* (1974). Terhune doubled Sterling Hayden on *The Iron Sheriff* (1957), Clint Walker on *Gold of the Seven Saints* (1961), and John Wayne on *Circus World* (1964). He served as Wayne's photo double on *The Greatest Story Ever Told* (1965).

He also worked on *Outlaw Country* (1949), *The Desert Fox* (1951), *Ride the Man Down* (1952), *Ten Wanted Men* (1955), *Pillars of the Sky* (1956), *Cowboy* (1958), *Rio Bravo* (1959), *The Unforgiven* (1960), *Seven Ways from Sundown* (1960), *How the West Was Won* (1962), *The Great Race* (1965), *Alvarez Kelly* (1966), *Smoky* (1966), *The King's Pirate* (1967), *Hostile Guns* (1967), *Welcome to Hard Times* (1967), *Camelot* (1967), *The Pink Jungle* (1968), *High Plains Drifter* (1973), *Earthquake* (1974), *The Towering Inferno* (1974), *Moving Violation* (1976), *St. Ives* (1976), *F.M.* (1978), *F.I.S.T.* (1978), *The Villain* (1979), *Prophecy* (1979), and *The Frisco Kid* (1979). TV credits include *Death Valley Days, State Trooper, Cheyenne, Sugarfoot, Lawman, The Texan, Cimarron City, Rawhide, Daniel Boone, Search, The Six Million Dollar Man,* and *Vega$*. Terhune is a member of the Stuntmen's Association.

See: "Daredevil Terhune." *Screen Thrills Illustrated*. Vol. 1, #4. April 1963; Lilley, Tim. *Campfire Conversations*. Akron, OH: Big Trail, 2010.

KEN TERRELL (1904–1966)

Kenneth Jones Terrell was born in Coolidge, Georgia. He excelled in sports at Georgia Tech and became interested in bodybuilding and adagio. In 1922 he entered the World's Most Perfectly Developed Man contest but lost to Charles Atlas. He later established the Terrell and Kemp stage show that played in vaudeville houses. He and his partner performed a balancing act and did acrobatic tumbling and feats of agility. Eventually he hooked up with the versatile Jimmy Fawcett and developed a popular slam-bang act that toured Australia and Europe. Terrell and Fawcett staged their knockabout act for twelve years and included Fawcett's athletic wife Helen Thurston. While performing in California, all three secured work in the motion picture industry as stunt personnel.

A superb high man, the 5'9", 170-pound Terrell specialized in fights that took place on catwalks, ladders, and rooftops. He was highly capable of swinging from fixtures and beams over open spaces and was trained in jiu jitsu. A "Stunt Cousin," Terrell doubled Humphrey Bogart, James Mason, Warner Baxter, Red Skelton, Ronald Colman, Douglas Fowley, John Carroll, and Duncan Renaldo. With his dark features, hawk nose, and feral face he made a perfect heavy and began appearing in countless bit parts, especially at Republic on the serials *Daredevils of the Red Circle* (1939), *Zorro's Fighting Legion* (1939), *Dick Tracy's G-Men* (19396), *King of the Royal Mounted*

Ken Terrell leaps onto catcher Jock Mahoney on *Money, Women, and Guns* (1958).

(1940), *King of the Texas Rangers* (1941), *Adventures of Captain Marvel* (1941), *Spy Smasher* (1942), *Perils of Nyoka* (1942), *King of the Mounties* (1942), *G-Men vs. the Black Dragon* (1943), *Secret Service in Darkest Africa* (1943), *The Masked Marvel* (1943), *Captain America* (1944), *Haunted Harbor* (1944), *The Tiger Woman* (1944), *et al*. In all, he made more than 250 films and over 125 television appearances, performing over 1,300 stunts. His most notable acting assignment came as the two-fisted butler on the sci-fi film *Attack of the 50 Foot Woman* (1958). Terrell broke a leg in 1958 and moved into acting roles the remainder of his career.

He also worked on *Conquest* (1937), *Seven Sinners* (1940), *Winners of the West* (1940), *All Through the Night* (1941), *The Spanish Main* (1945), *Detour to Danger* (1946), *Angel and the Badman* (1947), *Kansas Raiders* (1950), *The Thing from Another World* (1951), *His Kind of Woman* (1951), *Cripple Creek* (1952), *Scarlet Angel* (1952), *All the Brothers Were Valiant* (1953), *Desert Legion* (1953), *Tumbleweed* (1953), *Drums Across the River* (1954), *The Last Command* (1955), *The Conqueror* (1956), *The Ten Commandments* (1956), *Walk the Proud Land* (1956), *The Buccaneer* (1958), *Money, Women, and Guns* (1958), *Spartacus* (1960), *Elmer Gantry* (1960), and *How the West Was Won* (1962). A member of the Stuntmen's Hall of Fame and an honorary member of the Stuntmen's Association, Terrell died of arteriosclerosis at the age of 61.

See: Liederman, Earle. "A Well-Built Body Brought Success to Kenneth Terrell." *Strength & Health*. January 1960.

TEX TERRY (1902–1985)

Indiana-born Edward Earl Terry appeared in 300 films as a stuntman and bit player, often recognizable due to his bushy eyebrows. Terry worked in a coal mine and served with the U.S.

Cavalry, landing in Hollywood in 1922. As a stuntman he'd earn $2.50 a day, sometimes up to $7.50 depending on the stunt's difficulty. He was solidly built and very good with a bullwhip, first using it in on the Douglas Fairbanks film *Don Juan* (1924). He was likely Sunset Carson's whip double at Republic Studios in the 1940s. He worked on nearly all of Gene Autry's films and doubled sidekick Smiley Burnette on *Down Mexico Way* (1941) and *Cowboy Serenade* (1942).

As a B-western henchmen he put on a good fight with Autry on *Twilight on the Rio Grande* (1947). His best villainous roles were *The Maverick Queen* (1956) and *The Oregon Trail* (1959). Terry worked on ten films as a stuntman with John Wayne, the last being *The War Wagon* (1967). TV credits include *Death Valley Days, Gunsmoke,* and *Have Gun—Will Travel.* He often returned to Indiana to put on gun, whip, and rope demonstrations for local schools and later opened Tex's Longhorn Tavern in Coxville, Indiana. Terry died from a heart attack at the age of 82.

See: "Actor Tex Terry Dies at 82." *Ocala Star-Banner.* May 20, 1985; Buntain, Rex. "Movie Villain Tex Terry Recalls Many Roles." *Park City Daily News.* June 27, 1983; www.texterry.com.

ROBERT TESSIER (1934–1990)

Bob Tessier looked like the last guy anyone would want to meet in a dark alley. With his shaved head, tattoos, scowling visage, 50" chest, and nearly 19" biceps, he defined movie menace at a time when nobody else had that look. In *The Longest Yard* (1974) a shirtless Tessier practices his karate moves, and nobody doubts that he is indeed the baddest man on the cellblock. On *Hard Times* (1975) he went up against Charles Bronson in one of the screen's most memorable fight scenes. On *The Deep* (1977) he fought Mr. Universe Earl Maynard with a real outboard motor running perilously close to his face.

Robert W. Tessier was born in Lowell, Massachusetts, of French-Canadian, Senaca, and Algonquin Indian descent. He grew up on the Indian reserve performing sixty-foot somersault dives into the icy Merrimack River. During the Korean War he was a paratrooper with the 45th Thunderbird Division. Tessier was awarded two Bronze Stars, a Silver Star, and four Purple Hearts. He worked as a bouncer, toiled in construction, dabbled as a trapeze catcher and stunt cyclist for the Ringling Brothers Circus, and took up bodybuilding.

The 6'1", 230-pound Tessier arrived in Hollywood in 1962 working as a grip at Universal by day and a carpenter at CBS Studios in the evening. Whenever an extra was needed, Tessier stepped in. Between jobs he auditioned for stunt assignments, distinguishing himself as an expert at performing motorcycle jumps and high falls. He trained big cats and was capable on a horse, playing a number of Indians during 1960s westerns. His big break came as the stunt coordinator on *Born Losers* (1967), in which he also played a memorable heavy. Many motorcycle movies followed.

When fellow stuntmen created Stunts Unlimited in 1970, Tessier was one of the first members. He slid bikes into cars and under moving trailer trucks, jumped a bike onto a moving train, drove motorcycles and wagons off cliffs, and went off a ski jump on only one ski. As an actor-stuntman he worked on *Glory Stompers* (1967), *Run, Angel, Run!* 69), *Cry Blood, Apache* (1970), *The Jesus Trip* (1971), *Doc Savage* (1975), *Breakheart Pass* (1976), *Last of the Mohicans* (1977), *Hooper* (1978), *Steel* (1979), and the mini-series *Centennial* (1978). TV credits include *Cannon, Kung Fu, Starsky and Hutch, Buck Rogers, Hart to Hart, The Dukes of Hazzard, The Incredible Hulk, Vega$,* and *The Fall Guy.* Tessier died from cancer at the age of 56.

See: Brownstein, Bill. "Top Gun Tessier Shoots from the Hip." *Montreal Gazette.* April 20, 1985; Daniel, Gregg. "Bob Tessier: The Villain Who Turns Hero." *Easyrider.* December 1986; Doyle, James. "Soul of an Artist Behind the Cruel Smile." *San Diego Union.* October 25, 1981; "Toughness Seen as Part of Job for Local Stunt Man." *Boston Herald.* July 29, 1979.

HELEN THURSTON (1909–1979)

Helen Thurston was born in Oregon and gained acclaim as an athlete at Redding High. An aerialist and vaudeville acrobat, Thurston became an Olympic diving champ. She doubled Katharine Hepburn rolling down a hill on *Bringing Up Baby* (1938), Marlene Dietrich cat-fighting on *Destry Rides Again* (1939), Marilyn Monroe rafting down rapids on *River of No Return* (1954), and Eleanor Parker falling thirty feet on *Man with the Golden*

Charles Bronson fights Robert Tessier on *Hard Times* (1975).

Arm (1955). She also doubled Anne Baxter on *The Magnificent Ambersons* (1942), Kim Novak on *Jeanne Eagles* (1957), Ethel Merman on *It's a Mad, Mad, Mad, Mad World* (1963), and Lucille Ball and Vivian Vance on TV's *I Love Lucy*.

The 5'6" Thurston also worked on *Hold That Co-Ed* (1938), *Daredevils of the Red Circle* (1939), *Mysterious Doctor Satan* (1940), *Jungle Girl* (1941), *Perils of Nyoka* (1942), *Zorro's Black Whip* (1944), *The Spanish Main* (1945), *Pete Kelly's Blues* (1955), *The Guns of Fort Petticoat* (1957), *Spartacus* (1960), and *The Great Race*

(1965). She was the wife of stuntman Jimmy Fawcett, with whom she had a stunt-filled stage act. She was a charter member of the Stuntwomen's Association.

See: Hale, Mary. "Helen Plays Tag with Leopard, But Spider Makes Her Shudder." *Reading Eagle.* May 4, 1941; Moler, Murray. "Want Dainty Gal Bodyguard? Helen Thurston Can Qualify." *Waterloo Daily Courier.* February 7, 1945; "Helen Thurston, Stunt Girl, Likes Rough and Tumble Fights." *Reading Eagle.* January 12, 1957.

CASEY TIBBS (1929–1990)

Rodeo legend Casey Duane Tibbs was born in Fort Pierre, South Dakota, and began competing at the age of fourteen. The 1951 and 1955 World All-Around Rodeo Champ was the World Saddle Bronc Champ six times and the 1951 World Bareback Bronc Champion. In 1951 he was on the cover of *Life* magazine, attracting the attention of Hollywood. Tibbs doubled Don Murray on *Bus Stop* (1956) and Henry Fonda and Glenn Ford on *The Rounders* (1965). On the TV series *Stoney Burke* (1962–63) he was the technical advisor and doubled Jack Lord. He served as the rodeo coordinator for *Junior Bonner* (1972).

He also worked on *Bronco Buster* (1952), *The Lusty Men* (1952), *A Thunder of Drums* (1961), *Texas Across the River* (1966), *Gunpoint* (1966), *The Plainsman* (1966), *Firecreek* (1968), *Heaven with a Gun* (1969), *A Time for Dying* (1969), *The Cowboys* (1972), and *Breakheart Pass* (1976). TV credits include *Branded, The Rounders,* and *The Monroes.* A Golden Boot Award honoree and a member of the Pro Rodeo Cowboy Hall of Fame, Tibbs died from cancer at the age of 60.

See: Richards, Rusty. *Casey Tibbs: Born to Ride.* Wickenburg, AZ: Moonlight Mesa, 2010; www.caseytibbs.com.

LOUIS TOMEI (1910–1955)

Luigi "Louis" Tomei was born in Portland, Oregon, and is best known as an Indianapolis 500 race car driver. He finished in tenth place in 1937. As a car specialist, he comprised one of the famed "Stunt Cousins" that banded together at Universal in the late 1930s. Tomei died at the age of 45 from a cerebral hemorrhage incurred while working a fight scene on *Hell on Frisco Bay* (1955) when he struck his head on a boat's framework.

He worked on *Seven Sinners* (1940), *Invisible Agent* (1942), *Spy Smasher* (1942), *South Sea Sinner* (1950), *The Flame and the Arrow* (1950), *The Iron Mistress* (1952), *Jalopy* (1953), *The Charge at Feather River* (1953), *Johnny Dark* (1954), *A Star Is Born* (1954), *20,000 Leagues Under the Sea* (1954), *Prince Valiant* (1954), *The Egyptian* (1954), *The Silver Chalice* (1954), and *The Prodigal* (1955). Tomei was an honorary member of the Stuntmen's Association and an inductee of the Stuntmen's Hall of Fame.

See: "Luigi Tomei." *Variety.* May 18, 1955; "Surgery Fails to Save Films Stunt Driver." *Pittsburgh Post-Gazette.* May 17, 1955.

ROGER TORREY (1938–1985)

Roger Torrey was born Roger Pugmire in Pocatello, Idaho. Six-foot five and 240 pounds, the former lumberjack augmented his great natural size and strength by lifting weights. He won the Best Chest Award in the 1959 Mr. Idaho body-building contest. In Hollywood his horsemanship landed him a year-long job as the stunt double for James Arness on TV's *Gunsmoke.* His acting career received a boost when he was hired to play a heavy who fights Jeff Chandler on *The Plunderers* (1960). He was cast as a lumberjack on TV's *Iron Horse* (1966–67), battling series star Dale Robertson. His best fight came against Arness on the 1972 *Gunsmoke* episode "The River." Torrey died at the age of 47 from a cerebral hemorrhage.

See: Hall, Bill. "Roger Pugmire Got Tired of Cheese, So He Became a Movie Star." *Idaho State Journal.* December 6, 1960; Thomas, Bob. "Roger Pugmire Gets New Name, and Bright Future in Movies." *Moberly Monitor.* May 14, 1960.

DON TURNER (1910–1982)

Don Turner was born in Colorado, raised in California, and worked as a cowboy and lumberjack in the state of Washington. He was a standout track and field athlete for Occidental College and the University of Southern California, specializing in the mile and two-mile distance run. His overall athleticism, riding skill, and fencing ability made him a natural for stunt work on the many swashbuckling films popular during that era. He worked primarily at Warner Bros. and doubled Errol Flynn on *Captain Blood* (1935), *The Charge of the Light Brigade* (1936), *The Adventures of*

Robin Hood (1938), *Dodge City* (1939), *The Sea Hawk* (1940), *Santa Fe Trail* (1940), *Dive Bomber* (1941), *Adventures of Don Juan* (1948), *Silver River* (1948), and *Adventures of Captain Fabian* (1951).

Turner also doubled Gary Cooper, Ronald Reagan, and George Brent. At one point he was called Hollywood's best known stuntman, earning a reputation for safety at a time when some stuntmen were known for recklessness. Turner was out of the industry by the time he was fifty. He had already hinted at leaving. At the height of his earning power in the early 1940s, Turner and his wife left Hollywood to run a ranch in the Elysian Valley, only to return after two years. In the late 1940s Flynn's stand-in Jim Fleming announced he intended to produce low-budget westerns with Don Turner as the star, although no Turner cowboy films were ever released.

In the early 1950s, film extra Jules Garrison sued Warner Bros. when they claimed in a newsreel that anyone proving star Burt Lancaster didn't do all of his own hazardous stunts would be paid a million dollars. The extra said Turner doubled Lancaster on numerous occasions on *The Flame and the Arrow* (1950). The suit was ruled in favor of the studio, with a judge determining from film footage that the three scenes in which Turner was doubling Lancaster were not "hazardous."

He worked on *God's Country and the Woman* (1937), *Valley of the Giants* (1938), *Gold Is Where You Find It* (1938), *Heart of the North* (1938), *Secret Service of the Air* (1939), *Cloak and Dagger* (1946), *Slave Girl* (1947), *Fortunes of Captain Blood* (1950), *At Sword's Point* (1952), *High Noon* (1952), *The World in His Arms* (1952), *Valley of the Kings* (1954), *The Silver Chalice* (1954), *The Killing* (1956), *The Buccaneer* (1958), *The Hanging Tree* (1959), and *Spartacus* (1960). Turner retired to Lake Havasu, Arizona, where he died at the age of 71.

See: "New Film Project." *Milwaukee Sentinel.* December 19, 1947.

TOM TYLER (1903–1954)

Tom Tyler was born Vincent Markowski in Port Henry, New York, and raised in Hamtramck, Michigan. Active in scholastic sports, he began weightlifting to build his physique. In California he worked as a merchant seaman, lumberjack, and physique model. As a stunt extra his highest pro-file credit came as a chariot driver on the 1925 *Ben-Hur*. His lean, sturdy physique, engaging smile, and handsome features won him the new cowboy star gig for FBO. Rechristened Tom Tyler, he went on a crash horseback course for *Let's Go, Gallagher* (1925). Brawling came naturally, and he did his own fights. As his star ascended, Tyler became the AAU National Weightlifting Champion and qualified for the 1928 Olympic Games.

The 6'2", 200-pound Tyler headlined countless B-westerns while working small parts in the more prestigious *Gone with the Wind* (1939) and *Stagecoach* (1939). He had a highly regarded fight with Victor Jory on *The Light of Western Stars* (1940) in which both men did their own stunts, and followed with another big battle against Rod Cameron on *Boss of Boomtown* (1944). Tyler played the Mummy on *The Mummy's Hand* (1940) and starred in two of the industry's most popular serials *Adventures of Captain Marvel* (1941) and *The Phantom* (1943). Still, he would just as easily show up uncredited alongside a group of stuntmen for screen brawls on *Her Man* (1930) and *Brother Orchid* (1940).

Unfortunately, his muscular body began to fail him. Tyler was stricken with the genetic disease scleroderma, a degenerative arthritic condition that affects the skin, joints, and internal organs. He continued to act but was often relegated to playing stone-faced henchmen. By 1953 the painful disease had crippled him. He returned to Michigan to live his final days, dying of heart failure at the age of 50.

See: Chapman, Mike, & Bobby J. Copeland. *The Tom Tyler Story.* Culture House, 2005; Price, Bob. "Tom Tyler." *Screen Thrills Illustrated.* October 1963.

JACK TYREE (1943–1981)

Six-foot-two, 195-pound Tennessee-born John Hale Tyree served in the Marine Corps in Vietnam prior to working on TV's *The Virginian* at Universal Studios, where he did live shows. A professional scuba instructor and skin diver, he was married underwater at Marineland to stuntwoman Corna Day in 1967. Actor Doug McClure was his Best Man. Tyree died at the age of 37 performing an eighty-foot fall off a cliff on *The Sword and the Sorcerer* (1982), missing his air bag by two feet. The stunt was left in the film, which was dedicated to him. He worked on *Planet of the Apes*

(1968), *Flap* (1970), *Lost Flight* (1970), *The Don Is Dead* (1973), *Prophecy* (1979), *Stunt Seven* (1979), *The Nude Bomb* (1980), and the TV series *Men from Shiloh, Young Rebels, McCloud, Kojak, The Rockford Files, Police Story, Planet of the Apes,* and *How the West Was Won.* Tyree was a member of the Stuntmen's Association.

See: *San Diego Union.* "Couple Plunges into Matrimony." October 8, 1967; "Stuntman Killed in 80 Foot Jump." *Seattle Daily Times.* August 27, 1981.

DAN VADIS (1938–1987)

Constantine Daniel Vafiadis was born in Shanghai, China, of Chinese and Greek descent. He served in the U.S. Navy and was part of the Mae West bodybuilding line-up recruited from Muscle Beach. Known for his daredevil stunts and athleticism, he could do standing back-flips and perform handstands on the ledge of tall buildings. His leaping ability was unparalleled. He competed for the Marina Del Rey Outrigger Canoe Club, paddling to Catalina Island, and played football at L.A. City College. Six-foot-four and 225 pounds, he tested for Tarzan, but was deemed too muscular. He was also too big to convincingly double other actors so he entered European gladiator films under the name Dan Vadis.

Vadis was one of the few musclemen to stick around Europe through the spy and spaghetti western genres and often coordinated stunts. He had an excellent fight with Brad Harris on *Death Is Nimble, Death Is Quick* (1966) and did an impressive death fall on *The Stranger Returns* (1967). He's knocked into a campfire on *The Scalphunters* (1968). Vadis had solid supporting roles as menacing heavies opposite John Wayne on *Cahill—U.S. Marshal* (1973) and Clint Eastwood on *High Plains Drifter* (1973). Vadis fought Eastwood on screen often, getting knocked from a train on *The Gauntlet* (1977) and playing a comic biker on *Every Which Way But Loose* (1978) and *Any Which Way You Can* (1980). Eastwood gave him his best role, as the Indian snake dancer on *Bronco Billy* (1980). Vadis died under mysterious circumstances at the age of 49, found in the backseat of a car on the highway with a lethal combination of heroin and morphine in his body.

See: http://wconnolly.blogspot.com.

ALICE VAN (1918–2008)

Alice Grace Van Der Veen was born in Arvada, Colorado. After competing as a jockey, performing in rodeos, and entertaining in the 1932 Olympic ceremonies, she was crowned World Champion Trick Rider in 1933. This led to a career doubling Ann Sheridan, Bette Davis, Ava Gardner, Marion Davies, Susan Hayward, Jane Wyman, Ingrid Bergman, and Doris Day. Her best known assignments came doubling Olivia de Havilland on *The Adventures of Robin Hood* (1938) and Elizabeth Taylor on *National Velvet* (1944).

She was at Republic for many years, leading to a long association as the double for Dale Evans. While at Republic she also doubled Peggy Stewart and Estelita. Alice broke her back doubling Gail Davis on TV's *Annie Oakley* (1954–57). She married western director R.G. Springsteen and recovered from her injury to double Barbara Stanwyck on the TV series *The Big Valley* (1965–69). An inductee of the Cowgirl Hall of Fame, Van died from pneumonia at the age of 90.

See: Barnes, Mike. "Stuntwoman Alice Van Springsteen Dies." *Hollywood Reporter.* September 16, 2008.

FRANKIE VAN (1904–1978)

New York–born Frankie Van Hawten, a former featherweight contender, was a stand-in and double for Hugh Herbert and Lou Costello. He is best known as a boxing technical advisor, staging ring fights from *Kid Nightingale* (1939) and *Footlight Serenade* (1942) to *Flesh and Fury* (1952) and *The Square Jungle* (1956). Van was often seen as referees so he could manage the action up close. He shows up as a ref on *Rocky* (1976). When not filming, he was the head trainer at the Universal Studios gym, putting stars such as Rock Hudson, Jeff Chandler, and Tony Curtis through their paces. He appeared as stunt fighters on *Winner Take All* (1939), *There's One Born Every Minute* (1942), *Scarlet Angel* (1952), *Up Periscope* (1959), *Birdman of Alcatraz* (1962), and *Blazing Saddles* (1974).

See: "Ex-Pugilist Rebels at Feminine Togs for Picture Stunt." *Hartford Courant.* April 8, 1940.

JERRY VANCE

Jerry Vance was a member of the U.S. Olympic equestrian team and found a home in the late 1950s doing live shows at Corriganville. In 1959 he toured with Bob McCaw's Cavalcade performing famous movie stunts for live audiences. The 5'5", 130-pound Vance worked at Warner Brothers and Ziv, doubling women and small men. He drove the Black Beauty car for Bruce Lee on the TV series *The Green Hornet* (1966–67). On *Caprice* (1967) he doubled Ray Walston for a forty-seven–foot balcony fall. In the mid–1960s Vance spent weekends as a stunt performer at Apacheland Studios in Arizona. He also worked on *Ballad of a Gunfighter* (1964), *A Fine Madness* (1966), and *Hangfire* (1968).

See: Van Buskirk, Pam. "For a Hollywood Stuntman, Weekend Fun." *Arizona Republic*. December 11, 1966.

BEAU VANDEN ECKER (1930–2007)

Beau Vanden Ecker spent twelve years in Hawaii as a stuntman on the TV series *Hawaii Five-0* (1968–80). Primarily hired as James MacArthur's double, he often found himself in front of the camera playing thugs. He served as stunt coordinator for some episodes. When that series ended, he continued in Hawaii on the series *Magnum P.I.* (1980–88).

Born in Beverly Hills, Vanden Ecker served in the Korean War as a combat platoon sergeant. He assisted martial arts coordinator Gordon Doversola for the famous fight on *The Manchurian Candidate* (1962) and taught Dean Martin Okinawa Te moves for *The Silencers* (1966). Vanden Ecker was on the cover of the March 1965 issue of *Black Belt* magazine. He was a regular stuntman on the World War II TV series *Combat* (1962–67) and appeared on *The Man from U.N.C.L.E.* and *Star Trek*.

See: "Star Learns to Fight." *Dallas Morning News*. August 30, 1965.

BUDDY VAN HORN (1929–)

Buddy Van Horn is best known as the longtime double for Clint Eastwood. Born in Los Angeles as Wayne Van Horn, his father was a veterinarian who tended animals for Universal Studios.

Buddy and his brother Jimmy were raised on the back lot and attended North Hollywood High and Cal Poly. After service with the Army, he worked as a horse wrangler and riding extra for the studio, eventually following his brother into stunts. The 6'2", 185-pound Buddy made a name for himself doubling Guy Williams on the TV series *Zorro* (1957–61), excelling at fencing, fights, and leaps onto horses from heights.

With his rangy build, he doubled Gregory Peck on *Mirage* (1965), *Mackenna's Gold* (1969), *The Stalking Moon* (1969), *Marooned* (1969), and *I Walk the Line* (1970), Jimmy Stewart on *The Rare Breed* (1966), *Firecreek* (1968), *Bandolero!* (1968), and *Fools' Parade* (1971), Henry Fonda on *Stranger on the Run* (1967) and *The Cheyenne Social Club* (1970), and Richard Boone on *Big Jake* (1971). In the 1950s he doubled Lex Barker on *The Man from Bitter Ridge* (1955) and was supposed to be doubling Jock Mahoney for his Universal starring roles. On TV's *Laredo* (1965–67) he doubled William Smith for riding shots.

Van Horn began with Eastwood on *Coogan's Bluff* (1968) and continued through *Paint Your Wagon* (1969), *Two Mules for Sister Sara* (1970), *Dirty Harry* (1971), *The Beguiled* (1971), *Joe Kidd* (1972), *Magnum Force* (1973), *Thunderbolt and Lightfoot* (1974), *The Enforcer* (1976), *The Gauntlet* (1977), and *Every Which Way But Loose* (1978). He was cast as the marshal for the flashback scenes on *High Plains Drifter* (1973), adding to the ghostly angle of that film as many viewers were unsure if the character being whipped to death was meant to be Eastwood's brother or the mysterious Eastwood. He served as stunt coordinator and second unit director for *Pale Rider* (1985) and most of Eastwood's top action films, including the Oscar winners *Unforgiven* (1992) and *Million Dollar Baby* (2004). Eastwood rewarded him with directorial assignments on *Any Which Way You Can* (1980), *Dead Pool* (1988), and *Pink Cadillac* (1989).

He also worked on *Warpath* (1951), *Son of Paleface* (1952), *Gunsmoke* (1953), *Ride Clear of Diablo* (1954), *Taza, Son of Cochise* (1954), *Prince Valiant* (1954), *Destry* (1954), *Chief Crazy Horse* (1955), *Lady Godiva* (1955), *Escape to Burma* (1955), *Around the World in Eighty Days* (1956), *Giant* (1956), *Last of the Badmen* (1957), *Spartacus* (1960), *Swordsman of Sienna* (1962), *Kings of the Sun* (1963), *It's a Mad, Mad, Mad, Mad World* (1963), *Major Dundee* (1965), *The War Lord*

Buddy Van Horn doubles Clint Eastwood as Ernest Robinson overturns a car on *Dirty Harry* (1971).

(1965), *Our Man Flint* (1966), *Alvarez Kelly* (1966), *The Professionals* (1966), *Camelot* (1967), *The Cowboys* (1972), *Prime Cut* (1972), *The Great Waldo Pepper* (1975), *Bite the Bullet* (1975), *The Master Gunfighter* (1975), *Family Plot* (1976), *Swashbuckler* (1976), *The Last Remake of Beau Geste* (1977), *FM* (1978), *The Deer Hunter* (1978), *Stunt Seven* (1979), and *Heaven's Gate* (1980). TV credits include *Rawhide, Daniel Boone, Bonanza, Gunsmoke, Voyage to the Bottom of the Sea,* and *The Six Million Dollar Man.* A member of the Stuntmen's Association, Van Horn received a Taurus Lifetime Achievement stunt award, a Golden Boot, and induction into the Stuntmen's Hall of Fame. His brother Jimmy died doing a horse fall in 1965.

See: Davis, Laura. *Independent.* "Buddy Van Horn: My Life as Clint Eastwood's Stuntman." August 9, 2010.

DALE VAN SICKEL (1907–1977)

Dale Harris Van Sickel was born in Eatonton, Georgia. He was a standout football player and All-American end for the University of Florida in the late 1920s, leading the Gators to a 1928 NCAA scoring title and coming one point away from a Rose Bowl berth. He was the starting guard and captain of the basketball squad, played baseball, and boxed. The University named Van Sickel the most handsome man on campus. He turned down pro offers to move to California and made his screen debut playing football on *Spirit of Notre Dame* (1931).

Van Sickel found a home at Republic in the 1940s when he paired with Tom Steele as a fight partner on countless thrilling cliffhangers. His best Republic showcase came extensively doubling Dick Purcell on the serial *Captain America*

(1944). He doubled Robert Taylor, Clark Gable, Dana Andrews, Tyrone Power, Gilbert Roland, Joseph Cotten, John Carroll, Craig Stevens, Douglas Fowley, Kirk Alyn, Roy Barcroft, Bruce Cabot, Reed Hadley, Tom Neal, Richard Denning, David Janssen, and Mike Connors. On TV he doubled George Reeves on *Superman* (1952–53) and Robert Taylor on *The Detectives* (1959–62). A capable actor, he played many supporting roles and fought all the cowboy stars. In 1961 Van Sickel became the first president of the Stuntmen's Association. After suffering a hip injury he began to concentrate on automotive stunts, executing top driving for *On the Beach* (1959), *Bullitt* (1968), *The Love Bug* (1968), and the TV movie *Duel* (1971).

He worked on *Duck Soup* (1933), *Dante's Inferno* (1935), *High Tension* (1936), *Gone with the Wind* (1939), *Zorro's Fighting Legion* (1939), *Holt of the Secret Service* (1941), *Reap the Wild Wind* (1942), *Saboteur* (1942), *The Big Shot* (1942), *Pittsburgh* (1942), *G-Men vs. the Black Dragon* (1943), *Secret Service in Darkest Africa* (1943), *The Masked Marvel* (1943), *Zorro's Black Whip* (1944), *The Tiger Woman* (1944), *Haunted Harbor* (1944), *Saratoga Trunk* (1945), *Adventure* (1945), *The Purple Monster Strikes* (1945), *Manhunt of Mystery Island* (1945), *Federal Operator 99* (1945), *Jeep Herders* (1945), *The Crimson Ghost* (1946), *Canyon Passage* (1946), *Brute Force* (1947), *The Farmer's Daughter* (1947), *Bells of San Angelo* (1947), *Jesse James Rides Again* (1947), *Dangers of the Canadian Mounted* (1948), *Gallant Legion* (1948), *Adventures of Frank and Jesse James* (1948), *G-Men Never Forget* (1948), *Ghost of Zorro* (1949), *Mighty Joe Young* (1949), *The Fighting Kentuckian* (1949), *Tokyo Joe* (1949), *Radar Patrol vs. Spy King* (1949), *King of the Rocket Men* (1949), *Federal Agents vs. Underworld Inc.* (1950), *The Invisible Monster* (1950), *Flying Disc Man from Mars* (1951), *The Kid from Texas* (1950), *His Kind of Woman* (1951), *Soldiers Three* (1951), *Don*

Dale Van Sickel (left) struggles with Tom Steele on the serial *The Masked Marvel* (1943).

Daredevil Rides Again (1951), *The Greatest Show on Earth* (1952), *Scarlet Angel* (1952), *Cripple Creek* (1952), *Radar Men from the Moon* (1952), *Untamed Frontier* (1952), *The War of the Worlds* (1953), *Law and Order* (1953), *Thunder Bay* (1953), *All the Brothers Were Valiant* (1953), *The Mississippi Gambler* (1953), *20,000 Leagues Under the Sea* (1954), *Rogue Cop* (1954), *Man with the Steel Whip* (1954), *Seven Brides for Seven Brothers* (1954), *Rails into Laramie* (1954), *The Far Country* (1955), *Battle Cry* (1955), *The Searchers* (1956), *Around the World in Eighty Days* (1956), *The Last Hunt* (1956), *Giant* (1956), *Day the World Ended* (1956), *Flesh and the Spur* (1957), *The Wings of Eagles* (1957), *The Garment Jungle* (1957), *Omar Khayyam* (1957), *Gunsight Ridge* (1957), *Thunder Road* (1958), *North by Northwest* (1959), *Cast a Long Shadow* (1959), *Good Day for a Hanging* (1959), *Spartacus* (1960), *North to Alaska* (1960), *Seven Ways from Sundown* (1960), *Elmer Gantry* (1960), *Six Black Horses* (1962), *It's a Mad, Mad, Mad, Mad World* (1963), *Showdown* (1963), *Cattle King* (1963), *Viva Las Vegas* (1964), *The Great Race* (1965), *Town Tamer* (1965), *What Did You Do in the War, Daddy?* (1966), *Murderers' Row* (1966), *Johnny Reno* (1966), *The St. Valentine's Day Massacre* (1967), *Bonnie and Clyde* (1967), *The Flim-Flam Man* (1967), *Hot Rods to Hell* (1967), *Wild in the Streets* (1968), *The Wrecking Crew* (1969), *Magnum Force* (1973), *The Sugarland Express* (1974), and *Part Two, Walking Tall* (1975). TV credits include *The Lone Ranger, Roy Rogers, Wyatt Earp, Cheyenne, Zane Grey, Mike Hammer, Richard Diamond, Peter Gunn, Bronco, Trackdown, Johnny Ringo, Wanted—Dead or Alive, 77 Sunset Strip, Bonanza, Perry Mason, The Wild Wild West,* and *The Green Hornet.* An inductee of the Stuntmen's Hall of Fame and the College Football Hall of Fame, Van Sickel died at the age of 69 from injuries sustained in a 1975 car stunt for the film *No Deposit, No Return* (1976).

See: LeNoir, Bob. "Gator Great Van Sickel Dies at 69." *St. Petersburg Times.* January 26, 1977.

TURK VARTERESIAN (1923–2000)

Harry Varteresian was born in Los Angeles. A former Marine, Varteresian was a Muscle Beach bodybuilder who won the tall division of the 1946 Mr. Los Angeles contest. He served as bodyguard to Ronald Reagan and became a professional wrestler in the 1950s. The bearded, 6'4", 260-pound Hollywood strongman was known for his 19" biceps and prowess at arm-wrestling and surfing. He was the longtime proprietor of Turk's Tavern at Sunset Beach and later Dana Point, establishments frequented by John Wayne, Robert Mitchum, and Woody Strode.

As a stuntman he specialized in fight scenes, working on over sixty films including *Rhubarb* (1951), *Road to Bali* (1952), *The Ten Commandments* (1956), *Omar Khayyam* (1957), *One Eyed Jacks* (1961), *How the West Was Won* (1962), *The Bible* (1966), and *The King's Pirate* (1967). TV credits include *Laredo, The Virginian, Lost in Space, Get Smart,* and *The Man from U.N.C.L.E..* Varteresian died from a heart attack at the age of 76.

See: Roberts, Jerry. *Orange Coast.* "Still Crazy After All These Years." September 1998; Smith, T.D. *Los Angeles Times.* "Turk's Dana Wharf Namesake Is the Big Man on the Marina." November 5, 1992; Vida, Herbert J. *Los Angeles Times.* "Strong Arm Gives Leg Up to Part-Time Actor in the Tavern Business." September 9, 1986.

JACK VERBOIS (1942–)

Jack Marshall Verbois entered films after a rodeo career in his native Baton Rouge, Louisiana. First recruited for stunt work on *Alvarez Kelly* (1966), the 5'10", 170-pound Verbois did a variety of action on TV's *The Rat Patrol* (1966–68), made headway as Hugh O'Brian's double on *Search* (1972–73), and cemented his reputation getting knocked off a ladder and swinging from a banner through a glass window on *What's Up, Doc?* (1972). For Robert De Niro he fell seventy feet out of a helicopter into the River Kwai on *The Deer Hunter* (1978). Between stunts, Verbois was an archery expert hired to teach the stars.

He worked on *The Great Bank Robbery* (1969), *The Phynx* (1970), *99 and 44/100 percent Dead* (1974), *Earthquake* (1974), *The Towering Inferno* (1974), *The Master Gunfighter* (1975), *The Hindenburg* (1975), *Nickelodeon* (1976), *Swashbuckler* (1976), *Futureworld* (1976), *Outlaw Blues* (1977), *Butch and Sundance* (1979), and *Stunt Seven* (1979). TV credits include *The Man from U.N.C.L.E., Then Came Bronson, Young Rebels, The Streets of San Francisco, Kung Fu, The Rockford Files, Switch, Barnaby Jones,* and *Wonder*

Woman. Verbois is a member of the Stuntmen's Association.

See: Belehrad, Tim. "Monitor." *Advocate.* December 18, 1981.

RON VETO (1933–2005)

Filipino-American Ronald Barry Veto was a star sprinter and football running back for Los Angeles High and Valley College in the early 1950s. "Rapid Ron" appeared as a diver on *Fun in Acapulco* (1963) and also worked on *Around the World in Eighty Days* (1956), *Green Mansions* (1959), *Pork Chop Hill* (1959), *The Ugly American* (1963), *Donovan's Reef* (1963), *Von Ryan's Express* (1965), *Harper* (1966), *The Professionals* (1966), *A Fine Madness* (1966), *In Like Flint* (1967), and *Che!* (1969). He appeared on several episodes of TV's *Star Trek.* His son, also named Ron Veto, did stunt work in the 1970s.

SAILOR VINCENT (1901–1966)

William J. Vincent was born in Dracut, Massachusetts, and entered the Navy in his teens. He so loved the service of his country he had a U.S. flag tattooed on his chest. As a welterweight "Sailor" Billy Vincent held the Pacific Fleet Title and was the Navy Boxing Champ for twelve years. Out of 268 bouts he claimed to have lost only 25 of them, all professionally. His final pro line was 49–25–24. Although he wasn't championship material, Sailor was a popular fighter and gained entrance into the movie business as a stuntman and technical advisor on films such as *The Personality Kid* (1934).

Once he quit boxing, Sailor's body expanded noticeably and he chiefly doubled stocky, rough-hewn types such as Edward G. Robinson, W.C. Fields, Alan Hale, and Barton MacLane. He doubled Charles Laughton as Quasimodo on *The Hunchback of Notre Dame* (1939) and was the go-to man when any matronly middle-aged woman needed a stunt double. The colorful stuntman specialized in screen fights, amassing over 1,000 of them. Many were of a humorous nature. On *The Fuller Brush Girl* (1950) Lucille Ball hit him with a fistful of frozen bananas. He was killed on screen more than 500 times. His most notable acting role came as the humorously sleepy boxing trainer on *The Irish in Us* (1935).

He worked on *Her Man* (1930), *Seven Days Leave* (1930), *The Bowery* (1933), *King Kong* (1933), *Barbary Coast* (1935), *Captain Blood* (1935), *Professional Soldier* (1935), *God's Country and the Woman* (1937), *San Quentin* (1937), *Submarine D-1* (1938), *Mysterious Mr. Moto* (1938), *Valley of the Giants* (1938), *Each Dawn I Die* (1939), *Dodge City* (1939), *Flowing Gold* (1940), *Virginia City* (1940), *The Wagons Roll at Night* (1940), *Santa Fe Trail* (1940), *High Sierra* (1941), *Shadow of the Thin Man* (1941), *Sergeant York* (1941), *Manpower* (1941), *The Sea Wolf* (1941), *Lady Takes a Chance* (1943), *Destination Tokyo* (1944), *Saratoga Trunk* (1945), *The Spanish Main* (1945), *Wild Harvest* (1947), *Albuquerque* (1948), *South of St. Louis* (1949), *Montana* (1950), *Kansas Raiders* (1950), *The Flame and the Arrow* (1950), *The Kid from Texas* (1950), *Soldiers Three* (1951), *Abbott & Costello Meet Captain Kidd* (1952), *The Duel at Silver Creek* (1952), *Carson City* (1952), *Against All Flags* (1952), *The Lawless Breed* (1952), *The Man Behind the Gun* (1953), *Riding Shotgun* (1954), *Destry* (1954), *The Command* (1954), *Battle Cry* (1955), *Around the World in Eighty Days* (1956), *Walk the Proud Land* (1956), *No Time for Sergeants* (1958), and *Guns of the Timberland* (1960). In later years he worked as a TV extra. An honorary member of the Stuntmen's Association and an inductee of the Stuntmen's Hall of Fame, Vincent died from a heart attack at the age of 64.

See: Burton, Ron. "Sailor Vincent Has Had His 1,000th Movie Type Brawl." *Star News.* August 26, 1957; Kountze, Denman. "Sailor's Behind the Chair That Parts the Villain's Hair." *Omaha World Herald.* May 26, 1958; Wilson, Elizabeth. "Hollywood Hardpans." *Liberty.* October 20, 1945.

WENDE WAGNER (1941–1997)

Wende Wagner was born in New London, Connecticut, and grew up on California's Coronado Island. Her father was a Navy commander and former Olympic swimming and diving instructor. Her mother was a champion downhill skier. Wagner trained for the Olympics growing up, but by her teenage years became enamored with the sport of surfing. Discovered in the Bahamas by the makers of the TV series *Sea Hunt,* she began doing aquatic stunts for guest actresses. Marrying stuntman Courtney Brown, she doubled Joanne Dru on *Summertime* (1960) and stunted on the TV series *The Aquanauts* (1960–61) and *Malibu Run* (1961). The 5'6" Wagner was given a push toward stardom as an Apache maiden on *Rio Conchos* (1964) but was unable to stick with audiences despite her beauty. Her most visible assignment came as the secretary on the TV series *The Green Hornet* (1966–67). Never returning to stunt work, Wagner died from cancer at the age of 55.

See: Lisanti, Tom. *Drive-In Dream Girls.* Jefferson, NC: McFarland, 2003; Meade, James. *San Diego Union* "Wende Wagner Back in Movies." July 8, 1966; Shearer, Lloyd. *Albuquerque Journal.* "Navy Brat on Her Own." June 28, 1964.

FRANCIS "FRANK" WALKER (1910–1971)

Idaho-born Francis Walker toiled in more than 100 B-westerns ranging from *Law of the Plains* (1929) to *Return of the Durango Kid* (1945). He doubled for Harry Carey on *Wagon Trail* (1935). After serving with the Army during World War II, he left Hollywood to drive a truck. Credits include *Robinson Crusoe of Clipper Island* (1936), *The Spider's Web* (1938), and *Desert Hawk* (1944). Walker died at the age of 60.

GREG WALKER (1945–)

William Greg Walker was born in Bakersfield, California, the son of a rodeo announcer. He began competing in cowboy events at Canoga Park High. In 1964 he went to New York for the World's Fair and worked in a live stunt show. Joining the rodeo team at Pierce College, Walker entered films in the mid–1960s. He is best known as the double for David Carradine on the TV series *Kung Fu* (1972–75), where he did all the dangerous leaps and falls. Walker doubled Peter Strauss on *Soldier Blue* (1970).

The 5'11", 170-pound Walker also worked on *Justine* (1969), *MASH* (1970), *Wrath of God* (1972), *The Last American Hero* (1973), *Death Race 2000* (1975), *The Outlaw Josey Wales* (1976), *Silent Movie* (1976), *Cannonball* (1976), *Buffalo Bill and the Indians* (1976), *Black Sunday* (1977), *The White Buffalo* (1977), *F.I.S.T.* (1978), *Butch and Sundance* (1979), *More American Graffiti* (1979), *Heaven's Gate* (1980), and *The Long Riders* (1980). He was one of the title creatures in the cult TV movie favorite *Gargoyles* (1972) and

worked on the mini-series *Centennial* (1978) and *The Chisholms* (1979). Walker is a member of the Stuntmen's Association.

See: Hurst. P.B. *The Most Savage Film:* Soldier Blue, *Cinematic Violence, and the Horrors of War.* Jefferson, NC: McFarland, 2008; http://gregwalker.homestead.com.

NELLIE WALKER

Nellie Walker specialized in horse stunts and was president of the Rough Riders organization. She doubled Julie Bishop on *Tarzan the Fearless* (1933) and found a lasting home at Republic on Roy Rogers pictures. Put on a year-round contract, she doubled many actresses there during the 1940s. She was never able to branch out to bigger assignments. Among her credits are *Tank Girl* (1938), *In Old Oklahoma* (1943), and *Jesse James Rides Again* (1947). Actresses she doubled include Linda Stirling, Helen Talbot, Jean Parker, June Storey, and Carole Landis. Walker retired from stunts as she reached her forties.

See: Muir, Florabel. "They Risk Their Necks for You." *Saturday Evening Post.* September 15, 1945; "Western Sports Show Skedded at San Diego." *Billboard.* June 1, 1946.

ROCK WALKER

Five-foot-nine, 145-pound Rock Arlen Walker is the brother of Greg Walker and the son of stuntman–rodeo performer William A. Walker. Rock rode bulls and became a full-time stuntman in the late 1960s as a protégé of Everett Creach, who put him in the middle of the astounding stunts during the airstrip attack on *Tora! Tora! Tora!* (1970). Walker became equally skilled in all facets of stunt work and was chosen by his peers to represent them in the 1977 Sports Spectacular Stunt Competition against five other all-around stuntmen (Gary Combs, Gary McLarty, Buddy Joe Hooker, Dick Ziker, and Billy Burton). Walker doubled Dustin Hoffman and Kris Kristofferson.

He worked on *Will Penny* (1968), *Bandolero!* (1968), *Chubasco* (1968), *Hellfighters* (1968), *MASH* (1970), *Little Fauss and Big Halsey* (1970), *Conquest of the Planet of the Apes* (1972), *Gargoyles* (1972), *Electra Glide in Blue* (1973), *Earthquake* (1974), *The Master Gunfighter* (1975), *Marathon Man* (1976), *The Car* (1977), *F.I.S.T.* (1978), *1941* (1979), *Lady in Red* (1979), *Butch and Sundance* (1979), *The Electric Horseman* (1979), and *Tom Horn* (1980). Walker was once president of the Stuntmen's Association.

See: Silden, Isobel. *Australian Women's Weekly.* "Stunt Men." February 10, 1982; "Stuntmen Compete in Sports Spectacular." *Joplin Globe.* January 15, 1977.

MARVIN WALTERS (1938–)

Marvin James Walters was one of the first black stuntmen to emerge as an all-around professional. While working on TV's *Cowboy in Africa* (1967–68) he was trained for the profession by Mickey Gilbert and Fred Waugh. A founder of the Black Stuntmen's Association, he used his knowledge to train fellow members Tony Brubaker, Richard Washington, and Henry Kingi. Walters left the group a year later and became one of the first black members of the Stuntmen's Association. He doubled Richard Roundtree on *Shaft's Big Score* (1972) and *Earthquake* (1974), as well as Roger E. Mosely, Lou Gossett, and Brock Peters.

Walters resigned from the Stuntmen's Association in 1975 to concentrate on the Coalition of Black Stuntmen and Women. A champion of equal rights, Walters sought to end the practice of white stunt performers being painted down to double minorities. In 1975 he began as an affirmative action consultant for MGM. In 1977 he moved to Universal and obtained work for stunt performers worthy of being given a chance to coordinate. His credits include *Up Tight!* (1968), *What's Up, Doc?* (1972), *Across 110th Street* (1972), *The Front Page* (1974), *Black Samson* (1974), *Freebie and the Bean* (1974), *Blazing Saddles* (1974), *Smokey and the Bandit II* (1980), TV's *Star Trek,* and the first season of *Magnum P.I.* (1980–81) as stunt coordinator.

See: "MGM Hires Man for Minority Aid." *Colorado Springs Gazette.* December 17, 1975; www.aprofessionalanswer.com.

AUTRY WARD (1937–)

Air Force veteran Autry Ward was born in Red Hill, Texas, and raised in Linden. He made his film debut on *Merry Andrew* (1958) prior to establishing the Ward Brothers stunt team with siblings Troy, Steve, and Dennis. The brothers worked at Apacheland and Old Tucson Studios

and made live appearances. They worked together on *How the West Was Won* (1962), *Arizona Raiders* (1965), *Joe Kidd* (1972), *Junior Bonner* (1972), *Book of Numbers* (1973), *Bootleggers* (1974), *Mackintosh and T.J.* (1975), and *Rolling Thunder* (1977).

See: www.lindentexas.org.

BILL WARD (1926–)

Horseback specialist and wrangler Bill Ward is best known as the main double for Clayton Moore on *The Lone Ranger* (1949–56) and its 1956 big-screen version where he puts on a great fight scene. His stunt horse Traveler doubled for Silver, with the two working well together on mounts and falls. Traveler was a popular film horse in the 1950s and later became USC's Trojan Horse. Ward also doubled Jim Davis on *Badge of Marshal Brennan* (1957) and Roy Rogers on *The Roy Rogers Show.*

Raised in Vallejo, California, horse country, Ward played football for Pasadena City College. Cowboy work led him into stunts and he operated the Studio Ranch in Chatsworth, providing livestock for films. He worked on *The Merry Widow* (1952), *Buffalo Bill in Tomahawk Territory* (1952), *Son of the Renegade* (1953), *War Arrow* (1953), *The Black Whip* (1956), and *Snowfire* (1958). Ward was the director, writer, and producer of *Ballad of a Gunfighter* (1964). He left films in the early 1960s to train thoroughbred race horses. In the 1990s he tried to get a movie studio started in Oklahoma.

See: Beck, Ken. *The Encyclopedia of TV Pets.* Thomas Nelson, 2002; Menges, Jack. "Hollywood Dude a Top Trainer." *Oakland Tribune.* November 14, 1967; Moore, Clayton. *I Was That Masked Man.* Rowman & Littlefield, 1998; Reiger, Andy. "Bill Ward Has Dream of Studio." *Oklahoman.* April 11, 1994.

DEREK WARE (1938–)

Derek Arthur Ware worked extensively on British TV shows such as *The Avengers* and *Doctor Who* and doubled Michael Crawford on the series *Some Mothers Do 'Ave 'Em* (1973–78). Film credits include *Far from the Madding Crowd* (1967), *The War Game* (1967), *A Long Day's Dying* (1968), *Witchfinder General* (1968), and *The Italian Job* (1969). He ran the stunt agency Havoc and founded the Society of British Fight Directors. The 5'7", 155-pound Ware also authored a number of stunt-related books, most notably *Stunting in the Cinema* (1973).

DICK WARLOCK (1940–)

Five-foot-nine, 175-pound Dick Warlock was born Richard Anthony Lemming in Oakley, Ohio. He moved to Southern California at the age of thirteen and began writing letters to the studios offering his services as a stuntman for Dick Jones. Hooking up with speed skating champion Ralph Valledares, he trained at the Western Skating Institute. This led to a professional roller derby career with the Los Angeles Braves. Live stunt shows at Corriganville led to obtaining his SAG card on *Ballad of a Gunfighter* (1964), where he doubled Marty Robbins.

Under the professional name Dick Warlock he enjoyed a long association with Walt Disney Studios while doubling Dean Jones, Tim Conway, Joe Flynn, Buddy Hackett, Gary Crosby, and Richard Jaeckel. He mainly doubled Disney's teenage star Kurt Russell beginning with *The Computer Wore Tennis Shoes* (1969). This association lasted twenty-five years into Russell's adult career as a star on *Used Cars* (1980) and *Escape from New York* (1981). Warlock doubled Richard Dreyfuss in the shark cage on *Jaws* (1975), but gained his greatest notoriety playing Michael Myers on *Halloween II* (1981) and the assassin on *Halloween III* (1983).

He also worked on *Blackbeard's Ghost* (1968), *The Green Berets* (1968), *Chubasco* (1968), *The Love Bug* (1968), *Skin Game* (1971), *Soylent Green* (1973), *Blazing Saddles* (1974), *Mr. Majestyk* (1974), *Dirty Mary, Crazy Larry* (1974), *Earthquake* (1974), *The Ultimate Warrior* (1975), *The Hindenburg* (1975), *Lepke* (1975), *Lucky Lady* (1975), *Rollerball* (1975), *Silent Movie* (1976), *Herbie Goes to Monte Carlo* (1977), *The Cat from Outer Space* (1978), *1941* (1979), *Stunt Seven* (1979), *The Stunt Man* (1980), and *The Nude Bomb* (1980). TV credits include *The Rat Patrol, Emergency, Kolchak: The Night Stalker, The Rockford Files, Police Story, Police Woman,* and *The Six Million Dollar Man.* Warlock is a member of the Stuntmen's Association and an inductee of the Stuntmen's Hall of Fame.

See: www.dickwarlock.com.

RICHARD WASHINGTON (1940–)

Richard Washington worked in the fishing industry prior to beginning stunt work with the Black Stuntmen's Association. He specialized in underwater stunts and doubled Lou Gossett on *The Deep* (1977). A sideline was motorcycle racing, which stood him well doubling Richard Roundtree jumping a motorcycle through a hoop of fire on *Earthquake* (1974). Five-foot-ten, 185-pound Washington also doubled Marvin Gaye, Billy Dee Williams, and Richard Pryor.

He worked on *Escape from the Planet of the Apes* (1971), *Dirty Harry* (1971), *Chrome and Hot Leather* (1971), *What's Up, Doc?* (1972), *Conquest of the Planet of the Apes* (1972), *Cleopatra Jones* (1973), *Battle for the Planet of the Apes* (1973), *The Towering Inferno* (1974), *The Front Page* (1974), *The Gumball Rally* (1976), *Swashbuckler* (1976), *Drum* (1976), *Stunt Seven* (1979), and *The Nude Bomb* (1980). TV credits include *Silent Force, Ironside,* and *Buck Rogers.* A member of the Stuntmen's Association, he is the father of stunt woman Kym Washington.

See: "Black Stunt Men." *Sepia.* Vol. 20, #12, 1971; "Dad and Daughter Cheat Death for Their Livelihood." *Jet.* March 24, 1986.

CHUCK WATERS (1934–)

Five-foot-nine, 150-pound Chuck Waters was on the swim team at Waukegan High prior to service with the Marines. He began stunting in the mid-1960s and took part in some of the biggest stunts of the following decade, crashing a motorcycle on *The Grissom Gang* (1971), doubling Jason Miller for a long stair fall on *The Exorcist* (1973), falling off the Space Needle in Seattle for *The Parallax View* (1974), taking an 85-foot cliff fall with a wagon while doubling Genevieve Bujold on *Swashbuckler* (1976), and falling off a tower into a river with Terry Leonard on *Apocalypse Now* (1979). Waters doubled Jim Varney, Chevy Chase, Christopher Walken, John Savage, and Bradford Dillman. He holds the distinction of being on *Raiders of the Lost Ark* (1981), *Indiana Jones and the Temple of Doom* (1984), and *Indiana Jones and the Lost Crusade* (1989).

He also worked on *The Sweet Ride* (1968), *Che!* (1969), *The Molly Maguires* (1970), *There Was a Crooked Man...* (1970), *Conquest of the*

Chuck Waters is about to fall off the Seattle Space Needle as he is pursued by Paul Baxley on *The Parallax View* (1974).

Planet of the Apes (1972), *High Plains Drifter* (1973), *Magnum Force* (1973), *Battle for the Planet of the Apes* (1973), *The Towering Inferno* (1974), *Thunderbolt and Lightfoot* (1974), *Young Frankenstein* (1974), *The Hindenburg* (1975), *The Killer Elite* (1975), *Every Which Way But Loose* (1978), *The Deer Hunter* (1978), *The Manitou* (1978), *The In-Laws* (1979), *Stunt Seven* (1979), *Bronco Billy* (1980), and *Heaven's Gate* (1980). TV credits include *The Wild Wild West, Cannon,* and *Kolchak: The Night Stalker.* He is a member of the Stuntmen's Association.

FRED WAUGH (1932–2012)

Fred M. Waugh from Indiana was a high school gymnast and a trapeze artist in the circus. He began working on the TV series *Circus Boy* (1956–58) and learned stunts from Chuck Couch. Waugh doubled David McCallum on *The Man from U.N.C.L.E.* (1964–66) but is best known for his innovative doubling of Nicholas Hammond on *The Amazing Spiderman* (1977–

79). On this show he scaled the sides of buildings in ways that did not seem humanly possible. In the early 1970s the 5'10", 155-pound Waugh designed a camera to be worn by a stunt performer for point-of-view shots. He first utilized this on the rodeo film *J.W. Coop* (1972) and perfected its use on the *Spiderman* series. He was considered one of the foremost high men in the business and became one of the first members of Stunts Unlimited.

Waugh suffered a horrible injury during the making of the *UNCLE* series when he was run over by an out-of-control boat. The propeller gashed him open the entire length of his back. He suffered a broken back and required 500 stitches. He recovered quickly and went back to work. One of his best stunts came on *Caprice* (1967) doubling actor Richard Harris at Mammoth Mountain on a rope ladder underneath a helicopter while stuntwoman Julie Ann Johnson held onto him.

He also worked on *The Buccaneer* (1958), *Circus World* (1964), *The Undefeated* (1969), *Paint Your Wagon* (1969), *Little Big Man* (1970),

Monte Walsh (1970), *Sometimes a Great Notion* (1971), *Conquest of the Planet of the Apes* (1972), *Buck and the Preacher* (1972), *Bad Company* (1972), *Battle for the Planet of the Apes* (1973), *McQ* (1974), *The Towering Inferno* (1974), *The Front Page* (1974), *Night Moves* (1975), *The Killer Elite* (1975), *Hot Lead and Cold Feet* (1978), *Buck Rogers in the 25th Century* (1979), and *Stunts Unlimited* (1980). TV series credits include *The Girl from U.N.C.L.E., Mannix, The Invaders, Bearcats, S.W.A.T.,* and *Gemini Man*. Sons Scott and Ric became stuntmen. An inductee of the Stuntmen's Hall of Fame, Waugh died from cancer at the age of 80.

See: Blanchard, Nina. *How to Break into Motion Pictures, Television, Commercials, & Modeling*. NY: Doubleday, 1978; Heitland, Jon. *The Man from U.N.C.L.E. Book*. Macmillan, 1987.

GUY WAY (1924–2009)

Guy Gifford Way was born in Detroit, Michigan. The former Marine and World War II veteran played football as a tackle for UCLA and professionally for the Calgary Stampeders in 1952. Six-two and 220 pounds, he entered Hollywood as a stand-in for John Wayne. He is best known for Don Siegel films, performing great driving stunts on an unfinished freeway on *The Lineup* (1958) and fighting on an ore bucket over the Grand Canyon for Mickey Shaughnessey on *Edge of Eternity* (1959). Way was stunt coordinator on *Hell Is for Heroes* (1962) and doubled heavyset actors Jackie Gleason and Raymond Burr.

He worked on *Saturday's Hero* (1951), *Anne of the Indies* (1951), *Take the High Ground* (1953), *Trouble Along the Way* (1953), *China Venture* (1953), *From Here to Eternity* (1953), *The Shanghai Story* (1954), *The Atomic Kid* (1954), *The Long Gray Line* (1955), *The Boss* (1956), *Invasion of the Body Snatchers* (1956), *Baby Face Nelson* (1957), *Elmer Gantry* (1960), *Flaming Star* (1960), *Everything's Ducky* (1961), *The Honeymoon Machine* (1961), *Quick Before It Melts* (1964), *John Goldfarb, Please Come Home* (1965), *In Cold Blood* (1967), *Point Blank* (1967), *Skidoo* (1968), *Charley Varrick* (1973), *Doc Savage* (1975), and *One Man Jury* (1978). TV credits include *Lineup, Mr. Lucky, Perry Mason, The Man from U.N.C.L.E., The Girl from U.N.C.L.E., Batman, Mission: Impossible, Mannix, It Takes a Thief, Ironside, The Rockford Files,* and *Kojak*.

JESSE WAYNE (1941–)

Jesse Wayne was born in Los Angeles as Felix Francis Carbonneau. At sixteen he was a member of the Great Western Fast Draw Club and was working live stunt shows at Corriganville as Billy the Kid, making $6 a high fall. He gained notice for a fire stunt on *Hell Is for Heroes* (1962) and doubled Mickey Rooney on *Platinum High School* (1960), *It's a Mad, Mad, Mad, Mad World* (1963), and everything else the actor did up through *Black Stallion* (1979). Five-foot-four, 130-pound Wayne also doubled Red Buttons, Mel Brooks, Donald Pleasence, Arte Johnson, Mel Torme, Robert Morse, Frankie Avalon, and, on *Snow White and the Three Stooges* (1961) and *The Outlaws Is Coming* (1965), Moe Howard and Larry Fine. On TV he subbed for David McCallum on *The Man from U.N.C.L.E.* and Walter Koenig on *Star Trek*. Wayne's small size allowed him to double females and children such as Johnny Crawford on TV's *The Rifleman*, Kurt Russell on *Travels of Jamie McPheeters* (1963–64), Irene Ryan on *The Beverly Hillbillies,* and Helen Hayes on *Snoop Sisters* (1973–74).

He worked on *Walk Like a Dragon* (1960), *Everything's Ducky* (1961), *Ladies Man* (1961), *The Comedy of Terrors* (1963), *Quick Before It Melts* (1964), *Surf Party* (1964), *John Goldfarb, Please Come Home* (1965), *Young Fury* (1965), *What Did You Do in the War, Daddy?* (1966), *Follow Me Boys* (1966), *Hot Rods to Hell* (1967), *Wild in the Streets* (1968), *Darker Than Amber* (1970), *There Was a Crooked Man...* (1970), *The Grissom Gang* (1971), *Chrome and Hot Leather* (1971), *Unholy Rollers* (1972), *Blacula* (1972), *Super Fly* (1972), *Bless the Beasts and Children* (1972), *Hit!* (1973), *Battle for the Planet of the Apes* (1973), *99 and 44/100 percent Dead* (1974), *Young Frankenstein* (1974), *The Front Page* (1974), *The Master Gunfighter* (1975), *Hearts of the West* (1975), *Silent Movie* (1976), *King Kong* (1976), *Two-Minute Warning* (1976), *Great Scout and Cathouse Thursday* (1976), *Helter Skelter* (1976), *Herbie Goes to Monte Carlo* (1977), *Rollercoaster* (1977), *Black Oak Conspiracy* (1977), *The Manitou* (1978), *Meteor* (1979), *Lady in Red* (1979), and *Bronco Billy* (1980). TV credits include *Stagecoach West, Stoney Burke, Rawhide, The Outer Limits, Burke's Law, Combat, Bonanza, Laredo, Batman, I Spy, The Big Valley, The Rat Patrol, Young Rebels, The FBI, Ironside, Banacek, Faraday & Company,*

The Streets of San Francisco, Barnaby Jones, and *M*A*S*H.* A member of the Stuntmen's Association, Wayne worked on over 500 productions.

See: Batdorff, Allison. "Stuntman Recalls Glory Days of Films." *Billings Gazette.* January 4, 2005; Wayne, Jesse. *Confessions of a Hollywood Stuntman.* Self, 2013.

JOHN WAYNE (1907–1979)

Film legend John Wayne developed the modern screen punch with stuntman Yakima Canutt in the early 1930s. The Pass System came about because the participants were tired of bruising one another's arms and shoulders with blows. Wayne and Canutt began positioning themselves for the camera to give the illusion of punches connecting, that were actually harmless misses. Wayne went on to become the best known screen puncher in film history, logging epic fights against Randolph

Scott on *The Spoilers* (1942) and Victor McLaglen on *The Quiet Man* (1952). He fought Lee Marvin on *Donovan's Reef* (1963) and took part in monumental brawls on *Seven Sinners* (1940), *North to Alaska* (1960), and *McLintock!* (1963). Wayne did not require a double for fights and was still blocking out fight action as far along as *The War Wagon* (1967) and *Brannigan* (1975).

Six-foot-four, 235-pound Wayne was born Marion Morrison in Winterset, Iowa. He was raised in California and as Duke Morrison stood out playing football at Glendale High. While under scholarship at USC, he began working at the movie studios as a prop man and jack of all trades. A shoulder injury suffered body surfing at Newport Beach ended his football days and he began to focus on films. He was occasionally called into duty for stunt work. He doubled Francis X. Bushman, Jr., for football scenes on *Brown of Harvard* (1926) and dove off a boat into rough

John Wayne (top) and Yakima Canutt developed the modern fight scene on low-budget westerns such as *Paradise Canyon* (1934).

seas on *Men Without Women* (1930). He also logged stunt work during the flood on *Noah's Ark* (1928) and more football action for *Salute* (1929) and *Forward Pass* (1929). Raoul Walsh gave him a starring role on *The Big Trail* (1930). For that early western he was taught horsemanship by Jack Padjan and knife-throwing by Steve Clemente. The film failed at the box office, and Wayne was forced into B-westerns. On *Lucky Texan* (1934) Wayne put on villain Canutt's outfit so Canutt could double Wayne leaping from a horse to bulldog himself off a rail car. Wayne rode a log down a flume on *Lawless Frontier* (1934) and did a horse fall on *Randy Rides Alone* (1934).

Director John Ford gave him the starring role on *Stagecoach* (1939) and resurrected his career. Wayne was not called into service during World War II but starred in a number of patriotic war films such as *Sands of Iwo Jima* (1949). An outdoorsman, he was not known for his horse skills, although he did do his own horse jump over a fence on *True Grit* (1969). An honorary member of the Stuntmen's Association, Wayne died from lung cancer at the age of 72.

See: Davis, Ronald L. *Duke: The Life and Image of John Wayne.* Norman, OK: University of Oklahoma, 1998; Landesman, Fred. *The John Wayne Filmography.* Jefferson, NC: McFarland, 2004; Munn, Michael. *John Wayne: The Man Behind the Myth.* New York: New American, 2003.

JOHNNY WEISSMULLER, JR. (1940–2006)

Johnny Weissmuller, Jr., was the son of the famous Olympic champion swimmer and popular screen Tarzan. Born in San Francisco, the younger Johnny was a city swim champ at Hamilton High, but temporarily gave up the pool for the basketball court. He returned to the water to become a record-setting swimmer at Santa Monica City College. He picked up stunt assignments through his dad's pals Paul Stader and Stubby Krueger during the time he was a member of USC's swim team and doing underwater demolition for the Navy. Six-foot-six and 220 pounds, he worked on several TV westerns, among them *Gunsmoke, Lawman, Sugarfoot, Death Valley Days,* and *Wagon Train.*

John Jr. found obtaining work in Hollywood difficult due to his size. Many actors refused to share the screen with him, and he was often relegated to playing corpses or creatures. A great dis-

appointment was losing the role of Tarzan to Ron Ely. Weissmuller relocated to San Francisco where he found work as a longshoreman. He still managed to pick up acting and stunt work on *THX-1138* (1971), *What's Up, Doc?* (1972), *American Graffiti* (1973), *Magnum Force* (1973), *The Killer Elite* (1975), and the TV series *The Streets of San Francisco.* He died at the age of 65 from liver cancer.

See: "Johnny Weissmuller, Jr." *Variety.* August 1, 2006; Selna, Robert. "Johnny Weissmuller, Jr.: Dockworker, Actor, Yacht Racer." *San Francisco Chronicle.* July 31, 2006; "Tarzan's Gargantuan Son a Stuntman." *Lima News.* February 15, 1970; Weissmuller, Jr., Johnny. *Tarzan, My Father.* ECW, 2002.

JOHN WELD (1905–2003)

Writer John Weld was born in Birmingham, Alabama, and raised on a Colorado ranch. After military school he played football at Alabama Polytech and was crowned the Missouri Valley Champion Swimmer. In Los Angeles he swam competitively for the Ambassador Hotel. Fox Studios recruited Weld and Gordon Carveth to high dive off a 137-foot cliff into the ocean for $60 on *Folly of Vanity* (1924). Weld had business cards printed proclaiming himself a "world champion high diver." This began a three-year relationship with Hollywood that saw Weld double Tom Mix, Buck Jones, John Barrymore, Earle Fox, Gloria Swanson, Leatrice Joy, Zasu Pitts, Norma Shearer, Anna Q. Nilsson, Charlie Chaplin, and Laurel and Hardy.

Weld worked on *Iron Horse* (1924), *Peter Pan* (1924), *Man on the Box* (1925), and *Fighting Heart* (1925). He was a member of the Twenty-Eighty-Three Club, standing for the weekly sum of $20.83 stuntmen received as unemployment pay if they were injured on the job. Weld was often broken up from stunt work and left for adventures in Paris prior to becoming a reporter and screenwriter. He wrote about his stunt experiences in his autobiography. Weld died of natural causes at the age of 98.

See: Eyman, Scott. *Print the Legend: The Life and Times of John Ford.* John Hopkins University, 2001; "John Weld, 98; Newspaperman, Author, Screenwriter." *Los Angeles Times.* July 22, 2003; McLellan, Dennis. "Story Doesn't End at *Fly Away Home*." *Los Angeles Times.* February 21,

1991; Weld, John. *Fly Away Home: Memoirs of a Hollywood Stuntman.* Santa Barbara, CA: Mission, 1991.

TED WELLS (1899–1948)

Silent movie western star Ted Wells was born John Oscar Wells in Midlands, Texas. He was raised on a ranch in Montana and attended military school. After time on the rodeo circuit as a trick rider, he got his Hollywood start doubling Rudolph Valentino on *Son of the Sheik* (1926). He starred in the Pawnee Bill, Jr., films, and Universal advertised him as "Ted Wells, World's Champion Rider." In talkies he starred in *Phantom Cowboy* (1935) before moving permanently back into bits and stunt work. He doubled Tyrone Power on *Suez* (1938) and William Boyd on many Hopalong Cassidy films. Wells died from a heart attack at the age of 48.

See: Rainey, Buck. *The Strong, Silent Type.* Jefferson, NC: McFarland, 2004.

RED WEST (1936–)

Robert Gene West was born in Memphis, Tennessee. "Red" was a sports star at Humes High playing football, baseball, and basketball. He boxed Golden Gloves and played football for Jones Junior College, participating in the Junior Rose Bowl. While serving with the U.S. Marine Corps he began studying karate. Red hooked up with high school friend Elvis Presley while the singer was stationed in Germany, and through Presley's friend Nick Adams was introduced to Hollywood. The 200-pound, six-foot West began working stunts on TV's *The Rebel* and *Spartacus* (1960).

His first Elvis film was *Flaming Star* (1960), in which he played an Indian. Red was the most visible of Presley's Memphis Mafia and served as his chief bodyguard. On virtually all of Presley's films he'd have bit parts or double actors Elvis was fighting. His best fights with Elvis came on *Tickle Me* (1965) and *Live a Little, Love a Little* (1968). Red grabbed a regular stuntman gig on the TV show *The Wild Wild West* (1966–69) and fought Robert Conrad on many great action scenes playing thugs or, in one episode, doubling Ken Swofford. West appeared in nearly a hundred films and 200 TV shows as a stuntman and actor.

See: Beifuss, John. "At 73, In Lead at Last, Elvis Pal Red West an Overnight Success." *Commercial Appeal.* May 13, 2009; McCoy, Carolyn. "Elvis Presley's Staunchest Defender: Red West." *Fighting Stars.* April 1976.

SONNY WEST (1938–)

Delbert Bryant West was born in Memphis, Tennessee. "Sonny" engaged in football with his cousin Red and was involved in ROTC. Upon graduation he joined the Air Force and worked as a jet mechanic. Red introduced him to Elvis, and Presley liked the way Sonny handled himself on the roller skating rink in a violent game called War. Elvis offered Sonny a job as a member of his crew in 1960. He became one of the most visible of Presley's friends-bodyguards.

Six-foot-one, 190-pound Sonny did extra work, bit parts, and stunts on the Presley films. He doubled actors on *Tickle Me* (1965) and *Double Trouble* (1967) and fought Elvis on *Live a Little, Love a Little* (1968) and *Stay Away, Joe* (1968). Like his cousin, Sonny branched out into non–Presley films and TV. He had an extended gig as Richard Chamberlain's stand-in on the *Dr. Kildare* series and had leads on the biker films *Hellcats* (1968) and *Outlaw Riders* (1970). On TV he stunted on *Daniel Boone* and *The Six Million Dollar Man.* Between acting assignments he was a bar bouncer. In 1969 Sonny became the chief of security when Presley went back to live performing.

See: West, Sonny. *Elvis: Still Taking Care of Business.* Chicago, IL: Triumph, 2008.

WALLY WEST (1903–1984)

Wally West was born Theo Wynn in Gough, Texas. He grew up on a ranch acquiring horse-riding skills and starred as Tom Wynn on the low-budget westerns *Desert Mesa* (1935) and *Mormon Conquest* (1939). As Wally West he doubled Gene Autry on *The Phantom Empire* (1935) and Bob Livingston on *The Vigilantes Are Coming* (1936). He also doubled B-westerns stars Ken Maynard, Tim McCoy, Tex Ritter, George Houston, Bill Cody, and Buster Crabbe among his 300 films.

He worked on *The General* (1927), *Melody Ranch* (1939), *The Virginian* (1946), *Superman* (1948), *Ghost of Zorro* (1949), *Batman and Robin* (1949), *Roar of the Iron Horse* (1951), *A Lawless Street* (1955), and *Law of the Lawless* (1964). On TV he doubled Lee Aaker on *Adventures of Rin*

Tin Tin (1954–59), Richard Egan on *Redigo* (1963), and made multiple appearances on *Roy Rogers*.

See: Price, Bob. "Wally West." *Screen Thrills Illustrated*. Vol. 2, #3. February 1964.

BILL WESTON (1941–2012)

Bill Weston doubled Gordon Jackson on *Fighting Prince of Donegal* (1966), Keir Dullea on *2001: A Space Odyssey* (1968), and Michael Caine on *The Eagle Has Landed* (1976), the first film in a thirty-year partnership. The 6'1", 175-pound horse expert and SAS military veteran was a familiar stuntman to the Bond franchise, doubling villains Louis Jourdan on *Octopussy* (1983) and Christopher Walken on *A View to a Kill* (1985). On *The Living Daylights* (1987) he played a butler who engages in a surprising fight scene. He also doubled Peter O'Toole, Michael York, and David Warner.

He worked on *Mayerling* (1968), *On Her Majesty's Secret Service* (1969), *Moon Zero Two* (1969), *Dead Cert* (1974), *A Bridge Too Far* (1977), *Star Wars* (1977), *The Spy Who Loved Me* (1977), *Superman* (1978), *Raiders of the Lost Ark* (1981), *For Your Eyes Only* (1981), and *Never Say Never Again* (1983). TV credits include *Doctor Who, Benny Hill,* and *Blake's 7.* Weston died from cancer at the age of 70.

See: Autry, Jon. "Bill Weston: The Gentleman Stuntman." Retrieved on July 11, 2013 at www.issuu.com.

PAUL WESTON

Paul Weston left a career in engineering to be a model. This led to stand-in work for Roger Moore on TV's *The Saint*. Weston's athleticism and fitness soon had him doing stunt work for Patrick Macnee on *The Avengers*. He perfected his craft working live stunt shows throughout Europe. The six-foot, 175-pound Weston doubled Robert Redford and Ryan O'Neal on *A Bridge Too Far* (1977), Christopher Reeve flying on *Superman* (1978), Richard Kiel leaping from a cable car on *Moonraker* (1979), and Roger Moore running along the top of a train ducking oncoming bridges on *Octopussy* (1983). He was stunt coordinator for the Bond films *The Living Daylights* (1987) and *Licence to Kill* (1989), where he did the climactic fire stunt for Robert Davi.

He also worked on *The Dirty Dozen* (1967), *Casino Royale* (1967), *You Only Live Twice* (1967), *A Countess from Hong Kong* (1967), *Live and Let Die* (1973), *The Man with the Golden Gun* (1974), *Star Wars* (1977), *Escape to Athena* (1979), *Ashanti* (1979), *The Lady Vanishes* (1979), *Superman II* (1980), *Raiders of the Lost Ark* (1981), *For Your Eyes Only* (1981), and *Return of the Jedi* (1983). TV credits include *Doctor Who, Blake's 7, The Prisoner, The Professionals, The Baron,* and *Space 1999*. He doubled Pierce Brosnan on *Remington Steele*.

See: www.paulwestonstunts.com.

TED WHITE (1927–)

In addition to being a recognizable character actor, 6'4", 215-pound Ted White doubled many of Hollywood's big men, including John Wayne, Clark Gable, Rock Hudson, Victor Mature, Charlton Heston, Lee Marvin, Richard Boone, James Garner, Claude Akins, and Jack Palance. On TV he doubled John Bromfield on *Sheriff of Cochise* and Fess Parker on the entire run of *Daniel Boone* (1964–70).

White was born Ted C. Bayouth in Krebs, Oklahoma. At the University of Oklahoma he was a football, swimming, and boxing star, holding the Southwest Heavyweight Title. He served in the Marine Corps where he was awarded a Purple Heart and a battlefield commission. While in the Marines he worked on *Sands of Iwo Jima* (1949).

Years later he was on the set of *Born Reckless* (1958) and volunteered for a horseback roping job. The roping ability came in handy doubling Gable on *The Misfits* (1961). He was considered a top fight man based on his doubling of Don Murray on *These Thousand Hills* (1959). His best battle came in a nightclub against Lee Marvin on *Point Blank* (1967). White doubled John Wayne on *Rio Bravo* (1959), *The Horse Soldiers* (1959), and *The Alamo* (1960), where White and his falling horse Johnny Reb were part of the fourteen-man horse fall. White did all the doubling for Wayne and Bruce Cabot in Africa on *Hatari* (1962). He had a falling out with Wayne after publicity wrote a story about Wayne's double roping an escaped cape buffalo. At that time it was a cardinal sin for stuntmen to acknowledge they were a star's double. White never worked on another Wayne film. He did gain a measure of notoriety when he played the hockey-masked killer

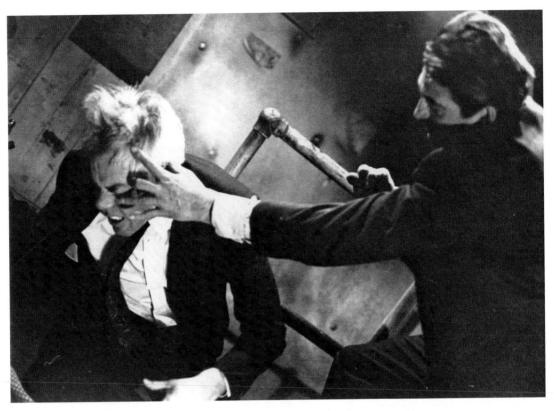

Lee Marvin is measured for a punch by Ted White on *Point Blank* (1967).

Jason on *Friday the 13th—The Final Chapter* (1984). Fans of the genre considered him the best in the role, though it was not a role White embraced due to the graphic violence.

He also worked on *Onionhead* (1958), *The Naked and the Dead* (1958), *One Foot in Hell* (1960), *Exodus* (1960), *Ship of Fools* (1965), *Cat Ballou* (1965), *Smoky* (1966), *What Did You Do in the War, Daddy?* (1966), *Camelot* (1967), *Planet of the Apes* (1968), *Support Your Local Sheriff* (1969), *They Call Me Mr. Tibbs* (1970), *Soylent Green* (1973), *The Don Is Dead* (1973), *Dirty Mary, Crazy Larry* (1974), *Black Oak Conspiracy* (1977), *The Manitou* (1978), *Comes a Horseman* (1978), *1941* (1979), and *Bronco Billy* (1980). TV credits include *Maverick, Bonanza, Rawhide, The Green Hornet, Mission: Impossible, Search, Kung Fu, Kolchak: The Night Stalker, The Rockford Files, Kojak, The Six Million Dollar Man,* and *The Fall Guy.* White is a member of the Stuntmen's Association, an inductee of the Stuntmen's Hall of Fame, and a Silver Spurs Award winner.

See: "Danger Lurks on Movie Sets." *El Paso Herald Post.* November 12, 1966; "Joplin Woman's Brother Has Role in *The Alamo.*" *Joplin Globe.* June 4, 1961; Lilley, Tim. *Campfire Conversations.* Akron, OH: Big Trail, 2007; www.baydogma. blogspot.com.

MARY WIGGINS (1909–1945)

Born in Tampa, Florida, Mary Wiggins won many diving and swimming titles and later entertained carnival audiences as a high diver doing precision jumps through rings of fire. She was also a barnstorming pilot, parachutist, and wingwalker. Considered a water and aviation stunt specialist by Hollywood, Wiggins was called America's Greatest Stunt Girl. She was the only female in her day qualified to roll over a car. For diving stunts she doubled Clara Bow on *Three Weekends* (1928), Norma Shearer on *Their Own Desire* (1929), Marlene Dietrich on *Blonde Venus* (1932), and Claudette Colbert on *It Happened One Night* (1934). She did tough mountain-climbing scenes for Barbara Stanwyck on *Shopworn* (1932) and doubled Stanwyck again on *Union Pacific* (1939).

Wiggins doubled Ruth Chatterton on *Frisco*

Jenny (1932) and *Female* (1933), Loretta Young on *Heroes for Sale* (1933), Ann Sothern on *Hell-Ship Morgan* (1936), Jane Wyatt on *Lost Horizon* (1937), Lupe Velez on *The Storm* (1938), Dorothy Lamour on *Spawn of the North* (1938), Annabella on *Suez* (1938), and Gracie Allen on *The Gracie Allen Murder Case* (1940). She also doubled Martha Raye and Fay Wray. Wiggins did print ads for Camel cigarettes and performed a stair fall for the stunt short *Spills for Thrills* (1940). Her only injury came on a vacation to her home state on the diving board on which she first learned. She broke her back and was in the hospital for twelve weeks. During World War II she served with the WASP as an Army ferry pilot. A member of the Stuntmen's Hall of Fame, Wiggins died at the age of 36 from a self-inflicted gunshot wound.

See: "Girl Who Isn't Afraid of Anything." *Oregonian.* May 18, 1941; "Veteran Stunt Woman Ends Life." *Los Angeles Times.* December 21, 1945.

GEORGE P. WILBUR (1942–)

Six-foot-two, 205-pound George Peter Wilbur was born in Connecticut and spent four years in the Navy. He got a job as a wrangler at a Tucson, Arizona, dude ranch and competed in rodeos. In Tucson he worked as a cowboy extra on *El Dorado* (1967) and was recruited to be the stand-in for John Wayne. Wilbur became friends with the stuntmen and moved to California to train at Paul Stader's Gym. When he met Peter Graves on the Paramount lot he convinced the *Mission: Impossible* star he would be a perfect double. Graves bought into the idea, and Wilbur spent the next five years working with Graves.

On the *Conquest of the Planet of the Apes* (1972) riot scene, Wilbur is the ape who throws a human onto an electrical board. On *The Poseidon Adventure* (1972) he tried climbing an upside down Christmas tree. Wilbur's favorite stunt ac-

Clint Eastwood throws a punch at George P. Wilbur on *Every Which Way But Loose* (1978).

tivity was fight scenes. He fought Clint Eastwood on *Every Which Way But Loose* (1978) and doubled Joe Don Baker on *Framed* (1975) for a vicious brawl with Roy Jenson. He doubled Charlton Heston and James Garner, but scored his greatest notoriety playing Michael Myers on the horror films *Halloween: The Return of Michael Myers* (1988) and *Halloween: The Curse of Michael Myers* (1995). Fans of the series liked the way he moved in the role and the punishment he absorbed, making Wilbur highly regarded in the horror genre.

He also worked on *Hombre* (1967), *Escape from the Planet of the Apes* (1971), *Blacula* (1972), *High Plains Drifter* (1973), *Battle for the Planet of the Apes* (1973), *Slaughter's Big Rip-Off* (1973), *Cleopatra Jones* (1973), *99 and 44/100 percent Dead* (1974), *Blazing Saddles* (1974), *The Towering Inferno* (1974), *Doc Savage* (1975), *Lepke* (1975), *The Hindenburg* (1975), *Death Journey* (1976), *Grizzly* (1976), *Futureworld* (1976), *Drum* (1976), *Silent Movie* (1976), *The White Buffalo*

(1977), *Black Oak Conspiracy* (1977), *Movie, Movie* (1978), *Beyond the Poseidon Adventure* (1979), *Stunt Seven* (1979), and *Mountain Men* (1980). TV credits include *The Monroes, Search, The Rockford Files, The Six Million Dollar Man, Switch, Delvecchio,* and the mini-series *Pearl* (1978). Wilbur is a member of the Stuntmen's Association and the Stuntmen's Hall of Fame.

See: www.georgewilburtheshape.com; www.rackandrazors.com/georgep.html.

GLENN WILDER (1933–)

Born in Los Angeles, Glenn R. Wilder entered the Navy and, after his discharge, made the USC football team. He excelled as an athlete and, as was typical of USC and UCLA football players, began to pick up stunt work on the side. In 1960 he was signed to play pro ball for the Los Angeles Chargers but a knee injury curtailed that career. He dabbled as a private detective and male model before pursuing stunt work full-time. Nicknamed

Glenn Wilder (left) doubles John Wayne behind the wheel for the high speed car chase on the beach on *McQ* (1974).

"Wild Man," the 6'1", 200-pound Wilder doubled Troy Donahue on *Palm Springs Weekend* (1963) and David Janssen on the TV show *The Fugitive* (1963–67). He later doubled Ron Harper on *Planet of the Apes* (1974) and Steve Forrest on *S.W.A.T.* (1975–76).

One of Wilder's first fights nearly turned out disastrously: Battling Elvis Presley on *Roustabout* (1964), his shoe caught Presley across the eye and opened a cut that needed nine stitches. Presley claimed it was his own fault, and a motorcycle wreck was written into the film to explain the injury so no days of shooting would be lost. *The Carpetbaggers* (1964) came shortly after and garnered Wilder a rep as a top fight man doubling George Peppard. Wilder was the double for Richard Crenna on *The Sand Pebbles* (1966) and *Wait Until Dark* (1967), executing a notable stair fall. He doubled John Wayne driving during the beach chase on *McQ* (1974) and Gene Hackman on *Night Moves* (1975) and *March or Die* (1977). As an actor he fought Burt Reynolds on *Shamus* (1973) and *White Lightning* (1973). In 1970 Wilder broke away from the Stuntmen's Association and co-founded Stunts Unlimited with Hal Needham and Ronnie Rondell.

He also worked on *Son of Flubber* (1962), *John Goldfarb, Please Come Home* (1965), *Our Man Flint* (1966), *The Devil's Brigade* (1968), *Ice Station Zebra* (1968), *The Boston Strangler* (1968), *The Love Bug* (1968), *The Good Guys and the Bad Guys* (1969), *The Arrangement* (1969), *Darling Lili* (1970), *Fuzz* (1972), *Cleopatra Jones* (1973), *Friends of Eddie Coyle* (1973), *The Longest Yard* (1974), *The Trial of Billy Jack* (1974), *Three the Hard Way* (1974), *Street People* (1975), *Mother, Jugs, and Speed* (1976), *Gator* (1976), *Logan's Run* (1976), *Two-Minute Warning* (1976), *Moonshine County Express* (1977), *Who'll Stop the Rain* (1978), *Convoy* (1978), *Hooper* (1978), *Blue Collar* (1978), and *Buck Rogers in the 25th Century* (1979). TV credits include *Batman, The Green Hornet, Mission: Impossible, Mannix, Mod Squad, Cannon, The Six Million Dollar Man, Vega$, CHiPs,* and the mini-series *Centennial* (1978). He was an inductee of the Stuntmen's Hall of Fame; his son Scott followed him into stunt work.

See: Fox, Charles. "Falls, Fractures, & Fortunes." *True.* January 1971; Hinman, Catherine. "Stuntman's Risky Business." *Orlando-Sentinel.* May 16, 1992.

BUSTER WILES (1910–1990)

Vernon Everett Wiles, the long-time friend and double of Errol Flynn, was born in Caruthersville, Missouri, and raised in Memphis, Tennessee. He won a Golden Gloves boxing tournament, played football for Messick High, and joined the Ringling Bros. Circus, where he worked as an apprentice on the trapeze with the Flying Codonas. While working as an extra on *The Last Days of Pompeii* (1935) he utilized his circus expertise for a stunt fall into a net. Buster met Flynn on *Captain Blood* (1935) and became a regular on his films. On *The Charge of the Light Brigade* (1936) he jumped a horse over a cannon and for *The Adventures of Robin Hood* (1938) he doubled Flynn's escape from the gallows by swinging over the castle gate. On *Valley of the Giants* (1938) he took a fifty-foot fall off a boulder into a shallow pool of water. On *Dodge City* (1939) he went off a second floor balcony with Red Breen. *They Drive By Night* (1940) saw him jump from a truck doubling George Raft. For Humphrey Bogart he did the tumble down a rocky ledge on *High Sierra* (1941). The 6'1", 180-pound Wiles also subbed for Gary Cooper, Alan Ladd, Dennis Morgan, Lloyd Nolan, Alan Hale, Douglas Fowley, Raymond Burr, and Van Heflin. He served with the Army during World War II and resumed his movie career at a less hectic pace, retiring from stunt work in the 1950s.

He also worked on *Another Dawn* (1937), *Heart of the North* (1938), *Gold Is Where You Find It* (1938), *Hell's Kitchen* (1939), *The Return of Doctor X* (1939), *The Private Lives of Elizabeth and Essex* (1939), *Virginia City* (1940), *The Sea Hawk* (1940), *Santa Fe Trail* (1940), *Tear Gas Squad* (1940), *River's End* (1940), *The Fighting 69th* (1940), *The Great Dictator* (1940), *The Wagons Roll at Night* (1941), *Out of the Fog* (1941), *Manpower* (1941), *Blues in the Night* (1941), *The Sea Wolf* (1941), *They Died with Their Boots On* (1941), *Desperate Journey* (1942), *Gentleman Jim* (1942), *The Desert Song* (1943), *Edge of Darkness* (1943), *Northern Pursuit* (1943), *Thank Your Lucky Stars* (1943), *Passage to Marseille* (1944), *Buffalo Bill* (1944), *Saratoga Trunk* (1945), *Objective, Burma* (1945), *Escape Me Never* (1947), *Wild Harvest* (1947), *The Paleface* (1948), and *The Brass Legend* (1956). He was an honorary member of the Stuntmen's Association and an inductee of the Stuntmen's Hall of Fame.

Errol Flynn tosses Buster Wiles (doubling Douglas Fowley) out a door on *Dodge City* (1939).

See: Thomas, William. "Stunt Man Fell into Fame." *Palm Beach Post.* February 3, 1984; "Vernon 'Buster' Wiles; Stuntman, 79." *New York Times.* July 26, 1990; Wiles, Buster, & William Donati. *My Days With Errol Flynn.* Santa Monica, CA: Roundtable, 1988.

BOB WILKE (1914–1989)

Thanks to his bullish build (6'3", 210 pounds) and unhandsome mug, Bob Wilke became one of the top heavies of the 1950s. Robert Joseph Wilke was born in Cincinnati, Ohio. He played football and baseball and was an avid swim-mer and recreational diver. This led to a spot as a high diver at the Chicago's World Fair in 1934. He was a lifeguard at New York's Coney Island and later in Miami Beach, entering Hollywood as a stuntman taking high falls into a net on *San Francisco* (1936). Gradually the stunt work developed into bit parts with time out for military service in World War II.

Wilke played dozens of snarling henchmen in westerns throughout the 1940s. His role as one of the outlaws on *High Noon* (1952) won him bigger and better projects and his own stuntman to handle at least some of the action for big fights on *20,000 Leagues Under the Sea* (1954), *Strange*

Lady in Town (1955), and *The Lone Ranger* (1956). He proved to be an effective character actor on *Spartacus* (1960) and *The Magnificent Seven* (1960). On TV he had big fights with Jock Mahoney on *The Range Rider,* and his battle with Forrest Tucker on the 1967 *Gunsmoke* episode "Cattle Barons" ignited one of the largest street brawls ever seen on the show. Wilke died of lung cancer at the age of 74.

CHUCK WILLCOX (1933–)

Born in Lancaster County, Pennsylvania, Charles E. Willcox was raised on an Amish farm. He ran off to join the Clyde Beatty Circus and spent time with a professional wrestling troupe, playing the shill they picked out of the audience. He became a baby-face wrestling hero but was stabbed in the chest by fans in Mexico. After recovering, he ended up as a stuntman on TV's *You Asked for It.* Utilizing his team-driving experience he worked on a number of westerns, specializing in crashing wagons. Willcox was accidentally stabbed in the jaw on a pirate picture and lost an eye. He later lost a hand due to a firearm accident, ending his stunt career.

Willcox doubled Richard Burton on *The Rains of Ranchipur* (1955) and James Dean on *Rebel without a Cause* (1955) and *Giant* (1956). He also doubled for Humphrey Bogart and acted under the stage name Tony Marshall. An honorary member of the Stuntmen's Association, Willcox worked on *Johnny Guitar* (1954), *Creature From the Black Lagoon* (1954), *I Was a Teenage Werewolf* (1957), *Speed Crazy* (1959), *Ben-Hur* (1959), and *Spartacus* (1960).

See: Greenwald, Charles. "Chuck Willcox— A True Valley Character." *Santa Ynez Valley Journal.* March 1, 2012.

MARVIN WILLENS (1934–2013)

Marvin Earl Willens was an All-Valley Gymnast while competing at George Washington Prep High and El Camino College. He became a competitive bodybuilder and a real-life Beverly Hills Cop. Willens doubled Phil Silvers on *It's a Mad, Mad, Mad, Mad World* (1963) and was poised to become one of the top stuntmen in the industry. Unfortunately, he broke his neck when he dove through a window and landed wrong while working on the TV series *The Man from U.N.C.L.E..*

He worked on *The Ten Commandments* (1956), *This Rebel Breed* (1960), *The George Raft Story* (1961), *Sweet Bird of Youth* (1962), *Confessions of an Opium Eater* (1962), *Kings of the Sun* (1963), *PT 109* (1963), and *4 for Texas* (1963). In the early 1960s he sponsored boxers along with fellow stuntman Paul Stader through a mutual gym partnership. He is an honorary member of the Stuntmen's Association and an inductee of the Stuntmen's Hall of Fame.

BILL WILLIAMS (1921–1964)

Bill Williams, a Colorado rancher's son, grew up competing in the rodeo. After World War II military service as a gunner's mate, he began a fifteen-year stunt career. He doubled Kirk Douglas on *The Indian Fighter* (1955) and Richard Widmark on *The Alamo* (1960). He primarily worked horse and wagon stunts on *Texans Never Cry* (1951), *Battle at Apache Pass* (1952), *Gunsmoke* (1953), *Column South* (1953), *Tumbleweed* (1953), *Ride Clear of Diablo* (1954), *Black Horse Canyon* (1954), *The Far Country* (1955), *Chief Crazy Horse* (1955), *Walk the Proud Land* (1956), *Night Passage* (1957), *The Young Land* (1958), *The Comancheros* (1961), *Two Rode Together* (1961), *Lonely Are the Brave* (1962), *Advance to the Rear* (1964), *Cheyenne Autumn* (1964), and *Major Dundee* (1965).

Williams died at the age of 43 when he was unable to jump clear of a wagon going over a cliff on *The Hallelujah Trail* (1965). The incident occurred in front of his wife and daughter who were visiting the Gallup, New Mexico location. No one present could figure out why an experienced stuntman such as Williams froze in his seat. Assistant director Robert Relyea was so shaken by the death that he never directed another second unit. The stunt remains in the film. Williams was a member of the Stuntmen's Association and an inductee of the Stuntmen's Hall of Fame.

See: "Movie Stuntman Killed in Leap." *Deseret News.* November 14, 1964; Relyea, Robert, & Criag Relyea. *Not So Quiet on the Set.* Bloomington, IN; IUniverse, 2008.

JACK WILLIAMS (1921–2007)

Jack Williams was born in Butte, Montana, and raised in Los Angeles. He was the son of stuntman George Williams and rodeo trick rider

Paris Williams. He first appeared on screen at age four when he was tossed between riders on *Flaming Forest* (1926). While a student at Burbank High he served as a horse rider on *The Charge of the Light Brigade* (1936), *Gone with the Wind* (1939), and a number of Errol Flynn films. Williams was on the polo team at USC and continued to perform stunts on the side. He gained notice doing a horse fall on *In Old California* (1943). After World War II service with the Coast Guard during the invasion of Okinawa, he was off and running with another great horse spill on *Red River* (1948) when shot by Montgomery Clift.

The six-foot, 170-pound Williams and his trained falling horse Coco worked on dozens of westerns; they were noted for their ability to rear straight up and go into spectacular falls. The western *The Last Outpost* (1951) is a treasure trove of horse falls by Williams and Chuck Roberson. Williams did many of the most noted falls on *The*

Conqueror (1956), in particular those for John Wayne, Leo Gordon, and Lee Van Cleef. Williams doubled Kirk Douglas on *20,000 Leagues Under the Sea* (1954), Eli Wallach on *The Magnificent Seven* (1960), Robert Preston on *How the West Was Won* (1962), and Christopher Plummer on *Fall of the Roman Empire* (1964). On TV he doubled Roy Rogers on *The Roy Rogers Show.*

He also worked on *Daniel Boone* (1936), *The Adventures of Robin Hood* (1938), *Dodge City* (1939), *Virginia City* (1940), *Santa Fe Trail* (1940), *They Died with Their Boots On* (1941), *Fort Apache* (1948), *Three Godfathers* (1948), *Tripoli* (1950), *Distant Drums* (1951), *The Lion and the Horse* (1951), *Bend of the River* (1952), *Bugles in the Afternoon* (1952), *The Naked Spur* (1953), *The Man from the Alamo* (1953), *Column South* (1953), *The Desert Song* (1953), *Hondo* (1953), *Tumbleweed* (1953), *Taza, Son of Cochise* (1954), *Border River* (1954), *Drums Across the*

Jack Williams does a saddle fall on *Gun for a Coward* (1957).

River (1954), *The Far Country* (1955), *Strange Lady in Town* (1955), *Backlash* (1956), *The Burning Hills* (1956), *Pillars of the Sky* (1956), *The Wings of Eagles* (1957), *Band of Angels* (1957), *Night Passage* (1957), *Joe Dakota* (1957), *The Left Handed Gun* (1958), *The Law and Jake Wade* (1958), *Man of the West* (1958), *Ride a Crooked Trail* (1958), *The Old Man and the Sea* (1959), *Rio Bravo* (1959), *Westbound* (1959), *Spartacus* (1960), *The Alamo* (1960), *El Cid* (1961), *The Comancheros* (1961), *Hatari!* (1962), *The Man Who Shot Liberty Valance* (1962), *Merrill's Marauders* (1962), *The Spiral Road* (1962), *Cheyenne Autumn* (1964), *Major Dundee* (1965), *Cat Ballou* (1965), *The Sons of Katie Elder* (1965), *The War Lord* (1965), *7 Women* (1965), *Smoky* (1966), *The Professionals* (1966), *Alvarez Kelly* (1966), *The War Wagon* (1967), *Camelot* (1967), *Welcome to Hard Times* (1967), *Will Penny* (1968), *The Scalphunters* (1968), *Mackenna's Gold* (1969), *The Wild Bunch* (1969), *Paint Your Wagon* (1969), *The Good Guys and the Bad Guys* (1969), *Beneath the Planet of the Apes* (1970), *Rio Lobo* (1970), *Ballad of Cable Hogue* (1970), *A Man Called Horse* (1970), *The Omega Man* (1971), *Soylent Green* (1973), *99 and 44/100 percent Dead* (1974), *The Master Gunfighter* (1975), and *Mountain Men* (1980). TV credits include *Maverick, Rawhide, Daniel Boone, Bonanza, Laredo, The Monroes, Lancer,* and *High Chaparral.* A member of the Stuntmen's Association and an inductee of the Stuntmen's Hall of Fame, he was honored with a Golden Boot and induction into Newhall's Walk of Western Stars. Williams died of natural causes at the age of 85.

See: "Empty Saddles." *Western Clippings.* #77, May-June 2007; Lilley, Tim. *Campfire Conversations.* Akron, OH: Big Trail, 2007; McLellan, Dennis. "Jack Williams, 85, Stuntman Known for Horse-Riding Skills." *Los Angeles Times.* April 16, 2007; Peeples, Stephen K. "Jack Williams, Stunt Double, Enjoys Newfound Tranquility." *SCV Signal.* April 25, 2005.

WILLARD WILLINGHAM (1915–)

Willard Willingham grew up on the Paramount Ranch in Malibu, California, and was breaking horses by his teens. He was a rodeo champ at Pendleton and Calgary. Due to his small stature he doubled Jane Russell on *The Paleface*

(1948) and Alan Ladd on *Branded* (1950). Willingham met Audie Murphy on *The Kid from Texas* (1950) and the two became close friends. Willingham doubled Murphy for the next decade and eventually began writing screenplays for his westerns while appearing in small parts.

He also worked on *Colorado Sunset* (1939), *Sierra* (1950), *The Cimarron Kid* (1952), *Son of Paleface* (1952), *The Duel at Silver Creek* (1952), *The Savage* (1952), *Gunsmoke* (1953), *Pony Express* (1953), *Arrowhead* (1953), *Column South* (1953), *Tumbleweed* (1953), *Drums Across the River* (1954), *The Far Country* (1955), *The McConnell Story* (1955), *Walk the Proud Land* (1956), *Santiago* (1956), *The Guns of Fort Petticoat* (1957), *Night Passage* (1957), *The Deep Six* (1958), *The Quiet American* (1958), *Ride a Crooked Trail* (1958), *The Badlanders* (1958), *Hell Bent for Leather* (1960), *Gunfight at Comanche Creek* (1963), *The Quick Gun* (1964), *Gunpoint* (1966), and *A Time for Dying* (1969).

HENRY WILLS (1921–1994)

Six-foot, 185-pound Henry Wills was born in Florence, Arizona, growing up on a cattle ranch and becoming a proficient rider. He was intrigued by a cousin working in Hollywood, and in his teens took summer breaks to California to find horse work movies. He earned up to $7.50 a day as a horse-riding extra on *Ali Baba Goes to Town* (1937) and *The Adventures of Marco Polo* (1938). An excellent football player at Florence High, he nevertheless decided to give moviemaking a shot. He was an extra at Republic on the Three Mesquiteers series, did stunts on *Stagecoach* (1939), performed a bulldog for Buck Jones on his last film *Dawn on the Great Divide* (1942), and doubled Jack Beutel on *The Outlaw* (1943). As his favorable reputation grew, Wills doubled Robert Taylor, Alan Ladd, Roy Rogers, Tex Ritter, Robert Preston, Dean Martin, Richard Widmark, Marlon Brando, Henry Fonda, William Holden, Dick Powell, Neville Brand, Anthony Caruso, Barry Sullivan, Jerry Lewis, and Bob Hope.

He was expert at horse and saddle falls and performed over 1400 for the camera, suffering injuries only on *The Fighting Kentuckian* (1949) and *One-Eyed Jacks* (1961). He was a top fight man, stunt coordinator, and second unit director specializing in westerns such as *Shane* (1953), *The Magnificent Seven* (1960), and *Major Dundee*

Henry Wills, Charles Horvath, and Bob Morgan execute horse falls on *Pillars of the Sky* (1956).

(1965), where he orchestrated a twenty-three man horse fall in a river. He further distinguished himself to western fans as the stunt coordinator for the TV series *High Chaparral* (1967–71) and as a double for Pernell Roberts on *Bonanza* (1959–65). His son Jerry became a stuntman.

He worked on *Hawk of the Wilderness* (1938), *Zorro's Fighting Legion* (1939), *Dark Command* (1940), *Winners of the West* (1940), *Adventures of Captain Marvel* (1941), *Reap the Wild Wind* (1942), *The Spoilers* (1942), *Perils of Nyoka* (1942), *Tall in the Saddle* (1944), *Buffalo Bill* (1944), *Along Came Jones* (1945), *Unconquered* (1947), *Angel and the Badman* (1947), *Fort Apache* (1948), *Joan of Arc* (1948), *The Paleface* (1948), *Samson and Delilah* (1949), *Kansas Raiders* (1950), *Across the Wide Missouri* (1951), *Westward the Women* (1951), *Cavalry Scout* (1951), *The Savage* (1952), *The Duel at Silver Creek* (1952), *The Redhead from Wyoming* (1953), *Houdini* (1953), *The Mississippi Gambler* (1953),

Ride, Vaquero! (1953), *Gunsmoke* (1953), *Saskatchewan* (1954), *Stand at Apache River* (1954), *Four Guns to the Border* (1954), *Black Horse Canyon* (1954), *Destry* (1954), *Chief Crazy Horse* (1955), *Run for Cover* (1955), *Wichita* (1955), *Rage at Dawn* (1955), *Lady Godiva* (1955), *Red Sundown* (1956), *Away All Boats* (1956), *A Day of Fury* (1956), *Night Passage* (1957), *Gunfight at the O.K. Corral* (1957), *Omar Khayyam* (1957), *The Law and Jake Wade* (1958), *Saddle the Wind* (1958), *The Saga of Hemp Brown* (1958), *Ride a Crooked Trail* (1958), *The Badlanders* (1958), *Seven Ways from Sundown* (1960), *Posse from Hell* (1961), *The Comancheros* (1961), *Six Black Horses* (1962), *Sergeants Three* (1962), *How the West Was Won* (1962), *Taras Bulba* (1962), *Showdown* (1963), *Mail Order Bride* (1964), *The Greatest Story Ever Told* (1965), *Shenandoah* (1965), *The Sons of Katie Elder* (1965), *Nevada Smith* (1966), *Texas Across the River* (1966), *Gunpoint* (1966), *Beau Geste*

(1966), *In Like Flint* (1967), *Rough Night in Jericho* (1967), *Return of the Gunfighter* (1967), *Red Tomahawk* (1967), *Chisum* (1970), *Shoot Out* (1971), *The Cowboys* (1972), *The Don Is Dead* (1973), *Oklahoma Crude* (1973), *99 and 44/100 percent Dead* (1974), *Zandy's Bride* (1974), *The Master Gunfighter* (1975), *Drum* (1976), *The Shootist* (1976), *F.I.S.T.* (1978), *Beyond the Poseidon Adventure* (1979), and *Mountain Men* (1980). TV credits include *Roy Rogers, The Cisco Kid, Cheyenne, Tales of Wells Fargo, Lawman, Wanted—Dead or Alive, Wagon Train, Zorro, Bat Masterson, Rawhide, Laramie, The Virginian, Laredo, The Rat Patrol, Mannix, Here Come the Brides, Mod Squad, Delphi Bureau, Kung Fu,* and *The Cowboys.* He was a member of the Stuntmen's Association, an inductee of the Stuntmen's Hall of Fame, and a recipient of the Golden Boot Award. Wills died from a heart attack at the age of 73.

See: "Carefully Plan All Mishaps in Action Film." *Springfield Union.* March 16, 1964; Creacy, Don. "Henry Wills: From Extra to Second Unit Director." *Under Western Skies.* #47, 1995; Lilley, Tim. *Campfire Conversations Complete.* Akron, OH: Big Trail, 2010; Macomber, Bill. "Stuntman Recalls Tough Tender Boyhood." *Casa Grande Dispatch.* September 11, 1992; Payne, William. "Movie Stunt Record Set By *Dundee* Fall." *Dallas Morning News.* April 16, 1964.

JERRY WILLS (1947–2010)

Five-foot-eleven, 165-pound Jerry Dea Wills grew up around horses and stuntmen. He got his professional start doubling Mark Slade and Rudy Ramos on the TV western *High Chaparral* (1967–71), a show his dad Henry was coordinating. On one episode he doubled Barry Sullivan, an actor his dad doubled on *The Woman of the Town* (1943). On TV's *Bonanza* he doubled David Canary. Horse fall specialist Wills doubled Tom Laughlin on *The Master Gunfighter* (1975) and George Segal on *The Duchess and the Dirtwater Fox* (1976).

He also worked on *Nevada Smith* (1966), *Warning Shot* (1967), *Planet of the Apes* (1968), *Chubasco* (1968), *The Don Is Dead* (1973), *99 and 44/100 percent Dead* (1974), *Blazing Saddles* (1974), *Dirty Mary, Crazy Larry* (1974), *Rollerball* (1975), *The Outlaw Josey Wales* (1976), *Every Which Way But Loose* (1978), *F.I.S.T.* (1978), *Tom Horn* (1980), *Mountain Men* (1980), *Bronco Billy* (1980), and *Heaven's Gate* (1980). TV credits include *Mission: Impossible, Gunsmoke, The Cowboys,* and *Little House on the Prairie.* He was a member of the Stuntmen's Association.

JAY WILSEY (1896–1961)

Wilbert Jay Wilsey was born in St. Francisville, Missouri. He was active as a rider in the rodeo and Wild West shows, leading him to Hollywood in 1924. Beginning with *Rarin' to Go* (1924) he starred in a series of B-westerns as Buffalo Bill, Jr., and continued headlining low-budget films into the sound era. The Poverty Row quickies paid so little that Wilsey started taking on stunt work to make ends meet. The 6'3" Wilsey doubled Tom Mix on *Hidden Gold* (1932) and also subbed for Ken Maynard, Johnny Mack Brown, Bob Allen, Bill Elliott, George Houston, Charles Starrett, and Russell Hayden. He worked on *Way Out West* (1930), *The Phantom Empire* (1935), and *Ali Baba Goes to Town* (1937). Wilsey died from lung cancer at the age of 65.

See: Russell, Bill. "Jay Wilsey aka Buffalo Bill, Jr." *Western Clippings.* #75/76 January-April 2007.

AL WILSON (1895–1932)

In the 1920s, Kentucky-born pilot Albert Pete Wilson was called the World's Most Sensational Stunt Player. Having organized the barnstorming Wild West Circus with fellow pilot Frank Clark, Wilson walked on wings, performed car-to-plane transfers, and staged fistfights on the wings of biplanes. He was the first man to execute a double plane transfer, ending up back in his original airplane. He worked stunts on *Eagle's Talons* (1923) and starred in a series of films such as *Air Hawk* (1924), *Cloud Rider* (1925), and *Phantom Flyer* (1928). Today he is best known for his piloting on Howard Hughes' *Hell's Angels* (1930), including a controversial crash in which Wilson bailed out but his passenger was killed. Once the flight instructor for Cecil B. DeMille; Wilson's Hollywood career ended due to the fatality. "Daredevil Al" died at the National Air Races in Cleveland, Ohio, when his Curtiss Pusher plane collided in midair with an autogiro. He was 36 years old.

HARRY WILSON (1897–1978)

Harry Wilson was a longtime stand-in and double for Wallace Beery and Broderick Crawford, battered character leads not known for their glamour shots. Bit player Wilson had one of the self-described ugliest mugs in Hollywood and played dozens of henchmen, pirates, and gangsters in nearly 1000 films. Wilson specialized in being killed on screen, and as a stuntman his bread and butter was quarterdeck brawls and fight scenes such as those seen in Beery's *Bad Man of Brimstone* (1937). His most humorous bit came in the big melee in *Wild Harvest* (1947), where he is continuously knocked over a railing.

Harry Wilson was born in London, England and embarked on a seafaring life as a merchant marine. During World War I he served with the U.S. Navy and thereafter dabbled as a professional wrestler before landing in Hollywood in the early 1920s. The 6'1", 210-pound Wilson was on a San Pedro dock watching a film crew when he volunteered to jump forty feet off a boat into the water for the cameras. There began a lengthy film career that saw him work on as many as three films in a single day. His meaty hands were often used for insert shots of someone being strangled. They even heisted jewelry in *Gone with the Wind* (1939) and rolled a scroll on *Samson and Delilah* (1949). Wilson played the monster on *Frankenstein's Daughter* (1958).

He worked on *Her Man* (1930), *Les Miserables* (1935), *Flash Gordon* (1936), *Big City* (1937), *God's Country and the Woman* (1937), *The Adventures of Marco Polo* (1938), *Mysterious Mr. Moto* (1938), *Stand Up and Fight* (1939), *Seven Sinners* (1940), *One Million B.C.* (1940), *Shadow of the Thin Man* (1941), *The Hairy Ape* (1944), *The Three Musketeers* (1948), *Wake of the Red Witch* (1948), *Fortunes of Captain Blood* (1950), *Lone Star* (1952), *Sign of the Pagan* (1954), *The Silver Chalice* (1954), *The Buccaneer* (1958), *Some Like It Hot* (1959), *How the West Was Won* (1962), and *The War Lord* (1965).

See: Bacon, James. "Ugliest Actor Frets on Ringo." *Abilene Reporter.* November 15, 1964; Day, John. "Professional Bad Guy." *Canandaigua Daily Messenger.* September 1, 1972; Goodwin, Fritz. "His Face Is His Fortune." *Colliers.* March 15, 1952; Harrison, Paul. "Meet the Movies Most Murdered Man." *Rock Hill Herald.* December 29, 1936.

JACK WILSON (1926–1999)

Fire specialist Jack Wilson was born in Chattanooga, Tennessee. He spent time as a professional roller derby player, motorcycle dirt track racer, sprint car driver, and sports car enthusiast. His biggest adrenaline rush came from fire, a talent Hollywood was happy to capitalize on after Wilson rollerskated through a fiery hoop on the TV show *You Asked for It*. His most famous fire stunt was a twenty-second burn for George Peppard on *Tobruk* (1967). He worked on *Ice Station Zebra* (1968), *The Great White Hope* (1970), *Raid on Rommel* (1971), *Johnny Got His Gun* (1971), *The Front Page* (1974), *Earthquake* (1974) and the TV shows *Combat, The Wild Wild West,* and *Bonanza.* Wilson died of a heart attack at the age of 73.

See: "Jack Wilson; Stuntman Known as Human Torch." *Los Angeles Times.* June 24, 1999; Taylor, Frank. "Jack Wilson Lights Up for Movie Cameras." *Rock Hill Herald.* November 10, 1971.

TERRY WILSON (1923–1999)

Six-foot-three, 190-pound Terry Wilson was born in Huntington Park, California and raised on a horse ranch. He excelled at football for Canoga Park and North Hollywood High, playing on scholarship at Cal Poly before joining the U.S. Marines to fight in World War II. He saw action at both Saipan and Okinawa in the Pacific Theatre. Wilson entered stunts upon his return thanks to his cousin being married to Allen Pomeroy, and he worked on seventy-five films his first three years in the business.

Known as a fight man, Wilson had top dust-ups on *Romance of Rosy Ridge* (1947), *Belle Starr's Daughter* (1948), *Panhandle* (1948), *Stampede* (1949), *Devil's Doorway* (1950), and *The Secret Fury* (1950), and crashed through the door during the John Wayne-Victor McLaglen fight on *The Quiet Man* (1952). He doubled Wayne on *Hondo* (1953) and *Legend of the Lost* (1957), Robert Mitchum on *Pursued* (1947) and *The Big Steal* (1949), Randolph Scott on *Colt .45* (1950), and Forrest Tucker on *Sands of Iwo Jima* (1949) and *Montana Belle* (1952). He put on a fat suit to double Orson Welles on *Man in the Shadow* (1957) and doubled Richard Egan, Brian Keith, Van Johnson, Howard Keel, Pedro Armendariz, and Andrew Duggan. Alongside Frank McGrath he became one of John Ford's regular stunt troupe on *Rio Grande* (1950), *The Searchers* (1956), and *The Wings of Eagles* (1957).

Wilson and McGrath joined the cast of the long-running TV series *Wagon Train* (1957–65). Wilson played trail scout Bill Hawks and served as the stunt coordinator for the show and the double for star Ward Bond. He was most proud of the fact that in 300 episodes of television, not a single person was injured. After *Wagon Train*, Wilson played character parts on *The War Wagon* (1967), *Support Your Local Gunfighter* (1971), and *Westworld* (1973), still taking punches and squib shots.

He also worked on *The Lady from Shanghai* (1948), *Silver River* (1948), *Tripoli* (1950), *Two Flags West* (1950), *Soldiers Three* (1951), *Westward the Women* (1951), *The Red Badge of Courage* (1951), *Scaramouche* (1952), *The Last Posse* (1953), *Seven Brides for Seven Brothers* (1954), *20,000 Leagues Under the Sea* (1954), *The Egyptian* (1954), *Prince Valiant* (1954), *It's Always Fair Weather* (1955), *The Prodigal* (1955), *The Last Frontier* (1955), *The Conqueror* (1956), *Designing Woman* (1957), and *The Young Land* (1958). He was an honorary member of the Stuntmen's Association and an inductee of the Stuntmen's Hall of Fame.

See: Hagner, John. "Profile." *Falling for Stars*. Vol. 1 #8 November-December 1965; Lilley, Tim. *Campfire Conversations*. Akron, OH: Big Trail, 2007; "Terry Wilson." *Citizen News*. March 21, 1949.

JOE "JAY" WISHARD

Jay Wishard had a gymnastic background in his native Maryland and became a successful rider on the rodeo circuit, developing a stunt where he'd dive from a galloping horse into an empty barrel. He wrestled professionally under the name J.J. White and doubled Leo Gordon on *Baby Face Nelson* (1957) and Kirk Douglas on *Gunfight at the O.K. Corral* (1957). He also worked on *The FBI Story* (1959), *The Horse Soldiers* (1959), *The Alamo* (1960), *Spartacus* (1960), and *Cimarron* (1960) among his eighty films and 200 TV appearances. In harness racing Wishard was known as "The Golden Hawk" for his flamboyant dress. He still worked on the occasional Hollywood film such as *Oklahoma Crude* (1973).

See: "Ex Hagerstown Meat Cutter Finds Success in Hollywood." *Morning Herald*. September 22, 1959; "Golden Hawk Returns to Bay Meadows." *San Mateo Times*. February 2, 1973; Menges, Jack. "Stuntman Wins Two Harness Races." *Oakland Tribune*. June 4, 1964.

BUD WOLFE (1910–1960)

Bud Wolfe was born Marion Wolfe in New York City. An automotive and fight specialist, he doubled Kent Taylor on *Wings Over Honolulu* (1937) and *Deadline for Murder* (1946), Boris Karloff on *Son of Frankenstein* (1939), Ralph Byrd on *Dick Tracy vs. Crime, Inc.* (1941), Raymond Burr on *Code of the West* (1947), and Steve Cochran on *Inside the Walls of Folsom Prison* (1951). One of the original "Stunt Cousins," during World War II he made military training films for Republic Studios.

Other credits include *Flash Gordon's Trip to Mars* (1938), *The Lone Ranger Rides Again* (1939), *Dick Tracy's G-Men* (1939), *Daredevils of the Red Circle* (1939), *Seven Sinners* (1940), *Mysterious Doctor Satan* (1940), *A Man Betrayed* (1941), *King of the Texas Rangers* (1941), *Spy Smasher* (1942), *Perils of Nyoka* (1942), *Haunted Harbor* (1944), *The Tiger Woman* (1944), *Flame of Barbary Coast* (1945), *The Crimson Ghost* (1946), *The Razor's Edge* (1946), *Detour to Danger* (1946), *The Farmer's Daughter* (1947), *Brute Force* (1947), *Wild Harvest* (1947), *Jesse James Rides Again* (1947), *Dangers of the Canadian Mounted* (1948), *The Fuller Brush Man* (1948), *Adventures of Frank and Jesse James* (1948), *G-Men Never Forget* (1948), *Mighty Joe Young* (1949), *The Fighting Kentuckian* (1949), *King of the Rocket Men* (1949), *Broken Arrow* (1950), *The Kid from Texas* (1950), *His Kind of Woman* (1951), *The Prisoner of Zenda* (1952), *Scarlet Angel* (1952), *Jalopy* (1953), *The War of the Worlds* (1953), *Seven Brides for Seven Brothers* (1954), *Tarantula* (1955), *Showdown at Abilene* (1956), and *Around the World in Eighty Days* (1956). He was a member of the Stuntmen's Hall of Fame.

RODD WOLFF (1947–)

Born in Bloomington, Illinois, Rodd Wolff was raised in Phoenix where he was active in football, basketball, and baseball at Cortez High. As a boy he was inspired by a meeting with Jock Mahoney, who became a lifelong friend and mentor. Wolff began riding horses and practicing stunts

Top horseman Rodd Wolff takes an impressive fall on *Mission to Glory* (1977).

at the age of eight and also befriended and learned from Ben Johnson. In time he became a top horseman and trainer of falling horses, working primarily on Arizona-filmed projects. Wolff was the riding double for Elvis Presley on *Charro* (1969) and a substitute for Jack Cassidy on an unsold television pilot. He later doubled Burt Reynolds and Terence Hill.

With his horses Sandy and Twerp he guest starred at numerous parades and rodeos, including the Rose Bowl Parade with Montie Montana. In 1977 he performed in the live show Buffalo Bill's Wild West & Congress of Rough Riders of the World. The 6'1", 190-pound Wolff has won both the Ron Nix Stuntman Competition and the Stunt Players Directory Photo Contest where he staged a horse fall while studiously reading a book. Wolff was hired as The Marlboro Man until the company discovered he was a non-smoker. In the early 1980s Jocko Mahoney and Rex Rossi tried to produce a movie about the life of Tom Mix starring Wolff.

He also worked on *Duel at Diablo* (1966), *A Time for Dying* (1969), *Rio Lobo* (1970), *Dirty Dingus Magee* (1970), *Soldier Blue* (1970), *Powderkeg* (1971), *Mark of Zorro* (1974), *The Outlaw Josey Wales* (1976), *Another Man, Another Chance* (1977), *Speedtrap* (1977), and *Mission to Glory* (1977). Wolff was on the Yuma, Arizona, stunt scenes on *Return of the Jedi* (1983) and performed notable horse work on *Rambo III* (1988). TV credits include *Death Valley Days, High Chaparral, Bonanza, Bearcats, Mission: Impossible, McMasters of Sweetwater, Mannix, Oregon Trail,* and *The New Dick VanDyke Show.* A member of the International Trick and Fancy Ropers Association and an inductee of the Stuntmen's Hall of Fame, he has served as SAG chair for Arizona's Stunt and Safety Committee.

See: Conley, Jr., John H. *Heart of a Cowboy.* CreateSpace, 2010; Fenster, Bob. "Pulling Stunts." *Arizona Republic.* July 5, 1992; Stephens, Marie. "Valley Stuntman Follows Dream into Hall of Fame." *Scottsdale Tribune.* May 2003; www.sagaftra.org/Arizona.

SUNNY WOODS

Acrobat and California surfer Sunny Woods was attending Glendale College when the circus came to town. She became a hire wire walker and aerialist with the Flying Viennas. Woods met Chuck Couch who began training her in stunt work. Her first stunt was surfing in a Beach Party film. She doubled Mary Ann Mobley as a trapeze artist on TV's *Mission: Impossible* and followed Couch to Hawaii for *Hawaii Five-O.* A martial arts student, she also doubled Elke Sommer and Britt Ekland. Her biggest assignment was doubling Jessica Lange on *King Kong* (1976). The 5'6" Woods also worked on *The Phynx* (1970), *Logan's Run* (1976), and the TV shows *The Girl from U.N.C.L.E., Wonder Woman, The Bionic Woman,* and *Charlie's Angels.* She was once president of the Stuntwomen's Association.

See: Holter, Peggy Magner. "Stuntwomen." *Playgirl.* April, 1976; Sobel, Stuart. "Dare Me!" *Fighting Stars.* July 1978.

BOB WOODWARD (1909–1972)

Oklahoma-born Bob Woodward never strayed from westerns during a thirty-year stunt career. He doubled Buck Jones, Gene Autry, Lash LaRue, Jimmy Wakely, and Dick Foran while playing henchmen in cowboy fare. Woodward was a top hand at riding and fighting and could drive a stagecoach. He was especially prevalent in TV westerns of the 1950s, doubling Autry regularly on *The Gene Autry Show.* Other credits include *Melody Ranch* (1939), *Stampede* (1949), *Stage to Tucson* (1950), *Texans Never Cry* (1951), *The Stranger Wore a Gun* (1953), *Westward Ho, the Wagons!* (1956), *7th Cavalry* (1956), and *Apache Territory* (1958). A member of the Stuntmen's Hall of Fame, Woodward died from a heart attack at the age of 62.

JACK WOODY (1896–1969)

Jack Woody was born Frank Bryan Woody in Elkhorn, Kansas. A veteran of the Marine Corps, Woody was a hunting and fishing guide in the High Sierras. He is remembered for a stormy marriage to actress Helen Twelvetrees that served as the basis for the plot of *I'm Still Alive* (1940). He had a knack for escaping serious injury or death. Woody was hit in the neck by a ricocheting bullet on *Thank You, Mr. Moto* (1937). A year later he was shot in the face by a blank charge while doubling J. Carrol Naish wrestling over a gun on *Hotel Imperial* (1939). Both accidents barely interrupted his work. Woody doubled Humphrey Bogart on *Racket Busters* (1938) and *Brother Orchid* (1940).

He also worked on *Her Man* (1930), *Mysterious Mr. Moto* (1938), *Passport Husband* (1938), *I Am the Law* (1938), *Road to Singapore* (1940), *Desperate Journey* (1942), *Samson and Delilah* (1949), *Springfield Rifle* (1952), *Carson City* (1952), *The Stranger Wore a Gun* (1953), *Thunder Over the Plains* (1953), *Riding Shotgun* (1954), *The Bounty Hunter* (1954), and *Day of the Outlaw* (1959). He was an honorary member of the Stuntmen's Association.

See: "Stunt Man Becomes Actor in Westerns." *State Times Advocate.* July 17, 1952.

HARRY WOOLMAN (1909–1996)

Harry Simon Woolman was born in Elkton, Maryland. "Dynamite Harry" was a motorcycle daredevil who found his way to Hollywood and worked as a double for Clark Gable, William Bendix, Charles Laughton, John Carradine, and James Whitmore, the latter on *Battleground* (1949). On TV he doubled Jack Webb on *Dragnet.* He became known for live auto thrill shows performing ramp-to-ramp motorcycle jumps and head-on collisions. In the 1950s he was the regular stunt artist on the TV show *You Asked for It.* He was still doing movie stunts up to *Ride in the Whirlwind* (1965) before turning to special effects work on *Executive Action* (1973) et al. Married to Alma Pappas, stand-in and double for Lupe Velez and Ida Lupino, Woolman died from heart failure at the age of 87.

See: "Stuntman Still Sound Specimen Despite His Crashes and Falls." *Los Angeles Times.* April 20, 1961; Mosby, Aline. "Fans Request TV Daredevils to Risk Necks." *San Mateo Times.* April 5, 1955.

TOMMY WORRELL (1936–)

Thomas Alfred Worrell was born in Sylvan, Arkansas, and earned a football scholarship to Trinity University in San Antonio, Texas. Joining local gun clubs, he won the San Antonio Fast Draw and the Northwest Fast Draw Championships. This led to performing live stunt shows at Oregon's Centennial Frontier Village. Returning to Texas, he landed stunt work on *The Alamo* (1960). The following season in Oregon, Worrell worked on several location episodes of the TV series *Have Gun—Will Travel.* He was offered a chance to go to Hollywood as a stuntman but returned to Texas to honor commitments as a football coach at Trinity and an athletic director at Sunshine Cottage School.

After a few years Worrell did journey to California, landing stunt work on *The Poseidon Adventure* (1972) and the TV shows *Gunsmoke, The Virginian,* and *Bonanza.* He once again returned to Texas where he worked on the local film *Adventures of Jody Shanan* (1978). His most highly visible assignment was a popular commercial for Pace Picante Sauce. Worrell put on cowboy shows at the Diamond W Ranch and entertained audiences with his trained longhorn Sundance.

See: www.tommycowboy.com.

AL WYATT (1917–1992)

Six-foot-four, 200-pound Allan Riley Wyatt was born in Mayfield, Kentucky. Wyatt was an expert horseman, and served his country in World War II. He entered films as a double for Jon Hall on *Last of the Redmen* (1947), Errol Flynn on *Silver River* (1948), and Charles Starrett as the Durango Kid. He was the catcher for a great Jock Mahoney dive on *Horsemen of the Sierras* (1949). Throughout the 1950s Wyatt was one of the most in-demand stuntmen in the business, regularly doubling Randolph Scott, Rock Hudson, and Jeff Chandler. All three stars had it written into their contracts that if Wyatt was available, he was to be their double. He was especially athletic for a big man and quite adept at fight scenes, doubling Rod Cameron, James Arness, James Coburn, Forrest Tucker, Fred MacMurray, Joseph Cotten, Wendell Corey, Phil Carey, and George Montgomery.

Wyatt dove through a window for Gregory Peck on *The World in His Arms* (1952), made a great bulldog leap off a horse for Joel McCrea on *Border River* (1954), performed the fire stunts for the title character on *Creature from the Black Lagoon* (1954), and doubled Henry Silva for the famous fight with Frank Sinatra on *The Manchurian Candidate* (1962). On the serial *Cody of the Pony Express* (1949) and the TV series *The Range Rider* (1950–53) he was on hand to double star Jock Mahoney, who wound up doing all his own stunts after Wyatt rehearsed them. He and Mahoney put together great fights with Wyatt doubling guest stars. Wyatt doubled Clint Eastwood and Eric Fleming on the TV series *Rawhide* (1959–66), Karl Malden on *The Streets of San Francisco*

Al Wyatt dodges a leaping stallion on *Black Horse Canyon* (1954).

(1972–77), and Buddy Ebsen on *Barnaby Jones* (1973–80). He served as stunt coordinator for *Blazing Saddles* (1974) and *Dirty Mary, Crazy Larry* (1974). His son Al Jr. played pro baseball and was a stunt double for John Schneider on the TV series *The Dukes of Hazzard*.

He also worked on *Coroner Creek* (1948), *Superman* (1948), *The Doolins of Oklahoma* (1949), *Cargo to Capetown* (1950), *The Flame and the Arrow* (1950), *Saddle Tramp* (1950), *Comanche Territory* (1950), *Whirlwind* (1951), *Texas Rangers* (1951), *Carson City* (1952), *Hangman's Knot* (1952), *Battle at Apache Pass* (1952), *The Lawless Breed* (1952), *The Mississippi Gambler* (1953), *Gun Fury* (1953), *Wings of the Hawk* (1953), *Seminole* (1953), *The Great Sioux Uprising* (1953), *Column South* (1953), *Border River* (1954), *Taza, Son of Cochise* (1954), *Battle of Rogue River* (1954), *Sitting Bull* (1954), *Lone Gun* (1954), *Ten Wanted Men* (1955), *Tall Man Riding* (1955), *Shotgun* (1955), *7th Cavalry* (1956), *The Far Horizons* (1955), *Wichita* (1955), *A Lawless Street* (1955), *Seven Angry Men* (1955), *Desert*

Sands (1955), *The Last Command* (1955), *The Lone Ranger* (1956), *Westward Ho, the Wagons!* (1956), *Walk the Proud Land* (1956), *The Guns of Fort Petticoat* (1957), *Gun for a Coward* (1957), *Gun Duel in Durango* (1957), *The Oklahoman* (1957), *Buchanan Rides Alone* (1958), *Toughest Gun in Tombstone* (1958), *Light in the Forest* (1958), *Tonka* (1958), *Man from God's Country* (1958), *Badman's Country* (1958), *The Jayhawkers!* (1959), *Night of the Quarter Moon* (1959), *King of the Wild Stallions* (1959), *The Plunderers* (1960), *The Canadians* (1961), *Ride the High Country* (1962), *Sergeants Three* (1962), *Mail Order Bride* (1964), *The Quick Gun* (1964), *The Rounders* (1965), *The Great Race* (1965), *Von Ryan's Express* (1965), *Not With My Wife You Don't* (1966), *Duel at Diablo* (1966), *Counterpoint* (1968), *Heaven with a Gun* (1969), *The Molly Maguires* (1970), *Flap* (1970), *Wild Rovers* (1971), *Valdez Is Coming* (1971), *The Great Northfield Minnesota Raid* (1972), *Freebie and the Bean* (1974), *Bound for Glory* (1976), *Fighting Mad* (1976), *The World's Greatest Lover* (1977), *The*

Manitou (1978), *The Fury* (1978), and *Meteor* (1979).TV credits include *Gene Autry, The Lone Ranger, Wyatt Earp, Tales of Wells Fargo, Boots and Saddles, Broken Arrow, Lawman, The Rifleman, Gunsmoke, The Virginian, The Wild Wild West, Batman, Star Trek, Hondo, Cimarron Strip,* and *Cannon.* Wyatt was a co-founder of the Stuntmen's Association and an inductee of the Stuntmen's Hall of Fame. He was the first stuntman honored by the Golden Boot Awards. Wyatt died of cancer in 1992 at the age of 75.

See: "Old-Time Stuntmen Gather Over Coffee." *Los Angeles Times.*

WALTER WYATT (1939–1986)

Born in Kern County, California, Walter Clarke Wyatt grew up on a dairy farm and played football in Bakersfield. He joined the Rodeo Cowboys Association in 1955, becoming Salinas steer wrestling champion in 1961 and Pendleton champ in 1966. Due to his size (6'1", 230 pounds) and strength he was valued as a catcher for bulldog stunts. Wyatt doubled John Wayne on *The Cowboys* (1972), Joe Don Baker on *The Pack* (1977), and Arnold Schwarzenegger on *The Villain* (1979).

He also worked on *The Great Race* (1965), *The Undefeated* (1969), *Little Big Man* (1970), *Westworld* (1973), *Cahill, U.S. Marshal* (1973), *Blazing Saddles* (1974), *The Trial of Billy Jack* (1974), *Animal House* (1978), *Convoy* (1978), *Hooper* (1978), *One Man Jury* (1978), *Tom Horn* (1980), and *Stunts Unlimited* (1980). His TV credits include *Gunsmoke, Laredo, Lancer, Custer, The Virginian, Mannix, The Quest,* and *Fantasy Island.* Plagued by injuries and several major sinus operations, Wyatt died from osteomyelitis at the age of 46.

See: "Movie Stuntman Has Fought Off Death for 30 Years." *Rock Hill Herald.* June 13, 1975.

BOB YERKES (1932–)

Five-foot-ten, 170-pound Brayton Walter Yerkes was born in Los Angeles and became enamored with the acrobats on Muscle Beach. When his parents divorced, he ran away from home at the age of fourteen to join the DeWayne Brothers Circus and learned the teeterboard with time out for the Korean War. He resumed his professional career with the Clyde Beatty Circus and the Rin-

gling Brothers, often working as the catcher for Faye Alexander. Yerkes later toured with an act called the Flying Artons. He was a skilled trapeze aerialist and tightrope walker and was mentored into stunt work by Russ Saunders. Yerkes later used his variety of experience to work as the trainer for TV's *Circus of the Stars.*

Yerkes popped in and out of Hollywood for stunts, most notably doubling Paul Newman, Robert Duvall, and David Nelson, the latter for trapeze work on *The Big Circus* (1959). By the 1970s he was stationed in Hollywood. Two of his best stunts are a high fall from a helicopter on *Breakout* (1975) and the hanging by one hand on the Statue of Liberty on *Remo Williams* (1985). Yerkes doubled Arnold Schwarzenegger swinging across the Sherman Oaks Galleria mall on *Commando* (1985), Christopher Lloyd hanging from the clock tower on *Back to the Future* (1985), and Eli Wallach being thrown off a train on *Tough Guys* (1986). He flew around for Boba Fett on *Return of the Jedi* (1983) and was still doing high falls into his seventies. Yerkes designed one of the first movie air bags and routinely trained stunt people in his backyard gym in Northridge, California. His home gym contained a trapeze outfit, a Russian Swing, a trampoline, air bags, and tumbling mats.

He worked on *Julia Misbehaves* (1948), *The Three Musketeers* (1948), *The Silver Chalice* (1954), *Airport* (1970), *The Towering Inferno* (1974), *Earthquake* (1974), *Airport '75* (1974), *Doc Savage* (1975), *Drum* (1976), and *The Amazing Dobermans* (1976). A longtime member of the Stuntmen's Association, Yerkes was inducted into the Stuntmen's Hall of Fame and received the World Acrobatic Society's Lifetime Achievement Award.

See: "He Falls for Scripture." *Los Angeles Times.* February 19, 1977; Hennessy, Leigh. "Bob Yerkes: A Life Stranger Than Fiction." *Inside Stunts.* Winter, 2006; Marelius, John. "High Flyer Has Swinging Time in Own Backyard." *Van Nuys Valley News.* February 10, 1970; Sullivan, Deborah. "Still Happy as Fall Guy: Northridge Man, 66, Marks 50 Years Doing Stunt Work." *Daily News.* November 5, 1998.

DUKE YORK (1908–1952)

Duke York was born Charles Everett Sinsabaugh in Danby, New York. The muscular swimmer and former lifeguard is best known for appearing as a villain opposite Buster Crabbe on the *Flash Gordon* (1936) serial and as monsters in several Three Stooges shorts. He fought the wolf dog Chinook in a series of adventure films. York doubled Huntz Hall on *Sea Raiders* (1941) but broke his back in an auto wreck. He began playing stoic cigar store Indians until he recovered enough to resume stunt work. Between jobs he ran the gym of his actor friend Greg McClure. York had a stormy marriage to stuntwoman Frances Miles.

He worked on *Island of Lost Souls* (1932), *Strike Me Pink* (1936), *Dick Tracy Returns* (1938), *Union Pacific* (1939), *Destry Rides Again* (1939), *When the Daltons Rode* (1940), *Texas* (1941), *Shadow of the Thin Man* (1941), *Two Yanks in Trinidad* (1942), *Destination Tokyo* (1943), *A Southern Yankee* (1948), *The Paleface* (1948), *Stampede* (1949), *The Gunfighter* (1950), *Winchester '73* (1950), *The Red Badge of Courage* (1951), *Texans Never Cry* (1951), *Fort Worth* (1951), and *Carbine Williams* (1952). TV credits include *The Lone Ranger, The Range Rider,* and *Wild Bill Hickok.* York died of an apparent suicide at the age of 43 after having an argument with his girlfriend.

See: "Tough Guy Kills Self." *Vancouver Sun.* January 26, 1952.

TERRY YORKE (1926–2003)

The media called British-born Terry Yorke "King of the Stuntmen" when he headed up the action of more than forty stunt performers during the making of *55 Days at Peking* (1963), but he was never able to capitalize on that brief shot of publicity. For the most part he remained a nondescript professional working behind the scenes. At one time Yorke was a prospective actor who was introduced to stunt work when he was hired to double Robert Taylor for jousting scenes on *Knights of the Round Table* (1953). Yorke determined that the stunt profession was a quicker way to earn a wage than a stage career and stuck with it. A highlight was doubling Hugh O'Brian for a terrific fight with Mario Adorf on *Ten Little Indians* (1965).

He worked on *Solomon and Sheba* (1959), *King of Kings* (1961), *The Guns of Navarone* (1961), *Lawrence of Arabia* (1962), *Circus World* (1964), *The Long Duel* (1967), *Casino Royale* (1967), *Where Eagles Dare* (1968), *The Pink Pan-*

ther Strikes Again (1976), and *Superman II* (1980). On TV he doubled Richard Greene on *Adventures of Robin Hood* (1957–60) and Tony Curtis on *The Persuaders* (1971–72), and he appeared on *The Saint, The Avengers,* and *The Prisoner.*

See: Gersdorf, Phil. "Chief Neck-Risker." *Omaha World Herald.* January 13, 1963.

JACK YOUNG (1926–)

Jack N. Young was born in Fincastle, Virginia, and boxed in his youth. During World War II he served in the U.S. Navy as a frogman with an underwater demolitions team completing over 100 missions. The aquatic experience aided him on *The Frogmen* (1951), *Beneath the 12 Mile Reef* (1953), *Underwater!* (1955), and the TV series *Sea Hunt,* although Young primarily worked on westerns. "BlackJack" Young was known for his resemblance to Clark Gable and worked with "The King" on *Across the Wide Missouri* (1951), *Lone Star* (1952), *The Tall Men* (1955), *The King and Four Queens* (1956), and *The Misfits* (1961). He doubled Gary Cooper for the classic fight with Jack Lord on *Man of the West* (1958) and also filled in for Richard Widmark, Robert Taylor, and doubled Jack Palance on *Shane* (1953). While filming *The Alamo* (1960) he was part of a mass horse fall that fractured his skull and left nearly sixty percent of his body broken up.

Young opted to move away from stunt work involving horses, taking live jobs at Frontier Village in Oklahoma City, Frontier Town in Wichita, Kansas, Apacheland in Arizona, and Alamo Village in Brackettville, Texas. He mixed in film work but decided to leave the business after seeing Bob Morgan losing a leg on *How the West Was Won* (1962). While filming *McLintock!* (1963) Young accepted a job offer from Bob Shelton at Old Tucson Studios and became the top cowboy for the park's gunfight shows. Buzz Henry talked him into doubling James Caan on *El Dorado* (1967) for the scene where the horses jump over him. Young eventually moved behind the scenes to handle public relations and work as a location manager. He was active in bringing the TV series *High Chaparral* (1967–71) to Old Tucson. He briefly moved to Santa Fe, New Mexico, in the late 1960s to work out of their film office but returned to Tucson to become a casting director and jack of all cinematic trades.

He worked on *The Street with No Name*

Publicity photo for BlackJack Young.

(1948), *She Wore a Yellow Ribbon* (1949), *Slattery's Hurricane* (1949), *D.O.A.* (1949), *Rio Grande* (1950), *Panic in the City* (1950), *Rawhide* (1951), *Westward the Women* (1951), *Springfield Rifle* (1952), *High Noon* (1952), *The Duel at Silver Creek* (1952), *The Naked Spur* (1953), *Hondo* (1953), *Law and Order* (1953), *City of Bad Men* (1953), *The Last Posse* (1953), *The Far Country* (1955), *The Fastest Gun Alive* (1956), *Tribute to a Bad Man* (1956), *The Conqueror* (1956), *The Last Wagon* (1956), *The Searchers* (1956), *Gun the Man Down* (1956), *The Man from Laramie* (1955) and *Man Without a Star* (1955), *Gunfight at the O.K. Corral* (1957), *The Guns of Fort Petticoat* (1957), *Night Passage* (1957), *The Tin Star* (1957), *Forty Guns* (1957), *Legend of the Lost* (1957), *3:10 to Yuma* (1957), *The True Story of Jesse James* (1957), *Saddle the Wind* (1958), *Buchanan Rides Alone* (1958), *The Law and Jake Wade* (1958), *Rio Bravo* (1959), *The Horse Soldiers* (1959), *The Wonderful Country* (1959), *The Comancheros* (1961), *Deadly Companions* (1961), and *Rio Lobo* (1970). TV credits include *Wyatt Earp, Cheyenne, Gunsmoke, Have Gun—Will Travel, The Rifleman, Wagon Train, Bonanza, Bronco, Wanted—Dead or Alive, Death Valley Days,* and *The Rat Patrol.* He was the subject of the documentary short *Unsung: The Ballad of BlackJack Young.*

See: Hull, Tim. "Cinematic Life of Black Jack Young. *Tucson Weekly.* April 19, 2001; "Young Named Head of SF Film Center." *Santa Fe New Mexican.* October 20, 1968.

BILL YRIGOYEN (1912–1976)

California-born Bill Yrigoyen was the brother of Joe Yrigoyen and a top-rated horseman. He doubled Gene Autry, Roy Rogers, Don "Red" Barry, and Bob Steele, working most often at Republic Studios. Yrigoyen did stunts on *The Painted Stallion* (1937), *Army Girl* (1938), *The Lone Ranger* (1938), *Zorro's Fighting Legion* (1939), *Man of Conquest* (1939), *They Died with Their Boots On* (1941), *In Old Oklahoma* (1943), *Daredevils of the West* (1943), and *The Crimson Ghost* (1946). For *Dark Command* (1940) Yrigoyen, his brother Joe, Cliff Lyons, and Yakima Canutt got their horses to jump thirty-five feet off a ledge into water with the riders accompanying them. He left stunt work to raise cattle. He was an honorary member of the Stuntmen's Association and an inductee of the Stuntmen's Hall of

Fame, Yrigoyen died at the age of 63.

See: Gunter, Norma. *The Moorpark Story.* Moorpark Chamber of Commerce, 1969.

JOE YRIGOYEN (1910–1998)

Five-foot-ten, 180-pound Basque stuntman Joe Yrigoyen was born in Ventura, California. He was a top horseman specializing in transfers from horse to wagon. He could drive a six-up team and handle a fight scene well enough to make Gene Autry look good on *Rim of the Canyon* (1949). He worked with his brother Bill at Republic in the 1940s. Among the actors he doubled were Roy Rogers, Rex Allen, and Richard Widmark. Yrigoyen was held in high regard, especially by stunt legend Yakima Canutt who hired him often. He took a horse off a cliff with Canutt on *Dark Command* (1940) and doubled Stephen Boyd for the chariot race on *Ben-Hur* (1959). He was cast on that as the Egyptian charioteer. The father of stuntman Joe Finnegan and father-in-law of Mickey Gilbert, Yrigoyen didn't do many acting parts and never became better known to the masses.

He worked on *Ali Baba Goes to Town* (1937), *The Painted Stallion* (1937), *Army Girl* (1938), *Man of Conquest* (1939), *Dick Tracy's G-Men* (1939), *Zorro's Fighting Legion* (1939), *Daredevils of the Red Circle* (1939), *Adventures of Red Ryder* (1940), *They Died with Their Boots On* (1941), *Secret Service in Darkest Africa* (1943), *The Masked Marvel* (1943), *In Old Oklahoma* (1943), *Daredevils of the West* (1943), *Captain America* (1944), *The Spanish Main* (1945), *The Crimson Ghost* (1946), *Angel and the Badman* (1947), *Adventures of Frank and Jesse James* (1948), *Ghost of Zorro* (1949), *Brimstone* (1949), *Montana Belle* (1952), *Wings of the Hawk* (1953), *Tall Man Riding* (1955), *Desert Sands* (1955), *The Last Command* (1955), *Walk the Proud Land* (1956), *Westward Ho, the Wagons!* (1956), *Gun Duel in Durango* (1957), *Warlock* (1959), *Seven Ways from Sundown* (1960), *Hell Bent for Leather* (1960), *Posse from Hell* (1961), *How the West Was Won* (1962), *Savage Sam* (1963), *4 for Texas* (1963), *A Distant Trumpet* (1964), *Shenandoah* (1965), *The Sons of Katie Elder* (1965), *The Great Race* (1965), *The Hallelujah Trail* (1965), *Alvarez Kelly* (1966), *Africa—Texas Style* (1967), *Camelot* (1967), *Will Penny* (1968), *The Wild Bunch* (1969), *Paint Your Wagon* (1969), *The Cowboys* (1972), *Blazing Sad-*

dles (1974), and *Prisoner of Zenda* (1979). TV credits include *Mike Hammer, Have Gun—Will Travel, Overland Trail, Bat Masterson, Whispering Smith, Laramie, Bonanza, Daniel Boone, Gunsmoke, The Virginian,* and *Cowboy in Africa.* He was a member of the Stuntmen's Association, an inductee of the Stuntmen's Hall of Fame, and a Golden Boot Award honoree.

See: Witbeck, Charles. "Men Like Joe Will Make TV Shows Wilder." *Salina Journal.* February 12, 1960.

FRED ZENDAR (1907–1990)

Manfred Volkmar Zendar was born in Switzerland but raised in France, a country he represented as a swimmer in the 1924 Paris Olympics. Zendar placed third in the Breast Stroke. He competed again at the 1928 Olympics in Amsterdam but failed to place. The 5'8", 170-pound Zendar became a sailor and traveled to the United States, where he worked as a lifeguard and newsreel cameraman. Zendar was a swimming partner of director Cecil B. DeMille, who often employed him on his films. His first film as a water specialist was *Mutiny on the Bounty* (1935). During World War II Zendar became a frogman and Master Diver for the U.S. Navy. His growing renown saw him land a number of special dive assignments. He raised the *Normandie* luxury liner out of New York Harbor and dove for the $14 million in gold the Philippine government dumped into the Bay of Corregidor during the war.

Zendar was hired by Hollywood as a marine coordinator handling all aspects of shooting on or underneath water. He designed his own fifty-foot submarine for underwater work and earned the nickname Ancient Mariner. His nautical talents can be seen on *20,000 Leagues Under the Sea* (1954), *River of No Return* (1954), *The Vikings* (1958), *The Old Man and the Sea* (1958), *Voyage to the Bottom of the Sea* (1961), *The Poseidon Adventure* (1972), *Jaws* (1975), and *Beyond the Poseidon Adventure* (1979). As a stuntman, Zendar doubled Bob Hope and was capable of diving off cliffs and wrestling alligators. He worked on *Strange Cargo* (1940), *Reap the Wild Wind* (1942), *O.S.S.* (1946), *Unconquered* (1947), *Joan of Arc* (1948), *Battleground* (1949), *Samson and Delilah* (1949), *Sealed Cargo* (1951), *The Greatest Show on Earth* (1952), *Son of Paleface* (1952), *The War of the Worlds* (1953), *The Ten Command-*

ments (1956), *The Buccaneer* (1958), *Spartacus* (1960), *Fantastic Voyage* (1966), *Butch Cassidy and the Sundance Kid* (1969), *Sometimes a Great Notion* (1971), *The Don Is Dead* (1973), *The Towering Inferno* (1974), and *Airport '77* (1977). TV credits include *Sea Hunt* and *Voyage to the Bottom of the Sea.* A member of the Stuntmen's Association, Zendar died from heart failure at the age of 82.

See: "Films Keep Him Dripping." *San Diego Union.* December 9, 1956; Johnson, Erskine. "Hollywood Today." *Sandusky Register.* June 13, 1958; "Manfred Zendar, Ex-Olympian, Water Stunts Expert." *Los Angeles Times.* May 12, 1990.

DICK ZIKER (1940–)

Richard John Ziker was raised in Casper, Wyoming, and was a Natrona County High athlete. He practiced high dives off the Alcova Resevoir and skied competitively while working construction jobs. He was on a surf vacation in Hawaii when he was recruited for *Ride the Wild Surf* (1964). They needed someone to dive off Waimea Falls and Ziker volunteered. This led to stand-in work for the 6'1", 190-pound Ziker for John Wayne on *In Harm's Way* (1965) and doubling Sean Connery on *Thunderball* (1965). In Hollywood, Ziker began on television, doubling Eric Braeden on *The Rat Patrol* (1966–68), Mike Connors on *Mannix* (1967–75), Peter Lupus on *Mission: Impossible* (1968–73), Lyle Waggoner on *Wonder Woman* (1975–79), and Robert Urich on *S.W.A.T.* (1975–76) and *Vega$* (1978–80). He also served as stunt coordinator on these shows, a post he handled on the early episodes of *Charlie's Angels* (1976–77).

Ziker became one of the highest paid stuntmen in Hollywood. He doubled Yul Brynner for the groundbreaking full burn on *Westworld* (1973), Sean Connery atop a speeding train on *The Great Train Robbery* (1979), F. Murray Abraham hanging from a helicopter on *Scarface* (1983), and Roger Moore aboard a speeding fire engine on *A View to a Kill* (1985). As a stunt coordinator he was known for his ability to pull off complicated stunts. He was in charge of orchestrating car wrecks involving 200 stuntmen on *Smokey and the Bandit 2* (1980). For a stuntmen's competition, he did a full burn fall of sixty feet.

He worked on *Tobruk* (1967), *Ice Station Zebra* (1968), *The Undefeated* (1969), *Strawberry*

Actor Richard Benjamin watches Dick Ziker double Yul Brynner for a record-setting full burn on
Westworld **(1973).**

Statement (1970), *The Night Stalker* (1972), *Trader Horn* (1973), *The Don Is Dead* (1973), *White Lightning* (1973), *The Stone Killer* (1973), *The Night Strangler* (1973), *Three the Hard Way* (1974), *Rafferty and the Gold Dust Twins* (1975), *Mitchell* (1975), *Jaws* (1975), *Carrie* (1976), *Gator* (1976), *Gable and Lombard* (1976), *Logan's Run* (1976), *Bound for Glory* (1976), *Black Sunday* (1977), *Smokey and the Bandit* (1977), *The Choir-* *boys* (1977), *Hooper* (1978), *Hot Lead and Cold Feet* (1978), and *Stunts Unlimited* (1980). A member of Stunts Unlimited, Ziker is an inductee of the Stuntmen's Hall of Fame.

See: Ciarfalio, Carl. "A Few Good Men." *Inside Stunts.* Spring, 2005; Drake, Kerry. "Casper Native Wins Emmy for Stunt Work." *Casper Tribune.* September 23, 2003; "Stuntmen Compete in Sports Spectacular." *Joplin Globe.* January 15, 1977.

Bibliography

Aaker, Everett. *Encyclopedia of Early Television Crime Fighters.* Jefferson, NC: McFarland, 2006.

Aaker, Everett. *Television Western Players of the Fifties.* Jefferson, NC: McFarland, 1997.

Armstrong, Vic, and Robert Sellers. *The True Adventures of the World's Greatest Stuntman.* London: Titan, 2012.

Baxter, John. *Stunt: The Story of the Great Movie Stuntmen.* Garden City, NY: Doubleday, 1973.

Brownlow, Kevin. *The Parade's Gone By.* Berkeley: University of California Press, 1968.

Canutt, Yakima, and Oliver Drake. *Stuntman.* New York: Walker, 1979.

Cline, William C. *In the Nick of Time.* Jefferson, NC: McFarland, 1984.

Conley, Kevin. *The Full Burn.* New York: Bloomsbury, 2008.

Crosse, Jesse. *The Greatest Movie Car Chases of All Time.* St. Paul: Motorbooks, 2006.

Emmons, Carol A. *Stuntwork and Stuntpeople.* New York: Triumph, 1982.

Greenwood, Jim, and Maxine Greenwood. *Stunt Flying in the Movies.* Blue Ridge, PA: Tab, 1982.

Hagner, John. *Falling for Stars.* 1964.

Ireland, Karin. *Hollywood Stuntpeople.* New York: Messner, 1980.

Kelly, Shawna. *Aviators in Early Hollywood.* Charleston, SC: Arcadia, 2008.

Larkins, Bob, and Boyd Magers. *The Films of Audie Murphy.* Jefferson, NC: McFarland, 2004.

Magers, Boyd. *Gene Autry Westerns.* Madison, NC: Empire, 2007.

Magers, Boyd, Bob Nareau, and Bobby Copeland. *Best of the Badmen.* Madison, NC: Empire, 2005.

Mathis, Jack. *Republic Confidential, Volume 2: The Players.* Barrington, IL: Jack Mathis, 1992.

Miklowitz, Gloria D. *Movie Stunts and the People Who Do Them.* New York: Harcourt, 1980.

Needham, Hal. *Stuntman! My Car-Crashing, Plane-Jumping, Bone-Breaking, Death-Defying Hollywood Life.* New York: Little, Brown, 2011.

Oliviero, Jeffrey. *Motion Picture Players Credits.* Jefferson, NC: McFarland, 1991.

Phillips, Mark, and Frank Garcia. *Science Fiction Television Series.* Jefferson, NC: McFarland, 1996.

Powell, Joe. *The Life and Times of a Fall Guy.* Brighton: Book Guild, 2007.

Roberson, Chuck, and Bodie Thoene. *The Fall Guy.* New York: Hancock House, 1980.

Ryan, Jim. *The Rodeo and Hollywood.* Jefferson, NC: McFarland, 2006.

Simmons, Bob. *Nobody Does It Better.* New York: Javelin, 1987.

Smith, Dean, and Mike Cox. *Cowboy Stuntman.* Austin: University of Texas Press, 2013.

Studio Directory of Stunt Men & Women. 1965.

Sullivan, George, and Tim Sullivan. *Stunt People.* New York: Beaufort, 1983.

Wayne, Jesse. *Confessions of a Hollywood Stuntman.* Jesse Wayne, 2013.

White, Patrick J. *The Complete Mission: Impossible Dossier.* New York: Avon, 1991;

Wiener, David Jon. *Burns, Falls, and Crashes.* Jefferson, NC: McFarland, 1996.

Wise, Arthur, and Derek Ware. *Stunting in the Cinema.* London: Constable, 1973.

Witney, William. *In a Door, Into a Fight, Out a Door, Into a Chase.* Jefferson, NC: McFarland, 1996.

Wynne, H. Hugh. *Motion Picture Stunt Pilots and Hollywood's Classic Aviation Movies.* Missoula, MT: Pictorial Histories, 1987.

Periodicals

Aftra/SAG Newsletter: Arizona Branch. Various issues featuring Rodd Wolff's "Stunt and Safety" articles.

British Stunt Registry. Spotlight, 1986–1990.

Falling for Stars. John Hagner, 1965–1981.

Hollywood Stuntmen's Hall of Fame Newsletter. John Hagner, 1982–1993.

Inside Stunts. John D. Ross, 2003–2009.

Stuntmen's Association of Motion Pictures Directory. SAMP, 1965–1981.

TV Guide, Triangle Publishing, Pennsylvania, 1953–1985.

Western Clippings. Boyd Magers, #1-

Websites

www.blackstuntmensassociation.com

www.b-westerns.com (Chuck Anderson's Old Corral)

www.boxrec.com (boxing record archive)

www.ctva.biz (TV episode database)

www.dannytitus.com (Black Stuntmen's Association site)

www.filesofjerryblake.com (Jerry Blake's serial site)

www.findagrave.com

www.hollywoodstuntmen.com (stuntman tribute site)

www.imdb.com (Internet Movie Database)

www.legendarysurfers.com (surfing history website)

www.memory-alpha.org/wiki (*Star Trek* site)

www.moabhappenings.com (site with stuntmen tributes)

www.monsterkidclassichorrorforum.com

www.movielocationsplus.com (Corriganville site)

www.oscars.org (Motion Picture Academy database)

www.planetoftheapes.wikia.com (*Planet of the Apes* site)

www.ponderosascenery.homestead.com (*Bonanza* site)

www.riflemanconnors.com; (*Rifleman* site)

www.serialexperience.com (Todd Gault's serial site)

www.stuntmen.com (Stuntmen's Association site)

www.stuntplayers.ws (memorial wall for stunt performers)

www.stuntsunlimited.com

www.tcm.com (Turner Classic Movies database)

www.thehighchaparral.com (*High Chaparral* site)

www.tv.com (TV episode database)

www.westernclippings.com (Boyd Magers' site with Neil Summers columns)

www.wikipedia.org

www.wildwildwest.org (*The Wild Wild West* site)

Index

Page numbers in **_bold italics_** indicate pages with illustrations.